ANDERSON'S
Law School Publications

Administrative Law Anthology
Thomas O. Sargentich

Administrative Law: Cases and Materials
Daniel J. Gifford

An Admiralty Law Anthology
Robert M. Jarvis

Alternative Dispute Resolution: Strategies for Law and
E. Wendy Trachte-Huber and Stephen K. Huber

The American Constitutional Order: History, Cases, and Philosophy
Douglas W. Kmiec and Stephen B. Presser

American Legal Systems: A Resource and Reference Guide
Toni M. Fine

Analytic Jurisprudence Anthology
Anthony D'Amato

An Antitrust Anthology
Andrew I. Gavil

Appellate Advocacy: Principles and Practice, *Third Edition*
Ursula Bentele and Eve Cary

Arbitration: Cases and Materials
Stephen K. Huber and E. Wendy Trachte-Huber

Basic Accounting Principles for Lawyers: With Present Value and Expected Value
C. Steven Bradford and Gary A. Ames

Basic Themes in Law and Jurisprudence
Charles W. Collier

A Capital Punishment Anthology (and Electronic Caselaw Appendix)
Victor L. Streib

Cases and Materials on Corporations
Thomas R. Hurst and William A. Gregory

Cases and Materials on the Law Governing Lawyers
James E. Moliterno

Cases and Problems in California Criminal Law
Myron Moskovitz

Cases and Problems in Criminal Law, *Fourth Edition*
Myron Moskovitz

The Citation Workbook: How to Beat the Citation Blues, *Second Edition*
Maria L. Ciampi, Rivka Widerman, and Vicki Lutz

Civil Procedure Anthology
David I. Levine, Donald L. Doernberg, and Melissa L. Nelken

Civil Procedure: Cases, Materials, and Questions, *Second Edition*
Richard D. Freer and Wendy Collins Perdue

Clinical Anthology: Readings for Live-Client Clinics
Alex J. Hurder, Frank S. Bloch, Susan L. Brooks, and Susan L. Kay

Commercial Transactions Series: Problems and Materials
Louis F. Del Duca, Egon Guttman, Alphonse M. Squillante, Fred H. Miller,
 Linda Rusch, and Peter Winship
  Vol. 1: Secured Transactions Under the UCC
  Vol. 2: Sales Under the UCC and the CISG
  Vol. 3: Negotiable Instruments Under the UCC and the CIBN

Communications Law: Media, Entertainment, and Regulation
Donald E. Lively, Allen S. Hammond, Blake D. Morant, and Russell L. Weaver

A Conflict-of-Laws Anthology
Gene R. Shreve

Constitutional Conflicts
Derrick A. Bell, Jr.

A Constitutional Law Anthology, *Second Edition*
Michael J. Glennon, Donald E. Lively, Phoebe A. Haddon, Dorothy E. Roberts,
 and Russell L. Weaver

Constitutional Law: Cases, History, and Dialogues, *Second Edition*
Donald E. Lively, Phoebe A. Haddon, Dorothy E. Roberts, Russell L. Weaver,
 and William D. Araiza

The Constitutional Law of the European Union
James D. Dinnage and John F. Murphy

The Constitutional Law of the European Union: Documentary Supplement
James D. Dinnage and John F. Murphy

Constitutional Torts
Sheldon H. Nahmod, Michael L. Wells, and Thomas A. Eaton

A Contracts Anthology, *Second Edition*
Peter Linzer

Contract Law and Practice
Gerald E. Berendt, Michael L. Closen, Doris Estelle Long, Marie A. Monahan,
 Robert J. Nye, and John H. Scheid

Contracts: Contemporary Cases, Comments, and Problems
Michael L. Closen, Richard M. Perlmutter, and Jeffrey D. Wittenberg

A Copyright Anthology: The Technology Frontier
Richard H. Chused

Corporate Law Anthology
Franklin A. Gevurtz

Corporate and White Collar Crime: An Anthology
Leonard Orland

Criminal Law: Cases and Materials, *Second Edition*
Arnold H. Loewy

A Criminal Procedure Anthology
Silas J. Wasserstrom and Christie L. Snyder

Criminal Procedure: Arrest and Investigation
Arnold H. Loewy and Arthur B. LaFrance

Criminal Procedure: Trial and Sentencing
Arthur B. LaFrance and Arnold H. Loewy

Economic Regulation: Cases and Materials
Richard J. Pierce, Jr.

Elder Law: Readings, Cases, and Materials
Thomas P. Gallanis, A. Kimberley Dayton, and Molly M. Wood

Elder Law: Statutes and Regulations
Thomas P. Gallanis, A. Kimberley Dayton, and Molly M. Wood

Elements of Law
Eva H. Hanks, Michael E. Herz, and Steven S. Nemerson

Ending It: Dispute Resolution in America
  Descriptions, Examples, Cases and Questions
Susan M. Leeson and Bryan M. Johnston

An Environmental Law Anthology
Robert L. Fischman, Maxine I. Lipeles, and Mark S. Squillace

Environmental Law Series
   Environmental Decisionmaking, *Third Edition*
   Robert L. Fischman and Mark S. Squillace

   Water Pollution, *Third Edition*
   Jackson B. Battle and Maxine I. Lipeles

   Air Pollution, *Third Edition*
   Mark S. Squillace and David R. Wooley

   Hazardous Waste, *Third Edition*
   Maxine I. Lipeles

Environmental Protection and Justice
  Readings and Commentary on Environmental Law and Practice, *Second Edition*
Kenneth A. Manaster

European Union Law Anthology
Karen V. Kole and Anthony D'Amato

An Evidence Anthology
Edward J. Imwinkelried and Glen Weissenberger

Family Law in Action: A Reader
Margaret F. Brinig, Carl E. Schneider, and Lee E. Teitelbaum

Federal Antitrust Law: Cases and Materials
Daniel J. Gifford and Leo J. Raskind

Federal Income Tax Anthology
Paul L. Caron, Karen C. Burke, and Grayson M.P. McCouch

Federal Rules of Civil Procedure
Publisher's Staff

Federal Rules of Evidence Handbook
Publisher's Staff

Federal Rules of Evidence: Rules, Legislative History, Commentary and Authority
Glen Weissenberger

Federal and State Civil Procedure Handbook
Jeffrey A. Parness

Federal Wealth Transfer Tax Anthology
Paul L. Caron, Grayson M.P. McCouch, Karen C. Burke

First Amendment Anthology
Donald E. Lively, Dorothy E. Roberts, and Russell L. Weaver

The History, Philosophy, and Structure of the American Constitution
Douglas W. Kmiec and Stephen B. Presser

Individual Rights and the American Constitution
Douglas W. Kmiec and Stephen B. Presser

International Environmental Law Anthology
Anthony D'Amato and Kirsten Engel

International Human Rights: Law, Policy, and Process, *Second Edition*
Frank C. Newman and David Weissbrodt

**Selected International Human Rights Instruments and
   Bibliography for Research on International Human Rights Law,** *Second Edition*
Frank C. Newman and David Weissbrodt

International Intellectual Property Anthology
Anthony D'Amato and Doris Estelle Long

International Law Anthology
Anthony D'Amato

International Taxation: Cases, Materials, and Problems
Philip F. Postlewaite

Introduction to the Study of Law: Cases and Materials, *Second Edition*
John Makdisi

Judicial Externships: The Clinic Inside the Courthouse, *Second Edition*
Rebecca A. Cochran

A Land Use Anthology
Jon W. Bruce

Law and Economics Anthology
Kenneth G. Dau-Schmidt and Thomas S. Ulen

The Law of Disability Discrimination, *Third Edition*
Ruth Colker and Bonnie Poitras Tucker

The Law of Disability Discrimination Handbook: Statutes and Regulatory Guidance
   Third Edition
Ruth Colker and Bonnie Poitras Tucker

Lawyers and Fundamental Moral Responsibility
Daniel R. Coquillette

Mediation and Negotiation: Reaching Agreement in Law and Business
E. Wendy Trachte-Huber and Stephen K. Huber

Microeconomic Predicates to Law and Economics
Mark Seidenfeld

Natural Resources: Cases and Materials
Barlow Burke

Patients, Psychiatrists and Lawyers: Law and the Mental Health System, *Second Edition*
Raymond L. Spring, Roy B. Lacoursiere, and Glen Weissenberger

Preventive Law: Materials on a Non Adversarial Legal Process
Robert M. Hardaway

Principles of Evidence, *Fourth Edition*
Irving Younger, Michael Goldsmith, and David A. Sonenshein

Problems and Simulations in Evidence, *Second Edition*
Thomas F. Guernsey

A Products Liability Anthology
Anita Bernstein

Professional Responsibility Anthology
Thomas B. Metzloff

A Property Anthology, *Second Edition*
Richard H. Chused

Public Choice and Public Law: Readings and Commentary
Maxwell L. Stearns

The Question Presented: Model Appellate Briefs
Maria L. Ciampi and William H. Manz

Readings in Criminal Law
Russell L. Weaver, John M. Burkoff, Catherine Hancock, Alan Reed, and Peter J. Seago

Science in Evidence
D.H. Kaye

A Section 1983 Civil Rights Anthology
Sheldon H. Nahmod

Sports Law: Cases and Materials, *Fourth Edition*
Ray L. Yasser, James R. McCurdy, C. Peter Goplerud, and Maureen A. Weston

State and Local Government Law: A Transactional Approach
John Martinez and Michael E. Libonati

A Torts Anthology, *Second Edition*
Julie A. Davies, Lawrence C. Levine, and Edward J. Kionka

Trial Practice
Lawrence A. Dubin and Thomas F. Guernsey

Unincorporated Business Entities, *Second Edition*
Larry E. Ribstein

FORTHCOMING PUBLICATIONS

The Best Kept Secrets of Evidence Law: 101 Principles, Practices, and Pitfalls
Paul R. Rice

Cases and Materials in Juvenile Law
J. Eric Smithburn

Civil Procedure for Federal and State Courts
Jeffrey A. Parness

First Amendment Law: Cases, Comparative Perspectives, and Dialogues
Donald E. Lively, William D. Araiza, Phoebe A. Haddon, John C. Knechtle, and Dorothy E. Roberts

Property Law: Cases, Materials, and Questions
Edward E. Chase

Taxation: A Skills Approach
Michael A. Livingston

Unincorporated Business Entities

Second Edition

Unincorporated Business Entities

Second Edition

Larry E. Ribstein

GMU Foundation Professor of Law
George Mason University School of Law

ANDERSON PUBLISHING CO.
CINCINNATI

NOTE TO USERS

To ensure that you are using the latest materials available in this area, please be sure to periodically check Anderson Publishing's web site for downloadable updates and supplements at www.andersonpublishing.com

UNINCORPORATED BUSINESS ENTITIES, SECOND EDITION
LARRY E. RIBSTEIN

Anderson Publishing Co.
2035 Reading Road / Cincinnati, Ohio 45202
800-582-7295 / e-mail lawschool@andersonpublishing.com / Fax 513-562-5430
www.andersonpublishing.com

ISBN: 1-58360-766-8

TABLE OF CONTENTS

PREFACE FOR THE SECOND EDITION

The fast-paced developments in partnerships, limited liability companies and other unincorporated firms have opened a gap in the law school curriculum. The traditional corporations and agency and partnership courses no longer adequately prepare law students for business practice today. This book is designed to fill this gap.

This book has three general goals. First, it focuses on the modern law of partnerships and other unincorporated firms. As a result, it emphasizes the issues that business lawyers are dealing with today rather than the arcane legal rules that traditionally have been the focus of the agency and partnership course.

Second, this book is intended as a business planning book. This means that it includes many notes and problems on planning and drafting issues. It also means that it draws together materials from disparate areas of the law, including tax, bankruptcy, securities and employment discrimination, that bear on business planning.

Third, this book is intended as a short gap-filler in the existing curriculum. I have taught this book in a two-semester-hour course in Unincorporated Businesses. However, the book is designed to be short enough to complement standard courses in Corporations and Agency and Partnership, or as a stand-alone or supplementary text in a Business Planning course.

These multiple goals drive my selection of materials. The chapter on agency is intended only to cover the basics rather than to duplicate the complete coverage of agency that is included in the many fine books that already exist on this subject. This leaves room, even within a shorter book, to cover the many detailed issues on contracting within partnerships and other unincorporated firms that get left out even of longer agency and partnership books. The book includes enough discussion of tax issues to indicate where some of the tax problems lie. However, the length constraints of this book, coupled with the inherent problems of trying to cover a subject as complex as partnership tax, necessitate leaving much tax discussion to a separate course.

As indicated above, drafting and planning coverage is implemented through notes, questions and problems. The "Chameleon" agreement in the Appendix provides the skeleton of a partnership or operating agreement for any of the forms of business discussed in this book. (The parties to the agreement are referred to as "memners"—that is, partner/members.) This agreement shows the topics that might be covered in a partnership or operating agreement and how the coverage might be organized. Notes throughout the book cross-reference the agreement, and the annotations in the agreement in turn cross-reference the book. There are also many notes throughout the book on additions or modifications to the skeletal agreement to deal with specific issues. Chapter 1 includes a global drafting and planning exercise that links together all of the material in the book.

The focus of the substantive coverage of the book is the general partnership. Much of this coverage also relates to the other business forms discussed in Chapters 11-14. These chapters cross-reference the partnership discussion where appropriate, as well as raising issues that are unique to each business form. Chapter 12 on limited liability companies includes many planning and drafting notes and questions that also relate to limited and general partnerships. I have put these materials in Chapter 12 because, as a practical matter, I expect the LLC to be a dominant form for sophisticated business planning, at least for non-professional firms. Even if this prediction is wrong, this discussion can easily be applied to other business forms.

Supplementing will continue to be done by the Web. Supplements can be accessed through my web page, mason.gmu.edu/~lribstei/index.htm.

Many thanks to the George Mason University School of Law students in my Unincorporated Businesses course who helped me both with the initial draft and with fine-tuning for the second edition, and to my colleague Claire Hill who went through the entire first draft and gave me some valuable tax advice (errors remain mine).

TABLE OF CASES

(Excerpted cases indicated in *italics*)

CHAPTER 1
INTRODUCTION

1.01 Why Study Unincorporated Firms?

This book treats subjects that have been orphaned by the rest of the law school curriculum—partnerships and other types of unincorporated businesses. These firms present a distinct set of issues and themes, which are discussed briefly in this Chapter and illustrated throughout this book. The basic business associations course, "corporations," usually either ignores these business forms, covers them briefly for comparison or uses them as hors d'oeuvres before the main course. The "agency and partnership" course, when it is taught at all, usually concentrates on agency rules, leaving little time for more modern and (I believe) interesting business planning issues and the nuances of partnerships and other unincorporated firms.

These curricular gaps are unfortunate. Partnerships and other types of firms are practically important in terms of the volume of business and legal work they involve. Also, because unincorporated firms rely heavily on customized contracts rather than default rules, they are well suited for teaching the techniques of planning, drafting and other aspects of business lawyers' work. This book contains numerous drafting and planning questions and exercises.

The law of business associations normally focuses on the internal organization of firms, leaving the law concerning relations between the firm and others to be covered in other courses. This segregation of issues is an inevitable by-product of the "cubbyhole" nature of the law school curriculum. This book shows how a variety of other subjects, including tax, employment discrimination and securities law, relate to drafting and planning and choice of business form.

This book deals not merely with *unincorporated* firms, but with all *closely held* firms. Close corporations are discussed in Chapter 11. Closely held firms present distinct issues that arise from the owners' inability to exit the firm by selling their shares in liquid securities markets. The absence of a market mechanism for exiting the firm increases the importance of owners' management rights and right to exit by selling their interests back to the firm or causing the firm to dissolve and liquidate. A study of partnerships and other unincorporated business forms that were designed especially for closely held firms provides valuable insights into these planning and drafting problems.

1.02 The Menagerie of Business Associations

This book discusses, among other types of statutory firms, general and limited partnerships, limited liability companies, and limited liability partnerships. It also covers variations among the states with respect to each type of firm. This section discusses some general questions raised by all of this variety.

A. The Functions of Business Association Statutes

Why all of these different statutes? Some possible explanations are presented in Ribstein, *Statutory Forms for Closely Held Firms: Theories and Evidence,* 73 WASH. U. L.Q. 369 (1995).

In the first place, it is not even clear why there are *any* statutes. As discussed below in this chapter and throughout this book, firms can contract around many of the applicable statutory provisions. One function of statutes is to provide "standard forms" in order to economize on contracting costs. Firms' costs of drafting their own special sets of customized terms can exceed their benefits from this activity, particularly if the firms involve relatively small amounts of money or if "off the rack" provisions can be standardized across many different types of businesses. But standard forms needn't be statutes. For example, courts supply agency law, as seen in Chapter 2. While statutes may be clearer and more accessible than case law, this is also true of forms provided by non-government individuals and groups. But private groups may not always be able to capture the benefits from promulgating standard forms that would benefit large numbers of firms. Also, a statute may have the advantage over private forms of being so notorious and widely available that it can encourage the development of a useful body of interpretative judicial opinions and lawyers' customs and forms.

Even if *some* statutory forms are necessary, why are there so *many* different types? This book shows that the rules for each business form provide a distinct structure of complementary rules. For example, the management, financial and dissolution provisions of the partnership statute follow logically from each other and from the partners' personal liability for partnership debts. By letting firms adopt particular structures, separate statutory standard forms help define the parties' expectations and give courts clues on how to fill gaps in the statute or the parties' contracts.

B. Linking Statutory Forms

This leads to the question of whether courts and legislatures should "link" standard forms. In particular, general partnership cases are applied to limited partnerships. *See* § 11.02. Courts might also apply general and limited partnership cases to limited liability companies and limited liability partnerships. The usefulness of statutes in encouraging the development of a body of case law and custom suggests that it may be even more useful to combine the cases and customs that apply to separate forms. Thus, in *Child Care of Irvine, L.L.C. v. Facchina*, 1998 WL 409363 (Del. Ch. July 15, 1998), at 6, the court pointed out

> Unlike the rich body of corporate law decisions that often provide members of this Court with at least an intuitive sense about the parties' likelihood of prevailing in this matter, in this dispute I do not enjoy the luxury of interpretive decisions upon which to make a reasoned judgment regarding who ultimately will prevail.

However, this would undercut the reasons for having separate standard forms. *See* Ribstein, *Linking Statutory Forms,* 58 LAW & CONTEMP. PROBS. 187 (Spring 1995). These considerations carry over to the ultimate linkage—that is, abolishing separate business association statutes and providing for one big statute which has many variations, something like a restaurant menu. This "unified business entity" approach is discussed in Chapter 14.

C. Choice of Form

Because there are so many types of business associations, firms are faced with the decision of deciding what type of business association they will be. One of the main themes in this book is how the various legal rules relate to the practical question of which type of business association a firm should be. In making this decision, a firm must consider whether the default rules suit its particular type of business, taking into account not only the rules of each business form, but also how the potential application of regulatory and tax statutes may turn on a firm's choice of default rules. Although firms mostly can contract around the rules in the form it selects, as discussed above, contracting may be costly, and contracts waiving statutory rules may not be fully enforced.

D. Choice of Law and Uniformity

The choice of *form* issue is closely related to choice of *law*. Firms must consider the state variations that are discussed throughout this book, particularly concerning limited liability companies and limited liability partnerships where there is the most variation. A firm whose business operations are located in State X may choose to organize under what it considers to be the more favorable statute in State Y as long as State X will enforce State Y's rules.

In contrast to corporations, partnerships and unincorporated firms could not always choose the applicable law so easily. While the courts have enforced provisions in partnership agreements for applying the law of a particular state, as discussed in more detail in Chapter 3 they have not always done so. In any event, choice of law was never much of an issue for partnerships because for most of this century state law has united around the *Uniform Partnership Act* (1914) and the *Uniform Limited Partnership Acts* (1916, 1976 and 1985). This is changing rapidly. Limited liability company, limited liability partnership and most limited partnership statutes now include specific provisions recognizing "foreign" firms of the same type and applying the laws under which those firms are organized. Moreover, the revised version of the *Uniform Partnership Act* includes a choice-of-law provision. As a result, even general partnership law may come to vary among the states.

These practical issues concerning choice of law raise legal and theoretical issues concerning whether firms *should be* able to choose the applicable law and whether the law should be uniform. A uniform law would make it more difficult for firms to evade mandatory provisions of state statutes and would reduce the costs that must be incurred by owners and third parties of learning the law of different states. On the other hand, competition among the states, and the evolutionary process that results when legislators and lawyers in different states come up with their own solutions to problems, may produce better laws. *See* Ribstein & Kobayashi, *Economic Analysis of Uniform State Laws,* 25 J. Leg. Stud. 131 (1996). Moreover, there may be a need for different types of statutes that suit different types of firms.

Evolution and legal change may, however, bring their own problems. In particular, changes in the law may cause changes in contracts that are based on current legal rules. For example, permitting firms to register as LLPs or to convert to LLCs may change the rights both of minority owners who oppose this sort of fundamental change and third party creditors whose rights may be affected by the fundamental change in the nature of the debtor.

E. Business Associations as Aggregates and Entities

The business associations discussed in this book are, in general, outgrowths of the partnership form of business, which traditionally has been regarded as an "aggregate" of the owners. By contrast, a corporation traditionally has been regarded as a separate legal "entity" that has rights, powers and liabilities separate from the owners. Because corporations are "entities," it seems to make sense that the corporation itself, and not the owners, is liable for the debts of the business. On the other hand, partners themselves comprise a partnership, which is consistent with the traditional partnership rule that the partners are personally liable for the debts of the firm. Other traditional consequences of the "entity" nature of the corporation include the continuation of the firm after the withdrawal or death of an owner, ownership of property and prosecution and defense of litigation in the corporate name, and taxation of income and losses at the firm rather than owner level.

Although "entity" and "aggregate" appear to describe certain features of business forms, these concepts should not be overused. An unincorporated business association is not necessarily best characterized as either an aggregate or an entity because it combines aggregate and entity features. For example, even a traditional general partnership may be an "aggregate" when it comes to partner liability, but an "entity" for purposes of holding property in partnership name. Indeed, even the method of asserting liability against partnerships, as discussed in Chapter 6, may be entity in nature in the sense that creditors may have to first assert the liability against the partnership assets before pursuing individual partners. It follows that it makes no sense to say that, because a partnership is on balance an "aggregate," it should necessarily have *only* "aggregate" features, such as personal liability or direct taxation of partners. Nevertheless, as discussed in Chapter 10, the tax distinction between partnerships and corporations appears to be based on just this sort of circular reasoning.

1.03 Tax Considerations

This is primarily a book about the non-tax aspects of unincorporated firms. In general terms, as discussed in more detail in Chapter 10, a partnership or other unincorporated firm is usually taxed on a "flow-through" basis which means that income and perhaps also losses are taxable directly at the member level rather than first at the level of the firm. The relevant tax rules are very complex and take up a course of their own. However, since so much of the law and business related to unincorporated firms is tax-related, it is impossible wholly to ignore tax considerations. Thus, the materials highlight tax issues where they are likely to be significant to planning or where (as with the classification rules discussed in Chapter 10) they explain the development of the non-tax law of this type of firm.

1.04 Lawyers' Roles

As discussed below, this book emphasizes planning and drafting problems in unincorporated firms. This raises important questions concerning the appropriate role of business lawyers. Some commentators, including Gilson (*see Value Creation by Business Lawyers: Legal Skills and Asset Pricing,* 94 YALE L.J. 239, 243 (1984)), contend that lawyers potentially have an important role in promoting their clients' *business* objectives by reducing transaction costs and thereby adding value to transactions. On the other hand, it is not clear why lawyers, as distinguished, for example, from business people and accountants, are best suited to perform these non-legal roles. Among other things, law school does not now offer the best training for this sort of work. Moreover, an expansive view of lawyers' roles may make it easier for lawyers to persuade clients to consume too much, or the wrong kind of, legal services.

In any event, this book focuses on lawyers' roles in giving *legal* advice—itself a full-time job. Among other things, lawyers advise on the legal implications of alternative business decisions and how best to effectuate these decisions from a legal standpoint. In giving this advice, the lawyer must know not only "black letter" legal rules, but also enough of the policy considerations underlying these rules to be able to determine how the rules will be applied to new situations. Legal advice includes drafting documents, advising on the underlying terms of transactions, and choosing the business form and the applicable law. For example, the lawyer may need to be able to advise the client that a particular management and control device the client suggests may have adverse tax or liability consequences, but that a different device that will accomplish the same objective will not. These planning and drafting issues are developed in notes and questions throughout the book and in the operating and partnership agreements in the Appendix.

1.05 Outline and Overview

This book discusses separately various forms of unincorporated firms. Chapter 2 discusses the sole proprietorship, focusing on the law of agency, and particularly on principals' liability for agents' acts, which is the most important law governing sole proprietorships.

Chapters 3-9 discuss in some detail the basic unincorporated firm, the general partnership. The book emphasizes the general partnership because these rules are the foundation of many of the rules regarding other types of unincorporated firms.

Chapter 10 is a transitional chapter that discusses the search for the "incorporated partnership"—that is, a business form that combines corporate-type limited liability with the flexibility and other features of the partnership. This chapter shows why the close corporation failed fully to accomplish this objective, leading to the growth of limited liability unincorporated business forms.

Chapters 11-13 discuss the main varieties of limited liability unincorporated firms—limited partnerships, limited liability companies and limited liability partnerships.

Chapter 14 ends the book by discussing new varieties of firms and significant new developments that are appearing on the horizon.

1.06 The Role of the Parties' Agreement

As already noted, the parties to a firm can waive many of the statutory rules that apply to their type of firm by provisions in their governance agreement, variously referred to as a "partnership" or "operating" agreement. An important underlying theme of this book concerns the considerations involved in drafting these agreements and the extent to which they are enforced. In order to provide a rough beginning point for discussing the drafting of these agreements, this book includes in the Appendix an all-purpose "Chameleon" agreement which contains a skeleton of the sort of provisions one might find in any firm's agreement. While courts usually hold that the agreement is enforceable, they may weaken the effect of agreements by interpreting them restrictively and filling resulting "gaps" with statutory or common law rules. Lawyers must understand these nuances in order to be able to draft agreements that courts will apply consistently with the parties' expectations.

The following problem is designed to focus your thinking on these issues. Write an annotated operating or partnership agreement for any one of the following types of firms. Assume in each case that the firm's business operations will be based in your home state:

(1) A law firm consisting of ten experienced lawyers who are leaving their current firms to form a new firm.

(2) A firm that will invest venture capital in high-technology start-up firms. The manager will have a minority ownership stake and will receive a management fee, while 20 passive investors will provide initial capital. *See* Gompers & Lerner, *The Use of Covenants: An Empirical Analysis of Venture Partnership Agreements,* 39 J.L. & ECON. 463 (1996).

(3) A firm that intends to develop new computer software products. The initial owners are ten computer programmers who have approximately equal programming experience and are contributing approximately equal small amounts of capital. The firm expects to attract more capital after developing its first products.

For each agreement, do the following:

(1) Select a particular form of unincorporated business and discuss why that form was selected for the particular type of firm.

(2) Select the state under whose law the business will be formed and discuss why that law was selected.

(3) Draft a complete governance agreement (i.e., an "operating" or "partnership" agreement, depending on the form of business).

(4) With respect to each provision in the agreement, discuss the considerations relevant to drafting or selecting that provision.

(5) State any facts about the business that you are assuming in drafting the agreement in addition to those listed above.

The Chameleon agreement provides some guidance in drafting this agreement, particularly in showing how the various provisions interrelate and in providing cross-references to the material. Notes throughout the book provide hints on drafting and planning that should be taken into account in customizing the agreement for the particular firm you select.

CHAPTER 2
AGENCY AND THE SOLE PROPRIETOR

2.01 The Sole Proprietorship

The basic unincorporated business is the sole proprietorship, in which a single owner (which may be another business association) "hires" capital, supplies and labor by employment, lease and loan agreements. A good example of a sole proprietorship is the business in the recent movie, *Grosse Pointe Blank,* "Pacific Trident Global Trading." John Cusack plays the owner, a professional hit man, and even looks a lot like his sole employee, his secretary (played by sister Joan). The fact that there is only one owner means that only one person receives the profits that accrue to the firm after paying those who provide capital, labor and credit the market rate for their contributions. (Principals' duty to compensate agents is discussed below in § 2.06). The proprietor's profits measure her value added in monitoring and coordinating these inputs. *See* Alchian & Demsetz, *Production, Information Costs, and Economic Organization*, 62 AM. ECON. REV. 777 (1972).

The relationships between the owner and the other inputs in a sole proprietorship are not covered in a separate business association statute (although such a statute is proposed in Chapter 14). This chapter discusses the most important body of case law that applies to this type of firm—the common law of agency, which is summarized in the Restatement (Second) of Agency. A third Restatement is underway. For the Reporter's preliminary prospectus, *see* DeMott, *A Revised Prospectus for a Third Restatement Of Agency,* 31 U.C. Davis L. Rev. 1035 (1998).

Agency law is also important because it underlies the other business associations discussed in this book. Moreover, the principal's liability for the wrongs of its agents (*see* § 2.04) is a necessary backdrop for understanding the limitations on this liability discussed in Chapters 11-14.

2.02 Formation of Agency

The threshold question is whether the parties are in an agency relationship. This presents some difficulty because agency is an informal relationship which may exist without a writing, filing or even explicit acknowledgment.

A.   The Definition of Agency

Restatement (Second) of Agency ("Restatement") § 1 provides:

Agency is the fiduciary relation which results from the manifestation of consent by one person to another that the other shall act on his behalf and subject to his control, and consent by the other so to act. The one for whom action is to be taken is the principal. The one who is to act is the agent.

Parsing this section shows that agency has the following main characteristics: (1) *consent* by both the principal and agent; (2) *control* by the principal; and (3) action by the agent *on behalf of* the principal. These elements are discussed below.

1. Consent

The consent element follows from the fact that agency is essentially a contractual relationship. However, the consent required is *not* the parties' explicit consent to be "agent and principal," but rather their consent to enter into a relationship which includes the "on behalf of" and "control" elements of agency. *See* Restatement § 1, comment b.

2. Control

The principal's ultimate power of control over the agent is an important element of agency. It supports attributing agents' acts to their principals. Other terms of agency relationships, such as the agent's duty to follow the principal's instructions (*see* § 2.05), also follow logically from the fact that the agent has contracted to be subject to the principal's control.

3. Action on Behalf of the Principal

An agent agrees to disregard her own interest and act for the principal's benefit. This is the basis for the agent's fiduciary duty of loyalty (*see* § 2.05) and supports holding a principal liable for her agent's acts. The "benefit" principle involves the agent's and the principal's *expectation* that the agent will produce a benefit for the principal, so that the agent's acts can be connected with the principal's enterprise. Agency can exist, however, even if the agent does not *actually* produce a benefit for the principal.

B.   Distinguishing Agency and Non-Agency Relationships

It is important to distinguish from agency relationships those which contain some, but not all, of the elements of agency. For example, a trust is not an agency because, although the trustee acts for the beneficiary, the trustee is not subject to the beneficiary's control.

Some relationships, such as purchase for resale (Restatement § 14J) and secured debt (Restatement § 14O), are not necessarily agency relationships but may become agencies under particular circumstances. A retailer or other person who buys goods for resale generally acts for her own benefit rather than for the benefit of the original seller, and generally has no duty to obey the instructions of the original purchaser. In this situation, there is no reason to assume that the parties should owe strong duties to each other or that the wholesaler should be liable as a principal if the retailer, for example, injures someone by using the product in a dangerous way. The original seller may be liable for its own misconduct in manufacturing a dangerous product, or the reseller may agree to control and benefit terms that constitute an agency.

As the following cases illustrate, the line between agency and non-agency in these types of relationships is not always clear.

Gay Jenson Farms Co. v. Cargill, Incorporated
309 N.W.2d 285 (Minn. 1981)

PETERSON, Justice.

Plaintiffs, 86 individual, partnership or corporate farmers, brought this action against defendant Cargill, Inc. (Cargill) and defendant Warren Grain & Seed Co. (Warren) to recover losses sustained when Warren defaulted on the contracts made with plaintiffs for the sale of grain. After a trial by jury, judgment was entered in favor of plaintiffs, and Cargill brought this appeal. We affirm.

This case arose out of the financial collapse of defendant Warren Seed & Grain Co., and its failure to satisfy its indebtedness to plaintiffs. Warren, which was located in Warren, Minnesota, was operated by Lloyd Hill and his son, Gary Hill. Warren operated a grain elevator and as a result was involved in the purchase of cash or market grain from local farmers. The cash grain would be resold through the Minneapolis Grain Exchange or to the terminal grain companies directly. Warren also stored grain for farmers and sold chemicals, fertilizer and steel storage bins. In addition, it operated a seed business which involved buying seed grain from farmers, processing it and reselling it for seed to farmers and local elevators.

Lloyd Hill decided in 1964 to apply for financing from Cargill. Cargill's officials from the Moorhead regional office investigated Warren's operations and recommended that Cargill finance Warren.

Warren and Cargill thereafter entered into a security agreement which provided that Cargill would loan money for working capital to Warren on "open account" financing up to a stated limit, which was originally set as $175,000. Under this contract, Warren would receive funds and pay its expenses by issuing drafts drawn on Cargill through Minneapolis banks. The drafts were imprinted with both Warren's and Cargill's names. Proceeds from Warren's sales would be deposited with Cargill and credited to its account. In return for this financing, Warren appointed Cargill as its grain agent for transaction with the Commodity Credit Corporation. Cargill was also given a right of first refusal to purchase market grain sold by Warren to the terminal market.

A new contract was negotiated in 1967, extending Warren's credit line to $300,000 and incorporating the provisions of the original contract. It was also stated in the contract that Warren would provide Cargill with annual financial statements and that either Cargill would keep the books for Warren or an audit would be conducted by an independent firm. Cargill was given the right of access to Warren's books for inspection.

In addition, the agreement provided that Warren was not to make capital improvements or repairs in excess of $5,000 without Cargill's prior consent. Further, it was not to become liable as guarantor on another's indebtedness, or encumber its assets except with Cargill's permission. Consent by Cargill was required before Warren would be allowed to declare a dividend or sell and purchase stock.

Officials from Cargill's regional office made a brief visit to Warren shortly after the agreement was executed. They examined the annual statement and the accounts receivable, expenses, inventory, seed, machinery and other financial matters. Warren was informed that it would be reminded periodically to make the improvements recommended by Cargill.[3] At

---

[3]   Cargill headquarters suggested that the regional office check Warren monthly. Also, it was requested that Warren be given an explanation for the relatively large withdrawals from undistributed earn-

approximately this time, a memo was given to the Cargill official in charge of the Warren account, Erhart Becker, which stated in part: "This organization (Warren) needs very strong paternal guidance."

In 1970, Cargill contracted with Warren and other elevators to act as its agent to seek growers for a new type of wheat called Bounty 208. Warren, as Cargill's agent for this project, entered into contracts for the growing of the wheat seed, with Cargill named as the contracting party. Farmers were paid directly by Cargill for the seed and all contracts were performed in full. In 1971, pursuant to an agency contract, Warren contracted on Cargill's behalf with various farmers for the growing of sunflower seeds for Cargill. The arrangements were similar to those made in the Bounty 208 contracts, and all those contracts were also completed. Both these agreements were unrelated to the open account financing contract. In addition, Warren, as Cargill's agent in the sunflower seed business, cleaned and packaged the seed in Cargill bags.

During this period, Cargill continued to review Warren's operations and expenses and recommend that certain actions should be taken.[4] Warren purchased from Cargill various business forms printed by Cargill and received sample forms from Cargill which Warren used to develop its own business forms.

Cargill wrote to its regional office in 1970 expressing its concern that the pattern of increased use of funds allowed to develop at Warren was similar to that involved in two other cases in which Cargill experienced severe losses. Cargill did not refuse to honor drafts or call the loan, however. A new security agreement which increased the credit line to $750,000 was executed in 1972, and a subsequent agreement which raised the limit to $1,250,000 was entered into in 1976.

Warren was at that time shipping Cargill 90% of its cash grain. When Cargill's facilities were full, Warren shipped its grain to other companies. Approximately 25% of Warren's total sales was seed grain which was sold directly by Warren to its customers.

As Warren's indebtedness continued to be in excess of its credit line, Cargill began to contact Warren daily regarding its financial affairs. Cargill headquarters informed its regional office in 1973 that, since Cargill money was being used, Warren should realize that Cargill had the right to make some critical decisions regarding the use of the funds. Cargill headquarters also told Warren that a regional manager would be working with Warren on a day-to-day basis as well as in monthly planning meetings. In 1975, Cargill's regional office began to keep a daily debit position on Warren. A bank account was opened in Warren's name on which Warren could draw checks in 1976. The account was to be funded by drafts drawn on Cargill by the local bank.

---

ings made by the Hills, since Cargill hoped that Warren's profits would be used to decrease its debt balance. Cargill asked for written requests for withdrawals from undistributed earnings in the future.

  [4]   Between 1967 and 1973, Cargill suggested that Warren take a number of steps, including: (1) a reduction of seed grain and cash grain inventories; (2) improved collection of accounts receivable; (3) reduction or elimination of its wholesale seed business and its speciality grain operation; (4) marketing fertilizer and steel bins on consignment; (5) a reduction in withdrawals made by officers; (6) a suggestion that Warren's bookkeeper not issue her own salary checks; and (7) cooperation with Cargill in implementing the recommendations. These ideas were apparently never implemented, however.

In early 1977, it became evident that Warren had serious financial problems. Several farmers, who had heard that Warren's checks were not being paid, inquired or had their agents inquire at Cargill regarding Warren's status and were initially told that there would be no problem with payment. In April 1977, an audit of Warren revealed that Warren was $4 million in debt. After Cargill was informed that Warren's financial statements had been deliberately falsified, Warren's request for additional financing was refused. In the final days of Warren's operation, Cargill sent an official to supervise the elevator, including disbursement of funds and income generated by the elevator.

After Warren ceased operations, it was found to be indebted to Cargill in the amount of $3.6 million. Warren was also determined to be indebted to plaintiffs in the amount of $2 million, and plaintiffs brought this action in 1977 to seek recovery of that sum. Plaintiffs alleged that Cargill was jointly liable for Warren's indebtedness as it had acted as principal for the grain elevator. * * *

The court determined that Cargill was the disclosed principal of Warren. It was concluded that Cargill was jointly liable with Warren for plaintiffs' losses, and judgment was entered for plaintiffs. * * *

1. The major issue in this case is whether Cargill, by its course of dealing with Warren, became liable as a principal on contracts made by Warren with plaintiffs. Cargill contends that no agency relationship was established with Warren, notwithstanding its financing of Warren's operation and its purchase of the majority of Warren's grain. However, we conclude that Cargill, by its control and influence over Warren, became a principal with liability for the transactions entered into by its agent Warren.

Agency is the fiduciary relationship that results from the manifestation of consent by one person to another that the other shall act on his behalf and subject to his control, and consent by the other so to act. [citations omitted] In order to create an agency there must be an agreement, but not necessarily a contract between the parties. Restatement (Second) of Agency § 1, comment b (1958). An agreement may result in the creation of an agency relationship although the parties did not call it an agency and did not intend the legal consequences of the relation to follow. * * *

Cargill contends that the prerequisites of an agency relationship did not exist because Cargill never consented to the agency, Warren did not act on behalf of Cargill, and Cargill did not exercise control over Warren. We hold that all three elements of agency could be found in the particular circumstances of this case. By directing Warren to implement its recommendations, Cargill manifested its consent that Warren would be its agent. Warren acted on Cargill's behalf in procuring grain for Cargill as the part of its normal operations which were totally financed by Cargill. Further, an agency relationship was established by Cargill's interference with the internal affairs of Warren, which constituted de facto control of the elevator.

A creditor who assumes control of his debtor's business may become liable as principal for the acts of the debtor in connection with the business. Restatement (Second) of Agency § 140 (1958). It is noted in comment a to section 140 that:

> A security holder who merely exercises a veto power over the business acts of his debtor by preventing purchases or sales above specified amounts does not thereby become a principal. However, if he takes over the management of the debtor's business either in person or through an agent, and directs what contracts

may or may not be made, he becomes a principal, liable as a principal for the obligations incurred thereafter in the normal course of business by the debtor who has now become his general agent. The point at which the creditor becomes a principal is that at which he assumes de facto control over the conduct of his debtor, whatever the terms of the formal contract with his debtor may be.

A number of factors indicate Cargill's control over Warren, including the following:

(1)   Cargill's constant recommendations to Warren by telephone;
(2)   Cargill's right of first refusal on grain;
(3)   Warren's inability to enter into mortgages, to purchase stock or to pay dividends without Cargill's approval;
(4)   Cargill's right of entry onto Warren's premises to carry on periodic checks and audits;
(5)   Cargill's correspondence and criticism regarding Warren's finances, officers' salaries and inventory;
(6)   Cargill's determination that Warren needed "strong paternal guidance";
(7)   Provision of drafts and forms to Warren upon which Cargill's name was imprinted;
(8)   Financing of all Warren's purchases of grain and operating expenses; and
(9)   Cargill's power to discontinue the financing of Warren's operations.

We recognize that some of these elements, as Cargill contends, are found in an ordinary debtor-creditor relationship. However, these factors cannot be considered in isolation, but, rather, they must be viewed in light of all the circumstances surrounding Cargill's aggressive financing of Warren.

It is also Cargill's position that the relationship between Cargill and Warren was that of buyer-supplier rather than principal-agent. Restatement (Second) of Agency § 14K (1958) compares an agent with a supplier as follows:

> One who contracts to acquire property from a third person and convey it to another is the agent of the other only if it is agreed that he is to act primarily for the benefit of the other and not for himself. Factors indicating that one is a supplier, rather than an agent, are: (1) That he is to receive a fixed price for the property irrespective of price paid by him. This is the most important. (2) That he acts in his own name and receives the title to the property which he thereafter is to transfer. (3) That he has an independent business in buying and selling similar property.

Restatement (Second) of Agency § 14K, Comment a (1958).

Under the Restatement approach, it must be shown that the supplier has an independent business before it can be concluded that he is not an agent. The record establishes that all portions of Warren's operation were financed by Cargill and that Warren sold almost all of its market grain to Cargill. Thus, the relationship which existed between the parties was not merely that of buyer and supplier.

A case analogous to the present one is *Butler v. Bunge Corporation,* 329 F. Supp. 47 (N.D. Miss. 1971). In *Butler,* the plaintiff brought an action to recover the price of a soybean crop sold to an elevator that was operated by Bayles, a purported agent of the defendant Bunge Corporation. Bayles had agreed to operate a former Bunge elevator pursuant to an agreement in which Bayles was designated as manager. Although Bunge contended that Bayles was an independent contractor, the court determined that the elevator was an agent of Bunge.[8]

In this case, as in *Butler,* Cargill furnished substantially all funds received by the elevator. Cargill did have a right of entry on Warren's premises, and it, like Bunge, required maintenance of insurance against hazards of operation. Warren's activities, like Bayles' operations, formed a substantial part of Cargill's business that was developed in that area. In addition, Cargill did not think of Warren as an operator who was free to become Cargill's competitor, but rather conceded that it believed that Warren owed a duty of loyalty to Cargill. The decisions made by Warren were not independent of Cargill's interest or its control.

Further, we are not persuaded by the fact that Warren was not one of the "line" elevators that Cargill operated in its own name. The Warren operation, like the line elevator, was financially dependent on Cargill's continual infusion of capital. The arrangement with Warren presented a convenient alternative to the establishment of a line elevator. Cargill became, in essence, the owner of the operation without the accompanying legal indicia.

The *amici curiae* assert that, if the jury verdict is upheld, firms and banks which have provided business loans to county elevators will decline to make further loans. The decision in this case should give no cause for such concern. We deal here with a business enterprise markedly different from an ordinary bank financing, since Cargill was an active participant in Warren's operations rather than simply a financier. Cargill's course of dealing with Warren was, by its own admission, a paternalistic relationship in which Cargill made the key economic decisions and kept Warren in existence.

Although considerable interest was paid by Warren on the loan, the reason for Cargill's financing of Warren was not to make money as a lender but, rather, to establish a source of market grain for its business. As one Cargill manager noted, "We were staying in there because we wanted the grain." For this reason, Cargill was willing to extend the credit line far beyond the amount originally allocated to Warren. It is noteworthy that Cargill was receiving significant amounts of grain and that, notwithstanding the risk that was recognized by Cargill, the operation was considered profitable.

---

[8]   In *Butler v. Bunge Corporation,* 329 F. Supp. 47 (N.D. Miss. 1971), the evidence revealed the following indicia of agency: (1) Bunge furnished all or practically all of the means and appliances for the work; (2) Bunge furnished substantially all funds received by Bayles; (3) Bunge controlled the destination of all grain handled by Bayles; (4) Bunge controlled the price, weights and grades of all grain handled by Bayles; (5) Bunge, on certain occasions, permitted Bayles to sell a limited quantity of grain to other buyers; (6) Bunge not only had the right to direct details important to grain buying but gave actual direction to Bayles through constant contact, quoting its price to him and consulting with him regarding prices for the farmers; (7) Bunge had a significant degree of control over the operation of the grain elevator at Roundaway in such areas as training Bayles' personnel, inspecting the premises and requiring maintenance of insurance against hazards of operation; (8) Bayles' grain transaction with farmers was the identical type of business activity that was regularly carried on by Bunge, and Bayles' transactions formed a substantial part of Bunge's business that was developed from the area in which Coahoma Grain Elevator operated; and finally (9) although the agreement formally specified a fixed term, the relationship between the parties had no viability apart from grain dealings that were wholly subject to Bunge's will. These findings make clear that Bunge did not consider Bayles an independent operator who was free to become Bunge's competitor in buying grain from the farmers in the region, but rather that he was effectually given authority to buy grain from Bunge. *Id.* at 61.

On the whole, there was a unique fabric in the relationship between Cargill and Warren which varies from that found in normal debtor-creditor situations. We conclude that, on the facts of this case, there was sufficient evidence from which the jury could find that Cargill was the principal of Warren within the definitions of agency set forth in Restatement (Second) of Agency §§ 1 and 140. * * *

Affirmed.

Notes and Questions

1.   **Control.** Should the control in *Cargill* have been deemed sufficient to establish agency for purposes of holding Cargill liable to the farmers who dealt with Warren? For criticism of *Cargill, see* Hynes, *Lender Liability: The Dilemma of the Controlling Creditor,* 58 TENN. L. REV. 635 (1991). In general, it is useful to distinguish the "negative" power to veto particular transactions and the "positive" power to dictate the details of the agent's business. Comment a to Restatement § 140, relied on by the court, says that a security holder becomes a principal when "he takes over the management of the debtor's business." Compare with *Cargill* the much more extensive control in *Butler* summarized in footnote 8 to the court's opinion. This distinction between positive and negative control is consistent with the reason why control is important for agency. The party who is making the basic decisions about running the business is normally the one who is in the best position to make cost-benefit decisions. One who has only a veto power has a only a sporadic opportunity to engage in this balancing process.

2.   **Benefit.** Did Warren act on behalf of Cargill? Although Cargill received grain for resale and interest and repayment on its loans, any commercial relationship produces benefits of this sort. The agency ingredient that is arguably missing is that Cargill did not share the *profits* from Warren's business. Thus, the court's rule would force Cargill to bear the costs but not the rewards of ownership. Recall the *amici curiae*'s contention that imposing liability will cause business lenders to decline to loan to county elevators. More broadly, imposing liability on lenders for business failures would, in effect, bar firms from borrowing money from those who do not want to become owners, which would increase firms' credit costs. Where, then, should the line be drawn? Should it be enough to satisfy the benefit test that Cargill was not only a substantial creditor but was also by far Warren's largest customer?

3.   **Negligent exercise of control.** Even a non-principal may be liable for negligence in exercising control over another. A prominent example is *Connor v. Great Western Savings and Loan Association,* 69 Cal. 2d 850, 447 P.2d 609, 73 Cal. Rptr. 369 (1969), in which a bank was held liable for negligence in financing a developer that had built faulty houses. Justice Traynor reasoned in part:

> Since the value of the security for the construction loans and thereafter the security for the permanent financing loans depended on the construction of sound homes, Great Western was clearly under a duty of care to its shareholders to exercise its powers of control over the enterprise to prevent the construction of defective homes. Judged by the standards governing nonsuits,

it negligently failed to discharge that duty. It knew or should have known that the developers were inexperienced, undercapitalized, and operating on a dangerously thin capitalization. It therefore knew or should have known that damage from attempts to cut corners in construction was a risk reasonably to be foreseen.

69 Cal. 2d at 864, 447 P.2d at 616, 73 Cal. Rptr. at 376. Does characterizing the issue as one of direct negligence eliminate the policy issue discussed in Note 2?

4.   **Apparent agency.** Restatement (Second) of Agency § 267 provides:

One who represents that another is his servant or other agent and thereby causes a third person justifiably to rely on the care or skill of such apparent agent is subject to liability to the third person for harm caused by the lack of care or skill of one appearing to be a servant or other agent as if he were such.

For a leading case on this theory, *see Gizzi v. Texaco*, 437 F.2d 308 (3d Cir. 1971). The related theory of agency by estoppel is discussed in Restatement (Second) of Agency, § 8B.

Problem

What would you have advised Cargill in the *Cargill* situation to do to minimize its risk of liability for Warren's debts?

2.03 Management Powers of Agent

Agents, including employees of sole proprietorships, may have significant management responsibilities. An agent's internal and external power to manage the principal's business may differ. Although the agent's internal power depends solely on her contract with the principal, externally this contractual power may be enlarged to meet a third party's expectations. An agent who acts beyond her internal authority but nevertheless binds the firm in a transaction with a third party may be liable to the principal (*see* § 2.03(a)).

The agent's power to bind the firm is based on her "authority." *See* Restatement (Second) of Agency § 7 (1965). The principal creates "actual" authority by manifesting to the agent the principal's consent to be bound by the agent's acts. *See id.* § 8. Real authority can be either *express* or *implied* from the course of dealings between the principal and agent. *Apparent authority* exists when the *principal's* acts create an appearance of authority from the perspective of third parties dealing with the agent whether or not the principal has consented to be bound by the agent's acts. *See id.* § 8A. *Inherent agency power* arises, among other ways, from the general power the principal has conferred on the agent. *Id.* § 8B.

The following cases illustrate these various types of authority and how they interrelate.

A.   Apparent and Actual Authority

Essco Geometric v. Harvard Industries
46 F.3d 718 (8th Cir. 1995)

BRIGHT, Senior Circuit Judge.

[Diversified Foam Products (Diversified), a materials supplier, sought damages from Harvard Industries, Inc. (Harvard), a manufacturer of office chairs, for, among other things, Harvard's failure to honor a written contract for materials. A jury awarded $400,000 on this contract. Harvard claims, among other things, that Diversified failed to make a submissible case that Harvard's purchasing agent, Michael Gray, had either actual or apparent authority to enter into this contract.] * * *

II. BACKGROUND

We present the relevant facts in the light most favorable to the nonmoving party, as is required in reviewing a denial of a motion for judgment as a matter of law. [citation omitted]

Harvard produces several products, but most importantly for purposes of this appeal, it manufactures chairs, and sells those chairs both to private and public entities. Diversified sells foam used in the chairs manufactured by Harvard. For over thirty years, Diversified supplied a large portion of Harvard's foam needs.

Prior to 1988, Harvard usually subcontracted with only two foam suppliers, Diversified being one of them.

To determine which companies would supply its foam, Harvard would issue bid requests to several potential suppliers, detailing Harvard's needs for a particular chair contract. The bids submitted did not contractually bind either party, but usually determined which two companies would have Harvard's business, what prices the suppliers would charge, and approximately the quantity sellers would deliver.

Once Harvard had locked-in its two suppliers for a given chair contract, it ordinarily issued cancelable purchase orders whenever it needed foam. The purchase orders contained standard terms and conditions, which stipulated that the agreement committed Harvard only to the quantities of foam found in that particular purchase order. Harvard's purchase orders always applied to a limited time period, usually requiring the supplier to deliver within a couple of weeks or months.

For over twenty years, Frank Best served as Harvard's purchasing manager. From the beginning of his tenure at Harvard, Best cultivated a close business relationship with Edsel Safron, the president of Diversified, ensuring a continuing business relationship between supplier and manufacturer. In 1987, it appeared that Harvard would win the 1988-1990 General Services Administration (GSA) "double shell" chair contract. Best again issued a request to Diversified for bids on Harvard's foam needs. After the bids came in and were reviewed, Harvard issued purchase orders to Diversified for some of the GSA chairs, but Harvard also issued purchase orders to American Excelsior and Dalco, foam suppliers in competition with Diversified.

In July 1988, Frank Best retired, and Michael Gray, the former purchasing agent, became the new purchasing manager for Harvard. JoAnn Ceresia became Harvard's new purchasing agent under Gray and became responsible for issuing purchase orders as Harvard's day-to-day needs demanded. In September 1988, Ed Kruske became Harvard's new president.

With this new management in place, Harvard began a program to cut costs and improve quality. This program became known as the "world class manufacturing plan." Pursuant to this plan, Harvard decided in late 1988 to offer Diversified, Dalco and American Excelsior each an opportunity to quote new prices for the remainder of Harvard's 1988-1990 GSA contract. Because American Excelsior quoted the lowest prices and because JoAnn Ceresia desired to diminish Harvard's perennial reliance on Diversified foam, American Excelsior became the primary supplier of Harvard's foam needs for the remainder of that contract. Diversified, however, did not receive another purchase order from Harvard for over a year.

When Diversified first learned that it no longer would supply foam for the GSA contract, Edsel Safron immediately contacted Harvard's new president, Ed Kruske, and claimed he had an oral agreement with Frank Best, guaranteeing Diversified 70% of the foam business. Kruske asked Safron whether Safron had anything in writing supporting his claim. Safron did not.

In the ensuing months, and throughout most of 1989, Harvard accelerated the implementation of its new world class manufacturing plan. Three aspects of that program are of particular note. First, Harvard had committed itself to reducing its vendor base and to working more closely with its foam suppliers so as to make the entire process of foam manufacturing and delivery more efficient. A principal part of this effort resulted in the collaboration of Harvard's and American Excelsior's engineering departments to consolidate and standardize foam parts.

A second dimension to the world class manufacturing plan was quality control. Under this part of the program, Harvard began gathering information on how each vendor manufactured its foam products and how each controlled the quality of the products produced. Throughout late 1989 and early 1990, Harvard visited several foam manufacturing plants, sent surveys out to its suppliers requesting information on their particular quality control measures, and met internally through a committee of Harvard managers to formulate a plan of quality control—which presumably would be imposed on their primary vendor.

In the fall of 1989, Ed Kruske implemented the third facet to Harvard's world class manufacturing plan. In an effort to cut costs, Kruske issued two internal memoranda. The first, issued on October 26, 1989, directed that all purchase orders (production and non-production) be initialed by Kruske prior to being sent out to a vendor. The second directive, issued on December 4, 1989, stipulated that all requisitions of fifty dollars or more have both the departmental manager's approval and Kruske's approval, unless an emergency arose. Michael Gray received both of these directives, but Harvard never notified anyone outside of the company that it had instituted these internal operating procedures.

At the same time that Harvard was implementing these reforms, it began requesting bids for its 1990-1992 GSA chair contract. JoAnn Ceresia was responsible for sending out the requests and sent them to Dalco and American Excelsior. She did not send one to Diversified, however. Michael Gray had elected not to participate in this bid request and did not know that Ceresia had not sent a request to Diversified.

When Edsel Safron learned that Harvard had cut Diversified out of the bidding process for this new GSA contract, he contacted Gray to discuss whether Diversified could get a chance to bid. Safron and Gray met four or five times in early September 1989. Ultimately, Gray allowed Safron to submit a bid for the 1990-1992 GSA contract, which he did on September 12th. Based on further discussion in late September and October, Gray orally agreed to give Diversified all of its foam business for the GSA contract, as well as all of its commercial contracts covering the same two-year period. At the time, Harvard's quality department had rejected hundreds of American Excelsior's foam products because of manu-facturing defects. Diversified, on the other hand, had never presented a "quality" problem, and its bids for the GSA contract were significantly lower than American Excelsior's. Gray had informed Kruske of Diversified's superiority, and believed Kruske would ultimately approve of his decision to make Diversified Harvard's primary vendor. Nevertheless, Kruske did not become aware of the agreement with Diversified until May 1990.

Pursuant to this oral agreement and mindful of Kruske's admonition that Harvard would only honor written contracts, Diversified's president Safron wrote and delivered a letter to Gray on January 9, 1990. The letter addressed to Harvard stated in part:

> We are with the understanding that our bids covers supplying the foam for the entire projectile 350,000 to 500,000 Double Shell office chairs as called for from 2/1/90 thru 1/31/92. Our pricing is to remain fixed throughout the stated time period. We are with the further understanding that Harvard would prefer that the firm enjoying the Lions share of its foam business also supply the foam on a contract by contract basis, for its other chairs, such as; Himco, Ergo, Commer-cials, wheel chairs, etc. In this regard, an agreement in principle exist[s] in which Diversified Foam Products will supply the foam for said chairs over the period of 2/1/90 thru 2/31/92 at fixed quoted prices. I trust you will find these understand-ings in keeping with our recent conversation. An extra copy of this letter is pro-vided for your signature and return.

Both Safron and Gray signified approval by each signing at the bottom of the letter. Both Safron and Gray testified at trial that they understood the letter to represent an exclusive multi-million dollar contract between Harvard and Diversified for all of Harvard's foam needs for all of its chairs for a two-year period.

Later Gray issued Diversified several purchase orders covering parts for the GSA con-tract. Although Gray made these requests on unofficial purchase order request forms, he later replaced them with standardized forms that circulated throughout Harvard's various departments. On January 12, 1990, three days after signing the letter, Gray took Kruske to visit both Diversified's and American Excelsior's plants to assess each company's quality control programs. On January 22, 1990, Harvard wrote its major suppliers requesting that they submit "quality program plans." The letter went to current and past (and potentially future) vendors.

In the ensuing months, Diversified received purchase orders for commercial and GSA contracts, delivered parts, and got paid. Additionally, representatives from Diversified periodically met with representatives from Harvard to discuss ways to render Diversified's foam delivery more efficient. Despite these ongoing relations between Diversified and Har-vard, Edsel Safron had become concerned by the receipt of what he believed was an abnor-mally low number of purchase orders. On April 3, 1990, Safron met with Gray to discuss his concerns. Gray explained that he was having some difficulties with his assistant JoAnn Cere-sia, who had been misdirecting purchase order requests away from Diversified and towards American Excelsior. On May 7, 1990, after again explaining to Kruske the problems Harvard was having with American Excelsior's quality and the better prices that Diversified offered, Gray directed Ceresia to issue all future purchase orders to Diversified. Additionally, Gray wrote a letter to American Excelsior, cancelling all of its orders.

Kruske within days thereafter put a hold on Gray's purchase orders to Diversified. Soon thereafter, American Excelsior submitted a new bid, unsolicited by Gray, that offered marginally lower prices than Diversified's on the 1990-1992 GSA contract. Three weeks later, Kruske decided to make American Excelsior Harvard's new principal supplier. This lawsuit followed. * * *

III. DISCUSSION

A. Submissibility on Actual or Apparent Authority

* * * [W]e conclude that the district court did not err in denying Harvard's motion for judgment as a matter of law.

1. Actual Authority

Under Missouri law, for an agent to have actual authority, he must establish that the principal has empowered him, either expressly or impliedly, to act on the principal's behalf. [citation omitted] The principal can expressly confer authority by telling his agent what to do or by knowingly acquiescing to the agent's actions. [citation omitted] Implied authority flows from express authority, and "encompasses the power to act in ways reasonably necessary to accomplish the purpose for which express authority was granted." [citation omitted] Missouri case law suggests that custom and the relations of the parties establish the parameters of implied actual authority. [citations omitted] Thus, evidence that an agent historically engaged in related conduct, without limitation, would be enough to support a jury question on the issue of actual authority.

a. Gray's Implied Authority

As an initial matter, both sides agree that no job description outlined the nature of Gray's responsibilities, let alone the scope of his authority. Despite the lack of express authority, however, other documentary evidence and testimonial evidence supports Diversified's claim. First, Gray's own testimony bore on his authority to bind Harvard to the January 9th agreement, and under Missouri law, this testimony alone is enough to make a submissible case. [citation omitted] On direct examination, Gray testified as follows:

> Q. And did you perceive and were you acting, signing this in your—as part of your job as a purchasing manager of Harvard?
> A. Yes. . . .
> Q. Did you believe Ed Kruske was in favor of your decision to go with Diversified as of January 1990?
> A. Yes. . . .
> Q. Did you have any doubt in your mind at all about your authority to sign that document?
> A. No.

Moreover, on re-direct, Gray testified that while the decision to enter the January 9th agreement with Diversified was risky, particularly in light of Kruske's management style, it was Gray's decision to make and Gray's risk to take as purchasing manager for the company.

Second, Gray's October 1989 performance evaluation establishes Harvard's express intention that Gray continue to take a more active role in managing his department and work on further reducing costs. Given the express nature of this evaluation, made only three months before Gray signed the January 9th letter, it would appear that Gray's negotiations with Diversified and the ultimate signing of the agreement furthered the company's objectives. Although not as explicit as a job description, the performance evaluation established enough express authority that a reasonable jury could conclude that Gray acted pursuant to it. * * *

A third evidentiary basis for Gray's actual authority is the custom and practice at Harvard and within the industry. Gray testified that he had observed for over fifteen or sixteen years Frank Best, Harvard's former purchasing manager, negotiate with vendors and ultimately select vendors who Best believed would benefit Harvard. Others similarly testified that purchasing managers within the industry customarily made unsupervised decisions as to who would be their company's suppliers.

Although an exclusive, non-cancelable requirements contract differs materially from a standard purchase order, the practical reality of Harvard's (and the rest of the industry's) GSA contracts suggests that when Harvard ultimately selects a vendor for its GSA contracts, that vendor will enjoy between 60% and 70% of Harvard's foam needs for the duration of the one or two year contract. To be sure, cancelable purchase orders constitute the daily and weekly routine, and usually Harvard will use more than one vendor. Nevertheless, cancellations have been few and far between, and with Harvard's new world class manufacturing plan, primary vendors have become exclusive vendors as Harvard seeks to cut down its vendor base. In fact, Brian McGuire, the St. Louis branch manager for American Excelsior, testified on cross-examination that American Excelsior was Harvard's exclusive foam supplier at the time of the trial.

Harvard maintains that its company's actions and its internal operating procedures in the weeks surrounding the signing of the January 9th letter negate any inference that Michael Gray had the authority to bind Harvard to an exclusive, non-cancelable requirements contract. We address these arguments.

b. Harvard's Express Limitations

As noted above, Harvard had never explicitly authorized Gray to bind the company to an exclusive, non-cancelable requirements contract. Harvard asserts that it had in fact explicitly limited, not impliedly expanded, that authority. Harvard bases this contention on two internal Harvard memoranda, issued months before January 9th, which stipulated that every purchase order and every requisition over fifty dollars required Ed Kruske's approval. Because the January 9th letter purportedly bound Harvard to millions of dollars of purchases and because the evidence unequivocally demonstrated that Gray never notified Kruske of the letter before signing it, Harvard contends that no one could reasonably believe that Gray had acted within the scope of his authority. Moreover, that Gray usually complied with Kruske's directives further suggests that when he did not comply, Gray knew he was acting beyond his authority.

To counteract Harvard's contention that Gray violated the very letter of Kruske's directives, Diversified paints a very different picture, suggesting that Gray had fully complied with the spirit of these mandates. According to Gray's own testimony, Kruske's directives were a mere formality. Kruske never refused to sign-off on a requisition or purchase order and the directives themselves did not explicitly limit Gray's authority to negotiate and enter into contracts. As for signing the January 9th agreement, Gray testified that he did not need Kruske's approval because Kruske would ultimately have to sign-off on purchase orders issued pursuant to the agreement.

Evidence about Harvard's world class manufacturing plan strongly suggested that Kruske had issued these directives because he wanted to cut costs and maintain high quality controls. A reasonable jury could thus conclude that Gray's decision to sign the letter fully comported with the purpose behind the directives. On January 9th, Diversified did have the cheapest prices and, if not the best quality foam, certainly foam of comparable quality to their competitors. Even Kruske, on cross-examination, acknowledged Diversified's superiority at the time.

Diversified also presented evidence which suggested that Gray's failure to have Kruske sign-off on the January 9th agreement was motivated not by a belief that he lacked the authority, but rather by problems he was having with Kruske's management style and with his assistant, JoAnn Ceresia. Marc Treppler, Harvard's former quality control manager, testified that Kruske would not give clear directions and would let his managers make decisions. Michael Gray testified that Kruske "could be led pretty easily." Meanwhile, JoAnn Ceresia admitted on cross-examination that she was having communication problems with Gray, her immediate supervisor, and was meeting regularly with Kruske to make her pitch for American Excelsior. The tension between Gray and Ceresia, the close working relationship between Ceresia and Kruske, and Kruske's pliability may explain why Gray chose to delay notifying Kruske of the January 9th agreement.

Gray ultimately believed that Kruske would agree to his decision to select Diversified. The price and the quality were right; it was just a matter of timing. The fact that Harvard repudiated Diversified's agreement, stopped issuing purchase orders to Diversified, and began issuing purchasing orders to American Excelsior—all less than a month after receiving a fractionally lower bid from American Excelsior—suggests that Harvard wanted the cheaper foam, not that it had no contract with Diversified.

In sum, the evidence regarding the limitations Harvard placed on Gray's authority and inferences therefrom are conflicting. Reasonable jurors could disagree in their interpretations of the nature of those limitations. Thus, the district court did not err in submitting the issue of Diversified's actual authority claim to the jury.

2. Apparent Authority

Under Missouri law, apparent authority is created by the conduct of the principal which causes a third person reasonably to believe that the purported agent has the authority to act for the principal, and to reasonably and in good faith rely on the authority held out by the principal. [citations omitted] An agent may have apparent authority to act even though as between himself and the principal, such authority has not been granted. [citation omitted] Apparent authority does not arise from the acts of the agent. [citation omitted]

There are essentially three ways to establish apparent authority. One way is by the principal expressly and directly telling a third person that a second person has authority to act on the principal's behalf. Missouri courts have also recognized two other methods of creating apparent authority—by prior acts and by position. * * * If a principal allows an agent to occupy a position which, according to the ordinary habits of people in the locality, trade or profession, carries a particular kind of authority, then anyone dealing with the agent is justified in inferring that the agent has such an authority. The principal may also create the appearance of authority by "prior acts." By allowing an agent to carry out prior similar transactions, a principal creates the appearance that the agent is authorized to carry out such acts subsequently. [citation omitted]

In the present case, a reasonable jury could conclude that Harvard created the appearance of authority through a combination of position and prior acts.

For over twenty years, Harvard had allowed its purchasing manager, Frank Best, to solicit bids from vendors, negotiate with vendors, and ultimately select vendors for Harvard's governmental and commercial contracts. For most of those years, Diversified provided a substantial amount of Harvard's foam needs. When Ed Kruske took over as president of Harvard and Michael Gray succeeded Best as Harvard's purchasing manager, no one ever advised Diversified that Harvard had instituted new internal operating procedures or that the purchasing manager would have less authority to negotiate on behalf of the company. Moreover, no one ever advised Diversified that Harvard would delay its vendor selection for the 1990-1992 GSA contract. The only information that Diversified did receive regarding a change in Harvard's method of operations was Ed Kruske's declaration in 1988 that Harvard would only honor written contracts.

Based on the prior relationship between Harvard and Diversified and other evidence, Diversified made out a submissible case of apparent authority. [citations omitted]

While Harvard's previous purchasing managers never before had entered an exclusive, non-cancelable requirements contract, and Diversified knew that Harvard had never before entered such a contract, several of Harvard's foam suppliers intimated that the industry custom presumed, without question, that the purchasing manager possessed the authority to bind the company. As to whether industry representatives would apply this same presumption to long-term, exclusive and non-cancelable requirements contracts, and not merely purchase orders, Safron testified that Diversified had entered exclusive oral agreements with some customers, covering all of their foam needs and further had received a single written purchase order with one company that extended over two years. As with actual authority, the evidence and inferences therefrom led to differing conclusions, and were matters for resolution by the jury.[2] * * *

IV. CONCLUSION

For the reasons stated above, we affirm. * * *

---

[2]   Harvard principally argues that Diversified should have been more suspicious of Gray's authority to negotiate such an agreement. Given the uniqueness of a long-range, exclusive and non-cancelable requirements contract, that Harvard visited Diversified's plant on January 12th to assess Diversified's quality control programs, and that Harvard sent Diversified a quality control survey on January 22nd, Diversified should have done more to investigate whether, in fact, Gray had the authority to sign the January 9th agreement. Missouri law, however, imposes no duty on a third party to investigate a purported agent's authority if "'a person of ordinary prudence, conversant with business usages and the nature of the particular business'" could reasonably believe that the agent had such authority. [citation omitted] Here, the jury could consider it reasonable for Edsel Safron and Diversified to have assumed that (1) Gray could speak for Harvard; (2) that the terms of the contract, while unusual, did require commitments that Diversified had had with other buyers; and (3) that the visit to Diversified's plant on January 12th and the receipt of the quality survey on January 22nd were simply part of Harvard's ongoing world class manufacturing plan, and designed to ensure that Diversified had the capability to handle the account.

Progress Printing Corporation v. Jane Byrne
Political Committee
235 Ill. App. 3d 292, 601 N.E.2d 1055, 176 Ill. Dec. 357 (1992)

Justice DiVITO delivered the opinion of the court:

In 1982-83, defendant Jane Byrne (the candidate), then mayor of Chicago, ran unsuccessfully in the Democratic mayoral primary election. Plaintiff Progress Printing Corporation (Progress) produced brochures and other materials for the campaign. Two years later, Progress filed this suit against the Jane Byrne Political Committee (the Committee) and the candidate (collectively, defendants), alleging joint and several liability for approximately $91,000 in unpaid campaign printing bills. * * * We affirm the judgment of the circuit court as to liability, but we remand for entry of an order with a lesser judgment amount. * * *

At trial, Stanley Gapshis (Stanley), chairman of Progress, testified that he met the candidate in front of her office at City Hall in November 1982, at which time she told him "you will have my campaign. * * * Mr. [William] Griffin will get in touch with you." Shortly thereafter, Griffin called Stanley and said "you have the Byrne campaign" and "you will get your copy from [Mary Elizabeth] Pitz." One week later, Stanley went to Pitz's office at her request. There, Pitz told him she would be "handling all the artwork and copy for the campaign." During the campaign, the general practice was that someone from Progress would pick up the artwork from Pitz along with a purchase order. Progress then would produce the order and deliver it to one of the campaign headquarters or a campaign worker would pick it up. Shortly after completion of each printing job, Progress prepared an invoice, which described the items printed and the quantity . . . .

On cross-examination, Stanley admitted that other than Pitz, neither Griffin nor the candidate had even mentioned the names of the people who had ordered materials, much less told him that they were authorized to do so. Stanley was unable to identify who had placed some orders or who had taken delivery of others because a number of the orders at issue had incomplete job tickets or were lacking purchase orders or delivery forms. * * *

Defendants began presentation of their case by calling Wanda Smolinski, who had served as the candidate's personal secretary at City Hall and, as such, received all visitors and telephone calls. She did not recall Pitz coming to more than one campaign staff meeting there and stated that in November 1982, the candidate had told Griffin to fire Pitz for "very unprofessional work." Kathy Byrne (Kathy), the candidate's daughter, testified that she met Pitz at a meeting at City Hall in November 1982 at which her mother and Griffin, among others, were present. She recalled only one other encounter with Pitz, which occurred at the main campaign headquarters where Kathy worked. Thomas Geary, the candidate's director of personnel, also testified. He remembered Pitz attending campaign staff meetings "once or twice, . . . no more than a handful," all of which were early in the campaign.

* * * [T]he candidate [testified that] [s]he herself placed no printing orders, and she had not given authority to anyone . . . to order printed materials. * * *

According to the candidate, after campaign staff meetings, which she did not attend, she would pre-approve printing jobs for known costs on the basis of the staff's recommendations. She acknowledged that she had approved some of the orders and that she signed Committee checks to Progress, but she denied having seen the bills for them, stating that she had rarely read bills for checks she signed because she did not have the time. * * *

On cross-examination, the candidate testified that she "certainly was in charge of the campaign" and that "as far as who has authority to do what in a campaign, [she] ha[d] the final word." * * *

In Progress's rebuttal case, Stanley . . . stated that he had provided printing for hundreds of political candidates for 50 years, starting with Mayor Kennelly, and that the custom and practice in Chicago mayoral campaigns was never to contact the candidate. * * *

II.

The circuit court found that all those who placed the orders had apparent or actual authority, and additionally that all of the orders were ratified. Defendants insist that even if the evidence discussed above were admissible, the burden of proof here was on Progress to establish authorization or ratification, not on them to refute it, and Progress failed to present sufficient proof that the unpaid orders were authorized. * * *

A.

Defendants point to Stanley's testimony of the sole conversation between the candidate and Stanley, in which he testified that she mentioned only Griffin's name when she told him Progress would do the campaign printing work, as proof that only Griffin had authority to place printing orders. An agent's authority must be based on the acts of a principal, they observe, and Progress presented no evidence whatsoever that the candidate gave such authority to anyone other than Griffin, who placed none of the orders. Moreover, they argue, Progress presented no evidence that Griffin had been authorized to delegate his authority to anyone, including Pitz or Roque. Thus, they reason, because Progress had been told only of Griffin's authority, it had a duty to ascertain the scope of authority for anyone else submitting an order; not having done so, in their view, Progress filled the orders at its peril.

Defendants' argument is predicated on its assumption that the lack of express authority from the candidate to place printing orders is dispositive. * * *

For the orders placed by Pitz and Roque, application of the doctrine of apparent authority controls. Even if we were to agree that Progress initially acted at its peril in filling orders placed by anyone other than Griffin, the person Progress had been told would oversee the account, having received payment expressly for orders placed by these two, Progress's belief that they had been authorized in some way to place orders became reasonable because . . . when the Committee reimbursed Progress for Pitz's and Roque's orders, it "create[d], through words or conduct, the reasonable impression that [Pitz and Roque] ha[d] been granted authority" to place similar orders. [citation omitted] * * * Without notice from their principal that these two lacked such authority, Progress had no duty to verify their authorization for subsequent orders of a similar nature. As a result, "having created the appearance of authority, [defendants are] estopped to deny it to the detriment of a third party," in this case, Progress. Thus, the circuit court's ruling that Pitz and Roque had apparent authority to place orders was not against the manifest weight of the evidence.

Similarly, the Committee may be held liable for the [orders placed by campaign workers or unidentified people] despite defendants' contention that acknowledgement of contractual obligations incurred by one purported agent will not excuse a lack of reasonable diligence in ascertaining the scope of another purported agent's authority. By not communicating to Progress that only particular persons had authority to place orders or that expenses had to be within certain limits, and then making a $50,000 lump sum payment for orders placed by a number of campaign workers in addition to Pitz and Roque, the Committee fostered a reasonable belief that campaign workers were authorized to place printing orders for campaign materials in reasonable amounts. Although we agree with defendants that third parties have a duty to verify an agent's authorization to enter contracts on behalf of its principal, the duty is one of reasonable diligence. Under the circumstances here, when every order was for the campaign and each order was placed, accepted, and used by campaign workers, when the turnaround time for the orders was often short, and when Stanley's unrebutted testimony was that it was customary not to contact a candidate directly, Progress committed no breach of duty in not inquiring further. Too, a third party's duty in this regard does not obviate a principal's own duty to third parties, which is to exercise reasonable diligence in monitoring its agents' activities so that they are not exceeding their authority, particularly when the information is as readily available as it was here. Were the circumstances different, if for example a campaign worker had placed an order that a vendor, in the exercise of reasonable prudence, should have suspected was for the worker's own benefit rather than the principal's, we would expect a higher level of scrutiny by the vendor. [citation omitted] That, however, is not the case here, where the orders by their nature were exclusively for the benefit of the candidate and were placed and accepted only by campaign workers. Consequently, the circuit court's finding that under the circumstances here, the orders in [this group] also were apparently authorized was not against the manifest weight of the evidence.

B.

The circuit court found alternatively that the orders had been ratified because they had been used without objection even though Griffin had the opportunity to repudiate the orders after he received the invoices within a few days of each order. Defendants contend that Progress did not meet its burden of proof on the issue of ratification of the unpaid orders because not only did Progress fail to present evidence that the candidate actually knew about each of the unpaid orders before the election, but the evidence is otherwise. * * *

Ratification is the equivalent of authorization, but it occurs after the fact, when a principal gains knowledge of an unauthorized transaction but then retains the benefits or otherwise takes a position inconsistent with nonaffirmation. [citations omitted] As with their objection to the Pitz and Roque orders, the essence of defendants' argument is the lack of evidence of express ratification by the candidate. Like authority, however, ratification need not be express; it may be inferred from surrounding circumstances, including long-term acquiescence, after notice, to the benefits of an unauthorized transaction. [citations omitted] Of significance here, although normally a principal's actual knowledge of the transaction is essential, "one whose ignorance or mistake was the result of gross or culpable negligence in failing to learn the facts will be estopped as if he had full knowledge of the facts." [citation omitted]

In her conversation with Stanley, the candidate indicated that Griffin was the person in charge of the printing arrangements. It was to Griffin that Progress sent its invoices. Thus Griffin was in the best position to discover any impropriety promptly, given that the invoices detailed the content and size of each order and thus contained sufficient information to permit repudiation even though they lacked the name of the orderer. Griffin, however, by his own admission rarely even opened the invoices and reviewed none of them. Any lack of actual knowledge of the unauthorized orders is therefore the result of his breach of the duty to gain knowledge of the transactions by simply reviewing the invoices, a breach that has the same legal effect as actual knowledge of the facts and which may be imputed to his principal. In addition, the benefits of the transactions were retained in that the campaign staff accepted the materials, which were then used without question. Thus, the circuit court's decision that the unpaid orders were ratified was not against the manifest weight of the evidence because the evidence demonstrated that defendants' designated agent had the opportunity to repudiate the orders and that defendants "took a position inconsistent with nonaffirmation" by accepting and using the products of those transactions without objection. To hold otherwise would permit a principal to foist liability onto third parties on the basis of its lack of actual knowledge of an unauthorized transaction even when its ignorance of the facts is the direct result of its expressly designated agent's neglect. * * *

For the reasons stated above, we affirm the circuit court's judgment on defendants' liability, but we vacate the judgment as to its amount and remand for entry of a judgment against defendants jointly and severally in the amount of $74,494.56.

Notes and Questions

1. **Policy basis of apparent authority.** Why should a principal ever be liable for a contract by an agent that is outside the agent's actual authority—that is, where the principal did not consent to being bound? Consider the effects of two types of extreme rules: (1) the principal is liable for all acts of agents, whether or not authorized; and (2) the principal is liable only for expressly authorized transactions. Either rule would deter the valuable use of agents by making principals wary of using agents or third parties wary of relying on them. For example, storekeepers would have to mind the counter themselves rather than attending to other work. Business people would want to try to capture some of the value of delegating responsibility by contracting out of rules that make using agents too onerous. If the legal rule always imposed liability on the principal, the principal would contract with third parties, possibly with some sort of a payment, to avoid liability in certain situations. Conversely, if the legal rule always put the risk of unauthorized transactions on third parties, principals might contract with third parties for a more moderate rule to encourage third parties to deal through agents. But these contracts are costly to negotiate and write. The law of agency can be viewed as a way to minimize these costs by providing the rules that most parties would contract for—a kind of "hypothetical bargain." The hypothetical bargain applied by agency law is to impose the risk of loss on the party who could most cheaply have prevented the agent from departing from the principal's will. This can be referred to as a "least cost avoider" approach. If the transaction looked to the third party like one the principal could not have agreed to, as where it benefits only the agent, the third party is the least cost avoider and the transaction should be not be enforceable against the principal. The principal, however, is often the least cost avoider because there is so much she could have done to control agents' errors through better monitoring, instructions, and selection of the agent. In such cases the law should bind the principal even if the agent departed from instructions. How well does this "least cost avoider" analysis explain the cases and rules in this section?

2.   **Implied vs. apparent authority.** Can you distinguish these concepts as applied in *Essco*? What differences in the facts would lead to different results on each theory?

3.   **Estoppel.** Like restitution and ratification discussed in the following notes, estoppel permits third parties to recover from principals as a result of *unauthorized* agent transactions or acts. Estoppel involves a principal's carelessly letting a third party rely to its detriment on the *agent's* assertion of authority (Restatement (Second) of Agency, § 8B). Unlike apparent authority, estoppel does not depend on the *principal's* having created an appearance of authority.

4.   **Restitution** involves recovery for a benefit a third party has conferred on the principal for which the principal should be required to pay (*id.* § 8C).

5.   **Ratification** occurs by the principal's "affirmance" of an earlier unauthorized act (*id.* § 82). This includes any conduct manifesting consent to be bound by the transaction (Restatement § 93). A principal may be held responsible for an unauthorized transaction by, for example, failing to say anything about it under circumstances in which silence may be interpreted as consent, even though the third party did not rely on the consent (or, indeed, even know about it) and did not confer a benefit on the principal. The Restatement provides "the best defense of ratification is pragmatic; that it is needed in the prosecution of business. It operates normally to cure minor defects in an agent's authority, minimizing technical defenses and preventing unnecessary law suits" (*Id.* § 82, comment d). Are you satisfied with this rationale?

6.   **Sorting out the theories.** Which of the above theories were involved in *Progress*? What would the result have been if the brochures were not used in the campaign, but rather had been delivered to campaign workers who used them as wallpaper in their apartments? What if the brochures had been used in the campaign, but Griffin had promptly objected to them after receiving them?

B.   Inherent Authority

Kidd v. Thomas A. Edison, Inc.
239 F. 405 (S.D.N.Y. 1917), *aff'd*, 242 F. 923 (2d Cir. 1917)

This is a motion by the defendant to set aside a verdict for the plaintiff on exceptions. The action was in contract, and depended upon the authority of one Fuller to make a contract with the plaintiff, engaging her without condition to sing for the defendant in a series of 'tone test' recitals, designed to show the accuracy with which her voice was reproduced by the defendant's records. The defendant contended that Fuller's only authority was to engage the plaintiff for such recitals as he could later persuade dealers in the records to book her for all over the United States. The dealers, the defendant said, were to agree to pay her for the recitals, and the defendant would then guarantee her the dealers' performance. The plaintiff said the contract was an unconditional engagement for a singing tour, and the jury so found.

The sole exception of consequence was whether there was either any question of fact involved in Fuller's authority, or a fortiori whether there was no evidence of any authority. In either event the charge was erroneous, and the defendant's exception was good. The pertinent testimony was that of Maxwell, and was as follows: He intrusted to Fuller particularly the matters connected with the arranging of these 'tone test' recitals. He told him to learn from the artists what fees they would expect, and to tell them that the defendant would pay the rail-road fares and expenses. He also told Fuller to explain to them that the defendant would book them, and act as booking agent for them, and would see that the money was paid by the deal-ers; in fact, the defendant would itself pay it. He told him to prepare a form of contract suit-able for such an arrangement with such artists as he succeeded in getting to go into it, and that he (Maxwell) would prepare a form of booking contract with the dealers. He told him to pre-pare a written contract with the artists and submit it to him (Maxwell), which he did. He told him that he was himself to make the contracts with the artists by which they were to be booked, that he was not to bring them to him (Maxwell), but that he should learn what fees they would demand, and then confirm the oral agreement by a letter, which would serve as a contract.

This is all the relevant testimony.

LEARNED HAND, District Judge (after stating the facts as above).

The point involved is the scope of Fuller's 'apparent authority,' as distinct from the actual authority limited by the instructions which Maxwell gave him. The phrase 'apparent authority,' though it occurs repeatedly in the Reports, has been often criticized (MECHEM, LAW OF AGENCY, Secs. 720-726), and its use is by no means free from ambiguity. The scope of any authority must, of course, in the first place, be measured, not alone by the words in which it is created, but by the whole setting in which those words are used, including the customary powers of such agents. [citations omitted] This is, however, no more than to regard the whole of the communication between the principal and agent before assigning its meaning, and does not differ in method from any other interpretation of verbal acts. In considering what was Fuller's actual implied authority by custom, while it is fair to remember that the 'tone test' recitals were new, in the sense that no one had ever before employed singers for just this pur-pose of comparing their voices with their mechanical reproduction, they were not new merely as musical recitals; for it was, of course, a common thing to engage singers for such recitals.

When, therefore, an agent is selected, as was Fuller, to engage singers for musical recitals, the customary implication would seem to have been that his authority was without limitation of the kind here imposed, which was unheard of in the circumstances. The mere fact that the purpose of the recitals was advertisement, instead of entrance fees, gave no intimation to a singer dealing with him that the defendant's promise would be conditional upon so unusual a condition as that actually imposed. Being concerned to sell its records, the venture might rightly be regarded as undertaken on its own account, and, like similar enterprises, at its own cost. The natural surmise would certainly be that such an undertaking was a part of the advertising expenses of the business, and that therefore Fuller might engage singers upon similar terms to those upon which singers for recitals are generally engaged, where the manager expects a profit, direct or indirect.

Therefore it is enough for the decision to say that the customary extent of such an authority as was actually conferred comprised such a contract. If estoppel be, therefore, the basis of all 'apparent authority,' it existed here. Yet the argument involves a misunderstanding of the true significance of the doctrine, both historically (*Responsibility for Tortious Acts: Its History,* Wigmore, 7 HARV. L. REV. 315, 383) and actually. The responsibility of a master for his servant's act is not at bottom a matter of consent to the express act, or of an estoppel to deny that consent, but it is a survival from ideas of status, and the imputed responsibility congenial to earlier times, preserved now from motives of policy. While we have substituted for the archaic status a test based upon consent, *i.e.,* the general scope of the business, within that sphere the master is held by principles quite independent of his actual consent, and indeed in the face of his own instructions. * * * It is only a fiction to say that the principal is estopped, when he has not communicated with the third person and thus misled him. There are, indeed, the cases of customary authority, which perhaps come within the range of a true estoppel; but in other cases the principal may properly say that the authority which he delegated must be judged by his directions, taken together, and that it is unfair to charge him with misleading the public, because his agent, in executing that authority, has neither observed, nor communicated, an important part of them. Certainly it begs the question to assume that the principal has authorized his agent to communicate a part of his authority and not to disclose the rest. Hence, even in contract, there are many cases in which the principle of estoppel is a factitious effort to impose the rationale of a later time upon archaic ideas, which, it is true, owe their survival to convenience, but to a very different from [sic] the putative convenience attributed to them.

However it may be of contracts, all color of plausibility falls away in the case of torts, where indeed the doctrine first arose, and where it still thrives. It makes no difference that the agent may be disregarding his principal's directions, secret or otherwise, so long as he continues in that larger field measured by the general scope of the business intrusted to his care. [citations omitted]

The considerations which have made the rule survive are apparent. If a man select another to act for him with some discretion, he has by that fact vouched to some extent for his reliability. While it may not be fair to impose upon him the results of a total departure from the general subject of his confidence, the detailed execution of his mandate stands on a different footing. The very purpose of delegated authority is to avoid constant recourse by third persons to the principal, which would be a corollary of denying the agent any latitude beyond his exact instructions. Once a third person has assured himself widely of the character of the agent's mandate, the very purpose of the relation demands the possibility of the principal's being bound through the agent's minor deviations. Thus, as so often happens, archaic ideas continue to serve good, though novel, purposes.

In the case at bar there was no question of fact for the jury touching the scope of Fuller's authority. His general business covered the whole tone test recitals; upon him was charged the duty of doing everything necessary in the premises, without recourse to Maxwell or any one else. It would certainly have been quite contrary to the expectations of the defendant, if any of the prospective performers at the recitals had insisted upon verifying directly with Maxwell the terms of her contract. It was precisely to delegate such negotiations to a competent substitute that they chose Fuller at all.

The exception is without merit; the motion is denied.

Notes and Questions

Apparent vs. inherent authority. Under Judge Hand's reasoning. when might there be inherent authority but not apparent or actual authority? Consider Judge Easterbrook, concurring in *Cange v. Stotler & Co.,* 826 F.2d 581, 598 (7th Cir. 1987):

> I do not understand my colleagues to add, to the categories of actual and apparent authority, the new brand of "inherent" authority. If a limit known to third parties confines the agent's actual authority, then there is also no authority at all. The third party (here, Cange) cannot get around this actual, known limitation by appealing to "inherent" authority. Neither agents nor third parties may engage in such bootstrapping.

Inherent authority as articulated in *Kidd* may be limited to situations in which the principal has given a managerial agent broad power to run the business and communicated no limit on authority to third parties. But wouldn't the principal's act of placing the agent in a managerial position also be *apparent* authority? Is it useful for courts to describe a subclass of apparent authority cases dealing with broadly authorized agents?

C.   Undisclosed Principals

Sometimes the principal is in the background, unknown to third parties who deal with the agent. That might be because the principal does not know it is one. *See Cargill,* § 2.02 (in which even Cargill did not know that it was a "principal"). Or, perhaps, the principal knows about its status but has its own reasons for refusing to come forward—as in the Martin Scorsese movie "Casino," where the mob "back home" was the silent partner in the Las Vegas casino. Should third parties who deal with the agent be able to recover from a party on whom they never relied in extending credit? Consider the following case.

Morris Oil Company, Inc. v. Rainbow Oilfield Trucking, Inc.
106 N.M. 237, 741 P.2d 840 (1987)

GARCIA, Judge.

* * * Defendant Dawn appeals from the judgment rendered against it in favor of Morris Oil Company, Inc. (Morris), based upon a determination that Rainbow Oilfield Trucking, Inc. (Rainbow) was Dawn's agent when it incurred indebtedness with Morris. We affirm the trial court.

FACTS

Appellant Dawn, the holder of a certificate of public convenience and necessity, is engaged in the oilfield trucking business in the Farmington area. Rainbow was a New Mexico corporation established for the purpose of operating an oilfield trucking business in the Hobbs area. Defendant corporations entered into several contracts whereby Rainbow would be permitted to use Dawn's certificate of public convenience and necessity in operating a trucking enterprise in Hobbs. Dawn reserved the right to full and complete control over the operations of Rainbow in New Mexico. Dawn was to collect all charges due and owing for transportation conducted by Rainbow and, after deducting a $1,000 per month "clerical fee" and a percentage of the gross receipts, was to remit the balance to Rainbow. Under a subcontract entered into by defendants, Rainbow was to be responsible for payment of operating expenses, including fuel; further, the subcontract provides that all operations utilizing fuel were to be under the direct control and supervision of Dawn. All billing for services rendered by Rainbow would be made under Dawn's name, with all monies to be collected by Dawn.

Defendants also entered into a terminal management agreement which provided that Dawn was to have complete control over Rainbow's Hobbs operation. The agreement further recited that Rainbow was not to become the agent of Dawn and was not empowered to incur or create any debt or liability of Dawn "other than in the ordinary course of business relative to terminal management." The agreement recited that Rainbow was to be an independent contractor and not an employee, and that liability on the part of Rainbow for creating charges in violation of the agreement would survive the termination of the agreement. Dawn was to notify Rainbow of any claim of such charges whereby Rainbow would assume the defense, compromise or payment of such claims.

Rainbow operated the oilfield trucking enterprise under these contractual documents, during which time Rainbow established a relationship with plaintiff Morris, whereby Morris installed a bulk dispenser at the Rainbow terminal and periodically delivered diesel fuel for use in the trucking operation. The enterprise proved unprofitable, however, and Rainbow ceased its operations and ultimately declared bankruptcy, owing Morris approximately $25,000 on an open account.

When Morris began its collection efforts against Rainbow, it determined that Rainbow had ceased its operations, everyone associated with Rainbow had moved back to Texas and it did not appear likely that the account would be paid. Morris was directed by Rainbow's representative in Texas to Dawn for payment of the account.

When Rainbow ceased its operations, Dawn was holding some $73,000 in receipts from the Hobbs operation. Dawn established an escrow account through its Roswell attorneys to settle claims arising from Rainbow's Hobbs operation. When Morris contacted Dawn with regard to the outstanding account, it was notified of the existence of the escrow account and was asked to forbear upon collection efforts, indicating that payment would be forthcoming from the escrow account. Dawn's representatives indicated that it was necessary to wait for authorization from Rainbow's parent Texas corporation before paying the account. At no time did Rainbow or Dawn question the amount or legitimacy of Morris' open account balance.

Dawn's principal further testified that the subcontract and terminal management agreement were cancelled by Dawn when he learned that Rainbow was incurring debts in Dawn's name. The charges owing to Morris, however, were incurred in the name of Rainbow and not Dawn.

Although some claims were paid from the attorneys' escrow account established by Dawn, there was no explanation at trial why the Morris claim was not paid. When Morris learned that the escrow funds had been disbursed without payment of its charges, it instituted this action and also sought to garnish the remaining $13,000 held by Dawn from the impounded funds. Rainbow did not defend, and the trial court entered a default judgment against Rainbow, from which it does not appeal.

DISCUSSION

* * * Dawn urges one point of error on appeal; that the trial court erred in finding liability based on a principal-agent relationship between the defendants. Dawn relies upon the language in the terminal management agreement which states:

4. Rainbow is not appointed and shall not become the agent of Dawn and is not empowered to incur or create any debt or liability of Dawn other than in the ordinary course of business relative to terminal management. Rainbow shall not enter into or cause Dawn to become a party to any agreement without the express written consent of Dawn.

5. Rainbow shall be considered an independent contractor and not an employee of Dawn.

Dawn's reliance upon these paragraphs of the agreement is unpersuasive for two reasons. First, the agreement specifically states that Rainbow may create liabilities of Dawn in the ordinary course of business of operating the terminal. There is no question that the liability to Morris was incurred in the ordinary course of operating the trucking business. Second, the recitation of the parties in their contractual documents need not bind third parties who deal with one of them in ignorance of those instructions. [citations omitted]

While Dawn argues from cases discussing apparent authority, we view this as a case of undisclosed agency. Rainbow contracted in its own name and not in the name of Dawn Enterprises, Inc. Thus, this case involves concepts relating to undisclosed agency rather than to apparent authority, and is governed by principles of undisclosed principal-agent contracts. [citation omitted]

It is well established that an agent for an undisclosed principal subjects the principal to liability for acts done on his account if they are usual or necessary in such transactions. Restatement (Second) of Agency § 194 (1958). This is true even if the principal has previously forbidden the agent to incur such debts so long as the transaction is in the usual course of business engaged in by the agent. *Id.*

The indebtedness in the instant case is squarely governed by well-established principles of agency where an undisclosed principal entrusts the agent with the management of his business. The undisclosed principal is subject to liability to third parties with whom the agent contracts where such transactions are usual in the business conducted by the agent, even if the contract is contrary to the express directions of the principal. Restatement (Second) of Agency § 195 (1958). * * *

Morris correctly observes that secret instructions or limitations placed upon the authority of an agent must be known to the party dealing with the agent, or the principal is bound as if the limitations had not been made. [citation omitted]

Dawn argues that Morris had constructive notice of the alleged limitations because the subcontract between the defendants was filed with the Corporation Commission. The filing of the subcontract does not constitute constructive notice to all third parties of an alleged limitation on an agent's authority. * * * The mere filing of a document with a public office does not constitute constructive notice of the contents of the document to the public unless the person to be charged with notice should reasonably anticipate that the information will be contained in the documents filed. [citation omitted]

Finally, Dawn asserts that Morris has made an election to hold Rainbow liable as the agent, and has taken judgment against it. Dawn argues that because Morris has made this election, it cannot now hold Dawn liable.

In *Amortibanc Inv. Co. v. Rampart Associated Management, Inc.,* 6 Kan. App. 2d 227, 231, 627 P.2d 389, 394 (1981), the Kansas appellate court succinctly explained the law in this area:

(1) Where a third party enters into a contract with an agent for an undisclosed principal, the third party, upon discovery of the agency, may bring action against both principal and agent.

(2) Once the agency has been established, either by admission or by evidence, the third party may be required to elect whether to proceed against the principal or the agent.

(3) The right to compel an election belongs to the principal and the agent, though the right to make an election belongs to the third party.

(4) If no motion to compel an election is made in the trial court before judgment is entered against either principal or agent, then the matter of election is waived.

(5) A judgment on a single contract, entered against both principal and agent, will support but a single recovery. In other words, satisfaction of the judgment by either principal or agent extinguishes the judgment against the other.

In this case, Dawn did not assert the right to compel an election at trial. For this reason, we consider any right was waived. [citation omitted] Additionally, we think it consequential that Dawn was in possession of the proceeds owing to Rainbow. Dawn was the entity making the decisions as to which creditors would be paid. While there were apparently sufficient funds to pay the amount owed to Morris on Rainbow's open account among Rainbow's proceeds, Dawn chose not to pay Morris, and in fact, to deduct some $25,000 of the proceeds as its own "clerical fee." In light of Dawn's control over Rainbow's proceeds, we decline to recognize Dawn's right to compel an election in this matter.

Moreover, assuming arguendo that Dawn was not responsible for the indebtedness to Morris for the reasons urged on appeal, it is clear that Dawn ratified the open account after learning of its existence when Morris contacted Dawn regarding payment. A principal may be held liable for the unauthorized acts of his agent if the principal ratifies the transaction after acquiring knowledge of the material facts concerning the transaction. [citation omitted]

It was undisputed that in several telephone conversations between the principals of Dawn and Morris, the material facts of the Morris open account were disclosed to Dawn. At no time did Dawn dispute the legitimacy or amount of the open account, and indeed assured Morris that payment would be forthcoming from the funds retained from Rainbow's revenues. Despite this, Dawn used the fund to pay itself a $1,000 per month clerical fee, to pay legal fees incurred as a result of its agency with Rainbow and to settle other claims arising from the Rainbow operations. Where the principal retains the benefits or proceeds of its business relations with an agent with knowledge of the material facts, the principal is deemed to have ratified the methods employed by the agent in generating the proceeds. [citations] The diesel fuel provided by Morris was used in Rainbow's trucking operation. Dawn collected the receipts due to Rainbow. Dawn seeks to retain the benefits of the agency with Rainbow, and yet at the same time disclaims responsibility for the business of the agent by which the benefits were generated. This it cannot do. [citation omitted]

In sum, for the foregoing reasons, we affirm.

Notes and Questions

1.   **The *Watteau* case.** An early leading case on undisclosed agency was *Watteau v. Fenwick,* 1 Q.B. 346 (1892). The "agent," Humble, had transferred to the defendant brewery firm a business he had carried on at the Victoria Hotel, after which Humble remained as defendants' manager. Humble's name was on the license and the door. Under his agreement with defendants, Humble lacked authority to buy any goods except bottled ales and mineral waters. Plaintiff was allowed to recover from defendant on cigars, bovril and other articles plaintiff sold only on Humble's credit.

2.   **A policy basis for liability.** Why hold the undisclosed principal liable even for *unauthorized* transactions? The basis of liability might be ratification or restitution, discussed in Notes 4-5 on p. 30. [Does the last part of the *Morris* opinion deal with ratification, as the court says, or does it more accurately deal with restitution of amounts improperly retained by Dawn?] Even if none of these theories is available, liability still might be justified on the theory that the principal is the least cost avoider. The third party may misjudge the credit risk because she mistakenly believes that the "agent" actually owns substantial business assets. Although perhaps the third party should have investigated further, it may not be clear when further investigation is necessary. The principal, on the other hand, knows that the agent is not really a proprietor and is in a good position to clarify the situation for the third party. Would this explain liability in *Morris?*

3.   **A counterargument.** Undisclosed principal liability thwarts the actual deal the parties have made for the third party to rely solely on the agent's credit. This actual

deal indicates that it was worth it to principals like Dawn to have third parties like Morris bear the cost of the Rainbow's credit risk—*i.e.*, that the third party, not the principal, was the least cost avoider. Moreover, the principal's disclosure costs may not be trivial. Parties like Dawn presumably could avoid liability only by disclosing to all third parties both their own non-liability and the agent's true capitalization. In *Morris*, simply filing the agreement with the Commission such communication did not accomplish this. Also, disclosure is not an answer for principals who for some reason want to keep secret their ownership.

4.   **Election and waiver.** An agent for an undisclosed principal is liable on the contract, consistently with the third party's expectations. *See* Restatement (Second) of Agency, § 322. As discussed in *Morris,* the plaintiff must *elect* remedies, and cannot proceed to judgment against both the agent and principal. *See id.* § 186. This rule arguably reflects some uneasiness with allowing the plaintiff to obtain recovery against the principal. The rule also may be based on the wasted litigation costs of circular action. A principal who is held liable can sue the agent for acting beyond his authority. If the third party was willing to pursue the agent, this suggests the agent was solvent and would ultimately bear the liability. Note, though, that the principal may *waive* the right to force an election by failing to raise the point. This may be based on the need to clarify whether the third party has made an election. Alternatively, the principal's failure to force an election may be a sort of ratification of the agent's act.

5.   **Partially disclosed principals.** If a third party has notice that an agent is or may be acting for a principal, but not of the principal's identity, the principal is "partially disclosed" as defined in Restatement § 4(2). The partially disclosed principal and the agent are both parties to the contract (*see* Restatement §§ 147 and 321). Does this meet the expectations of the agent, principal and third party? Apart from actual expectations, can you think of policy reasons for these rules?

Problem

Allen had long worked as a salesman in a jewelry store and wanted to go into business for himself. However, since he had few personal assets, he could not obtain the necessary financing. Allen's brother-in-law Peter decided to give Allen a chance. Peter advanced Allen enough money to buy inventory for and to operate a jewelry store, named Topkapi Jewelry, and permitted Allen to operate the store in a building owned by Peter. Allen agreed to work initially for a small salary and to pay to Peter the remaining net income of the store (*i.e.,* income remaining after payment of expenses and an additional amount representing rent on the store) until Allen repaid Peter's advance with 5% per year interest. After repayment, Peter was to be paid a fixed amount per month as rent for the store space. Allen dealt alone with wholesale suppliers and retail customers, but was to confer with Peter before making any purchase or sale over $2,000. Allen signed all receipts and checks on behalf of Topkapi Jewelry and obtained sufficient funds from

Peter to cover payments for jewelry. Allen signed and filed in the appropriate state office an "assumed name" certificate stating that Allen owned "Topkapi Jewelry."

During its first few months of business, Topkapi steadily lost money and Allen became disconsolate, believing his one big chance to be an independent business person was slipping away. Allen decided that it takes money to make money, and began purchasing jewels on credit in the over $2,000 range without conferring with Peter. These items moved no faster than the less expensive jewelry. Allen decided to abscond to Brazil with one of these items, a $10,000 platinum, diamond, ruby, gold and silver wedding ring, leaving Peter to pick up the pieces and ponder his sister's taste in men.

A jewelry wholesaler who sold the $10,000 ring to Allen on credit sues Peter to recover payment. The wholesaler had always dealt only with Allen and was unaware of Peter's existence. Allen's other purchases from this wholesaler were for less than $2,000 and had been billed and paid for before sale of the $10,000 ring. What result?

2.04 Principal's Liability for Agent's Torts

A principal may be liable for torts of, as well as contracts entered into by, agents. For purposes of tort liability, the question depends on whether the principal was a "master" and the agent a "servant." "Servant" generally means a full-time employee. Section A discusses the scope of a master's liability for the acts of servant agents. The precise distinction between "servants" and independent contractor agents is discussed in Section B.

A.   Scope of Employment

A master normally is not liable for the torts of a servant unless the conduct is within the "scope of employment." This is defined as follows in the Restatement (Second) of Agency § 228:

(1)   Conduct of a servant is within the scope of employment if, but only if:

    (a)   it is of the kind he is employed to perform;

    (b)   it occurs substantially within the authorized time and space limits;

    (c)   it is actuated, at least in part, by a purpose to serve the master; and

    (d)   if force is intentionally used by the servant against another, the use of force is not unexpectable by the master.

(2)   Conduct of a servant is not within the scope of employment if it is different in kind from that authorized, far beyond the authorized time or space limits, or too little actuated by a purpose to serve the master.

Under Restatement § 219, masters may be liable for torts committed by their servants outside the scope of employment if :

    (a)   the master intended the conduct or the consequences, or

    (b)   the master was negligent or reckless, or

(c)   the conduct violated a nondelegable duty of the master, or

(d)   the servant purported to act or to speak on behalf of the principal and there was reliance upon apparent authority, or he was aided in accomplishing the tort by the existence of the agency relation.

These principles are applied in the following cases.

Jackson v. Righter
891 P.2d 1387 (Utah 1995)

STEWART, Associate Chief Justice:

Plaintiff Jeffrey L. Jackson appeals the district court's grant of summary judgment in favor of defendants Novell, Inc., and the joint venture between Novell, Inc., and Unix Systems Laboratories, Inc., dba Univel. We affirm. * * *

Plaintiff and Marie Jackson were married August 14, 1987. In November 1988, Mrs. Jackson began working at Novell in Provo, Utah, as a secretary in the Software Engineering Department. At that time, defendant Grover P. Righter was Novell's Director of Software Engineering. As director, Mr. Righter was responsible for supervising several large engineering teams; managing a substantial budget; hiring, evaluating, promoting, and firing employees; and organizing employee functions. Mr. Righter was Mrs. Jackson's immediate supervisor between November 1988 and August 1991 and, over the course of her employment, promoted her to the positions of administrative assistant and project coordinator, authorized her to record unworked overtime hours as an unofficial raise, and gave her substantial bonuses. He also lavished gifts on her from his personal funds.

By November 1990, Mr. Righter had become attracted to Mrs. Jackson and thereafter began making overtures toward her which resulted in a romantic relationship between them. In early 1991, the two spent much time together in Mr. Righter's office during working hours discussing personal matters, hugging, and kissing. On the pretext of business, Mr. Righter took Mrs. Jackson to the Star Palace dance hall in Provo, the Excelsior Hotel in Provo, and the Little America Hotel in Salt Lake City, kissing, hugging, or fondling her on these occasions. Mr. Righter also took Mrs. Jackson on business trips during working hours to monitor Novell's office and team in Sandy, Utah, for which Mr. Righter was responsible, at times taking up to six hours to travel the one-half hour commute between Provo and Sandy. At some point, others at Novell became aware of Mr. Righter's and Mrs. Jackson's activities.

Mrs. Jackson terminated their romantic relationship in July 1991. That same month, Mrs. Jackson began a relationship with defendant Clay Wilkes, who was employed at that time as an engineering manager in Novell's Sandy office. Within weeks, Mr. Wilkes and Mrs. Jackson were involved in a sexual relationship.

In August 1991, Mr. Righter became Vice President of Univel and moved to the Sandy office. Mrs. Jackson transferred with him and remained under his direct-line supervision. In December 1991, Mr. Wilkes also became employed by Univel as a technical lead and worked in the same department with Mrs. Jackson at the Sandy office but never supervised her.

Plaintiff became aware of Mrs. Jackson's romantic involvement with both Mr. Wilkes and Mr. Righter in November 1991. The Jacksons attempted reconciliation and participated in marriage counseling. However, Mrs. Jackson resumed her sexual relationship with Mr. Wilkes shortly thereafter, and the Jacksons subsequently divorced.

Plaintiff then filed this action alleging that defendants Mr. Righter and Mr. Wilkes had alienated Mrs. Jackson's affections toward him, intentionally inflicted emotional and physical injury on him, and intentionally interfered with his marital contract. Plaintiff also alleged that defendants Novell and Univel were vicariously liable for these tortious actions and that Novell and Univel were directly liable for negligently supervising and retaining Mr. Righter and Mr. Wilkes. * * *

II. CLAIMS AGAINST NOVELL AND UNIVEL

Plaintiff argues that the trial court erred in granting summary judgment in favor of Novell and Univel because genuine issues of material fact exist regarding (1) whether Mr. Righter's conduct was within the scope of his employment, performed in his managerial capacity, or performed under his apparent authority, and (2) whether Novell and Univel negligently supervised and retained Mr. Righter and Mr. Wilkes. For the reasons discussed below, we hold that no genuine issues existed with respect to plaintiff's claims against Novell and Univel and that summary judgment was proper.

A. Vicarious Liability of Novell and Univel

Plaintiff claims that Mr. Righter's actions that allegedly alienated Mrs. Jackson's affections were within the scope of his employment and that summary judgment for Novell and Univel was improper because such a determination is a question of fact. We disagree. An employer may be vicariously liable under the doctrine of respondeat superior for the harmful actions of an employee if those actions are committed within the scope of the employee's employment. [citations omitted] To be considered within the scope of employment, an employee's conduct must (1) "be of the general kind the employee is employed to perform"; (2) "occur within the hours of the employee's work and the ordinary spatial boundaries of the employment"; and (3) "be motivated, at least in part, by the purpose of serving the employer's interest." * * *

In this case, Mr. Righter's romantic involvement with Mrs. Jackson was so clearly outside the scope of his employment that reasonable minds could not differ. Applying the *Birkner* criteria, we note, as Novell and Univel concede, that most of Mr. Righter's alleged tortious conduct occurred within the hours and spatial boundaries of his employment. However, Mr. Righter's conduct was not of the general type he was employed to perform, and neither was it intended to serve, nor did it serve, Novell's or Univel's purpose. Mr. Righter was not hired to perform acts of a sexual nature on, or make romantic overtures toward, an employee under his supervision. [citation omitted] Plaintiff argues that many of Mr. Righter's alleged tortious acts were part of the conduct he was hired to perform in connection with his authority to promote, evaluate, train, and give raises to Mrs. Jackson. For example, plaintiff asserts that the first time Mr. Righter expressed his attraction for Mrs. Jackson was while he held her hand during a formal employee evaluation in his office. Plaintiff's argument is without merit. Mr. Righter was not authorized to use his supervisory position to engage in a romantic relationship with his subordinates. His romantic advances were not a part of his duties but amounted to an abandonment of the supervisory and managerial responsibilities he was hired to perform.

In addition, while Mr. Righter used his company duties as a springboard for pursuing his relationship with Mrs. Jackson, he was not motivated by the purpose of serving Novell's or Univel's interests. An employee's conduct is usually not in the scope of employment where the employee's motivation for the activity is personal, even though some transaction of business or performance of duty may also occur. [citations omitted] Mr. Righter admits that his motives were entirely personal and were in no way directed at the accomplishment of Novell's or Univel's interests. Thus, although Mr. Righter used business activities as a forum for pursuing his romantic relationship with Mrs. Jackson, his acts were clearly an abandonment of employment and outside the scope of his employment. * * *

B. Negligent Supervision

Plaintiff claims that Novell and Univel were negligent in supervising and retaining Mr. Righter and Mr. Wilkes and that their negligence caused the alienation of Mrs. Jackson's affections. To recover for negligence, a plaintiff must show that the defendant owed the plaintiff a duty, the defendant breached the duty, the breach was a proximate cause of the plaintiff's injuries, and there was in fact injury. [citations omitted] Plaintiff has failed to allege facts establishing a duty on the part of Novell or Univel to protect him from his claimed injury.

In the context of a claim for negligent supervision or retention, a duty may arise when an employer could reasonably be expected, consistent with the practical realities of an employer-employee relationship, to appreciate the threat to a plaintiff of its employee's actions and to act to minimize or protect against that threat. [citations omitted] Plaintiff asserts that Mr. Righter's and Mr. Wilkes' acts which allegedly alienated Mrs. Jackson's affections were foreseeable because Novell and Univel knew that spousal affections could be alienated by romantic relations among employees and knew or should have known of Mr. Righter's and Mr. Wilkes' relationships with Mrs. Jackson. We disagree. The inquiry is not whether Novell or Univel could foresee that any marital relation may be damaged by any romantic relationship between two employees. A general knowledge that marital relations could foreseeably be damaged is not sufficient to impute to an employer a duty to protect its employees' spouses from a work-place romance. * * * Rather, the inquiry is whether Novell or Univel could reasonably be expected to foresee the threat of alienation of Mrs. Jackson's affections by Mr. Righter's or Mr. Wilkes' acts.

Nothing plaintiff alleges shows that Novell or Univel could reasonably be expected to foresee this threat. Plaintiff claims that Novell knew Mr. Righter promoted Mrs. Jackson, authorized her to record unworked overtime hours, and required her, as his administrative assistant, to spend a great deal of time in his office and accompany him on business trips. However, nothing in these acts would give Novell reason to foresee that the acts would alienate Mrs. Jackson's affections toward plaintiff.

Nor, as plaintiff claims, would a knowledge of Mrs. Jackson's romantic relationships with Mr. Righter or Mr. Wilkes give Novell or Univel reason to know that they should act to minimize or prevent plaintiff's injury. Unlike the foreseeability of a physical injury caused by an employee who has demonstrated violent or deviant propensities, a romantic relationship between employees may or may not give rise to a cause of action by an employee's spouse. Recovery for the alienation of affections depends upon the determination of the controlling cause of the injury and necessarily involves an analysis of the quality of the marriage relationship. [citations omitted] The tort will not lie when the personalities or inadequacies of the spouses, not the acts of third persons, caused the breakdown of the bonds that are essential to the consortium interests protected by law. [citation omitted] Romantic relationships between employees may only be incidental to, or result from, the primary causes of marital discord and loss of affections. [citation omitted] Thus, an employer's awareness of a romantic relationship between two of its employees does not give the employer sufficient knowledge to anticipate a claim for alienation of affections against an employee under its supervision. * * *

Policy considerations also preclude our imposition of a duty upon employers to police the private conduct of their employees for the protection of employees' spouses. * * *

[E]mployers have no duty to determine the marital status of their employees. It would be unreasonable to impose upon employers a duty to monitor romantic relationships among their employees to protect marital relations of which they may not even be aware. Indeed, absent some indication of harassment or intimidation, an employer who attempted, merely upon the basis of its knowledge of a romantic relationship, to police the personal conduct of its employees may expose itself to liability for interfering with private relationships.

Plaintiff has also failed to allege facts establishing that any act or omission on the part of Novell or Univel was the proximate cause of his injury. Nothing indicates that more rules or different supervision would have prevented Mr. Righter's or Mr. Wilkes' acts. First, Mr. Righter acknowledged that romantic relationships between supervisors and subordinates were improper and violated the employment rules of Novell and Univel. It is unreasonable to assume that different rules would have affected Mr. Righter's conduct. In addition, despite Novell's advice to Mrs. Jackson that she should distance herself from Mr. Righter and pursue a different career path at Novell, she chose to transfer to Univel, remain under Mr. Righter's supervision, and work in the same department with Mr. Wilkes. Finally, Mr. Wilkes and Mrs. Jackson continued their sexual relationship after taking a leave of absence and finally terminating their employment with Univel. Nothing plaintiff alleges indicates that different actions by Univel would have prevented that relationship.

For the foregoing reasons, we hold that no genuine issue of material fact exists and that Novell and Univel were entitled to judgment as a matter of law.

Mains v. II Morrow, Inc.
128 Or. App. 625, 877 P.2d 88 (1994)

DURHAM, Judge pro tem.

Plaintiff appeals from summary judgment for defendant II Morrow Corporation on plaintiff's claims for employment discrimination on the basis of sex, disability and filing a workers' compensation claim, for intentional infliction of emotional distress and for wrongful discharge. We reverse as to the claims for sex discrimination and for intentional infliction of emotional distress, and otherwise affirm. * * *

* * * A factfinder could infer from the record that plaintiff's supervisor, Berry, harassed her at work because of her gender and created an environment in which he and other employees sexually harassed plaintiff on a daily basis. Berry was defendant's shop supervisor. * * *

A factfinder could infer that defendant was aware of Berry's conduct and failed to correct it. Following an earlier sexual harassment complaint, the Bureau of Labor and Industries investigated and required defendant to place a warning letter in Berry's file. However, he retained his supervisory position. Moreover, plaintiff testified: "[W]hen I first started working there, all the women came up to me . . . and said, 'How can you work for [Berry]? He's terrible. He's horrible. He hates women. He puts them down like crazy. He's a male chauvinist pig.' * * * From my first day there, I heard about his reputation."

Ultimately, plaintiff reported Berry's behavior to defendant's personnel supervisor, who placed plaintiff on paid leave. Following an investigation, defendant terminated Berry and asked plaintiff to return to work. Defendant offered to "attempt to find other suitable and available employment" if plaintiff did not want to return to her former position. Plaintiff refused to return and filed this action.

The trial court granted defendant's motion for summary judgment on plaintiff's claims for intentional infliction of emotional distress, sex discrimination and wrongful discharge, because plaintiff did not "demonstrate the responsibility of Defendant II Morrow." The court also held that plaintiff's claims for employment discrimination stemming from the workers' compensation claim were barred by the statute of limitations. * * *

Defendant contends that, as a matter of law, it is not responsible for Berry's conduct. * * *

An employer is liable for an employee's tortious conduct if the employee acted within the "scope of employment." [citation omitted] To make that determination, we apply a three-part test: "(1) [W]hether the act occurred substantially within the time and space limits authorized by the employment; (2) whether the employee was motivated, at least partially, by a purpose to serve the employer; and (3) whether the act is of a kind which the employee was hired to perform." *Chesterman v. Barmon,* 305 Or. 439, 442, 753 P.2d 404 (1988). Vicarious liability is imposed, regardless of whether the employer committed a morally wrongful act, as a policy of risk allocation. [citation omitted]

The first element of the *Chesterman* test is satisfied, because defendant acknowledges that Berry's conduct occurred at work. Defendant argues that Berry was not motivated to serve defendant when he sexually harassed plaintiff and was not hired to engage in that behavior. Defendant defines the issue under the three-part scope of employment analysis too narrowly. The Restatement (Second) Agency, § 229(1) (1958) describes the type of conduct that is relevant to the three-part test: "To be within the scope of employment, conduct must be of the same general nature as that authorized, or incidental to the conduct authorized." The Restatement also provides: "An act, although forbidden, or done in a forbidden manner, may be within the scope of employment." Restatement, *supra,* at § 230. In *G.L. v. Kaiser Foundation Hospitals, Inc.,* 306 Or. 54, 60, 757 P.2d 1347 (1988), the Supreme Court quoted, with approval, section 245 of the Restatement, which provides: "A master is subject to liability for the intended tortious harm by a servant to the person or things of another by an act done in connection with the servant's employment, although the act was unauthorized, if the act was not unexpectable in view of the duties of the servant." Restatement, *supra,* at § 245. As the Ninth Circuit recently explained, in a diversity case involving Oregon law, "the specific egregious act giving rise to an intentional tort claim will itself rarely be 'of a kind which the employee was hired to perform'; the appropriate inquiry is whether the employee committed the tort while performing, or in connection with, his job responsibilities." * * *

Defendant argues that this case is controlled by *G.L. v. Kaiser Foundation Hospitals, Inc., supra,* and *Carr v. U.S. West Direct Co.,* 98 Or. App. 30, 36, 779 P.2d 154, *rev. den.* 308 Or. 608, 784 P.2d 1101 (1989), which held that the employees' acts of sexual assault could not reasonably be considered acts carried out for the benefit of the employer. Those cases are distinguishable, because they involved no allegation that the employer's agent acted with the intention of furthering the employer's business purposes.

In contrast, in this case, a factfinder could infer from the record that sexual harassment was a characteristic of Berry's method of supervising and controlling female subordinate employees in the workplace, and that defendant condoned this supervisory technique. Berry created a pervasive atmosphere of sexual harassment, was the subject of an earlier sexual harassment claim that the Bureau of Labor and Industries investigated, and was notorious within the company for discriminating against women. Despite the earlier complaint and his reputation, defendant retained Berry in a supervisory role. Berry told plaintiff that he harassed her because the male employees that he supervised expected that behavior. In a letter to the Employment Division after defendant fired him, Berry said that he "was discharged for something that my superiors condoned by participating in the same sort of conduct." The evidence is sufficient to create a factual question regarding the second and third parts of the test described in *Chesterman v. Barmon, supra.* The court erred in dismissing plaintiff's claim for intentional infliction of emotional distress. * * *

Reversed and remanded on claims for intentional infliction of emotional distress and statutory sexual discrimination; otherwise affirmed.

Notes and Questions

1. **Scope of employment.** Can the cases be reconciled? Can *Jackson* be explained solely by the nature of the plaintiff husband's injury? What if Righter had run a pedestrian over as he drove Marie to a motel several miles off the road between Provo and Sandy?

As discussed in Sykes, *Boundaries of Vicarious Liability: An Economic Analysis of the Scope of Employment Rule and Related Legal Doctrines,* 101 HARV. L. REV. 563 (1988), the question is whether employers' liability for employees' torts is an extra cost the business should bear. In general, whether liability is socially justified depends on whether the costs of reducing socially desirable activities outweighs the benefit of reducing accident costs. This depends in turn on whether *the business causes the wrong* and on whether the employer can *reduce the probability of its occurring* through incentive contracts with its employees. Thus, even if the firm can reduce the risk of harm by controlling the employee, perhaps it should not be liable if the employment did not increase the likelihood of the harm occurring. In this situation, liability might reduce business activities to below what is socially optimal. Even if the firm's business increased the risk of harm, perhaps the firm should not be liable if it could not reduce the risk of harm other than by curtailing its activities. For example, bringing male and female employees together in the workplace undoubtedly increases the probability of marital breakdown and sexual harassment. At the same time, liability rules that discourage firms from having offices or from mixed-sex staffing would involve significant social costs. Such rules would be more likely to have net benefits if they discouraged only specific employment practices that significantly increased workplace sexual costs. Does this analysis help to explain the results in the principal cases?

2. **Frolic and detour.** An important category of "scope of employment" issues involves "frolic and detour"—that is, the question of whether the employee was on her master's business at the time of the harm. If an employee truck driver runs an unforeseeably long personal errand, there is no liability under this doctrine. Should the length of the detour or the foreseeability of the particular tort matter under the policy analysis in Note 1?

3. **Principal's direct liability.** As *Jackson* indicates, a principal may be *directly* liable for her own acts or failure to act whether or not the agent's acts are within the scope of employment. This includes not only negligent supervision or retention, but also negligent selection of the agent (as where the employer hires an employee with a known history of engaging in sexual misconduct) or by giving the agent faulty tools or instructions.

4. **Liability under employment discrimination laws.** The Supreme Court has decided three cases that bear on employers' liability for employees' sexual harassment.

In *Meritor Savings Bank v. Vinson*, 477 U.S. 57 (1986), the Court recognized the application of agency principles in determining employers' responsibility for discrimination by supervisory employees, noting that the law defines "employer" to include "agents." The lower federal courts interpreted *Meritor* to mean that employers' were vicariously liable for so-called "quid pro quo" harassment that was accompanied by dismissal or other employment action against the employee. However, a negligence standard applied where the harassment merely created a "hostile environment" for the employee unaccompanied by employment action.

In *Burlington Industries, Inc. v. Ellerth*, 524 U.S. 742 (1998), and *Faragher v. City of Boca Raton*, 524 U.S. 775 (1998), the Court expanded on the standards applicable to employer's liability for their employees' sex discrimination. In *Ellerth,* an employee was subjected to sexual harassment, including unfulfilled threats of employment action, by one of her supervisors. The Court held that, while the distinction between quid pro quo and hostile environment harassment was relevant to proof of discrimination, it is not relevant on the issue of vicarious liability. With respect to vicarious liability, the Court held it would apply a federal standard as a matter of statutory interpretation, but one that is informed by the general state common law of agency. Under this standard, although sexual harassment by a supervisor is not within the scope of employment, the employer may be liable for conduct outside the scope of employment under Restatement (Second) of Agency § 219(2)(d) when the employee uses apparent authority or "was aided in accomplishing the tort by the existence of the agency relation." The latter phrase applies in the usual harassment case, which involves misuse of power, as when the supervisor makes a tangible employment decision. Without such an action, the use of the employee's agency power is unclear. While a supervisor's agency power necessarily makes harassment more threatening, it is not necessarily determinative. In any event, under *Meritor,* the employer cannot be absolutely liable for all acts of supervisors: "Congress' decision to define 'employer' to include any 'agent' of an employer, 42 U.S.C. § 2000e(b), surely evinces an intent to place some limits on the acts of employees for which employers under Title VII are to be held responsible." 477 U.S. at 72. *Meritor* also noted that "common-law principles may not be transferable in all their particulars to Title VII." *Id.* For example, federal law encourages the creation of anti-harassment policies and grievance procedures. Thus, the Court held that, in hostile environment cases unaccompanied by tangible employment action, the employer has an affirmative defense of showing that it exercised reasonable care to prevent and correct sexually harassing behavior, and that the plaintiff employee unreasonably failed to take advantage of any preventive or corrective opportunities provided by the employer or to avoid harm otherwise.

In *Faragher*, a lifeguard was sexually harassed by her supervisors without any threats against her job. The Court applied the rule adopted in *Ellerth*, noting that sexual harassment, or even sexual assaults, might under a broad view be anticipated by the employer and therefore charged against the employer as a cost of doing business. However, it concluded that there was no indication that Congress wanted to ignore the traditional distinction between frolic and detour, which has been recognized by the lower courts. The Court said that Restatement § 219(2)(d) is only the "starting point" because "our obligation here is not to make a pronouncement of agency law in general or to transplant § 219(2)(d) into Title VII. Rather, it is to adapt agency concepts to the practical objectives of Title VII." 534 U.S. at 803, n.3.

Is it clear after these cases how federal discrimination law differs from state agency law, and why?

B. Independent Contractors

A principal may not be liable even for acts that are within the scope of employment of an agent who is an independent contractor rather than a servant.

Restatement (Second) of Agency, § 220 provides:

§ 220. DEFINITION OF SERVANT
(1)   A servant is a person employed to perform services in the affairs of another and who with respect to the physical conduct in the performance of the services is subject to the other's control or right to control.
(2)   In determining whether one acting for another is a servant or an independent contractor, the following matters of fact, among others, are considered:
    (a)   the extent of control which, by the agreement, the master may exercise over the details of the work;
    (b)   whether or not the one employed is engaged in a distinct occupation or business;

(c)   the kind of occupation, with reference to whether, in the locality, the work is usually done under the direction of the employer or by a specialist without supervision;

(d)   the skill required in the particular occupation;

(e)   whether the employer or the workman supplies the instrumentalities, tools, and the place of work for the person doing the work;

(f)   the length of time for which the person is employed;

(g)   the method of payment, whether by the time or by the job;

(h)   whether or not the work is a part of the regular business of the employer;

(i)   whether or not the parties believe they are creating the relation of master and servant; and

(j)   whether the principal is or is not in business.

Anderson v. Marathon Petroleum Company
801 F.2d 936 (7th Cir. 1986)

POSNER, Circuit Judge.

This diversity personal-injury suit pits two residents of Illinois (Donald Anderson, who died while the case was on appeal, and his widow) against a nonresident corporation, Marathon Petroleum Company. The district judge granted a directed verdict for Marathon at the close of the plaintiffs' case on the ground that the plaintiffs had failed to show a breach of duty by Marathon.

Anderson was an employee of Tri-Kote, Inc., which had a contract with Marathon to clean the inside of Marathon's oil storage tanks by sandblasting. The evidence, viewed most favorably to the Andersons, shows that sandblasting in a confined space creates clouds of silicon dust, which if breathed in over a long period of time cause silicosis, a serious lung disease from which, in fact, Anderson died. Anderson had begun working for Tri-Kote in 1970 as a sandblaster, mostly on the Marathon contract, and quit in 1983 when he was diagnosed as suffering from silicosis. During this period he averaged three or four days a week sandblasting Marathon storage tanks. Until 1980 the only form of mask that Tri-Kote supplied Anderson to protect him from silicon dust was a so-called "desert hood." It had no fresh-air hose but only a wire mesh in front of the nose and mouth, and the dust could get in through the mesh. Supervisory personnel of Marathon often saw Anderson coming out of a storage tank with dust on his face after sandblasting and they knew that Tri-Kote had supplied him with just the patently inadequate "desert hood." Yet Marathon did nothing to try to get Tri-Kote to protect its workers better. The two employees of Tri-Kote who sandblasted Marathon's storage tanks before Anderson came on the scene also died of silicosis.

The issue is the tort duty of a principal to the employees of his independent contractor. The duty could be vicarious or direct: vicarious if the principal is not himself at fault in the accident to the employee, direct if he is. Mrs. Anderson makes both sorts of claim, though her emphasis is on the former, and that is the one we shall discuss first. The district judge rejected both claims, and our practice is to give some deference to determinations of the law of a state by a district judge sitting in that state. [citation omitted]

Generally a principal is not liable for an independent contractor's torts even if they are committed in the performance of the contract and even though a principal is liable under the doctrine of respondeat superior for the torts of his employees if committed in the furtherance of their employment. [citations omitted] The reason for distinguishing the independent contractor from the employee is that, by definition of the relationship between a principal and an independent contractor, the principal does not supervise the details of the independent contractor's work and therefore is not in a good position to prevent negligent performance, whereas the essence of the contractual relationship known as employment is that the employee surrenders to the employer the right to direct the details of his work, in exchange for receiving a wage. The independent contractor commits himself to providing a specified output, and the principal monitors the contractor's performance not by monitoring inputs— *i.e.,* supervising the contractor—but by inspecting the contractually specified output to make sure it conforms to the specifications. This method of monitoring works fine if it is feasible for the principal to specify and monitor output, but sometimes it is not feasible, particularly if the output consists of the joint product of many separate producers whose specific contributions are difficult (sometimes impossible) to disentangle. In such a case it may be more efficient for the principal to monitor inputs rather than output—the producers rather than the product. By becoming an employee a producer in effect submits himself to that kind of monitoring, receiving payment for the work he puts in rather than for the output he produces.

Since an essential element of the employment relationship is thus the employer's monitoring of the employee's work, a principal who is not knowledgeable about the details of some task is likely to delegate it to an independent contractor. Hence in general, though of course not in every case, the principal who uses an independent contractor will not be as well placed as an employer would be to monitor the work and make sure it is done safely. This is the reason as we have said for not making the principal vicariously liable for the torts of his independent contractors. *See* Calabresi, *Some Thoughts on Risk Distribution and the Law of Torts,* 70 YALE L.J. 499, 545 (1961).

The rule is not applied, however, when the activity for which the independent contractor was hired is "abnormally dangerous," *see* Restatement (Second) of Torts § 427A (1964), or in an older terminology "ultrahazardous," *see, e.g., Cities Service Co. v. State,* 312 So. 2d 799, 802 (Fla. Dist. Ct. App. 1975)—*i.e.,* if the activity might very well result in injury even if conducted with all due skill and caution. When an activity is abnormally dangerous, it is important not only that the people engaged in it use the highest practicable degree of skill and caution, but also—since even if they do so, accidents may well result—that the people who have authorized the activity consider the possibility of preventing some accidents by curtailing the activity or even eliminating it altogether. *See Bethlehem Steel Corp. v. EPA,* 782 F.2d 645, 652 (7th Cir. 1986); Shavell, *Strict Liability versus Negligence,* 9 J. LEGAL STUD. 1 (1980). On both scores there is an argument for making the principal as well as the independent contractor liable if an accident occurs that is due to the hazardous character of the performance called for by the contract. The fact that a very high degree of care is cost-justified implies that the principal should be induced to wrack his brain, as well as the independent contractor his own brain, for ways of minimizing the danger posed by the activity. And the fact that the only feasible method of accident prevention may be to reduce the amount of the activity or substitute another activity argues for placing liability on the principal, who makes the decision whether to undertake the activity in the first place. The electrical utility that has to decide whether to transport nuclear waste materials by motor or rail may be influenced in its choice by the relative safety of the modes—if it is liable for the consequences of an accident.

True, the principal would in any event be liable indirectly if the price it paid the independent contractor fully reflected the dangers of the undertaking; but this condition would be fulfilled only if the contractor were fully answerable for an accident if one occurred. And though fully liable in law, the independent contractor would not be fully liable in fact if a damage judgment would exceed his net assets. The likelihood of the independent contractor's insolvency is greater the more hazardous the activity; by definition, expected accident costs are greater. Another thing making them greater is that the contractor will be strictly liable for accidents caused by the abnormally dangerous character of his activity, *see* Restatement, supra, § 427A, comment a, and therefore his expected legal-judgment costs will be higher than those of a contractor liable only for negligence. With the exposure of the independent contractor to liability so great, it may be necessary to make the principal liable as well in order to ensure that there is a solvent defendant. This is important not only to provide compensation for accident victims but also to reduce the number of accidents. Without such liability a principal might hire judgment-proof independent contractors to do his dangerous jobs, knowing that the contractors would have an incentive to cut corners on protecting safety and health and that this would reduce the cost of the contract to him. *See* Sykes, *The Economics of Vicarious Liability*, 93 YALE L.J. 1231, 1241-42, 1272 (1984).

Is sandblasting abnormally dangerous? A district judge in Louisiana, in the only case we have found on the question, held not. *Touchstone v. G.B.Q. Corp.*, 596 F. Supp. 805, 815 (E.D. La. 1984). In the absence of any precedent establishing the abnormal dangerousness of sandblasting, the plaintiffs in this case were obliged to lay a factual basis for an inference that people engaged in sandblasting cannot prevent a serious risk of injury by taking precautions. They did not do this. * * *

Mrs. Anderson presses on us cases which suggest that something less than abnormal danger may be enough to take a case out of the rule that a principal is not liable for the torts of its independent contractors. An example is *Johnson v. Central Tile & Terrazzo Co.*, 59 Ill. App. 2d 262, 276-77, 207 N.E.2d 160, 167 (1965), which says that "if one employs another to do work which he should recognize as involving some peculiar risk to others unless special precautions are taken, the one doing the employing will remain liable if harm results because these precautions are not taken," even though the person "employed" is actually an independent contractor.

* * * [E]ven if the present case is within the "peculiar risk" or "inherent danger" exception as recognized by the Illinois cases, Mrs. Anderson must lose. With rare exceptions, some based on statutes such as the omnipresent scaffolding acts (*see, e.g.,* ILL. REV. STAT. ch. 48, ¶¶ 60 et seq.) that impose strict liability on contractors for injuries to their subcontractors' employees caused by hazardous working conditions, the cases that make principals vicariously liable for the torts of their independent contractors involve injuries to third parties rather than employees; and the general though not uniform view is that the employee has no common law tort right against his employer's principal in such a case. * * *

There is a reason for the distinction between the plaintiff who is an employee of the independent contractor and the plaintiff who is not. If a nuclear reactor blows up and thousands of people are irradiated, we would not allow the reactor company to slough off all liability for the accident onto a careless independent contractor, who, not having the resources to compensate the victims of his tort, had lacked adequate incentives to take care. Similarly, we would not want Marathon to be able to avoid liability to its neighbors caused by its hiring contractors, who turn out to be careless, to perform abnormally dangerous jobs. But the only people endangered in this case were the contractor's employees; and they are compensated for the risks of their employment by a combination of wages, benefits, and entitlement to workers' compensation in the event of an accident. The principal pays for the package indirectly, in the contract price, which is calculated to cover the contractor's labor as well as other costs. Moreover, as we shall see, if the contractor does not carry workers' compensation insurance and proves unable to pay benefits out of its own pocket, the principal must pay the benefits. The principal thus has every incentive to assure safe working conditions in order to reduce its contract costs and its contingent liability for workers' compensation; so there is no danger of the shell game that is played when the firm causing the accident is insolvent and its principal is not liable because the tortfeasor was an independent contractor rather than an employee.

Since the principal is the indirect employer of its contractor's employees, to make the principal liable in common law tort for the accidents befalling those employees would be inconsistent with the bedrock principle that workers' compensation rights are exclusive of common law tort rights. * * *

The position urged by Mrs. Anderson would bring about profound changes in liability for industrial accidents. Firms engaged in activities that are dangerous if proper precautions are not taken (and which activity is not?) would become the virtual insurers of their contractors' employees. Indeed, imagine a case where a homeowner hired a contractor to fix the roof, and one of his workers fell off the roof and was injured. The risk of falling would be in some sense inherent in or peculiar to the work; could the worker therefore sue the homeowner? That would be a revolution in liability. * * *

Up to now we have treated the case as one in which the principal is alleged to be vicariously liable for its contractors' torts, but Mrs. Anderson also argues that there was enough evidence of Marathon's negligence to make the directed verdict improper even if Tri-Kote's negligence cannot be imputed to Marathon. Supervisory employees of Marathon testified that on occasion they had seen Mr. Anderson coming out of the storage tanks with dust on his face, and they knew he did not have an adequate mask. Even so, this does not show that Marathon was negligent in hiring Tri-Kote initially; so this conventional avenue of principal's liability . . . is cut off.

But suppose that a principal, having hired an independent contractor after a careful investigation which showed that the contractor was careful and responsible, discovers that he is careless yet takes no steps to correct his unsafe practices or terminate him; can the victim of the contractor's carelessness get damages from the principal? We assume the answer is "yes" if the victim is a third party, but Mrs. Anderson has cited no case in which an Illinois court has allowed an employee of the independent contractor to recover damages on this basis. The majority view is that he may not. [citations omitted] Again the reason is that the employee is protected by his workers' compensation rights[.] * * *

AFFIRMED.

SWYGERT, Senior Circuit Judge, dissenting.

The majority's cost/benefit analysis does not provide an adequate basis for rejecting the holding in *Chicago Economic Fuel Gas Co. v. Myers,* 168 Ill. 139, 146, 48 N.E. 66, 68-69

(1897), in which the Illinois Supreme Court held that employers of independent contractors owe a nondelegable duty to the contractor's employees when those employees are involved in inherently dangerous work or work which carries with it a peculiar risk of injury. * * *

The majority suggests that the position taken by the Illinois Supreme Court in *Myers* is now untenable in light of recent developments, most notably the advent of worker's compensation. But other jurisdictions have continued to adhere to the rule reiterated in *Myers* even after worker's compensation developed, the reason being that there are policy considerations apart from worker's compensation coverage that come to play in cases such as the one at bar. [citations omitted]

* * * Thus, the question becomes whether sandblasting is "peculiarly or inherently dangerous." * * * At trial the plaintiffs presented the following expert testimony. Their medical expert testified that silica in the lungs is a toxic poison, and that in an area of really intense exposure, where there is not good ventilation, where the particle concentration is extremely high, the only acceptable kind of prevention is an external air source used throughout the procedure with a tight fitting hood [and] external oxygen source or backpack oxygen . . . [where the concentration of silica particles is intense], you have to use more and more rigorous methods to protect against exposure. In this case, there was also additional evidence that Anderson sandblasted three to four times a week in tanks no more than twelve feet in diameter and fifteen feet high, using approximately 2000-2500 pounds of sand, and that Anderson used only a tarpaulin head covering with no fresh air supply. In Illinois, the question of whether an activity is inherently or peculiarly dangerous is one for a jury, [citation omitted] and the Andersons certainly presented sufficient evidence to reach the jury on this issue.

Thus, because I agree with the majority that there was insufficient evidence of Marathon's negligent retention of the independent contractor, the order of the district court directing a verdict in favor of Marathon on the issue of its alleged breach of its nondelegable duty should be reversed and the cause remanded for a new trial.

Notes and Questions

1.   **The "independent contractor" rule and the economic theory of the firm.** The distinction between independent contractors and servants could be viewed as legal recognition for the economic theory of the "firm." *See* Coase, *The Nature of the Firm,* 4 ECONOMICA 386 (1937), *reprinted in* THE NATURE OF THE FIRM: ORIGINS, EVOLUTION, AND DEVELOPMENT (Williamson & Winter, eds. 1991); Masten, *A Legal Basis for the Firm,* 4 J.L. ECON. & ORG. 181 (1988). As discussed by Judge Posner, firms' contracts with employees differ fundamentally from those with independent contractors with regard to the type of monitoring and other matters. The law recognizes this difference by attributing to firms liabilities from those activities that they have chosen to embrace, but not for activities that they have chosen to delegate to other firms.

2.   **Independent contractors and agents.** Note that the test for independent contractors in Restatement § 220 includes control and benefit factors that are similar to the test for agency discussed above in § 2.01. Not surprisingly, the issues are often confused in the cases. For example, if Warren in *Cargill,* § 2.02(B), had committed a tort, the

issue might have been whether Warren was an independent contractor. Despite this potential confusion, the issues are separate: an independent contractor may or may not be an agent and an agent may or may not be an independent contractor. In *Anderson,* Tri-Kote was probably not even Marathon's agent. But even if the facts had been such as to support agency, the agent could still be independent enough from the principal's business that the principal should not be liable for the agent's tortious acts.

3.   **Abnormally dangerous activities.** Although *Anderson* shows that a principal may choose to delegate potential responsibility for torts to an independent business, this delegation is not determinative if it falls within one of the exceptions discussed in *Anderson.* The abnormally dangerous exception involves a situation in which the defendant might otherwise be tempted to delegate control solely to avoid tort responsibility. Apart from the fact that the plaintiff was an employee, why not characterize sandblasting as abnormally dangerous in light of the risks cited by the dissent?

Problem

Sam is a theoretical mathematician specializing in topology who is having trouble making ends meet. To help solve this problem he decided to take on a paper route for the Daily Planet. However, Sam knew that he could not get up before dawn every morning. Sam formed Rhomboloid Associates, Inc. (RAI) (Sam's paper route graphed as a rhomboloid) and hired one of his students, Sid, to make the deliveries with Sam's car three mornings a week and to handle some collections. RAI contracted with the Daily Planet to handle a paper route.

Paper deliverers for the Daily Planet buy their newspapers from the Planet and deliver them from their own cars along a route selected by the Planet. The Planet provides detailed instructions to its deliverers concerning how deliveries and collections are to be handled. Customers subscribe through the Planet, but pay the deliverer once a month. The Planet has the right under their contracts with their deliverers to terminate a deliverer at any time for any reason. The deliverers were compensated by the difference between what they paid the Planet and the amounts they collected from their customers.

Sid proved to be less than fully satisfactory at his job. During his first round of collections, Sid injured a customer by slamming a screen door in the customer's face when he became irritated that the customer had no formally logical reason for refusing to pay. The next morning, after Sid had finished his last delivery and was heading toward his house with the car where he intended to park it until the following morning's deliveries, he accidentally rammed Al's car, which was stopped at a stoplight.

Customer and Al sue (a) RAI; and (b) the Daily Planet. What result in each suit?

2.05 Duties of Agent to Principal

The agency relationship is "fiduciary" in nature. This means that the agent must exercise the powers described in this chapter primarily for the benefit of the principal. *See* Restatement (Second) of Agency, § 13. As this definition suggests, the fundamental fiduciary duty is the duty of *loyalty*—to act solely for the benefit of the principal. *See* Restatement § 387. The duty of loyalty includes the duties to account for profits arising out of the agency (*id.* § 388), not to act adversely to the principal without the latter's consent (*id.* §§ 389-92), and not to compete with the principal on matters relating to the agency (*id.* § 393).

The agent also owes what the Restatement calls "duties of service and obedience," including a duty of care (a paid agent must act with the ordinary skill of persons performing similar work in the locality under the Restatement § 379); to give information (*id.* § 381) and keep and render accounts (*id.* § 382), to act within the agent's authority (*id.* § 383) and to obey the principal's instructions (*id.* § 385).

As discussed at greater length in Chapter 8, fiduciary duties fill gaps in long-term contracts that involve delegation of discretion. As such, the duties vary with the context of the particular contract. Moreover, the general default fiduciary duties provided for by common law rules and statutes may be varied by contrary agreement.

Principals have a variety of remedies for agents' breaches of duty, listed in Restatement § 399, including liability for breach of the agent's contract (*id.* § 400) and tort liability for loss the agent causes to the principal (*id.* § 401). Thus, for example, if the agent's acts without actual authority impose liability on the principal, the principal may recover from the agent (*id.* § 401, comment d). Note, however, that the agent is liable only for liabilities that result from the agent's breach of duty to the principal. Thus, if the agent obeys instructions and acts carefully and loyally, the agent is not liable to the principal (although the agent may have direct liability to the third party).

2.06 Duties of Principal to Agent

A principal's duties to the agent, apart from liability to employees that arise under worker compensation, employee safety and other laws, are primarily a matter of contract between the agent and principal. The contract may provide for such things as compensation, job description and working conditions. If the agent was hired to work for the principal's benefit, a duty to compensate the agent is generally implied unless the circumstances indicate otherwise. If the amount of the compensation was not agreed on, the agent is compensated on a quantum meruit basis. The principal also has a default duty to indemnify the agent for amounts paid and liabilities the agent incurs on the principal's behalf. *See* Restatement (Second) of Agency, § 438.

2.07 Termination of Agency

Agency is inherently a consensual relationship and so continues only as long as that consent lasts. Accordingly, an agency relationship terminates when the parties mutually agree, or when either manifests to the other dissent to its continuation. *See* Restatement (Second) of Agency, §§ 117-119. Not surprisingly, the agency also terminates on death or loss of capacity of either party (*id.* §§ 120-123). Perhaps more surprisingly, agency also terminates on bankruptcy of the agency or principal (*id.* §§ 113-114).

Termination of an agent's actual authority does not necessarily terminate the agent's apparent authority. *See id.* § 124A. Also, an agent or principal may have only the *power* to terminate the agency relationship but not the *right* to do so, in the sense the termination (such as the firing of an employee) may be a breach of contract or may violate statutory protection of employees at will.

CHAPTER 3
FORMING THE PARTNERSHIP

3.01 Introduction: Application of Partnership Default Rules

This Chapter begins the discussion of an important variation on the agency relationship—the general partnership. More specifically, this chapter concerns when the parties will be deemed to be partners.

If a partnership exists (*see* § 3.02), then the default rules of the Uniform Partnership Act apply to the relationship unless they are waived by contrary agreement. This book will discuss both the original 1914 version of the Uniform Partnership Act (UPA) which is in effect in many states and the 1994 Revised Uniform Partnership Act (RUPA) which has been adopted by about half the states Because of this increasing state-to-state variation in partnership law, an important initial issue for many partnerships may be whether to contract for the application of a particular state's law—*i.e.*, for RUPA or UPA. *See* § 3.03, below. Even within a given state, a firm may have an option after the state's adoption of RUPA as to whether to adopt RUPA or to stay with the UPA. The state may eventually eliminate the UPA and automatically apply RUPA to all partnerships, thereby forcing revisions in existing partnership agreements. *See* RUPA § 1006; Vestal, *Should the Revised Uniform Partnership Act of 1994 Really be Retroactive,* 50 Bus. Law. 267 (1994).

The default rules supplied by the UPA and RUPA are best understood as interrelated sets. In this way, the law economizes on contracting costs by supplying the contract that the parties are most likely to have agreed to if they had gone beyond the bare bones and agreed on the details. *See* § 1.02(A). The default partnership rules make the most sense if one begins with the most important legal consequence of being co-owners—the partners' liability as co-principals of the business. Several implications follow from the partners' status as co-principals:

1. If partners are each liable for the debts of the business, they would certainly want a big say in the business. Partnership law makes each partner a co-manager with an equal vote on all matters and a power to veto important decisions and amendments to the agreement.

2. Co-management means, among other things, that no single partner may deal with specific partnership property as her own, but rather may use the partnership's property only for the firm's benefit.

3. Since the partners share liability and management they would expect to share equally in revenues and expenses—that is, profits and losses.

4. Given partners' significant rights and powers, each partner would expect to be able to veto the admission of new partners. A partner therefore cannot transfer her management rights or partner status without the other partners' consent.

5. Since partners cannot easily exit the firm by simply selling out, they would want some other escape mechanism—specifically, the power to dissolve the firm and put it up for sale.

3.02 Existence of Partnership: Partnership Law

The default partnership rules obviously apply only if the relationship is a partnership. Like agency, general partnership is traditionally an informal relationship, and so may arise unexpectedly. To understand the practical issues this may involve, consider the following fact situations:

1. Bob and Mary are married and together operate a "bed and breakfast" in their home. Bob owned the house before the marriage and the mortgage is in his name. Bob and Mary share all revenues and expenses from the business and apply business income to pay the mortgage. Bob dies suddenly with no will. Bob's heirs seek the property, claiming it was his, while the creditors of the B & B are more respectful of Mary's role, claiming she is a partner and therefore personally liable for the debts of the B & B. How should these claims be resolved?

2. First Bank finances a housing development by Acme Developers. Because the development is a significant credit risk, First Bank insists on being repaid the principal amount of the loan with interest at the market rate and

> on receiving a share of any profits on sale of the houses in the development. First Bank also contracts for the power to veto certain actions by Acme that might increase the loan's risk. When Acme goes bankrupt, suppliers of building materials seek repayment from First Bank as Acme's partner.

To make the partnership determination, it may be necessary to work backwards from the default rules analysis in § 3.01: If the parties have agreed to partnership default rules, it arguably follows that they are partners. But just because a contract provides for some of the default rules of partnership, it does not necessarily follow that the parties want other partnership default rules to apply. Conversely, even if the parties have agreed to many terms that differ from the partnership default rules, this may have little bearing on how the relationship should be characterized because even *partners* can contract around most of these rules.

UPA § 6 defines a partnership as "an association of two or more persons to carry on as co-owners a business for profit." RUPA uses similar language both to define a partner-ship (§ 101(4)) and to provide how a partnership is formed (§ 202). Most of the elements of this definition—multiple owners, business and profit—are relatively clear. But, as the above hypotheticals illustrate, it is much less clear when parties carry on a business *as co-owners*, or whether they are in another relationship, such as husband-wife or debtor-cred-itor. Unlike a simple agency, in which there is only one residual claimant (the principal), a partnership is a relationship of multiple ownership. Thus, unlike an agent, a partner does not work primarily on behalf of a co-partner, and may *share* management responsibility rather than agreeing to be subject to the other's direction.

The courts often ask whether the parties *intended* to be partners. Sometimes they ask in a generalized way whether the parties made statements or engaged in conduct indicating that they thought they were co-principals of a business. This is the "subjective intent" to be partners. At other times the courts determine whether the parties *acted* like partners, regardless of whether they seemed to think they were partners. This can be referred to as "objective intent," or the intent to engage in acts that make one a partner. One court called this the "duck" test—that is, just as something is a duck if it walks and quacks like one, par-ties are partners if they "acted like partners, worked like partners, and shared profits/losses as partners." *Johnson v. Wiley,* 613 N.E.2d 446, 451 (Ind. App. 1993).

UPA § 7 provides some guidance on when the parties act like partners by directing the courts to look for one critical element—profit sharing. If profit-sharing is present, the relationship is presumptively a partnership *unless* it also fits one of the specific categories listed in UPA § 7 and RUPA § 202. If the relationship is not in one of those categories, the fact of profit-sharing may be determinative if the evidence is equally balanced, and may get the proponent of partnership past a motion to dismiss or for summary judgment even in the absence of any other indication of partnership. If the relationship is in one of the specific categories, the special importance of profit sharing drops out of the case and the court must simply weigh the profit-sharing evidence against other evidence of objective and subjective intent.

In re Marriage of Hassiepen
269 Ill. App. 3d 559, 646 N.E.2d 1348 (1995)

Justice STEIGMANN delivered the opinion of the court:

In January 1991, Cynthia Hassiepen, petitioner, filed a petition to increase child support payments she received from Kevin Von Behren, respondent, for support of their three children. In May 1991, Kevin filed a petition to decrease those payments. In June and July 1993, the trial court held hearings on these motions and ultimately increased Kevin's child support payments. Cynthia also filed a petition requesting the court to order Kevin to pay her attorney fees. After a hearing in January 1994 on this motion, the court awarded Cynthia a small portion of the requested amount.

Cynthia appeals, arguing that the trial court erred by (1) increasing Kevin's child support obligation to only $1,500 per month, and (2) awarding her only a small portion of her attorney fees. * * *

I. BACKGROUND

In October 1984, Cynthia and Kevin were granted a dissolution of their seven-year marriage. During their marriage, they had three children, Kevin (born December 1978), Jacob (born August 1980), and Joshua (born October 1981). Cynthia was awarded custody of the children, and Kevin was ordered to pay $400 per month in child support. By agreement of the parties, the amount of child support was increased to $500 per month in June 1987. * * *

In 1985, Kevin began living with Brenda. At that time, Kevin ran a bait shop and archery business. In September 1985, Kevin was discharged in bankruptcy, but continued to attempt to run these businesses. Because these businesses continued to cause financial difficulties, he and Brenda decided to start an electrical contracting business, called Von Behren Electric. Kevin started this business with only an old pickup truck and a drill which his father had given him. Brenda's credit cards were used to purchase other business supplies and materials. Brenda handled the general office work, including taking phone calls, picking up mail, preparing bills, banking, and preparing bids. Kevin performed the electrical contracting work. When they began the business, Brenda was also a court reporter, and she continued to receive income from this job for about two years thereafter.

After Kevin and Brenda began living together, they opened a joint checking account, which they used for all personal and business transactions. They did not pay themselves wages or a salary, but instead withdrew money from the account for both personal or business reasons. They put any money received into this joint account. At the time of the 1993 hearings, they continued this practice for handling money.

Von Behren Electric proved to be quite prosperous. In November 1991, Kevin and Brenda incorporated Von Behren Electric upon the advice of their accountant, Carol Nelson. Nelson kept track of their expenses, separating all their transactions into personal and business categories. She also prepared a yearly profit and loss statement for the business. After incorporating, Kevin and Brenda paid themselves an annual salary of $12,000 each. However, if they needed any additional money for personal expenses, they would merely withdraw this from the joint checking account. * * *

II. ANALYSIS

A. Child Support

* * *

2. Were Kevin and Brenda Business Partners?

Cynthia first argues that the trial court erred in finding that Kevin and Brenda were partners in Von Behren Electric and Von Behren Properties. Essentially, Cynthia claims that Kevin is sole owner of the two businesses and that Brenda is one of his employees. As a result, Cynthia contends that all of the net income from Von Behren Electric and Von Behren Properties should be accorded to Kevin, not just half of this income as determined by the trial court based upon its finding that a partnership existed. Kevin responds that the court did not abuse its discretion by finding a partnership.

The existence of a partnership is a question of the parties' intent and is based upon all the facts and circumstances surrounding the formation of the relationship at issue. [citations omitted] As a result, the formalities of a written partnership agreement are unnecessary to prove the existence of a partnership. [citations omitted] A partnership arises when (1) parties join together to carry on a venture for their common benefit, (2) each party contributes property or services to the venture, and (3) each party has a community of interest in the profits of the venture. * * *

Cynthia points to the following facts which she claims support a conclusion that Kevin and Brenda were not partners in the Von Behren businesses: (1) prior to their marriage, Kevin and Brenda filed separate tax returns, in which Kevin reported all of the business income and Brenda reported only her court reporting income; (2) when they filed joint tax returns after their marriage, Brenda did not report any income from either business on her separate tax schedules; (3) Kevin put "sole proprietorship" on the top (in bold letters) of his tax return schedules for 1988 through 1991; (4) no written partnership agreement exists; (5) they never filed a partnership tax return; (6) they never informed Nelson, their accountant, that they were a partnership; (7) Brenda's name is not on any of the legal documents or deeds for the real estate known as Von Behren Properties; (8) all business vehicles are titled in Kevin's name; (9) no business signs indicated that either business was a partnership; (10) business cards for Von Behren Electric, Inc., state "Kevin Von Behren/Owner;" and (11) when Kevin answered interrogatories for this case, he stated that he was sole owner and that Brenda worked for him.

Kevin asserts that the following facts support his claim that he and Brenda were partners in the Von Behren businesses: (1) in 1987, he and Brenda verbally agreed to "start an electrical contracting business to see if they could make some money out of it;" (2) Brenda's credit cards were used to obtain credit when they began the electrical business because he had no credit available after going through bankruptcy; (3) all money earned by the electrical business was put into their joint checking account; (4) neither he nor Brenda received wages from the electrical business; (5) Brenda gave up her court reporting career to work full-time for the business; (6) Brenda was not paid separately for her work for the business; and (7) Brenda performed integral duties for the business, including paying all bills, managing the business, coordinating employees and equipment, handling the payroll, taking phone calls, and dealing with other important matters. Kevin further claims that the lack of proper written formalities for their electrical business does not negate their original agreement to "start a business and make some money together." Also, Kevin asserts that Von Behren Properties was handled in the same manner as the electrical business, and thus should be treated as a similar entity.

After reviewing the evidence, the trial court found that Brenda was involved with Kevin in the electrical contracting business when it began in 1987. Also, the court noted that "Brenda was substantially and integrally involved in the Von Behren electrical business and other enterprises and shared in the economic results of the business[es]," and concluded that their business relationship was a partnership. Based upon our review of the record, we cannot say that this conclusion was against the manifest weight of the evidence.

Obviously, Kevin and Brenda are not sophisticated business people. While the trial court should consider the absence of written formalities, that is only one factor to consider when determining if a partnership exists. The trial court must review all facts and circumstances surrounding the formation of the business. In this case, both Kevin and Brenda provided services for the businesses, Brenda provided credit for the initial operations of the business, and Kevin contributed assets to the business. Also, all the money earned by the business was put into their joint account and used for reinvestment in the businesses or for their personal needs. Accordingly, we conclude that the trial court did not err by finding that Kevin sustained his burden of proving that his businesses were partnerships with Brenda. Consequently, the trial court did not err in according Kevin only half of the income from the two businesses.

Martin v. Peyton
246 N.Y. 213, 158 N.E. 77 (1927)

ANDREWS , J.

[Creditors of the bankrupt firm of Knauth, Nachod & Kuhne are suing K.N. & K. as well as Peyton and others who had loaned money to K.N. & K. The lower courts had held that those who had loaned money to K.N. & K. were not partners.]

Much ancient learning as to partnership is obsolete. Today only those who are partners between themselves may be charged for partnership debts by others. Partnership Law (Consol. Laws, c. 39), § 11. [UPA § 7] There is one exception. Now and then a recovery is allowed where in truth such relationship is absent. This is because the debtor may not deny the claim. Section 27. [UPA § 16] * * *

Assuming some written contract between the parties, the question may arise whether it creates a partnership. If it be complete, if it expresses in good faith the full understanding and obligation of the parties, then it is for the court to say whether a partnership exists. It may, however, be a mere sham intended to hide the real relationship. Then other results follow. In passing upon it, effect is to be given to each provision. Mere words will not blind us to realities. Statements that no partnership is intended are not conclusive. * * *

In the case before us the claim that the defendants became partners in the firm of Knauth, Nachod & Kuhne, doing business as bankers and brokers, depends upon the interpretation of certain instruments. There is nothing in their subsequent acts determinative of or indeed material upon this question. And we are relieved of questions that sometimes arise. "The plaintiff's position is not," we are told, "that the agreements of June 4, 1921, were a false expression or incomplete expression of the intention of the parties. We say that they express defendants' intention and that that intention was to create a relationship which as a matter of law constitutes a partnership." Nor may the claim of the plaintiff be rested on any question of estoppel. "The plaintiff's claim," he stipulates, "is a claim of actual partnership, not of partnership by estoppel, and liability is not sought to be predicated upon article 27 of the New York Partnership Law."

Remitted then, as we are, to the documents themselves, we refer to circumstances surrounding their execution only so far as is necessary to make them intelligible. And we are to remember that although the intention of the parties to avoid liability as partners is clear; although in language precise and definite they deny any design to then join the firm of K.N. & K.; although they say their interests in profits should be construed merely as a measure of compensation for loans, not an interest in profits as such; although they provide that they shall not be liable for any losses or treated as partners, the question still remains whether in fact they agree to so associate themselves with the firm as to "carry on as co-owners a business for profit."

In the spring of 1921 the firm of K.N. & K. found itself in financial difficulties. John R. Hall was one of the partners. He was a friend of Mr. Peyton. From him he obtained the loan of almost $500,000 of Liberty bonds, which K.N. & K. might use as collateral to secure bank advances. This, however, was not sufficient. The firm and its members had engaged in unwise speculations, and it was deeply involved. Mr. Hall was also intimately acquainted with George W. Perkins, Jr., and with Edward W. Freeman. He also knew Mrs. Peyton and Mrs. Perkins and Mrs. Freeman. All were anxious to help him. He therefore, representing K.N. & K., entered into negotiations with them. While they were pending, a proposition was made that Mr. Peyton, Mr. Perkins, and Mr. Freeman, or some of them, should become partners. It met a decided refusal. Finally an agreement was reached. It is expressed in three documents, executed on the same day, all a part of the one transaction. They were drawn with care and are unambiguous. We shall refer to them as "the agreement," "the indenture," and "the option."

We have no doubt as to their general purpose. The respondents were to loan K.N. & K. $2,500,000 worth of liquid securities, which were to be returned to them on or before April 15, 1923. The firm might hypothecate them to secure loans totaling $2,000,000, using the proceeds as its business necessities required. To insure respondents against loss K.N. & K. were to turn over to them a large number of their own securities which may have been valuable, but which were of so speculative a nature that they could not be used as collateral for bank loans. In compensation for the loan the respondents were to receive 40 per cent of the profits of the firm until the return was made, not exceeding, however, $500,000, and not less than $100,000. Merely because the transaction involved the transfer of securities and not of cash does not prevent its being a loan, within the meaning of section 11 [UPA § 7]. The respondents also were given an option to join the firm if they, or any of them, expressed a desire to do so before June 4, 1923.

Many other detailed agreements are contained in the papers. Are they such as may be properly inserted to protect the lenders? Or do they go further? Whatever their purpose, did they in truth associate the respondents with the firm so that they and it together thereafter carried on as co-owners a business for profit? The answer depends upon an analysis of these various provisions.

As representing the lenders, Mr. Peyton and Mr. Freeman are called "trustees." The loaned securities when used as collateral are not to be mingled with other securities of K. N. & K., and the trustees at all times are to be kept informed of all transactions affecting them. To them shall be paid all dividends and income accruing therefrom. They may also substitute for any of the securities loaned securities of equal value. With their consent the firm may sell any of its securities held by the respondents, the proceeds to go, however, to the trustees. In other similar ways the trustees may deal with these same securities, but the securities loaned shall always be sufficient in value to permit of their hypothecation for $2,000,000. If they rise in price, the excess may be withdrawn by the defendants. If they fall, they shall make good the deficiency.

So far, there is no hint that the transaction is not a loan of securities with a provision for compensation. Later a somewhat closer connection with the firm appears. Until the securities are returned, the directing management of the firm is to be in the hands of John R. Hall, and his life is to be insured for $1,000,000 and the policies are to be assigned as further collateral security to the trustees. These requirements are not unnatural. Hall was the one known and trusted by the defendants. Their acquaintance with the other members of the firm was of the slightest. These others had brought an old and established business to the verge of bankruptcy. As the respondents knew, they also had engaged in unsafe speculation. The respondents were about to loan $2,500,000 of good securities. As collateral they were to receive others of problematical value. What they required seems but ordinary caution. Nor does it imply an association in the business.

The trustees are to be kept advised as to the conduct of the business and consulted as to important matters. They may inspect the firm books and are entitled to any information they think important. Finally, they may veto any business they think highly speculative or injurious. Again we hold this but a proper precaution to safeguard the loan. The trustees may not initiate any transaction as a partner may do. They may not bind the firm by any action of their own. Under the circumstances the safety of the loan depended upon the business success of K. N. & K. This success was likely to be compromised by the inclination of its members to engage in speculation. No longer, if the respondents were to be protected, should it be allowed. The trustees therefore might prohibit it, and that their prohibition might be effective, information was to be furnished them. Not dissimilar agreements have been held proper to guard the interests of the lender.

As further security each member of K. N. & K. is to assign to the trustees their interest in the firm. No loan by the firm to any member is permitted and the amount each may draw is fixed. No other distribution of profits is to be made. So that realized profits may be calculated the existing capital is stated to be $700,000, and profits are to be realized as promptly as good business practice will permit. In case the trustees think this is not done, the question is left to them and to Mr. Hall, and if they differ then to an arbitrator. There is no obligation that the firm shall continue the business. It may dissolve at any time. Again we conclude there is nothing here not properly adapted to secure the interest of the respondents as lenders. If their compensation is dependent on a percentage of the profits, still provision must be made to define what these profits shall be.

The "indenture" is substantially a mortgage of the collateral delivered by K. N. & K. to the trustees to secure the performance of the "agreement." It certainly does not strengthen the claim that the respondents were partners.

Finally we have the "option." It permits the respondents, or any of them, or their assignees or nominees to enter the firm at a later date if they desire to do so by buying 50 per cent or less of the interests therein of all or any of the members at a stated price. Or a corporation may, if the respondents and the members agree, be formed in place of the firm. Meanwhile, apparently with the design of protecting the firm business against improper or ill-judged action which might render the option valueless, each member of the firm is to place his resignation in the hands of Mr. Hall. If at any time he and the trustees agree that such resignation should be accepted, that member shall then retire, receiving the value of his interest calculated as of the date of such retirement.

This last provision is somewhat unusual, yet it is not enough in itself to show that on June 4, 1921, a present partnership was created, nor taking these various papers as a whole do we reach such a result. It is quite true that even if one or two or three like provisions contained in such a contract do not require this conclusion, yet it is also true that when taken together a point may come where stipulations immaterial separately cover so wide a field that we should hold a partnership exists. As in other branches of the law, a question of degree is often the determining factor. Here that point has not been reached. . . . The judgment appealed from should be affirmed, with costs.

Minute Maid Corp. v. United Foods, Inc.
291 F.2d 577 (5th Cir. 1961), *cert. denied*, 368 U.S. 928 (1961)

TUTTLE, CHIEF JUDGE.

This is an appeal from a judgment of the trial court, sitting without a jury, denying a recovery from United States Cold Storage Corporation by the appellant for the purchase price of commodities sold by it to the United Foods, Inc.

Appellant's theory of recovery was that United Foods, Inc., a direct purchaser from it, was engaged in a partnership operation with the Cold Storage Corporation, thus making Cold Storage liable for the unpaid purchase price.

There is no dispute about the fact that United Foods was indebted to Minute Maid Corporation in the sum of $143,141.66, representing the purchase price of frozen food products sold to United. The question whether Cold Storage is equally liable for this sum must be answered in the light of the following history of the relationship between the parties: Commencing November 1, 1956, United Foods was an authorized direct buyer of products packaged by Minute Maid; Minute Maid's terms of sale for retail size packages to authorized direct buyers, such as United Foods, included discounts based upon the volume of goods included in a single order, which discounts were generally referred to as "quantity allowances" or "freight allowances," or described in the price list as "truckload storage allowances" and "car-load storage allowances"; Minute Maid stored a substantial amount of frozen foods in Dallas, Texas, through arrangements with United Foods, paying United Foods at the rate of 20 cents per hundred-weight for such storage; at all times pertinent to this action Cold Storage owned and operated a cold storage warehouse in Dallas, Texas.

United Foods did not have the financial ability from its own resources plus normal credit sources to finance the carrying of a large inventory of frozen food products; that means that there were certain substantial price benefits that it could not get; Cold Storage did have and was willing to make funds available to assist United Foods in buying Minute Maid products in quantities that permitted the maximum discounts; the market conditions affecting frozen food products are such that the price of such goods tends to rise from the month of May to the end of the year, and such increases in price as to citrus food products is as high as 50% in years when weather conditions adversely affect citrus production; at all times pertinent to this action a direct buyer of frozen food products, such as United Foods, was protected against price declines to the extent of inventories representing goods received during the last thirty day period; United Foods, without the knowledge of Minute Maid, operated so as to obtain an additional thirty days protection against price declines by taking goods owned by Minute Maid from warehouses approximately thirty days prior to notifying Minute Maid of the withdrawal. The effect of this relationship made it possible for a direct buyer, by buying large quantities, to profit as much as 50% on inventories by receiving notice from Minute Maid of proposed price increases a considerable time in advance of the price increase, whereas there was practically no risk of a loss on such inventories by reason of the sixty days protection against price declines above referred to. It is undisputed that this made peculiarly attractive the speculation in inventories.

On May 1, 1957, United Foods and Cold Storage entered into an agreement which spelled out their relationship with each other. Since we conclude that the essential question presented by this appeal must be resolved by reference to this written agreement we consider it essential to print the relevant portions of it in full as follows:

Memorandum of Agreement
May 1, 1957
Between—United Foods, Inc., referred to as United and United States Cold Storage Corporation, referred to as U.S.
United is a broker of frozen foods in the Dallas, Texas, Area;
U.S. operates cold storage plants at Dallas and Fort Worth, and will extend finance services to United on the following basis:

1. Staple commodities bought by United, stored in U. S. plants, will be the collateral if acceptable to U.S., together with acceptable (to U.S.) accounts receivable resulting from sales of the commodities, for loans to be made by U.S. The aggregate amount of loans outstanding at both plants, taken together, shall not exceed $300,000.00.

2. The amount of loan to United on any lot of product shall be United's gross cost delivered to the warehouse of U.S. The amount of the loan on any of United accounts receivable shall be the amount of the invoices.

3. Notes to U.S. shall be given by United for each loan and shall bear interest at 6% until paid.

4. Notes for loans on commodities shall be paid when product is ordered from warehouse.

5. Notes for loans on accounts receivable shall be paid to U.S. by endorsement of check received from customer to U.S. provided that United will itself pay U.S. for any invoices not otherwise paid in 45 days from date of invoice.

6. Warehouse charges on staple product on which loans are made on these terms shall be 15¢/100 lbs. handling and 12¢/100 lbs. per month storage, based on the gross weight of package and contents, and a lot delivery charge of 50¢ as current at each plant. Interest, interest service charges and insurance charges shall be at the rates current at each plant. Tariff rates will apply on all other products stored.

7. All warehouse, interest and insurance charges shall be billed by U.S. monthly, and charged to the "Special Account" described below.

8. The "Special Account" on the books of U.S. is to be set up to accumulate charges as set forth in Paragraph 7 and to accumulate credits as follows:

    a. United shall pay to U.S. the 6¢ per dozen packer allowance on retail merchandise or any other quantity allowance, advertising, freight, allowance, incentive and profit to the Special Account;

    b. United shall pay to U.S. for the Special Account the incentive from any packer special proposals, as for instance, in forward buying, in anticipating of a price raise, or other inducements to move special product items, such as fish, shrimp, poultry and the like;

    c. United is paid 20¢/100 lbs./month by Minute Maid on institutional merchandise and this allowance will be paid to U.S. for the Special Account to which also U.S. will debit the warehouse charges on this product; * * *

9. At the end of the calendar year, the Special Account shall be closed, and

    a. If there is a credit balance, 1/2 thereof shall be paid by U.S. to United within 20 days and the remainder shall be retained by U.S. as its property.

    b. If there is a debit balance, U.S. shall so notify United, who will pay U.S. 1/2 of the amount of such debit balance within 20 days of notification. * * *

11. In case of pending price increase, U.S. and United may agree on the volume to be purchased by United, and U.S. will loan, upon receipt of product in storage, the cost to United. When the price increase is effective, U.S. will loan United an additional amount equivalent to the price increase, and such amount shall be paid by United to U.S. for credit to the Special Account, as set forth in Paragraph 8 b.

12. This agreement shall terminate January 1, 1958, but may be extended by written agreement of the parties hereto.

On June 24, 1957, the foregoing agreement was amended only to the extent of providing that instead of $300,000 the aggregate amount of loans outstanding was increased to $500,000.

All of the sales for which the purchase price is here in litigation were made while this contract was in effect. Subsequently, on December 9, 1957, at which time there was a credit balance of approximately $22,000 in the "special account," referred to in the contract, the parties entered into a termination agreement terminating the contract effective December 31, 1957. This contract further provides:

> Any amounts due by United States Cold Storage Corporation to United Foods, Inc. under said contract and the provisions of paragraph nine thereof shall be retained by United States Cold Storage Corporation to apply against future storage and financing charges that may accrue on products stored with them by United Foods, Inc.

United Foods, as a food broker engaged in the business of selling Minute Maid products, during the year 1957 handled in excess of $1,000,000 of these products. This business was carried on by United Foods at its own office, with its own employees, and at its own expense.

During the life of the contract, Cold Storage did advance 100% of the invoice price of Minute Maid products purchased and stored by United Foods in Cold Storage's warehouse; and United Foods deposited in the "special account" all of the allowances referred to in the written contract. This account, which was held by Cold Storage, paid Cold Storage interest at 6% on all advances and paid its warehouse and insurance charges monthly. At the end of the year the profits from the accumulated credits exceeded these expenses by some $22,000.

Minute Maid did not know of the relationship between United Foods and Cold Storage. It does not contend that it was misled into extending credit to United by reason of such relationship. It contends that the agreement between the parties and the course of dealing thereunder created a partnership relationship between United and Cold Storage and that Cold Storage became liable with United Foods for all debts of the partnership. Minute Maid distinguishes between the regular sales business of United Foods in selling Minute Maid products to the trade from what it considers to be the subject of the partnership. It says that the partnership consisted of a joint endeavor by United Foods and Cold Storage under which United Foods would take advantage of its position as a direct purchaser of Minute Maid products and of the financing afforded it by Cold Storage to buy products in the quantities that would yield the greatest amount in allowances and discounts and if the market appeared right, to speculate on a possible price increase; that in return for Cold Storage's agreement to finance the transaction to the extent of advancing 100% of the purchase price of the products it would store the products in Cold Storage's warehouse at a profitable rate, it would pay interest of 6% on all advances and it and Cold Storage would share equally the profits that could thus be anticipated from the discounts and from profitable speculation, if indulged in.

Cold Storage, on the other hand, contends that the agreement created only a relationship at most of debtor and creditor between it and United, or that the relationship was an ambiguous one which the trial court, on disputed evidence, found as a fact not to be a partnership.

The essential facts are not in dispute. A decision, therefore, whether the relationship shown by the undisputed facts to exist, constituted a partnership or only that of debtor and creditor is one for the court to make as a matter of law. We thus approach the question not as a reviewer of the facts, but to determine whether the trial court properly applied the law to the facts.

A critical examination of the foregoing facts, most of which are made the basis of formal findings by the trial court, necessarily leads to the following conclusions:

(1) Cold Storage was to be repaid the principal amount of its advances to United regardless of the success or failure of the enterprise.

(2) Cold Storage was to receive its warehouse charges, its interest at 6% and reimbursement for the cost of insurance out of the "special fund" set up under the contract. It seems plain that there could be no failure of the special fund to provide sufficient sums to meet these obligations and provide a profit, because the parties could in advance know exactly how much by way of special allowances and discounts would be paid into the special fund, and, of course, the charges would bear a direct relation to these same items. However, if there was a deficit in this special fund, it was to be shared by the parties equally.

(3) The advance of 100% of the invoice price of the merchandise was not a normal credit arrangement which would be available to United by the payment of legal rates of interest.

(4) Both United and Cold Storage would profit by increasing the purchases of United made possible by the arrangement between the two parties. United's profit would come from its 50% participation in the profits in the special fund and Cold Storage's profit would come from the increasing of the inventory for which it received substantial warehouse fees, an increase in inventories for which it received its 6% interest and the anticipated profit arising by reason of the fact that it could be computed in advance that the special allowances and discounts paid into the fund would exceed the carrying charges. Cold Storage became the owner of one half of this excess.

(5) Cold Storage was undoubtedly in the relation of a creditor of United; it was also in the relation of a bailee for hire.

(6) It is also clear, however, that the operation that here produced the sale of the volume of Minute Maid products to United would not have occurred by reason of Cold Storage's willingness to engage in either or both of these two activities standing alone, and on normal terms—that is as a creditor receiving a legal rate of interest and a warehouseman receiving its stated warehouse charges.

(7) It is plain that Cold Storage was interested in assisting United to create a larger indebtedness on which it would receive its interest and a larger volume of inventory on which it would receive its warehouseman's fees and that in order to assist in creating this larger volume of business for itself it participated with United in making possible the larger purchases of Minute Maid products than United could otherwise have accomplished.

Does this analysis cause us to conclude that the two parties, acting to their mutual interest to make possible an increased purchase of Minute Maid products, created a joint venture or partnership between them? * * *

Appellee is too preoccupied, we think, with its insistence that the relationship between United and Cold Storage was that of debtor and creditor. This is undoubtedly correct, but it is equally undoubtedly indecisive. Appellee also relies strongly on the contention that there was no express obligation assumed under the written contract whereby Cold Storage was to share in the overall losses of the enterprise. This, of course, is the very question that this Court has to decide, for if the relationship between the parties constituted them partners, then the law imposes upon them the obligation to pay the losses. No case has been cited from Texas or elsewhere to the effect that the mere failure to agree in the formal contract that the parties will share the losses prevents the relationship from being that of partners. * * *

It is the burden of appellee's argument here that if there is nothing more than a lender relationship, coupled with an agreement that compensation for the loan is to be in the form of a sharing in profits, either in lieu of or in addition to normal interest, these facts are sufficient to rebut the presumption that arises by the profit sharing agreement. Appellee contends that additional indicia of an intent to create a partnership must be shown either in the nature of joint control by the person sought to be bound as a partner, or an express agreement to share in losses.

Assuming this position to be correct, we think it is undeniably true here that control over the particular enterprise in which these two parties were engaged was jointly held by United and Cold Storage. We must bear in mind exactly what this enterprise was. It was not the commission food business carried on by United. It was the arrangement whereby Cold Storage furnished the financing and warehouse facilities to make possible United's use of its relationship as a direct buyer of Minute Maid products in such quantities and under such terms as would turn a profit for both of them. There can be no question but that the parties had joint control over this enterprise. This follows from the fact that United initially determined how much to buy but such determination was subject to Cold Storage's right to determine whether the proposed collateral would be "acceptable." Also, it was provided that in case of pending price increases, which the court found would offer the opportunity to speculate on inventory, the parties would agree on the volume to be purchased. In point of fact the responsible officer for United testified that, "they [Cold Storage] could have stepped in and written me [United] off pretty damned fast."

Appellee argues that the retention of warehouse receipts by Cold Storage in its name as joint depositor and the assignment of invoices to it for its protection were normal security measures taken by the lender on a warehouse stock. This, it seems to us, misses the whole point. Whether or not such security measures amounted by themselves to "control" of the partnership affairs, we think the operation heretofore outlined was clearly within the joint control of the parties. * * *

We conclude that the relationship established by the written contract of the parties and by their conduct thereunder constituted a legal partnership or joint enterprise under the Texas law. * * *

The judgment of the trial court is reversed and the case is remanded to the trial court for further proceedings not inconsistent with this opinion.

JOSEPH C. HUTCHESON, CIRCUIT JUDGE (dissenting).

* * * It seems indisputable to me under the facts as found by the district judge, indeed under the undisputed facts, that there is no basis for finding a partnership, and, therefore, for setting aside and reversing the judgment of the district court.

* * * [T]he question of whether or not a partnership is created depends entirely upon the intent, of the parties to the agreement, to create a partnership . . . not, however, their secret subjective intent but the intent manifested in what they agreed to, and did do. Here there was no such indication whatever of such an intent on the part of either United States Cold Storage or United Foods, Inc.

Second, in Texas it is settled law that "In order for there to be a partnership, the parties must not only participate in the profits but *they* must have an interest in the profits, as profits, and share them as joint owners or principals of the business or venture, as distinguished from having an interest therein as compensation under a profit sharing agreement" (emphasis added). *LeBus v. LeBus*, Tex. Civ. App., 269 S.W.2d 506, 511. Here there was no agreement between United States Cold Storage and United Foods, Inc., that they should go into any kind of business together to share the profit thereof. The agreement was specifically that the United States Cold Storage, in connection with its warehousing business would lend money to United Foods and the money loaned would be paid back to United States Cold Storage at all events, primarily out of the special account provided for in the agreement, if there was accumulated enough in it to pay it, with the further understanding, however, that there was a chance that after the loan, with interest, was paid back by United Foods, there would be additional compensation to United States Cold Storage out of one-half of the special account, if there was a balance left in it after paying the proper expenses chargeable against it.

Notes and Questions

1. **Subjective vs. objective intent.** How important were "subjective" and "objective" intent in these cases? Why might the evidence of "subjective" intent not have been persuasive in *Hassiepen*? Subjective intent alone may be controlling where the parties' agreement explicitly characterizes the relationship as either a partnership or a non-partnership (as in *Martin*). For a loan case in which the parties' characterization of the relationship as a partnership was controlling despite the absence of objective indicia of partnership, *see Rolfe v. Varley,* 860 P.2d 1152 (Wyo. 1993). *As between the alleged partners*, there may be little reason why such a provision should not be enforced, since it is a clear signal as to how parties wanted to fill the gaps in their contract.

2. **Partnership characterization and third parties.** Suppose the parties to a relationship contract for all of the elements of partnership, including management, profit-sharing and the like, but include a provision in their agreement that says that the relationship is *not* a partnership. Even if this provision would be controlling between the parties, should the provision be applied so as to preclude vicarious partner liability as to those who are unaware of the provision? It follows from both UPA § 7(1) and RUPA § 308(e) that the relationship would no more be a partnership as to third parties than it is among the alleged "partners" (*see* Note 10, below). These provisions reject a "quantum theory" of partnership in which the firm may be simultaneously a partnership and a non-partnership, depending on who looks at it. This makes sense, because in drafting their agreement the supposed "partners" take into account whether or not they will be deemed to be partners as to third parties.

3. **Objective indicia of partnership.** In *Martin* and *Minute Maid*, the courts weighed evidence for and against the parties' objective intent to be co-owners. Why do you suppose the courts reached different results in those cases? Consider the following notes concerning the objective indicia of partnership.

4. **The importance of profit sharing.** Why is profit-sharing, rather than some other feature such as joint control, singled out as triggering a presumption of partnership? Recall from Chapter 2 the significance of the principal's power of control to the existence of an agent-principal relationship. Because partners share control, this factor is more ambiguous in partnership than in agency. Profit-sharing is an important indicator of partnership because it strongly suggests that the parties would want the other default partnership rules to apply. In particular, those who share profits have incentives also to share management responsibilities in order to maximize both the revenue and expense components of profit. But note that Delaware now recognizes partnerships that are formed not for profit if the parties intend to form a partnership. DEL. CODE ANN., tit. 6, § 15-202. How would proof of such intent be shown in the absence of profits to share? How might such a partnership differ from that provided for in the statutory default provisions?

5. **What is profit-sharing?** The reasons discussed in Note 4 why profit-sharing is important help determine when there is profit-sharing for purposes of supporting the existence of partnership. Sharing gross revenues alone does not indicate partnership under the UPA and RUPA because a gross-sharer, such as a salesperson working on commission, has no incentive to control expenses. If a bank lender agrees to be compensated in part by sharing the gains on resale of property that is financed by a loan, should this qualify as profit-sharing? Given the potential for gain from the property, the bank would have an incentive to monitor the borrower's use of the property. On the other hand, the property value may depend more on market factors and therefore may not indicate much about the bank's participation in the business. Moreover, there is a need for certainty so that the parties can have some idea at the outset of their relationship and whether it will be characterized as a partnership. Accordingly, it makes sense to make only sharing of profits in the traditional accounting sense of net income, rather than any kind of benefit-sharing, an indicator of partnership.

6. **Control.** Although the control factor may not be quite as important to partnership as to agency, it is an important indicator of partnership. *Martin* shows that, as with respect to agency (*see* Note 1, p. 17), active participation in management may be a stronger indicator of partnership than a mere veto power.

7. **Liability as risk-allocation.** Apart from control as a specific indicator of partnership, a court may find that a controlling party is a partner where it concludes that this party should bear the risks from dealings with third parties. Does this explain the *Minute Maid* decision?

8. **Loss-sharing.** Like profit-sharing, loss-sharing, strongly indicates the extent of the sharer's incentive to monitor the business. When is there the requisite loss-sharing? For example, a lender who makes a "non-recourse" loan that precludes recovery out of the borrower's non-partnership assets shares in the risks of the borrower's business. However, analogous to the discussion of profit-sharing in Note 5, there is a danger of uncertainty and unpredictability in making anyone who somehow shares business risk a partner. It follows that only loss-sharing in the traditional accounting sense of sharing in the excess of expenses over revenues should support the existence of a partnership relationship.

9. **Protected relationships**. Certain profit-sharing relationships, such as the debtor-creditor relationships involved in *Martin* and *Minute Maid*, are singled out in the UPA and RUPA as not being presumptive partnerships. This reflects a legislative judgment that people in such relationships are likely to share profits without wanting the other elements of partnership, such as joint control. But as *Minute Maid* makes clear, debtors and creditors and others in protected relationships *can* be partners. The significance of finding one of these "protected relationships" is that the proponent of partnership must show something more than profit-sharing in connection with this relationship in order to prevail. There may be protected relationships other than those listed in the statute. In particular, some courts have hesitated to recognize partnerships between profit-sharing co-managing spouses on the theory that such indicia as commingled accounts and participation in con-

trol may indicate a family rather than a partnership relationship. *See* BROMBERG & RIBSTEIN ON PARTNERSHIP, § 2.10. Why do you suppose the court was nevertheless willing to find a partnership in *Hassiepen*?

10. **Partnership by estoppel**. Even a non-partnership may be a purported or estoppel partnership on the basis of representations to third parties. *See* UPA § 16; RUPA § 308. One of the main questions is what kinds of representations create this estoppel. In *Atlas Tack Corp. v. DiMasi*, 37 Mass. App. Ct. 66, 637 N.E.2d 230 (1994), the court held that there might be a partnership by estoppel where plaintiff was billed on stationery which included defendant's name in the name of "a professional association," relying partly on an ethics opinion that characterized the term as possibly implying a partnership. In *Kansallis Finance Ltd. v. Fern*, 40 F.3d 476 (1st Cir. 1994) the court held a law firm might be an *actual* partnership despite the fact that the firm's letterhead described it as a "professional association." In *Armato v. Baden*, 71 Cal. App. 4th 885, 84 Cal. Rptr. 2d 294, 302 (1999), doctors whose names were listed on a medical corporation's office door, appointment cards and prescription pads, but used separate receptionists, were not as a matter of law ostensible partners, and therefore not vicariously liable for the negligence of the corporation's employee.

Problem

Your client, Airwalker Ventures, a venture capital fund, has been approached by Michael Blomoni, a producer-director of movies whose past projects have had good reviews, but who has a reputation for budget overruns and a record of box office failures. Having been unable to get either studio or bank financing for his latest project, Blomoni is trying Airwalker. Airwalker thinks the project, tentatively entitled "Big Bang," an epic about the destruction of the universe, might be a good investment. However, Airwalker wants to make sure that the contract includes significant control provisions to help ensure that the movie is successful and does not seriously overrun its budget. Among other things, Airwalker is concerned about costly location filming, the use of stars with limited "box office" potential particularly in the lucrative foreign market, and Blomoni's propensity for depressing endings that turn off audiences. At the same time, Airwalker wants to be sure that its exposure to risk on this project does not exceed the amount of its financial investment. Airwalker also wants to be adequately compensated for the significant risks it would be taking in financing this venture. Airwalker seeks your advice on how the financing agreement may be structured to meet these objectives. What would you suggest in light of both the partnership cases in this section and the agency cases in § 2.02?

3.03 Existence of Partnership: Other Law

The determination of whether a partnership exists may interrelate with non-partnership law. Section A discusses a situation in which the partnership determination to some extent depends on other law, while Section B discusses the potential impact of the partnership determination on application of other law.

A.   Employment Discrimination

The employment discrimination laws clearly apply to partnership employment decisions regarding non-partner employees, including the "up or out" decision to promote or terminate a law firm associate. *See Hishon v. King & Spalding*, 467 U.S. 69 (1984). In a concurring opinion in this case, Justice Powell noted that the employment discrimination laws probably do not regulate employment decisions involving bona fide partners. *Id.* at 79. One case ordered the admission of an associate upon a finding of discrimination, thereby holding that employment discrimination law may override partnership law. *See Hopkins v. Price Waterhouse*, 920 F.2d 967 (D.C. Cir. 1990). However, the court noted that the case involved "only an employee's elevation to partnership" rather than her retention or the regulation of the partners' relations. *Id.* at 979. The following case deals with the question left open in these cases—who is a "partner."

Simpson v. Ernst & Young
850 F. Supp. 648 (S.D. Ohio 1994)

Steinberg, United States Magistrate Judge.
  * * * Plaintiff P. LaRue Simpson brings this action against Ernst & Young alleging claims under the Age Discrimination in Employment Act (ADEA), 29 U.S.C. § 621 *et seq.*; Age Discrimination By Employers, Ohio Revised Code § 4101.17; the Employee Retirement Income Security Act (ERISA). * * *
  Simpson contends that he was Ernst & Young's employee; therefore, this Court has jurisdiction over his ADEA, Ohio age discrimination, and ERISA claims. Ernst & Young contends that Simpson was a partner, and, because these statutes apply only to employees, he has no claim as a matter of law. * * * Based on the trial evidence, the parties agreed there are no disputed questions of material fact on the jurisdictional issue and resubmitted it to the Court for summary judgment. The parties also submitted for summary judgment the issue whether Simpson was an employee within the meaning of ERISA.

UNDISPUTED FACTS

  * * * Ernst & Young is a large accounting firm created in 1989 by the merger of the Ernst & Whinney and Arthur Young accounting firms. Prior to his relationship with Ernst & Young, Simpson was the Managing Partner for Arthur Young's Cincinnati, Ohio office. * * *

VI. Simpson's Discharge

At the time of the merger, an analysis of the merged firms' retirement benefit plans showed that the accumulated benefit obligations were $290,000,000 higher than the funding then available. Despite representations that the merger was not expected to result in a reduction in "partners" the Management Committee had concluded that a substantial number of "partners" would have to be discharged. * * *

Ernst & Young Management Committee member Jesse Miles stated that the firm engaged in a "process of resignations and retirements" to reduce the number of "partners" . . . "in order to protect the firm from substantial reduction in profits." * * *

The Management Committee had the right to request Simpson to terminate his relationship with Ernst & Young U.S. by giving him six months written notice. Simpson had no right to appeal his discharge or the discharge of any other Party. Upon discharge, the Management Committee determined the net amount owing to a Party. That determination was final and binding. * * * In May 1990, Ernst & Young U.S. requested Simpson's resignation. He refused, and on June 19, 1990, he was given written notification that he was discharged effective December 19, 1990. He was then 46 years old. * * *

OPINION

I. The Court Should Apply Traditional Partnership Law Concepts In Determining Whether Simpson Was A Partner Or An Employee

Pursuant to 29 U.S.C. § 623(a)(1), it is "unlawful for an employer . . . to discharge any individual . . . because of such individual's age." The Act defines an employee as "an individual employed by any employer." 29 U.S.C. § 630(f). An employer is defined as "a person engaged in an industry affecting commerce who has twenty or more employees . . . ." 29 U.S.C. § 630(b). * * * These definitions are circular and explain nothing. * * *

Ernst & Young asserts that neither Simpson nor any other Party discharged during 1990 and 1991 is entitled to the protection afforded by the employment discrimination laws because these individuals are not employees, but partners. The inescapable logic of this position is that Ernst & Young claims to be free to discriminate against hundreds of its accountants due to age, race, sex, religion, national origin, and handicap because it asserts they are not employees.

Simpson, who considered himself to be a partner during his employment with Ernst & Young, now contends that he was actually an employee, as that term is defined in the law, and did not meet the legal definition of partner. He seeks the protection of the age discrimination laws. * * * Simpson contends that the Court should use an "economic reality" test rather than traditional legal concepts in determining whether he was a partner or employee. The Sixth Circuit has described this test as "a loose formulation, leaving the determination of employment status to case-by-case resolution based on the totality of the circumstances." *Lilley v. BTM Corporation*, 958 F.2d 746, 750 (6th Cir.), *cert. denied*, 113 S. Ct. 376, 121 L.Ed.2d 287 (1992).

Ernst & Young contends that an economic reality test is not the appropriate means to determine whether an individual is a partner or employee and that Simpson's status must be determined by the application of traditional partnership law concepts. Ernst & Young claims Simpson possessed both "essential and non-essential" attributes of a partner. It argues that whatever partnership characteristics Simpson lacked, he voluntarily delegated them to the Management Committee and their absence did not destroy his partner status. Therefore, it claims, the Court has no jurisdiction over his age discrimination claims. * * *

In *Nationwide Mutual Insurance Co. v. Darden*, [112 S. Ct. 1344, 1348, 117 L. Ed. 2d 581 (1992),] . . . decided after the aforementioned cases, the Supreme Court unanimously ruled that traditional agency law criteria should be used to determine whether the plaintiff was an independent contractor or an employee under ERISA. * * *

The Court distinguished the economic reality test applied in [Fair Labor Standards Act] cases [citations omitted], because unlike ERISA, FLSA contained an "expansive" definition of the verb employ to mean "suffer or permit to work." *Darden*, 112 S. Ct. at 1350. * * *

Although neither the Supreme Court nor the Sixth Circuit has addressed the proper test to be used to distinguish partners from employees, *Darden* strongly counsels the use of traditional legal principles to determine this issue rather than a broader test. * * *

We do not view the *Darden* analysis as a quantitative test where the Court simply adds up employee and employer attributes a claimant possessed. Rather, it must be a qualitative test to determine whether the claimant actually met the traditional legal definition. In order to determine whether Simpson was a bona fide partner, we must examine the traditional legal concepts of partnership.

II. Traditional Partnership Law Concepts

The parties agree that New York law applies to the Ernst & Young organization. Both the Partnership Agreement and the U.S. Agreement state that their construction is in accordance with the laws of the State of New York. In New York, traditional partnership concepts are codified in N.Y. PARTNERSHIP LAW § 1 *et seq.* (McKinney 1988) and are set forth in the state's case law. * * * [The court here reviews New York law on the characteristics of partnerships.]

The Uniform Partnership Act (UPA) has been adopted by most states, including New York in 1919, as the governing body of partnership law. It sets forth, among others, the following characteristics of a partner: unlimited liability (§ 15); the right to share in profits and participate in management (§ 18(a), (e)); the right and duty to act as an agent of the other partners (§ 9); shared ownership (§ 6); and fiduciary relationship among partners (§ 21). The drafters of the UPA used the term "co-owners" to indicate that each partner has "the power of ultimate control." UNIF. PARTNERSHIP ACT § 6 official cmt., U.L.A. (1969).

The concurring opinion in *Hishon v. King & Spaulding*, 467 U.S. 69, 104 S. Ct. 2229, 81 L. Ed. 2d 59 (1984), also provides some guidance as to the nature of partnership. There, Justice Powell reasoned that the relationship among partners should not be characterized as an employment relationship to which Title VII may apply: The relationship among law partners differs markedly from that between employer and employee. * * * The essence of the law partnership is the common conduct of a shared enterprise. The relationship among law partners contemplates that decisions important to the partnership normally will be made by common agreement . . . or consent among the partners. *Id*. at 79-80, 104 S. Ct. at 2236. Critical to this concept of a professional partnership is the partners' authority to make decisions important to the partnership. The mere labeling of an individual as a partner does not make him so. * * *

III. Simpson Was An Employee Subject To ADEA Protection

A. Simpson Did Not Make A True Capital Contribution To The Firm

Simpson never established a capital account with Ernst & Young. Therefore, we give no weight to the Partnership Agreement's reference to a Capital Account.

Simpson established an Ernst & Young U.S. Capital Account. Simpson's "capital" payment into this account was arranged by Ernst & Young and financed by Citibank. This "capital contribution" generated interest payments from Ernst & Young U.S. rather than a pro rata share of the profits. The Capital Account was not the basis for a Party's pro rata share of either profits or firm assets. Thus, Simpson's payment to Ernst & Young U.S. was more akin to a loan than a capital contribution.

Gary Stewart, a CPA and expert in the field of CPA business organizations, testified at trial that Simpson did not contribute capital but rather loaned money to Ernst & Young U.S. Stewart's opinion was based on several factors: 1) the definition of "firm capital" in Section 7 of the U.S. Agreement indicates that "amounts owing to Parties" are treated as a firm liability rather than as owner's equity; 2) when a Party withdraws from the firm, he receives only what he paid in plus interest, rather than a percentage of the value of the firm; and 3) the firm paid interest to the Parties on their Capital Accounts.

We view Simpson's Capital Account as a paper transaction designed to give him the appearance, but not the reality, of a partner. On its face, his substantial payment ($84,000) appears to be a capital contribution to the firm. However, Simpson did not invest one cent of his own money in the firm. The firm arranged the bank loan that Simpson signed and paid the interest on his behalf. He made no payments on the principal. Although the U.S. Agreement bound him to begin reducing the principal in his third year with Ernst & Young U.S., he was discharged before then. Although he was liable to the bank for the principal, his Capital Account at the firm was available to, and ultimately did, satisfy the debt. His yearly earnings and discharge payment were not based on the proportion the $84,000 contribution had to total capital investment in the firm. It appears that the primary significance of his Capital Account was not to establish Simpson's ownership interest, but to generate funds for the firm. As of the date of Simpson's termination, he had not made a true capital contribution to the firm.

B. Simpson Did Not Share In The Firm's Profits and Losses

Simpson received no compensation from Ernst & Young. Therefore, we give no weight to the reference in the Partnership Agreement that its profits be allocated among its Partners.

Simpson received an annual salary from Ernst & Young U.S., as determined by the Management Committee. The U.S. Agreement does not identify Simpson as a partner and specifically refers to his compensation as "salary." For state tax purposes, Ernst & Young U.S. treated Simpson's compensation as salary. For federal tax purposes, however, it treated it as a partnership distribution of earnings. This is of little significance, because under Internal Revenue Code regulations, a partnership is considered to be anything which is not a corporation, trust, or estate. 26 C.F.R. § 301.7701-3(a). Simpson's salary did not vary based on the rise and fall of firm profits. There was no evidence that Simpson or any other Party were required to return any amount of salary due to declining profits. Nor was there evidence that his salary was calculated as a proportionate share of the firm's profits.

In addition to his salary from Ernst & Young U.S., Simpson was eligible to receive an "allocation" each year, also determined by the Management Committee. Neither party discussed in their memoranda the relative amounts of Simpson's salary compared to his allocation or its significance. Pursuant to the U.S. Agreement, a Party could receive advances against his/her allocation, but would have to return any advances in the event that they exceeded the allocation. The separate denominations and treatment of salary and allocation indicate that the two items are different. There is no evidence, however, that allocations were calculated from net profits or even from gross receipts. Nor is there evidence that Simpson's allocation was calculated as a proportionate share. The U.S. Agreement fails to set forth any formula for calculating allocations, leaving the determination instead to the Management Committee. Since Simpson had no right to an accounting as to how his allocation was calculated, he did not have the ability to offer evidence on this issue. It is fair to infer that, had Simpson's allocation been calculated from his proportionate share of net profits, Ernst & Young would have introduced that favorable evidence. Therefore, we conclude the allocation was comparable to a periodic bonus paid to an employee at the firm's discretion from the firm's gross revenues. [citation omitted] * * *

C. Simpson Had No Other Indicia Of An Ownership Interest In The Firm

Ernst & Young contends that Simpson's ownership rights in the firm are demonstrated by his UBT [unbilled time and uncollected fees] account. The UBT account, however, is not indicative of his relationship with Ernst & Young since this account was a carry-over from his prior relationship with Arthur Young. Neither Ernst & Young nor Ernst & Young U.S. utilized UBT accounts. Their failure to continue a UBT arrangement demonstrates that the firms, rather than their members, owned the accounts receivable.

Ernst & Young also contends that Simpson had a contingent undivided interest in all firm assets, citing the U.S. Agreement, Section 18. That section, however, applies only upon dissolution or liquidation of the firm. When Simpson left the firm, Ernst & Young U.S. calculated his compensation in December, nine months prior to the firm's fiscal year end, using an estimate based on the prior year's figures. Thus, Simpson's discharge compensation was not measured by any ownership interest in the firm's assets but was a salary. Furthermore, Section 18 states that, upon dissolution or liquidation, the amount owing to each Party shall be computed pursuant to Section 11. The latter does not provide for a distribution of an undivided interest in firm assets. Rather, it awards a Party the amount of his Account, as determined by the Management Committee; any allocations or interest the firm owes the Party; and the Party's proportionate allocation for the current fiscal year, less any liability the Party owes the firm, plus an "earnings charge" pursuant to Section 9 computed by the Management Committee. Simpson did not possess an undivided interest in firm assets.

Ernst & Young claims that Simpson's ownership interest in the firm is shown by his rights regarding the firm's operations. It points to the fact that Simpson could vote for amendments to the Partnership Agreement and the U.S. Agreement, dissolution of the firm, certain mergers, and members of the Advisory Council. Simpson's voting rights, however, were illusory because the Advisory Council had the right to approve and thus, implicitly, to veto any vote put to the Parties. Simpson's right to vote for members of the Advisory Council was perfunctory since the candidates were unopposed and selected by the Nominating Committee which, in turn, was selected by the Management Committee. Furthermore, the Advisory Council had no direct authority to act, serving only in an advisory capacity to the Management Committee. The Chairman selected the members of the Management Committee without any vote of the Parties, and the Management Committee selected the Chairman. The Chairman and the Management Committee managed the firm. Thus, as a practical matter, the Parties had no power to alter decisions of the Chairman and the Management Committee.

Even more illuminating are the issues for which Simpson had no vote. He had no vote for Management Committee membership. He had no vote for the admission of new partners. He had no vote on the discharge of existing partners, including himself. Finally, he had no vote on how firm members were to be compensated. * * *

D. Simpson Had No Right To Examine The Firm's Books And Records

Simpson did not have the unconditional right to examine the firm's books and records, and he was denied access to them regarding the UBT accounts. He had no right to learn the other Parties' compensation. A basic tenant of a bona fide partnership is that every partner shall at all times have access to and may inspect and copy partnership books. [citations omitted] Although some other emoluments of partnership are, under the New York Partnership Act, implicitly delegable, this section is not subject to variation by agreement of the parties. [citation omitted]

E. Simpson Had Little, If Any, Management Authority

Contrary to Ernst & Young's conclusory contentions, Simpson had few rights regarding Ernst & Young U.S.'s operations. He did not have the authority to hire, fire, or transfer even clerical workers within or without his department. The operations strategy of his department was determined by a superior. Simpson was subject to annual performance reviews. To the extent involvement in a firm's operations is indicative of being a bona fide partner, the evidence shows that Simpson's partnership interest in Ernst & Young U.S. was slim, at best. [citation omitted]

F. There Was No Fiduciary Relationship Between The Management Committee And Simpson

Partners bear a fiduciary relationship to each other. [citations omitted] The main elements of fiduciary duty are the utmost good faith, the highest fidelity, fairness, and loyalty. [citations omitted] Ernst & Young's refusal to permit Simpson to examine books and records regarding UBTs and to obtain its attorney's opinion regarding Simpson's discharge demonstrate an absence of a fiduciary relationship between the Management Committee and Simpson.

The Management Committee's act, at the time of the merger, of privately planning to "lay-off" Parties, while at the same time assuring them good increases in 1990 and 1991, equal or better benefits, and no reduction in partners, is a vivid example of the absence of a fiduciary relationship. Simpson's discharge and that of 126 other Parties was done for two stated economic reasons: 1) to protect the continued profit of firm members who were not discharged; and 2) to encourage recruitment and retention of younger accountants, who were generally paid less, were farther away from retirement, and needed assurance they would rise to partnership status. The failure of Ernst & Young to choose other options, such as not admitting as many new accountants, or reducing Parties' compensation, belies its contention that Simpson was a bona fide partner to whom the Management Committee owed a fiduciary duty. Since bona fide partners share in profits and losses proportionately, N.Y. PARTNERSHIP LAW §§ 26, 40(1), a reduction in all Parties' compensation would have been consistent with the existence of a fiduciary relationship. "Layoff" of Parties to preserve other Parties income is not. The fact that the Management Committee was simultaneously considering hiring accountants and terminating Parties is also indicative of the absence of a fiduciary relationship.

There is a degree of permanence associated with the status of partner that is absent from the status of employee. [citation omitted] The element of co-ownership of the firm and consequent fiduciary relationship and employment security inherent therein is absent when some Parties can be discharged, without any voice in the matter, in order to insure the financial gain of other Parties.

G. The Firm Did Not Actually Consider Simpson A Co-Owner

We are not persuaded by Ernst & Young's contention that Simpson delegated certain management responsibilities. We acknowledge that the N.Y. PARTNERSHIP LAW, § 40(5), permits delegation of such duties, and we agree that the larger the partnership, the more delegation is to be expected. [citation omitted] Simpson, however, could not delegate rights he never possessed. Furthermore, at some point, delegation destroys partner status. While it may have been "normal business caution" to prevent Simpson from binding the firm to promissory notes by his signature and from pledging firm assets, or to require reviews of certain audits or the engagement of new clients, it was not "normal business caution" to prevent him from voting on substantive matters, to deny him a proportionate share of firm profits, to eliminate his share in the firm's accounts receivable, to deny him personnel authority, to prevent him from examining the firm's books, and to prevent him from learning what legal advice the firm's attorneys provided.

H. Simpson Agreed To Unlimited Liability For Partnership Losses

The U.S. Agreement and the Partnership Agreement provide that Simpson was jointly and individually liable for the losses of Ernst & Young U.S. and Ernst & Young respectively. On its face, this is a characteristic of partnership. It certainly cannot, however, be considered a benefit of partnership. Furthermore, there is no evidence that Simpson or any other Party was ever called upon to accept responsibility for losses of Ernst & Young U.S. or Ernst & Young. We question the enforceability of this provision in light of the apparent lack of consideration therefor. It seems inequitable to hold an individual liable for the losses of his "partners" when that individual has no choice in determining who his partners are, no power to control the risks his "partners" take, and no right to examine the firm's books to determine what his liabilities might be. With these qualifications, Simpson's unlimited liability is a partnership attribute.

I. Simpson Was Not A Bona Fide Partner; He Was An Ernst & Young Employee

* * * Ernst & Young U.S. . . . did not refer to Simpson as a partner, but rather as a "Party." While labeling a person "partner" does not make him so, the failure to term Simpson a partner, when he had been thus denominated at Arthur Young, is an indication that he was not intended to be a partner. Simpson lacked any meaningful control and voting rights in Ernst & Young U.S., did not share in the firm's profits and losses, did not enjoy a fiduciary relationship with the Management Committee members, and had no other ownership rights therein.

In view of all the factors analyzed *supra*, with no one factor being dispositive, we find, under a traditional partnership law analysis, that Simpson has many qualitative characteristics of an employee and few, if any, attributes of a bona fide partner. Therefore, we find Simpson was an employee protected against age discrimination under ADEA.

In addition to our finding being directed by traditional legal principles, it is also an equitable result, putting Simpson on par with other business executives and professionals who have held positions of greater responsibility in their firms than Simpson and who were found to be protected by ADEA. [citations omitted] * * *

J. It Is Not Necessary To Resolve Simpson's Contention That Ernst & Young Is Not Actually A Partnership

Simpson also contends that both the U.S. Agreement and the Partnership Agreement fail to establish bona fide partnerships; therefore, he is not a partner. Simpson has presented substantial evidence in this regard, much of which has been discussed above. Simpson contends that the Partnership Agreement has no specific provision regarding the distribution of earnings; it does not result in the establishment of a capital account; it provides no voting procedure for the election of the Chairman or Management Committee; and it specifically restricts the rights of the Partners to sign promissory notes or to examine the firm's books. With regard to the U.S. Agreement, Simpson contends that it has been carefully crafted to avoid creating a partnership because it includes non-CPAs as parties and state laws prohibit CPAs and non-CPAs from representing themselves as partners. The fact that we have found Simpson to be an employee does not, in and of itself, justify the conclusion that Ernst & Young and Ernst & Young U.S. are not partnerships.[6]

Because we have resolved the jurisdictional issue by finding Simpson to be an employee, it is not necessary to go further to decide whether either the entities Ernst & Young or Ernst & Young U.S. are in actuality partnerships. * * *

CONCLUSION

Simpson had few, if any, meaningful attributes of a partner. For all practical purposes, he was an employee with the additional detriment of having promised to be liable for the firm's losses. Ernst & Young was free to draft its Partnership Agreement and U.S. Agreement in such a way as to generate the belief in its employees that they enjoyed partnership status and to permit them to represent themselves as partners. However, because these individuals actually had no bona fide ownership interest, no fiduciary relationship, no share in the profits and losses, no significant management control, no meaningful voting rights, no meaningful vote in firm decisions, and no job security, they were not bona fide partners. Therefore, Ernst & Young was obligated not to discriminate against them because of their age, sex, race, religion, national origin, or handicap. * * *

Notes and Questions

1. **The court's test.** Did the *Simpson* court apply a different definition of partnership from the one discussed in § 3.02? Note, for example, the court's conclusion that Simpson did not have certain fiduciary and inspection rights that cannot be waived by partnerships (on this point, *see* § 8.06, below), and skepticism that Simpson was really liable as a partnership for partnership debts. If Simpson would have these rights and obligations as a partner under state law, it seems to follow that the court deemed Simpson not to be a partner under state law. Is that the case? If Simpson was a partner under state law, then why would not be one under federal law? If the court in effect applied special criteria applicable to the age dis-

---

[6]   Although we do not answer the question, it is possible that the Management Committee constitutes a partnership, with the remaining Parties being employees of the partnership. It is also possible that Ernst & Young or Ernst & Young U.S. are non-partnership business associations.

crimination laws, how is this different from the "economic realities" test the court purportedly rejected? For a case similar to *Simpson, see Strother v. Southern California Permanente Medical Group*, 79 F.3d 859 (9th Cir. 1996), holding that the district court wrongly determined that plaintiff was not an "employee" based solely on the complaint, the attached partnership agreement, and the fact that plaintiff was labeled a "partner." Although the partnership agreement provided for partnership rights, including the rights to be elected to the firm's board of directors, which managed the firm, to vote on amendments to the partnership agreement, board representatives, partner discharges, and termination of the partnership, plaintiff had little control over the board, was compensated based on her performance, was subject to discipline for poor performance, and was one of 2400-2500 "partners," suggesting rights comparable to those of an employee. The court reasoned that it was appropriate to look beyond labels at the true relationship, including the method of compensation, responsibility for partnership liabilities, management structure and the "partner's" role, to determine if an individual should be treated as a partner or an employee for the purpose of employment discrimination laws.

2. **Choice of form considerations.** Under the *Simpson* test, does it matter whether the firm purported to be a corporation, a partnership or some other type of business? Note that, for employment discrimination purposes, shareholders in professional *corporations* have been treated both as employees (*see Hyland v. New Haven Radiology Assocs.*, 794 F.2d 793 (2d Cir. 1986)) and as partners (*Wells v. Clackamas Gastroenterology Associates, P.C.*, 2000 WL 776416 (D. Or., May 05, 2000); *Fountain v. Metcalf, Zima & Co., P.A.*, 925 F.2d 1398 (11th Cir. 1991); *E.E.O.C. v. Dowd & Dowd*, 736 F.2d 1177 (7th Cir. 1984)). Conversely, *Simpson* shows that even one who is designated as a partner in a partnership but has employee-like characteristics may be treated as an employee under the employment discrimination laws. *See also Caruso v. Peat, Marwick, Mitchell & Co.*, 664 F. Supp. 144 (S.D.N.Y. 1987), 717 F. Supp. 218 (S.D.N.Y. 1989).

3. **"Partners" as non-employees.** Those styled as partners in large firms may be treated as such for employment discrimination purposes. *See Wheeler v. Hurdman*, 825 F.2d 257 (10th Cir. 1987), *cert. denied*, 484 U.S. 986 (1987) (reasoning that despite some similarities between partners in very large partnerships and corporate employees, there are significant differences between partners and employees, including liability for loss, profit sharing, and selectivity of admission); *Ehrlich v. Howe*, 848 F. Supp. 482 (S.D.N.Y. 1994) (plaintiff was jointly and severally liable for partnership debts, shared profits and losses, voted as a partner, had a sufficient voting interest to be able to block partnership decisions with one other partner, participated in hiring decisions and could be terminated only by unanimous vote of the other partners); *Rhoads v. Jones Financial Companies*, 957 F. Supp. 1102 (E.D. Mo. 1997) (despite lack of full control indicating employee status, plaintiff was a partner rather than an employee of a brokerage firm, distinguishing *Simpson* on the basis that plaintiff was liable for the loan she received to buy her interest, shared in profits and losses according to her interest in the firm, had meaningful partner powers to vote on partnership matters, remove the managing partner and examine partnership books, and was referred to and treated as a general partner in all partnership documents). Did the courts in these cases apply a different test than in *Simpson*?

4. **Drafting and planning considerations.** In light of *Simpson*, how should the agreement have been drafted in order to minimize the likelihood that Simpson would be protected as an employee under federal law? Is there a way to achieve this end consistent with the other purposes served by the agreement? Note, in addition to the internal governance and financial objectives of the agreement, the state law problem of avoiding a partnership with non-C.P.A.s.

B.   Application of the Federal Securities Laws

The federal securities laws—in particular, the Securities Act of 1933 and the Securities Exchange Act of 1934—provide a wide range of anti-fraud and affirmative disclosure protection for investors in connection with the purchase or sale of a "security." The 1933 Act requires substantial disclosure in connection with the sale of a security by an "issuer" or controlling person, which theoretically could include a partner or a partnership. The 1934 Act provides for, among other things, continuous disclosure by larger issuers and, more importantly in the present context, broad antifraud liability under § 10(b) and Securities and Exchange Commission Rule 10b-5.

As discussed in the following case, a "security" includes an "investment contract." The Supreme Court has held that whether a transaction involves an "investment contract" should depend on the underlying "economic realities" that relate to whether the plaintiff needs the protection of the disclosure laws. The leading case is *Securities & Exchange Commission v. W.J. Howey Co.*, 328 U.S. 293 (1946), which looks at, among other things, whether the investor is relying on "the efforts of others." The intuition underlying this test is that one who has invested in another's ability to deliver profits needs the sort of information required by the securities laws in order to evaluate the enterpreneur's abilities.

The definition of "investment contract" is particularly hard to apply to partnerships and other unincorporated firms whose owners may have significant control powers and yet also have delegated management functions to others. Accordingly, it may not be clear when the transaction has crossed the line into an "investment contract." In making this determination, the courts rely on "economic realities." But, as indicated by the following case, this does not necessarily mean that the courts wholly disregard the form of the transaction. In other words, the fact that the relationship is a partnership under state law may play a substantial role in determining whether it is a "security" under the securities laws.

Rivanna Trawlers Unlimited v. Thompson Trawlers, Inc.
840 F.2d 236 (4th Cir. 1988)

Before POWELL, Associate Justice (Retired); United States Supreme Court, sitting by designation; ERVIN, Circuit Judge; and BUTZNER, Senior Circuit Judge.

POWELL, Associate Justice:

The dispositive issue presented in this case is whether the district court correctly concluded that appellants' general partnership interests in Rivanna Trawlers Unlimited are not securities within the meaning of the federal securities laws. We hold that these interests are not securities, and affirm.

The appellate record indicates that the Virginia general partnership, Rivanna Trawlers Unlimited ("RTU"), was formed in August 1982 when twenty-three parties executed an agreement for the purpose of forming a general partnership, "which will acquire, own, lease and operate multi-purpose fishing vessels and otherwise engage in the commercial fishing business . . . ." At some point, not disclosed by the record, Joseph W. May, M.D. also joined the partnership. On August 30, 1982 RTU purchased four fishing boats and entered into several agreements for their management and maintenance with Thompson Management, Inc. By the spring of 1983 the partners were expressing concern over the partnership's operations and they were considering management alternatives. Operation of the fishing boats had not been meeting the partners' financial expectations. The partners subsequently replaced RTU's external managers twice and removed RTU's original managing partner Walter B. Salley, Sr., who was a general partner of GMS, and replaced him with a managing partnership committee.

In August 1984 RTU and a number of its partners filed a complaint against Thompson Trawlers, Inc., Thompson Management, Inc. and various other companies and individuals. * * * These plaintiffs alleged that their interests in the general partnership were "investment contracts" as defined in the federal securities laws, and that appellees had violated these laws. * * *

II

Appellants contend that issues of material fact exist as to whether their general partnership interests fall within the scope of the term "investment contract" as used in section 2(1) of the 1933 Securities Act, 15 U.S.C. § 77b(1), and in section 3(a)(10) of the 1934 Securities Exchange Act, 15 U.S.C. § 78c(a)(10). * * *

B

We address first appellants' claim that their interests in the RTU partnership were investment contracts, and therefore were securities within the meaning of the federal securities laws. The Supreme Court has defined an investment contract as "a contract, transaction or scheme whereby a person invests his money in a common enterprise and is led to expect profits solely from the efforts of the promoter or a third party. . . ." *Securities & Exchange Commission v. W.J. Howey Co.*, 328 U.S. 293, 298-99, 66 S.Ct. 1100, 1102-03, 90 L.Ed. 1244 (1946). The critical issue on this appeal is whether appellants' general partnership interests in RTU meet the third prong of the *Howey* test—that is, the expectation of profits derived solely from the efforts of others. General partnerships ordinarily are not considered investment contracts because they grant partners—the investors—control over significant decisions of the enterprise. *Williamson v. Tucker*, 645 F.2d 404, 422 (5th Cir.), *cert. denied*, 454 U.S. 897, 102 S.Ct. 396, 70 L.Ed.2d 212 (1981) [other citations omitted]. In *Williamson*, a leading case, the Fifth Circuit identified a narrow exception to the strong presumption that a general partnership is not a security. The court stated that . . . a partnership can be an investment contract only when the partners are so dependent on a particular manager that they cannot replace him or otherwise exercise ultimate control. *Id.* at 424. Only when this degree of dependence by the partners exists is there an investment contract. *Id.* at 423. Moreover, the court emphasized that "[t]he delegation of rights and duties—standing alone—does not give rise to the sort of dependence on others which underlies the third prong of the *Howey* test." *Id.* In other words, the mere choice by a partner to remain passive is not sufficient to create a security interest. The critical inquiry is, "whether the powers possessed by the [general partners] in the [partnership agreement] were so significant that, regardless of the degree to which such powers were exercised, the investments could not have been premised on a reasonable expectation of profits to be derived from the management efforts of others." *Id.* at 419.

We agree with the Fifth Circuit, as well as the other circuits that appear to have embraced the *Williamson* reasoning,[6] that only under certain limited circumstances can an investor's general partnership interest be characterized as an investment contract. A court must examine the partnership agreement and circumstances of a particular partnership to determine the reality of the contractual rights of the general partners. When, however, a partnership agreement allocates powers to the general partners that are specific and unambiguous, and when those powers are sufficient to allow the general partners to exercise ultimate control, as a majority, over the partnership and its business, then the presumption that the general partnership is not a security can only be rebutted by evidence that it is not possible for the partners to exercise those powers.[7]

As the district court stated, "[e]ven when general partners do not individually have decisive control over major decisions, they do have the sort of influence which generally provides them with access to important information and protection against a dependence on others." In a case of this kind, it also is important to bear in mind that Congress, in enacting the securities laws, did not intend to provide a federal remedy for all common law fraud. *Marine Bank v. Weaver*, 455 U.S. 551, 556, 102 S.Ct. 1220, 1223, 71 L.Ed.2d 409 (1982).

C

The RTU Partnership Agreement confers broad authority on the partners to manage and control the business. It provides that the partnership can be dissolved by a concurrence of 60% in interest of the partners. It also states that, "[c]oncurrence of sixty percent (60%) in interest of the partners should be required with respect to policy and management decisions on [sic] the partnership business. . . ." Policy and management decisions include: (i) the power to sell and convey, lease, mortgage, or encumber partnership assets; (ii) the power to borrow or lend sums on behalf of the partnership when in excess of $5000; (iii) the power to hire agents to manage or operate the business of the partnership; (iv) and the power to appoint a successor to the man-

---

[6]   *See, e.g.*, *Deutsch Energy Co. v. Mazur*, 813 F.2d 1567 (9th Cir. 1987); *Odom v. Slavik*, 703 F.2d 212 (6th Cir. 1983); *Gordon v. Terry*, 684 F.2d 736 (11th Cir. 1982), *cert. denied*, 459 U.S. 1203, 103 S.Ct. 1188, 75 L.Ed.2d 434 (1983). *But see, Goodwin v. Elkins & Co.*, 730 F.2d 99, 103-04 (3d Cir.) (Opinion of Garth, J.), *cert. denied*, 469 U.S. 831, 105 S.Ct. 118, 83 L.Ed.2d 61 (1984). Judge Garth, in an interesting opinion, concluded that in view of the powers expressly conferred on general partners by New Jersey law, he would hold that a partnership interest could not be considered a security as a matter of law. In view of the broad powers conferred by the RTU partnership agreement, we have no occasion to consider the effect of Virginia law. *See infra* note 8.

[7]   If and to the extent that *Williamson* and other cases may be read to require a court to look to the actual knowledge and business expertise of each partner in order to assess his or her individual ability intelligently to exercise the power of a general partner, we do not agree. Such an inquiry would undercut the strong presumption that an interest in a general partnership is not a security. It also would unduly broaden the scope of the Supreme Court's instruction that courts must examine the economic reality of partnership interests. *See infra* note 10. We note that no such specific argument is made in this case. Appellants' complaint and briefs properly speak only in terms of the rights and authority of the partners as a group.

aging partner named in the agreement. Moreover, at all times, each partner has reasonable access to the partnership's books of account and has the right to demand an audit of the partnership. Unanimous consent of the partners is required to transfer legal ownership of partnership interests, and additional partners can be added only with the unanimous consent of the partners. Finally, unanimous consent of the partnership also is required to distribute profits other than in proportion to the partners' respective interests.[8]

As the district court found, the express powers granted to the partners are sufficient, on their face, to give them the authority to manage their investments. Normally, such authority renders unnecessary the protection of the federal securities laws. The Eleventh Circuit has stated that, "[a]n investor who has the ability to control the profitability of his investment, either by his own efforts or by majority vote in group ventures, is not dependent upon the managerial skills of others." *Gordon v. Terry*, 684 F.2d 736, 741 (11th Cir. 1982), *cert. denied*, 459 U.S. 1203, 103 S.Ct. 1188, 75 L.Ed.2d 434 (1983). In this case, the partners not only had the authority under the agreement to manage the business, they exercised this authority and demonstrated that they were not dependent on the irreplaceable skills of others.[9] Members of the partnership negotiated with external management groups, inspected the boats on behalf of the partnership, and reviewed partnership insurance material and financial information. Significantly, on two separate occasions the external managers were replaced. Moreover, as previously mentioned, by vote of the partners, one of the promoters, Walter Salley, Sr., was removed as managing partner of RTU and replaced with a management committee of partners. Partners also participated in settlement discussions.[10]

---

[8]   In addition to the terms of the partnership agreement, Virginia law provides that, subject to any agreement between the parties, all partners have equal rights in the management and conduct of the partnership, Va. Code Ann. § 50-18(e) (1986); no persons can become a member of a partnership without the consent of all partners; *id.* at § 50-18(g); and that no act in contravention of any agreement between the partners may be done rightfully without consent of all the partners, *id.* at § 50-18(h). Moreover, section 50-19 of the Virginia Code provides that "every partner shall at all times have access to and may inspect and copy any of [the partnership's books]," and section 50-24 of the Virginia Code provides that included among the property rights of a partner are, "his right to participate in the management." *See supra* note 6.

[9]   This is not a case like *SEC v. W.J. Howey Co.* where the "individual development of the plots of land that [were] offered and sold would seldom be economically feasible due to their small size," and therefore investors were, in reality, unable to exercise individual management and control over their plots of land. 328 U.S. at 300, 66 S.Ct. at 1103. The general partners of RTU all had a realistic opportunity to manage, control and supervise the operation of the partnership through the exercise of substantial partnership powers. In fact, the record indicates that many of the partners, to a varying extent, have done just that. *See, e.g.*, App. at 509-514, 1316-17, 1553-54, 1555, 1564-65, 1570 for examples of partner participation.

[10]   The fact that some of the general partners may have remained passive or lacked financial sophistication or business expertise does not affect the result. General partners who are capable of exercising significant managerial powers cannot convert their partnership interests into a security merely by remaining passive. *See supra*. Moreover, members of a general partnership who lack financial sophistication or business expertise nevertheless may exercise intelligently the powers conferred on them by the partnership agreement and state law. They are entitled to receive financial reports and have the right to inspect and obtain copies of partnership books and records. *See supra* note 8. To the extent a partner needs advice or assistance in the exercise of his powers, he is of course free to consult with more knowledgeable partners or third persons, or to employ accountants and lawyers. In a word, a general partner is not dependent only on the degree of his own business sophistication in order to exercise intelligently his partnership powers.

The real gravamen of appellants' complaint lies in common law fraud. As previously mentioned, the securities laws were not intended to be a substitute for state fraud actions. We affirm the district court's finding that appellants' partnership interests are not securities within the meaning of the Securities Act of 1933 or the Securities and Exchange Act of 1934. * * *

Notes and Questions

1. **The Williamson test.** The *Williamson* test for whether a partnership interest is a "security" asks whether the investors have the traditional powers of partners under the partnership agreement and whether the investors are able to exercise those powers. The latter question involves two components—investor sophistication, and their practical ability to replace the promoter. As *Rivanna* indicates, not all courts have accepted the need for investor sophistication. *See* notes 7 and 10 to the court's opinion. As for investors' ability to replace the promoter, *see* note 9 to the court's opinion. One may be able to replace a manager without knowing enough to be a manager. *See Holden v. Hagopian*, 978 F.2d 1115 (9th Cir. 1992), which held that a horsebreeding partnership was not a "security" despite the investors' lack of expertise about horsebreeding because the investors did not show that they could not have replaced the manager with someone else of similar expertise. However, an investment may be a "security" where the investors have little practical power over the promoter. *See Koch v. Hankins,* 928 F.2d 1471 (9th Cir. 1991), which held that there was a question of fact whether partners in 35 partnerships, each of which was a part of a larger jojoba plantation, could meaningfully exercise control over the overall enterprise. *See also SEC v. Shreveport Wireless Cable Television Partnership*, 1998 WL 892948 (D.D.C. October 20, 1998) (denying summary judgment on "security" issue where the partners' powers under the agreement resembled those of limited partners or shareholders, partners' input was limited by sale of 700-1000 interests, almost half as fractional interests, and there was evidence that the partners were precluded from participating in essential managerial decisions).

2. **Application of *Howey* to partnership interests.** Based on *Rivanna* and Note 1, do the courts seem to be applying an "economic reality" test to partnership interests, as *Howey* seems to require, or do they instead assume that the securities laws do not usually apply to general partnerships irrespective of economic reality? Can the two approaches be reconciled? *See* Ribstein, *Private Ordering and the Securities Laws: The Case of General Partnerships,* 42 CASE W. RES. L. REV. 1 (1992).

3. **Relevance of business form to the definition of a "security."** It makes a difference under the securities laws whether the firm is a corporation or a partnership, since "stock" is expressly enumerated as a "security." *See Landreth Timber Co. v. Landreth,* 471 U.S. 681 (1985), where the Court noted the need for some predictability in determining when the securities laws would apply. Interestingly, Justice Powell, who decided *Landreth,* wrote *Rivanna* as a retired Justice sitting on the Fourth Circuit. Note that a limited partnership interest is usually treated as a security. It is still an open question whether interests in other types of unincorporated firms, including LLCs, will be treated like corporations or

partnerships. This, along with the general question of form vs. substance in the definition of a security, is considered further in § 12.02(G).

4. **The role of the partnership agreement.** *Williamson* and *Rivanna* suggest that, to avoid being characterized as a "security," the partnership agreement must give partners the substantial governance powers normally associated with partnership. This is obviously significant in drafting the agreement. But there is some authority for ignoring not only individual investor characteristics but also the terms of the partnership agreement. See the discussion of *Goodwin v. Elkins* in note 6 to the court's opinion. Under this approach, the default and mandatory terms of the partnership statute are enough to ensure that investors who are partners under state law do not need the protection of the securities laws. The partnership agreement may be relevant in ways other than concerning the partners' powers. For example, suppose the agreement provides that the partners may not transfer partnership interests so as to jeopardize the availability of the private or limited offering *exemptions* of securities transactions from 1933 Act registration requirements. Does this suggestion that the partnership interests' need of some exemption imply that they *are* securities?

3.04 Choice of Law

A potentially important issue the parties must consider in forming a partnership is deciding which state's law will apply. As discussed in Chapter 1, choice of law has not historically been much of an issue for partnerships because of the widespread adoption of the Uniform Partnership Act. However, the parties may want to choose to be governed by the relatively developed case law of a particular jurisdiction. Moreover, choice of statutory law may become increasingly important as the spread of limited liability partnership provisions and the Revised Uniform Partnership Act makes the law increasingly non-uniform.

Choice of law for corporations is a relatively simple matter of determining where the articles of incorporation have been filed. Under the so-called "internal affairs" rule, the law of the state of organization applies concerning the governance, financial rights, and other matters within the firm. *See* Restatement (Second) of Conflicts § 302(2) (1971). By contrast, choice of law in partnerships is complicated by the fact that there is not necessarily a formal filing that easily fixes the law of the state of organization, and partnerships have been treated like ordinary contracts.

General choice-of-law principles apply to UPA partnerships that do not choose the applicable law. While the Uniform Partnership Act does not include a choice of law rule, UPA § 5 says that "rules of law and equity" apply, probably including the common law of conflict of laws. *See* Vestal, *Choice of Law and the Fiduciary Duties of Partners under the Revised Uniform Partnership Act,* 79 IOWA L. REV. 219 (1994). Restatement (Second) of Conflicts, § 294, provides that "[t]he rights and duties owed by partners to each other are determined by the local law of the state which, with respect to the particular issue, has the most significant relationship to the partners and the transaction under the principles stated in § 6. This law is selected by application of the rules of §§ 187-188."

These rules and their application to partnerships and other firms are discussed in Ribstein, *Choosing Law By Contract,* 18 J. CORP. L. 245 (1993). In brief, § 187(1) provides for enforcement of the law chosen in the parties' contract as to interpretation issues the parties could have resolved by contract. On the other hand, under § 187(2) the contract is not enforced as to issues such as validity if:

(a) the chosen state has no substantial relationship to the parties or the transaction and there is no other reasonable basis for the parties' choice, or (b) application of the law of the chosen state would be contrary to a fundamental policy of a state which has a materially greater interest than the chosen state in the determination of the particular issue and which, under the rule of § 188, would be the state of the applicable law in the absence of an effective choice of law by the parties.

Under § 6(2), which applies in the absence of an effective choice of law by the parties, the contacts to be taken into account in applying the principles of § 6 to determine the law applicable to an issue include: (a) the place of contracting, (b) the place of negotiation of the contract, (c) the place of performance, (d) the location of the subject matter of the contract, and (e) the domicile, residence, nationality, place of incorporation and place of business of the parties. Under § 188(2), these contacts are to be evaluated according to their relative importance with respect to the particular issue. Section 188(3) provides that the law of the state in which the contract is negotiated and performed is usually applied.

Under these principles, the law selected in the partnership agreement usually is applied. For example, in *Exxon Corp. v. Burglin,* 4 F.3d 1294 (5th Cir. 1993), the court held under Texas law that a clause in the partnership agreement which applied Alaska law was enforceable where the oil leases, the subject of the partnership, were located in Alaska, so that Alaska bore a reasonable relation to the partnership agreement, although the Agreement was predominately negotiated, drafted, and executed in Texas and the partnership involved several Texas companies. Nevertheless, a court might refuse to apply the law of a state other than the forum if the partnership has no substantial relationship with that state or the matter, such as the partners' liability, concerns a fundamental policy of the forum. It is not clear what circumstances *should* be enough to justify not enforcing the parties' contract. For example, the parties may have strong reasons to select the law of a particular jurisdiction that has a well-developed partnership law even if that jurisdiction is quite remote from the transaction and does not seem to have any "interest" in the transaction other than in attracting partnership litigation to its courts. Indeed, this may be a "reasonable basis" for the selection that would validate it under Restatement § 187(2)(a).

RUPA § 106 for the first time provides a specific default choice of law provision for partnership: "[t]he law of the jurisdiction in which a partnership has its chief executive office governs relations among the partners and relations between the partners and the partnership." This provision may not apply RUPA on matters relating solely to relations between the partners and third parties, such as the "exhaustion" rule in RUPA § 307 that is discussed below in § 6.01. *Cf. Cornerstone Realty, Inc. v. Dresser Rand Co.,* 993 F. Supp. 107 (D. Conn. 1998) (disputed issue of whether New York pleading requirement for exhaustion applied where parties disagreed whether the place where the agreement for the partnership property was made or the place where the partnership agreement was made should control). For an article critical of the RUPA provision and arguing for a principal place of business rule for unregistered entities *see* Johnson, *Risky Business: Choice of Law and the Unincorporated Entity*, 1 J. SM. & EM. BUS. LAW 249 (1997).

RUPA § 106 is not one of the nonwaivable provisions under § 103, and so appears to be subject to contrary choice-of-law agreements. However, this may be qualified by RUPA § 103(b)(9), which provides that the partnership agreement "may not . . . restrict rights of third parties under this [Act]." Moreover, the Official Comment to § 106 says that the choice of law is "subject to generally applicable conflict of laws requirements," suggesting that restrictions on contracting for choice of law may apply. The Texas Revised Partnership Act makes clear that the law of a state selected in the contract is applied only "if that state bears a reasonable relation to the partners or to the partnership business and affairs under principles that apply to a contract among the partners other than the partnership agreement." *See* TEX. REV. CIV. STAT. ANN. art. 6132b-1.05 (West 1995).

CHAPTER 4
PARTNER'S FINANCIAL RIGHTS

4.01 Partners' Financial Rights in General

The default financial rules governing partnerships are simple: Partners share equally in partnership profits, and share losses equally (or in proportion to profits if the partners agree to share profits unequally). UPA §18(a); RUPA § 401(b). Profits and losses are divided up on dissolution of the partnership, which occurs, among other times, when a partner leaves. UPA § 40; RUPA § 807. Partners have no statutory default right to distributions during the firm's operation, although the partnership agreement may provide for such a right. *See* paragraph 4.4 of the Chameleon agreement. Chapter 9 discusses distributions to and contributions by partners when the firm dissolves.

The equal-division rule means, among other things, that partners receive no extra compensation for contributions of money or services unless they agree otherwise. The equal profit sharing rule works well where the partners' total contributions in terms of labor, capital and credit are approximately equal, but this is rarely the case. However, partners frequently contribute significantly different amounts of time and money to the firm. In such firms, the equal division rule may surprise the partners. In "The Treasure of the Sierra Madre," a film about a gold-mining "partnership" that went bad, Humphrey Bogart's character Fred C. Dobbs, who made the biggest capital contribution, pointed out that "in any civilized place the biggest investor gets the biggest return." Even the partners' liability for the firm's debts may not balance out their contributions in firms where liabilities are not a big issue (as in the gold-mining partnership) or where some partners are richer than others. Yet despite potential inequalities, the equal sharing rule is an appropriate *default* rule because it is difficult or impossible to design a rule that will better suit a large number of firms. Indeed, Fred, in the gold-mining partnership, had initially agreed to an equal division because he said if they struck it rich the differences in capital contributions, given the partners' huge labor investment, would not matter much.

Sections 4.02 and 4.03 show how the equal-division and no-compensation rules may be qualified by express or implied agreements. Section 4.04 discusses the role of the partners' accounting in interpreting their agreements concerning financial rights. Section 4.05 discusses the default rules concerning loss-sharing.

4.02 Financial Contributions

Partners can make two general types of financial contributions to a partnership—by capital contribution and by loan. The latter normally involves scheduled repayment and periodic interest payments. The former is more of a commitment to the firm that may not be repaid until dissolution and that is taken into account in determining the partner's profit share. Partners are not required to make financial contributions to a partnership. Indeed, service-only partners are common. Financial contributions raise both tax issues, which are discussed at various places below, and two types of partnership issues. Section A discusses how courts determine which property has actually been contributed to the firm as opposed to retained by the partner who originally owned it. Section B discusses the rules for compensating partners for their financial contributions. Section 4.04 discusses accounting issues associated with property contributions. Chapter 7 discusses the legal incidents of the partnership's ownership of property.

The partners may or may not have continuing obligations to make financial contributions. *See* paragraph 3.3 of the Chameleon agreement and § 9.06(B), below.

A.   Partnership and Individual Property

In a formal firm, the partnership property, including the partners' contributions to the firm, are normally clarified in the agreement. *See* paragraph 3.1 of the Chameleon agreement. In informal partnerships, it may not be clear whether the partnership itself, or one or more individual partners, owns property that the partnership uses. This may be significant both to the partners themselves, who try to take back "their" property, and to creditors of the partnership or of individual partners.

UPA § 8 and RUPA § 204 establish logical presumptions to help courts determine what property the partnership owns. The UPA and RUPA presumption that the partnership owns property purchased with partnership funds, and the RUPA counter-presumption that property titled in individual partners is not partnership property, are both logical. The provision in RUPA § 204(c) that the partnership is presumed to own property purchased with partnership funds even if the property is held in the partners' names individually is somewhat more controversial. This rule may frustrate the expectations of creditors who reasonably relied on record title and could not know that the property was purchased with partnership funds. Also, does it make sense for RUPA § 204 to provide that purchase in the partnership name is stronger evidence of partnership ownership than purchase in individual name is of non-partnership ownership?

Where the partnership's main business is the ownership and operation of an asset such as real estate, the question of what the partnership owns is closely related to whether there is a partnership at all. In *Matter of Woolston*, 147 B.R. 279 (M.D. Ga. 1992), the court held that a mobile home park, development of which was the partnership's sole business, was the property of individual partners based on the partners' use of individual funds, loans, and deeds in individual names, and strong evidence of partners' belief that they owned property as individuals. But if the property that is the subject of the firm's only business is owned individually, can the individual owners be co-owners of the business?

B.   Compensation for Financial Contributions

The partnership statutes assume that partners are compensated for capital contributions, as for contributions of credit and services, through their equal profit share. However, contributions in addition to capital are characterized as loans for which partners may get extra compensation in the form of interest. *See* paragraph 3.5 of the Chameleon agreement. For a case that struggles with the issue of whether the parties had waived the default rule of no compensation for capital, *see Skretvedt v. Kouri,* 445 S.E.2d 481 (Va. 1994).

4.03 Service Contributions

Partners often contribute their services as well as their financial capital. Unlike agents (*see* § 2.06), partners have no default right to extra compensation for their services. As discussed in § 4.01, the partnership statutes assume that services, like financial contributions, are part of what partners pay in return for their profit shares. Section A discusses the operation of this default rule, while Section B discusses explicit agreements for partner compensation.

A.   Default Rules and Implied Agreements

In some firms the equal division default rule fails even to roughly approximate the partners' *very* different investments of both time and capital. The courts sometimes imply agreements to vary the UPA default in these situations. *See Walker v. Walker*, 854 F. Supp. 1443 (D. Neb. 1994), in which the court awarded fees partly because of the size and complexity of the farming operation managed by one of the partners. In *Warren v. Warren*, 784 S.W.2d 247 (Mo. App. 1989), the court held that partners who provided substantial time and vital services deserved extra compensation. The court also relied on an agreement based on the co-partner's knowledge of compensation and failure to object.

Should the courts assume that the parties implicitly agreed to vary the statute solely because they worked differing amounts, or should it apply the statutory default rule because the parties did not explicitly change it? The answer depends on whether the default rule is intended to define the result in the ordinary case or to force the parties explicitly to contract for any alternative rule they want to be applied. Even if strictly applying the default rule frustrates the parties' subjective expectations in a particular case, overall it may be the right rule because it reduces litigation costs and forces parties to reveal information during negotiations.

The parties can eliminate uncertainty on this issue by clearly providing that the partners are not entitled to compensation even if they make disparate service contributions. *See* paragraph 4.3 of the Chameleon agreement. Note also that partners may be immediately taxed on certain types of partnership interests they receive as compensation for services.

B.   Alternative Compensation Arrangements

Partners are free to contract for compensation schemes that vary the statutory default rules. Interesting variations occur in professional, real estate, venture capital and investment partnerships. *See* Gompers & Lerner, *The Use of Covenants: An Empirical Analysis of Venture Partnership Agreements,* 39 J. Law & Econ. 463 (1996) (discussing covenants that have been used to motivate and constrain managers of venture capital partnerships). This section discusses business considerations that underlie compensation arrangements in professional firms, as well as legal considerations that complicate contracting for compensation.

1.   Business Considerations

In contracting for compensation in professional firms, the partners must try to minimize several types of costs, particularly including *shirking, risk bearing, administrative* and *opportunism* costs. These costs, and methods of reducing them through compensation arrangements, are discussed below. *See* Ribstein, *A Theoretical Analysis of Professional Partnership Goodwill*, 70 Neb. L. Rev. 36 (1991) (*"Partnership Goodwill"*).

Shirking. Shirking is an inherent problem of working in "teams." It may be difficult to measure each team member's contribution to the firm's profits. In a law firm, for example, everybody contributes in many ways to attracting clients, winning cases and doing the other things necessary to increase profits. If partners are not precisely rewarded according to their contributions, each may try to "free ride" on the others' efforts. This would make everybody worse off. Shirking is constrained not only through appropriate compensation arrangements, but also by the market for lawyers' services and expulsion provisions in the partnership agreement. Expulsion is a crude remedy that is normally reserved for the most serious disagreements or misbehavior. The market operates in a more subtle way by rewarding harder-working, more successful, partners.

As suggested above, the most direct way to discipline shirking in professional firms would be to align partners' profit share and other compensation with their contributions to the firm's profits in the preceding accounting period. McChesney, *Team Production, Monitoring and Profit-Sharing in Law Firms: An Alternative Hypothesis*, 11 J. LEG. STUD. 379 (1982), argues that law partners' compensation reflects how much new business they produce. However, a new client may join the firm only partly because of recruitment by a given partner, and mostly because of the firm's general reputation. Lawyers may add to this reputation in hard-to-measure ways such as publicizing the firm in continuing legal education presentations, winning cases and training associates. If lawyers are compensated only for actually bringing clients through the door, this may discourage them from working to bolster the other important elements of a firm's reputation. Law firms have experimented with compensation schemes in order to calibrate compensation with lawyers' contributions to profits.

Risk-bearing costs. Some methods of disciplining shirking by rewarding partner effort may not work because they expose partners to substantial risks to their earning potential over which they have no control. If, for example, a partner is compensated strictly by billable hours, her compensation is subject to economy-wide fluctuations in demand for work in the partner's specialty, such as securities offerings. Gilson & Mnookin, *Sharing Among the Human Capitalists: An Economic Inquiry into the Law Firm and How Partners Split Profits*, 37 STAN. L. REV. 313 (1985), state that some large law firms address this problem by paying partners a profit share based solely on their seniority in the firm. This ensures that income produced by securities lawyers in a rising economy balances bankruptcy lawyers' slow times. At the same time, this encourages shirking by letting less productive partners free ride off the efforts of their more productive colleagues. Gilson and Mnookin argue that shirking can be minimized, among other ways, by developing through training and recruitment a firm "culture" of conscientiousness and that seniority-based compensation encourages lawyers to work for the good of the firm's reputation rather than solely to keep their "own" clients happy.

Administrative costs. A compensation system that perfectly rewards partners' contributions would probably involve administrative costs that exceed the benefits in terms of partner productivity. Not only is it inherently difficult to determine exactly how much each partner adds to the firm's profits, but also the inevitable uncertainty would encourage disputes and costly litigation.

Opportunism costs. A compensation system that minimizes the other costs discussed above may cause problems because it allows partners to act opportunistically—that is, to take advantage of their co-partners. For example, partners who benefit from seniority-based compensation when their specialty is out of favor may decide to leave for another firm with clients in tow as soon as their specialty becomes "hot." Gilson & Mnookin, *supra,* argue that professional firms can address this problem by tying client relationships to the firm's reputation rather than to particular partners. But it is not easy for the firm to encourage the partners to sacrifice development of their own client base to the cause of developing the firm's own reputation when this would make it harder for them to seek higher incomes at other firms.

Evaluate some of the following alternative methods of compensation (discussed in BROMBERG & RIBSTEIN ON PARTNERSHIP, § 6.02(b)(1), in light of the above discussion:

(1) Assigning varying "points" or "units" of profit participation to the partners based on several indicia of partner productivity.

(2) Having a managing partner or committee of partners allocate profits based on their evaluation of each partner's contribution.

(3) Pay that rises with a partner's seniority in the firm.

(4) A "profit center" approach that bills and credits to the partners their shares of revenue and expense items.

2.   Legal Considerations

Even if the partners are able to design a perfect compensation system, they must put this into an enforceable contract. This involves not only anticipating contingencies, but also drafting the agreement so that it is enforced according to the parties' expectations. Among other problems, as illustrated by the following case, the courts may imply fiduciary or good faith duties that the parties may or may not have anticipated. These duties are discussed further in Chapter 8. The following case illustrates the problems involved in effectuating the parties' expectations.

Starr v. Fordham
20 Mass. 178, 648 N.E.2d 1261 (1995)

NOLAN, Justice.

The plaintiff, Ian M. Starr, was a partner in the Boston law firm Fordham & Starrett (firm). After the plaintiff withdrew from the firm, he commenced this action to recover amounts to which he claimed that he was entitled under the partnership agreement. The plaintiff also sought damages for breach of fiduciary duty and fraudulent misrepresentation. The defendants, his former partners at the firm, counterclaimed that the plaintiff had violated his fiduciary duties to his partners and breached the terms of the partnership agreement.
* * *

The founding partners and Attorneys Fordham and Starrett, in their individual capacities, cross appeal from the judge's finding that they violated their fiduciary duties and the implied covenant of good faith and fair dealing. In addition, Attorney Fordham appeals from the judge's finding that he engaged in fraudulent misrepresentation. We affirm.

1. Facts. We summarize the judge's findings of fact. In 1984, the plaintiff was a partner in the Boston law firm Foley, Hoag & Eliot (Foley Hoag). The plaintiff specialized in corporate and business law. Although the plaintiff had become a partner at Foley Hoag in 1982, he was actively seeking to leave the firm in early 1984. During this time, the founding partners were also partners at Foley Hoag. Both men enjoyed outstanding professional reputations among their colleagues. Nevertheless, they agreed that they would withdraw from Foley Hoag in early 1985 in order to establish a new law firm with another established Boston attorney, Frank W. Kilburn.

Fordham invited the plaintiff to join the new law firm Kilburn, Fordham & Starrett in January, 1985. At first, the plaintiff was somewhat hesitant to accept the offer because he was not known as a "rainmaker" (*i.e.*, an attorney responsible for significant client origination) at Foley Hoag. Fordham, however, assured the plaintiff that business origination would not be a significant factor for allocating the profits among the partners. Relying on this representation, the plaintiff withdrew from Foley Hoag on March 1, 1985. The founding partners and another attorney, the defendant Brian W. LeClair, withdrew from Foley Hoag on March 4, 1985.

Prior to executing the partnership agreement, the plaintiff informed Fordham that certain provisions in the agreement disturbed him. The source of the plaintiff's disquiet was Paragraph 1 of the partnership agreement which vested in the founding partners and Kilburn, the authority to determine, both prospectively and retrospectively, each partner's share of the firm's profits. Despite his concern, the plaintiff did not claim at this time that the agreement contradicted Fordham's representations to him that rainmaking would not be a significant factor in distributing the firm's profits. Fordham summarily dismissed the plaintiff's concerns, telling him, in effect, to "take it or leave it." On March 5, 1985, the founding partners, Kilburn, and LeClair each executed the partnership agreement for Kilburn, Fordham & Starrett. The plaintiff also signed the agreement without objection and without making any revisions. The defendant Barry A. Guryan joined the new firm on March 11, 1985.

In August of 1985, Kilburn withdrew from the firm. Subsequently, the firm assumed the name Fordham & Starrett. In September, 1985, the partners met to consider entering into a ten-year lease for office space. The partners were anxious about both the length of the lease and the additional cost; the new lease rate was double the rate that they had been paying. After individually confirming their commitment to shoulder the additional burden, the partners agreed to enter into the lease.

The founding partners had divided the firm's profits equally among the partners in 1985. Each of the five partners received $11,602. In 1986, the firm's financial fortunes improved significantly. On December 31, 1986, the firm's profits were $1,605,128. In addition, the firm had $1,844,366.59 in accounts receivable and work in progress.

The plaintiff withdrew from the firm on December 31, 1986. The partners remaining in the firm were the founding partners, LeClair, and Guryan. When the plaintiff withdrew from the firm, the sum of the plaintiff's accounts receivable and work in process was $204,623. The firm eventually collected $195,249 of the plaintiff's total receivables. The founding partners determined the plaintiff's share of the firm's profits for 1986 to be 6.3% of the total profits. In allocating the firm's profits among the partners, the founding partners did not consider any of the firm's accounts receivable or work in process. In addition, the founding partners refused to assign any of the firm's accounts receivable or work in process to the plaintiff when he withdrew from the firm. * * *

3. 1986 profits. * * * The founding partners assert several arguments on appeal from the judge's finding that they violated their fiduciary duties and the implied covenant of good faith and fair dealing when they allocated to the plaintiff only 6.3% of the firm's profits for 1986. We address each in turn.

A. The burden of proof. The founding partners claim that the judge erroneously imposed on them the burden of proving the fairness of their profit distribution to the plaintiff. We disagree. * * * The founding partners were responsible for dividing the partnership's profits and assigning to each partner his respective share of the profits. Thus, the founding partners had some self-interest in designating each partner's respective share of the profits because the percentage of profits which they were assigning to the other partners had a direct effect on their own percentage of the profits. [citation omitted] As a result, we conclude that there was no error in the judge's imposing on the founding partners the burden of proving that their distribution of the firm's profits to the plaintiff was fair and reasonable. *See Meehan v. Shaughnessy*, supra.

B. The business judgment rule. The founding partners argue next that the judge erred in concluding that the business judgment rule does not preclude judicial review of their determination of the plaintiff's share of the 1986 profits. There was no error.

* * * Having properly concluded that the founding partners had engaged in self-dealing when they assigned to the plaintiff his share of the profit, the judge made no error in concluding that the business judgment rule did not apply to the founding partners' actions.

C. Fiduciary duties and covenant of good faith. The founding partners argue that the judge's conclusion that they had violated both their fiduciary duties and the implied covenant of good faith and fair dealing when they allocated only 6.3% of the firm's profits for 1986 to the plaintiff was clearly erroneous. We disagree.

An implied covenant of good faith and fair dealing exists in every contract. [citation omitted] Thus, an unfair determination of a partner's respective share of a partnership's earnings is a breach not only of one's fiduciary duty, [citation omitted] but also of the implied covenant of good faith and fair dealing. [citation omitted] A court has the power to determine whether a partner's share of the profits is fair and equitable as a matter of law. [citation omitted] In the present case, the judge "vigorously scrutinized" the founding partners' determination of the plaintiff's share of the profits. [citation omitted] The judge then made extensive findings concerning the fairness of the plaintiff's share of the profit distribution. The judge found that the plaintiff had produced billable hour and billable dollar amounts that constituted 16.4% and 15%, respectively, of the total billable hour and billable dollar amounts for all of the partners as a group. The judge noted, however, that the founding partners distributed only 6.3% of the firm's 1986 profits to the plaintiff. Meanwhile, the other partners received substantially greater shares of the profits.[4]

---

[4]   The plaintiff received $101,025.60. Meanwhile, the defendants Guryan and LeClair each received 18.75% ($301,025.60) of the firm's total profits. As a result, each of the managing partners kept for himself a 28.1% share of the profits, or $451,025.60 each. The judge did note, however, that the founding partners were not unfair in allocating to the plaintiff 7.2% of the firm's expenses in 1986.

The judge concluded, therefore, that the founding partners had decided to exclude billable hour and billable dollar totals as a factor in determining compensation. The judge determined that this decision to exclude billable hour figures was unfair to the plaintiff and indicated that the founding partners had selected performance criteria in order to justify the lowest possible payment to the plaintiff.[5]

The judge also noted that Fordham had fabricated a list of negative factors that the founding partners had used in determining the plaintiff's share of the firm's profits. As a result, the judge concluded that the founding partners had violated their respective fiduciary duties to the plaintiff as well as the implied covenant of good faith and fair dealing. The judge also concluded that the plaintiff was entitled to 11% of the firm's profits for 1986 and awarded the plaintiff $75,538.48 in damages.[7]

* * * [W]e conclude that the judge's ultimate finding of liability was not clearly erroneous. * * *

4. Misrepresentation. Fordham argues that the judge's conclusion that he had misrepresented to the plaintiff the basis on which the firm's profits would be allocated among the firm's partners was clearly erroneous. We disagree.

Statements of present intention as to future conduct may be the basis for a fraud action, if "the statements misrepresent the actual intention of the speaker and were relied upon by the recipient to his damage." [citation omitted] In the present case, the judge found that Fordham had represented to the plaintiff that business origination would not be a significant factor in determining the plaintiff's share of the firm's profits. The judge also noted that Fordham had made this representation to the plaintiff in January, 1985, while the plaintiff was still working at Foley Hoag. The judge found that the plaintiff had relied on this representation when he had left Foley Hoag to join Kilburn, Fordham & Starrett. Nevertheless, the judge decided that Fordham had intended client origination to be the dominant factor for allocating profit shares when he made his representation to the contrary to the plaintiff. In addition, the judge determined that the founding partners had assigned profit shares for 1986 based primarily on each partner's contribution to business origination. As a result, the judge concluded that Fordham had tortiously misrepresented to the plaintiff the basis on which the founding partners would distribute the firm's profits to the partners. * * *

In the present case, the judge found that the partnership agreement did not contradict Fordham's prior representations that business origination would not be a significant factor in allocating the firm's profits. Thus, the provisions of the partnership agreement are not

---

[5]   The judge compared the plaintiff's work performance directly to the work performance of the defendants Guryan and LeClair. The judge concluded that the plaintiff's "billable hours by working attorney" were 85% of the total billable hours that Guryan had worked and 77% of the total billable hours that LeClair had worked. The plaintiff's share of the profits, however, was only 34% of the amount which Guryan and LeClair each had received.

[7]   The judge found that 11% of the profits was a more accurate reflection of the plaintiff's contribution to the firm's 1986 profits after considering the plaintiff's billable hour and billable dollar totals. In addition, the judge noted that Starrett had recommended that the plaintiff receive an 11% profit share in the fall of 1986 when the plaintiff first had informed his partners of his intention to withdraw from the firm. Eleven percent of the firm's total profits for 1986 amounted to $176,564.08. The judge then subtracted the 6.3% of the profits, which the plaintiff had already received, from $176,564.08 to arrive at $75,538.48.

"clearly at variance" with Fordham's representation. [citation omitted] There was no clear error, therefore, in the judge's conclusion that the plaintiff was reasonable in his reliance on Fordham's representation.

Fordham argues next that the judge erred in concluding that the plaintiff was not unreasonable in relying on Fordham's representations because the plaintiff was a sophisticated corporate attorney. We reject this argument. The plaintiff's sophistication did not relieve Fordham of his obligation to deal with the plaintiff in an honest manner. * * *

Notes and Questions

1. **Interpreting the contract.** Did the court's interpretation reflect the parties' probable intentions? Doesn't the agreement clearly grant discretion to the managers despite their obvious conflict of interest? If so, should they have the burden of proving that the allocation was fair?

2. **Business considerations.** Would the agreement as interpreted by defendants have been a bad deal for the plaintiff? The other partners would have had little incentive not to fully reward plaintiff for his contribution if he was doing a good job because he might leave if he became disgruntled. However, the case concerned the payment to plaintiff on his voluntary departure from the firm, when the other partners had little incentive to be nice to him.

3. **The role of misrepresentation.** Even if the defendants *said* that profit allocation would not depend on business origination, should they be held to this in light of the language of the agreement and the refusal to change the language to meet plaintiff's concerns during negotiation?

Problem

Assume that plaintiff in this case had retained you, an expert in partnership law, to advise him at the time of his joining the firm. Plaintiff lays out the circumstances, including his concerns about compensation, and asks you to propose a compensation provision that both he and the others can live with. What advice would you give?

4.04. The Role of Partnership Accounting

Formal partnerships almost always establish partnership accounts to guide their financial affairs. One important device is the use of *capital accounts*. These initially reflect cash and the fair market value of property contributed by the partners. Over time, they are adjusted upward to reflect the partners' shares of profits and additional partner contributions and downward to reflect the partners' shares of losses and distributions to and withdrawals by the partners. *See* paragraph 4.3 of the Chameleon agreement and the illustrations in § 4.05, below. A partner who contributes property to the partnership does not at that time have to pay tax on appreciation in the value of property since she bought it (*see* Internal Revenue Code (I.R.C.) § 721). Instead, under I.R.C. § 723, the partner continues to have the same tax basis in the property—*i.e.*, the amount that is used for determining any eventual taxable gain on the property—even after contributing it to the partnership. When the property is sold, appreciation over this basis is taxed to the partner.

The partners often agree in the partnership agreement on how to allocate money and tax consequences. As illustrated by the following case, the partners may agree on their accounting method, and on distributions to partners prior to dissolution. Although the partners can allocate distribution rights and contribution obligations differently from how they allocate tax consequences, tax law requires the tax consequences to accord substantially with non-tax financial rights. The partners' capital accounts are important in showing how the partners divide the money and so how they should allocate tax consequences. *See* I.R.C. § 704. However, as shown in the Chameleon agreement, the parties may have a "sharing ratio" for dividing control and financial rights that differs from the ratios of their capital accounts.

Darr v. D.R.S. Investments
232 Neb. 507, 441 N.W.2d 197 (1989)

RIST, District Judge.

This is an action for the dissolution of a partnership and for an accounting with respect to such dissolution.

On August 2, 1976, the plaintiff and defendants James Stephens and Erwin Rung entered into an agreement creating a partnership known as D.R.S. Investments (DRS). Each partner contributed $1,500 in cash to the partnership.

The purpose of the partnership as stated in the agreement was to own, build, rent, sell, or otherwise dispose of real or personal property. The partnership in fact built a building upon land owned by J.E.D. Construction (JED), a corporation, in which corporation all the partners were equal stockholders, the partnership leasing the land from the corporation for 35 years with a 10-year renewal option and leasing back some of the building space to JED. Funds were borrowed by the partnership for the construction of the building, the corporation and partnership mortgaging the land and building to secure the same.

The partnership agreement provided for equal sharing of the partners in net profits and net losses, the same to be credited or charged to the drawing account of each partner. The agreement further provided that the books of the partnership were to be maintained on a cash basis and closed on December 31 of each year.

Paragraph 10 of the agreement provided: Any partner may retire from the partnership at the end of a calendar year, provided he has given sixty (60) days advance written notice of his intention to the other partners. Such a retirement shall cause a dissolution of the partnership, but the remaining partners shall have the right to continue the partnership business provided the continuing partnership pays to the retiring partner the value of his interest in the partnership. For this purpose the value of the interest of a retiring partner shall be the amount of his capital account, plus or minus any credit or debit balance in his drawing account, all determined at the end of such calendar year in accordance with the accounting methods regularly used by the partnership.

During 1976, all accounting appears to have been done on a cash basis. Beginning in 1977, however, on the recommendation of its accountant, the partnership accounting for income tax purposes was done on an accrual basis, resulting in tax losses in all subsequent years, which the partners reported on their respective income tax returns. The record shows the purpose of using accrual accounting was to provide income tax losses that would exceed any such losses if reported on a cash basis.

The partnership agreement was prepared by an attorney for the partnership, the record not reflecting whether any partner or partners had any particular input into it. The record shows the parties considered the agreement, after it was prepared, without any detailed study or consideration and signed it.

On May 10, 1982, plaintiff wrote the defendant partners, giving notice of his intention to retire from the partnership at the end of 1982 because of a disability, and asked whether they elected to pay his interest in the partnership or whether they wished to liquidate the assets and make final distribution. Later that year the defendant partners wrote plaintiff, accepting his retirement and advising him that they intended to continue the partnership and that they would pay him the value of his interest as determined under paragraph 10 of the partnership agreement. They further advised that a meeting would be held January 11, 1983, to determine that value as of the end of 1982. Such meeting was held, but the plaintiff did not attend. Subsequent thereto, defendant partners offered plaintiff $1,500 for his interest in the partnership, which he rejected.

At some point during this period, plaintiff also disposed of his interest in JED.

On March 1, 1985, plaintiff commenced this action for dissolution and accounting. The defendants in their answer pleaded the provisions of paragraph 10, that plaintiff had a negative balance in his capital account in the amount of $7,866.66, and that he owed the partnership this amount for which they counterclaimed against him. Plaintiff, in his reply, denied defendants' determination of his interest, alleged that paragraph 10 of the partnership agreement did not express the intent of the parties and should be reformed to reflect the correct intent and that it was unconscionable, denied the counterclaim, and renewed the prayer of his petition. * * *

On appeal, plaintiff assigns as error (1) the failure of the trial court to reform the partnership agreement, and (2) the trial court's award of judgment to defendants in the absence of a partnership provision authorizing such award. * * *

Reformation is decreed in order to set forth the real agreement of the parties when the written instrument does not represent their true intent. Such reformation may be decreed with respect to a mutual mistake, and in that situation the erroneous written agreement is conformed to the antecedent agreement of the parties entered into prior to the execution of the erroneous written agreement. [citation omitted]

An examination of the record reflects that until plaintiff's retirement, there was no expression by any of the parties as to what a retiring partner should receive. There is no evidence that the defendant partners ever understood or agreed to plaintiff's conception of what his retirement rights were. From the beginning of the partnership to the time of plaintiff's retirement, the only evidence of what the parties intended is what is expressed in the partnership agreement. The partners now differ over its meaning. The evidence supports the trial court's finding that there is no mutual mistake warranting reformation of the contract.

Plaintiff asserts that reformation should be had because the agreement with respect to the valuation of his interest as a retiring partner is unconscionable. His claim is the parties did not contemplate any system of accounting that would result in a negative amount being due from a retiring partner and that equity requires the valuation of his partnership interest by taking into account the appreciated value of the partnership assets. What constitutes appropriate accounting will be dealt with later in this opinion. Suffice it to say at this point that parties creating a partnership have a wide selection of methods to value a retiring partner's interest. If they choose one that does not include a determination of appreciated value, that is a choice they are free to make.

In this case, the partnership agreement makes no reference to such appreciated value but, rather, provides for a capital account plus or minus profits or losses of the partnership upon a cash basis accounting.

We take note of the testimony of the accountants who testified in effect that unless an agreement specified an accounting with appreciated asset values, such values would not be considered in any normal accounting practice or procedure.

In *G & S Investments v. Belman*, 145 Ariz. 258, 700 P.2d 1358 (1984), the estate of a deceased partner disputed the valuation of that partner's interest under a buy-out provision by the remaining partners. The partnership agreement called for payment of the deceased partner's capital account with certain adjustments. The deceased partner's estate claimed a right to share in the appreciated value of the partnership assets. The Arizona Court of Appeals disagreed, holding that the words "capital account" were not ambiguous where the contract called for cash basis accounting, as such words have a recognized meaning that does not include appreciated value, and that a buy-out provision may involve a different amount than might be realized in a total dissolution and sale of assets. The court said,

> Because partnerships result from contract, the rights and liabilities of the partners among themselves are subject to such agreements as they may make. * * * Partnership buy-out agreements are valid and binding although the purchase price agreed upon is less or more than the actual value of the interest at time of death. * * *

> * * * We do not have the power to rewrite [the buy-out provision] based upon subjective notions of fairness arising long after the agreement was made or because the agreement did not turn out to be an advantageous one. Modern business practice mandates that the parties be bound by the contract they enter into, absent fraud or duress. * * * It is not the province of this court to act as a post-transaction guardian for either party.

145 Ariz. at 267-68, 700 P.2d at 1367-68. Such holding is applicable to the situation in this case.

We find from the record that all the partners of DRS were experienced businessmen and that they saw and had opportunity to read the partnership agreement and to discuss it before signing it. Plaintiff cannot now have changes in it because he was inattentive to what he signed. We further find there is no evidence of fraud or overreaching.

Regardless of what appreciation of the assets may have accrued, it was proper for the parties at the inception of the partnership to have determined the method of accounting which did not include any such future appreciation. The trial court correctly held that the partnership contract was not unconscionable and that appreciated values were not appropriate in this case.

Plaintiff's argument that the agreement provides only for the payment of a positive amount to a retiring partner and that the contract is silent with respect to any negative balance appears to suggest that the agreement is incomplete in this regard and that the provisions of the Uniform Partnership Act, NEB. REV. STAT. §§ 67-301 *et seq.* (Reissue 1986), may apply. The trial court found paragraph 10 of the agreement clear and unambiguous in this regard, and we agree. The agreement requires profits and losses to be credited or debited to a partner's capital account through the use of a drawing account. It follows that if losses exceed the original capital account investment of a partner, there is an amount due and owing the partnership from a retiring partner for losses exceeding the original capital account balance. No recourse to the Uniform Partnership Act is necessary.

The remaining issue is whether the use of accrual accounting was appropriate under the partnership contract to determine the plaintiff's interest in the partnership. The agreement calls for the use of cash basis accounting. * * *

The record is clear that the partnership accountant recommended accrual accounting for specific use with respect to income tax reporting, since it would give greater deductions to the partners on their individual returns than would cash basis accounting. All of the parties accepted this with respect to income tax reporting. We also determine from the testimony of the accountants that individuals or entities are entirely at liberty to select one method of accounting for income tax purposes and another method of accounting for other purposes.

Since the partnership agreement provided for cash basis accounting, a proper construction of the agreement would require this method of accounting to apply unless the parties by their subsequent actions evidenced a clear choice to have the partnership accounting done on an accrual basis for all purposes. Given the uncontradicted record that accrual accounting was solely motivated by income tax considerations, that the partnership could lawfully and properly use accrual accounting for that purpose only and cash basis accounting for other purposes, that the agreement provides for the use of cash basis accounting for partnership purposes, and that prior to this dispute accrual accounting was used only for income tax purposes, we find the valuation of a retiring partner's capital account should be determined upon a cash basis as provided in the agreement. With respect to what constitutes cash basis accounting, we hold the same is to be done in accordance with accepted accounting procedures and the terms of the agreement.

We therefore find that the trial court erred in accepting an accounting of plaintiff's capital account on an accrual basis and that the same should be determined upon a cash basis.

We reverse and remand this cause to the trial court for determination of plaintiff's interest as a retiring partner under appropriate cash basis accounting as of December 31, 1982, and for disposition accordingly.

REVERSED AND REMANDED WITH DIRECTIONS.

WHITE, Justice, dissenting.

* * * The case is a classic example of otherwise business-wise persons signing an agreement containing words whose meanings are not readily known to them, and whose application, except in the case of the lone survivor, is disastrous.

It is obvious that the partnership was not formed in anticipation of a yearly profit. The partnership was intended to lose money (whether real or bookkeeping money), and the anticipated gain was to be made in liquidation, consisting of asset appreciation and recovery of claimed depreciation costs.

Two phrases in the agreement are the source of the trouble: "capital accounts" and "cash basis" accounting.

Capital generally consists of the difference between the book value of assets and liabilities. We know that each partner contributed $1,500 to the partnership, that no withdrawals were made, and that a fair reading of the record supports a finding that the difference between asset value and liabilities is in the $60,000 range.

We note that the rules for the cash basis accounting were not specified in the agreement, but consisted of charges to partnership income as determined by the firm's accountant. The elimination of two items alone would establish a plus figure for the value of appellant's interest; neither is a cash item, *i.e.*, depreciation of the partnership building and a charge of accrued debts to a corporation wholly owned by the partners. (The propriety of the last item as an allowable deduction was sharply disputed by the two accountants who testified.)

The fairness of a system whereby depreciation is charged against a capital account but appreciation is not aside, the suggestion that there is not a mutual mistake proven when three partners enter into a pact, which as interpreted provides for financial suicide on the part of two of them, is not realistic.

In the absence of a meeting of the minds as to dissolution, I would remand the matter to the district court for dissolution proceedings in accordance with the Uniform Partnership Act.

Notes and Questions

1. **Cash and accrual accounting.** "Cash" accounting generally records revenues and costs when money is received or paid. "Accrual" accounting records transactions when the firm has done the work necessary to be paid or entered into a commitment to pay. "Accrual" accounting realistically reflects the current economic status of most firms and gives them less leeway to shift revenues and expenses from year to year. Not surprisingly, therefore, tax law requires accrual accounting for many firms. Cash accounting is, however, common and permitted in some partnerships, including professional firms, in which it may not be clear when revenue is earned. Under I.R.C. § 448, a partnership that does not have a C corporation partner can use the cash method of accounting unless, generally speaking, it is a "tax shelter." The definition of "tax shelter" is intricately cross-referenced and depends, among other things, on whether the firm's members will actively engage in the business.

2. **Interpreting the agreement.** Do you agree with the court's interpretation of the agreement? The problem in *Darr* is that the partners used the capital accounts as the basis of a distribution to a leaving partner prior to the sale of the property on dissolution. This brought up the question of how to treat appreciation that is not normally reflected in the capital account. Is it enough to support an interpretation the agreement that the language is clear and would result in a simple method for determining the amount to be paid a withdrawing partner, even if the interpretation would result in "financial

suicide" for some partners? Dissociation agreements are also discussed below in Section 9.06.

For an often-cited case involving partners' duty to make up negative capital accounts balances *see Park Cities Corp. v. Byrd*, 534 S.W.2d 668 (Tex. 1976) (partner liable for negative balance attributable to depreciation where that partner got all the tax benefits of depreciation). *Wadsworth v. WWDM, Ltd.*, 162 Or. App. 622, 986 P.2d 1197 (1999), held that a partner was not required to restore the deficit, noting that, unlike in *Park Cities*, the agreement provided for the alternative remedy of reducing the partner's interest in the firm. The agreement should clarify this issue. For example, *Moran, Shuster, Carignan & Knierim v. August*, 43 Conn. Sup. 431, 657 A.2d 736 (1994), *aff'd.*, 232 Conn. 756, 657 A.2d 229 (1995), required the partner to make up the balance under a provision that "[i]f a Partner's capital account decreases to less than Ten Thousand ($10,000.00) Dollars then the Partner shall contribute the additional amount necessary to make the account Ten Thousand ($10,000.00) Dollars."

4.05 Losses and Partner Capital Accounts

An important element of partnership law is that creditors may seek payment out of partnership assets. One implication of this is that partners must share the losses. Under UPA § 18(a) and RUPA § 401(b), in the absence of a contrary agreement the partners share losses equally, or in proportion to profits if profits are shared unequally. "Losses" refers to the excess of liabilities over assets on final accounting. Thus, "losses" under the UPA and RUPA must be distinguished from accounting losses in the sense of the excess of expenses over revenues in a particular accounting period. Under UPA §§ 18(b) and 40, a partner who contributes capital to the firm gets this back on dissolution as a kind of debt owed by the firm, standing in line after the debts owed other than on account of capital. As discussed in the Notes following the principal case, the result may differ under RUPA.

It is important to understand how the partnership statutes operate in the context of partnership capital accounts. Consider the following simple example. A and B form a partnership. A makes a capital contribution of property with a fair market value of $10,000 (for simplicity, assume that this is also the partner's own tax basis in the property), while B contributes no capital but will work in the business. A simple capital account in this firm may look like this:

A	B
$10,000	0

Assume in Year 1 that the firm has expenses of $10,000 and revenues of $5,000, for a loss of $5,000—$2,500 for each partner. At the end of this year, the capital accounts would look as follows, with the parentheses in B's account indicating a deficit (which, incidentally, the partner may have a tax obligation to restore):

A	B
$10,000	0
-$2,500	-$2,500
$7,500	($2,500)

Assume in Year 2 the firm sells the property originally contributed by A for $15,000. Since A contributed this property to the firm, the appreciation belongs to the firm, to be divided equally among the partners in the absence of contrary agreement. Assume also that during this year the firm's other expenses equal the firm's other revenues.

A	B
$7,500	($2,500)
+$2,500	+$2,500
$10,000	$0

Note that, although the property was sold for $15,000, the balance sheet shows a total of $10,000 in assets because this reflects the operating loss from the prior year.

Assume that during Year 3 the firm dissolves, that the value of its remaining property is $10,000 and that it has liabilities to its non-partner creditors of $5,000. Since the net value of the firm was reduced from $10,000 in Year 2 to $5,000 in Year 3, it must have lost $5,000 in Year 3, which is divided equally between A and B. The final capital accounts would look like this:

A	B
$10,000	0
-$2,500	-$2,500
$7,500	($2,500)

The practical effect of the loss would be that the firm would pay off a total of $12,500—that is, $5,000 to "outside" creditors and $7,500 to A to compensate for what is left of A's capital contribution. The payment would come from the $10,000 proceeds from the sale of property and $2,500 from B's pocket.

Keeping the accounts in this way would constitute a kind of agreement by the partners on how to divide up profits and losses on dissolution. In informal partnerships there may be no precise accounts each year, and only one accounting at the end that produces a final gain or loss. In this situation the firm would simply see a surplus or deficit of assets as compared to liabilities that the partners must be divide in some way. A court probably would reconstruct the accounts as illustrated above to determine a surplus or deficit that is then divided among the partners. RUPA §§ 401 and 807 assume the existence of such accounts in every partnership and therefore apparently would require the construction of some sort of accounts, although probably not a reconstruction of what happened during each year of the partnership's existence.

Note that in the above example B, who contributes services, may not only get nothing in return, but may have to ante up out of her own pocket to repay A's capital contributions when the firm fails. As the following case indicates, the courts are not always happy with this result, even in the absence of a contrary agreement.

Kessler v. Antinora
279 N.J. Super. 471, 653 A.2d 579 (1995)

KING, P.J.A.D.

I

Plaintiff Robert H. Kessler and defendant Richard Antinora entered into a written agreement for the purpose of building and selling a single-family residence on a lot in Wayne in Passaic County. The concept of the agreement seemed simple: Kessler was to provide the money and Antinora was to act as general contractor. Profits would be divided—60% to Kessler, 40% to Antinora—after Kessler was repaid. No thought was given to losses. The venture lost money. Kessler sued Antinora to recover 40% of his financial losses or $65,742. The Law Division judge ruled in Kessler's favor on summary judgment. The judge denied Antinora's cross-motion for summary judgment of dismissal. We disagree, reverse the judgment in Kessler's favor, and order judgment in Antinora's favor.

II

On April 15, 1987 Kessler and Antinora executed a seven-page written agreement titled "JOINT VENTURE PARTNERSHIP AGREEMENT." The agreement contemplated a single venture: buying a lot in Wayne and building and selling a residence on it. Under the agreement Kessler agreed to "provide all necessary funds to purchase land and construct a one-family dwelling and disburse all funds to pay bills." Antinora agreed to "actually construct the dwelling and be the general contractor of the job."

The agreement provided for distribution of the proceeds of the venture:

> 9. Distribution. Upon or about completion of the dwelling it shall be placed for sale. Upon sale of same, and after deducting all monies expended by Robert Kessler plus interest at prime plus one point and/or including interest or any funds borrowed for the project, not to exceed prime plus one point, engineering fees, architectural fees, legal fees, broker fees, if any, and any other costs connected with the project, the parties, Robert Kessler and Richard Antinora, shall divide the net profits as follows: . . . Robert Kessler—sixty (60%) percent Richard Antinora—forty (40%) percent

The agreement was silent about losses. There was no provision to compensate Antinora for any services other than the 40% profit clause.

Both parties complied with the agreement. Kessler provided the funds; Antinora supervised and delivered the finished house. This took over three years. Meanwhile, the real estate market soured. The house sold on September 1, 1991 for $420,000. The cost incurred in building and selling the house was $498,917.

Kessler was repaid all but $78,917 of the money he advanced pursuant to the contract. He also claimed unreimbursed interest of $85,440 for his self-characterized "loan" to the partnership. This claim for interest is disputed as to amount. Kessler thus claimed a total loss of $164,357. He sought and obtained his summary judgment in the Law Division for 40% of this amount, or $65,742.80. No amount was presented on the value of Antinora's services over the three-year period as general contractor.

Antinora contended that the agreement was basically for a joint venture, silent as to losses, and that both parties risked and lost their unrecovered contributions—Kessler's money and Antinora's labor. The Law Division judge disagreed and found that statutory partnership law governed. The judge ruled that N.J.S.A. 42:1-18a required each partner to "contribute towards the losses, whether of capital or otherwise, sustained by the partnership according to his share in the profits." N.J.S.A. 42:1-18a. The judge ruled that Antinora was liable for 40% of Kessler's monetary losses and inferentially rejected any recognition of Antinora's "in kind" loss.

III

We conclude that New Jersey's allegedly applicable section of the Uniform Partnership Law, N.J.S.A. 42:1-18a, does not control here because of the specific terms of the agreement between the parties. The pertinent statutory section states: 42:1-18. Rights and duties of partners The rights and duties of the partners in relation to the partnership shall be determined, subject to any agreement between them, by the following rules: a. Each partner shall be repaid his contributions, whether by way of capital or advances to the partnership property and share equally in the profits and surplus remaining after all liabilities, including those to partners, are satisfied; and must contribute towards the losses, whether of capital or otherwise, sustained by the partnership according to his share in the profits. * * * [N.J.S.A. 42:1-18a.]

We find the agreement controlling over the statute. The agreement said that upon sale of the house "and after deducting all monies expended by Robert Kessler plus interest," fees, and other costs the "parties [Kessler and Antinora] shall divide net profits" 60% and 40%. We conclude that the agreement evinced a clear intent that Kessler would be repaid his investment from the sale of the house only, not by Antinora. There is no suggestion in the agreement that any of Kessler's risked and lost money would be repaid in part by Antinora. Nor is there any suggestion that Antinora's risked labor would be repaid in part by Kessler.

We find particularly persuasive the reasoning of the California Supreme Court in *Kovacik v. Reed*, 49 Cal.2d 166, 315 P.2d 314 (1957). There the parties orally agreed to participate in a kitchen remodeling venture for Sears Roebuck & Company. Kovacik agreed to invest $10,000 in the venture and Reed agreed to become the job estimator and supervisor. They agreed to share the profits on a 50-50 basis. Possible losses were not discussed. Despite their efforts, the venture was unsuccessful and Kovacik sued Reed to recover one-half the money losses he endured. Kovacik prevailed in the trial court and recovered $4,340, or one-half the net monetary loss of $8,680.

The California Supreme Court acknowledged the general rule of partnership law that in the absence of an agreement, "the law presumes that partners and joint adventurers intended to participate equally in the profits and losses of the common enterprise, irrespective of any inequality in the amounts each contributed to the capital employed in the venture, with the losses being shared by them in the same proportions as they share the profits." *Id.*, 315 P.2d at 315-16, citing CAL. CORP. CODE § 15018, which is identical to N.J.S.A. 40:1-18.

The California court then observed that this "general rule" did not obtain where one party contributed the money and the other the labor, stating:

However, it appears that in the cases in which the above stated general rule has been applied, each of the parties had contributed capital consisting of either money or land or other tangible property, or else was to receive compensation for services rendered to the common undertaking which was to be paid before computation of the profits or losses. Where, however, as in the present case, one partner or joint adventurer contributes the money capital as against the other's skill and labor, all the cases cited, and which our research has discovered, hold that neither party is liable to the other for contribution for any loss sustained. Thus, upon loss of the money the party who contributed it is not entitled to recover any part of it from the party who contributed only services. [*Id.* at 316.]

The rationale which the California decision and the earlier cited cases adopted was where one party contributes money and the other services, in the event of a loss, each loses his own capital—one in the form of money, the other in labor. *Id.* A corollary view was that the parties have implicitly agreed, by their conduct and contract, to share profits and that their contributions of money and sweat equity have been valued in an equal ratio. Thus, upon the loss of both some money and labor, the loss falls upon each proportionately without any legal recourse. Thus, Kovacik lost $8,680 of his $10,000 while Reed lost all of his labor.

Likewise, in the case before us, Kessler lost some of his money—$65,472, plus disputed interest, but Antinora lost all of the value of his labor on the three-year project. The Arizona Court of Appeals in *Ellingson v. Sloan*, 22 Ariz. App. 383, 527 P.2d 1100 (1974), has also recognized that in a joint venture "[t]he term 'losses' is not limited to monetary losses, but includes time expenditures and out-of-pocket expenses, especially where one party in a joint venture furnishes property and the other only services." *Id.*, 527 P.2d at 1103, citing *Kovacik v. Reed*, supra. The point of the Arizona case is that rendering services to an ultimately losing venture represents a valuable contribution, even though the laboring venturer risked no money capital. * * *

We conclude that the "JOINT VENTURE PARTNERSHIP AGREEMENT" here did contemplate repayment to Kessler of his investment but only from the proceeds of the sale of the house, not from his coventurer Antinora. This is what the parties said, the only truly reliable evidence of what they intended. Our interpretation of the agreement between the parties accords with the result reached under the common-law cases discussed, and with our overall sense of fairness. Each party shoulders a loss, one in determinative dollars; the other in labor, difficult, if not impossible, to quantify. The parties did not think about losses in casting their agreement and any attempt by the law now to reconstruct their then non-existent intent on the subject would be speculative.

Reversed for entry of summary judgment for the defendant Antinora.

Notes and Questions

1. **Application of the UPA and interpretation of the agreement.** Under the UPA default rule, the difference between Kessler's contribution of $498,917 and the $420,000 sale price of the house apparently would be a loss of $78,917, which under the 60-40 sharing agreement would be divided $47,350 for Kessler and $31,566 for Antinora. Did the agreement vary the statutory default, or was it simply silent? If the latter, wouldn't

the statute control? Should the court have characterized Kessler's investment as a loan, which would have triggered an additional interest obligation of the partnership?

2. **Capital losses under RUPA.** Would *Kessler* have been decided differently under RUPA? Section 807(b) provides that partners shall contribute to the partnership the excess of charges over credits in their accounts. RUPA § 401 provides how the accounts are to be constructed—that is, by crediting contributions and profits and debiting distributions and losses. Under this approach, the difference between what Kessler contributed ($498,917) and what he received on sale of the house ($420,000) would be charged in the profit-sharing proportions (here, 60-40) to each of the partners. It follows from this analysis that, as under the UPA, Kessler would receive the $420,000 sale price plus a contribution from Antinora of $31,566. However, unlike the UPA, RUPA does not make clear that losses include *capital* losses. The official comment to RUPA § 807 confuses matters by stating:

> RUPA eliminates the distinction in UPA Section 40(b) between the liability owing to a partner in respect of capital and the liability owing in respect of profits. * * * The partners may, however, agree to share "operating" losses differently from "capital" losses, thereby continuing the UPA distinction.

The first part of the above quote refers to what the *partnership owes* to the partners on account of capital and profits. The second part of the quote refers to what the *partners owe* when the firm has lost money. It appears to say that RUPA treats capital losses the same as operating losses. Contrary to the comment's assertion, this is the rule under UPA.

3. **What should the default rule be?** Should the default rule provide for different treatment of capital and service contributions by requiring service partners to pay for capital losses? On the one hand, this different treatment is arguably inconsistent with the general valuation-simplifying assumption for compensation purposes that partners' contributions balance each other (*see* § 4.01). On the other hand, the market value of service contributions is generally less than that of financial contributions because service contributions are specialized to particular firms. Also, subjecting service contributions to the risk of the enterprise gives labor partners like Antinora an incentive to perform carefully and loyally that is not necessary for capital contributors. It has been argued that default rules should not necessarily be what the parties could be expected to agree to. Rather, they should be designed in some circumstances to force the party disadvantaged by the default rule to disclose information to the other party. *See* Ayres & Gertner, *Filling Gaps in Incomplete Contracts: An Economic Analysis of Default Rules,* 99 YALE L.J. 87 (1989). One commentator argues against applying the Ayres & Gertner in the *Kessler*-type situation because "default" general partnerships are likely to be so informal that the parties probably won't bargain over the agreement, and in any event it is not clear whether the service or capital partner has the relevant information. Bainbridge, *Contractarianism in the Business Associations Classroom: The Puzzling Case of* Kovacik v. Reed *and the Allocation of Capital Losses in Service Partnerships,* 34 GA. L. REV. 631 (2000). Interestingly, Professor Bainbridge bases his

assumption of informality on the growing use of LLCs and LLPs (*see* chapters 12 and 13, below) for more formal firms. Bainbridge also argues for the UPA default on the ground that most parties would find that equal sharing makes sense. As to whether there should be a special exception for the non-standard situation where one party does all the work and contributes no capital, Bainbridge notes the benefits of clear and simple rules rather than case-by-case exceptions.

4. **Loss-sharing, indemnification and contribution.** Allocating partnership losses among the partners also depends on the rules concerning indemnification and contribution, which correlate the partners' joint and several liability to third parties with their proportionate obligations among themselves. These rules are discussed in Chapters 6 and 9 below.

Problem

Draft financial provisions for the joint venture involved in *Kessler* in light of the law and facts in the opinion. Consider the following alternatives:

(1) A straight payment to Antinora without a profit or loss percentage. Would this be a partnership? Why do you suppose the parties agreed to a profit percentage?

(2) Allocating some or all of the capital loss to Antinora under specific circumstances, as where Antinora exceeds a specified limit on expenses.

(3) Allocating more than 60% of the capital loss to Kessler to reflect the fact that Antinora is receiving no payment on account of his services.

CHAPTER 5
MANAGEMENT AND CONTROL

5.01 Management Rights Among the Partners

Since the partners make substantial contributions of money, time and credit they would want to have some role in making sure their investments are used wisely. At the same time, the members do not want to become so involved in management and watching their partners that this takes away from more valuable ways to spend their time. "Treasure of the Sierra Madre," provides an illustration here, as it did for financial rights (*see* § 4.01). When the gold-miners have gotten their gold, they end up spending a lot of time guarding it from the other members, including getting up in turns in the middle of the night to check on their "stashes." At one point, Howard, the old prospector, says "I won't take my turn if you guys will stop worrying and go to bed. We've got work to do." At another point, when the relationship has further deteriorated, Fred C. Dobbs (Humphrey Bogart) says, "Betcha $105,000 [the amount of the hoard] you go to sleep before I do." Perhaps the partners should have taken Howard's earlier suggestion to just let him manage the cash because he's the most "trustworthy." (He points out that that doesn't mean the most "honest"—just that he can't run as fast as the others.) In general, the choice of management and monitoring devices can make a big difference in the overall wealth of the firm. In the end, the gold-mining partnership ends with the whole hoard of gold dust being blown by a "norther" back into the mountain it came from.

There are two categories of partner management rights and powers: those that apply among the partners themselves, and those that apply vis a vis third parties. These categories follow the agency categories of actual and apparent authority discussed in § 2.03. This section discusses partners' actual authority under the partnership statute, while § 5.02 discusses partners' apparent authority. Section 5.03 discusses the scope of the partnership's liability for partners' wrongful acts, which is analogous to the vicarious tort liability of principals discussed in § 2.04. Section 5.04 discusses the impact of the partnership agreement on partners' actual and apparent authority.

In general, partners' management rights under the partnership statutes include the following:

1. **The right to manage.** Under UPA § 18(e) and RUPA § 401(f), all partners may participate in the governance of the firm. This differs from a corporation, in which the board manages and shareholders vote.

2. **Equal voting rights.** Partners have *equal* rights to participate in management—that is, each partner gets one vote. This rule contrasts with the corporate "one-share-one-vote" rule that allocates voting power according to the extent of the shareholders' capital contributions. While a shareholder's contribution in the standard form corporation is limited to a financial investment, a partner's contribution also includes services and credit (unlimited liability).

3. **Vote required to take action: statutory rules.** In the event of a disagreement over ordinary business, a majority vote controls under UPA § 18(i), RUPA § 401(j). For example, only a majority of the partners, and not a single partner, can sue to enforce a partnership claim. *See Nogueras v. Maisel & Associates of Michigan,* 142 Mich. App. 71, 369 N.W.2d 492 (1985). (Partnership litigation is discussed below in Chapter 8.) However, a single partner does have the right to veto major partnership decisions. This balances the potentially high decision-making costs of giving each partner a veto power against the potentially high costs to partners of letting the majority decide issues that may have significant consequences. UPA § 18(h) provides that, while a majority controls as to "ordinary matters," acts "in contravention of any agreement between the partners" must be decided unanimously. This implies that unanimity is required for extraordinary acts, as is made clear by RUPA § 401(j). UPA § 18(g) and RUPA § 401(i) provide for a default right to veto a particular type of major decision—the admission of a partner. This is discussed further in Chapter 7. Note that a partner's power to dissociate and dissolve at will, discussed in Chapter 9, may operate something like a veto power, although a partner may pay a high cost for voting with her feet.

4. **Applying the statutory rules.** The question of which matters individual partners can veto under the above statutory provisions depends on the parties' express and implied agreement. In the absence of an explicit agreement a court might assume that the parties would have adopted an economically "reasonable" agreement that balances the expected decision-making costs of a high-vote rule against the expected costs to dissenting partners of being outvoted. "Extraordinary" clearly would include changing the form of the business from a partnership to a corporation. *See Fortungno v. Hudson*

Manure Co., 51 N.J. Super. 482, 144 A.2d 207 (1958). *Paciaroni v. Crane,* 408 A.2d 946 (Del. Ch. 1979), is a closer case. Two of three partners who owned a race horse wanted to race him despite an injury, while the third owner, the trainer, objected. In a Solomonic decision, the court held that the threat to the partnership's only asset made this an extraordinary matter requiring a unanimous vote, but that the partnership should be deemed to have dissolved and that the majority partners may race the horse in connection with winding up upon posting of a bond.

   5. **Fiduciary duties and management rights.** Partners' management rights are closely related to their fiduciary duties and remedies discussed below in Chapters 8 and 9. In order to vote and participate in management, partners need information. Hence, partners' have a fiduciary right to disclosure. *See* § 8.02. Also, members' right to participate in management may translate into a right to damages if they are excluded from management. *See* § 9.02(D).

5.02 Partners' Authority to Bind the Partnership

   Section 5.01 deals with partners' management and control rights among themselves. Like non-partner agents (*see* Chapter 2), partners may have more extensive power to bind the partnership in transactions with third parties than they do among their co-partners. UPA § 9 and RUPA § 301 state the general principle that each partner is an agent. They also define each partner's power as one to bind the firm when the partner is "apparently carrying on in the usual way" the partnership business (RUPA substitutes "ordinary course" for "usual way"). This is the scope of the partners' *apparent* authority, at least to the extent that third parties are not notified of any limitation of the partners' power. Under UPA § 9(2) and RUPA § 301(2), a partner can bind the partnership even in transactions that are not "usual" or "ordinary" if they are *actually* authorized by the partnership. A partner who binds the firm without actual authority may be subject to sanctions within the firm, including liability to the other partners and inability to obtain indemnification from the other partners for payments they make to third parties. The UPA rules on authority are applied in the following case.

Patel v. Patel
212 Cal. App. 3d 6, 260 Cal. Rptr. 255 (1989)

CHANNELL, Associate Justice.
   Appellants P.V. and Kirit Patel sued for specific performance of a real estate contract and incidental damages from respondents and sellers L.G., S.L., and Rajeshkumar Patel. The sellers successfully defended the specific performance action at trial, although they were ordered to compensate P.V. and Kirit for all expenses incurred to execute the contract. P.V. and Kirit Patel appeal, contending that (1) as bona fide purchasers for value, they were entitled to specific performance and (2) the trial court should have awarded them damages, costs, and attorney fees. We affirm the judgment.

I. FACTS

Respondents L.G. and S.L. Patel, husband and wife, own and operate the City Center Motel in Eureka. Appellants P.V. and Kirit Patel, father and son, own and operate another motel in the same community. On April 16, 1986, Rajeshkumar, the son of L.G. and S.L., formed a partnership with his parents and became owner of 35 percent of the City Center Motel. The partnership agreement required that Rajeshkumar approve any sale of the motel. Record title to the motel was not changed to reflect his interest.

On April 21, L.G. and S.L. listed their motel for sale with a real estate broker. On May 2, P.V. and Kirit Patel made an offer on the motel, which L.G. and S.L. accepted. Neither the broker nor the purchasers knew of the son's interest in the motel. When L.G. and S.L. notified Rajeshkumar of their plans, to their surprise, he refused to sell his 35 percent of the motel. On May 4, L.G. and S.L. notified P.V. and Kirit that they wished to withdraw their acceptance. They offered to pay $10,000 in damages and to give them a right of first refusal for five years.

Instead, on May 29, P.V. and Kirit filed an action for specific performance and incidental damages. L.G., S.L., and Rajeshkumar responded that the contract could not lawfully be enforced. After trial, the court found that, but for Rajeshkumar's undisclosed partnership interest, P.V. and Kirit would be entitled to specific performance of the contract. However, the trial court found the sale, which would make it impossible to continue the partnership business, was barred unless all partners agreed to it. The trial court held the contract unenforceable and denied specific performance. * * *

II. SPECIFIC PERFORMANCE

First, P.V. and Kirit contend that they met the prerequisites for specific performance. They contend that the trial court erred when it refused to grant specific performance because Rajeshkumar did not approve his parents' sale of the motel. P.V. and Kirit assert that the trial court should have concluded that the sellers were estopped by their conduct from asserting that anyone other than L.G. and S.L. Patel were sole owners of the motel.

Generally, every partner is an agent of the partnership for the purpose of its business, and the act of every partner to carry on the business of the partnership binds the partnership. [UPA § 9(1)] However, partners acting without the approval of the remaining partners may not do any act which would make it impossible to carry on the ordinary business of the partnership. [UPA § 9(3)(c)] These provisions distinguish between acts of a partner which bind the partnership without the express authority of the remaining partners and acts binding on the partnership only after express authorization by all partners. A contract executed by less than all of the partners to sell partnership real estate binds the other partners if the partnership is in the business of buying or selling real estate and the property covered by the contract is part of the stock held for sale. [citation omitted] Enforcement of the contract for sale of the motel, executed by L.G. and S.L. without the approval of their partner Rajeshkumar, would result in the sale of all of the partnership assets, making it impossible for the partnership to continue, in violation of [UPA § 9(3)(c)].

Historically, partnerships were divided into two types: commercial or trading partnerships and noncommercial or nontrading partnerships. Although this distinction has been rejected in California, it remains a valuable tool in considering whether L.G. and S.L. exceeded their statutory authority by entering into the real estate sale contract, thus making it impossible to carry on the ordinary business of the partnership. [citation omitted] In the case of a commercial or trading partnership in which the usual partnership business is to hold and sell real property, a contract such as that involved in this case—to sell the sole partnership asset—would be enforceable. [citation omitted] By contrast, when—as in the present case—the usual partnership business is to run a business, rather than to hold it in anticipation of its eventual sale, the partnership is not bound by a contract selling that business without the approval of all partners. [citation omitted] Under these circumstances, the trial court properly denied specific performance of the unauthorized contract in order to prevent destruction of the partnership, in compliance with [UPA § 9(3)(c)].

Nevertheless, P.V. and Kirit contend that the trial court should have applied [UPA § 10(3)] instead of [UPA § 9(3)(c)]. [UPA § 10(3)] states: "Where title to real property is in the name of one or more of the partners, whether or not the record discloses the right of the partnership, the partners in whose name the title stands may convey title to such property, but the partnership may recover such property unless the partner's act binds the partnership under the provisions of subdivision (1) of Section 15009, or unless the property has been conveyed to a bona fide purchaser for value without knowledge that the partner in executing the conveyance has exceeded his authority." P.V. and Kirit contend that they are bona fide purchasers for value because they had no knowledge of Rajeshkumar's unrecorded interest in the motel. They contend that this statute must be applied even though contrary to [UPA § 9(3)(c)].

The trial court found the provisions of [UPA § 9(3)(c)] to prevail over those of [UPA § 10(3)]. To enforce the contract of sale without Rajeshkumar's approval would frustrate the purpose of [UPA § 9(3)(c)] by making it impossible for the partnership to continue. We have found no cases with similar facts which discuss the conflict between these two provisions of the Uniform Partnership Act. However, as the purpose of the partnership is to operate a motel, rather than to hold it for eventual sale, we believe that the better result would be to preserve the partnership and hold the contract unenforceable. * * *

The judgment is affirmed.

Notes and Questions

1. **The scope of partner authority.** Several factors may determine the scope of partner authority under the UPA and RUPA, including the type of partnership and the customs and practices of the specific partnership and of other partnerships in the general locale. For example, consider whether the result in *Patel* would have differed if motel partnerships in Eureka, or in California, customarily bought and sold motels.

2. **Presumptively unauthorized transactions.** The UPA categories of presumptively unauthorized transactions, one of which is applied in *Patel*, are not included in RUPA. Some of these categories, such as arbitration clauses, are commonplace today and so probably should not be considered presumptively unauthorized. But the general idea of carving out particular types of transactions as unauthorized arguably provides helpful predictability.

3. **Real property transfers.** The general rules on authority also apply to real property transfers. But even if the transfer was not authorized under UPA § 9, perhaps it should nevertheless bind the partnership because of the way record title to the property was held. This distinctive aspect of real property transfers is covered by UPA § 10, which is discussed in *Patel*. UPA § 10(3) provides that title passes where all titleholders join in a transfer *unless* the transaction is unauthorized under UPA § 9(1) *and* the purchaser is *not* "a holder for value without knowledge." Should § 10(3) have controlled in *Patel* over § 9(1), given that § 10 deals specifically with the relevance of record title to real property? Even if the transaction was extraordinary, perhaps it should have bound the partnership if the third party reasonably believed based on record title that all owners had joined in the transfer. If § 10 does apply in *Patel*, what should be the result if: (1) record title was in the "City Center Motel Partnership"? or (2) the son had approved of the transaction? Note that, in the second situation, the transferee is not "without knowledge" and the transaction is not binding under § 9(1) (the only subsection cross-referenced in § 10(3)), although it is binding under § 9(2).

4. **RUPA.** RUPA § 302 applies the same basic philosophy as UPA § 10 except that, among other things, it eliminates the awkward provisions on transfer of *equitable* title, applies to property other than real property, and cross-references all of § 301, the analogue to UPA § 9 (thereby eliminating the anomaly referred to at the end of Note 3). For an application of RUPA in another motel case involving people named Patel, *see In re Swaffar*, 222 B.R. 326 (Bankr. E.D. Ark. 1998). The court held under the Arkansas version of RUPA that neither the purchaser nor a subsequent transferee had "constructive or inquiry notice" of transferring partner's lack of authority based on the partnership agreement since the agreement could not be considered in the chain of title. The court also held that even if the purchaser had seen the agreement it could not have determined transferring partner's lack of authority because the withdrawing partner whose consent was supposedly required was not a partner at time of the sale.

5. **Notice to the partnership.** The partners' power to bind the firm goes beyond entering into contracts on behalf of the partnership. Under UPA § 12 and RUPA § 102, notice to or knowledge of a partner may constitute notice to or knowledge of the partnership. Compare the detailed rules on partner notice and knowledge in the UPA with RUPA § 102(f). In both cases, notice to or knowledge of a partner is ineffective as to the partnership if the partner is defrauding the partnership. Should a third party bear a loss that results from a partnership's not having notice from a fraudulent partner if the third party does not know about the fraud? Also, compare the effect under the UPA and RUPA of information a person learns about before becoming a partner.

6. **Partner admissions.** A partner's statement may bind the partnership as an admission. This is explicit in UPA § 11, and an admission is probably an "act" covered by RUPA § 301. What is the effect under each statute of an admission of partnership liability by a partner whose job covered the subject matter of the statement but not speaking for the firm?

5.03 Partners' Wrongful Acts

Partners may bind the partnership not only as to contracts but also as to fraudulent, tortious or other misconduct. *See* UPA §§ 13-14 and RUPA § 305. Liability generally depends on whether the activity is within the ordinary course of the partnership's business. There is a special rule, applied in the following cases, for misapplication of funds.

Zimmerman v. Hogg & Allen, Professional Association
286 N.C. 24, 209 S.E.2d 795 (1974)

Plaintiff, an officer and employee of Holly Farms Poultry Industries, Inc. (hereafter referred to as Holly Farms), sued defendant, Hogg & Allen, Professional Association (P.A.), successor to Greene, Hogg & Allen, P.A. (hereafter referred to as Professional Association) and defendant Glenn L. Greene, Jr., individually (hereafter referred to as Greene) for breach of contract and breach of trust with regard to the handling of a certain stock purchase transaction. Holly Farms had engaged Professional Association to represent it in labor relations and to act as labor counsel for the corporation. Professional Association had sought to limit its practice of law to this area. The charter of the Association, however, issued under Florida law, contained no such limitation. To the contrary, it granted very broad powers to the entity, as evidenced by the following excerpt from the Charter:

ARTICLE II—GENERAL NATURE OF BUSINESS AND POWERS
The general nature of the business to be transacted by this corporation shall be as follows: (a) To engage in every phase and aspect of the practice of law and to render professional legal services to any and all persons, firms, corporations, and other entities, and to the general public, in the State of Florida and all of (sic) otherwise, throughout the world, unless prohibited by law; (b) To invest its funds in real estate, mortgages, stocks, bonds or other types of investments, and to own real or personal property necessary for the rendering of the aforesaid professional services; (c) In general, to do all things and perform all acts necessary and proper for the accomplishment of the aforesaid purposes or necessary or incidental to the achievement of the objectives of the corporation, and to have and exercise all powers of any nature whatsoever permitted or conferred by law upon corporations in general, unless specifically prohibited by the Professional Services Corporation Act of the State of Florida, including and (sic) subsequent amendments thereto; (d) The foregoing clauses shall be construed both as objects and powers, and it is hereby expressly provided that the foregoing enumeration of special powers shall not be held to limit or restrict in any manner the powers of this corporation.

Defendant Greene, allegedly acting as agent for Professional Association, entered into a contract with plaintiff whereby Greene was to obtain for, and sell, transfer, and deliver to, plaintiff three thousand shares of the common stock of Kentucky Fried Chicken, Inc., for $24,000. When he received the money, Greene wrote the following letter to plaintiff:

LAW OFFICES GREENE, HOGG & ALLEN PROFESSIONAL
        ASSOCIATION
SUITE 602 - 607
THE MUTUAL OF OMAHA BUILDING
1201 BRICKELL AVENUE
MIAMI, FLORIDA 33131

May 3, 1971

Mr. Sam Zimmerman
c/o Holly Farms Poultry Industries, Inc.
Monroe, North Carolina

Dear Sam:

This is to acknowledge receipt of your check in the amount of $24,000.00 and
also receipt of Mr. Garmon's check in the amount of $3600.00. This will enti-
tle you to 2,000 shares of Kentucky Fried Chicken, and Mr. Garmon will be entitled to 300 shares. It now appears that the merger between Kentucky Fried
Chicken and Heublein is official, and you will receive .53 of Heublein's stock for
each share of Kentucky Fried Chicken stock. It will take approximately 90 to 120
days to get the Heublein stock after the merger is formally approved by the SEC.
If you have any questions concerning this matter, please let me know.

Sincerely,
s/ GLENN
Glenn L. Greene, Jr.

GLG: rw

Although plaintiff demanded delivery of the stock, he never received it, and he
demanded delivery of stock or payment of fair market value of the stock, as of the date of
merger between Kentucky Fried Chicken and Heublein, which value was $22 per share. Plain-
tiff alleged in his second claim for relief that Greene, acting as agent of Professional Association, had received the sums here involved to be held in trust by defendants for the
purpose of purchasing Kentucky Fried Chicken stock. He further alleged that defendant Association breached this trust when, through its agent Greene, it disposed of the moneys
received and so held in trust in violation of the terms of the trust agreement made by
Greene. The complaint then stated substantially identical allegations against defendant
Greene individually. In addition, the complaint contained additional claims for relief based
upon a substantially identical transaction between defendants and one Garmon and alleged
that plaintiff had purchased from Garmon all of his right, title, and interest in any chose in
action resulting from the breach of contract or the breach of trust.

Defendant Professional Association moved for summary judgment. After considering
the affidavits and exhibits submitted on this motion, Judge Rousseau rendered summary judgment in favor of defendant Professional Association. Plaintiff appealed. On appeal to the Court
of Appeals, the judgment of the Superior Court was affirmed, Judge Vaughn dissenting.

BRANCH, Justice. * * * The question of liability of a professional association of attorneys for investment of client's funds by an officer or director of the professional association
is one of first impression in this jurisdiction. In fact, we find very little authority even as
to a partner's liability in a general partnership engaged in the practice of law. Since plain-

tiff's claims are based on the premise that defendant Greene was acting as an agent for the professional association at the times complained of, we first look to the general law of agency, particularly the law of apparent authority. * * *

All parties appear to agree that the crucial question on this appeal is whether the receipt of funds for investment purposes falls within the scope of the practice of law, and therefore within the scope of the apparent authority of Greene.

We are guided to some degree by a very few cases which have considered the liability of a Partner when another member of the firm accepts funds for investment and then misappropriates the funds. We find two cases in this country which stand for the general proposition that the acceptance of money for investment in undesignated securities is not generally within the orderly scope of a partnership organized for the practice of law, and therefore another partner will not be charged with liability for misconduct of the person accepting the money for investment unless there be knowledge of, consent to, or ratification of the transaction by the other partners. [citations omitted]

In *Blackmon v. Hale*, 1 Cal. 3d 548, 83 Cal. Rptr. 194, 463 P.2d 418, a client entrusted funds to an attorney for the purpose of clearing a title on real estate and purchasing a note secured by a mortgage on the real estate. The attorney deposited the funds in a partnership trust account during the existence of the partnership and subsequently misappropriated the funds after the partnership was dissolved. The court held that the receipt of this money was within the ordinary course of legal business for which the other parters were accountable. In reaching its decision, the Supreme Court of California, in part, stated: "Every partner is an agent of the partnership for the purpose of its business, and the act of every partner . . . for apparently carrying on in the usual way the business of the partnership of which he is a member binds the partnership." [citation omitted] The apparent scope of the partnership business depends primarily on the conduct of the partnership and its partners and what they cause third persons to believe about the authority of the partners. Ostensible agency or acts within the scope of the partnership business are presumed "where the business done by the supposed agent, so far as open to the observation of third parties, is consistent with the existence of an agency, and where, as to the transaction in question, the third party was justified in believing that an agency existed." [citations omitted] The partnership will be relieved from liability for the wrongs of its partners acting individually when the third person has knowledge of the fact that he is dealing with the partner in his individual capacity. [citation omitted] *Cf. Smith v. Travelers Indemnity Co.*, 343 F. Supp. 605 (M.D.N.C.), and *Douglas Reservoirs Water Users Ass'n v. Maurer & Garst*, 398 P.2d 74 (Wyo.), each of which declined to impose liability upon a partner because of misapplication of funds received, where the investment was isolated and clearly unrelated to the practice of law.

Because of the paucity of American case law on the question before us for decision, we briefly discuss pertinent English authority.

Willett v. Chambers, Cowp. pt. 2, 814, 98 Eng. Rep. 1377, considered the question of liability of partners for misappropriation of funds received for investment by another partner. There the Court allowed recovery from the other partners on the ground that it was a customary and usual practice for attorneys to receive and lend money so as to obtain profit from the fees and charges collected for drawing the legal instruments. * * *

In order to apply the above-stated principles of law to the facts of this case, it becomes necessary to summarize the evidence presented at the hearing on the motion for summary judgment by movant. In support of its motion for summary judgment, movant Professional Association, in summary, presented the following evidence:

(1.) The sworn statement of defendant Glenn L. Greene, Jr., who averred that all matters in suit were "purely personal matters between myself and plaintiff. Other than that, that is all I am going to say about that." He further stated that all correspondence with plaintiff was signed by him personally, not as an attorney, and there was no agreement concerning the matter in suit between plaintiff and Professional Association.

(2.) Affidavits of Jesse H. Hogg and W. Reynolds Allen to the effect that neither the Professional Association or either of the affiants had engaged in the practice of receiving or holding money or securities for investment or profit. Affiants each stated that the law practice of the Professional Association was limited to the practice of labor law.

(3.) The deposition of Amie Ferro, personal secretary to Greene, who stated that all of the practice of the Professional Association was labor-oriented and that she knew of nothing which indicated that any attorney in the Professional Association was aware that Greene was receiving money for investment. Neither was she aware of any file or transaction indicating that any member of the Professional Association had ever represented Sam Zimmerman, Frank Rhodes, or Pruitt Garmon. She knew that Greene was selling stock to other people, but she did not know that he was receiving funds for the purpose of buying stock. She further stated that Greene handled all the finances of the firm and that no one else saw any mail until it was called to his attention. In fact, no one in the firm ever went into the "Big Chief's" office.

(4.) The deposition of Robert Louis Norton, an associate in the Professional Association, who averred that he invested money through Greene in a Kentucky Fried Chicken transaction upon the express understanding that he should not tell other members of the Professional Association about it. He did recall having a conversation at a breakfast meeting concerning this stock with Frank Rhodes.

At this point, in our opinion, movant's evidence that Greene was not acting as the agent of the Professional Association within the scope of his authority at the times complained of carried the burden placed upon it by Rule 56(c) by showing the absence of one of the essential elements of plaintiff's claim.

Plaintiff, in order to carry the burden thereby imposed upon him to show that a material issue of fact did exist, offered the following evidence:

(1.) Affidavit of Bonnie Rhodes, in which she averred that she was the personnel director of Holly Farms and in that capacity had dealt with defendants. She stated that the letter which embodied the contract in suit was typed on the same letterhead and was signed in the same manner as letters received from Greene concerning legal matters. She further averred that Greene made all decisions involving legal matters for Holly Farms and that she had personally discussed the Kentucky Fried Chicken transactions with other employees of the Professional Association who were aware of the transaction.

(2.) Affidavit of plaintiff Sam Zimmerman, who stated that he was operations manager of Holly Farms and that to his knowledge Greene, the senior member of the Professional Association, completely controlled it, made all decisions concerning fees, and handled the bulk of Holly Farms' legal work; that in the past Greene had advised him concerning personal legal matters, particularly as to investments in a beer franchise, domestic difficulties, and the making of a will; that he had previously delivered to Greene $12,000 to invest, which had been returned together with a substantial profit; that he requested Greene to handle the Kentucky Fried Chicken transaction through the firm and Greene told him it would be so handled; and that he had discussed the Kentucky Fried Chicken transaction with other members and employees of the Professional Association in the presence of Greene. He further stated that one of the other directors and stockholders in the Professional Association, Hogg, had also volunteered to furnish legal services to him in a domestic matter. Affidant had actually discussed the transaction in suit with Hogg at a breakfast meeting.

(3.) The deposition of Frank E. Rhodes, Director of the North Carolina Division of Holly Farms, who stated that he had known Greene for several years and that prior to the transaction in suit, Greene had invested $25,000 for him for which Greene received a commission, and that Greene was supposed to get a commission for the transaction involving Kentucky Fried Chicken stock. In the latter transaction Greene had agreed to obtain 3,000 shares of Kentucky Fried Chicken for the sum of $36,000. He forwarded a check to Greene in the amount of $36,000, and he had been reimbursed by two checks in the amount of $750 each. He further stated that he had talked with Norton, an associate in the Professional Association, about the Kentucky Fried Chicken transaction, but he could not say whether it was before or after he entered into the agreement with Greene. By an affidavit Rhodes also stated that before he delivered the money for investment, Greene told him that he could get the Kentucky Fried Chicken stock at a reduced price because a close friend who was having domestic difficulties wanted to sell to prevent his wife from getting additional stock.

The checks for the purchase of stock were made to Greene personally.

It is reasonable to infer from this evidence that the investment services rendered by Greene to the employees of Holly Farms might have been for the purpose of obtaining the good will of the corporation to insure the continuance of a profitable association between the corporate client and the Professional Association. This inference would suggest a striking analogy to the practice of receiving funds for investment in order to generate fees for drawing legal instruments, a practice which has been recognized by both our courts and the English courts as being within the scope of the usual practice of law.

The evidence in this case, when construed most indulgently in plaintiff's favor, as Rule 56 requires, tends to show that the powers granted to the Professional Association by its charter were very broad powers, the exercise of which was principally in the hands of Greene; that defendant Greene, while he was on business trips to attend to the legal business of Holly Farms, accepted funds for investment purposes from employees of the corporate client; that these corporate employees were assured that such moneys would be handled through the Professional Association; that such activities by Greene, the president and principal stockholder of the Professional Association, had occurred over a period of several years; and that other employees of the Professional Association had knowledge of such dealings.

Under these particular circumstances, we are of the opinion that plaintiff's evidence was sufficient to justify a reasonable and prudent belief by plaintiff Sam Zimmerman that the Professional Association had conferred authority upon Greene to receive the funds from him for investment while acting as its agent. Thus plaintiff's evidence raised a genuine material issue for trial as to whether Greene acted within the scope of his authority and as agent for the Professional Association at the times complained of. * * *

The decision of the Court of appeals is reversed, and this cause is remanded to that Court with direction that the cause be remanded to the Superior Court of Wilkes County for proceedings consistent with this opinion.

Heath v. Craighill, Rendleman, Ingle & Blythe, P.A.
97 N.C. App. 236, 388 S.E.2d 178 (1990)

COZORT, Judge.

* * * This lawsuit has its origins in the relationship between plaintiff M. Lee Heath, Jr., and Francis O. Clarkson, Jr., formerly a lawyer and member of Craighill, Rendleman, Clarkson, Ingle & Blythe, P.A. Clarkson had been a partner in the firm and became an officer, director, and employee when it incorporated as a professional association in July 1972. Beginning in 1977 Clarkson performed for Heath various legal services, including the preparation of a will, codicils, and a continuing power of attorney. Another member of the firm, Robert B. Blythe, handled real estate matters for Heath.

In September or October 1982, Clarkson telephoned to solicit Heath's investment "in some type of oil-related venture." When Heath returned the call, Clarkson told him that another investor had been found. In the winter and spring of 1983 Clarkson proposed two other investments to Heath. The first offer involved a client in need of operating funds who would pay Heath "five percent per month for thirty to ninety days" until a pending insurance settlement was approved. The second offer also involved a short-term loan, this time until funds were disbursed from an estate in probate. Heath declined both offers because he did not have funds available.

In August 1983 Clarkson, promising a "two-to-one return," persuaded Heath to invest in an "Arab oil deal" with a "group of American investors" represented by Richard Seaman of Florida. Heath testified that when he asked about the risk, Clarkson replied: "I will minimize the risk by giving you my own promissory note." On 16 August 1983, in return for $25,000 Clarkson gave Heath a note for $50,000 payable on 30 September 1983. When the note came due, Clarkson promised an additional $12,500 in return for a two-week delay. Heath agreed to the new date and collected $62,500, representing a return on his money of one hundred and fifty percent in sixty days. In the meantime in early October, by letter dated 30 September 1983, effective the same day, Clarkson resigned from his firm. The firm allowed him to remain in its offices for about two months until he negotiated a lease on an office condominium.

Heath's final investments with Clarkson were made in November 1983. Again Clarkson proposed investment in foreign oil exploration which would yield investors a one hundred percent return. On 4 November 1983, Heath gave Clarkson $50,000 and took a note for $100,000 payable 19 December 1983. * * *

Soon afterward Clarkson solicited a final $25,000 from Heath, who declined the invitation until promised a "three-to-one return on this last phase . . . ." On 19 November 1983 Heath exchanged $25,000 for Clarkson's note in the amount of $75,000 payable 19 December 1983 . . . .

Shortly after the notes came due, Clarkson wrote personal checks to pay them. His checks were dishonored. In February 1984, Clarkson paid Heath $50,000. Subsequently that payment was identified as a preference by Clarkson's trustee in bankruptcy, and $37,500 was reclaimed in the bankruptcy proceedings.

Plaintiff Heath initiated this action on 15 April 1986 with a complaint alleging that Clarkson converted plaintiff's funds and that defendants are liable for the conversion. Plaintiff made four claims, each of which set out a distinct theory for the recovery of damages: agency, breach of fiduciary duty, negligence, and violation of N.C. GEN. STAT. Chap. 78A (North Carolina Securities Act). * * *

Plaintiff contends that the trial court erred in granting defendants' motion for JNOV on the first claim and in granting defendants' motion for a directed verdict on the second, third, and fourth claims. We disagree. * * *

A professional corporation like the firm in the case below is liable on the same basis and to the same extent as a partnership. *Zimmerman v. Hogg & Allen*, 22 N.C. App. 544, 546, 207 S.E.2d 267, 269, *rev'd on other grounds*, 286 N.C. 24, 209 S.E.2d 795 (1974). A partnership is liable for loss or injury caused "by any wrongful act or omission of any partner acting in the ordinary course of business of the partnership or with the authority of his copartners . . . to the same extent as the partner so acting or omitting to act." N.C. GEN. STAT. § 59-43 (1989). Thus, the question presented upon the trial court's grant of JNOV turns on whether, as a matter of law, there was insufficient evidence to justify a verdict that Clarkson's dealings with Heath were within the scope of authority or apparent authority conferred on Clarkson by his firm. * * *

Plaintiff submits that apparent authority to solicit money may be attributed to Clarkson from a variety of transactions and circumstances. Plaintiff alleges principally that Clarkson's letter of 4 November 1983 was written on firm stationery, and he asserts that "[o]n one occasion, James Craighill, a partner [sic] in the firm, was present with two staff members and overheard a discussion between Clarkson and Heath concerning the transactions."

Plaintiff fails to note that he was never billed by the firm for any aspect of his investments with Clarkson, including the letters of 4 November and 19 November 1988, which plaintiff characterizes as "legal opinions." The letter of 19 November was written on Clarkson's personal stationery. James Craighill testified that on or about 30 September 1983 the firm instructed its "secretaries [to] run a line through [Clarkson's] name to indicate that he was no longer with the firm . . . ." Clarkson's letter of 4 November 1983 on firm stationery was not typed by a secretary; it was written entirely in his hand.

Regarding the discussion between Clarkson and plaintiff, at which James Craighill, Janice Burton and Elizabeth Carr were present, plaintiff testified as follows:

I made what you would call, I guess, a jestful comment, in the presence of all these people, and I said, "I'd better be careful. Frank will have me signing over all my assets to him so he can invest it with his Arab clients," to which Mr. Clarkson responded, "Yes. They're having cash flow problems in Jidda,["] to which I responded, "Yes. Those poor Arabs are only making millions instead of billions." * * * Everybody heard it. Everybody laughed. Mr. Clarkson chuckled, and Mr. Craighill grinned, and the girls sort of grinned, too, knowing that basically my comment was a jestful comment.

Ms. Burton testified that secretaries "were allowed to do personal work for the attorneys whose legal work they did." She testified further that, to the extent she knew of Clarkson's meetings with Heath, she never discussed them with other lawyers in the firm. Neither plaintiff's testimony, nor that of Ms. Burton supports his claim that other lawyers at the firm knew or "should have known about Clarkson's soliciting and accepting the money."

Finally, plaintiff cites *Zimmerman v. Hogg & Allen* in support of his argument for reinstating the verdict below. * * *

In the case below, the charter of Craighill, Rendleman, Clarkson, Ingle & Blythe, P.A., limited it to rendering legal services. Clarkson was not the principal stockholder of the professional association, nor principally in charge of its operation. He gave no assurances that money invested with him would be handled through his law firm, and plaintiff presented no credible evidence that other shareholder-employees knew or had reason to know of Clarkson's transactions with Heath. Given these facts, plaintiff's reliance on *Zimmerman* is misplaced. * * *

We hold that the trial court ruled correctly on the defendants' motions for directed verdict and JNOV. * * *

Notes and Questions

1. **Scope of partnership's vicarious liability for co-partners' wrongful acts.** Can *Heath* be reconciled with *Zimmerman*? Did Heath reasonably believe that the lawyer's activities were connected with the firm? If so, should the firm be liable? For criticism of *Heath, see* DeMott, *Our Partners' Keepers? Agency Dimensions of Partnership Relationships,* 58 J. LAW & CONTEMP. PROB. 109, 118-19 (Spring 1995).

2. **Breach of trust vs. wrongful act.** *Zimmerman* involves the situation covered by UPA § 14 rather than that covered by § 13. Under the former section, the breach of trust itself, such as the failure to turn over the stock in *Zimmerman*, need not be within the scope of the business. This is not surprising, since it is the rare partnership in which breach of trust is part of the ordinary course of business. Rather, the breach must occur in connection with an ordinary course transaction.

3. **Planning and drafting implications.** Note how the partnership agreement's definition of the scope of the partnership's business was relevant in the principal cases. This suggests the need for care in drafting such provisions. DeMott, *supra*, criticized *Heath* partly on the ground that a private charter cannot limit the firm's liability to a

client. But the *Heath* court might simply have held that the charter was not a sword for the plaintiff (as it was in *Zimmerman*) rather than that it was a shield for the firm.

5.04 Management and Control Agreements

So far this Chapter has been concerned with the default management and control rights that are provided by the partnership statutes. This section shows that these rights may, and often should, be altered by contrary agreement. As discussed in section C, the most difficult problem is making these agreements effective against third parties.

A.   Allocating Management and Voting Rights

The partners may agree to concentrate management power in one or more managing partners. *See* paragraphs 6.1 and 8.2 of the Chameleon agreement. This is commonly done in professional and other large partnerships that are too big for all members to participate effectively in daily decision-making. *See, e.g., Day v. Avery,* 548 F.2d 1018 (D.C. Cir. 1976), *cert. denied,* 431 U.S. 908 (1977), which involved the power of a law firm's executive committee. In capital-intensive firms such as real estate partnerships passive owners might provide the capital and delegate management functions to experts. The partners may also agree to unequal voting rights. This is common in professional firms in which there is wide variation in the experience levels and other matters bearing on the value of the human capital contributions of the members.

Variations from the statutory default rules may, however, be strictly interpreted. In particular, courts may assume that partners, who are vicariously liable for the firm's debts, wanted some decision-making role and some reins on managers even if the agreement literally seems to provide otherwise. For example, in *Wilzig v. Sisselman,* 182 N.J. Super. 519, 535, 442 A.2d 1021, 1030 (1982), the court held that the four survivors of five managing partners of an 11-person partnership did not continue as managing partners in a firm that was reconstituted on the death of one managing partner and admission of five new partners. The court expressed concern about long-term concentration of control in one surviving manager, resulting in an imbalance in representation of various factions. The court added:

> [T]he right of a partner to be heard on fundamental and vital aspects of the partnership enterprise, matters that could substantially affect the investment and liability of a partner, should not be deemed surrendered unless the intention to do so is clearly expressed. Management rights are extremely important since partners are generally liable jointly for all obligations arising from the conduct of partnership business.

A court might also hold that merely designating one partner as the manager does not justify wholly excluding others from management unless the agreement explicitly provided for such exclusion.

Contractual alteration of partners' management rights raises practical as well as legal questions. As noted in § 5.01, while delegating management power may lower the firm's decision-making costs, it also creates a risk that the manager will act contrary to the interests of the other partners. Accordingly, the partners may agree to constraints on the manager's exercise of discretion while not hemming the manager in so much as to defeat the purpose of delegating managerial power.

This balancing act underlies the provisions of the partnership agreement that determine the matters on which the managers may act without partner approval. Partnership agreements typically provide that the manager has the power to act without partner vote except as to certain designated matters. How should these exceptional matters be defined? A general distinction between "day-to-day" and "extraordinary" matters creates much uncertainty and potential for litigation. The agreement might make narrow exceptions, such as for asset sales or admission of new partners. *See* paragraph 8.1 of the Chameleon agreement. However, this might leave a significant amount of business to the managers' discretion. One possibility would be to require the managers to prepare annually a business plan that is approved by the partners, and then to permit the managers to engage in acts that appropriately effectuate the business plan without further partner approval. However, it might not be clear what happens if the managers neglect to prepare a plan.

Provisions directly limiting the managers' freedom to act are not the only way to control the managers' exercise of discretion. The managers' incentive to act consistently with partner interests is affected by, among other things, the partners' power to remove managers, how much information partners are entitled to receive, managers' fiduciary duties and remedies for breach, how the managers are compensated and the partners' power dissolve the partnership or demand that the firm buy out their interests. These rights are discussed below in Chapters 8 and 9.

B.   Variations on Partners' Veto Power

A partner's right to veto extraordinary decisions and amendments also may be varied by the partnership agreement. *See* paragraph 8.1 of the Chameleon agreement. One common type of provision reduces the uncertainty involved in distinguishing ordinary and extraordinary acts (*see* § 5.01) by identifying certain matters as requiring the approval of all or a supermajority of the partners. For example, the agreement may provide that the partners must consent to the sale or mortgaging of the partnership's real property.

Other types of provisions are aimed primarily at reducing the high costs of having to get unanimous partner consent. For many reasons, it may be difficult to get a significant number of people to agree on anything. Among other problems, a unanimity requirement invites partners to hold out in order to get something that they want before they will consent to something the others want. The costs of a unanimity requirement are illustrated by *Wilf v. Halpern*, 194 A.D.2d 508, 599 N.Y.S.2d 579 (1993), in which a partner had to be enjoined to execute his consent to a proposed refinancing of the partnership debt. The court held that a unanimity provision in the partnership agreement did not give the partner an absolute right to impede a cash buyout and possibly trigger foreclosure solely for personal gain.

As with respect to limitations on delegation of management power, a provision limiting a partner's power to veto an extraordinary act or act in contravention of the agreement may be subject to strict interpretation because it alters an important partner right under the UPA. For example, in *McCallum v. Asbury,* 238 Ore. 257, 393 P.2d 774 (1964), partners in a medical partnership agreed that "all decisions pertaining to the partnership . . . including amendment of this contract, shall be decided by a majority vote of the partners." Over plaintiff's objection, the majority created an executive committee. The court upheld the amendment because the committee's power was sufficiently limited, including by an override power in the partners, that it was within the scope of the original agreement. However, the court said:

> Fundamental changes in a partnership agreement may not be made without the consent of all the parties. This is true even though the agreement may provide that it can be amended by majority vote. The power to amend is limited by the rule that, unless unanimous, no amendment may be in contravention of the agreement.

238 Ore. at 260-61, 393 P.2d at 775-76. The court's statement that partners necessarily have a veto power over all "fundamental changes" whatever the agreement says appears inconsistent with the lead-in to UPA Section 18 and with case law enforcing non-unanimity provisions. For example, *Day v. Avery,* 548 F.2d 1018 (D.C. Cir. 1976), *cert. denied,* 431 U.S. 908 (1977), held that a partnership merger could be approved by majority vote pursuant to the partnership agreement despite its significant effect on the plaintiff's status. Also, *Vinson v. Marton & Assocs.,* 159 Ariz. 1, 764 P.2d 736 (Ariz. App. 1988), held that an agreement permitting all business to be conducted by majority vote authorized the majority to sell the partnership's sole asset. On the other hand, a court might strike down a majority-approved action even if it were arguably within a general majority-rule provision, if it is not clear whether the provision applies and the act significantly damages the objecting partner or indicates at least a borderline fiduciary breach by the majority.

The parties may choose to deal with the deadlock problem of unanimity provisions illustrated by *Wilf, supra,* by means of a provision authorizing a buyout of an objecting partner. Some logistical problems involved in such an agreement are illustrated by *Larken Minnesota, Inc. v. Wray,* 881 F. Supp. 1413 (D. Minn. 1995). In that case, a limited partnership agreement provided that, in event of a deadlock in connection with a major decision, each side could submit a price for which it would be willing to sell its interest to the other or buy the other's interest. The higher bidder had to buy the other's interest for price equal to the average of both sides' bids. A limited partner submitted a high bid but then was unable or unwilling to raise the money to close the sale. The court let the other party buy the property at its bid price, which the court determined had become the "average price" under the agreement. The court reasoned that this was the best way to effectuate the parties' intent to have an orderly divorce in the event of deadlock, since otherwise a party could thwart the process by submitting a high bid it had no intention of performing. The court noted that the agreement did not require that the final buyout price approximate fair market value.

C.   Varying Partners' Authority to Bind the Firm

Whatever the partners' rights to alter the default rules on management and control among themselves, additional complications are involved in enforcing these alterations vis a vis third parties. Partners often want to make sure that only certain people—*i.e.*, those with expertise or judgment—will be able to create partnership liabilities.

Consider the situation in *Patel* in § 5.02. Suppose that, when Rajeshkumar joined the partnership, he was concerned about his parents' encroaching feeble-mindedness and lack of business acumen, and so wanted to make sure that his parents could not transfer the motel without his consent. Suppose further that he was not willing to assume that a court would refuse to bind the partnership under UPA § 9(1) or that UPA § 10(3) would not apply to protect a third party. How could Rajeshkumar protect himself by a provision in the partnership agreement? Paragraph 8.1 of the Chameleon agreement probably is not enough protection under the UPA because third parties may not be deemed to have "knowledge" of this restriction on any authority the parents have under UPA § 9(1). For the same reason, paragraphs 6.1 and 8.2 of the Chameleon agreement would not necessarily protect Rajeshkumar if he were the manager of the partnership. Third parties who actually see the agreement containing the restriction may be bound, but Rajeshkumar cannot necessarily count on his parents to show the agreements to third parties.

Conversely, the third party may want to make sure that a transaction like the one in *Patel*, which is *not* within § 9(1), is binding. The third party may try to get the consent of all partners. But *Patel* illustrates one of the problems with this approach—who are the partners? Even a written agreement may not definitively identify the partners or describe what they have agreed to.

To deal with these situations, RUPA § 303 permits partnerships to file statements of partnership authority. Consider how such a statement might have confirmed the authority to transfer in the *Patel* situation—*i.e.*, what it would have to say, and what formalities the partnership would have to comply with. Conversely, how could such a statement ensure that the parents would not have authority to transfer without Rajeshkumar's consent? What if the transfer had involved a partnership automobile instead of a motel? What about office equipment?

It may be appropriate to include provisions in the partnership agreement that deal with a RUPA-type statement of partnership authority. For example, the agreement might require the managers to file a statement that restricts their authority as provided in the partnership agreement and that empowers only identified partners to transfer property and take other action. The agreement also might *require* the managers to send statements to the partners and may provide for amendment of the statement periodically and on the occurrence of such events as admission and dissociation of partners.

Problem

Five musicians have decided to form a rock band and to hire a manager who will handle the business end. The manager and the performers recognize that the performers are best left to their music, and may not be able to make cogent business decisions. For the same reason, they want to make sure that individual band members cannot bind the band to business decisions. At the same time, the performers want to have some artistic control over where and how they play. Draft the management and voting provisions of a partnership agreement that would accomplish these objectives. For inspiration, see the Alan Parker movie and Roddy Doyle book "The Commitments." For a theoretical discussion, *see* Cameron & Collins, *Transaction Costs And Partnerships: The Case Of Rock Bands*, 32 J. ECONOMIC BEHAVIOR AND ORGANIZATION 169 (1997).

CHAPTER 6
PARTNERS' VICARIOUS LIABILITY

6.01 Partners' Liability for Partnership Debts

Under traditional default rules, if the *partnership* is liable for a debt (*see* Chapter 5), then the creditor may recover both from the partnership and from the individual partners. *See* UPA § 15; RUPA § 306. At least in very closely held owner-managed firms, the partners resemble principals in an agency relationship in the sense that they share profits and are in a good position to monitor the firm and protect against loss. As discussed in Chapter 10, the monitoring rationale may not hold for all firms, particularly large professional firms. Indeed, Chapters 11-13 show that the law now broadly permits owners of closely held unincorporated firms to limit their liability.

The rules for collecting from partners have traditionally been set forth in non-partnership procedural statutes. RUPA § 307 now includes such rules. In general, the creditor has to sue and serve the individual partners to collect from them and may have to do so to collect from the partnership. More importantly, as discussed in the following case, the creditor may have to "exhaust" its remedies by first trying to collect the debt out of the partnership assets before suing the individual partners.

Thompson v. Wayne Smith Construction Company, Inc.
640 N.E.2d 408 (Ind. App. 1994)

SULLIVAN, Presiding Judge.

In 1986, Wayne Smith Construction Company, Inc., (Wayne Smith), procured a judgment on a contract against the partnership of Wolman Duberstein and Thompson, (the Partnership). During the intervening time, Wayne Smith has tried to collect on the judgment in South Carolina, Ohio, and Indiana. The South Carolina Court of Appeals, the Supreme Court of Ohio, and now the Court of Appeals of Indiana all have been involved in this dispute. This well-traveled case raises two issues for our review, which we restate as: I. Whether the trial court, in granting summary judgment to Wayne Smith, erred by failing to apply the doctrines of full faith and credit and res judicata to the South Carolina judgment regarding the liability of the individual partners; and II. Whether the trial court erred by failing to apply the doctrines of full faith and credit and res judicata to the Ohio judgment regarding damages.

The genesis of this dispute arose in South Carolina when the Partnership hired Wayne Smith to build two homes on Hilton Head Island. After a dispute arose between the parties regarding payment, Wayne Smith sued the Partnership and the individual partners for breach of contract in the South Carolina Court of Common Pleas. The South Carolina trial court entered judgment against the Partnership and each partner individually. The court calculated the damages plus interest at $107,381.65. On appeal, the South Carolina Court of Appeals affirmed the judgment against the Partnership, but vacated the judgment against the individual partners. *Wayne Smith Constr. Co. v. Wolman, Duberstein, and Thompson* (1987) S.C. App., 294 S.C. 140, 363 S.E.2d 115 (*Wayne Smith I*). Wayne Smith did not appeal this decision, and the time for appeal has expired.

Two years later, Wayne Smith registered the South Carolina judgment in Ohio, where it believed Partnership assets existed. After recovering $2,582.31, the Partnership assets were exhausted. Wayne Smith then instituted a new action in Ohio against the Partnership and the partners individually for the balance of the judgment. The partners defended the suit, claiming that because the South Carolina appellate court vacated the judgment against the individual partners, the doctrines of full faith and credit and res judicata dictated that Ohio could not enter a judgment against them. Nevertheless, the Ohio trial court entered judgment for the balance against the partners individually. The Partnership and the individual partners eventually appealed to the Ohio Supreme Court.

While the Ohio judgment was on appeal to the Ohio Supreme Court, Wayne Smith filed suit against Kenneth E. Thompson (Thompson), a resident of Marion County. At all relevant times Thompson was a general partner of the Partnership. The Indiana trial court granted Wayne Smith's motion for summary judgment and entered judgment against Thompson for the full amount of the unpaid South Carolina judgment, $157,703.01. Almost six months after the Indiana trial court's decision, the Ohio Supreme Court handed down its decision, which affirmed the judgment against the individual partners, but limited each partner's total liability to a pro rata share. *Wayne Smith Constr. Co. v. Wolman, Duberstein & Thompson* (1992) 65 Ohio St.3d 383, 604 N.E.2d 157 (*Wayne Smith II*). As there were three partners in the Partnership, the Ohio court held that each partner was liable only for one-third of the South Carolina judgment. Thompson now appeals the Indiana judgment against him individually, and alternatively the judgment against him for the full amount of the debt.

Before addressing the merits of this case, we note our concurrence with Professors Bromberg and Ribstein who write, "The enforcement of partnership obligations is the least uniform—and most confusing—of all aspects of American partnership law." 2 Alan R. Bromberg & Larry E. Ribstein, BROMBERG AND RIBSTEIN ON PARTNERSHIP 5:53 (1994).

I. Partnership Assets

Thompson contends that because the South Carolina appellate court vacated the judgment against the individual partners, full faith and credit and res judicata prevent either Ohio or Indiana from reaching the partners' individual assets. We disagree.

The South Carolina court held that a partnership is its own entity, separate and distinct from the individual partners. *Wayne Smith I, supra* 363 S.E.2d at 117. This is consonant with the modern view of partnership law.[2]

Accordingly, the court held that a suit upon a contract with a partnership cannot give rise to a suit against the partners in their individual capacities on such contract.[3] The court went on to state that Wayne Smith would have to prove a contract with each individual partner in his individual capacity to recover against each one individually.

A. Individual Liability

At first blush, the posture of Thompson's argument is persuasive. He argues that South Carolina conclusively established the lack of individual liability on the part of the partners. However, this argument necessarily presupposes that the only way to reach a partner's individual assets is to show that the partner, in his individual capacity, entered into a separate contract with the creditor.

This supposition ignores that, under the law of South Carolina and of most other states which impose joint liability for partnership obligations, there are two ways to establish the individual liability of a partner. One way is to prove a separate contract. The second way is to prove that partnership assets have been exhausted.[5]

---

[2] Historically, a partnership could not be sued in its own name because it was considered an "inseparable collection of individuals." BROMBERG & RIBSTEIN, *supra* at 5:68, 5:89. South Carolina has adopted the more modern view that a partnership is a distinct entity with regard to the legal relationships and liabilities of the partners. [citation omitted] However, South Carolina still retains the requirement that a partnership may be sued only by naming all of the partners. [citation omitted]

[3] In reaching this result, the South Carolina court relied upon an earlier decision, *Broom v. Marshall* (1984) S.C. App., 284 S.C. 530, 328 S.E.2d 639. At least one commentator has criticized *Broom* as an "arbitrary distinction." BROMBERG & RIBSTEIN, *supra* at 5:67.

[5] Bromberg and Ribstein recognize a third method of establishing the partners' liability. BROMBERG & RIBSTEIN, *supra* at 5:55. A creditor may reach individual assets by showing that the partnership is insolvent at the time suit is brought on the partnership debt. *Id.* To rely upon such a method, Wayne Smith would have had to raise this issue at trial. Accordingly, any allegations of solvency or insolvency would be barred by res judicata. However, the Partnership was not insolvent at the time of suit, as evidenced by the fact that Wayne Smith collected at least $2,582.31 of partnership assets after the judgment. In any event, the basis for claiming individual liability does not rest upon a claim that the Partnership is insolvent. Rather, it rests upon grounds that the partnership assets have been exhausted, which is a separate allegation.

Under South Carolina law, a partnership creditor must try to satisfy his judgment from partnership property before reaching individual property; whereas an individual creditor may attach any property the partner owns at any time.[citation omitted][6]

This exhaustion rule is recognized in most jurisdictions in which partnership liability is joint. BROMBERG & RIBSTEIN, *supra* at 5:59. Once partnership assets have been exhausted, however, a partnership creditor becomes a creditor of the individual partner with the same rights and upon the same level as the partner's other individual creditors. * * * By vacating the judgment against the individual partners, the South Carolina appellate court merely established that, at the time judgment was entered, Wayne Smith was still a creditor of the partnership and not of each partner individually.

Some authorities characterize this deferred liability as a transition from joint liability to joint and several liability. * * *

To reach a contrary holding would be to conclude that South Carolina has abolished the general partnership form of business. It is basic hornbook law that the major difference between corporations, limited partnerships, and general partnerships is the liability of the officers. [citation omitted] People form limited partnerships or corporations mainly to avoid the full liability of a general partner and to protect their individual assets. We refuse to believe that South Carolina has tacitly done away with general partnerships, especially in light of the many South Carolina statutes regulating such partnerships. [citation omitted]

B. Execution

At oral argument, Thompson provided an alternative argument, which must also fail. Thompson points out that Wayne Smith first registered the South Carolina judgment against the partnership in Ohio and executed upon it. When the execution failed to yield sufficient assets, Wayne Smith filed a complaint against the individual partners. Thompson argues that because Wayne Smith already had executed upon the South Carolina judgment, the second action in Ohio was not an attempt to enforce the same judgment. Rather, it was an attempt to relitigate the individual partners' liability. If the second Ohio complaint alleged a contract between each individual partner, we would agree that this complaint was barred by res judicata. But that is not the case.

The second Ohio complaint was also based upon the South Carolina judgment against the partnership. The only difference between the first Ohio action and the second Ohio action was that the first sought execution against partnership assets, while the second sought exe-

---

[6]   This rule originated to protect individual creditors from partnership creditors. A partnership creditor has "two funds," the partnership property and individual property. An individual creditor has only one fund. [citation omitted] Accordingly, an individual creditor may force a partnership creditor to seek satisfaction from partnership assets first. [citation omitted] While these cases could be read as holding that the exhaustion rule only applies at the option of an individual creditor, we decline to do so. The law is properly concerned with economy and equity. Where there is enough property to satisfy both partnership and individual creditors, a partnership creditor should not be allowed to satisfy his debt out of individual property, leaving the individual creditor with no remedy. This rule is sound whether the individual creditor has the foresight to insist upon its application or not. Indeed many cases leave out the 'option' requirement. [citation omitted]

cution against the partners' individual assets. This progression, of course, is in line with the general rule that a partnership creditor must first exhaust partnership assets before pursuing individual assets. In fact, the Ohio courts treated the second Ohio action as an execution. The Ohio Supreme Court as well as Ohio appellate courts have applied Ohio Civil Rule 69, which pertains to "'[t]he procedure on execution, in proceedings supplementary to and in aid of a judgment, and in proceedings on and in aid of execution . . . .'" *Wayne Smith II, supra*, 604 N.E.2d at 164. The Ohio Supreme Court went on to outline the Ohio procedure "to be followed to subject the individual property of partners to the satisfaction of a judgment obtained against the partnership in the firm name." *Id.* Thompson's argument, though ingeniously wrapped, is merely an assertion that partners' individual property cannot be used to satisfy a partnership debt. We have rejected that argument.

We note that as the law of partnership progresses, the imposition of joint liability has fallen from favor. After *Wayne Smith I* was decided, South Carolina followed the national trend and made partners jointly and severally liable for all partnership obligations. See S.C. CODE ANN. § 33-41-370.

II. Share of Liability

Thompson argues that if he is personally liable for the judgment, he is only liable for a one-third share. Although this issue was never presented in the Ohio litigation or the subsequent appeal, the Ohio Supreme Court sua sponte determined that because Thompson is a joint debtor, he is liable only for a pro rata share of the judgment. *Wayne Smith II, supra*, 604 N.E.2d at 161. Thompson argues that this holding must be given full faith and credit. Again, we disagree.

A. The Law of Joint Liability

The Ohio Supreme Court cites no authority for its proposition that a joint debtor is liable only for a pro-rata share. We have found no such authority. Such limitation is not an incident of joint liability. Thompson cites no authority in support of Ohio's position, nor have we found any.

The authorities agree that each joint debtor is responsible for the entire amount of the debt. * * *

The difference between joint liability and joint and several liability is merely procedural and does not affect substantive law.[11] [citations omitted] The major difference between the two types of liability is that in joint liability all joint parties must be sued, whereas in

---

[11]   The Uniform Partnership Act (UPA) imposes joint and several liability upon the partners for breaches of trust, wrongful acts, and torts, but imposes only joint liability for debts, obligations, and contracts. This is a codification of the common law. BROMBERG & RIBSTEIN, *supra* at 5:55. The UPA gave no reason for preserving the common-law distinction, merely explaining that the distinction was only procedural. Official Comment, 6 UPA 175 (1969). This position has been criticized by some commentators who recognize substantive consequences flowing from the different types of liability. BROMBERG & RIBSTEIN, *supra* at 5:55. For example, in joint liability, a release from one joint party extinguishes the liability of all other joint parties. Several states, including South Carolina, have departed from the UPA and have imposed joint and several liability for all partnership obligations. *Id.* Although the UPA stated that its distinction would not affect the Act's uniformity, one version of the revised UPA would impose joint and several liability for all partnership obligations. UPA § 306 (1991 revised proposed draft).

joint and several liability, just one party may be sued.[12] BROMBERG & RIBSTEIN, *supra* at 5:55. However, under joint liability, once all of the joint debtors are named in the suit and judgment is entered against them, the creditor may force any one of the debtors to pay all of the judgment. This rule has long been recognized in South Carolina and in Indiana. * * *

Pursuant to the Full Faith and Credit Clause of the United States Constitution, a foreign judgment is conclusive as to the merits of the action. [citation omitted] The determination of the amount due on a debt is a judgment upon the merits. [citation omitted] The South Carolina court determined that Wayne Smith was due $107,381.65, and that the partners were jointly liable for this amount. It is beyond the power of this or any other foreign court to add to or subtract from that judgment. If South Carolina limited joint debtors to a pro rata share, we would be bound by such a holding and only could allow Wayne Smith to satisfy one-third of the judgment from Thompson's individual assets. However, the facts are otherwise. [citation omitted]

Although the Ohio Supreme Court has the power to determine the meaning of joint liability under Ohio law, it may not engraft this meaning onto a final judgment of a sister state. The Ohio decision is a definition of the legal term, "joint liability," which we are not bound to follow. Any requirements, procedures, or limitations which Ohio places upon creditors seeking execution in Ohio are not binding upon Indiana or any other state.[15] The Ohio decision, although bearing upon the amount due, is not a decision upon the merits of the South Carolina judgment, because only the South Carolina court had the authority to decide those merits.[16] * * *

Notes and Questions

1. **When is exhaustion required?** As in *Thompson,* most courts require exhaustion only in cases of "joint" liability, which is, generally speaking, liability based on contract. On the other hand, most courts hold that exhaustion is not required for "joint and several" liability, which UPA § 15 imposes for liability based on partner wrongdoing under §§ 13 and 14. *See* BROMBERG & RIBSTEIN ON PARTNERSHIP, § 5.08. This means, in effect, that creditors contract by default for an exhaustion requirement, although they may opt out by contracting for the liability of individual partners. Tort-type creditors,

---

[12]   This dovetails with South Carolina's requirement that a partnership may be sued only by naming all of the partners and may not be sued in it's own name. *See supra* note 2.

[15]   As is the case here, creditors must often pursue debtor assets in several states in order to satisfy a judgment. If the procedures of every state in which execution was sought attached to the judgment, a bizarre and unworkable situation would result. While the first state in which execution is attempted might require the creditor to whistle Dixie as a prerequisite to execution, the second state might require the creditor to stand on his head. Worse yet, a third state might require the creditor to have never whistled Dixie or stood on his head as a condition precedent to proceeding. Repetitive or perhaps contradictory procedural requirements would proliferate to no purpose.

[16]   If Wayne Smith were attempting to execute upon the Ohio judgment instead of the South Carolina judgment, our decision might be different.

who often have not had the opportunity to bargain for contractual protection, get direct liability by default.

2. **What is exhaustion?** In order to exhaust remedies, the creditors may need to execute against the partnership and have the sheriff or other officer make a return of execution showing that assets were not found. *See British Land (B of C), Inc. v. 43 West 61st Street Assocs.,* 177 A.D.2d 458, 576 N.Y.S.2d 554 (1991), *leave to appeal dismissed,* 79 N.Y.2d 1040, 584 N.Y.S.2d 449, 594 N.E.2d 943 (1992), in which plaintiff satisfied its obligation by delivering six executions to the Sheriff, followed by the partner's failure to turn over partnership assets to the Sheriff within the applicable 60-day period. On the other hand, in *U.S. Trust Co. of New York v. Bamco 18,* 183 A.D.2d 549, 585 N.Y.S.2d 186 (1992), the court held that the plaintiff need not pursue partnership assets as a prerequisite to reaching the partner's assets, but rather need only show that the partnership cannot or will not satisfy the judgment.

3. **The effect of partnership bankruptcy.** If the partnership enters bankruptcy, this ordinarily indicates that the partnership is unable to satisfy a creditor's judgment. RUPA § 307(d) accordingly exempts creditors of bankrupt partnerships from having to exhaust remedies against the partnership. But at this point the creditors have another problem—they may be unable to proceed even against solvent partners because the bankruptcy court handling the partnership's bankruptcy may stay all actions against partners under Bankruptcy Code § 362 or enjoin such actions under Bankruptcy Code § 105. *See In re Litchfield,* 135 Bankr. 797 (W.D.N.C. 1992). The trustee in bankruptcy of the bankrupt partnership can sue individual partners on behalf of all creditors to recover the deficiency of partnership liabilities over partnership assets. *See* Bankruptcy Code § 723. But then stronger creditors may be worse off than they would have been if they had been able to collect on their own.

4. **The future of exhaustion.** As noted in the principal case, RUPA § 306(a) makes all partner liability joint and several. Moreover, as discussed below in Chapter 13, partners in limited liability partnerships have no joint and several liability at all for co-partner misconduct. It is not clear what effect these developments, coupled with the bankruptcy law discussed in Note 3, will have on the exhaustion requirement. They may mean that partners, when they are liable at all, will be directly liable without exhaustion, or conversely that creditors always will have to exhaust partnership assets whenever they seek to recover from partners.

5. **Determining the applicable law after RUPA.** As illustrated by *Thompson,* a creditor who must collect from partners in different states may face daunting problems. RUPA attempts to remedy these problems of non-uniformity but, in some respects, may make them worse by adding a new substantive rule on exhaustion to the interstate mix. Thus, to use the colorful language in note 16 to the *Thompson* opinion, while a creditor needed to "whistle Dixie" in some states and "stand on his head" in others in order to collect a judgment from a partner, now creditors need to stand on their heads in RUPA states only if they refuse to whistle Dixie (*i.e.,* if the debtor partnership is not within one of the RUPA exceptions to the exhaustion requirement). RUPA further complicates

matters both by including its own choice-of-law provision in § 106. Thus, a creditor may not even be sure if the RUPA "Dixie-whistling" rule applies.

6.02 Creditors' Contracts with Partners

Creditors may try to avoid the partnership and bankruptcy law barriers to collecting partnership debts from individual partners by contracting for direct partner liability. This was certainly true for law firms' lessors in the wake of recent large judgments against and bankruptcies of large law firms. Conversely, partners may attempt to contract with creditors to limit their liability. The following cases illustrate how these conflicting objectives may collide.

Regional Federal Savings Bank v. Margolis
835 F. Supp. 356 (E.D. Mich. 1993)

GADOLA, District Judge.

Plaintiff Regional Federal Savings Bank ("Regional") claims that defendants Harold Margolis, Stephen Hoffman, Isadore Goldbaum, and Louis Goldfaden are personally liable on the entire amount still outstanding on a loan made to defendant Eckles Road Investments ("ERI") that is now in default. Before the court is the defendants' motion for summary judgment. For the reasons discussed below, the court will grant defendants' motion.

I. Background Facts

In April of 1975, the individual defendants filed an application for a loan with the American Savings Association in the amount of $420,000 for the purchase of some commercial property. The defendants filed another application on July 21, 1975. Both applications stated that the loan would be secured by "personal guarantees" executed by "all principals and their respective wives on the top Thirty Percent (30%) of the loan."

The loan application was processed by American Savings and on July 31, 1975, the commercial loan officers recommended approval of the application to the commercial loan committee subject to certain stated terms. The recommendation stated that "[t]he proposed borrowers shall be personally liable for the first Thirty Percent (30%) of the loan." On August 11, 1975, American Savings sent a five-page commitment letter to the four individual partners setting forth the terms it was offering. The twelfth condition of the letter reads as follows: 12. Repayment of the top Thirty Percent (30%) of the loan shall be jointly and severally, personally guaranteed by Isadore Goldbaum and his wife; Harold Margolis and his wife; Stephen M. J. Hoffman and his wife; Louis Goldfaden and his wife; and all other principals and their respective wives. On September 23, 1975, defendant ERI filed a certificate of co-partnership with the Wayne County Clerk. The partners of ERI were listed as defendants Goldbaum, Margolis, Hoffman, and Goldfaden.

On October 1, 1975, defendant Goldbaum signed a mortgage note on behalf of ERI. The note makes no mention of a limitation of the personal liability of the partners. On the same day, the four partners and their wives signed a guaranty of the mortgage note. The guaranty provides as follows:

In the event of default by Borrower [ERI] in the payment of any sums due to Lender [American Savings], . . . Guarantors agree to pay or perform the same on demand; provided, however, that anything herein contained to the contrary notwithstanding, Isadore Goldbaum and Adrienne Goldbaum, his wife, Harold Margolis and Rachel Margolis, his wife, Stephen M. J. Hoffman and Barbara Hoffman, his wife and Louis Goldfaden and Sarah Goldfaden, his wife shall be liable only to the extent of first One Hundred Twenty Six Thousand and No/100 Dollars ($126,000.00) becoming due hereunder.

Pursuant to the note, the parties also executed a security agreement and a mortgage. Subsequently, plaintiff Regional, through the Resolution Trust Company and a predecessor to Regional, Union Federal Bank, acquired ERI's note to American Savings. Plaintiff alleges that ERI defaulted on the loan on October 1, 1990, and now owes in excess of $290,000 plus accrued interest.

On September 10, 1992, plaintiff filed its complaint in this court. Plaintiff claims that based on the express terms of the note, the partners are personally liable for the outstanding balance of the debt in excess of any assets held by ERI. According to plaintiff, the only asset held by ERI is the property securing the mortgage note. Plaintiff alleges that the property is worthless because of environmental contamination.

All of the defendants filed counter-claims against Regional, alleging mutual mistake in the formation of the contract. Defendants ask the court for reformation of the contract as originally intended by the parties. Defendants Hoffman, Goldfaden, Margolis, and ERI also filed a cross claim against defendant Goldbaum alleging negligence and malpractice. These defendants claim that Goldbaum negligently negotiated the note for the loan, mistakenly leaving out the agreed limitation of liability clause.

Defendant Goldbaum filed a motion for summary judgment on Regional's claim on July 14, 1993. The other three individual defendants and ERI have since joined in Goldbaum's motion. Defendants claim that they are no longer personally liable for any of ERI's remaining liability on the mortgage note. The partners argue that they were only personally liable for the first thirty percent of the loan, or $126,000. Since at least that portion of the loan has already been paid off, defendants claim that Regional can only recover from the assets held by ERI. * * *

III. Analysis

The issue before the court is whether the defendants are personally liable on the remaining indebtedness of the mortgage note. The court must examine the language of the contract in order to determine the liability of the partners. If the court finds that the language of the contract is plain and unambiguous, then the court must implement the clear terms of the agreement. [citation omitted] The threshold question of whether the contract is unambiguous is a question of law for the court to determine. [citation omitted]

In this case, defendants allege that the language of the contract is unambiguous in limiting the personal liability of the partners to the first thirty percent of the loan. In the alternative, however, defendants argue that if the court finds that the terms of the contract are ambiguous, then the court must examine parol evidence to determine the true intent of the parties to the original contract. Plaintiff claims that because the mortgage note contains no limitation of liability, the individual members of the partnership are fully liable for all remaining indebtedness.

Even where the terms of a contract appear to be unambiguous, the court may examine extrinsic evidence that demonstrates a latent ambiguity. [citation omitted] On its face, the note appears to hold the partnership liable for the entire amount. Since each partner is liable jointly and severally for the debts of the partnership, it would appear that the defendants are liable for the entire note. Defendants claim, however, that once the court examines the parol evidence, it will find that, in fact, the note is ambiguous.

In order to prove their claim, defendants present several different extrinsic authorities. The extrinsic evidence consists of two types, documents relating to the negotiation of the loan and the affidavits of employees of American Savings. In terms of documents, defendants point to the two loan applications, the commercial loan committee recommendation, the letter of commitment by American Savings to ERI, and the loan guaranty executed contemporaneously with the note. In each case, the personal liability on the loan of the individual defendants was limited to the first thirty percent. Similarly, defendants present five uncontradicted affidavits from American Savings personnel who were involved in the negotiation, approval, and execution of the note. All of the affidavits support defendants' position that the parties to the original note intended that the members of the partnership would only be personally liable on the first thirty percent of the indebtedness. Even given the nature of partnership liability, the parties to the contract agree that the liability of the individual partners was intended to be so limited.

Defendants' position is further bolstered by the fact that each of the partners signed the guaranty. If plaintiff's interpretation of the contract were true, there would be no reason for the partners to sign the guaranty. As members of the partnership, the defendants would already be liable for the full amount of the note, even without the guaranty. Thus, the fact that the partners executed a guaranty indicates that thirty percent of the loan was the intended extent of their liability. Otherwise, the partners' execution of the guaranty would have been superfluous. The clear implication is that the guaranty reflected the true extent of the total personal liability on the note.

After examining all of the extrinsic evidence presented by defendants, the court finds that the terms of the contract are ambiguous. Furthermore, based on the parol evidence, the court finds that it was the clear intent of the parties to the loan that the members of the partnership would only be personally liable for the first thirty percent, or $126,000, of the note. As plaintiff agrees that at least the first thirty percent of the loan has already been paid, the individual defendants cannot be held liable for the remainder of the note. Plaintiff will have to recover the outstanding portion of the loan from the assets still held by defendant ERI, including the property securing the mortgage. Defendant ERI's motion for summary judgment will be granted to the extent that the personal assets of its partners cannot be reached by plaintiff to satisfy the partnership's remaining indebtedness. * * *

Commons West Office Condos, Ltd. v. Resolution Trust Corporation
5 F.3d 125 (5th Cir. 1993)

EMILIO M. GARZA, Circuit Judge:

Clinton Weilbacher was found liable by the district court for 100% of the outstanding indebtedness on a promissory note that he executed as general partner, on behalf of Commons West Office Condos, Ltd. (the "partnership"). Weilbacher appeals, claiming that he executed a guaranty agreement which limited his liability to 25% of the indebtedness. Finding no error, we affirm.

I

On behalf of the partnership, Weilbacher, a general partner, executed a promissory note (the "Note") in the amount of $936,000.00 to Bexar Savings Association ("Bexar Savings"). The Note was secured by a deed of trust, which granted to Bexar Savings a lien on property owned by the partnership. The partnership, by and through Weilbacher as its general partner, also entered into a loan agreement with Bexar Savings. Contemporaneously, Weilbacher, in his individual capacity, executed a guaranty agreement (the "Guaranty"), guarantying payment of 25% of the principal of the Note, as well as 100% of all interest, expenses, and costs associated with the guarantied indebtedness. The partnership and Weilbacher defaulted on the Note and Guaranty. Subsequently, Bexar Savings posted the property securing the note for foreclosure, and the trustee auctioned the property for $256,500.00, leaving a deficiency of $913,983.97. The partnership brought suit against Bexar Savings, seeking a declaration that it had not defaulted. Subsequently, Bexar Savings was placed into receivership. The Resolution Trust Corporation ("RTC"), as receiver for Bexar Savings, filed a counterclaim against the partnership and a third party action against Weilbacher, individually and as general partner of the partnership, seeking a deficiency judgment for the amounts due under the Note and Guaranty, as well as attorney's fees. * * *

II

Weilbacher argues that the district court erred in finding him liable for 100% of the deficiency balance under the Note because the Guaranty limited his liability to 25% of the deficiency balance. The district court found that, under state law, Weilbacher was "liable for 100% of the deficiency balance as general partner of the borrower, independent of his 25% liability as guarantor." We review the district court's interpretation of state law de novo. [citation omitted]

Weilbacher argues that the Guaranty is ambiguous, and that therefore, we should interpret the Guaranty in a manner most favorable to the guarantor. * * *

We find no ambiguity in the language of the Guaranty. The Guaranty states that "the personal liability of the Guarantor[ ] is hereby expressly limited to twenty-five percent (25%) of the principal balance of the 'Guaranteed Indebtedness'. . . ." The Guaranty is silent as to the Texas statute imposing joint and several liability on partners for partnership debts, see infra, and makes no mention, or reference to Weilbacher qua general partner. The Guaranty mentions Weilbacher only in his capacity as guarantor. In addition, the Note does not state that Weilbacher limited his liability as general partner under the Note. The Guaranty is reasonably susceptible to only the meaning that Weilbacher, in his capacity as guarantor, was limiting his liability to 25%. Consequently, we find no ambiguity in the language of the Guaranty. Therefore, Weilbacher's contention that he intended the limitation of liability clause in the Guaranty to limit his liability as general partner under the Note is irrelevant. [citation omitted]

* * * The Guaranty did not reduce or alter the separate and distinct liability of Weilbacher in his capacity as general partner. By executing the Guaranty in addition to the Note, Weilbacher incurred liability in two separate and distinct capacities—as general partner under the Note and as guarantor under the Guaranty. *See Nance v. Resolution Trust Corp.*, 803 S.W.2d 323 (Tex.App.—San Antonio 1990, writ denied) (where general partner of a partnership, on behalf of the partnership, executed a promissory note in favor of a bank, and signed a guaranty of payment in his individual capacity, which limited his liability under the guaranty to 50% of the principal of the promissory note, court stated: "Nance is liable for one hundred percent (100%) of the deficiency balance as General Partner of the Borrower, independent of his fifty percent (50%) liability as Guarantor.");[3] *FDIC v. Singh*, 977 F.2d 18 (1st Cir. 1992) ("[T]he non-recourse provision limits the liabilities incurred under the 1987 Note by the appellants acting as partners of Bandon Associates; it does not limit the separate and distinct liabilities incurred by the appellants in their capacities as guarantors."). The district court correctly found that Weilbacher was 100% liable for the entire deficiency as general partner of the partnership, independent of his 25% liability as guarantor.

III

For the foregoing reasons, we AFFIRM the district court's judgment.

Notes and Questions

Interpretation of liability limitations and guarantees. In analyzing these cases, it *is* important to keep in mind that there is a technical difference between a partner guaranty, which allows the creditor to pursue the partner directly without exhausting remedies against the partners, and a partner's statutory vicarious liability that may entail an exhaustion requirement. In light of that difference, does the language in the *Regional Federal* agreement support the contention that the agreement was intended to limit the partners' vicarious liability as well as their liability under the guaranty? How might the agreements in the principal cases have been drafted to more clearly accomplish the parties' objectives?

---

[3]   In *Nance*, the court found that Nance incurred two separate and distinct liabilities apparently because the guaranty specifically stated that the obligations of the guarantor (Nance, individually) were independent of the obligations of the borrower (the partnership). *See Nance*, 803 S.W.2d at 334. Although the guaranty in this case did not specifically state that Weilbacher's obligations as guarantor were independent of the partnership's as borrower, we find *Nance* indistinguishable, because a guaranty obligation is, by its very terms, an obligation independent of the obligation of the borrower under a note. * * *

6.03 Indemnification and Contribution

Sections 6.01 and 6.02 discuss the partners' liability to third parties. This section discusses how these liabilities are shared among the partners.

A.   Indemnification

UPA § 18(b) and RUPA § 401(c) provide that, in the absence of contrary agreement, partners may be indemnified by the partnership for payments made and liabilities incurred in the partnership business. Thus, while a single partner may have to pay the entire amount of a partnership debt to third parties, indemnification provides a way to adjust loss sharing among the partners.

The scope of indemnification under the UPA and RUPA is unclear. What does it mean for the payments and liabilities to be made or incurred in "the ordinary and proper conduct" (UPA) or "ordinary course" (RUPA) of the partnership business? The partner's act must be at least apparently authorized or within the scope of the partnership business to trigger a *partnership* liability under the rules discussed in Chapter 5. However, the *partner's* right to indemnification may be either broader or narrower than the partnership's liability. Consider the following variations:

1. In order to secure a customer's goodwill, a partner pays a customer for damage done by an errant employee for which the partnership would not have been held liable because the act was outside the employee's scope of employment.
2. The payment or liability related to a contract that was within the partner's apparent authority but was outside the partner's actual authority. Does it matter whether the partner was *reasonably* mistaken about the scope of her authority?
3. The payment or liability related to the paying partner's act that triggered a partnership liability. Does it matter whether the act was negligent or intentionally wrong or fraudulent?

One way to resolve these questions is to treat partners' default indemnification rights as related to their fiduciary duties discussed in Chapter 8. In other words, a partner arguably should be able to recover for indemnification only if the partnership would not have been able to recover damages from the partner for breach of fiduciary duty for incurring the liability. The policy considerations relating to the default rules on indemnification would then be similar to those regarding the scope of the partners' fiduciary duties.

B.   Contribution

In an ongoing partnership, the partnership's indemnification of a partner is like any other partnership payment in the sense that it reduces the firm's profits. Thus, partners of a profitable firm incur detriments in proportion to their profit shares. On dissolution, the partnership's liability for indemnification, like any other liability, is also paid out of partnership assets. If there aren't enough business assets to pay this and other liabilities, partners must *contribute* to make up the resulting deficit under UPA § 40 and RUPA § 807 according to their loss shares. *See* Chapter 9. In short, indemnification is a *partnership* obligation, while individual partners pay contribution. The distinction was relevant in *Wallerstein v. Spirt*, 8 S.W.3d 774 (Tex. App. 1999), where the court interpreted an agreement requiring indemnification by the "Partnership (but not the Partners individually)" as not releasing the general partner from liability for the *partnership's* indemnification debt. Courts and partners sometimes ignore this fine distinction and, in effect, telescope indemnification and contribution into a one-step process by simply allowing one partner to recover directly from the other or others any payment she made to creditors in excess of what the others paid.

Other partnership rules impact indemnification and contribution. If the creditor has already exhausted remedies against the partnership, there might seem to be little reason for the paying partner to pursue an indemnification claim. However, the partner may be able to seek contribution from the individual partners (unless, as discussed in Chapter 13, the partnership is a limited liability partnership).

C.   Drafting the Partnership Agreement

The partners may want to clarify indemnification and contribution obligations in the partnership agreement. Note that the partners' agreement in this regard affects their responsibility for partnership liabilities, and therefore their ability to take partnership deductions and losses for tax purposes. The indemnification provision may cover not only liability to third parties, but also liability to the partnership for breach of fiduciary duty. The indemnification provision also may cover fees and other costs of defending actions. The policy considerations relating to the enforceability of such agreements are discussed in Note 4, p. 210.

CHAPTER 7
PARTNERS' PROPERTY RIGHTS

7.01 Description of Partners' Property Rights

Chapter 4 considered what property was owned by the partnership. This Chapter discusses the partners' rights in that property. Under UPA § 24, partners have three types of property rights—(1) in specific partnership property; (2) in the partnership as a whole; and (3) in management.

A. Partner's Interest in Specific Partnership Property

Partner's rights to partnership property are related to their financial and management rights in the firm discussed in Chapters 4 and 5 above. If a particular piece of property is devoted to firm use, partners should not be able to transcend their agreed management rights or take more than their agreed share by unilaterally dealing with the property as their own. UPA § 25 confirms that partners can use this property only on behalf of the firm and have no individual interest that they can sell or that is available to the partners' creditors or heirs. One of many implications of this general rule is that, when a partner becomes bankrupt, specific property of the partnership does not become part of the partner's bankruptcy "estate" (*see* Note 4, p. 159, below). Partners' rights in specific partnership property under the UPA are so tenuous that they are really a fiction devised to maintain the "aggregate" nature of partnership. See § 1.02(E). RUPA

§ 501 abolishes the fiction of partners' individual ownership of property. This is consistent with § 201, which defines the partnership as an "entity" separate from the partners.

B.   Partner's Interest in the Partnership

Although partners do not really own specific partnership property, they do own a financial interest in the partnership entity. The partner's interest in the partnership is defined in UPA § 26 as "his share of the profits and surplus" and along similar lines in RUPA § 502. This right is transferable to the partners' assignees, creditors and heirs. However, the transferee is not a partner, and accordingly does not have the financial, management or fiduciary rights of partners discussed in Chapters 4, 5 and 8. Rather, the assignee has only rights that derive from the assignor partner—that is, the right passively to receive whatever the partnership decides to distribute to partners. The assignee's only independent right is that under UPA § 32(2) and RUPA § 801(6) to have an "at will" partnership judicially dissolved. For further discussion of assignees' rights, *see* Note 3, p. 152.

C.   Partner's Interest in Management

As discussed in Chapter 5, a partner has a right to participate in managing the partnership entity. This is not much of a "property" right since it cannot be transferred without the consent of all of the partners. *See* UPA § 18(g) and § 27, RUPA § 401(i) and 503(a)(3). This follows from the fact that partners normally would want to be able to choose their co-managers, particularly in a relatively small partnership, and particularly since partners can create debts for which all partners can be held personally liable. So in "Treasure of the Sierra Madre" (*see* §§ 4.01 and 5.01), the gold-mining partners have a big decision to make when an interloper (Cody) finds them and wants to be admitted into the "firm."

7.02 Transfer of Partnership Interests

Perhaps the most important question concerning partner property rights is the extent to which these rights can be voluntarily transferred. As discussed in § 7.01, that depends on which of the three rights is being transferred—specific property, interest in the firm or management rights. The following case illustrates the importance of distinguishing these property rights for purposes of interpreting the partnership agreement.

Sunshine Cellular v. Vanguard Cellular Systems, Inc.
1993 WL 212675 (S.D.N.Y. 1993)

ROBERT L. CARTER, District Judge.

Plaintiff Sunshine Cellular ("Sunshine") moves for partial summary judgment on three counterclaims asserted by defendant Vanguard Cellular Systems, Inc. ("Vanguard"). Sunshine also moves pursuant to Rule 41(d), F.R.Civ.P., for costs it incurred defending a previously-dismissed action in which the same three claims were asserted against Sunshine by a wholly-owned Vanguard subsidiary, Northeast Pennsylvania Cellular Telephone Corporation ("NPCT").

The facts relevant to Sunshine's motion are as follows: On July 16, 1991, Sunshine general partner Arthur V. Belendiuk accepted an offer made by NPCT the previous day to purchase his fifteen percent "interest in the partnership" for $2.6 million subject to the other Sunshine partners' right of first refusal. Belendiuk and NPCT agreed that the closing date for the assignment of his interest would be no later than August 9, 1991. The agreement provided that Belendiuk could not assign his "rights or obligations under this Agreement without prior written consent" of NPCT. * * *

On August 13, 1991, NPCT commenced an action in the United States District Court for the District of Columbia against Sunshine, Belendiuk, Estess and Kerrigan partners.[†]
* * *

NPCT's second claim was for a declaratory judgment that NPCT must be made a 15 percent partner of Sunshine because having failed to exercise their right of first refusal in the Sunshine Partnership Agreement, Estess and Kerrigan had no remaining right to object to the transfer of Belendiuk's interest to NPCT. * * *

* * * On September 10, 1991, NPCT voluntarily dismissed its suit pursuant to Rule 41(a)(1)(i), F.R.Civ.P.

In the present antitrust action commenced by Sunshine against Vanguard on May 4, 1992, Sunshine alleges that NPCT's suit against it in the District of Columbia constituted "baseless and sham litigation." On November 19, 1992, Vanguard filed its Answer and Counterclaims. The first three counterclaims it asserts against Sunshine are identical to those asserted by NPCT in the District of Columbia suit.

Discussion

Vanguard's first three counterclaims are premised on its belief that Arthur V. Belendiuk had the authority to sell Vanguard subsidiary NPCT all his property rights in Sunshine, including the right to participate fully in the management of Sunshine, without obtaining the consent of the other Sunshine partners. Sunshine claims the only right Belendiuk was entitled to sell without the consent of the other Sunshine partners was his interest in receiving a 15 percent share of Sunshine's profits and surplus.

Sunshine is a Maryland general partnership, and Sunshine's Agreement of General Partnership ("Partnership Agreement") states that it should be construed under and in accordance with Maryland law. Therefore, this dispute is governed by Maryland law. *Woodling*

[†]   Editor's note: The latter two defendants are Belendiuk's co-partners in Sunshine.

v. Garrett Corp., 813 F.2d 543, 551 (2d Cir. 1987) (in diversity action, district court should look to New York choice-of-law rules which honor a contract's choice-of-law provision). * * *

Sunshine claims that under Maryland UPA § 9-401(7) (UPA § 18(g)) and § 9-504(a) (UPA § 27(1)) in order for Belendiuk to have had the right to sell his management or voting rights to NPCT such that NPCT would take his place as a partner of Sunshine, there must be an "express" provision in Sunshine's Partnership Agreement allowing the partners to make such conveyances. Sunshine moves for summary judgment on the ground that there is no such provision in its Partnership Agreement. Vanguard counters that the Sunshine partners did agree in their Partnership Agreement to allow conveyances like the one made by Belendiuk to NPCT, or that they agreed to do so through an "implied agreement" evidenced by a course of dealing among the partners.

The rules in § 9-401(7) and § 9-504(a) serve as "standard form" contract provisions controlling the rights and duties among the partners in the absence of an agreement among them to the contrary. *See* 2 Bromberg and Ribstein on Partnership, § 6.01(b) at 6:2 (1991). Under § 9-504(a) and § 9-401(7) unless the partners have an agreement to the contrary, a partner may convey his "interest in the partnership" without first consulting his fellow partners, but must obtain the unanimous vote of the partners in order to transfer management rights. [citation omitted]

Thus, the court must determine whether Sunshine's partners made an agreement to override the standard form rules in § 9-401(7) and § 9-504(a). On summary judgment, if such an agreement clearly and unambiguously does not exist, the court must read the rules in § 9-401(7) and § 9-504(a) into Sunshine's Partnership Agreement as express provisions. [citation omitted]

Although courts may at times imply aspects of the partnership relationship not embodied in a written partnership agreement,[6] Vanguard's argument that Sunshine's partners "impliedly agreed" to override the rules in § 9-401(7) and § 9-504(a) must be rejected outright. Since serious consequences flow from admitting a new partner,[8] or transferring management rights to the assignee of a partner's interest,[9] there must be a provision in the written partnership agreement in which the partners have agreed to override the standard

---

[6]   *See* 1 Bromberg, § 2.05(d) at 2:41 (discussing UPA §§ 6, 7); 2 Bromberg, § 6.01(c) at 6:3-6:4 (same).

[8]   The unanimous consent rule in § 9-401(7) guarantees a fundamental right of partnership law, the right to choose one's partners. This right is crucial in light of other aspects of partnership law such as the power of each partner to create partnership liabilities, the personal liability of partners for partnership debts, and the partners' equal participation in the management and conduct of partnership business. 2 Bromberg, § 6.03 at 6:49.

[9]   If management rights may be transferred to a non-partner without the unanimous consent of the other partners, the assignee in effect becomes a new partner in violation of the consent rule in § 9-401(7). *See Thomas v. Price*, 975 F.2d 231, 236-237 (5th Cir. 1992) (interpreting a state uniform partnership provision identical to Maryland UPA § 9-504 and UPA § 27); *Thomas v. American Nat'l Bank*, 704 S.W.2d 321, 323 (Tex. 1986) (same). Thus, the standard form rule in § 9-504(a) prevents the end-run around § 9-401(7) by allowing a partner to transfer only his interest in the partnership and not his management rights. [citation omitted]

form rules. *See* 2 BROMBERG, § 6.01 at 6:4-5, § 6.03 at 6:50; 59A AM.JUR.2D § 504 (1987). A provision purporting to allow partners to transfer their management rights to non-partners should be interpreted strictly. 2 BROMBERG, at 6:50; *see, e.g., Rapoport v. 55 Perry Co.*, 50 A.D.2d 54, 376 N.Y.S.2d 147, 149-150 (1975). Such a provision, however, need not contain an "express" agreement to eliminate the unanimous vote requirement or the limitations on assignees, but it must clearly authorize such action.

There is much support for Sunshine's contention that there is no provision of the Partnership Agreement in which the partners have agreed to override the standard form rules in § 9-401(7) and § 9-504(a). Like those rules, the Partnership Agreement on its face clearly distinguishes between the transfer of a partner's interest and the admission of new partners. Transfer of an interest is dealt with in ¶ 16 concerning the "transfer of ownership interests," in ¶ 17 regarding the timing of such transfers, and in ¶ 18 pertaining to the transferees or assignees of such interests. The admission of new partners is governed by a separate paragraph, ¶ 20. (*Id.*). Moreover, ¶ 20 is silent as to how many partners must agree, or the percentage of votes required, to allow a new partner to be admitted into the partnership. As discussed above, if the Partnership Agreement is clearly silent as to the degree of consent required for admission of a new partner, the "standard form" rule in § 9-401(7) of unanimous consent must be read into the Agreement as if parties expressly provided for it. [citation omitted]

Vanguard points to ¶ 16 of Sunshine's Partnership Agreement, which concerns "transfers of ownership interests," as the provision in which the partners agreed to override the standard form rules in § 9-401(7) and § 9-504(a). The only relevant restriction ¶ 16 places on a partner's transfer of his "ownership interest" is that the transferring partner must give the non-transferring partners a right of first refusal.[13] Vanguard claims that by "ownership interest," Sunshine's partners mean the "indivisible bundle of partnership rights that include voting rights, profit-sharing, and risk-sharing." Thus, under Vanguard's definition a partner could transfer his "entire bundle" of rights to a non-partner provided he offered his fellow partners a right of first refusal.

Vanguard offers its own definition of "ownership interest" because it claims the term is not defined in Sunshine's Partnership Agreement. If this were so, the court would be inclined to disagree with Vanguard's proposed definition, for it flatly contradicts the Maryland UPA definition of a partner's "interest in the partnership" in § 9-503. Moreover, under the Maryland UPA, the right to participate in the management of the partnership and partner's "interest in the partnership" are viewed not as an "indivisible bundle," but as distinct property rights. Of the two rights, under the Maryland UPA only a partner's "interest in the partnership" is regarded as a partner's personal property which he may freely transfer; management rights are transferable only in connection with admission of a new partner unless the partnership agreement provides otherwise. 1 BROMBERG, § 3.05(c)(3) at 3:59.

---

[13]   Paragraph 16(a) contains a few other restrictions on transfer which are not pertinent to this case. The paragraph provides as follows: TRANSFERS OF OWNERSHIP INTERESTS. (a) No partner may transfer its ownership interest in violation of any rule or regulation of the FCC or state regulatory commission or if to do so would be deemed by the Partnership to be a violation of this Agreement. . . . (b) No partner may transfer any part of its ownership interest in the Partnership without first offering such interest to the other partners, by providing the other Partners with a copy of a bona fide offer which the selling Partner desires to accept. The other Partners or any of them may thereupon elect within twenty days to purchase said ownership interest themselves by so notifying the selling partner. . . .

However, the partners may have defined the term "ownership interest" indirectly in ¶ 1 of the Partnership Agreement, which discusses formation of the partnership. Paragraph 1 states, "Each party shall initially own the percentage interest stated in Exhibit A, in terms of profits, losses and voting."[17] This sentence is the only other part of the Partnership Agreement which addresses ownership. If by "own," the partners agreed that voting rights were to be personal property just the same as profits and losses, then they may have intended for "ownership interest" to have a different meaning than "interest in the partnership" as defined in Maryland UPA § 503. If so, ¶ 16 may well authorize a Sunshine partner, who offers his fellow partners a right of first refusal, to transfer not only his right to profits and surplus but also his voting rights to a non-partner even if the other partners disapprove.

The serious consequences of Vanguard's interpretation warrant strict construction of ¶ 16 and the definition of "ownership interest." Nonetheless, as a result of the sentence in ¶ 1 of the Partnership Agreement, summary judgment in favor of Sunshine must be denied because there is some ambiguity in Sunshine's Partnership Agreement as to the rights partners may transfer to third parties without the consent of the other partners. * * *

Notes and Questions

1. **Drafting transfer restrictions.** This case illustrates the importance of drafting the partnership agreement in light of the partnership statute. How should the partners have drafted the agreement in this case to eliminate any reasonable doubt that only the partner's interest in the partnership was subject to the first option?

2. **Planning considerations: restricting transfer.** When might the partners want to prevent transfer of partners' financial rights? One example is in order to prevent an accidental termination of the partnership for tax purposes under Internal Revenue Code § 708 by sale or exchange of 50% of the capital and profits interests within twelve months. Termination can cause a constructive liquidation and recontribution of assets to a reconstituted partnership, which in turn can trigger important tax consequences, including recognition of gain or loss for tax purposes. Paragraph 9.1 of the Chameleon agreement is an example of a provision that guards against this result.

3. **Assignees' rights: in general.** As noted in § 7.01, an assignee of financial rights is technically not a partner, and accordingly lacks partners' financial, management, information and fiduciary rights. Although assignees would seem to be quite vulnerable to partners' self-benefiting acts to exclude them from partnership benefits, there is arguably no contractual relationship between the assignees and the non-assignor partners that would give rise to fiduciary duties to the assignee. *See Bauer v. The Bloomfield Company/Holden Joint Venture,* 849 P.2d 1365 (Alaska 1993), which held that an assignee could not question the partners' decision to pay a large commission to a co-partner that stopped income payments to assignee. The assignee relies, in effect, on her con-

---

[17]   The meaning of the term "percentage interest," although not expressly defined in the Partnership Agreement, is unambiguous. The term refers to each partner's percentage contribution to the capital of the partnership.

tract with the assignor partner, who may agree to exercise her own rights on behalf of the assignee. Even if the assignor does not explicitly agree to protect the assignee, a court might hold that such a duty is implicit in an assignment of economic rights, since the rights would be worthless without it. A deceased partner's estate or heir or a foreclosing creditor of a partner, while technically an assignee, is in a different position from other assignees because it cannot necessarily rely on a contract with the assignor. Courts might hold that the surviving or non-debtor partners have duties not to hurt or to inform estates or creditors. The partners could clarify these rights in the partnership agreement by, for example, giving assignees an explicit power to veto actions that would materially affect the assignee where there is no corresponding assignor partner with consent rights. Estates' rights are also discussed below in § 9.02(B), while partners' creditors' rights are discussed in the next section.

7.03. Rights of Partners' Creditors

It follows from the fact that partners can voluntarily transfer only their financial interest in profits or distributions that this is all that their creditors or heirs can reach. They can do so by applying for a "charging order" under UPA § 28 and RUPA § 504. Most courts have held that the charging order is the only way for a partner's individual creditor to reach the partner's interest—that is, it replaces garnishment and other remedies. RUPA § 504(e) makes this clear. The UPA and RUPA make a charging order available only to a "judgment creditor" of a partner (and a partner's assignee under RUPA), although courts have also granted orders to others, including spouses seeking alimony or child support. *See Baum v. Baum*, 51 Cal. 2d 610, 335 P.2d 481 (1959).

As indicated by the following case, it is not clear exactly what a creditor gets when it obtains this order or when it takes the further step of "foreclosing" on this order.

Hellman v. Anderson
233 Cal. App. 3d 840, 284 Cal. Rptr. 830 (1991)

SIMS, Associate Justice.

In this case, we hold that a judgment debtor's interest in a partnership (meaning the right to share in the profits and surplus) may be foreclosed upon and sold, even though other partners do not consent to the sale, provided the foreclosure does not unduly interfere with the partnership business.

Judgment debtor John B. Anderson (Anderson) appeals from the trial court's order authorizing the foreclosure and sale of Anderson's interest in a California general partnership known as Rancho Murieta Investors (RMI). The foreclosure and sale was requested to enforce a money judgment against Anderson in his individual capacity by judgment creditors Fred N. Hellman, Peter N. Hellman, Lesleigh A. Hellman, Judith S. Johnson, and D. James Fajack (hereafter collectively referred to as "Hellman"). Intervenors Eureka Federal Savings and Loan Association (Eureka) and Eric J. Tallstrom (Tallstrom) have also appealed the trial court's order. Eureka is Anderson's largest creditor. Tallstrom is Anderson's partner in RMI.

Appellants contend (1) the foreclosure sale is not authorized by law where the partnership is not the judgment debtor and (2) sale cannot be ordered where, as here, the "innocent" partner does not consent. Anderson additionally argues the trial court abused its discretion in ordering foreclosure in this case. We will conclude that such foreclosure is authorized by law and, while consent of nondebtor partners is not an inflexible requirement, the trial court should consider whether foreclosure of a charged partnership interest will unduly interfere with partnership business before the court exercises its equitable powers to order foreclosure. Because the parties in this case relied on authority requiring nondebtor partner consent, no evidentiary showing was made on the effect of foreclosure on partnership business. We therefore reverse the trial court's order directing foreclosure and remand for the trial court to make a finding whether foreclosure will unduly interfere with partnership business.

FACTUAL AND PROCEDURAL BACKGROUND

In 1985 and 1986, Hellman filed lawsuits against Anderson for accounting, breach of contract, breach of fiduciary duty, mandatory injunction, recission, and fraud. In 1987, Anderson and Hellman settled the suits. Anderson failed to make any of the payments required by the settlement agreements, and in October 1987, stipulated judgments totaling more than $440,000 were entered against Anderson and in favor of Hellman. In July 1988, after various unsuccessful attempts to enforce the judgments, Hellman obtained an "Order Charging Debtor John B. Anderson's Partnership Interest" in RMI pursuant to Corporations Code section 15028. Anderson owns 80 percent of RMI; Tallstrom owns the other 20 percent and is the managing partner of RMI. The charging order stated that Anderson's interest in RMI was charged with the unsatisfied judgment in the amount of $494,885 plus interest. Thus, all profits or other monies due Anderson by virtue of the charged partnership interest were thereafter to be conveyed to Hellman.

Despite the above orders, Hellman has not received any monies in satisfaction of the judgments. Anderson testified in an October 1988 debtor's examination that RMI had not generated profits and was not expected to do so in the near future.

In December 1988, Hellman filed a motion for an order authorizing and directing a foreclosure sale of Anderson's charged partnership interest in RMI, based on the unlikelihood that the charging order would result in satisfaction of the judgment within a reasonable time. On December 15, 1989, the trial court ordered that the interest of the judgment debtor in the profits and surplus of RMI would be sold at a public sale by the Sheriff of Yolo County. The trial court retained jurisdiction over all phases of the sale.

All appellants assign error to the trial court's order directing foreclosure and sale of the partnership interest.

DISCUSSION

I. California's Uniform Partnership Act (§ 15001 et seq.) Authorizes Foreclosure of a Partner's Charged Interest Without the Consent of the Other Partners.

Appellants contend foreclosure of Anderson's charged interest in RMI is contrary to law. Anderson argues foreclosure was improper because a partnership interest is statutorily exempt from execution. All appellants argue that the trial court cannot order foreclosure unless the nondebtor partners consent.

A. The applicable statutes authorize the foreclosure of a charged partnership interest.

In *Crocker Nat. Bank v. Perroton* (1989) 208 Cal. App. 3d 1, 255 Cal. Rptr. 794, the First District recently addressed the question whether a charged partnership interest was subject to foreclosure and sale. *Crocker*'s analysis begins with a summary of the background of the adoption of relevant provisions of the Uniform Partnership Act:

"A creditor with a judgment against a partner but not against the partnership ordinarily cannot execute directly on partnership assets or on the partner's interest in the partnership." [citation omitted] The reasons for the rule were discussed at some length in *Taylor v. S & M Lamp Co.* [(1961)] 190 Cal. App. 2d 700, 707-708 [12 Cal. Rptr. 323]:

"Prior to California's adoption of the Uniform Partnership Act (Corp.Code, § 15001 et seq.) a judgment creditor of a partner whose personal debt, as distinguished from partnership debt, gave rise to the judgment, could cause a sale at execution of partnership assets, including specific items of partnership property, to satisfy his judgment." [citation]

* * * Lord Justice Lindley gave the following reason for the English rule forbidding execution sale of a partner's interest in the partnership to satisfy his nonpartnership debt:

"When a creditor obtained a judgment against one partner and he wanted to obtain the benefit of that judgment against the share of that partner in the firm, the first thing was to issue a *fi. fa.* [*"fieri facias"*—term used to describe writ of execution commanding the sheriff to levy on goods and chattels], and the sheriff went down to the partnership place of business, seized everything, stopped the business, drove the solvent partners wild, and caused the execution creditor to bring an action in Chancery in order to get an injunction to take an account and pay over that which was due the execution debtor. A more clumsy method of proceeding could hardly have grown up." (28 Wash. L. Rev. 1; *see also* 9 Cal. L. Rev. 117.)

It was to prevent such "hold up" of the partnership business and the consequent injustice done the other partners resulting from execution against partnership property that the quoted code sections and their counterparts in the Uniform Partnership Act and the English Partnership Act of 1890 were adopted. As we view those code sections they are not intended to protect a debtor partner against claims of his judgment creditors where no legitimate interest of the partnership, or of the remaining or former partners is to be served.

Therefore, a judgment creditor must seek a charging order to reach the debtor partner's interest in the partnership. (*See* CORP. CODE, §§ 15028, 15522, 15673; CODE CIV. PROC., §§ 699.720, 708.310-708.320; *Advising California Partnership, supra*, § 6.88, pp. 428-429.) Through a charging order, the court may charge the debtor's interest in the partnership with payment of the unsatisfied judgment, plus interest. The court may

also appoint a receiver of subsequent profits or other money due to the
debtor partner. (Corp. Code, § 15028, subd. (1).)

(*Crocker, supra*, 208 Cal. App. 3d at pp. 5-6, 255 Cal. Rptr. 794, fns. omitted.)

Crocker concluded the trial court could order the "sale of a judgment debtor partner's
partnership interest as distinct from the property of the [ ] partnership, where the creditor
has shown that it was unable to obtain satisfaction of the debt under the charging order, and
where the remaining partner [ ] has consented to the sale." (*Id.* at p. 7, 255 Cal.Rptr. 794.)

Crocker's requirement of nondebtor partner consent will be discussed below. Before
reaching that question, we must re-examine another question resolved in *Crocker*: whether
foreclosure is authorized at all. Our re-examination is necessary because appellants tender
some statutory arguments not considered by *Crocker*. We therefore begin with the basics,
discuss the applicable statutes, and conclude *Crocker* correctly decided that court-ordered
foreclosure and sale of a charged partnership interest is statutorily authorized.

First, we clarify the nature of the property interest at issue in this case, i.e., Anderson's interest in the partnership, not in the partnership property.

"A partner's right in specific partnership property is not subject to enforcement
of a money judgment, except on a claim against the partnership . . . ." (§ 15025,
subd. (2)(c).)

However, a partner's right in specific partnership property is different from his interest in the partnership. "The property rights of a partner are (1) his rights in specific partnership property, (2) his interest in the partnership, and (3) his right to participate in the
management." (§ 15024.) "A partner's interest in the partnership is his share of the profits and surplus, and the same is personal property." (§ 15026.) * * *

Section 15028 [UPA § 28] authorizes a charging order on the debtor partner's partnership interest and further allows the trial court to "make all other orders . . . which the
circumstances of the case may require." The statute clearly implies judicial authority to order
foreclosure and sale of the charged interest because it further says the interest charged may
be redeemed "at any time before foreclosure, or in case of a sale being directed by the court"
may be purchased by nondebtor partners without causing a dissolution of the partnership.
(§ 15028, subd. (2)) * * * We cannot imagine why the statute would give advice about
redemption prior to foreclosure and sale unless foreclosure and sale were contemplated.

Foreclosure sales of charged partnership interests are also implicitly recognized in section 15032 [UPA § 32] which deals with partnership dissolutions and makes reference to
"the purchaser" of a partner's interest under section 15028. * * *

As we have mentioned, the statutory authority for the sale of a partnership interest in
satisfaction of a debt of an individual partner was recognized in *Crocker Nat. Bank v. Perroton, supra*, 208 Cal. App. 3d 1, 255 Cal. Rptr. 794. Courts from other jurisdictions have
agreed that the charging order provision of the Uniform Partnership Act authorizes sale of
a charged partnership interest. * * *

Eureka mentions Georgia law as precluding a forced sale; however, the cited law review
article merely indicates that Georgia's statute, by not providing for foreclosure, differs from
the Uniform Partnership Act. (Ribstein, *An Analysis of Georgia's New Partnership Law*
(1985) 36 Mercer L. Rev. 443, 490.) The Georgia statute says a charged interest "is not
liable to be seized and sold by the judgment creditor under execution." (Ga. Code Ann. §

14-8-28(b).) We are presented with no persuasive authority or argument that the Georgia statute compels a prohibition against foreclosure and sale otherwise authorized in California by section 15028.

Other commentators, though cited by *Eureka*, support Hellman's position that the Uniform Partnership Act's charging order provision is widely accepted as authorizing the sale of the charged partnership interest. (Gose, *The Charging Order Under the Uniform Partnership Act* (1953) 28 WASH. L. REV. 1, 6-7, 10-12, 16 [partnership interest may be sold if charging order ineffectual]; Lewis, *The Uniform Partnership Act* (1915) 24 YALE L.J. 617, 634 [charging order avoids undue interference with rights in partnership business and property].)

Anderson is concerned that the sale will detrimentally affect his other creditors, whose interests are subordinate to Hellman. However, the priority of creditors' interests is not a legitimate concern. Creditors with subordinate interests are always subject to the interests of prior creditors.

We conclude section 15028 authorized the trial court's order directing foreclosure and sale of the charged partnership interest. (*Crocker, supra*, 208 Cal. App. 3d at pp. 8-9, 255 Cal. Rptr. 794.)

B. The consent of nondebtor partners is not invariably required.

In *Crocker*, the nondebtor partner effectively consented to the foreclosure and sale of a limited partnership interest. *Crocker* concluded a trial court "may authorize sale of the debtor partner's partnership interest even in the absence of fraud, where three conditions are met: first, the creditor has previously obtained a charging order; second, the judgment nevertheless remains unsatisfied; and third, all partners other than the debtor have consented to the sale of the interest." (*Crocker, supra*, 208 Cal. App. 3d at p. 9, 255 Cal. Rptr. 794.)

* * * [W]e disagree with *Crocker*'s requirement that other partners must invariably consent to a foreclosure sale. * * *

First, the statutes do not say that nondebtor partner consent is required for foreclosure on a charging order. Yet section 15028, subdivision (2)(b) expressly requires the consent of nondebtor partners before partnership property may be used to redeem the charged interest. Plainly, if the Legislature wants to make partner consent a condition, it knows how to do so. Thus, the very code provision authorizing foreclosure expressly requires consent of nondebtor partners in connection with redemption but is silent on the question of nondebtor partner consent in connection with foreclosure. * * *

A second consideration is the policy underlying the Uniform Partnership Act of avoiding undue interference with partnership business. (*Crocker, supra*, 208 Cal. App. 3d at p. 9, 255 Cal. Rptr. 794.) However, we do not think that foreclosure of a partner's interest will always unduly interfere with the business of the partnership. This is because the statutory scheme itself limits the interest subject to foreclosure and sale. As we have mentioned, a partner's "interest in the partnership" is a personal property right separate and distinct from the partner's (1) rights in specific partnership property and (2) right to participate in management. (§§ 15024, 15026.) The "interest in the partnership" means only the partner's share of profits and surplus. (§ 15026.) Foreclosure entails no execution upon partnership assets, and the interest acquired by foreclosure does not include the right to participate in management. * * *

We conclude that since the interest acquired by the purchaser of a partnership interest is limited by operation of law to the partner's share of profits and surpluses, with no acquisition of interest in partnership property or management participation, the foreclosure and sale of the partnership interest will not always unduly interfere with the partnership business to the extent of requiring consent of the nondebtor partners. In some cases, foreclosure might cause a partner with essential managerial skills to abandon the partnership. In other cases, foreclosure would appear to have no appreciable effect on the conduct of partnership business. Thus, the effect of foreclosure on the partnership should be evaluated on a case-by-case basis by the trial court in connection with its equitable power to order a foreclosure.

Because we believe the effect of foreclosure on the partnership should be determined on a case-by-case basis, we respectfully disagree with *Crocker*'s inflexible requirement of partners' consent in order for the court to authorize a sale of a charged partnership interest.

Since we disagree with *Crocker*'s consent requirement, remand is required in order for the trial court to make a finding, upon such evidence as may be presented by the parties, on the question whether foreclosure in this case will unduly interfere with partnership business of the nondebtor partnership.

On remand, the burden of proving undue interference with partnership business will be upon defendant and appellant Anderson. * * * Here, because knowledge about (and evidence of) the effect of foreclosure upon the partnership is peculiarly known to defendant and appellant Anderson, in his capacity as a partner, the burden of proving undue interference as a consequence of foreclosure is properly placed upon him. * * *

Notes and Questions

1. **The rights of a charging creditor.** Under UPA § 28 and RUPA § 504, a charging creditor may request the court to order that payments, including any distributions of earnings or capital, that would otherwise go to the debtor partner should be made to the creditor instead, and to appoint a receiver for the charged interest. The debtor continues to be a partner in all other respects. The charging creditor has none of the management rights of partnership and is not owed fiduciary duties. Thus, the creditor must simply wait until the non-debtor partners decide to make distributions.

2. **Foreclosure of charged interest.** To get more rights and priority from the charging order, the charging creditor could, as discussed in *Hellman*, foreclose on the charged interest. By foreclosure, the charging creditor becomes an assignee of the debtor partner—that is, would own the partner's financial interest in the partnership, including amounts ultimately due the partner on dissolution. As an assignee, the charging creditor still has no management rights and still is owed no fiduciary duties (*see* Note 3, p. 152). However, the foreclosing creditor may be able to force some distributions by exercising an assignee's power to seek a judicial dissolution under UPA § 32(2) or RUPA § 801(6). In order to protect the non-debtor partners, some courts, such as the *Crocker* case discussed in *Hellman*, have been more restrictive in permitting foreclosure than *Hellman*. *See* Hynes, *The Charging Order: Conflicts Between Partners and Creditors,* 25 PAC. L.J. 1 (1993). Note that the non-debtor partners can deal with the assignee by

redeeming the charged interest before foreclosure or by dissolving the firm and buying the assets on liquidation.

3. **Planning and drafting considerations.** The above notes make clear that a partner's creditor has little access to partnership assets through a charging order. A creditor might avoid this problem by making the loan to the partnership. If the loan actually benefits a single partner, the creditor must be careful to get the consent of the other partners, since otherwise the loan may not be deemed to be an "apparently . . . usual" transaction which binds the partnership under UPA § 9(1) or RUPA § 301. Also, if the applicable statute prohibits foreclosure, the partnership agreement might give partners' creditors a foreclosure right. If the statute provides that the creditor *can* foreclose on the charged interest, the firm probably could not *restrict* that right by drafting around it in the partnership agreement unless third parties were somehow made parties to the partnership agreement. This suggests that a no-foreclosure rule may be the best default rule.

Note that a no-foreclosure rule may make partnerships useful in thwarting creditors. For example, a family partnership may be used as a kind of "spendthrift trust" for profligate kids by agreeing not to make any distributions on account of any foreclosed partnership interest. The creditor might try to avoid a debtor's conveyance of property to such a partnership as a fraudulent conveyance because of the debtor's intent to hinder or delay creditors.

4. **Bankruptcy.** A bankruptcy trustee who has charge of the property of a bankrupt partner does not control the partner's interest in specific *partnership* property, any more than do the creditors whom the trustee represents. *See, e.g., Matter of Minton Group, Inc.*, 46 B.R. 222 (S.D.N.Y. 1985). However, the partner's interest in the partnership is part of the debtor's bankruptcy estate. *See, e.g., Matter of Buckman*, 600 F.2d 160 (8th Cir. 1979). The trustee may or may not be able to sell the interest, depending on whether the partnership agreement restricts such sales and on whether these restrictions are enforceable in bankruptcy. Bankruptcy Code (11 U.S.C.) §§ 363 and 541 appear to give the trustee power over property of the debtor free of restrictions triggered by the bankruptcy. *See Connolly v. Nuthatch Hill Assocs. (In re Manning)*, 831 F.2d 205 (10th Cir. 1987) (agreement gave a partner only 75% of the value of his capital account constitutes a modification); *In re Grablowsky*, 180 B.R. 134 (E.D. Va. 1995) (first-refusal option).

7.04 Rights of Divorced Spouse

By analogy to assignees, creditors and heirs, the divorced spouse may have community property rights in or be entitled to equitable distribution on account of the partner's interest in the partnership. However, the spouse's award may be based on the full value, including goodwill, of the partnership interest, rather than merely distributions to the spouse by the partnership. *Stern v. Stern*, 66 N.J. 340, 331 A.2d 257, 74 A.L.R.3d 613 (1975). *See* Ribstein, *A Theoretical Analysis of Professional Partner-*

ship Goodwill, 70 Neb. L. Rev. 36 (1991). The award may include even amounts that are based to some extent on the partners' skills, including those of the partner spouse, rather than elements of value that inhere in the business and are separable from the partners. *See Dugan v. Dugan,* 92 N.J. 423, 457 A. 2d 1 (1983). Other courts have denied the spouse rights that are inseparable from the partner-spouse's ability to practice. *See Powell v. Powell,* 231 Kan. 2d 456, 648 P.2d 218 (1982). For two contrasting cases on this issue, *see Strauss v. Strauss,* 101 Md. App. 490, 647 A.2d 818 (Md. App. 1994) (rejecting expert testimony as to value of goodwill of husband's dental practice because it did not exclude the personal goodwill attributable to husband's name and reputation), and *Traczyk v. Traczyk,* 891 P.2d 1277 (Okla. 1995) (holding that the goodwill of a podiatry practice could be taken into account based on evidence based on the so-called "Goodwill Register" which was rejected in *Strauss* where the expert determined the proportion of the gross income that could be expected to remain with the new doctor based on evidence in the Register of the average percentage of patients who continue after a sale to a new doctor).

Like charging creditors, the spouse's right may be restricted to what the partner is entitled to receive under the partnership agreement. *See, e.g., McDiarmid v. McDiarmid,* 649 A.2d 810 (D.C. App. 1994) (husband's interest in law firm's goodwill should have been given no value as marital property in view of partnership agreement making goodwill nonsalable and absence of other factors making it valuable). *But see Burns v. Burns,* 84 N.Y.2d 369, 618 N.Y.S.2d 761 (1994), in which the court held that the partner's wife was not limited to the value of the husband's capital account to which he would be entitled on withdrawal because the husband continued to be a partner. But *should* a partner's spouse get more money on account of professional partnership goodwill than the partner himself or herself would be entitled to take out of the firm at the time of the divorce?

A spouse may have some trouble collecting an award against the partner, given that the partner's assets remain tied up in the partnership. A spouse who is the partner's judgment creditor might get a charging order against the partnership, foreclose under the standards discussed in § 7.03 above and then perhaps even cause a judicial dissolution of the firm.

Question

How might professional partners draft their partnership agreement to minimize their spouses' rights to obtain marital awards based on the value of the practice? Would partners be likely to include such provisions despite their potential benefits in limiting spousal awards?

CHAPTER 8
FIDUCIARY DUTIES AND REMEDIES

8.01 The Nature of Partners' Fiduciary Duties

Courts imply fiduciary duties where a "fiduciary"—a general term that includes trustees, agents, partners or corporate directors—is empowered to exercise discretion on behalf of a "beneficiary"—*e.g.*, a principal, co-partner or shareholder. *See* DeMott, *Beyond Metaphor: An Analysis of Fiduciary Obligation,* 1988 DUKE L.J. 879, 909-10: "Courts impose fiduciary constraints whenever one person's discretion ought to be controlled because of characteristics of that person's relationship with another." These duties are based on the logical assumption that one would not entrust her property to another without an assurance that the other will manage it in the owner's interest. Because it would be very costly if not impossible to specify in advance exactly what this obligation entails, courts apply a fiduciary duty on a case-by-case basis. Although fiduciary duties are present in many types of relationships, they pose particular problems in the law of partnerships and unincorporated firms because of the many variations in types of firms and because of the emphasis on customized contracting within each type of firm. The following case is the most famous expression of partners' fiduciary duties.

Meinhard v. Salmon
249 N.Y. 458, 164 N.E. 545 (1928)

CARDOZO, CH. J.

On April 10, 1902, Louisa M. Gerry leased to the defendant Walter J. Salmon the premises known as the Hotel Bristol at the northwest corner of Forty-Second Street and Fifth Avenue in the city of New York. The lease was for a term of twenty years, commencing May 1, 1902, and ending April 30, 1922. The lessee undertook to change the hotel building for use as shops and offices at a cost of $200,000. Alterations and additions were to be accretions to the land.

Salmon, while in course of treaty with the lessor as to the execution of the lease, was in course of treaty with Meinhard, the plaintiff, for the necessary funds. The result was a joint venture with terms embodied in a writing. Meinhard was to pay to Salmon half of the moneys requisite to reconstruct, alter, manage and operate the property. Salmon was to pay to Meinhard 40 per cent of the net profits for the first five years of the lease and 50 per cent for the years thereafter. If there were losses, each party was to bear them equally. Salmon, however, was to have sole power to "manage, lease, underlet and operate" the building. There were to be certain pre-emptive rights for each in the contingency of death.

The two were coadventurers, subject to fiduciary duties akin to those of partners. [citation omitted] As to this we are all agreed. The heavier weight of duty rested, however, upon Salmon. He was a coadventurer with Meinhard, but he was manager as well. During the early years of the enterprise, the building, reconstructed, was operated at a loss. If the relation had then ended, Meinhard as well as Salmon would have carried a heavy burden. Later the profits became large with the result that for each of the investors there came a rich return. For each, the venture had its phases of fair weather and of foul. The two were in it jointly, for better or for worse.

When the lease was near its end, Elbridge T. Gerry had become the owner of the reversion. He owned much other property in the neighborhood, one lot adjoining the Bristol Building on Fifth Avenue and four lots on Forty-Second Street. He had a plan to lease the entire tract for a long term to some one who would destroy the buildings then existing, and put up another in their place.

In the latter part of 1921, he submitted such a project to several capitalists and dealers. He was unable to carry it through with any of them. Then, in January, 1922, with less than four months of the lease to run, he approached the defendant Salmon. The result was a new lease to the Midpoint Realty Company, which is owned and controlled by Salmon, a lease covering the whole tract, and involving a huge outlay. The term is to be twenty years, but successive covenants for renewal will extend it to a maximum of eighty years at the will of either party. The existing buildings may remain unchanged for seven years. They are then to be torn down, and a new building to cost $3,000,000 is to be placed upon the site. The rental, which under the Bristol lease was only $55,000, is to be from $350,000 to $475,000 for the properties so combined.

Salmon personally guaranteed the performance by the lessee of the covenants of the new lease until such time as the new building had been completed and fully paid for. The lease between Gerry and the Midpoint Realty Company was signed and delivered on January 25, 1922. Salmon had not told Meinhard anything about it. Whatever his motive may have been, he had kept the negotiations to himself. Meinhard was not informed even of the bare existence of a project. The first that he knew of it was in February when the lease was an accomplished fact. He then made demand on the defendants that the lease be held in trust as an asset of the venture, making offer upon the trial to share the personal obligations incidental to the guaranty. The demand was followed by refusal, and later by this suit. A referee gave judgment for the plaintiff, limiting the plaintiff's interest in the lease, however, to 25 per cent. The limitation was on the theory that the plaintiff's equity was to be restricted to one-half of so much of the value of the lease as was contributed or represented by the occupation of the Bristol site. Upon cross-appeals to the Appellate Division, the judgment was modified so as to enlarge the equitable interest to one-half of the whole lease. With this enlargement of plaintiff's interest, there went, of course, a corresponding enlargement of his attendant obligations. The case is now here on an appeal by the defendants.

Joint adventurers, like copartners, owe to one another, while the enterprise continues, the duty of the finest loyalty. Many forms of conduct permissible in a workaday world for those acting at arm's length, are forbidden to those bound by fiduciary ties. A trustee is held to something stricter than the morals of the market place. Not honesty alone, but the punctilio of an honor the most sensitive, is then the standard of behavior. As to this there has developed a tradition that is unbending and inveterate. Uncompromising rigidity has been the attitude of courts of equity when petitioned to undermine the rule of undivided loyalty by the "disintegrating erosion" of particular exceptions. [citation omitted] Only thus has the level of conduct for fiduciaries been kept at a level higher than that trodden by the crowd. It will not consciously be lowered by any judgment of this court.

The owner of the reversion, Mr. Gerry, had vainly striven to find a tenant who would favor his ambitious scheme of demolition and construction. Baffled in the search, he turned to the defendant Salmon in possession of the Bristol, the keystone of the project. He figured to himself beyond a doubt that the man in possession would prove a likely customer. To the eye of an observer, Salmon held the lease as owner in his own right, for himself and no one else. In fact he held it as a fiduciary, for himself and another, sharers in a common venture. If this fact had been proclaimed, if the lease by its terms had run in favor of a partnership, Mr. Gerry, we may fairly assume, would have laid before the partners, and not merely before one of them, his plan of reconstruction. The pre-emptive privilege, or, better, the pre-emptive opportunity, that was thus an incident of the enterprise, Salmon appropriated to himself in secrecy and silence. He might have warned Meinhard that the plan had been submitted, and that either would be free to compete for the award. If he had done this, we do not need to say whether he would have been under a duty, if successful in the competition, to hold the lease so acquired for the benefit of a venture then about to end, and thus prolong by indirection its responsibilities and duties. The trouble about his conduct is that he excluded his coadventurer from any chance to compete, from any chance to enjoy the opportunity for benefit that had come to him alone by virtue of his agency. This chance, if nothing more, he was under a duty to concede. The price of its denial is an extension of the trust at the option and for the benefit of the one whom he excluded.

No answer is it to say that the chance would have been of little value even if seasonably offered. Such a calculus of probabilities is beyond the science of the chancery. Salmon, the real estate operator, might have been preferred to Meinhard, the woolen merchant. On the other hand, Meinhard might have offered better terms, or reinforced his offer by alliance with the wealth of others. Perhaps he might even have persuaded the lessor to renew the Bristol lease alone, postponing for a time, in return for higher rentals, the improvement of adjoining lots. We know that even under the lease as made the time for the enlargement of the building was delayed for seven years. All these opportunities were cut away from him through another's intervention. He knew that Salmon was the manager. As the time drew near for the expiration of the lease, he would naturally assume from silence, if from nothing else, that the lessor was willing to extend it for a term of years, or at least to let it stand as a lease from year to year. Not impossibly the lessor would have done so, whatever his protestations of unwillingness, if Salmon had not given assent to a project more attractive. At all events, notice of termination, even if not necessary, might seem, not unreasonably, to be something to be looked for, if the business was over and another tenant was to enter. In the absence of such notice, the matter of an extension was one that would naturally be attended to by the manager of the enterprise, and not neglected altogether. At least, there was nothing in the situation to give warning to any one that while the lease was still in being, there had come to the manager an offer of extension which he had locked within his breast to be utilized by himself alone. The very fact that Salmon was in control with exclusive powers of direction charged him the more obviously with the duty of disclosure, since only through disclosure could opportunity be equalized. If he might cut off renewal by a purchase for his own benefit when four months were to pass before the lease would have an end, he might do so with equal right while there remained as many years. [citation omitted] He might steal a march on his comrade under cover of the darkness, and then hold the captured ground. Loyalty and comradeship are not so easily abjured.

Little profit will come from a dissection of the precedents. None precisely similar is cited in the briefs of counsel. What is similar in many, or so it seems to us, is the animating principle. Authority is, of course, abundant that one partner may not appropriate to his own use a renewal of a lease, though its term is to begin at the expiration of the partnership. [citation omitted] The lease at hand with its many changes is not strictly a renewal. Even so, the standard of loyalty for those in trust relations is without the fixed divisions of a graduated scale. * * * To say that a partner is free without restriction to buy in the reversion of the property where the business is conducted is to say in effect that he may strip the good will of its chief element of value, since good will is largely dependent upon continuity of possession. *Matter of Brown's Will*, 242 N.Y. 1, 7, 150 N.E. 581, 44 A.L.R. 510. Equity refuses to confine within the bounds of classified transactions its precept of a loyalty that is undivided and unselfish. Certain at least it is that a "man obtaining his locus standi, and his opportunity for making such arrangements, by the position he occupies as a partner, is bound by his obligation to his copartners in such dealings not to separate his interest from theirs, but, if he acquires any benefit, to communicate it to them." *Cassels v. Stewart*, 6 App. Cas. 64, 73. * * *

We have no thought to hold that Salmon was guilty of a conscious purpose to defraud. Very likely he assumed in all good faith that with the approaching end of the venture he might ignore his coadventurer and take the extension for himself. He had given to the enterprise time and labor as well as money. He had made it a success. Meinhard, who had given money, but neither time nor labor, had already been richly paid. There might seem to be something grasping in his insistence upon more. Such recriminations are not unusual when coadventurers fall out. They are not without their force if conduct is to be judged by the common standards of competitors. That is not to say that they have pertinency here. Salmon had put himself in a position in which thought of self was to be renounced, however hard the abnegation. He was much more than a coadventurer. He was a managing coadventurer. [citation omitted] For him and for those like him the rule of undivided loyalty is relentless and supreme. [citation omitted] A different question would be here if there were lacking any nexus of relation between the business conducted by the manager and the opportunity brought to him as an incident of management. [citation omitted] For this problem, as for most, there are distinctions of degree. If Salmon had received from Gerry a proposition to lease a building at a location far removed, he might have held for himself the privilege thus acquired, or so we shall assume. Here the subject-matter of the new lease was an extension and enlargement of the subject-matter of the old one. A managing coadventurer appropriating the benefit of such a lease without warning to his partner might fairly expect to be reproached with conduct that was underhand, or lacking, to say the least, in reasonable candor, if the partner were to surprise him in the act of signing the new instrument. Conduct subject to that reproach does not receive from equity a healing benediction.

A question remains as to the form and extent of the equitable interest to be allotted to the plaintiff. The trust as declared has been held to attach to the lease which was in the name of the defendant corporation. We think it ought to attach at the option of the defendant Salmon to the shares of stock which were owned by him or were under his control. The difference may be important if the lessee shall wish to execute an assignment of the lease, as it ought to be free to do with the consent of the lessor. On the other hand, an equal division of the shares might lead to other hardships. It might take away from Salmon the power of control and management which under the plan of the joint venture he was to have from first to last. The number of shares to be allotted to the plaintiff should, therefore, be reduced to such an extent as may be necessary to preserve to the defendant Salmon the expected measure of dominion. To that end an extra share should be added to his half. * * *

ANDREWS, J. (dissenting).

A tenant's expectancy of the renewal of a lease is a thing, tenuous, yet often having a real value. It represents the probability that a landlord will prefer to relet his premises to one already in possession rather than to strangers. Less tangible than "good will" it is never included in the tenant's assets, yet equity will not permit one standing in a relation of trust and confidence toward the tenant unfairly to take the benefit to himself. At times the principle is rigidly enforced. Given the relation between the parties, a certain result follows. No question as to good faith, or injury, or as to other circumstances is material. * * *

At other times some inquiry is allowed as to the facts involved. Fair dealing and a scrupulous regard for honesty is required. But nothing more. It may be stated generally that a partner may not for his own benefit secretly take a renewal of a firm lease to himself. [citation omitted] Yet under very exceptional circumstances this may not be wholly true. [citation omitted] In the case of tenants in common there is still greater liberty. * * * In short, as we once said, "the elements of actual fraud—of the betrayal by secret action of confidence reposed, or assumed to be reposed, grows in importance as the relation between the parties falls from an express to an implied or a quasi trust, and on to those cases where good faith alone is involved." *Thayer v. Leggett*, 229 N.Y. 152, 128 N.E. 133.

Where the trustee, or the partner or the tenant in common, takes no new lease but buys the reversion in good faith a somewhat different question arises. Here is no direct appropriation of the expectancy of renewal. Here is no offshoot of the original lease. * * * The issue, then, is whether actual fraud, dishonesty, or unfairness is present in the transaction. If so, the purchaser may well be held as a trustee. [citation omitted]

With this view of the law I am of the opinion that the issue here is simple. Was the transaction, in view of all the circumstances surrounding it, unfair and inequitable? I reach this conclusion for two reasons. There was no general partnership, merely a joint venture for a limited object, to end at a fixed time. The new lease, covering additional property, containing many new and unusual terms and conditions, with a possible duration of 80 years, was more nearly the purchase of the reversion than the ordinary renewal with which the authorities are concerned. * * *

Under these circumstances the referee has found and the Appellate Division agrees with him, that Mr. Meinhard is entitled to an interest in the second lease, he having promptly elected to assume his share of the liabilities imposed thereby. This conclusion is based upon the proposition that under the original contract between the two men "the enterprise was a joint venture, the relation between the parties was fiduciary and governed by principles applicable to partnerships," therefore, as the new lease is a graft upon the old, Mr. Salmon might not acquire its benefits for himself alone.

Were this a general partnership between Mr. Salmon and Mr. Meinhard, I should have little doubt as to the correctness of this result, assuming the new lease to be an offshoot of the old. Such a situation involves questions of trust and confidence to a high degree; it involves questions of goodwill; many other considerations. As has been said, rarely if ever may one partner without the knowledge of the other acquire for himself the renewal of a lease held by the firm, even if the new lease is to begin after the firm is dissolved. Warning of such an intent, if he is managing partner, may not be sufficient to prevent the application of this rule.

We have here a different situation governed by less drastic principles. I assume that where parties engage in a joint enterprise each owes to the other the duty of the utmost good faith in all that relates to their coristol property. Very likely the matter had been earlier discussed between them. The $5,000 advance by Mr. Meinhard indicates that fact. But it has been held that the written contract defines their rights and duties. Having the lease, Mr. Salmon assigns no interest in it to Mr. Meinhard. He is to manage the property. It is for him to decide what alterations shall be made and to fix the rents. But for 20 years from May 1, 1902, Salmon is to make all advances from his own funds and Meinhard is to pay him personally on demand one-half of all expenses incurred and all losses sustained "during the full term of said lease," and during the same period Salmon is to pay him a part of the net profits. There was no joint capital provided.

It seems to me that the venture so inaugurated had in view a limited object and was to end at a limited time. There was no intent to expand it into a far greater undertaking lasting for many years. The design was to exploit a particular lease. Doubtless in it Mr. Meinhard had an equitable interest, but in it alone. This interest terminated when the joint adventure terminated. There was no intent that for the benefit of both any advantage should be taken of the chance of renewal—that the adventure should be continued beyond that date. Mr. Salmon has done all he promised to do in return for Mr. Meinhard's undertaking when he distributed profits up to May 1, 1922. Suppose this lease, nonassignable without the consent of the lessor, had contained a renewal option. Could Mr. Meinhard have exercised it? Could he have insisted that Mr. Salmon do so? Had Mr. Salmon done so could he insist that the agreement to share losses still existed, or could Mr. Meinhard have claimed that the joint adventure was still to continue for 20 or 80 years? I do not think so. The adventure by its express terms ended on May 1, 1922. The contract by its language and by its whole import excluded the idea that the tenant's expectancy was to subsist for the benefit of the plaintiff. On that date whatever there was left of value in the lease reverted to Mr. Salmon, as it would had the lease been for thirty years instead of twenty. Any equity which Mr. Meinhard possessed was in the particular lease itself, not in any possibility of renewal. There was nothing unfair in Mr. Salmon's conduct.

I might go further were it necessary. Under the circumstances here presented, had the lease run to both the parties, I doubt whether the taking by one of a renewal without the knowledge of the other would cause interference by a court of equity. An illustration may clarify my thought. A. and B. enter into a joint venture to resurface a highway between Albany and Schnectady. They rent a parcel of land for the storage of materials. A., unknown to B., agrees with the lessor to rent that parcel and one adjoining it after the venture is finished, for an iron foundry. Is the act unfair? Would any general statements, scattered here and there through opinions dealing with other circumstances, be thought applicable? In other words, the mere fact that the joint venturers rent property together does not call for the strict rule that applies to general partners. Many things may excuse what is there forbidden. Nor here does any possibility of renewal exist as part of the venture. The nature of the undertaking excludes such an idea.

So far I have treated the new lease as if it were a renewal of the old. As already indicated, I do not take that view. Such a renewal could not be obtained. Any expectancy that it might be had vanished. What Mr. Salmon obtained was not a graft springing from the Bristol lease, but something distinct and different—as distinct as if for a building across Fifth Avenue. I think also that in the absence of some fraudulent or unfair act the secret purchase of the reversion even by one partner is rightful. Substantially this is such a purchase. Because of the mere label of a transaction we do not place it on one side of the line or the other. Here is involved the possession of a large and most valuable unit of property for eighty years, the destruction of all existing structures and the erection of a new and expensive building covering the whole. No fraud, no deceit, no calculated secrecy is found. Simply that the arrangement was made without the knowledge of Mr. Meinhard. I think this not enough.
* * *

Notes and Questions

1. **Justice Cardozo's view: The absolute nature of fiduciary duties.** Justice Cardozo's statement that partners owe a duty of "[n]ot honesty alone, but the punctilio of an honor the most sensitive" is one of the most often-quoted statements in the law of business associations. It reflects the principle that a fiduciary should not be deterred by self-interest from the most faithful service of the beneficiary's interests. Cardozo's opinion

also reflects the view that strict duties inevitably attach to any trust-like relationship. As a result, Cardozo pays little attention to the fine distinctions between a lease *renewal* and the transaction involved in *Meinhard*, saying "[u]ncompromising rigidity has been the attitude of courts of equity when petitioned to undermine the rule of undivided loyalty by the 'disintegrating erosion' of particular exceptions . . . ." With respect to the absolute nature of the duty Justice Cardozo imposes, consider whether he would have decided the case differently if (a) the initial deal had been only for a year; (b) the subsequent deal involved a Gerry property on the other side of town; or (c) Salmon had disclosed Gerry's offer to Meinhard but then outbid him rather than accepting the offer on behalf of the joint venture? As to (b), note that the structure that resulted from Salmon's deal ended up as the imposing 59-story skyscraper known as 500 Fifth Avenue.

2. **The contextual nature of fiduciary duties.** Justice Andrews' dissent is more consistent with an alternative view that fiduciary duties depend on the precise nature of the relationship. For example, Judge Andrews would distinguish between a mere joint venture, like that between Meinhard and Salmon, which is limited to a particular project, and a "general partnership." More generally, as one writer says,

> Described instrumentally, the fiduciary obligation is a device that enables the law to respond to a range of situations in which, for a variety of reasons, one person's discretion ought to be controlled because of characteristics of that person's relationship with another.

DeMott, *Beyond Metaphor: An Analysis of Fiduciary Obligation,* 1988 DUKE L.J. 879, 915.

3. **Economic theory of fiduciary duties.** Contextual variations in fiduciary duties can be explained with reference to the costs and benefits of fiduciary duties in particular firms. Constraining fiduciaries' actions encourages them to exercise power consistently with the beneficiary's interests. But fiduciary duties also may discourage fiduciaries from exercising discretion or from scouting out favorable business opportunities for fear of having to pay for mistakes or to give up all of the fruits of their efforts. The parties therefore may want to substitute less costly ways of constraining fiduciaries. For example, the beneficiary might retain the power to vote on all of the fiduciary's business decisions, as do partners under the partnership default rule discussed in Chapter 5. A partnership in which owners share management may have a lower level of fiduciary duties than a *Meinhard*-type firm which has a single managing partner. Also, partners' power to remove their investments from the firm at any time (*see* Chapter 9, below) might justify a lower level of fiduciary duties than, for example, in a close corporation where owners may be "stuck."

4. **Contractual theory of fiduciary duties.** The economic explanations for variations in fiduciary duties discussed in Note 3 are often identified with a *contractual* theory of fiduciary duties. The economic and contractual theories are similar, since economic considerations often support enforcing contracts. The theories may diverge to the extent that, for example, contracts are enforced in order to respect the autonomy

of the contracting parties regardless of whether this is economically efficient. These issues are significant for the gap-filling discussion in Note 5, below, and for the waiver issue discussed in § 8.07. For discussions of the contractual theory of fiduciary duties, *see* Butler & Ribstein, *Opting out of Fiduciary Duties: A Response to the Anti-Contractarians,* 65 WASH. L. REV. 1 (1990); Easterbrook & Fischel, *Contract and Fiduciary Duty,* 36 J. LAW & ECON. 425 (1993). For discussions that to some degree reject the contractual approach *see* Brudney, *Corporate Governance, Agency Costs, and the Rhetoric of Contract,* 85 COLUM. L.REV. 1403 (1985); DeMott, *Beyond Metaphor: An Analysis of Fiduciary Obligation,* 1988 DUKE L.J. 879; Dickerson, *From Behind the Looking Glass: Good Faith, Fiduciary Duty and Permitted Harm,* 22 FLA. STATE U. L. REV. 955 (1995); Frankel, *Fiduciary Law,* 71 CALIF. L. REV. 795, 805 (1983).

5. **Fiduciary duties as contractual gap-fillers: The hypothetical bargain.** The contractual view of fiduciary duties lends itself to approaching fiduciary duties as a kind of "gap-filler." From this standpoint, fiduciary duties are a "hypothetical bargain"—*i.e.,* the terms the parties themselves would have drafted if detailed contracting were not so costly. The emphasis is on what the parties to the relationship are likely to have done, because under the contractual view the parties can waive default duties they do not like, and applying duties the parties probably will contract out of would simply impose extra contracting costs.

6. **When is there a "gap"?** Accepting the general logic of gap-filling does not answer many questions that might arise regarding fiduciary duties. In the first place, merely because the parties have not explicitly addressed the precise issue in the case does not mean that the court should assume that the contract is silent and proceed to fill in the default fiduciary duty terms. In fact, the contract might have spoken, if only in a negative sense. On the other hand, the parties' silence may mean that they assumed that the court would provide a duty in the unprovided for case. The difficulty of determining the existence of a "gap" can be seen in *Jordan v. Duff & Phelps, Inc.,* 815 F.2d 429 (7th Cir. 1987), *cert. denied,* 108 S. Ct. 1067 (1988), in which Judge Frank H. Easterbrook, a noted adherent to the economic and contractual views of fiduciary duties, held that a default duty to disclose an impending merger to shareholders who were selling their stock to the firm was not waived by a contract which apparently denied employee-shareholders the usual rights of shareholders. Judge Richard A. Posner—another noted advocate of the contractual and economic views—argued in dissent that the actual contract should control. Indeed, Judge Easterbrook himself later appeared to adopt a more restrictive view of gap-filling in *Continental Bank, N.A. v. Everett,* 964 F.2d 701 (7th Cir. 1992), in which the court refused to require a bank to disclose to a guarantor that loan collateral was inadequate. Judge Easterbrook observed (964 F.2d at 705): "People write things down in order to assign duties and allocate risks—functions vital to economic life yet defeated if courts prefer hypothetical bargains over real ones or use the ambiguities present in all language to frustrate the achievement of certainty."

7. **What should the default rule be?** When the parties have not made their deal clear, what deal should the court supply? One possible approach is to ask what most or all similarly situated parties would want. Another is to design the default rule so as to

force the party disadvantaged by the default rule to disclose information to the other party. *See* Note 3, § 4.05. Also, it may be more important how costly it is to contract around a particular default rule. *See* Charny, *Hypothetical Bargains: The Normative Structure of Contract Interpretation,* 89 MICH. L. REV. 1815 (1991). For example, other things (such as information costs) being equal, it may be harder to waive a strict default duty like the one Justice Cardozo imposes than to fill in duties when the default rule is more lenient or fact-sensitive, like the one Justice Andrews would have applied.

8. **Was *Meinhard* correctly decided?** Evaluate *Meinhard* in light of the above analysis. If parties could have contracted cheaply for all eventualities, what would they have done? Would they have allocated the benefit of this sort of deal to Salmon? Since Salmon would have to pay Meinhard for this benefit, it might be worth asking whether this sort of speculation was worth more to Salmon than to Meinhard. Or, apart from what the parties wanted, should Meinhard win in the absence of an explicit contract to the contrary on the ground that it would have been cheaper for Salmon to draft around this rule, or appropriate to force Salmon to disclose what he knew about the potential for a follow-up deal with Gerry?

For a defense of *Meinhard, see* Georgakopoulos, Meinhard v. Salmon *and the Economics of Honor,* 1999 COLUM. BUS. L. REV. 137. For what it is worth, this article reports, *id.* at 144, n. 11:

> Salmon retained majority control of the expanded project, which due to the depression was not successful, and anecdotally, only the cash infusion of Meinhard saved Salmon from ruin during the lean years. Salmon felt so grateful that he sent Cardozo a bouquet of flowers on each anniversary of the opinion. Moreover, when Meinhard died, his share was sold to the Salmon family at the depressed prices of the day. *See* Correspondence with C. Robert Morris, Professor of Law at Minnesota Law School, Feb. 2, 1998 (on file with author) (relating facts extracted and generously shared by Professor Morris from Walter Salmon Jr. in 1983-84). Furthermore, Professor Craig Albert, who examined the record at the New York City Bar while on a breather from correcting exams, claims that Meinhard was trying to force Salmon into giving him a better deal than 50% participation by dragging his heels (he transferred his interest to his wife, and when Salmon accepted in principle a 50% participation of Meinhard but not of his wife, Meinhard brought suit). *See* E-mail from Craig Albert, Associate Professor, Seton Hall Law School, Feb. 9, 1999 (on file with author).

9. **Who is owed fiduciary duties?** Not everybody who is involved with a partnership is owed partner-like fiduciary duties. For example, a debtor has the power to use property loaned by its creditors in ways that are contrary to the creditors' interests. Nevertheless, debtors owe no general fiduciary duty to their creditors. *See* DeMott, *supra,* at 914-15. Unlike partners, creditors normally *can* specify precise duties—that is, to repay the loan with interest—and so need not rely on a general duty of unselfishness. Duties to assignees are discussed in Note 3, p. 152.

10. **Statutory provisions on partners' fiduciary duties.** UPA § 21 and RUPA § 404 reflect the unselfishness standard applied by Justice Cardozo. As discussed below in § 8.06, the two statutes may differ regarding the effect of a waiver of fiduciary duty. Moreover, both statutes may permit some selfish conduct. It is not clear under UPA § 21 when a partner is deriving a "benefit" from the partnership, and RUPA § 404(e)-(f) makes clear that partners *can* act selfishly to some extent.

8.02 Disclosure

All contracting parties have some protection from misrepresentations by the other party to the contract. However, contracting parties do not necessarily have a right to *affirmative* disclosure of information. This right depends largely on the existence of a fiduciary duty, discussed in this section. Note that an affirmative disclosure obligation may also apply under the securities laws (*see* § 3.03(B)).

In order for partners to be able to monitor those who manage the firm they must have some right to demand accurate information relating to the partnership. They probably also have a right to affirmative disclosure from their co-partners in specific dealings, such as paying off an exiting partner. Partners' default disclosure rights are set forth in UPA §§ 19-20 and RUPA § 403. In general, these involve access to specific records (*see* II BROMBERG & RIBSTEIN ON PARTNERSHIP § 6.05) and the more open-ended right to other information (*id.* § 6.06). These default rights are discussed in this Section. Section 8.06 discusses variation of these default rights in the partnership agreement.

Walter v. Holiday Inns, Inc.
985 F.2d 1232 (3d Cir. 1993)

SLOVITER, Chief Judge.

Plaintiffs are several individuals and a corporation who formed a 50-50 partnership with Holiday Inns, Inc. (Holiday) in 1979 to develop and operate Harrah's Marina Hotel and Casino in Atlantic City, New Jersey. In 1981, plaintiffs sold their 49% interest in the partnership to Holiday. In 1983, plaintiffs sold their remaining 1% interest to Holiday. In 1985, four years after the first sale, by which time the hotel/casino complex had become highly profitable, they filed this suit claiming that in the buy-out transaction Holiday committed common law fraud, violated federal securities laws, and breached the fiduciary duty it owed to plaintiffs. After plaintiffs presented their case, the district court granted Holiday's motion for judgment as a matter of law on the breach of fiduciary duty claim. *See Walter v. Holiday Inns, Inc.*, 784 F. Supp. 1159 (D.N.J. 1992). At the conclusion of the trial, the jury decided for Holiday on the remaining claims. Plaintiffs appeal.

I. FACTS AND PROCEDURAL HISTORY

In August 1978, shortly after New Jersey legalized gambling, the plaintiffs purchased a tract of land with the intent of developing a hotel and casino complex at a marina in Atlantic City. Plaintiffs then created two New Jersey corporations (L & M Walter Enterprises, Inc. and Bayfield Enterprises, Inc.) and had both entities form a general partnership known as

Marina Associates. After looking for a suitable partner to develop the casino, plaintiffs sold Bayfield Enterprises to Holiday on January 30, 1979 and entered into a 50-50 Partnership Agreement with the hotel chain. Both parties agreed to make an initial capital contribution of $2 million each to the partnership business.

The partners successfully obtained a $75 million loan for the project from Midlantic National Bank, which later advanced an additional $20 million to the partnership. Construction commenced in early 1980 and proceeded at a rapid pace.

While the construction of the casino was progressing, the partners executed several documents that defined the nature of their relationship. Pursuant to a Memorandum of Understanding dated June 6, 1980, the partners agreed to advance in equal shares additional capital to the casino on an as-needed basis to cover project development (pre-opening) or operating (post-opening) cash shortfalls. If one partner was unable to meet its share, the other could advance the funds and then serve a written "cash call" letter on the non-contributing partner. The Memorandum provided that a failure to comply with a strict timetable for repayment of the cash call would result in a dilution of the non-contributing partner's interest in the casino, with the degree of dilution linked to the total amount of the cash call. The conditions for relief from dilution because of failure to meet a project development cash call were more formidable than those for an operating cash call.

A second Memorandum of Understanding dated June 20, 1980 set forth how the casino was to be managed. The day-to-day operations were turned over to Harrah's, Inc., a subsidiary of Holiday. The more important management and financing decisions remained with the partnership's Executive Committee, which was composed of two Holiday executives and two of the plaintiffs, Louis Walter and Lance Walter. The Executive Committee's decision-making power included, inter alia, overseeing the completion of the casino's construction and development, approving capital expenditures for replacement and expansion that exceeded 4% of total revenues for any year, the creation of long-term debt, and the creation of short-term debt for working capital in excess of $2 million.

The hotel and casino complex opened its doors to the public on November 22, 1980, before all of the construction was completed. However, construction costs rose substantially over budget, and financial concerns mounted. At a meeting of the Executive Committee in January 1981, the plaintiffs were presented with financial projections for the casino. Walter Haybert, the Chief Financial Officer of Marina Associates, presented "a 'worst case' projection of profit and loss for 1981 with related projections of monthly cash flow." He explained the need to substantially supplement working capital in the project development budget.

Shortly thereafter, two separate cash call letters were issued formally demanding that plaintiffs make equity contributions to the project. The first letter advised that an equity contribution of $18.8 million was required to cover expenditures in connection with the project development budget (plaintiffs' half being $9.4 million). The second letter, which cited Marina Associates' negative cash flow, was a call for cash increments due from November 1980 to May 1981 totaling $15.7 million (plaintiffs' share being $7.85 million) to cover operating shortfalls for the project.

Plaintiffs determined not to supply their share of the funds requested, allegedly relying on Holiday's pessimistic predictions about the financial prospects of the Marina. As a result, Holiday advanced its own funds to cover the shortfalls, and plaintiffs' partnership interest was diluted pursuant to the formula specified in the partners' prior agreements.

At the same January 1981 Executive Committee meeting, the partners also approved an Information Flow Agreement that specified the items of partnership financial data, such as financial statements and internal audit reports, that would be provided to the plaintiffs.

The financial situation presented at the January 1981 Executive Committee Meeting apparently precipitated plaintiffs' efforts to sell their interest in the casino to outside investors. However, there is some evidence in the record that in 1980 plaintiffs had approached Holiday and others to purchase plaintiffs' partnership interest. After the January 1981 meeting, negotiations with Holiday resumed at plaintiffs' request. They continued until the parties agreed on the terms of a buy-out on May 9, 1981, whereby Holiday agreed to acquire plaintiffs' 49% interest in the partnership for payments to plaintiffs of $1.75 million per year for twenty years, which plaintiffs calculate had a present value of $10.9 million. In July 1983, plaintiffs sold their remaining 1% interest to Holiday for an additional $1.8 million.

Sometime after the 1981 buy-out, the casino became a profitable enterprise. Under New Jersey law, the casino's profits and losses were a matter of public record and plaintiffs implicitly concede that they were aware of the highly profitable operations of Marina from 1982 to 1984. Nevertheless, plaintiffs did not challenge the buy-out transaction until this suit was brought in 1985. In that period, they sold their remaining 1% interest to Holiday and continued to do business with Holiday elsewhere. Louis Walter claims he was prompted to file this action by a newspaper article in which Donald Trump, the owner of another casino, suggested that Holiday had taken advantage of the plaintiffs in connection with the 1981 buy-out. * * *

* * * [T]he essence of plaintiffs' claims is that Holiday failed to provide them with certain information that they needed to negotiate the buy-out transaction from an equal position with Holiday. They also assert that Holiday had designed a "cash call strategy" to force the buy-out on terms unfavorable to plaintiffs.* * *

II. DISCUSSION

A. Asserted Fiduciary Duty

* * * We . . . focus . . . on the heart of this case—the nature of the obligations, if any, owed by Holiday to plaintiffs in connection with the negotiations leading to Holiday's buy-out of plaintiffs' interest. * * *

Since the mid-19th century, New Jersey courts have recognized that in order to set aside the sale of a partnership interest on the ground of breach of fiduciary duty, "it is essential that the misrepresentation or concealment should be . . . in regard to a fact material to the contract." * * * Even if Holiday had some fiduciary obligation to plaintiffs and Holiday had the burden of proving that this duty was not breached, if the evidence plaintiffs produced at trial showed that under the circumstances none of the alleged misstatements or omissions would have been material to their decision to sell their partnership interest to Holiday or that Holiday had no obligation to do more than it did, we must affirm.

B. Applicable Legal Principles

Materiality cannot be determined in a vacuum. In business transactions, what is material must be evaluated in the context in which the statements or omissions occurred. *See TSC Indus., Inc. v. Northway, Inc.*, 426 U.S. 438, 449, 96 S. Ct. 2126, 2132, 48

L.Ed.2d 757 (1976) (omitted fact is material if there is a "substantial likelihood that, under all the circumstances, the omitted fact would have assumed actual significance in the deliberations of the reasonable shareholder"). This is true as well in partnership buy-outs. 2 Alan R. Bromberg & Larry E. Ribstein, BROMBERG AND RIBSTEIN ON PARTNERSHIP § 6.06, at 6:64 (1988) (in partnership buy-out transactions, "[e]ven if a partner was subject to a duty of full disclosure and failed to disclose every fact in connection with a particular transaction, there is no liability unless the nondisclosed facts were such as might be expected to have induced action or forbearance by the other partners—that is, were material").

As a general proposition courts and commentators have recognized that in determining whether a fiduciary duty has been breached by a material misstatement or by a failure to disclose a material fact, the sophistication of the complaining partner and the degree of access to partnership records are key factors to be considered. [citations omitted]

As leading commentators in the law of partnerships have stated, "The extent of the duty to disclose depends on the circumstances of the individual case . . . [and] may depend on the degree to which the parties have access to accurate financial records, on whether the nondisclosing partner managed the business and thus was familiar with the relevant information, and on the knowledgeability or degree of expertise of the party to whom the duty of disclosure is owed." 2 Alan R. Bromberg & Larry E. Ribstein, BROMBERG & RIBSTEIN ON PARTNERSHIP § 6.06, at 6:64 (1988) (citation and footnote omitted); see also id. § 6:05, at 6:55-56 ("[I]f the partners have equal access to the books, and if full information is disclosed in them, they may be bound by interpartner transactions even without direct disclosure.") * * *

The plaintiffs stipulated that at the relevant times "each of the plaintiffs was a highly sophisticated and experienced investor," and the record amply bears that out.[5] In light of this concession we need only examine the extent of plaintiffs' access to the partnership records.

Plaintiffs contend that they were passive partners while Holiday was the managing partner with exclusive control over all financial information concerning the casino. If that were in fact the case, we believe that New Jersey would hold Holiday to a more stringent fiduciary standard in connection with the buy-out than if the partners bargained from equal positions. [citations omitted] However, we find insufficient evidence in the record to support plaintiffs' factual assertion, even viewing the facts in the light most favorable to the plaintiffs.

Those portions of the record that plaintiffs have cited to support their claim of passivity reveal that although the day-to-day operations of the casino were under Holiday's control through its subsidiary, Harrah's, Inc., the most important decisions regarding the planning and financial management remained with the partnership's Executive Committee on which plaintiffs served equally with defendants. For example, although plaintiffs note letters from Holiday executives referring to Harrah's as the managing partner of Marina Associ-

---

[5]   Louis Walter is an experienced developer and operator of hotels. At the time of trial he owned two hotels in California, which he managed as Holiday Inn franchises. He also developed a hotel and casino in Las Vegas, Nevada which was later leased to Holiday and another corporation. Lance Walter, who has a Bachelor of Science and a Master of Business Administration from the University of Southern California, testified that he was actively involved in the Walter Group's search for the optimal location for a hotel and casino in Atlantic City. Herbert Sturman testified that he was the founding partner of his law firm, Fierstein & Sturman, and had been certified by the State of California as a specialist in tax law since 1973.

ates, these simply reiterate the terms of the June 20, 1980 Memorandum of Understanding setting forth the division of responsibility between the Executive Committee and Harrah's. Holiday does not deny its role in that respect. However, Holiday's management of the daily operations of the casino does not demonstrate that plaintiffs were merely passive partners, as Herbert Sturman testified, or that plaintiffs were not given access to the information necessary to put them in a position where they could bargain fairly in the buy-out transaction.

The documents and testimony cited by Holiday overwhelmingly demonstrate the active role played by plaintiffs in every aspect of the partnership's business. * * * This active involvement continued throughout the Spring of 1981, when the parties were negotiating the buy-out. For example, at the final meeting of the Executive Committee on March 18, 1981, Louis Walter approved certain change orders relating to the casino's remaining construction needs, and Herbert Sturman discussed and approved a procedure for accounting for the operating and project development shortfalls.

The record also shows that plaintiffs requested and received volumes of financial data pursuant to the Information Flow Agreement that provided them with ample data by which to assess the partnership's financial situation. * * *

In fact, plaintiffs' access to the partnership's records was specifically assured by Section 5.1 of the 1979 Partnership Agreement which states: The Partnership will at all times maintain, at the Hotel, complete and accurate books of account. * * * Such books and records shall be made available for inspection and copying by the Partners, or their duly authorized representatives, during business hours.

Plaintiffs produced no evidence that they were ever denied access to any information on the casino's past or present financial situation. On the contrary, there is evidence that they were specifically notified that their independent auditors could examine the partnership records. * * *

Holiday refers us to unrebutted evidence produced by plaintiffs in their case-in-chief demonstrating plaintiffs' open access to all relevant financial records of the operation of the casino. We therefore proceed on the basis that plaintiffs had unrestricted access to all past and current information regarding the partnership and its financial operations. * * *

With these general principles in mind, we proceed with an item by item analysis of the specific facts that plaintiffs claim would have been material to their decision to sell their half share of the casino to Holiday. We do so mindful of our prior assertion that "[o]nly when the disclosures or omissions are so clearly unimportant that reasonable minds could not differ should the ultimate issue of materiality be decided as a matter of law." *Craftmatic Sec. Litig. v. Kraftsow*, 890 F.2d 628, 641 (3d Cir. 1989) (citation omitted).

C. The Alleged Misrepresentations and Nondisclosures

1. The Boxer Report

Plaintiffs have devoted considerable argument to Holiday's failure to provide them with copies of the financial projections contained in the Boxer Report. The Report, prepared prior to the 1981 buy-out, was a 35 year financial forecast prepared by the defendants, based on the current financial statements and projected growth, which projected large cash flows and high profits for the hotel/casino project. It also contained two ten-year projections of substantial, albeit differing, profits.

To support their assertion that this was an omission material to their buy-out decision, plaintiffs point to Sturman's testimony that "the Holiday projections would have been very, very meaningful to me[.] I would recognize that it is a projection but it would have been the best guess of a very sophisticated gaming entity and . . . so I would have given them some credibility." * * *

As for the relevance of the Boxer Report to the plaintiffs' decision, nothing indicates that plaintiffs would have placed any greater reliance on the Boxer projections than on the numerous other forecasts that Holiday had previously disclosed or that plaintiffs themselves had prepared through their independent auditors. Herbert Sturman and Charles Solomonson, a senior Vice President and Chief Financial Officer at Holiday, testified to Louis Walter's disdain for financial projections, such as the two 10-year financial projections that Holiday had previously commissioned in the spring of 1979 and which it provided to plaintiffs. Moreover, the Boxer Report was simply a projection based on the volumes of financial information already in plaintiffs' possession. Plaintiffs have not shown why the forecast prepared for them by their independent auditor in June 1980 was not an equally reliable predictor.

Of course, we recognize that every negotiator would like to have all the information upon which his or her counterpart is proceeding, but that is a far cry from materiality in the legal sense. That depends, instead, on whether plaintiffs had access to the raw data upon which they could make their own projections. The record shows they did. * * *

In light of the applicable law and all of the evidence presented, we hold that no reasonable jury could have concluded that Holiday's failure to make the Boxer Report available to plaintiffs was a breach of any fiduciary duty owed by Holiday.

2. Failure to Disclose 1981 Cash Flow Projection

We reach a similar result with respect to plaintiffs' assertion that Holiday failed to disclose a 1981 cash flow projection for the casino that was prepared by Marina Associates and presented to the Gaming Committee of Holiday's Board of Directors in January 1981. * * *

Sturman's statements demonstrate that Holiday's failure to disclose the 1981 cash flow projection was not a material omission. As with the Boxer Report, it would be unrealistic to require a partner to disclose every internal projection in its possession, particularly when its co-partner had equal access to the partnership records, had received the foundational facts upon which the projection was based, and was sufficiently knowledgeable to develop its own projection from those facts.

3. Transaction Audit Review Group Report

Plaintiffs contend that Holiday failed to disclose its Transaction Audit Review Group Report, which was completed on May 28, 1981. This review was undertaken to establish the reasons for the multi-million dollar project development cost overrun. The Report revealed that mismanagement by casino employees under Holiday's control was a significant cause of the cost overruns that precipitated Marina Associates' cash calls on plaintiffs. Plaintiffs claim that they would have had a stronger negotiating position against Holiday had they known of the Report, and could have resisted Holiday's dilution threats. * * *

Even if we infer, as plaintiffs ask us to do, that the study and analysis were done before the buy-out, plaintiffs had the opportunity to discover the relevant facts regarding the cost overruns but failed to avail themselves of this opportunity. Thus, they have no basis to complain that the Report was not provided to them when it was completed after the buy-out. * * *

6. Cash Calls

Plaintiffs place considerable importance in what they have labeled Holiday's "cash call strategy." According to plaintiffs' view of this purported scheme, Holiday intended to force a buy-out of plaintiffs' interest on unfavorable terms by inflating the cash calls made to plaintiffs, thereby threatening them with dilution of their interest in the partnership. * * *

* * * [P]laintiffs never made the promised audit that would have informed them of the factual basis for Holiday's requests. Had they done so they would have discovered what Holiday had already informed them: that the contributions required of the partners was substantially smaller than the projections contained in the cash call letters. Even without such an inspection, plaintiffs knew that a portion of the shortfalls were no longer projections but immediate demands for cash, yet they refused to advance any additional funds to cover their share of the shortfalls. In light of plaintiffs' failure to discover facts that were placed at their call, their breach of fiduciary duty claim against Holiday on this ground must fail as a matter of law. * * *

We conclude . . . that the record fails to support plaintiffs' argument that Holiday made any material misrepresentations or omitted providing material facts that it had a duty to disclose to plaintiffs. Thus we conclude that the district court did not err in granting judgment as a matter of law on plaintiffs' claim of breach of fiduciary duty. * * *

Appletree Square I Limited Partnership v. Investmark, Inc.
494 N.W.2d 889 (Minn. App. 1993)

CRIPPEN, Judge

Appletree Square One Limited Partnership purchased a commercial office building which is contaminated with asbestos fireproofing materials. Purchasers sued the sellers on various theories of fraud for failing to disclose the presence and hazards of asbestos. Purchasers appeal from summary judgment dismissing each of their claims. We reverse.

FACTS

Appletree Square I Limited Partnership was formed September 21, 1981, to purchase and operate One Appletree Square, a 15-story office building. The partnership was organized under the 1976 Uniform Limited Partnership Act, MINN. STAT. §§ 322A.01-.87 (1980). Appellants represent the partnership and its affiliates who purchased the property (purchasers). Respondents represent the builders and sellers of the property (sellers), who held interests in the partnership when sale transactions occurred.

This suit is based on two transactions. The building sale occurred in 1981. In 1985, a further acquisition was made by sale of a 25 percent interest in the Appletree partnership. An affiliate of the purchasers, CRI, represented them in both transactions; CRI is a real estate syndication firm. During negotiations for the sale of the property in 1981, CRI wrote a letter to sellers requesting "any information that you have not already sent to us which would be material to our investors' participation in this development." In response, CRI was told to inspect the building and the records, because the sellers "had no way of knowing what information would be material to your investors' participation."

In 1986, the purchasers learned that the structural steel in the building had been coated with asbestos-based fireproofing, which was deteriorating and releasing fibers. The cost of abatement was estimated at ten million dollars. In their subsequent suit, the purchasers alleged that the sellers were liable for failing to disclose the presence and danger of asbestos. The purchasers sought recovery of damages under theories of breach of contract; violation of the Limited Partnership Act, MINN. STAT. § 322A.17 (1990); violation of the Deceptive Trade Practices Act, MINN. STAT. § 325D.44 (1990); fraud and misrepresentation; and negligent misrepresentation. * * *

ANALYSIS

This appeal turns on whether respondents had a fiduciary duty to disclose to appellants the presence and danger of asbestos. * * *

1. Common Law Duty of Disclosure

Absent a fiduciary relationship, one party to a transaction has "no duty to disclose material facts to the other." [citation omitted] In this case, appellants and respondents were partners in a limited partnership. The relationship of partners is fiduciary and partners are held to high standards of integrity in their dealings with each other. [citation omitted] Parties in a fiduciary relationship must disclose material facts to each other. [citation omitted] Where a fiduciary relationship exists, silence may constitute fraud. [citation omitted] Under the common law, respondents had a duty to disclose information regarding asbestos if they knew about it.

Uniform Limited Partnership Act and Duties of Disclosure

The trial court held that the Uniform Limited Partnership Act changed the common law duties of disclosure. MINN. STAT. § 322A.28(2) (1990) states that limited partners have the right, "upon reasonable demand," to obtain information from the general partners. This statute mirrors the disclosure requirement in the Uniform Partnership Act and should be interpreted similarly. See MINN. STAT. § 323.19 (1990). The trial court held that because appellants did not demand information about asbestos, respondents had no obligation to disclose the information.

The trial court's holding is contradicted by a proper interpretation of the disclosure statute. MINN. STAT. § 322A.28(2) addresses the narrow duty of partners to respond to requests for information. It does not negate a partner's broad common law duty to disclose all material facts. [citation omitted]

Contractual Duties of Disclosure

The trial court also held that the parties limited their duties of disclosure in their contract. The contract stated that the general partners would "provide the partners with all information that may reasonably be requested." Again, appellants never requested information.

Partners may change their common law and statutory duties by incorporating such changes in their partnership agreement. See MINN. STAT. § 322A.33. [citation omitted] However, where the major purpose of a contract clause is to shield wrongdoers from liability, the clause will be set aside as against public policy. [citation omitted] Additionally, while "partners are free to vary many aspects of their relationship . . . they are not free to destroy its fiduciary character." [citation omitted]

To hold that partners may replace their broad duty of disclosure with a narrow duty to render information upon demand would destroy the fiduciary character of their relationship, and it would also invite fraud.

Unless partners knew what questions to ask, they would have no right to know material information about the business. In this case, if respondents knew the building was contaminated with asbestos and if they reasonably should have known their partners did not know about the asbestos, they may have breached their fiduciary duty of disclosure. [citation omitted]

2. Knowledge of Sellers

The evidence here is sufficient to create a genuine fact issue of whether respondents knew of the presence of asbestos in the building and knew before the 1985 transaction of the danger now associated with this use of the substance. * * *

Justifiable Reliance

The trial court determined that any alleged breach of a partner's duty to disclose was defeated by evidence that the purchasers inadequately investigated the transaction. The trial court held as a matter of law that appellants were not justified in relying on respondents to disclose the presence and danger of asbestos. The court based its decision on the fact that respondents told appellants to conduct their own investigation and on its finding that appellants were sophisticated buyers. A fiduciary's duty is defined "with reference to the experience and intelligence of the person to whom the duty is owed." [citation omitted]

The record here does not permit the holding as a matter of law that appellants were not justified in relying on respondents. The sellers designed and built the building and thus may have had superior knowledge about the asbestos. The buyers' expertise appears to have been in the area of finance and marketing. In an affidavit, respondent's former vice president who had supervised the construction of the building stated:

> CRI and its affiliates were involved in only the financial aspects of development and they would have looked to Ellerbe companies for information regarding asbestos or any other information about construction materials or hazards in One Appletree Square.

The unique qualifications of the buyers and sellers in this case create questions of fact regarding the relative sophistication of the parties. The fact-finder must weigh this evidence to determine whether the buyers' reliance on disclosures was reasonable.

There is no compelling evidence that either the building specifications or a visual inspection of the building should have revealed the asbestos. Moreover, although the purchasers had partnership authority over management of the building prior to the 1985 partnership interest buyout, respondents were managers in fact from 1972 (when the building was constructed) to 1985. To discover asbestos on their own, appellants would have had to know enough to ask about it or know enough to have various building materials tested.

Finally, the fact that respondents told appellants to investigate did not make appellants' reliance unreasonable as a matter of law. Respondents' statement did not specifically tell appellants not to rely on them. Moreover, even if respondents had told appellants not to rely on them, that statement would not necessarily make reliance unreasonable. Evidence in the record permits a finding that respondents had superior knowledge and knew appellants did not know about the asbestos. These are fact questions which must be answered to determine whether respondents neglected their fiduciary duty to inform appellants. [citation omitted] * * *

Notes and Questions

1. **When must partners disclose?** The statute and the contract in *Appletree* made disclosure contingent on demand. Did the court hold that demand was never required? Such a rule could impose an open-ended burden on the other partners. If demand is sometimes or usually required, what circumstances may have prompted the affirmative disclosure duty in *Appletree*? *Compare Walter. See also Newton v. Aitken,* 260 Ill. App. 3d 717, 633 N.E.2d 213, 198 Ill. Dec. 751 (Ill. App. 1994), holding that, because plaintiff and defendant had equal access to records and documents, plaintiff knew, or could have learned through ordinary prudence, what defendants knew and so had no right to rely on defendant's representations. RUPA § 403(c) compromises on the demand issue by requiring certain information to be disclosed without demand and other information only on demand. How would *Appletree* have been decided under RUPA § 403? For a discussion of the RUPA disclosure rules, *see* Vestal, *The Disclosure Obligations of Partners Inter Se under the Revised Uniform Partnership Act of 1994: Is the Contractarian Revolution Failing?* 36 WM. & MARY L. REV. 1559 (1995). For a case applying both *Appletree* as to the duty to disclose despite the absence of demand, and *Walter* as to the factors relevant to the scope of the duty, *see TSA Intern. Ltd. v. Shimizu Corp.,* 92 Hawai'i 243, 990 P.2d 713 (1999).

2. **What must partners disclose?** As discussed in the principal cases, the disclosure duty between partners, as in other contexts, is limited by the concepts of *materiality* (*i.e.,* that the information be important to a reasonable person), *reliance* (*i.e.,* that the information have been important to the plaintiff) and *scienter* (*i.e.,* that the defendant knew or should have known of the misrepresentation or omission). "Justifiable reliance" as applied in *Appletree* is close to materiality in requiring analysis of whether a reasonable person would have relied. Consider what differences in these elements might have led to the different results in *Appletree* and *Walter. See also* Note 4, below.

3. **Disclosure in formation.** Whether a partnership-based disclosure duty exists on formation and winding up of the partnership ought to depend on whether the underlying reason for the duty discussed at the beginning of this section applies—that is, the function of disclosure in constraining the exercise of partners' agency power. As also discussed in Note 7, p. 189, imposing fiduciary duties while the parties are still negotiating at arms' length over the terms of the partnership would be inconsistent with the non-existence of a fiduciary relationship at that time. *See Phoenix v. Shady Grove,* 734 F. Supp. 1181, 1191 (D. Md. 1990), *aff'd,* 937 F.2d 603 (4th Cir. 1991).

There is an argument for a pre-formation duty to disclose. *See* Vestal, *"Ask Me No Questions and I'll Tell You No Lies": Statutory and Common-Law Disclosure Requirements within High-Tech Joint Ventures,* 65 TUL. L. REV. 705 (1991). If A and B are planning to enter into a long-term relationship, perhaps the law should save them from having to engage in sharp questioning at the outset of the relationship. But such a duty would be difficult to waive, and so may impose high costs in situations in which the duty is inappropriate. Although the partners could agree in the partnership agreement that results from the negotiations that no fiduciary duties arose prior to the agreement, this tactic will not work if the negotiations break down prior to an agreement or if the court holds that this provision is itself vitiated by pre-agreement non-disclosure. Conversely, under a no-duty default rule the parties could affirmatively contract, as through a binding "letter of intent," for specific duties during the preformation period. For example, in *Newharbor Partners, Inc. v. F.D. Rich Co., Inc.*, 961 F.2d 294 (1st Cir. 1992), the parties entered into a letter of intent proposing a real estate venture which created some obligations but stated that it did not create legally binding obligations in other respects. The court held that the document did not create a mutually intended obligation to act in good faith.

Even if there is no special *partnership* duty to disclose before formation, there may still be some other kind of fiduciary relationship or a *good* faith obligation to disclose (*see* § 8.05, below). Indeed, as indicated in Note 5, the good faith obligation may explain the result in *Appletree*. The partners' pre-formation statements also may be actionable misrepresentations, which may shade into active concealment. Or the statements may help define the contractual obligations that eventually bind the parties.

4. **Duties on winding up.** When the partners are winding up the business, or when one or more of the partners is dissociating but the partnership will continue as a going concern, the parties are clearly still partners and the courts generally hold that fiduciary duties continue to apply. *See Walter*, above, and Chapter 9, below. Although the parties may be at odds or negotiating as adversaries rather than as colleagues at this point, for the same reasons that managers of the firm should be required to share information while the firm is continuing, they also should have to disclose it in connection with winding up or a buyout when the information may be most valuable. If the duty did not apply in this situation, partners would have a greater incentive to squelch the information earlier in the relationship.

5. **Contextual variation of the duty.** Even during the going-concern phase of the business, there may be some question about the scope of the disclosure duty. As discussed in § 8.01, fiduciary duties are "gap-fillers" that depend on the context of the particular relationship in which the duty is applied. *See* Note 5, p. 169. In general, the more control the partners delegate to managers, the more they would rely on the managers for information. Thus, in a limited partnership, the limited partners not only do not, but *may not*, participate in control. *See* § 11.05(B). It follows that the limited partners generally could be expected to want a higher level of disclosure than would partners in general partnerships. Moreover, as *Walter* indicates, there are gradations in control, and therefore in the disclosure duty, even among general partnerships. By extension, a non-manager may have no fiduciary disclosure duty. Why, then, was a disclosure duty imposed on *limited* partners in *Appletree*? Was this a fiduciary duty, or one of good faith (*see* § 8.05)?

8.03 Duty of Loyalty

As discussed in § 8.01, property owners who delegate control over their property to others expect that control to be exercised for the owner's benefit. Consistent with this principle, UPA § 21 requires partners to account for benefits derived without co-partner consent from transactions with the partnership or from use of its property. The cases under UPA § 21, as well as UPA § 404, articulate this duty as one to refrain from self-dealing in partnership transactions, selfish use of partnership property, competition with the partnership and use of partnership opportunities. *Meinhard* (*see* § 8.01) as well as the following case, indicate the scope of this duty.

Labovitz v. Dolan
189 Ill. App. 3d 403, 136 Ill. Dec. 780, 545 N.E.2d 304 (1989)

Justice SCARIANO delivered the opinion of the court:

We have for decision in this case the issue, as posited by the plaintiffs, of whether management discretion granted solely and exclusively to a general partner in a limited partnership agreement authorizes the general partner to use economic coercion to cause his limited partner investors to sell their interests to him at a bargain price.

Plaintiffs as limited partners invested over $12 million dollars in a cablevision progamming limited partnership sponsored and syndicated by defendant general partner Dolan. In 1985 the partnership reported earnings of over $34 million dollars, and in 1986 it had earnings of just under $18 million dollars, as a result of which each of the limited partners was required to report his pro rata share on his personal income tax returns for those years.

Plaintiffs claim that although the partnership had cash available to fund the limited partners' tax obligations, Dolan elected to make only a nominal distribution of cash to cover such liability; accordingly, in 1985 and in 1986 the limited partners were required to pay taxes almost entirely from their own funds on income retained by the partnership. In late November of 1986 an affiliate owned and controlled by Dolan offered to buy out the interests of the limited partners for approximately two-thirds of their book value. Over 90% of the limited partners accepted the offer, but simultaneously filed suit claiming Dolan's tactics to be a breach of his fiduciary duty to them. The circuit court dismissed plaintiffs' complaint with prejudice pursuant to Section 2-619(a)(9) of our Code of Civil Procedure, holding that Dolan's acts were within the broad discretion granted him under the terms of the partnership agreement. Plaintiffs appeal from that ruling.

The limited partnership in this case, Cablevision Programming Investments (CPI) was organized for the purpose of investing in entities that produce and acquire programming for marketing and distribution to cable and other pay television services. Dolan and the Dolan-owned and controlled Communications Management Corporation of Delaware (CMC) were the general partners in this venture. In 1980, CPI sold 85 limited partnership units at a per unit price of $200,000; plaintiffs purchased 62.4595 of those units for a collective price of $12,491,900 and constituted 73% of all investors. The 263 page Private Placement Memorandum (PPM) explained that the proceeds of the CPI offering would be used to purchase 100% of the Class A limited partnership interests in another entity (Rainbow) that was organized for the same purpose as CPI; that Rainbow would fund subsidiary partnerships that would produce a variety of programming for distribution to cable TV systems and would have the same general partners as CPI; and that Rainbow would fund another Dolan-controlled entity, Rainbow Programming Services Company, which would distribute "affiliated and unaffiliated cable programming."

The PPM also advised investors that their rights and obligations "are governed by the Articles of Limited Partnership" (the Articles), which were bound as an exhibit to the PPM, and added, in a section entitled "Projected Results of Operations of Cablevision Programming Investments," that: "The Partnership, Cablevision and its affiliates' intended policy is to make cash distributions to partners each year in an amount approximating the amount of taxable income reflected each year, after providing for adequate working capital requirements deemed necessary by the General Partners. Although the projections assume that this policy can be followed in the future, there are significant contingencies relating to many factors which, from time to time, may prohibit any distributions, including, but not limited to cash, cash availability, general working capital requirements, lending restrictions and revised costs and capital requirements."

The Articles provided that Dolan will have "full responsibility and exclusive and complete discretion in the management and control of the business and affairs of the partnership"; that "Dolan in his sole discretion shall determine the availability of Cash Flow for distribution to partners"; that they "contain the entire understanding among the partners and supersede any prior understanding and/or written or oral agreements among them"; and that Dolan would be liable to the limited partners for his willful misconduct but not for "errors in judgment or for any acts or omissions that do not constitute willful misconduct."

CPI limited partnership interests were offered and sold only to "wealthy and sophisticated investors." * * * Prospective investors were apprised in the PPM, that the "offering and the operations of the entities summarized [therein] are complex," and that a "thorough understanding of such matters is essential in order for prospective investors to evaluate the merits and risks of the offering." * * *

An examination of a limited partner's "K-1" tax form reveals that from 1980 through 1984 CPI provided no cash to the limited partners but did afford them some tax benefits. In 1985, each partner was required to report a taxable income of $415,331 per unit, while Dolan distributed only $12,000 per unit; and in 1986 the partners were required to report a taxable income of $216,750 per unit, while again receiving a distribution of only $12,000 per unit.

On November 25, 1986, Cablevision Systems Corporation (CSC), owned and controlled by Dolan, made an offer to purchase all of the CPI limited partnership interests for $271,870 per unit, payable $90,623 in cash and the remainder was to be paid either in 9% notes due on June 30, 1988, and June 30, 1989, or in CSC Class A common stock. The offer disclosed that "Dolan and his affiliates would derive substantial benefits in connection with the offer" and that "although the partnership was potentially very valuable . . . it was extremely difficult to determine its true value since it was likely that current assumptions would not materialize and that unanticipated events and circumstances would occur." The offer further disclosed that although the partnership had incurred an operating loss of $96,000 per unit in 1986, proceeds from extraordinary and nonrecurring sales of assets would result in sizable taxable income to those limited partners who retained their interests. However, the offer continued, by selling their interests, limited partners would realize not only an added $71,870 per unit in cash profits on their initial investment in addition to the $24,000 previously distributed, but they could also convert their position in 1986 from that of having large taxable income to that of showing a sizable tax loss. This was because, as the offer explained, each limited partner's capital account had been inflated for tax purposes by proceeds from extraordinary and non-recurring sales to the extent that the book value of a limited partnership interest was shown at $405,000. The "business reasons" given for making the offer were that "the buyout would avoid conflicts since both the operating and the programming entities would be under the same ownership, and would provide a needed source of funds for the development of the programming companies." The articles provided that a limited partner could not sell or otherwise transfer his interest in the partnership without the prior written consent of the general partners. More than 90% of the limited partners elected to accept CSC's offer and sold their interests in CPI to CSC.

On December 1, 1986, plaintiff Joel Labovitz, who had owned three units, filed a class action complaint, but after other former owners joined in his suit as individual plaintiffs, that complaint was withdrawn and this action was substituted. * * * In their complaint plaintiffs sought the imposition of "a constructive trust upon the funds held by Dolan, the Partnership and Rainbow which were not required to meet current obligations, to maintain a sound financial position or establish reasonable reserves, and distribute these funds to plaintiffs," and for damages for breach of fiduciary duty. Plaintiffs appeal the order of dismissal, contending that since "'discretion' can never be exercised in breach of a fiduciary duty," the trial court erred in holding that the PPM and the Articles granted Dolan the discretion to treat his limited partners as he did, without permitting a trial that would inquire into his intent regarding the fairness of the transactions at issue. * * *

Plaintiffs point out that the PPM provides that:

> Distributions of Cash Flow of the Partnership and Cablevision will be made at such times and in such amounts as Charles F. Dolan, as the individual General Partner of both partnerships, in his sole discretion shall determine, subject to any restrictions on distributions to partners contained in loan agreements which may be entered into by Cablevision as a condition to its borrowings and which restrictions are not ascertainable at this time.

* * *

> The Partnership, Cablevision and its affiliates' intended policy is to make cash distributions to partners each year in an amount approximating the amount of taxable income reflected each year, after providing for adequate working capital requirements deemed necessary by the General Partners.

Thus, plaintiffs argue, Dolan made it clear in the PPM that he intended to distribute cash flow annually when not required to meet current obligations; accordingly his "discretion" to distribute cash flow was limited by his fiduciary duties to his partners.

Defendants respond that the Articles "unambiguously" support the trial court's conclusion that Dolan had the sole discretion to determine the availability of cash for distribution to the limited partners, pointing to section 7.3 of the Articles which provides that: "Dolan in his sole discretion shall determine the availability of cash flow for distribution to partners." Defendants maintain with great insistence that plaintiffs do not and cannot point to any provision in the Articles which expressly or impliedly limited Dolan's discretion to determine whether partnership funds were needed for partnership purposes or could be distributed as cash to the limited partners; instead, defendants interpret plaintiffs' argument as being that certain statements contained in the PPM dilute that discretion. However, defendants assert, this argument is seriously impaired by the fact that the Articles, and not the PPM defined the partners' rights and obligations, pointing to Section 15.10 of the Articles which provides in pertinent part: "These Articles contain the entire understanding among the partners and supersedes [sic] any prior understandings and/or written or oral agreements among them respecting the within subject matter."

Defendants claim that although the "rights and obligations of the Investors are governed by the Articles," the PPM was merely "intended to furnish information to the proposed investors with respect to the investment described." Thus, defendants contend, the PPM is entirely consistent with the Articles' grant of sole discretion to Dolan to determine how partnership proceeds should be allocated. * * *

Defendants' further response to plaintiffs is that the general partner's specific authority to determine how partnership proceeds should be allocated was not inconsistent with any fiduciary duty owed by Dolan to the plaintiffs, insisting that partners have the right to establish among themselves, by a partnership agreement, their rights, duties and obligations. [citation omitted] * * *

In construing a partnership agreement, defendants urge, a court should consider the object, purpose and nature of the agreement [citation omitted], and that the constraints plaintiffs now seek to place on Dolan's sole discretion are antithetical to the nature and purpose of the limited partnership formed in this case, which was designed, they argue, "to offer wealthy and sophisticated investors a unique investment opportunity—access to a family of related entities in an emerging industry, guided by a pioneering and immensely successful talent." Dolan was given, they continue, "the sole discretion to determine whether partnership proceeds were needed to fund related entities or could be distributed as cash to the limited partners so that he would have the flexibility needed to meet and anticipate the ever-changing business conditions in the industry," and in deciding how to allocate partnership proceeds, "Dolan was called upon to exercise his business judgment in anticipating future needs, expanding profitable areas and exploring promising new fields." Plaintiffs now attempt, defendants claim, "to second-guess Dolan's business judgment with respect to whether proceeds withheld from distribution were needed for the sound operation of CPI's business affairs and to have the court do likewise."

OPINION

It is abundantly clear, as defendants point out, that Dolan was granted rather wide latitude in deciding whether or not to distribute cash to the limited partners; the Articles grant him "sole discretion" in the matter, and do not mention any distribution for the purpose of meeting the limited partners' tax obligations. Even in the PPM, where distributions of cash approximating the amount of taxable income each year are projected in tabulated form, the language is far from precise and gives the general partner rather liberal discretionary powers as to such distribution.

It is also clear, however, that despite having such broad discretion, Dolan still owed his limited partners a fiduciary duty, which necessarily encompasses the duty of exercising good faith, honesty, and fairness in his dealings with them and the funds of the partnership. [citation omitted] It is no answer to the claim that plaintiffs make in this case that partners have the right to establish among themselves their rights, duties and obligations, as though the exercise of that right releases, waives or delimits somehow, the high fiduciary duty owed to them by the general partner—a gloss we do not find anywhere in our law. On the contrary, the fiduciary duty exists concurrently with the obligations set forth in the partnership agreement whether or not expressed therein. Indeed, at least one of the authorities relied upon by defendants is clear that although "partners are free to vary many aspects of their relationship inter se, . . . they are not free to destroy its fiduciary character." [citation omitted]

Thus, the language in the Articles standing alone does not deprive plaintiffs of the trial they seek against Dolan for breach of fiduciary duty. We therefore agree with plaintiffs that the trial court did not give due consideration to Dolan's duty as general partner to exercise the highest degree of honesty and good faith in his handling of partnership assets, and instead treated the parties as arm's length strangers [citation omitted] holding that no inquiry could be made into the fairness of the transactions at issue because of the language in the Articles regarding Dolan's discretion. Yet "in any fiduciary relationship, the burden of proof shifts to the fiduciary to show by clear and convincing evidence that a transaction is equitable and just." [citation omitted] Indeed, cases cited and relied upon by defendants hold that "where there is a question of breach of a fiduciary duty of a managing partner, all doubts will be resolved against him, and the managing partner has the burden of proving his innocence." [citation omitted] * * *

* * * Plaintiffs' complaint in essence charges that Dolan, as general partner, owed plaintiffs, his limited partners, a fiduciary duty "to distribute available cash flow to his partners in 1983 through 1986," which duty he breached because "he never intended to pay cash flow to the limited partners," thus "forcing or squeezing his limited partners into accepting his below book value offer" to buy out their interests, to their financial damage. The complaint goes on to allege that by Dolan's selling of the 85 limited partnership units at $200,000 per unit, $17,000,000 was realized as capital for the partnership. After deducting $2,000,000 to pay fees to Dolan and to reimburse him for attorney and accounting fees and other costs incurred in the preparation of the PPM, the sum of $15,000,000 remained as the partnership's capital. In addition to the cash flow generated by operations, the partnership and its related entities realized cash as follows: $20,000,000 in 1983 by selling interests in two related entities to a subsidiary of The Washington Post. In 1985 there was a $31,600,000 gain upon the sale of an interest in a related entity to a subsidiary of CBS, Inc., plus $50,000,000 when a lawsuit against Ted Turner and MGM was settled. In 1986 approximately $20,000,000 was paid to the partnership by MGM/UA Home Entertainment Group in exchange for a license option agreement, and $3,500,000 in exchange for the termination of a distribution agreement.

In 1985 the partnership showed income of $2,778,000 exclusive of the gain on the sale of assets, and after allowing for depreciation of $1,289,000. During 1986 the balance in the partnership cash account increased $11,000,000; receivables from parties "related" to Dolan and the partnership increased $3,600,000; and long term notes receivable increased $9,000,000. For the year ending December 31, 1986, partnership net income was $17,658,000 and working capital increased by $10,220,000. A footnote to the financial statement for the year ended December 31, 1985, discloses that Dolan retained significant amounts of money within the partnership which were loaned to "related parties"; more specifically, that Rainbow had advanced funds to Rainbow Programming Services Company "which, at December 31, 1985 & 1984, amounted to approximately $13,417,000 and $19,139,000 respectively," besides Rainbow's having made a capital contribution of $8,800,000 to RPSC.

We can think of no reason as to why these allegations should not be found to be sufficient to encompass the claim raised on this appeal, and sufficient also to apprise defendants thereof. * * *

As Professor Daniel S. Reynolds of the Northern Illinois University School of Law states in his article, *"Loyalty and Limited Partnership,"* 34 KANSAS L. REV. 1, (1985), "Self-dealing and conflicts of interest are endemic to the limited partnership. Limited partnerships 'are born in conflicts of interest, live in conflicts of interest, and sometimes poof out of existence in conflicts of interest.' [Quoting from 16 Sec.Reg. & L.Rep. BNA 1559 (1984).] The general partners are typically the organizing entrepreneurs or promoters. They may be affiliated with the sellers of the enterprise's assets, and are frequently involved in multiple, potentially competing related enterprises. This may be good, bad, or indifferent. Categorical prohibitions of conflicting interests might be a coherent response to all this, but a potentially fatal one as well for whatever assumed benefits of flexibility in capital formation the form provides. Categorical permission for conflicting interests might also be a coherent response, but one running all the risks that 'fiduciary ideology' is supposed to prevent. What is desired is a scheme for containing conflicts, a fairness-promoting regime that ensures, to the extent possible, that investors in the limited partnership are not being exploited, overreached, or taken advantage of by the managers of their money."

Defendants prevailed in the trial court on their Section 2-619(a)(9) motion on the ground that the claim is defeated by affirmative matter, namely, Dolan's sole discretion in the matter of distributing cash flow. As to such affirmative defense, defendants choose to remain completely oblivious to the fact that although the Articles clearly gave the general partner the sole discretion to distribute cash as he deemed appropriate, that discretion was encumbered by a supreme fiduciary duty of fairness, honesty, good faith and loyalty to his partners. Language in an agreement such as "sole discretion" does not metamorphose the document into an unrestricted license to engage in self-dealing at the expense of those to whom the managing partner owes such a duty. Defendants cite no authority, and we find none, for the proposition that there can be an a priori waiver of fiduciary duties in a partnership—be it general or limited. Nor is the practice of imposing purported advance waivers of fiduciary duties in limited partnership enterprises to be given judicial recognition on the basis of the facts developed in this case. Defendants' argument that the good faith doctrine protects only the reasonable expectations of the contracting parties is, we think, aptly answered by plaintiffs' statement to the trial judge at the hearing on defendants' motion to dismiss: ". . . the risk we took was that the business would not succeed. We did not take the risk that the business would succeed so well that the general partner would squeeze us out and take the investment for himself," an argument, by the way, that sets forth a precise formulation of the exact issue in this case.

Our courts are not bound to endow it as doctrine that where the general partner obtains an agreement from his limited partner investors that he is to be the sole arbiter with respect to the flow that the cash of the enterprise takes, and thereby creates conditions favorable to his decision that the business is too good for them and contrives to appropriate it to himself, the articles of partnership constitute an impervious armor against any attack on the transaction short of actual fraud. That is not and cannot be the law. [citation omitted] And that is precisely the gravamen of plaintiffs' complaint: that the general partner refused unreasonably to distribute cash and thereby forced plaintiffs to continually dip into their own resources in order to pay heavy taxes on large earnings in a calculated effort to force them to sell their interests to an entity which Dolan owned and controlled at a price well below at least the book value of those interests. Such a claim plainly presents an issue for the finder of fact, namely, whether or not Dolan was serving his own interests or those of the partnership. Although defendants state in their brief that Dolan allocated the partnership's funds to meet its needs and to serve its purposes, and although in oral argument defendants represented that the partnership was continually short of cash, the record at this stage is totally devoid of any such evidence. To be sure, all of the allegations made by plaintiffs in their complaint and noted above stand, according to the record made in this case, as unrebutted, undenied, unexplained and uncontroverted.

Plaintiffs therefore correctly maintain that they "were entitled to a trial in which Dolan must prove he acted fairly and not as his limited partners' business adversary." Accordingly, we hold that the trial judge incorrectly granted the defendants' Section 2-619(a)(9) motion, and that plaintiffs were entitled to a trial on the issues formulated in this case.

REVERSED AND REMANDED.

Notes and Questions

1. **Self-dealing and discretionary power.** For another recent case applying self-dealing concepts to an agreement which explicitly delegated power to managing partners *see Starr v. Fordham* in § 4.03(B). The question in both cases is whether the agreement left a "gap" for the court to fill with fiduciary duties (*see* Note 6, p. 169).

2. **General and limited partnerships.** Note that *Labovitz* involved a limited partnership. While general partnership duties literally apply pursuant to RULPA §§ 403 and 1105 and UPA § 6(2), the contextual nature of fiduciary duties discussed in § 8.01 also comes into play. The extensive delegation of discretion to general partners discussed in *Labovitz* arguably necessitates stronger constraints on that delegation than, for example, in a "standard form" general partnership between co-equal members. This may have influenced the court's decision in *Labovitz* to constrain the general partner's power over distributions. The fiduciary duties of general partners in limited partnerships are discussed below in § 11.08(A).

3. **Partnership opportunities.** *Meinhard v. Salmon* in § 8.01 involves a specific type of partnership fiduciary duty—the duty not to appropriate partnership opportunities—that is implicit in UPA § 21 and explicit in RUPA § 404.

4. **Use of partnership information.** In *Tri-Growth Centre City, Ltd. v. Silldorf, Burdman, Duignan & Eisenberg*, 216 Cal. App. 3d 1139, 265 Cal. Rptr. 330 (1989), the court held that it was a breach of fiduciary duty for a partner to use confidential information, including knowledge that the partnership would not soon be able to close its deal, to bid against the partnership in buying property. The defendant might have had this duty even if he were not a partner since he was also a member of the partnership's law firm.

5. **Competition**. Partners also have a duty not to compete with their firms. Once again, this is implicit in UPA § 21 and explicit under RUPA § 404. The duty not to compete is often an issue on dissolution. For example, in *Meehan v. Shaughnessy,* § 9.06(C) below, the court held that, while law partners can *plan* to compete with the firm and arrange to leave while still working for the firm, they could not secretly solicit clients while still working at the firm. *See generally* Hillman, *Law Firms and Their Partners: The Law & Ethics of Grabbing and Leaving,* 67 TEX. L. REV. 1 (1988).

6. **Remedy for breach.** The remedy for breach of fiduciary duty may be the *benefit* to the breaching partner rather the damage to the partnership. This is frequently the case in partnership opportunity and competition cases. *See, e.g., Jennison v. Bierer,* 601 F. Supp. 1167 (D. Vt. 1984) (partner entitled to share in amount copartner received for secret employment contract negotiated in connection with sale of partnership assets); *Prince v. Harting,* 177 Cal. App. 2d 720, 2 Cal. Rptr. 545 (1960) (defendant liable for difference between his cost and resale price to partnership). In these cases, a strict remedy may be necessary to deter fiduciary breaches because of the difficulty of detecting partner wrongdoing. Rather than determining whether a partner has turned up every opportunity she could for the partnership, the partner is given an incentive to do so by being denied a profit from taking the opportunities. *See* Cooter & Friedman, *The Fiduciary Relationship: Its Economic Character and Legal Consequences,* 66 N.Y.U. L. REV. 1045 (1991).

7. **Pre-formation duties.** Because unincorporated and other closely held firms involve preliminary negotiations and end in the formation of a fiduciary relationship, it may not be clear at precisely what moment the fiduciary duty arose. UPA § 21 provides for fiduciary duties in the "formation" of the partnership. This may refer to formation of the *business* by those who have already agreed to be partners. In any event, RUPA § 404 clarifies matters by recognizing a duty only in "the conduct and winding up" of the partnership. As discussed above in Note 3, p. 180-81 regarding the duty to disclose, the duty arguably should not apply when the parties are still negotiating over whether to form a partnership relationship because this would be logically inconsistent with the non-existence of a fiduciary relationship. Pre-formation substantive duties going beyond the mere duty to disclose also would raise daunting practical issues. How can the court determine the "gap" in the agreement that the fiduciary duty is to fill when the parties have not yet agreed on any terms? For example, whether a partner should refrain from taking partnership opportunities may depend on whether the partners will agree to delegate exclusive management powers to one partner or on the extent of the exit rights they negotiate.

Problem

A, B and C are three equal partners in an advertising agency. From the beginning, A and B have also owned the small office building in which the partnership has its offices. The partnership agreement provides that any action can be taken only by a majority vote of the partners. There are no other relevant provisions in the agreement. A and B, acting on behalf of their office building partnership, decide to raise the advertising agency partnership's rent. C insists that the agency find other office space, but A and B refuse. Does C have a cause of action against A and B for breach of fiduciary duty?

8.04 Duty of Care

Should partners be liable for making mistakes in managing the firm even if they act unselfishly? Such a duty may not induce much additional care in partners who are already personally liable for the firm's debts and operate under the close scrutiny of their co-partners. But a duty of care may make sense in some partnerships. Partners' liability for the firm's debts does not necessarily ensure full effort. In general, the greater the separation of management and ownership, the greater the managers' incentive to "cheat" on the amount of time they spend to maximize the firm's profits. However, the direct litigation costs of potential liability, as well as the indirect costs of constraining the partners' exercise of discretion, may outweigh the benefits in deterring poor decisions.

RUPA § 404(c) recognizes liability only for gross negligence or recklessness. This is consistent with the case law under the UPA. *See, e.g., Wirum & Cash Architects v. Cash,* 837 P.2d 692 (Alaska 1992); *Duffy v. Piazza Construction, Inc.,* 62 Wash. App. 19, 815 P.2d 267 (1991). Firms may want to contract for a stronger, or for no, duty of care in some circumstances. *See* Note 8, p. 203-04.

8.05 Good Faith

In addition to fiduciary duties, partners, like all contracting parties, owe an obligation of "good faith." Good faith differs from fiduciary duties. *See* RUPA § 404(d), which defines good faith as an obligation separate from fiduciary duties (but nevertheless includes it in the same section that also defines partner fiduciary duties). All contracting parties have a duty of "honesty in fact" to refrain from misrepresentations. This may explain the limited partner's obligation to disclose the latent defect in *Appletree,* § 8.02. More broadly, good faith can be viewed as an aspect of contract interpretation. This sense of the good faith duty was articulated as follows in *Oregon RSA No. 6, Inc. v. Castle Rock Cellular of Oregon Ltd. Partnership,* 840 F. Supp. 770 (D. Ore. 1993), *aff'd,* 76 F.3d 1003 (9th Cir. 1996) (holding that a limited partner's first refusal right to buy a limited partnership interest could not be evaded by structuring the sale as a transfer of the limited partner):

> If in each contract the parties had to expressly describe and prohibit every artifice by which the parties could potentially deprive each other of the fruits of their agreement, then contracts would soon become as long as the tax code, as difficult to interpret, and (like the tax code) still contain innumerable loopholes available to a party that wished to avoid the spirit of its bar-

gain. The better approach . . . is to treat a contract for what it is—an exchange of solemn promises—and enforce the objectively reasonable expectations of the parties. The transaction in question here is an artifice intended to thwart plaintiff's legitimate contractual expectation that it would have a right of first refusal before the partnership interest owned by CRCO could be transferred to someone outside the Cellular family of companies. As such, the Purchase Agreement violates the covenant of good faith and fair dealing that Oregon law implies in every contract. * * * [T]he doctrine of good faith is not a new material term created by the court, but rather a term implied by law in every contract to give effect to the legitimate expectations of the parties that were created by the language of their contract.

See also In re Schick, 235 B.R. 318, 327 (Bankr. S.D.N.Y. 1999) (applying good faith rather than fiduciary duty to general partner's withholding of consent to transfer of limited partnership interests).

Good faith is, then, basically a way of interpreting the contract to meet the expectations of the contracting parties. Although non-fiduciary contracting parties may act selfishly, their actions are limited by the contract as interpreted in accordance with good faith principles discussed in the above excerpt. Thus, for example, one may not be able to seize on contract language, as in *Oregon RSA,* or use one aspect of the contract, such as the power to dissolve the firm at will, to defeat another, such as the duty to share equally in partnership property. *See Page v. Page,* § 9.02(A), below.

Fiduciary and good faith duties may be difficult to distinguish in practice. As discussed in § 8.01, fiduciary duties, like the good faith obligation, may vary with the particular relationship. Even non-fiduciaries may have fiduciary-type obligations, as where "honesty in fact" involves a duty to disclose. Moreover, "good faith" in non-fiduciary contracts may approach fiduciary duties, as in distributorship or similar agreements that require one of the contracting parties to use "best efforts." *See* Dickerson, *From Behind the Looking Glass: Good Faith, Fiduciary Duty and Permitted Harm,* 22 FLA. STATE U. L. Rev. 955 (1995). Conversely, even partners may not be strict fiduciaries and may be able to act selfishly, as RUPA § 404(e)-(f) recognizes.

8.06 Waiver

The general issue of the contractual nature of fiduciary duties (*see* § 8.01) really comes to a head on the specific questions of whether and to what extent these duties can be waived. This is explored in the following cases and notes.

Labovitz v. Dolan (see p.182)

Exxon Corporation v. Burglin
4 F.3d 1294 (5th Cir. 1993)

JERRY E. SMITH, Circuit Judge:

Cliff Burglin, Charles Hamel, Thomas J. Miklautsch, Weldtest, Inc., and CFM Corp., former limited partners in a limited partnership in which Exxon Corporation ("Exxon") was the general partner, appeal summary judgment in an action by Exxon for declaratory judgment concerning its 1989 purchase of the defendants' interests. Finding no genuine issue of material fact regarding the limited partners' claim that Exxon breached its duty to disclose certain information vital to the evaluation of their interests, we affirm except as to the district court's award of full attorneys' fees.

I.

A.

Miklautsch acquired two North Slope oil and gas leases in the Point McIntyre Field of Alaska, ADL 34622 and 34623 (the "leases"), in 1967 for $4,787. He subsequently assigned partial interests in the leases to each of the defendants.

The defendants sold partial interests in the leases to various third parties over the years. In 1968, Miklautsch and Burglin sold partial interests to General American Oil Company of Texas, which assigned part of its interest to Humble Oil Company (now Exxon). In 1975, the defendants sold an undivided one-half interest to Gulf Oil Company ("Gulf") pending resolution of disputes over the parties' ownership rights. The lawsuits arising from these disputes resulted in the 1977 settlement (the "Settlement Agreement") at issue in this case.

One aspect of the Settlement Agreement was the creation of a limited partnership (the "Partnership Agreement") known as "Gulf MBH-Alaska, Ltd.," consisting of Gulf as general partner with 80% beneficial ownership and Miklautsch, Burglin, and Hamel as limited partners with ownerships of 14.4%, 3.6%, and 2%, respectively. Through 1978, Gulf drilled two wells on the leases, Point McIntyre Wells No. 1 and No. 2, neither of which proved productive.

Chevron Oil Company ("Chevron") acquired Gulf in 1985 and sold its interest as general partner to Exxon in 1987. Exxon offered to purchase the limited partners' interests at that time, but the offer was rejected. Nevertheless, the limited partners consented to Exxon's assuming the role of general partner, provided Exxon assumed Chevron's existing duties.[2]

In April 1988, after completing the third well on the field ("Well No. 3"), ARCO filed a "Statement of First Discovery of Oil and Gas in Commercial Quantities in a Geological Structure" (the "Statement"). Exxon confirmed that it was a participant in this find. The

---

[2]   Section 9.07 of the Partnership Agreement states that "[w]ithout the consent of all of the Limited Partners, the General Partner may not assign its managerial rights . . . ." In a December 29, 1987, letter to the Limited Partners, Exxon stated, "Exxon seeks your consent to this Assignment and substitution of General Partner in order to consolidate ownership of these Leases, which we feel is essential to facilitate exploratory drilling operations. Exxon is prepared to assume and agrees to fulfill Chevron's role as General Partner."

initial findings indicated Well No. 3 was capable of producing 1,500 barrels of oil per day. Subsequent testing in February and March 1989 indicated a productive capacity of 3,700 barrels per day. Exxon informed Burglin that it was "encouraged" by Well No. 3 but did not disclose the filing of the Statement, the well's productivity, or estimates of the reserves.

On July 18, 1988, Burglin indicated that he might sell his interest in the leases. On August 12, he requested that Exxon make an offer for his interest or permit him to solicit other offers, pursuant to section 9.02(b) of the Partnership Agreement. For the next seven months, Exxon and Burglin were unable to agree on a purchase price, and Burglin sought outside offers and consulted experts regarding the value of the leases.

On April 7, 1989, Exxon offered Burglin $1.21 million for his interest and proportional amounts for each of the other limited partners' interests. This offer stipulated that the parties entered the transaction "based on data available today without knowing the results" of Well No. 4 then in progress. The offer also granted the limited partners the option (the "Third-Party Option") to "select a mutually acceptable consultant to make an independent assessment of Exxon's offer," the cost of which would be shared by Burglin and Exxon.

Burglin, Miklautsch, and Hamel accepted Exxon's offer without obtaining an independent valuation of their interests or awaiting the results of Well No. 4, which Exxon completed in July 1989. The success of this well significantly increased the expected value of the field.

B.

The limited partners brought suit in Alaska, alleging, inter alia, misrepresentation and fraud and charging that Exxon had breached its fiduciary duty by failing to disclose information necessary for the valuation of their interests. Exxon then brought a declaratory action in Texas pursuant to the Texas Uniform Declaratory Judgments Act ("TUDJA"), TEX. CIV. PRAC. & REM. CODE §§ 37.001-.011 (West 1985), to determine its duties under the Partnership Agreement. The limited partners removed the case to federal court and, after extended discovery, Exxon moved for summary judgment. The district court granted summary judgment, holding that Exxon had no duty to disclose information it considered confidential. The court also awarded full attorneys' fees to Exxon.

II.

* * *

A.

Our first concern in this partnership dispute is to determine the applicable law. Where federal court jurisdiction is based solely upon diversity of citizenship, we must follow the forum state's choice of law rules. *Klaxon Co. v. Stentor Elec. Mfg. Co.*, 313 U.S. 487, 61 S.Ct. 1020, 85 L.Ed. 1477 (1941). Texas choice of law rules recognize the parties' autonomy to select the law to be applied to their contract. [citation omitted] Section 11.02 of the Partnership Agreement specifically provides that Alaska law governs all rights and liabilities between the parties. Pursuant to this clause, the district court correctly applied Alaska law to the substantive claims.

B.

Under Alaska law, a general partner stands in a fiduciary relationship with the limited partnership and thereby owes "a fiduciary duty . . . to disclose information concerning partnership affairs." [citation omitted] ALASKA STAT. § 32.05.150 ("Partners shall provide on demand true and full information of all things affecting the partnership to any partner . . . ."). The partnership agreement, however, will determine the extent of disclosure required between partners and whether a failure of disclosure constitutes fraud or breach of the agreement.

"Partner fiduciary duties are aspects of the 'standard form' of partnership. As with respect to the other rights and duties among the partners, the partners may alter the standard form fiduciary duties to suit their particular relationship." 2 Alan R. Bromberg & Larry E. Ribstein, BROMBERG AND RIBSTEIN ON PARTNERSHIP § 6.07(h), at 6:89 (1991); *id.* § 6.06, at 6:67 (arguing that "parties could at least circumscribe the right to information"); *id.* § 6.05(d), at 6:59 (partners can bargain over access to information).

Courts should allow parties to define the means of disclosure as the management of a partnership necessarily involves "the weighing and balancing of disparate considerations to which the court does not have access." *Betz v. Chena Hot Springs Group*, 657 P.2d 831, 835 (Alaska 1982). In *Betz*, a provision in a partnership agreement allowed a majority of the general partners to "involuntarily retire" a fellow general partner without dissolving the partnership if they found "that it is in the best interests of [the partnership] that a general partner be required to retire." *Id.* at 834 n.4. Instead of receiving a proportional share of the partnership, the involuntarily retired partner would receive compensation based upon an elaborate valuation formula stated in the partnership agreement. *Id.* at 836 n.5. Upholding the provision, the court declared that "[a]bsent bad faith, breach of a fiduciary duty, or acts contrary to public policy, [Alaska courts] will not interfere with the management decisions of the firm." *Id.* at 835.

The settlement between the limited partners and Gulf sought to prescribe the General Partner's duty to disclose information to the limited partners in a manner consistent with the effective development of the leases. Section 4.02(a) of the Partnership Agreement gives the general partner the sole authority to manage and control the business of the partnership. As an aspect of this control, section 4.02(b) restricts the limited partners' access to information, stating that "no Limited Partner shall have the right to any confidential information concerning the Leases."

Section 8.03 defines the limits on the general partner's duty to disclose information: "The General Partner shall not be obligated to furnish any information concerning surface structure, reserves or other information concerning the Leases which the General Partner believes would be in the best interest of the Partnership or the General Partner to be kept confidential." The second sentence of section 8.03, however, places some constraints on the General Partner's control over information: "However, at least annually, the General Partner will furnish to the Limited Partners all nonconfidential information relevant to the evaluation of the Partnership Interest of each Limited Partner, such as reserves, projected rate of production, etc."

The first sentence of section 8.03 protects the interests of the partnership and the general partner. This provision recognizes not only the partnership's inherent need for secrecy to protect itself from outside competition but also the general partner's individual need to protect its interests from the limited partners. This is apparent in light of section 4.03, granting the limited partners the right to "engage in or own an interest in other business ventures engaged in the same or similar business as the Partnership." Since this provision abrogates the fiduciary duty of loyalty by allowing partners to compete with their partnership, it is reasonable to expect some limitation on the fiduciary duty of disclosure.

The Partnership Agreement was negotiated by highly sophisticated parties who bargained for the terms of the agreement at arm's length with the assistance of counsel. The limited partners received substantial sums of money for the relinquishment of their right to full disclosure. Under Alaska law, a court must give effect to the terms of the Partnership Agreement that unambiguously limit the duty of disclosure owed by the general partner to the limited partners.

C.

Under Alaska law, a general partner stands as a fiduciary to the limited partners; the contractual abrogation of some fiduciary duties does not relieve the general partner from other basic fiduciary duties, such as the duty of good faith and fair dealing. [citation omitted] Exxon does not dispute this point; it merely asserts that there can be no violation of these implied fiduciary duties where a party's actions are authorized by the contract. [citation omitted] As the terms of the Partnership Agreement do not violate public policy and are not illegal or unconscionable, the only question is whether Exxon's actions were in accordance with the provisions of that agreement.

D.

Exxon's offer to buy out the limited partners was consistent with its contractual duty to provide nonconfidential information. Furthermore, the offer did not violate any implied duties, such as the duty of good faith and fair dealing.

1.

The terms of the Partnership Agreement do not obligate Exxon to disclose nonconfidential information. Section 4.02(b) of the Partnership Agreement provides,

> Subject to Section 5.03(b) [sic], no Limited Partner shall have the right to any confidential information concerning the status of the Leases.

Section 8.03 states,

> [T]he General Partner shall not be obligated to furnish any information concerning subsurface structure, reserves or other information concerning the Leases which the General Partner believes would be in the best interest of the Partnership or of the General Partner to be kept confidential. However, . . . the General Partner will furnish to the Limited Partners all nonconfidential information relevant to the evaluation to the Partnership Interest of each Limited Partner, such as reserves, projected rate of production, etc.

Only one possible meaning of these sections makes sense: The general partner must furnish the limited partners with information necessary to evaluate their interests, unless the general partner believes the information is confidential.[6]

---

[6] One could read the list of items following the words "such as" as a list of nonconfidential items relevant to the evaluation to the partnership interest. Thus, all items on the list would be defined as nonconfidential. But this interpretation contradicts the first sentence of § 8.03, listing these items as examples of confidential information. The items on the list following "such as" are examples of relevant information. Thus, each item of information, although relevant, was subject to the restriction of confidentiality: Only nonconfidential relevant information will be supplied.

The general partner's belief is subject to the "reasonable discretion" requirement of section 3.02(a): For purposes of this Agreement, the determination of what is in the best interest of the Partnership shall be made by the General Partner in the exercise of its reasonable discretion and in light of its fiduciary capacity. Thus, only in good faith may the general partner exercise its discretion to determine the best interests of the partnership. Under this interpretation, Exxon had no duty to disclose, prior to the offer, the information regarding Well No. 4.

The limited partners sought to introduce extrinsic evidence concerning the meaning of these provisions of the Partnership Agreement. The extrinsic evidence is irrelevant, though, since the Partnership Agreement allows Exxon to define what information is confidential, subject only to a reasonable discretion standard. What the parties thought the term "confidential" meant is not relevant, as the contract allows Exxon to decide what information is in its best interest to keep confidential. Although this provision gives Exxon tremendous power, it is not inconsistent with its fiduciary responsibilities as the general partner, and a court must give effect to contract terms that unambiguously define the parties' rights under the contract.

Thus, Exxon did not breach the Partnership Agreement in its purchase of the limited partners' interests. The terms of the agreement allow Exxon to determine the confidentiality of information, and Exxon was under no duty to disclose nonconfidential information.

2.

The limited partners claim that Exxon's offer violated the implied duties of good faith and fair dealing, honesty, and the duty to pay a fair price. We disagree. Exxon's offer to purchase the limited partners' interests was consistent with its implied fiduciary duties.

The Third-Party Option gave the limited partners the choice to await the results of Well No. 4 or to have an independent third-party consultant analyze Exxon's offer. Exxon described the Third-Party Option as a "no-lose" proposition for the limited partners. Exxon agreed to pay the purchase price by April 15, as agreed, but the consultant would have until June 30 to analyze the offer. If the consultant found the offer to be inadequate, the limited partners had the right, but not the obligation, to return the purchase price and rescind the sale.

The limited partners claim that the "no-lose" proposition was deceptive and unfair. The analysis of Exxon's offer involved the release of the confidential information concerning Well No. 3 and No. 4 and therefore was subject to ARCO's approval. Under the terms of the Third-Party Option, after the limited partners agreed to have a third-party consultant evaluate the lease interests, Exxon would be obligated to seek, in good faith, ARCO's approval of the release of the confidential information.

If ARCO would not agree to release confidential information, however, the limited partners thereby would have stipulated that the purchase price was fair. In other words, if the limited partners exercised the option, they assumed the risk that ARCO would not agree to release the information and that the purchase price, accordingly, would be declared fair without a third party's evaluation.

The Third-Party Option presented the limited partners with four choices: They could exercise the option and hope that ARCO agreed to release the data; they could wait until the results of Well No. 4 were available; they could accept the offer and waive their right to a third-party evaluation or the results of Well No. 4; or they could reject the offer. The fact that the limited partners were financially inclined to accept the offer without the delay of the evaluation or of awaiting the results of Well No. 4 is irrelevant. Such a motivation for accepting the offer does not amount to coercion, unfair dealing, or bad faith by Exxon.

The limited partners were free to reject the offer. Likewise, the fact that the Third-Party Option may have subjected the limited partners to an unfavorable stipulation, had ARCO refused to reveal the confidential information, does not make the offer unfair. They still were free to reject the offer or await the results of Well No. 4. Taking advantage of a party's inclination to accept an offer does not transform an unfavorable offer into an unfair one.

Also, the standard of conduct for a general partner is somewhat lower when acting in an adversarial relationship with the limited partners. In regard to the buyout offer, Exxon was not acting on behalf of the partnership, representing both its and the limited partners' interests. If it were, the duty of good faith and fair dealing necessarily would be high, to avoid the problem of a general partner's self-dealing.

In this case, however, Exxon was buying out the limited partners' interests. It is logical to expect that the relationship would be somewhat adversarial. The limited partners must have realized that Exxon would try to secure the best deal it could and that this goal was adverse to their interests.

The limited partners further contend that Exxon's offer and subsequent purchase of their interests violated the fiduciary duty to pay a fair price. This argument is also without merit. The duty to pay a fair price was abrogated specifically by section 9.02(b) of the Partnership Agreement, which provides, "[I]f the General Partner is interested in acquiring [the] interest, both shall negotiate in good faith in an attempt to arrive at mutually agreeable terms of purchase." Thus, Exxon was required only to bargain in good faith; when parties negotiate in good faith and reach a mutually agreeable purchase price, the result of such a transaction cannot be upset by appeal to the concept of an objectively "fair" price.

If the price was not fair, the limited partners need not have accepted the offer. Exxon did not violate its obligation to negotiate in good faith by allegedly withholding valuable information that it was under no duty to disclose.

Thus, the offer was in conformance with the terms of the agreement. No provision of the agreement was violated by Exxon in its dealings with the limited partners. Moreover, Exxon breached no implied duty in its purchase of the limited partners' interests.

We express no opinion, however, on the limited partners' claims of affirmative misrepresentation and fraud, pending in their Alaska lawsuit. No part of this opinion should be read as sanctioning fraudulent conduct or misrepresentation. We read the district court's final judgment as reserving these issues. Summary judgment therefore is affirmed, preserving the issues of misrepresentation and fraud. * * *

Notes and Questions

1. **Waiving fiduciary duties: policy considerations.** *Labovitz* appears to say that fiduciary duties may not be wholly waived. Contrast the *Exxon* case on this issue. RUPA § 103(b) provides for some specific limitations on enforceability of waiver. The Official Comment to this section cites *Labovitz* (*see* Note 3, below). The drafting questions below in Notes 6-9 raise specific issues concerning the interpretation of these lim-

itations. Are restrictions on waiver appropriate? In most partnership cases, the fiduciary duty waiver has been included in a document that was actually signed, if not also negotiated, by the partner or other owner. This contrasts with the public corporation setting, in which any contract is the seemingly artificial one that is created when a shareholder buys shares in the anonymous market. (Even in this situation, there are strong arguments for recognizing and enforcing the contract. *See* Butler & Ribstein, *Opting out of Fiduciary Duties: A Response to the Anti-Contractarians,* 65 WASH. L. REV. 1 (1990)). There are strong arguments and significant case law support for enforcing waivers in general partnerships. *See* Ribstein, *Fiduciary Duty Contracts In Unincorporated Firms,* 54 WASH. & LEE L. REV. 537 (1997). For policy and legal arguments on the other side, *see* Dickerson, *From Behind the Looking Glass: Good Faith, Fiduciary Duty and Permitted Harm,* 22 FLA. STATE U. L. REV. 955 (1995); Dickerson, *Is it Appropriate to Appropriate Corporate Concepts: Fiduciary Duties and the Revised Uniform Partnership Act,* 64 U. COLO. L. REV. 111 (1993); Vestal, *Advancing the Search for Compromise: A Response to Professor Hynes,* 58 LAW & CONTEMP. PROB. 55 (Spring 1995); Vestal, *The Disclosure Obligations of Partners Inter Se Under the Revised Uniform Partnership Act of 1994: Is the Contractarian Revolution Failing?,* 36 WM. & MARY L. REV. 1559 (1995); Vestal, *Fundamental Contractarian Error in the Revised Uniform Partnership Act of 1992,* 73 B.U. L. REV. 523 (1993); Donald J. Weidner, *RUPA and Fiduciary Duty: The Texture of Relationship,* 58 LAW & CONTEMP. PROB. 81 (Spring 1995). Evaluate the following arguments against permitting waiver, and some possible responses to these arguments:

(a) *Partners cannot foresee the risks of conduct they would be permitting by a waiver.* However, partners also know that they cannot foresee these risks, and can take this knowledge into account in negotiating agreements. Moreover, this argument could apply to virtually any term in a partnership agreement.

(b) *Partners suffer from judgment errors that would cause them to treat the risks of fiduciary duty waivers too lightly. See* Eisenberg, *The Limits of Cognition and the Limits of Contract,* 47 STANFORD L. REV. 211 (1995). Once again, however, this could apply to many terms in partnership agreements, including rules on management, compensation and exit. Perhaps the argument here is that clearly irrational contracts should not be enforced. But there is already a legal rule of unconscionability to deal with such contracts. Should any fiduciary duty waiver be deemed to be irrational and, therefore, unconscionable?

(c) *In a typical limited partnership syndication, the interests may be marketed to unsophisticated investors without any real bargaining.* But even if this is a problem, it does not justify applying the same no-waiver rule in one-on-one deals. Note, also, that the securities laws provide some protection in this situation. *See* § 11.12.

(d) *Partners are unable or unwilling to bargain carefully even regarding risks they are aware of.* For example, they may be worried about "queering the deal." Anti-contractarians have noted bargainers' inclination to trust each other rather than risking aggressive negotiations that may "queer" the deal. *See* Klein & Coffee, BUSINESS ORGANIZATION AND FINANCE, 64-66 (6th ed., 1996). Or one attorney may represent all of the parties. But this suggests only that partners may too readily accept *default* rules—which include fiduciary duties.

(e) *Fiduciary duties are necessary to protect a helpless partner from managing partners who hold decision-making power. See* Dickerson, *supra*; Frankel, *Fiduciary Law,* 71 CALIF. L. REV. 795 (1983). But this is an argument for *default* fiduciary duties once the relationship is created, and not necessarily for protecting one who freely decides to delegate power to another implicitly from the terms of the delegation itself.

(f) *Enforcing waivers permits partners to "unfairly," "unjustly" or "unethically" harm their co-partners.* But is the "unfairness" separate from the problems discussed above? If so, what is it? Society might be a better place if everyone were "good," but we do not necessarily have a legal duty to be good because the costs of such duties sometimes outweigh the benefits.

Even if the above arguments against waivers are sound, there are some affirmative reasons for enforcing waivers.

(a) *Contracting is inevitable, and parties barred in one way will seek another.* For example, a fiduciary who is prevented from waiving fiduciary duties could use her supposedly superior bargaining power to seek a rise in the price. *See* Easterbrook & Fischel, *Contract and Fiduciary Duty,* 36 J. LAW & ECON. 425 (1993). Or the "fiduciary" could contract for the application of a permissive state law (*see* Note 5, below), or contract as an outsider rather than a partner. Keep in mind, however, that the existence of such contracting alternatives does not make the enforceability of fiduciary duty waivers a trivial issue, since there remains the question of how difficult the law should make it for the parties to avoid fiduciary duties.

(b) *There may be significant benefits from waiving fiduciary duties.* The arguments against waiver consider only the potential harm from "bad" waivers. But fiduciary duty waivers may save the parties from the costs of "bad" duties in some cases. Default fiduciary duties may be unnecessary given other constraints on the fiduciary's conduct, including monitoring by other partners and partners' ability to exit the partnership or remove the partner. Because of these other constraints, it may not be worth it to the partners to pay the fiduciary for her undivided fealty to the partnership, as by giving up all outside opportunities. Litigation to enforce fiduciary duties may be costly and disruptive, and courts can make mistakes. Thus, a partner might rationally curtail legitimate activities more than the duty literally requires in order to avoid the chance of a costly and an erroneous judgment. More generally, the reason for enforcing a fiduciary duty waiver, like any other contract, is that, even if the contract did not seem to work out in the particular case, there are benefits to letting the parties allocate risks and establish the rules for their relationship at the beginning. If the courts undo these waivers, this suggests that they can do a better job in setting these rules than the parties can, so that the parties should not try. Yet as discussed in Notes 2-8 on p. 168-70, fiduciary duties are highly contextual because they fill gaps in particular, highly differentiated transactions. Moreover, the courts may not have very good information as to what rule would best suit the parties' needs. The courts therefore may not often be able to do a better job than the parties and should let their waivers stand. Indeed, the same considerations apply even if fiduciary duty waivers would be viewed as "unconscionable." *See* Craswell, *Property Rules And Liability Rules In Unconscionability and Related Doctrines,* 60 U. Chi. L. Rev. 1 (1993).

2. **Defining the scope of fiduciary duties.** The partnership agreement can steer a middle course short of waiver of fiduciary duties by defining the actions that constitute breach of fiduciary duties. This is permitted to some extent even by RUPA § 103(b). For example, in *Singer v. Scher,* 761 F. Supp. 145 (D.D.C. 1991), law partners orally agreed that investment opportunities, including stock options, the partners received from clients were not to be shared with the other partners. The court criticized the firm for its oral agreement, saying that "[t]he uncertainties of contemporary legal practice make it imperative for partners to set forth their agreements in writing." 761 F.Supp. at 150.

3. **Interpreting waivers.** Interpretation, rather than enforcement, may be the most important issue concerning fiduciary duty waivers. Consider *Labovitz*, § 8.03. The comment to RUPA § 103 cites *Labovitz* as follows:

> * * * [A] very broad provision in a partnership agreement in effect negating any duty of loyalty, such as a provision giving a managing partner complete discretion to manage the business with no liability except for acts and omissions that constitute willful misconduct, will not likely be enforced. *See, e.g., Labovitz v. Dolan,* 189 Ill. App. 3d 403, 136 Ill. Dec. 780, 545 N.E.2d 304 (1989).

But is *Labovitz* a case in which a fiduciary duty waiver was not enforced, or instead one in which the court reasonably held that the grant of "sole discretion" to a managing partner came with default fiduciary duties attached unless these were waived? *Compare Adler v. William Blair & Co.,* 245 Ill. App. 3d 57, 613 N.E.2d 1264, *reconsidered on other grounds,* 153 Ill. 2d 534, 180 Ill. Dec. 300, 607 N.E.2d 194 (1993) (holding that the general partner could invest in property consistent with disclosures in the partnership agreement, that the purpose of the partnership was to invest for capital appreciation and not primarily for tax losses, that the tax laws might be changed, and that the general partners may have conflicts of interest. The court distinguished *Labovitz* as a squeezeout case).

For a case based squarely on interpretation of the scope of the waiver, *see BT-I v. Equitable Life Assurance Society of the United States*, 75 Cal. App. 4th 1406, 76 Cal. App. 4th 684E, 89 Cal. Rptr. 2d 811, 817-18 (1999). The court held that a general partner in a limited partnership could not buy and foreclose on a loan on the partnership's sole asset, an office building, even after giving the partnership an opportunity to participate in the purchase, despite provisions in the agreement that the general partner did not have to act to prevent a lender's foreclosure, the general partner had the right "to compete, directly or indirectly, with the business of the Partnership," and that the limited partners' had no right to vote on conflict transactions. The court said: "In view of the rule against waiving fundamental fiduciary duties, we cannot stretch these general provisions to include giving Equitable a free hand to act for its own self-interest." But the court enforced a provision in the agreement that the partner did not have to take affirmative action to protect the partnership property from foreclosure, observing that "[i]t is one thing simply to do nothing and suffer the consequences equally with all other partners. It is another to step out of the role of partner and into that of an aggressive (and apparently greedy) lender in the marketplace."

4. **The no-duty agreement.** In light of Notes 2 and 3, the only real issue regarding fiduciary duty waivers may be whether the partners can wholly waive fiduciary duties. As a practical matter, this question simply has not arisen. If it were raised, there may be an interpretation issue as to whether the parties really meant what they seemed to say. To be sure, the parties might want a fiduciary *relationship* without the costly judicial contests over *legal duties*? On the other hand, one must wonder why the parties contracted for a fiduciary relationship if they did not want any of the duties that go with it.

5. **Choice of law and fiduciary duty waiver.** As discussed in Note 1, the parties may, in effect, opt out of fiduciary duties by choosing to be bound by the law of a state, such as Delaware, which has strong law enforcing fiduciary duties. The Delaware Limited Partnership Act, DEL. CODE, tit. 6, § 17-1101 provides "[t]o the extent that . . . a partner has duties (including fiduciary duties) and liabilities relating thereto to a limited partnership or to another partner, (1) any such partner acting under a partnership agreement shall not be liable to the limited partnership or to any such other partner for the partner's good faith reliance on the provisions of such partnership agreement, and (2) the partner's duties and liabilities may be expanded or restricted by provisions in a partnership agreement." Note, however, that if the partnership lacks significant contacts with Delaware or some other chosen state and the forum state has a strong policy against enforcing fiduciary duty waivers, the forum court may not enforce the chosen law. *See* § 3.04.

6. **Drafting issues: Disclosure.** As *Exxon* illustrates, the parties can define their disclosure obligations in the partnership agreement. What provisions of the *Exxon* agreement reinforced the court's conclusion that the basic disclosure duty had been waived? Consider the various elements of the disclosure duty that should be covered in

the agreement, and the enforceability and interpretation of these provisions, particularly under RUPA § 103(b)(2).

(a) What books and records must be kept? *See* BROMBERG & RIBSTEIN ON PARTNERSHIP, § 6.05(b).

(b) What access do partners have to the books and records? *See id.* § 6.05(c). Note that restrictions on access may be interpreted strictly, since the restrictions may be a significant limitation on the partners' ability to participate in management. *See id.* § 6.05(d).

(c) Should the agreement provide that no additional disclosure obligations shall be deemed to be imposed by any other duties, such as the duty of good faith? What would be the effect of such a provision under RUPA § 103(b)?

(d) How, if at all, should the default duty to disclose other information on demand be restricted in the agreement?

(e) To what extent should the managers or other partners have a general duty to disclose information even if it is not demanded—for example, through annual reports?

7. **Drafting issues: Duty of loyalty.** Consider what the agreement should say about the duty of loyalty, and the issues that might arise concerning enforceability under the case law and RUPA § 103(b)(3).

(a) In light of the discussion in the above Notes and RUPA § 103(b)(3), parties that want to broadly shed fiduciary duties might be better advised to negate as precisely as possible the duties they are concerned about. The parties might waive only duties regarding business opportunities and competing opportunities, or define the particular types of business opportunities and competition that the partners may, or may not, engage in. For example, an agreement to develop and operate a shopping center might permit the partners to engage broadly in other opportunities except particular types of shopping centers or shopping centers that include one of the partnership's tenants. The agreement might also state that the list of permitted activities either is, or is not, intended to be exclusive. The parties' task is to avoid a waiver that is too broad or "manifestly unreasonable" under RUPA § 103(b)(3), while also ensuring that the partners are not exposed to duties they do not want.

(b) Would it help if the agreement adds that the parties agree that the waiver is reasonable? Or to give the partners' reason for the waiver, such as to maximize the partners' incentives to search for partnership opportunities? What other kinds of reasons might help persuade a court to enforce the waiver, or provide guidance as to interpretation?

(c) Instead of attempting to specify the activities partners may engage in, the agreement might provide for partner authorization pursuant to RUPA §

103(b)(3)(ii). The agreement could let the partners engage in any business they want if the other partners, or a majority or supermajority of them, do not object within a certain amount of time of being notified of the partner's intention, or waive objections at a meeting after notice. What kinds of problems might such provisions cause? What considerations might bear on whether to require a meeting or to permit waiver by silence? Is such a waiver likely to be enforced under RUPA § 103(b)(3)(ii).

(d) Partners in a UPA partnership may want to include the RUPA § 404(e) type of language that a partner does not violate fiduciary duties merely by acting in her own interest. But it is not clear what this language means. For example, it probably should not apply to a managing partner who does have default fiduciary duties unless the agreement negates these duties. The parties could eliminate this ambiguity by defining what sort of selfishness is permitted—for example, in voting as a partner, acting as a lender, exercising rights under a loan agreement or buying property at a foreclosure. On the other hand, as with the clauses discussed in (b), a narrow provision may leave partners with duties they do not want. Adding a clause that the listed acts of selfishness are not exclusive helps solve this problem while at the same time adding interpretation and enforceability questions.

(e) In order to try to clarify the meaning of a grant of discretion to a managing partner, the agreement could add that the partner has full power to resolve any conflicts between her own and the partnership's interests in any way she sees fit. Would this be enough to eliminate the possibility of fiduciary duty liability for self dealing or other abuse of discretion?

8. **Drafting issues: Duty of care.** Consider what the agreement might say about the duty of care.

(a) In a manager-managed partnership, the partners might tighten the duty of care, as by requiring the manager to conform to industry standards of management.

(b) The agreement could define the gross negligence standard, as by explicitly permitting partners to rely on advice or reports of others as in many LLC and corporation statutes.

(c) The parties might attempt to reduce the partners' standard of care below the gross negligence level. When might this "unreasonably reduce" the duty of care under RUPA § 103(b)(4)? Although it might seem that partners would never want to contract for recklessness, they may want to eliminate the potential for litigation over what this involves. For example, if "recklessly" is defined to include self-interested conduct, liability under this standard might be inconsistent with a waiver of a duty not to self-deal.

(d) Rather than leaving managers' duty to a vague duty of care, the agreement could specify that the managers owe a particular time commitment to the partnership—full- or part-time, depending on the circumstances. Note that this provision might also impact the partners' duty of loyalty, as by expanding or contracting the types of opportunities that the partner can take.

9. **Drafting issues: Good faith.** As discussed in § 8.05, the good faith obligation operates in the background of every contract, and thus may exist even after fiduciary duties of care and loyalty are waived. *See* DeMott, *Fiduciary Preludes: Likely Issues for LLCs,* 66 U. COLO. L. REV. 1043 (1995). Indeed, "good faith" in the context of a managing partner's conduct may be closely equivalent to a fiduciary duty. Accordingly, the partners might want to limit good faith duties as well, particularly if RUPA § 404(d) applies. For example, the partners might provide that certain activities do not violate the duty, such as exercising a partner's power to dissolve the firm or expel a partner. Or they might define the duty as non-fiduciary and consisting solely of "honesty in fact" and conformity with commercial standards of fair dealing. How are such provisions likely to be interpreted? Would they be enforceable under RUPA § 103(b)(5)?

Drafting Problems

Redraft the partnership agreement in *Labovitz* to increase the likelihood that the general partner's discretion regarding distribution and withholding of funds would be upheld. How might it affect your answer if the Revised Uniform Partnership Act rather than the UPA applies?

8.07 Partners' Remedies: Accounting Actions

The remedy for breach of fiduciary duty is ordinarily an "accounting" under UPA § 22. This differs from a corporate-type derivative suit in that the remedy is technically one sought by individual partners rather than a cause of action on behalf of the partnership entity. As discussed in the following case, an accounting is not a simple review of finances by an auditor, but rather a type of judicial proceeding in which all matters pending between the partners are adjudicated. *See, generally,* II BROMBERG & RIBSTEIN ON PARTNERSHIP, § 6.08. This may involve determinations of what the partnership owns and owes and how to allocate profits and losses among the partners. The determinations must take into account, among other things, partnership claims for indemnification against partners, partners' claims for indemnification against the partnership, and the partnership's claims against individual partners for contribution to partnership losses. Thus, a partner who claims to be owed for services rendered to the partnership, or that a manager owes the partnership for breach of fiduciary duty, may end up a debtor rather than a creditor once claims for indemnification and contribution are taken into account. The traditional rule, which is not explicit in UPA § 22, is that an accounting is the partners' *exclusive* remedy, meaning that they cannot bring an individual action against the partnership or their co-partners apart from an overall wrap-up of all disputes. As indicated by the following case and notes, this rule is under attack. It has been abolished in RUPA § 405.

Sertich v. Moorman
162 Ariz. 407, 783 P.2d 1199 (1989)

GORDON, Chief Justice.

Nancy J. Sertich and C. William Sundblad (plaintiffs) seek review of a court of appeals' decision affirming summary judgment against them. The court of appeals agreed that this action could not proceed without an accounting and that plaintiffs lacked standing to seek an accounting. *Sertich et al. v. Moorman et al.*, 159 Ariz. 311, 767 P.2d 34 (Ariz. Ct. App. 1988). * * * We now vacate the court of appeals opinion, reverse the trial court's grant of summary judgment and remand for further proceedings consistent with this opinion.

Facts and Procedural History

One Civic Center Plaza Ltd. Partnership (hereinafter "CCP") was formed in 1983 to develop a commercial building in Scottsdale, Arizona. Gilbert Wilson, Steve Moorman and Steven Bunch were general partners. The sole limited partner was One Civic Center Associates, another limited partnership in which defendant Brent Osborn was general partner.

In 1984, Steven Bunch assigned to plaintiffs his right to repayment of a loan he made to CCP while retaining his partnership interest. In 1985, Moorman, Wilson and CCP filed a separate action to force Bunch to execute a certificate of cancellation on the limited partnership. The court found that CCP had been dissolved and that winding up had begun. It then ordered Bunch to sign and execute the certificate of cancellation, which became effective March 19, 1985.

Prior to the effective date of CCP's dissolution, plaintiffs filed a complaint against CCP, Moorman, Wilson, Osborn, and their respective spouses, seeking payment of the debt owed by CCP to Bunch. The parties do not dispute that as of July 31, 1984, CCP was indebted to Bunch in the sum of $55,535.17. Sundblad claimed an assignment in the amount of $20,000 and Sertich claimed an assignment in the amount of $27,500. Defendants assert, however, that CCP set off its debt to Bunch against the claims of Bunch's creditors, including general partners Wilson and Moorman, before plaintiffs filed their complaint. The dissolution and winding up were accomplished without an accounting among the partners.

The trial court granted defendants' motion for summary judgment and dismissed the action for failure to state a claim upon which relief could be granted. It found that the assignee-plaintiffs stood in no better position than the assignor-partner and that, under the general accounting rule, the assignor-partner could not sue on the debt without first seeking an accounting from CCP. In addition, the trial court found that plaintiffs lacked standing to seek an accounting because they were not assignees of a partnership interest.

Plaintiffs appealed from the summary judgment and the court of appeals affirmed. Because the accounting rule had been adopted as the law of this jurisdiction, the court of appeals did not consider plaintiffs' policy arguments in support of abolishing the rule.

Moreover, the court held that the facts of this case did not invoke any of the recognized exceptions to the accounting rule and that the plaintiffs lacked standing to sue for an accounting.

We accepted review to examine the continuing validity and applicability of the accounting rule in Arizona. A review of the historical origins of the rule and the evolution of our procedures leads us to conclude that the accounting rule should be abolished in Arizona.

Historical Origin of the Accounting Rule

One common statement of the general accounting rule is that "[i]n the absence of statutory authority, partners ordinarily may not maintain actions at law among themselves, as opposed to equitable actions, where the subject of the action relates to partnership transactions, unless there is a prior accounting or settlement of the partnership affairs." [citation omitted] The rule establishes a condition precedent to a partner's right to maintain an action at law concerning partnership matters. A formal accounting is more than a presentation of financial statements; it is a comprehensive investigation of transactions between the various partners and an adjudication of their relative rights. A. Bromberg, CRANE AND BROMBERG ON PARTNERSHIP § 72, at 410 (1968).

The accounting rule affects the remedy available, not the right. Its origins lie in the mutual fiduciary obligations of the partners. *Id.* The rule, rooted in our early jurisprudence, was transported to the United States from England, where separate courts existed for equity and law.

Early English common law recognized the remedy known as an "action in account." This action was established at a time when the courts of law did not recognize a simple contract action and, initially, it merely compelled a bailiff to account for his stewardship. *See generally*, D. Dobbs, REMEDIES § 4.3 at 252-53 (1973). Later, courts extended the action to simple debt transactions between partners because of the analogous fiduciary relationship. With the development of assumpsit at law and the emergence of equitable accounting action, however, the action fell into disuse. *Id.*

Many claims for money damages on simple contracts became actionable following the development of assumpsit at law. Relief was not available at law for complex transactions, however, because a jury could not be expected to work out the details of complex accounts. Claims involving complex transactions between partners, therefore, required equity's intervention and thus the action for an accounting in equity emerged. *Id.* This action evolved, in part, because of the unique availability of the masters of the Chancery Court who served as auditors and reported complex accountings to the court. Moreover, the Chancellor had the power to compel the actual parties' testimony, a discovery device forbidden the judge at law. Finally, parties standing in fiduciary relationship to each other could challenge a breach of that relationship only in a court of equity. For complex transactions between partners, therefore, the only remedy available was in equity. *Id.*

In the United States, the rationale underlying the rule became further defined as it applied to remedies between partners during the continuance of the partnership. Our early jurisprudence did not recognize a partnership as a separate legal entity and, consequently, all proceedings to enforce partnership rights or partnership obligations were cognizable only against the partners individually. J. Story, COMMENTARIES ON THE LAW OF PARTNERSHIP (1841) (reprinted in HISTORICAL WRITINGS IN LAW AND JURISPRUDENCE 322-25 (1980)).

No partner could sue another for moneys paid or liabilities incurred on behalf of the partnership for several reasons. Under the principles of common law pleading, a party could not be both plaintiff and defendant in the same suit. *Id.* If partners sued copartners, they technically would be suing themselves. In addition, early courts were concerned that until all of the partnership concerns were ascertained and adjusted, it was impossible to determine whether a particular partner was a debtor or creditor of the firm. A settlement of the partnership concerns was unavailable at law, in part, because of the "serious inconvenience" of sorting out the potential cross claims. Also, an action at law to determine each partner's share of the final balance effectively changed the original contract from a joint contract between all partners to a several contract. J. Story, *supra*, at 322-35.

Even in equity, an accounting ordinarily was not enforced except upon dissolution of the partnership. This practice reflected equity's reluctance to use its injunctive powers to enforce the positive covenants between partners. *Id.* at 326-27. Thus, specific performance of the partnership contract was not an available remedy due to the potential for ongoing court involvement in the continuing partnership. A. Bromberg, *supra*, § 69. If, however, the negative covenants were breached and the fiduciary relationship jeopardized, equity would consider the relationship severed and order a partnership accounting and dissolution. J. Story, *supra*, at 328-332.

Despite the merger of law and equity in most jurisdictions, the early commentators noted that abolishing the distinctions between law and equity did not create a new cause of action at law. A suit could not be maintained "unless the case made by the pleadings and proof is such as would formerly have called for the interposition of a court of equity." [citation omitted]

Over the years, this judicially created rule of convenience and restriction on the forum available to enforce the remedies became a bar to a cause of action. In some instances, the rule was interpreted to stand for the broad proposition that no suit could be maintained between partners and partnerships. [citation omitted] In others, the rule was applied to reach absurd results. *See, e.g., State v. Quinn*, 245 Iowa 846, 64 N.W.2d 323 (1954) (partner could not be charged with obtaining money by false pretenses because an accounting is necessary to determine whether the taking was wrongful).

Some commentators urged that the rule, properly applied, merely prohibited a partner from suing a partnership, or a partnership suing a partner, at law on a joint right or obligation without an accounting. *See, e.g.*, A. Bromberg, LAW OF PARTNERSHIP § 70 (1968). Thus, if the partnership obligation was joint and several, the partner could maintain an action at law against the copartners. *Id.* Another view was that the accounting requirement was the exception, not the rule. In other words, the general rule was that one partner may sue another at law, but if a claim arises out of a complex, unliquidated partnership transaction, the action must be brought in equity where the complex transaction could be liquidated.
* * *

Nevertheless, most courts applied the rule pro forma to hold that an accounting or settlement of partnership affairs was a prerequisite or condition precedent to a right of action at law among partners with regard to partnership affairs. [citation omitted] Courts requiring an accounting gave various justifications, including: (1) the rule avoided premature and piecemeal judgments among partners; (2) a partner did not become a debtor or creditor of the copartner but of the firm in partnership transactions and, until a final settlement, no debt was due from one partner to another; (3) a party could not be both plaintiff and defendant; (4) one partner did not own or have a right to any specific portion of the partnership property; and (5) the complicated accounting required to establish the rights of partnership parties was not a proper subject for jury consideration and was better left to a court of equity. [citation omitted]

Development of the Rule in Arizona

In Arizona, this Court first applied the accounting rule in an action between partners, where one alleged the other had converted partnership property. * * *

Subsequent decisions of this Court and our court of appeals found exceptions to the general rule. [citations omitted]

In fact, the only circumstances to which our courts have applied the rule somewhat consistently to bar a cause of action involved claims for conversion or for a share of partnership assets. [citations omitted]

Continuing Validity of the Accounting Rule in Arizona

Plaintiffs argue that the accounting rule has outlived its usefulness in Arizona and, because of changed conditions, its continued enforcement is illogical, impractical, or inequitable. To the extent that the rule has created a condition precedent to maintaining a cause of action at law between partners or a partner and the partnership, we agree. When the original justifications for the rule are reviewed in light of our rules of procedure as they have evolved and the substantive provisions of the Arizona Uniform Partnership Act, we believe that changed conditions render the substantive and procedural bases for the rule obsolete.

The merger of law and equity in our courts of general jurisdiction eliminates the procedural problems associated with the accounting rule. Today, trial courts in Arizona enjoy all of the powers formerly vested in the separate courts and the trial judge sits as both chancellor in equity and judge at law. The merger of law and equity eliminates the distinction upon which the rationale that a party cannot be both plaintiff and defendant was based. [citation omitted] Moreover, our liberal pleading rules, particularly Rule 18 "Joinder of Claims and Remedies," alleviate the procedural problems associated with the distinct remedies available under law and equity as well as the concern for avoiding premature and piecemeal judgments between parties. Today, the joinder rule allows a party to bring any and all claims and request any and all remedies in one action in our courts of general jurisdiction. [citation omitted]

Our rules of procedure also remedy the concern that a jury cannot be expected to sort out complex partnership transactions and that such matters are best left to the court sitting in equity. Rules 38(b), 39(a)(1) and 53, Ariz. R. Civ. P. 16 A.R.S., preserve equitable procedures, adapt them to modern practice, and allow the court to appoint a master to sort out complex transactions if needed.

The legislature's enactment of the Arizona Uniform Partnership Act changed the common law and eliminated the substantive bases for the general accounting rule. By statute, the legislature declared that the partners' liability for tortious conduct, breach of fiduciary duty, and all other debts and obligations of the partnership is joint and several. A.R.S. § 29-215. The "oneness" concern, originally creating a substantive barrier to a cause of action at law because equity provided the only remedy for a breach of the fiduciary relationship at law, was eliminated.

The remaining justifications are addressed adequately by A.R.S. §§ 29-221 and 29-222. Every partner is accountable to the partnership as a fiduciary and retains an inherent partnership right to a formal accounting as to partnership affairs under certain circumstances. Thus, if the transactions between partners are such that any debts owed cannot be determined without an accounting, or if they involve apportioning partnership property, any partner can demand a formal accounting under the circumstances described in A.R.S. § 29-222. By enacting the Arizona Uniform Partnership Act, the legislature eliminated the substantive principle differentiating actions of an equitable nature and imposing a barrier in the common law yet protected and provided for the right to maintain the action for an equitable accounting in appropriate circumstances.

This case illustrates that continued enforcement of the accounting rule is indeed illogical, impractical, and inequitable. The partnership was dissolved, the affairs wound up, and a certificate of cancellation executed. The alleged debt is of an ascertainable amount, evidenced by two promissory notes, and does not involve a partnership share. Defendants basically assert that they set off any debt to the original obligee. Due solely to the enforcement of the accounting rule, plaintiffs were barred from establishing that a debt was owed. However, the only complexity involved here is a determination of the amount of set-off. Plaintiffs should be free to assert their claim and prove a debt is owed and defendant may prove set-off in accordance with Ariz. R. Civ. P. 13(a), 16 A.R.S. The court may appoint a master if it determines that an accounting is necessary to sort out the evidentiary claims. Ariz. R. Civ. P. 53, 16 A.R.S.

As Judge Jacobson observed in his special concurrence in *Catron v. Watson*, "[t]he substance of the rule having been removed in Arizona, we should no longer be required to do worship to the empty form." 12 Ariz.App. 132, 136, 468 P.2d 399, 403 (1970). Given modern pleading rules, all legal and equitable claims may be joined in the same action. In addition, requiring a partner to bring an action for a formal accounting before suing to enforce a debt owed runs counter to the purposes of our rules of procedure. Under the appropriate circumstances, a formal accounting may be required to establish whether, in fact, a debt is owed, but this should be viewed as an evidentiary issue rather than an impairment of a right to maintain a cause of action in the first instance.

We find that the reasons for the accounting rule no longer apply in Arizona and, therefore, hold that the general accounting requirement as a condition precedent to an action at law between partners or a partner and the partnership is abolished.

Conclusion

Having abolished the accounting rule in Arizona, we turn to the disposition of this case. The trial court dismissed plaintiffs' suit on summary judgment because no accounting had taken place. As assignees of a partner's debt, plaintiffs were subject to all defenses that could be asserted against the partner. We have determined that the accounting requirement may no longer be raised as a defense. The trial court also determined that plaintiffs lacked standing to request an accounting because they did not acquire a partnership interest but only an assignment of the debt. Our determination of the continuing validity of the accounting rule moots the standing issue. * * *

The decision of the court of appeals is vacated and the cause is remanded to the trial court for further proceedings consistent with this opinion.

Notes and Questions

1. **The abolition of exclusivity.** RUPA § 405 would change current law along the lines of *Sertich* by explicitly permitting actions apart from an accounting. Thus, the *Sertich* rule may become widespread. It is important, then, to consider what it means. The modern irrelevance of the historical basis of the rule discussed in *Sertich* does not alone eliminate practical considerations that may justify the rule. For one thing, the partners need to resolve all claims and cross-claims they have against each other in order to determine what each is owed or owes. For another, the rule serves the purpose of deterring costly or opportunistic litigation in partnerships. *See* Levmore, *Love It or Leave It: Property Rules, Liability Rules, and Exclusivity of Remedies in Partnership and Marriage,* 58 LAW & CONTEMP. PROB. 221 (Spring, 1995). It follows that, even in a jurisdiction that has abolished exclusivity, a court may require something like an accounting. On the other hand, even in a jurisdiction that continues to follow the traditional rule, relatively simple and discrete claims that do not require a balance are among the many exceptions to the exclusivity rule. *See* BROMBERG & RIBSTEIN, § 6.08(c). *Sertich* and RUPA § 405 therefore may not signal much of a change in existing law.

2. **Derivative suits.** A particularly troublesome aspect of the abolition of exclusivity concerns individual partners' suits for breach of fiduciary duty. Such litigation may be costly and time-consuming and therefore opposed even by partners who are not involved in the alleged wrongdoing. The abolition of exclusivity might mean that a partner can sue individually to pursue the partnership claim without seeking the approval of disinterested partners. While this may be appropriate for publicly held firms, where the burden of seeking for co-owner approval may block valuable claims, the same considerations do not justify permitting derivative claims in closely held firms such as general partnerships. *See* BROMBERG & RIBSTEIN, § 5.05.

3. **Drafting considerations.** Partners may be able to waive the default accounting right under the UPA. Conversely, as indicated by Note 2, in a partnership governed by RUPA the parties may wish to draft *for* an accounting exclusivity rule or some other restriction on partner litigation. Or the agreement may simply clarify that the partners have certain remedies against co-partners who breach their express or implied obligations under the agreement, including suits for damages, specific performance, accounting or buyout of a breaching partner. Should the agreement add that this list is, or is not, exclusive?

4. **Indemnification.** UPA and RUPA statutory provisions concerning partner indemnification (*see* UPA § 18(b) and RUPA § 401(c), discussed above in § 6.03) do not make clear the extent to which partners may be indemnified for legal expenses and liabilities triggered by their breaches of duty to the partnership. The partnership agreement may clarify this by, for example, providing broadly for indemnification, or by providing that partners are entitled to indemnification only if they have not breached duties to the partnership. Would an open-ended right to indemnification be enforceable under RUPA § 103(b)? Note that such a right arguably undercuts duties of care and loyalty, which under this provision may not be wholly negated. On the other hand, even *with-*

out liability, the *duties* would remain and would perhaps justify judicial dissolution or an injunction remedy.

5. **Arbitration.** The agreement may provide for a broad duty to have claims tried by an arbitrator rather than in court. Such clauses are widely enforced and broadly interpreted. *See* BROMBERG & RIBSTEIN, § 6.08(e). A supposed advantage of arbitration is that it is a relatively streamlined trial before experts. However, arbitration may not do much to reduce litigation costs, since some arbitrations are quite long and involved.

CHAPTER 9
DISSOCIATION AND DISSOLUTION

9.01 Introduction

Given the partners' usual inability to sell all of their rights in the partnership (*see* Chapter 7), they need to substitute another form of exit. This section sketches the UPA and RUPA rules on dissolution and dissociation that will be discussed in greater detail throughout this chapter.

A.   UPA

Under the traditional law embodied in UPA §§ 29 and 31, the partnership dissolves at the will or upon the departure of any partner. At that point, one of two things happens—continuation or liquidation. If there is no unexpired agreed term or uncompleted agreed undertaking, the partnership is liquidated under UPA § 38(1) unless all of the partners, including the partner whose express will or departure dissolved the partnership, agree to continue the business. If they agree to continue, the leaving partner is paid off under UPA § 42. If not, the business is wound up under UPA § 37 and the assets are sold and distributed according to UPA § 40.

On the other hand, if there is an unexpired term or agreed undertaking, the dissolution may be wrongful under UPA § 31(2). In that event, the partnership may be continued without liquidation under UPA § 38(2) if all of the partners *other than* the one who wrongfully dissolved the firm agree to continue. If the firm continues, the dissolving partner is paid the value of his interest less damages caused by the premature dissolution and not including "goodwill." If the firm is liquidated, UPA §§ 37 and 40 apply as in the non-wrongful dissolution situation.

Whether the partnership continues or is liquidated, UPA §§ 33-36 determine the partners' continuing liability for pre-dissolution debts and potential liability for post-dissolution debts.

B. RUPA

RUPA retains the critical UPA rule of dissolution at will of a partnership that is not for a particular term or undertaking. Unlike the UPA, RUPA provides for partner dissociation separately from dissolution. RUPA § 601 outlines causes of terminating the partner's continued association with the partnership (*i.e.*, dissociation). RUPA § 603 is a "switching" provision that summarizes the main effects of dissociation—buyout under Article 7, and dissolution and winding up under Article 8. Article 7 outlines the procedures for buying out a partner and the rules for continuation and termination of the partner's authority to bind the partnership and liability for partnership debts. Article 8 outlines the rules for dissolving and winding up the partnership. In contrast to the UPA, these rules come into play only when the partnership is ending. Note, however, that a partnership may wind up by selling its assets as a going concern to a third party.

Apart from the general structure of the dissociation and dissolution provisions, RUPA also differs from the UPA in making it more likely that the partnership will continue rather than dissolve when a partner leaves. Unlike the UPA, RUPA § 801(2) provides that the partnership does not dissolve, and therefore does not liquidate, upon wrongful dissociation or dissociation by death or related events unless at least half agree to wind up or dissociate within 90 days after the dissociation. Also, RUPA § 802 provides that the partners may waive dissolution and retroactively undo the winding up at any time prior to termination. RUPA § 103 clarifies that the partners may avoid dissolution under § 801 by contrary provision in the partnership agreement, except that the partners may not contract to avoid judicial dissolution or dissolution for unlawfulness under subsections 801(4)-(6).

C. Policy Considerations

Statutory dissolution and dissociation provisions attempt to balance the costs of partners' illiquidity (that is, of partners' inability to exit the firm by selling their interests) against the costs of partnership discontinuity (that is, of allowing partners to escape the firm through buyout or dissolution). RUPA § 801(2)(i) has been amended to provide that partner dissociation from a term partnership does not cause dissolution unless within 90 days at least half of the partners by number agree to wind up.

Illiquidity may be costly for several reasons. Locking partners into the firm amplifies their disagreements, leading to deadlock and litigation. For example, some owners may prefer to retain earnings in the business for expansion, while others want distributions, particularly since they must pay tax on partnership earnings whether or not these are distributed. The partners' ability to withdraw their investments is a potentially powerful constraint on self-dealing by managing partners. And the partners may want to be able to move their investments (including their own human capital) to higher valued uses.

The UPA's dissolution-at-will also can be costly. Dissolution can disrupt ongoing relationships with third parties by, for example, terminating executory contracts. Making it easy for partners to leave the firm means that the firm may have to sell crucial assets to pay off the partners, and that the exiting partners can easily withdraw skills, clients and credit that are critical to the firm's future. Buyout or dissolution rights may even let partners take property such as ongoing litigation of a law firm that was developed partly at the expense of the other partners. Although partners who wish to continue can try to outbid a dissolving partner at the liquidation sale, the dissolving partner may have insurmountable advantages of credit, wealth, or special information. The "non-wrongful" partners' power to continue a partnership that is for an uncompleted term or undertaking is only a partial remedy, since there may be other circumstances in which permitting liquidation at will can be costly to the other partners, as illustrated by *Page*, below. *Page* also illustrates the extent to which courts and legislatures have recognized the need to preserve the business by facilitating the continuation of the business and even the partnership entity itself.

For analyses of dissolution and continuation under the UPA and RUPA, *see* Ribstein, *The Revised Uniform Partnership Act: Not Ready for Prime Time,* 49 Bus. Law. 45, 69-75 (1993), and *A Statutory Approach to Partner Dissociation,* 65 Wash. U. L.Q. 357 (1987).

D. Overview of Chapter

The following sections discuss important aspects of the statutory default provisions on dissolution and dissociation as well as issues connected with drafting partnership agreements on these issues. Section 9.02 reviews the statutory causes of dissolution and dissociation. Sections 9.03 and 9.04 discuss the major consequences of dissolution and dissociation—liquidation and winding up (§ 9.03), and buyout and continuation (§ 9.04). Section 9.05 discusses the liabilities of dissolved partners and partnerships. Finally, § 9.06 discusses some important issues concerning dissolution and dissociation provisions in partnership agreements. Throughout this chapter, it is important to keep in mind how the various legal rules address the important balance discussed in Section C of the costs of partner illiquidity and of partnership discontinuity.

9.02 Dissolution and Dissociation Causes

This section discusses the causes of partner dissociation and dissolution and their major consequences under the UPA and RUPA—*i.e.*, liquidation of the partnership or buyout of a dissociating partner and continuation of the firm. Other sections below in this chapter elaborate on each of these major consequences.

A.   Dissolution at Will: Term and At-Will Partnerships

Page v. Page
55 Cal. 2d 192, 359 P.2d 41, 10 Cal. Rptr. 643 (1961)

TRAYNOR, JUSTICE.

Plaintiff and defendant are partners in a linen supply business in Santa Maria, California. Plaintiff appeals from a judgment declaring the partnership to be for a term rather than at will.

The partners entered into an oral partnership agreement in 1949. Within the first two years each partner contributed approximately $43,000 for the purchase of land, machinery, and linen needed to begin the business. From 1949 to 1957 the enterprise was unprofitable, losing approximately $62,000. The partnership's major creditor is a corporation, wholly owned by plaintiff, that supplies the linen and machinery necessary for the day-to-day operation of the business. This corporation holds a $47,000 demand note of the partnership. The partnership operations began to improve in 1958. The partnership earned $3,824.41 in that year and $2,282.30 in the first three months of 1959. Despite this improvement plaintiff wishes to terminate the partnership.

The Uniform Partnership Act provides that a partnership may be dissolved "By the express will of any partner when no definite term or particular undertaking is specified." CORP.CODE, § 15031, subd. (1) (b). The trial court found that the partnership is for a term, namely, "such reasonable time as is necessary to enable said partnership to repay from partnership profits, indebtedness incurred for the purchase of land, buildings, laundry and delivery equipment and linen for the operation of said business . . . ." Plaintiff correctly contends that this finding is without support in the evidence.

Defendant testified that the terms of the partnership were to be similar to former partnerships of plaintiff and defendant, and that the understanding of these partnerships was that "we went into partnership to start the business and let the business operation pay for itself,—put in so much money, and let the business pay itself out." There was also testimony that one of the former partnership agreements provided in writing that the profits were to be retained until all obligations were paid.

Upon cross-examination defendant admitted that the former partnership in which the earnings were to be retained until the obligations were repaid was substantially different from the present partnership. The former partnership was a limited partnership and provided for a definite term of five years and a partnership at will thereafter. Defendant insists, however, that the method of operation of the former partnership showed an understanding that all obligations were to be repaid from profits. He nevertheless concedes that there was no understanding as to the term of the present partnership in the event of losses. He was asked: "[W]as there any discussion with reference to the continuation of the business in the event of losses?" He replied, "Not that I can remember." He was then asked, "Did you have any understanding with Mr. Page, your brother, the plaintiff in this action, as to how the obligations were to be paid if there were losses?" He replied, "Not that I can remember. I can't remember discussing that at all. We never figured on losing, I guess."

Viewing this evidence most favorably for defendant, it proves only that the partners expected to meet current expenses from current income and to recoup their investment if the business were successful.

Defendant contends that such an expectation is sufficient to create a partnership for a term under the rule of *Owen v. Cohen* , 19 Cal.2d 147, 150, 119 P.2d 713. In that case we held that when a partner advances a sum of money to a partnership with the understanding that the amount contributed was to be a loan to the partnership and was to be repaid as soon as feasible from the prospective profits of the business, the partnership is for the term reasonably required to repay the loan. It is true that *Owen v. Cohen, supra*, and other cases hold that partners may impliedly agree to continue in business until a certain sum of money is earned (*Mervyn Investment Co. v. Biber*, 184 Cal. 637, 641-642, 194 P. 1037), or one or more partners recoup their investments (*Vangel v. Vangel*, 116 Cal. App. 2d 615, 625, 254 P.2d 919), or until certain debts are paid (*Owen v. Cohen, supra*, 19 Cal.2d at page 150, 119 P.2d at page 714), or until certain property could be disposed of on favorable terms (*Shannon v. Hudson*, 161 Cal. App. 2d 44, 48, 325 P.2d 1022). In each of these cases, however, the implied agreement found support in the evidence.

In *Owen v. Cohen*, supra, the partners borrowed substantial amounts of money to launch the enterprise and there was an understanding that the loans would be repaid from partnership profits. In *Vangel v. Vangel, supra*, one partner loaned his co-partner money to invest in the partnership with the understanding that the money would be repaid from partnership profits. In *Mervyn Investment Co. v. Biber, supra*, one partner contributed all the capital, the other contributed his services, and it was understood that upon the repayment of the contributed capital from partnership profits the partner who contributed his services would receive a one-third interest in the partnership assets. In each of these cases the court properly held that the partners impliedly promised to continue the partnership for a term reasonably required to allow the partnership to earn sufficient money to accomplish the understood objective. In *Shannon v. Hudson, supra*, the parties entered into a joint venture to build and operate a motel until it could be sold upon favorable and mutually satisfactory terms, and the court held that the joint venture was for a reasonable term sufficient to accomplish the purpose of the joint venture.

In the instant case, however, defendant failed to prove any facts from which an agreement to continue the partnership for a term may be implied. The understanding to which defendant testified was no more than a common hope that the partnership earnings would pay for all the necessary expenses. Such a hope does not establish even by implication a "definite term or particular undertaking" as required by section 15031, subdivision (1)(b) of the Corporations Code. All partnerships are ordinarily entered into with the hope that they will be profitable, but that alone does not make them all partnerships for a term and obligate the partners to continue in the partnerships until all of the losses over a period of many years have been recovered.

Defendant contends that plaintiff is acting in bad faith and is attempting to use his superior financial position to appropriate the now profitable business of the partnership. Defendant has invested $43,000 in the firm, and owing to the long period of losses his interest in the partnership assets is very small. The fact that plaintiff's wholly-owned corporation holds a $47,000 demand note of the partnership may make it difficult to sell the business as a going concern. Defendant fears that upon dissolution he will receive very little and that plaintiff, who is the managing partner and knows how to conduct the operations of the partnership, will receive a business that has become very profitable because of the establishment of Vandenberg Air Force Base in its vicinity. Defendant charges that plaintiff has been content to share the losses but now that the business has become profitable he wishes to keep all the gains.

There is no showing in the record of bad faith or that the improved profit situation is more than temporary. In any event these contentions are irrelevant to the issue whether the partnership is for a term or at will. Since, however, this action is for a declaratory judgment and will be the basis for future action by the parties, it is appropriate to point out that defendant is amply protected by the fiduciary duties of co-partners.

Even though the Uniform Partnership Act provides that a partnership at will may be dissolved by the express will of any partner (CORP.CODE, § 15031, subd. (1)(b)), this power, like any other power held by a fiduciary, must be exercised in good faith.

We have often stated that "partners are trustees for each other, and in all proceedings connected with the conduct of the partnership every partner is bound to act in the highest good faith to his co-partner, and may not obtain any advantage over him in the partnership affairs by the slightest misrepresentation, concealment, threat, or adverse pressure of any kind." [citations omitted]

A partner at will is not bound to remain in a partnership, regardless of whether the business is profitable or unprofitable. A partner may not, however, by use of adverse pressure "freeze out" a co-partner and appropriate the business to his own use. A partner may not dissolve a partnership to gain the benefits of the business for himself, unless he fully compensates his co-partner for his share of the prospective business opportunity. In this regard his fiduciary duties are at least as great as those of a shareholder of a corporation.

In the case of *In re Security Finance Co.*, 49 Cal.2d 370, 376-377, 317 P.2d 1, 5 we stated that although shareholders representing 50 per cent of the voting power have a right under Corporations Code § 4600 to dissolve a corporation, they may not exercise such right in order "to defraud the other shareholders [citation omitted], to 'freeze out' minority shareholders [citation omitted], or to sell the assets of the dissolved corporation at an inadequate price [citation omitted]."

Likewise in the instant case, plaintiff has the power to dissolve the partnership by express notice to defendant. If, however, it is proved that plaintiff acted in bad faith and violated his fiduciary duties by attempting to appropriate to his own use the new prosperity of the partnership without adequate compensation to his co-partner, the dissolution would be wrongful and the plaintiff would be liable as provided by subdivision (2)(a) of Corporations Code § 15038 (rights of partners upon wrongful dissolution) for violation of the implied agreement not to exclude defendant wrongfully from the partnership business opportunity.

The judgment is reversed.

Notes and Questions

1. **Partnership for a term or undertaking: Drafting implications.** If the partnership is for an agreed term or undertaking, it logically follows that the parties have concluded that it would be particularly damaging to end the partnership prior to the expiration of the term. Accordingly, the UPA and RUPA fill in the blanks by providing for penalties against the prematurely departing partner and for continuation by the other partners. A court must decide whether the partnership agreement is one for an agreed term or undertaking. The drafting lesson is that seemingly innocuous provisions may

bear on this interpretation. Providing for a particular purpose, such as building and leasing a building, may be interpreted as defining an undertaking. Providing that the partnership shall dissolve on a certain date may be interpreted as stating a *minimum* term.

2. **Judicially qualifying the power to liquidate: "Bad faith" dissolution.** Since the *Page* partnership was not for a term, it would seem to follow that plaintiff can compel liquidation of the partnership pursuant to UPA § 38(1) and buy the business at a liquidation sale. However, this may impose significant costs on a partner who, like the defendant in *Page*, wants to continue the firm. Thus, as in several other cases (*see* BROMBERG & RIBSTEIN ON PARTNERSHIP § 7.11(f)) the *Page* court suggested that liquidation may not be required even if dissolution is technically not wrongful under the UPA. What might be a "bad faith" dissolution discussed in the last section of Justice Traynor's opinion? As discussed above in § 8.05, the good faith obligation can be viewed as a way to interpret the contract. So interpreted, the "bad faith" qualification may ensure that the plaintiff cannot use a power to dissolve the firm to gain an advantage that is otherwise prohibited by the contract or the default provisions of the UPA. Specifically, the court was concerned that plaintiff was using dissolution to take a disproportionate share of the partnership property, which the court characterized as "the new prosperity of the partnership." But does this "new prosperity" legitimately belong to plaintiff because of his irreplaceable skills as manager of the business? One possible response is that plaintiff implicitly promised not to dissolve until defendant had an opportunity to earn back his investment in the firm. The court, however, explicitly rejected this argument in holding that this was not a partnership for a term.

What should be defendant's remedy if the court does find "bad faith"? Would allowing defendant to buy out plaintiff do the defendant much good? Should the court set a buyout price of defendant's interest? If so, how would the court go about valuing the partnership's "new prosperity"?

3. **Fiduciary duties on dissolution.** Even if the dissolution itself is not in bad faith, the court may hold that the dissolving partner breached her fiduciary duties by appropriating partnership property in the dissolution. These duties continue after dissolution through winding up. *See* § 9.04(B), below. This is yet another way of attempting to achieve the right balance of the costs of discontinuity against the costs of illiquidity. Thus, in *Rosenfeld, Meyer & Susman v. Cohen,* 146 Cal. App. 3d 200, 194 Cal. Rptr. 180 (1983), *on appeal after remand*, 191 Cal. App. 3d 1035, 237 Cal. Rptr. 14 (1987), the court held withdrawing law partners liable for appropriating a major antitrust case. Similar considerations apply to partners' sharing of work in process (*see* § 9.06(C)).

4. **Effect of RUPA.** What would have been the result in the *Page* situation under the RUPA dissolution and dissociation provisions? In particular, how would a court determine whether a "majority in interest" of the partners agreed to continue the firm?

B.   Partner Death

A partner's death dissolves a partnership under UPA § 31(4). However, it is less clear whether the surviving partners have the right to continue the business after the death of a co-partner. As a policy matter, the estate's rights again raise the issue of balancing illiquidity and discontinuity costs (*see* § 9.01(C)). A partner's death can occur unexpectedly, increasing the costs of liquidation for the surviving partners. But inability to force a sale leaves the estate with an illiquid interest and exposed to the partnership's pre-dissolution debts. The costs to the surviving partners of giving the estate the power to liquidate the firm depend on, among other things, how hard it will be for them to buy the business as a going concern at auction, or negotiate with the estate for a buyout.

Continuation is arguably consistent with UPA §§ 37 and 38(1), which give the right to force liquidation only to a "partner," as distinguished from the representative of a deceased's estate. But UPA § 41(3) implies that the estate's consent is required for continuation, and the estate's legal representative can obtain judicial winding up under UPA § 37.

RUPA § 601(7) provides that the death of a partner who is an individual causes the partner's dissociation from the firm. Subsections 601(8)-(10) provide for the figurative "death" of partners who are business associations or trusts by termination or distribution. Unlike the UPA, these events do not dissolve the partnership for a term or undertaking under RUPA § 801(2) unless a majority in interest of the partners agrees to wind up or dissociate within 90 days after the dissociation.

C.   Bankruptcy

Bankruptcy of a partner or the partnership causes dissolution under UPA § 31(5). Dissolution on bankruptcy of a partner follows logically from the fact that the non-bankrupt partners, who continue to be personally liable, may not want to continue in partnership with a partner who is no longer financial responsible. Since bankruptcy is not a cause of wrongful dissolution, in the absence of contrary agreement any partner, including the bankrupt partner, can compel liquidation under UPA § 38(1). However, subject to the bankruptcy rules discussed below, the parties can agree that, following the bankruptcy of a partner, the firm may purchase the interest of the bankrupt partner and continue the partnership's business.

RUPA § 601(6) provides that a partner's becoming a debtor in bankruptcy, executing an assignment for the benefit of creditors, or seeking, consenting, or acquiescing in the appointment of a trustee, receiver, or liquidator is a cause of the partner's dissociation. RUPA § 602(b)(2)(iii) provides that this dissociation is wrongful if it occurs prior to the expiration of a definite term or completion of particular undertaking, which may trigger a right to damages. Under RUPA § 801(2), such a dissociation does not dissolve the partnership unless a majority of the partners agree to wind up the firm or dissociate within 90 days after the dissociation.

Federal bankruptcy law may "trump" these state law rules and the parties' agreements. Some bankruptcy cases hold that, despite state law to the contrary, a partner's or partnership's Chapter 11 proceeding does not dissolve the partnership because dissolution would interfere with the reorganization of the bankrupt partner or partnership. *In re Hawkins,* 113 B.R. 315 (N.D. Tex. 1990); *In re Safren,* 65 B.R. 566 (C.D. Cal. 1986). This reasoning is questionable since dissolution would not prevent sale of the bankrupt partner's interest or of a dissolved partnership's business as a going concern. *Safren* also reasoned that this result was consistent with the UPA, which antedated Chapter 11. Yet the UPA also could be interpreted as referring to federal bankruptcy law as thereafter amended. *See Matter of Phillips,* 966 F.2d 926 (5th Cir. 1992), which is one of several cases that hold that a partner's bankruptcy does dissolve the partnership, consistent with state law.

Whether or not a partner's bankruptcy dissolves the partnership, there is a further question whether the partner (as "debtor-in-possession" of his bankruptcy estate) or the estate's trustee in bankruptcy, can continue as partner. Most courts hold under Bankruptcy Code (11 U.S.C.) § 365 that the bankrupt partner who is a "debtor in possession" continues as such notwithstanding a bankruptcy that might otherwise terminate the interest under the partnership statute or a partnership agreement. *See In re Clinton Court,* 160 B.R. 57 (E.D. Pa. 1993); *In re Rittenhouse Carpet, Inc.,* 56 B.R. 131, 131-32 (E.D. Pa. 1985). *See also* Bankruptcy Code §§ 541(c)(1) and 363(1) which provide, respectively, that the bankrupt partners' partnership rights are part of the debtor's bankruptcy estate and that they may be used or sold by the bankruptcy trustee. However, the non-debtor partners may not have to continue with a bankrupt partner's *trustee* in bankruptcy, in which case the trustee would have only the power to sell the partner's interest in the firm discussed in Note 4, p.159, above.

Note that this bankruptcy law could cause real problems for non-debtor partners by forcing them to shoulder the partnership debts alone while they must continue in business with a bankrupt partner. The partners might try to deal with this by expelling the insolvent partner. However, this might violate the bankruptcy stay under Bankruptcy Code (11 U.S.C.) § 362. It might also violate Code § 525, which makes illegal actions against bankrupt parties because of their bankruptcy.

D.   Judicial Dissolution

UPA § 32 provides for several judicially-determined grounds for a decree of dissolution under UPA § 31(6). The main significance of these judicial causes is that a partner in a partnership for a term or undertaking, or that is governed by an agreement which restricts liquidation at will, can avoid the adverse consequences of causing a wrongful dissolution by obtaining a judicial dissolution.

RUPA §§ 601 and 801 provide both for judicial *dissociation* (*i.e.,* expulsion) of errant partners and judicial *dissolution*. Some of the UPA dissolution causes are *dissociation* causes under RUPA. The RUPA approach avoids dissolving an entire partnership merely because of wrongful conduct or incapacity of a single partner.

The grounds for judicial dissolution and dissociation under the UPA and RUPA potentially interrelate with other provisions of the partnership statute. For example, one type of wrongful conduct that justifies judicial dissolution under UPA § 32(1)(d) and RUPA § 801(5) could be excluding another partner from participation in the partnership business in violation of the partnership agreement or the partners' default rights under UPA § 18(e) and RUPA § 401(f). *See* § 5.01, above. Other dissolution grounds relate to external effects on the partnership business, such as failure or illegality of the business. For example, UPA § 32(1)(e), provides for judicial dissolution when "[t]he business of the partnership can only be carried on at a loss."

9.03 Winding Up and Liquidation

Liquidation of the partnership means the assets must be sold rather than distributed in kind to the partners. This effectuates a complete separation of the partners, which is one of the main functions of dissolution and liquidation. Thus, for example, in *Hill v. Brown,* 166 Ill. App. 3d 867, 520 N.E.2d 1038 (1988), the court said that the partnership's breeder cow had to be sold and the proceeds from the sale distributed to the partners, rather than simply selling the cow "in halves" so that a partner could bid on only a half interest in the cow. Sale "in halves" would have amounted in effect to a continuation of the partnership with an auction of partnership interests. Although the assets must be sold rather than distributed in kind, this does not necessarily mean that the assets must be sold piecemeal. Rather, they can be auctioned as a going concern—including to one of the partners.

In addition to collecting assets, the dissolving firm must pay its debts. If the operating assets of the firm are not enough, the partners must contribute toward payment of debts in the proportion in which they share losses. Under UPA § 40, the partners' contribution obligation is, in effect, an asset of the firm. The partners' contribution obligation under the UPA and RUPA is discussed in § 6.03 above, and the partners' obligation to share "capital" losses through contributions is illustrated above on pp. 106-07. To give another example of partner contributions, suppose that a three-member partnership's assets are 5,000, two of the partners, A and B, each have made capital contributions of $2,500 and there are $12,000 of debts to "outside" creditors. Under UPA § 40, the three partners would contribute equally toward the excess of liabilities (including those to repay capital contributions) to assets. When the smoke clears, A and B would each have to come up with $1,500 ($4,000 – 2,500), while C would have to come up with $4,000 to pay A and B and the outside creditors. The result is probably the same under RUPA § 807, except that as discussed in § 4.05, RUPA does not make absolutely clear the partners' obligation to repay out of their own pockets their co-partners' capital contributions.

Under both the UPA and RUPA, the partners can provide for their own liquidation scheme in the partnership agreement. For example, in *Smith, Keller & Associates v. Dorr & Associates,* 875 P.2d 1258 (Wyo. 1994), the court upheld an arbitrator's award and granted an accounting based on an agreement that gave the partners on dissolution the assets and liabilities each brought to the partnership, including work in process, accounts receivable, accounts payable and miscellaneous assets based on the separate offices each partner contributed to the partnership. The partners may also provide that payout to the partners is subject to establishing a reserve for unpaid obligations so that individual partners are not later exposed for the full amount of these obligations.

9.04 Continuation and Buyout of Dissociating Partner

When the partnership continues, UPA § 42 provides by default that the firm must pay the outgoing partner for her share of the partnership, plus profits or interest for the partners' use of this share from the time of dissolution until the time of payment. Under UPA § 38, "wrongful" partners are not paid for goodwill and must pay damages caused by prematurely dissolving the firm. RUPA § 701 also provides for payment to outgoing partners, but elaborates on how this value is determined and does not provide either for the UPA profit-or-interest election or the UPA goodwill penalty against "wrongful" partners. The following sections discuss important issues that arise in connection with these default provisions.

A.   Valuation

The price a continuing partnership must pay for an outgoing partner's interests again raises the issue of the appropriate balance between illiquidity and discontinuity costs discussed in § 9.01(C). UPA § 42 does not provide for a specific approach to valuation, although cases under the UPA provide some guidance. RUPA § 701 elaborates on the standard for determining the value of the outgoing partner's interest by providing that a dissociated partner is entitled to the "amount that would have been distributable to the dissociating partner under Section 807(b) if, on the date of dissociation, the assets of the partnership were sold at a price equal to the greater of the liquidation value or the value based on a sale of the entire business as a going concern without the dissociated partner and the partnership were wound up as of that date." Some specific valuation issues are discussed in the following subsections.

1.   The minority discount

There is an issue whether the price the leaving partner receives depends on the value of the *entire firm* or on the partner's *interest* in the firm. This can make a significant difference because the market value of the partner's interest is affected by the marketability of the interest itself. Since buyout is supposed to address the problem of illiquidity, it arguably follows that the price should be based on the value of the entire firm. On the other hand, a rule that provides for a lower buyout price would reduce discontinuity costs by discouraging partners from leaving.

The case law under the UPA is mixed. *Shopf v. Marina Del Ray Partnership,* 549 So. 2d 833 (La. App. 1989), held that an appraiser should have taken into account offers for plaintiff's interest but should apply a minority discount to reflect the fact that the third party was a majority owner acquiring a minority stake for which an outsider would have paid less. On the other hand, *Hewitt v. Hurwitz,* 227 Ill. App. 3d 616, 169 Ill. Dec. 726, 592 N.E.2d 213 (1992), held that the trial court should not have rejected expert testimony and relied on the sale price of a minority (25%) interest in the partnership to a third party to establish the property's fair market value, reasoning in part that the sale of a partnership *interest* does not necessarily establish the fair market value of the *underlying asset.*

RUPA § 701 settles the issue of the minority discount by providing for liquidation valuation, which assumes a valuation of the assets and liabilities of the entire firm. Note, however, that the difference between "going concern" and "liquidation" value may not be clear. "Liquidation" could mean a variety of different types of asset sales, while the sale price of productive assets necessarily depends on how they are to be used—that is, their "going concern" value.

2. Wrongful dissolution

Wrongful dissolution or dissociation—in particular, leaving the firm prior to the expiration of an agreed term or undertaking—may have two effects on valuation in addition to its impact on continuation of the firm discussed in § 9.02. Under UPA § 38(2) and RUPA § 602 the wrongful partner must pay damages caused by the premature departure. This may entail a determination of the profits the firm would have made if the partner had stayed or the firm had not been dissolved. *See Hill v. Brown,* 166 Ill. App. 3d 867, 520 N.E.2d 1038 (1988), refusing to speculate from the breeding history of a cow's mother as to the profits that plaintiff would have made if he had not been denied possession of an unproved breeder cow.

Note that RUPA § 602 applies only to partner *dissociation.* RUPA does not literally provide for a right to damages for wrongful *dissolution. See Horizon/CMS Healthcare Corp. v. Southern Oaks Health Care, Inc.,* 732 So. 2d 1156 (Fla. App. 1999). The reason for the distinction is not clear, since the disruption caused by partner dissociation may be similar to that caused by a partner act that triggers dissolution.

UPA § 38(2) also penalizes the wrongful partner by denying her a share in the firm's goodwill. In *Marched v. Murky,* 27 Mass. App. 611, 614, 541 N.E.2d 371, 373-374 (1989), the court held that this did not necessarily deny the departing partner a share in the firm's permits, licenses, franchise agreement, and arrangements to enter into a favorable lease, because these were "assets of value which do not fit comfortably within this description of goodwill." On the other hand, in *Pav-Saver Corp. v. Vasso Corp.,* 143 Ill. App. 3d 1013, 97 Ill. Dec. 760, 493 N.E.2d 423 (1986), the court held that goodwill from which the wrongful partner was denied a share could include a patent. RUPA § 602 does not include the goodwill-denial penalty. As discussed in the Comments to RUPA § 602, there may be an element of double penalty in the UPA approach.

On the other hand, as discussed below in subsection 4, goodwill may be very difficult to value, particularly in professional partnerships. Accordingly, there is some justification for refusing to speculate as to the value of goodwill on behalf of a wrongful partner.

3. Partnership liabilities

As discussed below in § 9.05, partners continue to be liable for pre-dissolution liabilities even after they leave the firm until the creditors release them. However, the partnership has a default duty to indemnify the leaving partner against these liabilities. The leaving partner pays for the indemnification by means of a reduction in the buyout price to reflect the firm's liabilities. This reduction in price can be somewhat tricky with respect to contingent liabilities, such as tort or malpractice claims that have not been reduced to judgment. Yet evaluating this type of contingency may not be much harder than valuing assets such as good will.

4. Goodwill

The "goodwill" of a firm—in the loose sense of its value as a going concern—may be the firm's most important asset, particularly in professional and other service firms. On the other hand, it may not be clear whether this asset actually belongs to the firm. In the film "Casablanca," when Humphrey Bogart finally sells Rick's to Sydney Greenstreet, Bogart tells Greenstreet that the latter has to keep Abdul, Karl, Sasha, and Sam. Greenstreet says sure—it wouldn't be Rick's without them. If that's the case, and these employees are not slaves, what is Greenstreet paying Bogie for? Consider the following case.

Spayd v. Turner, Granzow & Hollenkamp
19 Ohio St. 3d 55, 482 N.E.2d 1232 (1985)

HOLMES, Justice.
In his appeal to this court, plaintiff Spayd contends both lower courts erred in their determination that, due to ethical considerations, there could be no accounting for goodwill upon the dissolution of a law partnership. Plaintiff further argues that the facts presented herein clearly establish a measurable element of goodwill within the operation of this particular law firm. * * *

We must consider whether, upon the dissolution of a law partnership, a partner is entitled to demonstrate . . . that goodwill is an asset of the partnership in the absence of a provision in the partnership agreement to the contrary. Unique to this issue is the query of whether the rules of ethics within this profession preclude the existence of goodwill in a law partnership. * * *

The comprehensive definition of "goodwill" is "the advantage or benefit, which is acquired by an establishment, beyond the mere value of the capital, stock, funds, or property employed therein, in consequence of the general public patronage and encouragement, which it receives from constant or habitual customers, on account of its local position, or common celebrity, or reputation for skill or affluence, or punctuality, or from other accidental circumstances or necessities, or even from ancient partialities or prejudices." STORY, COMMENTARIES ON THE LAW OF PARTNERSHIP (6 Ed.1868) 170, Section 99. * * *

Generally, a partnership business may build goodwill as an asset, and upon dissolution of the business by one or more of the partners, courts have recognized that measurable goodwill is a proper asset for consideration in an accounting between the partners where its disposition is not otherwise controlled by the partnership agreement, and the dissolution was not occasioned by the wrongful act of the one who sought the accounting. [citations omitted]

Traditionally, the prevailing rule relative to professional partnerships was that goodwill did not exist at dissolution as the reputation of the business entity was dependent on the individual skills of each member. [citations omitted]

There appears, however, to be a growing trend throughout the country which recognizes that a professional service partnership possesses goodwill. An ever-increasing number of jurisdictions have held that goodwill may lawfully exist in a professional partnership, and the actual existence of this asset in a particular partnership is a question of fact. [citations omitted] The rationale for many of these cases is that the reputation for skill and learning in a particular profession often creates an intangible but valuable asset by gaining the confidence of clients who will speak well of the business.

As to partnerships formed for the practice of law, courts have historically relied on two theories in holding that goodwill is not a measurable or distributable asset. One, as previously mentioned, the amount of goodwill that exists is attributable to the professional skill and reputation of each member of the partnership; and, two, the existence of ethical prohibitions against distributable goodwill in law partnerships. *See Siddall v. Keating* (1959), 8 App.Div.2d 44, 185 N.Y.S.2d 630, *aff'd* (1959), 7 N.Y.2d 846, 196 N.Y.S.2d 986, 164 N.E.2d 860. [citations omitted]

In *Siddall, supra*, which both lower courts apparently relied upon herein, the New York court denied an allowance of goodwill to a retiring partner of a law firm because such asset would have been calculated upon future earnings of the continuing law firm in which the retiring partner would have no active part or responsibility stemming therefrom. Thus, any distribution of a share of goodwill would have been in violation of Canon 34 of the Canons of Professional Ethics, the predecessor of DR 2-107 of the Code of Professional Responsibility. Canon 34 provided, "[n]o division of fees for legal services is proper, except with another lawyer, based upon a division of service or responsibility."

As with other professions, the legal profession has produced some rather dramatic changes in the last two decades since the *Siddall* case. Traditionally, attorneys were more apt to practice as sole practitioners, or within two- or three-person firms. More recently, law firms have grown extensively in size and scope, with firms of over one hundred attorneys not uncommon. Our profession has not only increased in terms of numbers, but other related factors have materially altered its complexion. The use of computers for clerical and administrative tasks has significantly increased, while office managers who are specifically schooled in the field are being employed; departmentalization of the larger firm is becoming the norm; branching of the firm within the same community, or beyond the county and state lines, has become the trend; and mergers of law firms are taking place in order to provide a broader service to clients on a more cost-effective basis.

All of these factors evidence the trend of law firms becoming more business-oriented. * * * Therefore, we believe the current status of law firms reasonably suggests that the existence of goodwill in a law partnership should not be precluded as a matter of law.

Based on the foregoing, we hold that where the evidence establishes that a professional partnership, including a law partnership, has generated measurable goodwill, it is not against public policy to include that amount of goodwill as an asset upon dissolution of the business.

A review of the relative ethical standards governing the bar does not mandate a different result. As previously stated, the *Siddall* court based its determination upon Canon 34 of the Canons of Professional Ethics which was the forerunner of DR 2-107.[6] The current rule prohibits the division of a fee for legal services with another lawyer who is not a partner or associate within the law firm, with certain well-defined exceptions. However, subsection (B) of the precept provides that the rule "does not prohibit payment to a former partner or associate pursuant to a separation or retirement agreement."

The underlying philosophy of both the old Canon and the existing Disciplinary Rule is aimed at the impermissive sharing of future fees where there is a lack of services performed, or responsibility to the client. However, this philosophy is unwarranted in relation to goodwill, which does not completely entail future earnings. While future earnings may be considered in the measure of goodwill, the latter, by contrast, is an intangible asset which the partnership possesses, and is in existence at the time of the dissolution. * * *

Therefore, we conclude that as a matter of law the ethical standard within DR 2-107(B) does not preclude a finding that goodwill exists in a law partnership upon dissolution of that association. * * *

From the record, it is evident that the partnership was dissolved through a voluntary departure of one of the partners, a situation provided for within the partnership agreement. Accordingly, plaintiff's partnership rights and interests must be determined by the provisions of the agreement, rather than any statutory enactment under the Uniform Partnership Law.

Pursuant to Section XII, the value of each partner's interest upon dissolution of the partnership is computed upon the basis of cash "equal to the amount of his capital account (contributed capital plus undrawn profits), as shown on the audit report, and shall be entitled to nothing other than said cash." The agreement is certainly expressive as to that amount to be paid to a retiring or terminating partner which represents his interest in the partnership. Significantly, the provision does not provide for payment of goodwill in the partnership. In addition, there was no evidence that the accounting practice within this partnership was to carry goodwill as an asset, nor was there evidence that any previously retiring partner under a similar provision had been paid for goodwill.

---

[6]   DR 2-107 states as follows: "A) A lawyer shall not divide a fee for legal services with another lawyer who is not a partner in or associate of his law firm or law office, unless: '(1) The client consents to employment of the other lawyer after a full disclosure that a division of fees will be made. '(2) The division is made in proportion to the services performed and responsibility assumed by each. '(3) The total fee of the lawyers does not clearly exceed reasonable compensation for all legal services they rendered the client. "(B) T'is Disciplinary Rule does not prohibit payment to a former partner or associate pursuant to a separation or retirement agreement."

A partnership agreement will generally not be disturbed by the courts in the absence of extenuating circumstances. [citation omitted] Furthermore, we believe the provision of goodwill to a retiring or terminating partner is a matter of contract which must be assented to by all parties involved. We hold, therefore, that the provision for goodwill as an asset of a partnership which is to be distributed upon dissolution of the business is a matter of contract between the partners and must be specifically set forth in the partnership agreement.

Accordingly, we conclude that the judgment of the court of appeals must be reversed and the judgment of the trial court reinstated but for reasons other than set forth in the judgment of the trial court and for the reasons set forth in this opinion.

Judgment reversed.

CELEBREZZE, Chief Justice, concurring.

* * * I part company with the majority in their dictum which allows payment for goodwill "upon dissolution of the business" if agreed to by the contracting law partners. * * *

Although I believe goodwill exists and is therefore ascertainable, I nevertheless agree with the lower courts' determinations that it may not ethically be compensable to a withdrawing partner in Ohio. Although DR 2-107(B) allows for payment to a retiring partner or associate pursuant to a separation agreement, I do not believe it permits a former partner to receive a portion of future services rendered by the firm in settlement of goodwill. [citation omitted] Rather, I believe this section of the Code of Professional Responsibility was intended to allow a firm to gradually pay off a partner's tangible interest in a firm and to allow for reasonable retirement payments. I find that the policy and ethical concerns of the court in *Siddall v. Keating* (1959), 8 App.Div.2d 44, 185 N.Y.S.2d 630, *aff'd* (1959), 7 N.Y.2d 846, 196 N.Y.S.2d 986, are equally valid today. *See, e.g., In re Silverberg* (1980), 75 App.Div.2d 817, 427 N.Y.S.2d 480, which found that an agreement that provided, inter alia, for payment for goodwill, between former partners, was an unethical division of legal fees without regard to services actually rendered and was void as against public policy.

In a strikingly similar case to the one at bar the Supreme Court of Iowa recently recognized that in some cases (such as divorce) the goodwill of a law practice may properly be valued. However, it held that "the transfer or withdrawal of a portion of a law practice . . . is not such a situation." *Bump v. Stewart, Wimer & Bump, P.C.* (Iowa 1983), 336 N.W.2d 731, at 737. I agree with the Iowa court, and the authorities it cites in support of the proposition that "placing a 'price tag on the goodwill of a law practice' is contrary to public policy . . . ." *Id.*

Based on the foregoing, I believe today's majority has taken one step forward in contract law and two steps backward in the realms of legal ethics and public policy by expressing approbation of goodwill bargains between attorneys.

Notes and Questions

1. **Other cases.** For a case reaching a similar conclusion, *see Dawson v. White & Case,* N.Y.2d 666, 672 N.E.2d 589, 649 N.Y.S.2d 364 (1996), involving expulsion of a partner from a law firm. The court held that goodwill, if any, is presumptively an asset

of the firm that must be accounted for. The court also held that accounting for good-will was permitted by the ethical rule authorizing sale of a law practice by a lawyer retiring from practice or the firm. It said that prior authority to the contrary "has been superseded by the economic realities of the contemporary practice of law, illustrated by attorney advertising, internationalization of law firms, and other professional developments," citing *Spayd*. However, the court held that the agreement may exclude goodwill. In the present case, "new White & Case partners never paid anything for goodwill; departing partners never received a payment for goodwill; and goodwill was not listed as an asset in the firm's financial statements." Moreover, the partnership agreement provided that "[i]t is expressly understood and agreed that no consideration has been or is to be paid for the Firm name or any good will of the partnership, as such items are deemed to be of no value" and that "[t]he computation of the amount with which a Former Partner shall be charged or credited . . . shall exclude any value for the good will of the partnership or the Firm name, as such items are deemed to be of no value." Rather than limiting these provisions to the specific sale/purchase, and withdrawal/death situations covered by the agreement, the court held that the "partnership agreement reflects the binding written expression of the terms under which these partners assented to associate with each other and evinces their intention that goodwill be deemed 'of no value.'"

However, in the *Cadwalader, Wickersham & Taft v. Beasley* case, excerpted below in § 9.06(B), the court held that the oldest continuous law firm in the U.S., Cadwalader, Wickersham & Taft, had no goodwill.

2. **What "goodwill" belongs to a leaving partner?** *Spayd* notes the traditional rule that the firm itself has no goodwill because the firm's reputation depends on the members themselves. Yet why shouldn't a leaving partner share in the value of what is left, even if that value depends on the continuing efforts of the remaining partners? This happens all the time when a shareholder sells out of a firm that is managed by others. Perhaps the result is justified by the difficulty of valuing goodwill based on human capital. *See* Ribstein, *A Theoretical Analysis of Professional Partnership Goodwill*, 70 NEB. L. REV. 36 (1991). The rule may also impact the firm's continuity. Since the partners may not be able easily to agree on valuation, the threat of a very conservative valuation of a partner's interest by the court may lead the leaving partner or estate to insist on liquidation. Note that *Spayd* does not settle the goodwill question because it leaves undecided precisely how professional firm goodwill is valued. For a recent case on valuation of goodwill in a professional partnership *see Salinas v. Rafati*, 948 S.W.2d 286 (Tex. 1997), which denied a partner leaving a medical partnership value attributable solely to the reputations of the other partners rather than name or location, primarily because of the problem of continuing claims after the parties wished to sever their relationship. For a discussion of the cases, arguing that law partners should be deemed to share their firm's goodwill, *see* Rosin, *The Hard Heart of The Enterprise: Goodwill and The Role of the Law Firm*, 39 S. TEX. L. REV. 315 (1998).

The question of whether "goodwill" belongs to the partners individually rather than the firm can also arise outside the professional context. For example, in *Active Asset Recovery, Inc. v. Real Estate Asset Recovery Services, Inc.*, 1999 WL 743479 (Del. Ch., Sep 10, 1999) the firm traded media advertising for assets such as inventories of unsold Cheap Trick CDs. The business relied on the partners' ability to accurately determine the value of the assets and to buy advertising time cheaply. The court noted: "The Partnership was not McDonald's (home of the Egg McMuffin); its name has no discernible economic value. There were no binding contracts prohibiting the Partners from competing with the Partnership after dissolution; therefore, no Partner is receiving exclusive rights to pursue the Partnership's former clients. There appear to have been no contracts prohibiting former employees from competing with the Partnership after termination and before dissolution. In fact, the Partnership did not even have employment agreements with its staff. No reasonable third-party buyer would pay the Partners for the good will of this Partnership in a sale absent some limitation on the selling Partners' right to continue to pursue barter contracts within the province of the Partnership. Since no such limitation exists on the exploitation of the Partnership's clients or method of doing business, there is no goodwill a third-party would be willing to buy and none upon which I can place a dollar value. As such, there is none to distribute to the Partners in this dissolution proceeding."

3. **Divorce cases.** Courts often hold that professional firms have goodwill for purposes of determining the amount owed a partner's divorced spouse. *See* § 7.04, above. Is this situation distinguishable from the division of assets among partners on dissolution?

4. **The effect of ethical rules.** See, in addition to *Spayd* and *Dawson*, Rule 1.5, Model Rules of Professional Conduct and *Fraser v. Bogucki,* 203 Cal. App. 3d 604, 250 Cal. Rptr. 41 (1988) (denying law partner's claim against his former partners for appropriation of client relationships). The "public policy" that might be offended by allowing leaving partners to cash in on goodwill is putting a price tag on clients, which appears inconsistent with the professional nature of the relationship. This issue is discussed further below in § 9.06(D).

5. **Effect of RUPA.** RUPA § 701(b) may change the valuation rules applied under the UPA. First, by providing for payment of going concern value determined "without the dissociated partner," § 701(b) implies that the reputations of the non-dissociating partners *are* taken into account. Second, because the valuation standard under UPA § 701(b) is based on a sale of the underlying assets, it does not reflect a minority or control discount.

B.   The Long Goodbye: The Rights of Partners Who Are Being Bought Out

There may be a substantial time lag between a partner's dissociation and the final settlement of the partner's interest. This again raises the policy issue of the appropriate balance between partner liquidity and partnership continuity. Requiring the continuing partners to immediately pay off the leaving partner could substantially burden the firm and cause it to sell critical assets. On the other hand, the continuing partners have an incentive to run the firm during the lag time for their own benefit, delaying buyout and skimping on the buyout price.

UPA § 42 provides some protection by giving a leaving partner an election between "interest, or . . . the profits attributable to the use of his right in the property of the dissolved partnership" which accrues during the period between dissolution and payment to the partner. This compensates partners for use of their invested capital and discourages continuing partners from inefficiently prolonging the business instead of winding it up. *See* II BROMBERG & RIBSTEIN ON PARTNERSHIP § 7.13(f). For an application of the profits-or-interest election in a case where it made an almost $900,000 difference in damages, *see Beasley,* excerpted p. 247 below. RUPA eliminates this right. RUPA § 701 does, however, provide specific buyout procedures that address some of the potential delay in buyout. Note that under both UPA § 38(2) and RUPA § 701(h), the firm may defer payment of the buyout price to a partner who leaves prior to an agreed term. This is consistent with the fact that the firm's unexpired term or undertaking suggests that it would be particularly costly to wind up the firm as soon as the partner leaves.

The continuing partners may owe fiduciary duties to a dissociated partner. Although the leaving partner is technically an assignee (*see* paragraph 10.2 of the Chameleon agreement), she differs from other assignees in that she has no assignor partner to whom she can look to protect her interests in the firm. *See* Note 3, p. 152-53. Until the dissociated partner is fully cashed out, the "old" partnership that included the dissociated partner is technically winding up. UPA § 21 and RUPA § 404 provide that fiduciary duties continue during winding up. This means at least that continuing partners owe affirmative disclosure duties in negotiating the buyout price. But the dissociated partner probably has no claim for post-dissociation mismanagement. *See Bane v. Ferguson,* 707 F. Supp. 988 (N.D. Ill. 1989) (holding that there was no fiduciary duty liability to retired partner for dissolution of firm that caused cessation of retirement benefits), *aff'd,* 890 F.2d 11 (7th Cir. 1989); *Finkelstein v. Security Properties, Inc.,* 888 P.2d 161 (Wash. App. 1995) (continuing partners have no fiduciary duty to withdrawn partners to refrain from self-dealing). Denial of fiduciary rights makes sense where the partner's buyout price is fixed as of the date of dissociation, so that the leaving partner is technically in a creditor's position of being owed a definite sum. It makes less sense when the partner's interest is being liquidated for a share of fluctuating profits (*see* section D, below).

C.   Work-in-Process in Professional Firms

Partners may be entitled to share in "work-in-process" such as pending law cases or uncompleted software. The main issue in these cases is whether departing or continuing partners who complete the work should be entitled to the full amount they received for the work after dissolution without having to share with their former partner who began the case or project. UPA § 18(f) provides for remuneration to partners for acting in the partnership business only when a "surviving partner" winds up the partnership's affairs. Under this rule, most courts have split the fee according to the partners' pre-dissolution profit share without allowing extra compensation to the completing partner, at least when the firm is dissolved other than by a partner's death. This raises a significant incentive problem since the completing partner does all of the work for only part of the fee. It also reduces the liquidity of partnership interests because a partner who wishes to withdraw must choose between developing a new workload or completing cases on behalf of the partnership without compensation for extra work. On the other hand, if partners can keep the earnings from completing post-dissolution work they have a greater incentive to compete for files, clients and projects and to withdraw when they get them. Unlike the UPA, RUPA § 401(h) provides for a default right to compensation of all winding up partners no matter how the dissolution was caused.

The partners can decide how to allocate work in process in their partnership agreement. *See* § 9.06(C), below. The important question, therefore, is which rule—UPA or RUPA—is the best default rule. This depends partly on which rule the parties are likely to have adopted if they had anticipated the issue in their agreement. Dividing fees on the pre-dissolution basis is a rough approximation that leaves the task of devising more detailed, case-specific formulae to the parties themselves.

D.   Tax Consequences of Withdrawal and Dissolution

Tax considerations may be important in connection with planning for withdrawal or dissolution. From a tax standpoint, it can make a difference whether the partner sells her interest to the other partners or to a third party or has her interest *liquidated* by the partnership. If she *sells* her interest, the partner is taxed on any gain at capital gains rates except to the extent that the sales proceeds represent accounts receivable or substantially appreciated inventory, which are taxed at ordinary income rates. *See* IRC §§ 741, 751. The buyer gets no deduction. If the partner's interest is *liquidated* by the partnership under IRC § 736, the result is the same for the leaving partner. However, this method can be a big advantage for a service-type partnership such as a law firm, which gets to deduct the amounts paid against its income. This is based on the assumption that the withdrawing partner remains a partner until her share is fully liquidated.

Dissolution of the partnership under partnership law does not necessarily have tax significance. If, however, no part of the venture continues in a partnership form, or 50% or more of the partnership interests are conveyed within a one-year period, the partnership "terminates" pursuant to IRC § 708 whether or not the firm dissolves under partnership law.

9.05 Liabilities of Dissolved and Continuing Firms

Dissolution raises several questions concerning partners' and partnerships' responsibilities for liabilities incurred prior to and after the dissolution. In general, it is helpful to keep in mind that a partnership's dissolution creates a technically new entity. With some exceptions noted below, partners in the "old" partnership continue to be liable for "old" liabilities, while partners in the "new" partnership are personally liable for "new" liabilities and exposed to old liabilities to the extent of their investments in the firm. This causes some complications, particularly in continuing firms in which the dissolution is only a technical one and the business continues as before. Even lawyer partners may not realize when they walk into their 200-partner firm on Tuesday that it is technically a different firm from what it was on Monday when a single partner dissolved the firm by resigning.

A.   Former Partners' Liability for Pre-Dissolution Debts

The former partnership, of course, remains liable for pre-dissolution debts after the dissolution. Dissolution also does not necessarily end the "old" partners' individual liability for partnership debts. *See* UPA § 36 and RUPA § 703. There may, however, be some uncertainty about what these liabilities are. For example, in *In re Judiciary Tower Associates,* 175 B.R. 796, 809 (D.D.C. 1994), the court held a former partner liable for a contract that was substantially performed over an 18-month period while he was a partner but that was not completed until two months after he left. The court reasoned that the partnership's obligation to perform the contract was the joint liability of all of the partners at the time of the contract, and that "[a] creditor contracting with a general partnership does so in the rightful expectation that all of the general partners stand behind that contract, and that a partner's withdrawal will not release that partner's responsibility on the contract except as set forth in [UPA § 36]." Also, in *8182 Maryland Associates, Ltd. Partnership v. Sheehan*, 14 S.W. 3d 576 (Mo. 2000), partners were liable for a lease entered into while they were partners but breached after they left. RUPA § 703 provides for continuing liability for a pre-dissociation "obligation." The Comment says that "[t]he word 'obligation' . . . is intended to include broadly both tort and contract liability incurred before dissociation." This apparently would include debts like that involved in *Judiciary Tower* and *8182 Maryland.*

These rules suggest the need for drafting and planning by partners and creditors. Creditors may want to bind partners individually to a lease or other long-term contract in order to avoid ambiguity about whether a partner continues to be liable on the lease after leaving the firm. Conversely, a partner who is nearing retirement may want to think twice about continuing with the firm and becoming obligated on the lease, and a new partner may hesitate before joining a firm that has entered into a burdensome office lease.

Under UPA § 36 and RUPA § 703, a creditor may agree to *release* an outgoing partner either expressly or implicitly by agreeing to an alteration in payment of the debt knowing that the partner has dissociated. Thus, a creditor needs to be careful about a modification of long term obligations that may have the effect of releasing departed partners.

The partner who is not released and must pay the debt can seek *indemnification* from the other partners or the partnership. UPA § 38 and RUPA § 701 both provide for full indemnification against past liabilities, although the UPA applies only to wrongful and expelled partners, apparently presuming that rightfully dissolving partners can negotiate for indemnification as the price of permitting the other partners to continue. This may not work for liabilities that were unknown at the time of the departure. But there is some uncertainty inherent in limiting indemnification to liabilities "known" at the time of the departure. Note also that the leaving partner does not get the benefit of later-discovered positive elements of value such as an oil well that suddenly gushes under the partnership's land after a partner leaves.

B.   Former Partnership's Liability for Post-Dissolution Debts

Liabilities that arise after the dissolution are covered under UPA § 33-35 and RUPA §§ 702, 804, which deal with several different scenarios:

1.   If the partnership continues after a partner's dissociation, the continuing partners have the power to bind the "new" firm just as they did prior to the dissociation and dissolution.

2.   The "old" firm continues for purposes of winding up, during which time the partners have the real authority to bind the firm only in "winding up" transactions such as compromise and release of claims, and not in transactions that are aimed at keeping the firm going.

3.   Suppose the partnership is continuing, but creditors do not know that it is technically a different partnership? This may particularly be an issue for clients of a continuing law firm. In this situation the creditor may be able to hold a partner of the pre-dissolution firm. *See Redman v. Walters,* 88 Cal. App. 3d 448, 152 Cal. Rptr. 42 (1979), which held a dissociated law partner liable for malpractice to a client that occurred after the lawyer's departure where the client retained the firm prior to the lawyer's leaving. Although the court's rationale is unclear, the liability would seem to be based on the theory that the leaving partner continued to be a part of the firm that represented the client until the client was informed of the lawyer's departure. Compare the UPA and RUPA provisions on this issue, and particularly the effect of statements of dissociation and dissolution under RUPA §§ 704 and 805. Similarly, although a partner who has dissociated from the old firm ceases to have any management role in the firm and, accordingly, any *real* authority to bind the firm (*see* RUPA § 603), the former partner may retain some *apparent* authority to bind the firm as to creditors who lacked knowledge or notice of the partner's dissociation. In this situation the partnership is in a good position to provide at least some notice to creditors, perhaps by a filing under RUPA or by publication under the UPA.

C.   New Partnership's Liability for Pre-Dissolution Debts

As noted above, liabilities of the new partnership generally belong to that firm and its new partners. However, the partnership and the new partners may have some responsibility for old liabilities, just as the old partners may have some responsibilities for new liabilities (*see* Section B). If a partnership dissolves and one or more of the original partners carry on its business, UPA § 41 provides that the new *partnership* is liable for the debts of the original partnership. UPA § 17 and RUPA § 306(b) provide that new *partners* are liable only to the extent of their investments in the firm. These provisions apply to new partners admitted to existing partnerships whether or not the partnership has dissolved. Also, RUPA Article 9 provides for *merger and conversion* of partnerships. The issues concerning these provisions are discussed separately below.

1. New Partners

The restriction on new partners' liability raises issues comparable to those involved in *Judiciary Tower,* discussed in section A, concerning allocating debts to the pre- and post-dissolution partnerships. In *Conklin Farm v. Leibowitz,* 274 N.J. Super. 525, 644 A.2d 687 (1994), the court reversed summary judgment for a new partner as to interest on a pre-admission promissory note that accrued following her admission into the partnership. The court reasoned that this was analogous to post-admission rental payments due on a lease or delivery of goods on preexisting contract. It noted that interest on the debt continued only as to amounts not paid and that the partnership had the option of prepaying the loan without penalty.

On the other hand, in *Citizens Bank of Massachusetts v. Parham-Woodman Medical Associates,* 874 F. Supp. 705 (E.D. Va. 1995), the court held that partners who entered the partnership after the date of a construction loan agreement were liable for partnership's debt only to the extent of partnership property, although the loan agreement provided for disbursement in installments and some disbursements had occurred after the partners joined partnership. The court reasoned that, despite contingencies concerning disbursements, the bank's obligation under the agreement was fixed when the agreement was executed. Under these circumstances, the creditor's expectations as to repayment were based on the partners as of the time of the loan agreement. The court rejected the reasoning of *Conklin Farm* because that case ignored the fact that the preexisting contract created the obligation. The court said (874 F. Supp. at 710):

> The interpretation of Section 17 reflected here is consistent with the language of the statute, with commercial reality as evinced by the applicable documents, and with the articulated purposes which Section 17 was enacted to achieve. This rule enables potential creditors of the partnership to know that what they see of a partnership is what they can reach and it permits potential incoming partners to avoid surprise liabilities. Creditors, of course, can construct and administer loans to partnerships in such a fashion as to reach the personal assets of partners admitted during the disbursement of term payments. However, absent such a basis, the personal assets of an incoming partner are not available to satisfy post-admission advances under the terms of a pre-admission contract.

If the default rule provides that a new partner is not liable on a pre-admission contract, creditors may want to contract directly with new partners to ensure that they are on the debt. Also, the former partners may want to contract with new partners to ensure that the latter have contribution liability on account of contracts (such as leases) in effect as of when the new admittees join the firm.

2.   Successor Partnerships

As noted above, UPA § 41 provides that successor partnerships are liable for the debts of the old firm. This provision applies when a partnership is continuing the business of a prior partnership with some continuity of partners. It does not apply when a wholly new "person," such as a corporation, continues the partnership business, or after a partnership has dissolved and wound up. *See Gillespie v. Seymour,* 876 P.2d 193, 201 (Kan. App. 1994), in which the court held that a successor accounting partnership was not liable for the acts of an accountant while he was a partner in the predecessor firm because UPA § 41 does not apply where a firm liquidates instead of continues.

UPA § 41 raises the question of when a firm is deemed to be continuing a prior partnership. Suppose, for example, that a 10-member professional firm breaks up and each partner goes to a different firm. Are all of these firms "successors," which are now liable for the previous firm's debts? *See* Woo, *The Business of Law,* WALL ST. J., September 2, 1994, p. B3, col. 4, noting that, on the dissolution of Lord, Day, & Lord, Barrett Smith, "because Morgan Lewis expects to hire Lord Day lawyers individually, subject to a vote of that firm's partners, it wouldn't have to pay the debts of the dissolving firm."

RUPA does not deal with successor firms. Rather, under RUPA § 801 the partnership does not dissolve at all following a partner's dissociation in some circumstances (*i.e.,* with the requisite vote to continue). Since the firm continues, there is no "successor" firm. *See* the Official Comment to RUPA § 703. But what do you suppose will happen if a RUPA partnership dissolves and its assets are sold as a going concern to some of the original partners? A creditor may have to pursue the separate assets of each partner of the original firm by obtaining charging orders (*see* § 7.02, above). But creditors may not be able to do even that without exhausting the assets of the old firm under RUPA § 307(d), discussed above in Chapter 6. Courts may find some way to allow recovery against *partnership* successor firms, whatever RUPA says, just as they have imposed liability on *corporate* successors of partnerships under a variety of theories, including fraudulent conveyances, disregarding the legal entity, bulk sale law, and implied assumption of liability. *See* BROMBERG & RIBSTEIN ON PARTNERSHIP § 7.19.

The partnership agreement may limit the liability of partners and successor firms and will be enforced among the parties to the agreement. *See* Note 2, § 6.02.

3. Partnership Merger

There is no formal method for merging partnerships under the UPA. Thus, partnerships have had to invent procedures involving admission of partners and combination of assets and liabilities. Presumably under this procedure partners of each firm are personally liable only for the liabilities that arise after the merger under UPA § 17.

RUPA § 905 provides a way to merge partnerships with other partnerships or limited partnerships. Under RUPA § 906, a merger combines the property and obligations of the constituent companies and a partner of the surviving partnership is personally liable for and must contribute toward the obligations for which he was liable before the merger. A partner is not, however, personally liable for pre-merger liabilities of any other constituent. RUPA § 908 provides that this is not the exclusive method for merging partnerships. Under this provision, what do you suppose would be the effect of a transaction which is styled a "merger" under RUPA but in which the formalities required under RUPA § 905 concerning the "plan" of merger are not complied with?

Mergers and conversions are discussed further below in Chapter 12 in connection with converting partnerships to limited liability companies.

9.06 Buyout and Continuation Agreements

The difficulty of determining the appropriate balance between illiquidity and discontinuity costs is compounded by the differences among partnerships that can affect this balance. As a result, many firms may want to vary the default statutory provisions in their partnership agreements. In particular, the partners may want to (1) provide that the partnership business continues notwithstanding the occurrence of an event of dissolution under the statute, particularly including a partner's dissociation in order to avoid the problems involved in *Page*; and (2) vary the default provisions concerning the valuation of the exiting partner's interest, having in mind the peculiarities of the default rules on valuation under UPA § 42 and RUPA § 701. Although the partners can agree on these matters when a partner dissociates or dissolves the firm, the end of a relationship is usually not the best time for the parties to work things out. Section A will discuss general dissolution and buyout provisions, while the remaining sections discuss some specific problems in connection with dissolution and buyout agreements.

A. General Considerations

Starr v. Fordham
420 Mass. 178, 648 N.E.2d 1261 (1995)

[See excerpt in § 4.03(B) for additional facts.]

* * *

5. Accounts receivable and work in process. The plaintiff claims that the judge's interpretation of Paragraph 3 of the partnership agreement improperly denied him his right to a "fair share" of the net value of the firm's accounts receivable and work in process minus liabilities, reasonable reserves, and allowances.[10]

---

[10]   Paragraph 3 of the partnership agreement provides:

Except as hereinafter provided, upon retirement from the practice of law or withdrawal from the firm without such retirement each partner shall be entitled to a fair share of the net value of unrealized accounts receivable and work in process of the firm, less liabilities.

The plaintiff argues that the judge's conclusion that the term "liabilities," as it appears in Paragraph 3 of the firm's partnership agreement, includes the aggregate sum of the firm's future lease payments, was clearly erroneous. We disagree.

We have stated that "[c]ontract interpretation is largely an individualized process, with the conclusion in a particular case turning on the particular language used against the background of other indicia of the parties' intention." * * *

In the present case, the judge . . . [concluded] that "[a] contractual obligation to pay monies is a liability." [citation omitted] The judge then decided that the firm's long-term office lease constituted a "liability" because it was a contractual obligation to pay money. The judge concluded, therefore, that the plaintiff was not entitled to any percentage of the firm's work in process or its accounts receivable because the "[f]irm's existing liabilities, including a long term lease, exceeded the [f]irm's work in process and accounts receivable by nearly [a] two to one margin without any reserves and allowances."

The plain meaning of the word "liabilities," in the context of the partnership agreement, certainly encompasses the firm's office lease. A partner is jointly liable for all debts and obligations of the partnership. G.L. c. 108A, § 15(b) (1992 Ed.). The partnership's office lease was indisputably a monetary obligation for which each partner was jointly liable. *See id.* We conclude, therefore, that the judge's conclusion that the office lease constituted a liability within the meaning of the firm's partnership agreement was not clearly erroneous.

* * * According to the plaintiff, the judge's interpretation of Paragraph 3 denies it the effect of a rational business instrument because a withdrawing partner would rarely be granted a share of the work in process and accounts receivable. We reject this argument.

At dissolution, a partner is entitled to firm profits only after all of the partnership's creditors have been satisfied and all capital contributions have been repaid. G.L. c. 108A, § 40(b) (1992 Ed.). Similarly, if the partnership's liabilities exceed its assets, then each partner must contribute toward the losses. G.L. c. 108A, §§ 18(a) & 40(d) (1992 Ed.). The judge's interpretation of Paragraph 3 of the partnership agreement has the same effect as G.L. c. 108A, §§ 18(a) & 40(b) (1992 Ed.). The plaintiff, as a withdrawing partner, is entitled to share in the partnership's accounts receivable and work in process which exceed the sum of the amounts owed to creditors and to contributors of capital as well as reasonable reserves and allowances. The lessor of the partnership's offices is a creditor of the firm. [citation omitted] If the partners had "woundup" the affairs of the partnership, the partnership's creditors would have to be ranked in the order of their priority. *See* G.L. c. 108A, § 40. The judge's interpretation of the term "liabilities" properly places the lessor's interest in the accounts receivable and work in process in a position that is superior to the withdrawing partner's interest. If the judge construed the term "liabilities" to exclude the lease, then the lessor would be the only creditor of the partnership whose interest in the partnership assets would be junior to a partner's interest. *See* G.L. c. 108A, § 40. Instead of denying Paragraph

---

Such share shall be determined by the Founding Partners, taking into account such factors as they deem meet and proper, and shall be paid in not more than twenty-four (24) monthly installments.

Thus, Paragraph 3 expressly authorized the founding partners to calculate a departing partner's "fair share" of the net value of the unrealized accounts receivable and work in process less liabilities.

3 the effect of a rational business instrument, the judge's interpretation properly enforces its intended logic.

The plaintiff claims next that the judge's interpretation of the term "liabilities" to include the lease was unreasonable and inequitable because it precluded him from sharing in the accounts receivable and work in process to which he was "entitled." We disagree.

The plaintiff acquiesced to the terms of Paragraph 3 when he signed the partnership agreement. As a result, the plaintiff agreed that his interest in accounts receivable and work in process at withdrawal would be junior to the claims of creditors. If the business of the partnership had been "wound up" after dissolution, the plaintiff would have been jointly liable, with his partners, for the monetary obligation due on the lease. G.L. c. 108A, § 15(b). The judge found that the amount due on the lease alone exceeded the firm's accounts receivable and work in process, without considering the partnership's additional liabilities at dissolution. The judge's interpretation of the term "liabilities," therefore, was neither unreasonable nor inequitable. The plaintiff was "entitled" only to a "fair share" of the accounts receivable and work in process which exceeded the firm's liabilities, reserves, and allowances.

* * *

Notes and Questions

1. **Enforcing the agreement.** Under the UPA the agreement cannot avoid *dissolution*. Thus, even if the agreement provides that the firm does not dissolve, the courts usually interpret these agreements as providing that the partnership business continues after dissolution. *See, e.g., Finkelstein v. Security Properties, Inc.,* 888 P.2d 161, 166 (Wash. App. 1995). Consider, in this light, how the Chameleon agreement would have to be modified for use with a UPA partnership. RUPA, however, provides that the partners may avoid dissolution by contrary agreement. Both the UPA and RUPA allow the partners to vary the *consequences* of dissolution. It is not clear whether an agreement that provides that neither party can withdraw would be enforced. *Infusaid Corp. v. Intermedics Infusaid, Inc.,* 739 F.2d 661 (1st Cir. 1984), indicates that the right to withdraw does not exist in all cases under the UPA. *Compare* RUPA § 103(b)(6). An agreement not to dissociate subjects a partner to open-ended exposure to the debts of the business. But why not allow partners to agree even to onerous provisions? Should a prohibition on withdrawal for a certain period (say, two years) be enforceable? Would it be under RUPA § 103(b)(6)?

Even if the agreement can avoid dissociation, it is necessary to draft clearly for this result given the costs of illiquidity discussed above in Section 9.01(c). In *Active Asset Recovery, Inc. v. Real Estate Asset Recovery Services, Inc.,* 1999 WL 743479 (Del. Ch., Sep 10, 1999), the court noted: "Where parties fail to hammer out a written partnership agreement or reach an accord about their right to walk away, it would be anomalous to interpret them as having entered into an indissoluble bond. * * * Implying such a bond in the absence of an agreement would encourage commercial parties to behave as AMS and REARS have done [breaching duty of loyalty], an incentive system that is irrational."

2. **Drafting the agreement: providing for the "trigger."** Dissolution and buy-out agreements generally contain at least two important elements: the "trigger," which states that certain events cause either dissolution or buyout of the partners' interests (*see* paragraph 10.1 of the Chameleon agreement); and the consequences that follow from the trigger (*see id.* paragraphs 10.2 and 10.3). The agreement might provide for buy-out or dissolution triggers such as deadlock that are not provided for in the statute. Conversely, the agreement might try to avoid UPA consequences for UPA dissolution or buyout causes. In doing this, the parties have to be careful to cover all UPA events. For example, a partner might try to "dissolve" the firm under the UPA in order to escape the consequences of "withdrawal" or "retirement" under the agreement. *See Hunter v. Straube,* 273 Or. 720, 543 P.2d 278 (1975) (which blocked this gambit). Apart from the UPA, the agreement itself might create confusion on triggers and consequences. In *Moran, Shuster, Carignan & Knierim v. August,* 232 Conn. 756, 657 A.2d 229 (1995), a partner was held not entitled to *retirement* compensation under the partnership agreement because he withdrew and started his own firm, thereby triggering a separate provision for *withdrawal* compensation.

In general, the partnership agreement, like the partnership act (*see* § 9.01), must balance the need for partner liquidity against the threat to the firm's continuity if it has to buy out anyone who wants to leave. The consequences of various triggers will vary with the type of partnership. For example, a professional partnership may want to provide liberally for buyout but permit liquidation only on supermajority vote. The parties to a two-person joint venture, on the other hand, want to try to prohibit withdrawal, at least for a certain period, and then give either an option to sell to or buy out the other. But they may want to provide for dissolution if either of the parties dies or becomes bankrupt or incompetent, if the venturers are deadlocked on an important business matter, or on expiration of a term.

3. **Valuation provisions.** When the agreement provides for buyout rather than liquidation, it should also include some provision for fixing the buyout price. Consider when each of the following alternatives might be appropriate from a planning standpoint, and what drafting problems they might raise:

(a) Return of the parties' capital accounts (*see* § 4.04) as in the *Spayd* case (§ 9.04(B)) and paragraph 10.3 of the Chameleon agreement, perhaps adjusted for profits and losses not allocated to the account and debts due to or owed by the partner.

(b) Return of the partner's share of receivables and work in process. *See Starr.* Note that that court's interpretation of "liabilities" results in all liabilities being subtracted from *some* assets—*i.e.*, only accounts receivable and work in process—rather than all of the profits the future lease payments will help produce. Also, should the liability under the lease be computed by simply adding up the total of all lease payments due? How might the disputed clause have been drafted to better deal with these issues?

(c) The current year's profits plus x times the partner's share of the firm's average annual earnings for the last y years.

(d) X times the average annual distribution to the partner over the past y years.

(e) The price determined by the partners or, if they cannot agree, the last agreed valuation of partnership assets or, if none, the firm's net assets per its balance sheet.

(f) The value determined by appraisers selected per the agreement, taking into account factors enumerated in the agreement, including the firm's inventory, real estate, and goodwill.

(g) The price an unaffiliated third party was willing to pay for the interest.

(h) In a two-person partnership, letting a partner who decides to leave propose a price at which the other partner may elect to be either the buyer or the seller.

4. **Other buyout terms.** In addition to the amount of payment, the agreement may need to include other provisions concerning buyout, including:

(a) Whether payment is in cash or by a note and, if the latter, if and how the note is to be secured. *See* paragraph 10.3 of the Chameleon agreement.

(b) The scope of indemnification against partnership liabilities. If the leaving partner's buyout price is generous, perhaps the indemnification right should be more restrictive that the default right discussed in § 9.05. Consider what the appropriate indemnification right should have been in the situation in *Starr*.

B.   Expulsion or Forced Buyout

Sometimes the partners may want not merely to plan for a partner's departure but also to make sure that they can get rid of an errant, recalcitrant or incompetent partner. UPA § 31(1)(d) provides that agreed expulsion is a cause of dissolution, and UPA § 38(1) provides by default for continuation of the business with a cash payment to the expelled partner. RUPA § 601(3) also provides for expulsion pursuant to the partnership agreement, and this is not a cause of dissolution under RUPA § 801.

It is important to provide for expulsion in the partnership agreement because partners may not be easy to get rid of in the absence of such a provision. They may be able to obtain a judicial decree of dissolution for cause under UPA § 32(1). In this event, the wrongdoing partner may be deemed to have wrongfully dissolved, so that the partners may buy out the partner and continue the firm under RUPA § 38(2). RUPA § 601(5), which provides for judicial expulsion for cause of wrongdoing partners, reaches a similar result by a different route. But the partners may be in trouble if they try to expel a partner on their own without support in the agreement. If they simply exclude the partner from the partnership, that partner may have a right to judicial dissolution on the ground of wrongdoing by the excluding partners, who then may find themselves out in the cold. If they try to expel one or more partners by dissolving the firm by express will, purchasing the assets at a liquidation sale, and continuing the business without the "expelled" partner, this may be deemed to be a bad faith freezeout or breach of fiduciary duty under the principles discussed in *Page v. Page* and related Notes in § 9.02(A).

The following cases show the consequences of expulsion pursuant to and without an expulsion provision in the agreement.

Chandler Medical Building Partners v. Chandler Dental Group
175 Ariz. 273, 855 P.2d 787 (1993)

JACOBSON, Presiding Judge.

Plaintiff-appellant Chandler Medical Building Partners ("CMBP") appeals from the trial court's judgment dismissing its complaint against defendants-appellees. The primary issue on appeal is whether the terms of the partnership agreement provided an exclusive remedy for Defendants' failure to pay capital contribution assessments, thereby precluding CMBP from maintaining a cause of action for damages pursuant to A.R.S. § 29-238.

FACTS AND PROCEDURAL BACKGROUND

CMBP is an Arizona general partnership ("the partnership") formed pursuant to the Uniform Partnership Act as adopted in Arizona, A.R.S. §§ 29-201 *et seq.*, by agreement dated June 3, 1983 ("the partnership agreement"). Chandler Dental Group ("CDG") is an Arizona general partnership, and, for purposes of this appeal, is deemed to be a general partner of CMBP. Defendants-appellees Kevin Cook, Gerald DiQuattro, Gail Goodman, and their respective spouses, are all general partners of CDG (collectively "Defendants"), who are bound by the terms of the partnership agreement.

The partnership was formed for the purpose of developing, constructing, operating, leasing, or selling a two-story medical office building in Chandler, Arizona. The partnership constructed the building, but incurred substantial debt, including more than $3 million in bonded indebtedness. The partnership was unable to pay its debt obligations and its necessary operating expenses. Therefore, pursuant to the partnership agreement, a majority of the partners on November 21, 1988, and again on September 26, 1989, by resolutions, voted to make capital call assessments against all partners based upon each partner's percentage interest in the partnership. The resolutions authorized three assessments for periods ending in 1988, 1989, and 1990. Although CDG paid the 1988 assessment, it did not pay the 1989 and 1990 assessments.

Effective April 1, 1990, a majority of the partners voted to treat CDG as having withdrawn from the partnership for failure to pay the assessments. Sixty percent of the remaining partners then elected to continue the partnership. The partnership then filed an action against Defendants pursuant to A.R.S. § 29-238 for breach of the agreement and for a declaratory judgment, alleging that Defendants had defaulted under the partnership agreement by failing to pay the capital contribution assessments and were liable for damages to the partnership as a result of the breach.

Defendants filed a motion to dismiss the complaint pursuant to Rule 12(b)(6), Arizona Rules of Civil Procedure. They alleged that the partnership agreement permitted a partner to withdraw from the partnership for failure to make capital contribution assessments and therefore they were not in default under it. They also argued that, even if there was a default, the partnership agreement provided specific procedures and exclusive remedies for such a default, and these exclusive remedies foreclosed an action under A.R.S. § 29-238. The court . . . entered judgment in favor of Defendants, dismissing the complaint and granting attorneys' fees. CMBP appealed, raising the following issues: 1. Did the trial court err in finding as a matter of law that Defendants were not in default under the partnership agreement when they failed to pay the capital contribution assessments? 2. Did the trial court err in finding that the partnership agreement provides an exclusive remedy for the partnership when Defendants failed to pay the capital contribution assessments, thus precluding an action for damages pursuant to A.R.S. § 29-238?

DISCUSSION

A. Default Under Partnership Agreement

CMBP argues that section 10 of the partnership agreement unambiguously requires that each partner contribute additional capital when requested to do so by a majority of the partners. Alternatively, CMBP argues that the partnership agreement sets forth a "particular undertaking" for the partnership, which prevents a partner from dissolving the partnership until the undertaking is completed. CMBP alleges that, when Defendants failed to pay the required assessment, a default occurred under the agreement.

Defendants argue that sections 10 and 14 of the partnership agreement unambiguously give a partner the right to withdraw from the partnership by refusing to pay a capital assessment, without any subsequent liability of that partner to the partnership. Defendants thus allege that no default occurred under the agreement as a matter of law. To resolve the dispute, we first examine the relevant portions of the agreement.

1. Applicable provisions of the partnership agreement.

Section 5(a) of the partnership agreement requires each partner to make an initial capital contribution to the partnership. Section 5(b) provides that "[e]xcept as provided above and in Section 10 hereof, no partner shall be obligated to contribute any additional capital . . . ."

Section 10 provides, in pertinent part:

> In the event that the cash of the partnership is insufficient to pay the necessary cash operating expenses and debt service obligations of the partnership as and when they become due . . . then the partnership, on the determination of a majority in interest of the partners, may make a call upon each partner for such sums as (in the discretion of a majority in interest of the partners) shall be necessary for the payment of such obligations as and when they become due. Each partner shall thereupon be obligated to contribute his pro rata share thereof within thirty (30) days after the date such call is made. Any such amounts which are paid by a partner to the partnership under this section shall be due within thirty (30) days after call and shall be a loan by the partner to the partnership, and not a capital contribution (unless otherwise determined by a majority in interest of the partners). * * * In the event a partner fails to provide his pro rata share as requested by this Section he shall be treated as having withdrawn from the partnership (*see* Section 14).

Section 14(a) of the partnership agreement provides:

A partner may withdraw from the partnership at any time. If a partner declines to meet any call to pay any necessary cash operating expenses and debt service to the partnership in accordance with Section 10 hereof, he shall be treated as having elected to withdraw from the partnership.

Section 14(c) provides that the partnership shall be dissolved inter alia by the withdrawal of a partner, but provides that sixty percent in interest of the remaining partners may elect to continue the partnership notwithstanding the withdrawal, and, in that event, the interest of the withdrawing partner shall remain under the control of the partnership.

Section 17 of the partnership agreement provides, in pertinent part:

Upon dissolution of the partnership because of the withdrawal, expulsion, or bankruptcy of a partner or issuance of a charging order against a partnership interest, as specified in subsection 14(c) for the election to continue the business of the partnership, the partnership itself, acting by a majority in interest of its partners, shall have the option, at any time during the thirty-six (36) months period following the date of dissolution . . . to purchase such former partner's interest by giving written notice of exercise of such option to the other prior to the expiration of such thirty-six (36) months period. * * * If such notice is not given within such period such option shall terminate and be of no further force and effect; provided, however, such former partner or his successor in interest shall, during the six (6) months period following the expiration of the partnership's thirty-six (36) months option period, have the option to require the continuing partnership to purchase such former partner's interest by giving written notice of exercise of such option to the partnership prior to the expiration of such six (6) months [period]. * * *

Finally, section 18 of the partnership agreement provides:

Any provision of this Agreement notwithstanding, if a partner or partner's affiliate is in default . . . under any term or provision of this Agreement, such partner or such partner's successor shall not be entitled to exercise any rights or options during the period such default continues to which such partner or his successor would be entitled under this Agreement. The partnership shall have a prior lien, security interest, charge and right of off-set against the interest of each partner or former partner for all obligations . . . which arise under this Agreement. All such obligations shall be fully paid and satisfied before a partner or former partner shall be entitled to receive any distribution on account of profits, partnership capital or because of the purchase of his interest by the partnership. * * *

3. Obligations and default under section 10.

Section 10 of the partnership agreement . . . provides that "[e]ach partner shall thereupon be obligated to contribute his pro rata share thereof within thirty (30) days after the date such call is made." The plain meaning of the word "obligate" is "to bind to the observance or performance of a duty; to place under an obligation. To bind one's self by an obligation or promise; to assume a duty." BLACK'S LAW DICTIONARY 1073 (6th ed. 1990). In addition, the agreement provides that any amounts paid under section 10 "shall be due within thirty (30) days after call . . . ." This language clearly indicates that Defendants had a mandatory duty under the agreement to pay the capital assessments.

Defendants argue that other portions of the agreement indicate otherwise. In particular, section 10 provides that in the event a partner fails to provide his pro rata share as requested he shall be treated as having withdrawn. Section 14(a) provides that a partner may withdraw from the partnership at any time and that, if a partner fails to meet a capital call, he shall be treated as having withdrawn and shall have no further interest in the partnership. Section 14(c) provides that withdrawal of a partner causes a dissolution of the partnership unless 60% in interest of the remaining partners agree to its continuation. Defendants allege, therefore, that under the plain language of the agreement a partner has a right to withdraw by failing to pay a requested capital contribution and may cause a dissolution of the partnership at any time without liability to the partnership. In response, CMBP argues that section 14 of the agreement reflects only that a partner cannot be forced to remain in the partnership relationship against his will.

In this regard, we recognize a distinction between the power to dissolve a partnership and the right to dissolve it in that any partner has the power to dissolve a partnership, even if the dissolution is in contravention of the agreement. [citation omitted] Section 31 of the Uniform Partnership Act (1969) (U.P.A.) recognizes such power although the agreement might limit the right to dissolve the partnership and the dissolution may constitute a breach. U.P.A. § 31; A.R.S. § 29-231. As the comment to § 31 states: The relation of partners is one of agency. The agency is such a personal one that equity cannot enforce it even where the agreement provides that the partnership shall continue for a definite time. The power of any partner to terminate the relation, even though in doing so he breaches a contract, should, it is submitted, be recognized. [citation omitted]

Attempting to harmonize the language of section 10 with the language of section 14, we think the most reasonable construction of the phrase "may withdraw" in section 14 is that a partner has the power to withdraw from the partnership at any time, and that such withdrawal causes an automatic dissolution of the partnership. To construe section 14 as Defendants suggest would render the obligatory language of section 10 meaningless and superfluous. Furthermore, in our view, the word "requested" in section 10 does not nullify the "shall be obligated" and "shall be due" language of that section; it simply refers to the fact that, when the partnership requests a specific amount from each partner, that partner must pay it within the time specified, or suffer the consequences. Because Defendants had a contractual duty to pay the assessments under section 10 and failed to do so, we believe the non-payment constituted a "default" under its terms. Thus, the trial court erred in finding no "default" under the terms of the agreement. However, we will affirm if the court reached the right result for the wrong reason. [citation omitted] We therefore examine whether dismissal was justified on the other grounds argued.

B. Remedies Available to the Partnership on Default

Defendants argue that, even assuming a default, the agreement sets forth the sole and exclusive remedies of the partnership; thus, the partnership is precluded from bringing an action for damages pursuant to A.R.S. § 29-238. CMBP argues that the options available to the partnership under the agreement are not exclusive remedies; thus, an action for damages under A.R.S. § 29-238 is appropriate.

We first note that A.R.S. § 29-218 provides that "[t]he rights and duties of the partners in relation to the partnership shall be determined, subject to any agreement between them . . . ." "Because partnerships result from contract, the rights and liabilities of the partners among themselves are subject to such agreements as they may make." * * *

Although this agreement provides a partner with a contractual obligation to pay a capital call assessment under section 10 of the agreement, the remedies for a default by failure to pay are provided in sections 14 and 18, and include the withdrawing partner's forfeiture of any right to participate further in the partnership, a loss of interest in its profits and assets, and the loss of a right to exercise any options or receive any distribution of his capital contribution while the default continues. In our view, section 10 provides a partner with a choice about payment of a capital contribution call: if a partner chooses to pay it, he remains in the partnership; if he fails to pay it, he is treated as withdrawn, with the resulting consequences. Because such a dissolution of the partnership is explicitly provided for under the terms of the agreement, it is not "caused in contravention of the partnership agreement" for which a cause of action for damages would arise under A.R.S. § 29-238.

We also believe such an agreement makes good business sense. Such a "pay or walk" provision leaves a partner free to withdraw from an investment that incurs increasing expenses, with nothing to lose but his existing capital contribution and no future liability. It leaves the remaining partners free to continue the venture as a new partnership with control of the withdrawn partner's interest, and under no obligation to return his capital contribution under any of the buy-out provisions until his default is cured. By providing all parties with choices in the face of increasing capital costs, the agreement has provided remedies for a default that are limited by the terms of the contract and which would be inconsistent with an action for damages. We therefore hold that the trial court correctly dismissed the suit for monetary damages. * * *

[The court also held that there was no wrongful dissolution prior to the expiration of a term or undertaking because the partnership was not one for a particular undertaking, *i.e.*, leasing the office building. Although the partnership agreement provided that this was part of the purpose of the partnership, there was no limit on how long the partnership would operate the building.]

CONCLUSION

For the reasons discussed above, we affirm the judgment of the trial court dismissing the action.

Cadwalader, Wickersham & Taft v. Beasley
District Court of Appeal of Florida, Fourth District.
1998 WL 904065 (1998)

POLEN, Judge.

* * * [James] Beasley laterally transferred to become a partner at CW & T [Cadwalader, Wickersham & Taft] in its Palm Beach office in 1989. After his arrival, the Palm Beach office suffered from internal discord and, by 1994, the office was operating at a loss. In response to this situation, the firm's management committee began discussions regarding the ter-

mination of up to 30 partners nationwide, including the Palm Beach partners. During this time, and allegedly unbeknownst to CW & T, Beasley was planning to leave the firm. He met secretly with associates in CW & T's Palm Beach office about leaving with him.

The management committee eventually held a day-long meeting on August 7, 1994. Prior to the meeting, the committee members were asked to submit lists of less productive partners to be considered for possible termination. All of the Palm Beach partners were identified on the lists actually submitted. A tentative vote was reached at that meeting and, later that month, the committee formally decided to close its Palm Beach office by year-end 1994. It informed its partners, including Beasley, of its decision on August 30, 1994.

After the announcement, Beasley retained Professor Robert Hillman, who opined that CW & T, pursuant to the partnership agreement, lacked the legal authority to expel him from the partnership. In response to this opinion, CW & T sent a memorandum to Beasley informing him that he was still a partner in the firm. It then offered Beasley either relocation within the firm but in the New York or Washington, D.C. offices, or, a compensation/severance package which included his return of capital, departure bonus, and full shares through December 31, 1994. He was presented with a written withdrawal agreement confirming the same. Beasley, a member of both the Florida and New York bars, rejected the same as impractical.

Settlement negotiations between CW & T and Beasley then continued. On November 9, he sued the firm for fraud and breach of fiduciary duty, among other counts. On November 10, 1994, CW & T sent a letter to Beasley informing him to vacate the premises by 5:00 p.m. the next day. The letter specifically prohibited him from continuing to represent himself as associated with the firm.

After a nine-day bench trial, Judge Cook authored a meticulous and, we believe, exceptionally well-reasoned final judgment. He found that CW & T was authorized to close the Palm Beach office pursuant to the partnership agreement, and that Beasley would have voluntarily left CW & T by year-end 1994 in any event. Nevertheless, since the partnership agreement lacked provisions for the expulsion of a partner except in one limited situation, he found that CW & T had anticipatorily breached the partnership agreement when it announced its plans to close the Palm Beach office in August, and then actually breached the agreement when it sent him the November 10, 1994 letter. The final judgment awarded Beasley his paid-in capital plus interest (which CW & T does not dispute), his percentage interest in the firm's accounts receivables and assets and interest thereon, and punitive damages, all totaling $2.5+ million. The later judgment awarded Beasley's attorneys fees and costs.

* * * [The damages included $867,110.00 for Beasley's interest in the firm, $884,000.00 for the firm's use of Beasley's rights in partnership property, and $500,000 punitive damages.]

I. WHETHER BEASLEY WAS EXPELLED OR VOLUNTARILY WITHDREW

Under New York Partnership Law's adoption of the Uniform Partnership Act (UPA), partners have no common law or statutory right to expel or dismiss another partner from the partnership; they may, however, provide in their partnership agreement for expulsion under prescribed conditions which must be strictly applied. *Gelder Med. Group v. Webber,* 41 N.Y.2d 680, 394 N.Y.S.2d 867, 363 N.E.2d 573 (N.Y. 1991); N.Y. Partnership Law § 62(1)(d)(McKinney 1993). Absent such a provision, as here, the removal of a partner may be accomplished only through dissolution of the firm. *Dawson v. White & Case*, 88 N.Y.2d 666, 649 N.Y.S.2d 364, 672 N.E.2d 589 (N.Y.1996).

The evidence supports Judge Cook's finding that CW & T intended to remove Beasley as a partner in the firm when it announced it was closing its Palm Beach office by year-end 1994. This finding, in turn, supports the conclusion that CW & T anticipatorily expelled Beasley from the firm. [citations omitted]

In reaching this conclusion, we necessarily reject CW & T's argument that Beasley voluntary withdrew from the firm rather than having been expelled. Beasley had been practicing exclusively in South Florida for 22 years, where he built a substantial client base. As the trial court observed, to suddenly uproot to New York or Washington and leave his clients and contacts behind, as the court suggested, would have severely diminished his rainmaking abilities. Under these circumstances, we conclude that his rejecting the offer as impractical was not tantamount to a voluntary withdrawal. [citations omitted]

Even assuming that CW & T did not anticipatorily breach the agreement on August 29, 1994, we conclude that the November 10, 1994 letter actually expelled him. Even though CW & T notes that Beasley planned on eventually leaving the firm even before it announced the decision to close the Palm Beach office, and that he most likely would not have stayed past 1994, the record does not reflect that he actually had definite plans to leave.

We further reject CW & T's argument that Beasley's suing the firm on November 9, 1994 was tantamount to a voluntary withdrawal. Since CW & T does not dispute the lack of frivolousness of Beasley's lawsuit, but merely takes issue with its allegations, we find its argument unpersuasive. [citation omitted]

II. THE AWARD OF INTEREST

CW & T then argues the trial court erred in finding that a dissolution occurred and contends that, as a "withdrawn partner" pursuant to the agreement, Beasley was entitled to only his paid-in capital. Even if dissolution had occurred, it argues he still only would be entitled to an amount significantly less than that awarded to him. Beasley disputes that he was a "withdrawn" partner pursuant to the agreement, and contends that dissolution was mandated.

Under the partnership agreement, a "withdrawn Partner" is anyone "who was a Partner under this or a prior Firm Agreement." More specifically, the agreement provides that a partner, upon 60 days written notice, may withdraw from the firm at the end of any fiscal year. CW & T argues that, under these provisions, Beasley was technically a withdrawn partner and, thus, was only entitled to his capital contribution plus interest under Paragraph F(2)(a)(i) of the agreement. We, instead, agree with Judge Cook that the term "withdrawn" neither contemplated nor encompassed a partner expelled in the same manner as Beasley, especially since Beasley never provided any written notice of a voluntary withdrawal, and since CW & T conceded at trial that it did not treat Beasley as a "withdrawn partner" after his departure.

Antidissolution Provision

CW & T then argues that concluding a dissolution occurred would conflict with that portion of the agreement which states, "Neither withdrawal of a Partner nor the death of a Partner, *nor any other event* shall cause dissolution of the Firm [unless 75% of the remaining partners agreed in writing]." (Emphasis added.) It reasons that expulsion of a partner, however wrongful, is an "event" for purposes of this antidissolution clause. We disagree, for to construe this anti-dissolution provision strictly would recognize an implicit expulsion provision where no provision exists. Such an interpretation would be inconsistent with existing law. *See Dawson, supra; Empire Properties Corp. v. Manufacturer's Trust Co.*, 288 N.Y. 242, 43 N.E.2d 25 (N.Y.1942).

Even if the provision were broad enough to cover expulsions, we believe Beasley would still be allowed to seek dissolution of the partnership. Under New York law, any partner has the right to a formal accounting as to partnership affairs if he is wrongfully excluded from the partnership business or possession of its property by his co-partners, or "[w]henever other circumstances render it just and reasonable." N.Y. Partnership Law § 44 (McKinney 1993). Thus, a wrongful exclusion of one partner by a co-partner from participation in the conduct of the business may be grounds for judicial dissolution. [citations omitted]

Since Beasley was expelled, his damages are to be assessed under § 71 of New York Partnership Law, and not under the partnership agreement. Since there is competent, substantial evidence in the record to support both the method and result used to calculate his interest in the firm's assets, we affirm the award of interest in the amount of $867,110.00.

III. THE AWARD OF PROFITS

Under New York law, when a partnership continues following the expulsion of a partner, that partner has the right to receive the value of his partnership interest as of the date of dissolution, either with interest from the date of dissolution, or, at his election, the profits attributable to the use of his right in the property of the dissolved partnership. N.Y. Partnership Law § 73 (McKinney 1993).

Strictly construing this statute, Beasley was entitled to either interest on the value of his interest in the dissolved partnership ($867,110) or profits attributable to the use of his right in the property of the firm on top of the $867,110. Beasley elected to receive the profits attributable to his use through the date of judgment instead of interest at 3% over prime (as defined in the agreement). Based on his expert, Mr. Burgher, having calculated the profits attributable to the use of his right in the property based on the firm's total earnings to reflect what Beasley's total income would have been had he stayed at the firm from November, 1994 through May, 1996, the court awarded Beasley profits in the amount of $935,261.52.

CW & T argues that, as a matter of law, awarding Beasley $935,261.52 in "profits" based on this calculation was incorrect. Relying on *Kirsch v. Leventhal*, 181 A.D.2d 222, 586 N.Y.S.2d 330 (App.Div.1992), it reasons that Beasley should not be entitled to profits resulting from the postdissolution services of the remaining partners. We agree. To the extent that some of the firm's postdissolution profits may be attributable to the postdissolution efforts, skill, and diligence of the remaining partners, the firm's fee as a result of those services should not be proportionately attributable to the use of the departing partner's right in the property of the dissolved partnership. [citations omitted] As the record does not clarify what portion, if any, of the postdissolution profits earned on services (as opposed to firm assets) was attributable to Beasley, we find that Beasley failed to carry his burden of showing what the quantum meruit value of his services was after he left the firm.

Beasley tries to distinguish *Kirsch* and the other cases upon which CW & T relies based on the fact that the partners in those cases were not wrongfully expelled. If recognized, this distinction may help justify the court's award, but it would seem to be an impermissible extension of § 73. As an equitable consideration, although the facts underlying Beasley's departure appear much more egregious than in the cases CW & T cites, Beasley still had "dirt under his fingernails." While CW & T should not be unjustly enriched through its wrongful expulsion of Beasley, neither should Beasley be unjustly enriched by reaping the rewards of other partners' individual efforts. Accordingly, we reverse this portion of the award and remand the case to the trial court to calculate Beasley's interest on $867,110 at 3% over prime, the defined rate pursuant to the agreement, under § 73.

IV. THE IMPOSITION OF PUNITIVE DAMAGES

CW & T then argues that the court's award of punitive damages was both unwarranted and erroneous as a matter of law. It asserts that the court's failure to award Beasley compensatory damages on his breach of fiduciary duty claim barred an award of punitive damages under New York law. Under New York law, the nature of the conduct which justifies an award of punitive damages is conduct having a high degree of moral culpability, or, in other words, conduct which shows a "conscious disregard of the rights of others or conduct so reckless as to amount to such disregard." [citations omitted] CW & T is correct in arguing that punitive damages are generally recovered only after compensatory damages have been awarded; [citations omitted] however, since the purpose of punitive damages is to both punish the wrongdoer and deter others from such wrongful behavior, as a matter of policy, courts have the discretion to award punitive damages even where compensatory damages are found lacking. [citations omitted]

We believe CW & T should not be insulated from the consequences of its wrongdoing simply because Beasley suffered no compensatory damages. As the court found, CW & T "was participating in a clandestine plan to wrongfully expel some partners for the financial gain of other partners. Such activity cannot be said to be honorable, much less to comport with the 'punctilio of an honor.'" Because these findings establish that CW & T consciously disregarded the rights of Beasley, we affirm the award of punitive damages.
* * *

Dawson v. White & Case
Court of Appeals of New York
88 N.Y.2d 666, 672 N.E.2d 589, 649 N.Y.S.2d 364 (1996)

In 1988, the law firm of White & Case dissolved and then re-formed without one of its partners, Evan R. Dawson. This appeal presents two questions arising from an accounting pursuant to Partnership Law § 74 of Dawson's interest in White & Case: (i) whether the law firm possesses goodwill that can be distributed in an accounting proceeding; and (ii) whether the law firm's unfunded pension plan is a liability of the firm. Based on the facts presented, we conclude that, for purposes of the White & Case partnership accounting, goodwill was not a distributable asset of the partnership and the pension payments were not a partnership liability. * * * [For the court's holding on goodwill, see Note 1, p.229 above.]

Before turning to the specific issues on appeal, it is useful to review certain elemental principles of partnership law. Foremost among these, indeed "at the heart of the partnership concept," is "the principle that partners may choose with whom they wish to be associated" (*Gelder Medical Group v. Webber*, 41 N.Y.2d 680, 684). In recognition of this principle, we have held that a partnership agreement may contain a termination provision or some other mechanism by which to remove a partner (*see id.*, at 683). Absent such a mechanism, however, the removal of a partner can be accomplished only through dissolution of the firm, defined as a "change in the relation of the partners caused by any partner ceasing to be associated in the carrying on . . . of the business" (Partnership Law § 60). The White & Case partnership agreement did not contain an express termination provision, and so, in order to remove Dawson, the partners voted to dissolve the firm and then to immediately re-form without him.

This act of dissolution conferred on Dawson the "right to an account of his interest . . . as against the partnership continuing the business" (Partnership Law § 74; *see*, Partnership Law § 52). When, as in this case, the partnership business is continued after dissolution, the accounting is performed by computing the firm's assets less its liabilities, with the balance hypothetically apportioned among the partners to fix the former partner's share of the partnership (see, Partnership Law § 71[c]; *see generally* 2 BROMBERG AND RIBSTEIN, PARTNERSHIP § 7.13[b], at 7:121). At issue on appeal is whether, in the White & Case partnership accounting, goodwill was properly included as an asset of the firm and the pension payments were properly disallowed as a partnership liability.

Notes and Questions

1. **Interpreting the agreement.** Do you agree with the court's interpretation of the agreement in *Chandler*? The agreement provided for an assessment only when the partnership is in poor financial condition. Doesn't it therefore follow that the partners normally would have little to lose by following the "walk" option of "pay or walk"? If so, the capital call provision may be toothless, which would suggest that the partners must have intended the capital contribution obligation to be absolute. But there was another possible penalty of walking—the other partners could respond by liquidating the partnership, which would require payment of the firm's liabilities. Might other drafting alternatives have better accomplished the parties' objectives in *Chandler*?

2. **Expulsion other than pursuant to the partnership agreement.** Compare *Beasley* and *Dawson* on the issue of whether a partner may be expelled when there is no expulsion provision in the agreement. Would the *Beasley* court have permitted expulsion if the firm had used the dissolution-and-reformation device used in *Dawson*? If so, should the expulsion be considered wrongful just because the firm did not use that procedure? Was Beasley even expelled? Did it make a difference to his damages whether he was expelled or left voluntarily?

3. **Bad faith expulsion.** When should expulsion, whether or not pursuant to the agreement, be considered in bad faith? For a discussion of interpretation of and judicial standards of good faith in the enforcement of expulsion provisions, *see* Hillman, *Misconduct as a Basis for Excluding or Expelling a Partner: Effecting Commercial Divorce and Security Custody of the Business*, 78 N.U. L. REV. 527, 559-81 (1983); Ribstein, *Law Partner Expulsion*, 55 BUS. LAW. 845 (2000); Vestal, *Law Partner Expulsions*, 55 WASH. & LEE L. REV. 1083 (1998). On the one hand, expulsion might seem

to result from the firm ganging up on a helpless partner. On the other hand, expulsion might be viewed as a necessary disciplinary mechanism for the firm that would be unduly hampered by bad faith qualifications.

As *Beasley* indicates, an expulsion may be in bad faith if its purpose was solely to benefit the expelling partners. *See also Waite on Behalf of Bretton Woods Acquisition Co. v. Sylvester,* 131 N.H. 663, 560 A.2d 619 (1989) (holding that partners could remove a co-partner in accordance with the partnership agreement where they had a legitimate business purpose, to resolve a disagreement among partners, rather than merely a motive to gain financially). However, this test is potentially quite broad since the expelling partners presumably would not vote for expulsion unless they would benefit in some way, perhaps by making the "firm" better off. The effect of the downsizing at Cadwalader was apparently a significant increase in efficiency. *See* Barrett, *Putsch and Shove: A Once-Stodgy Firm Makes a Flashy Return, But at What Cost?* WALL ST. J. August 17, 1998 at A1. How can the "firm" be separated from the expelling partners?

Should it make a difference if the expulsion is done at the behest of a powerful partner who would reap a special benefit? In *Winston & Strawn v. Nosal,* 664 N.E.2d 239, 215 Ill. Dec. 842 (Ill. App. 1996), the court found a triable issue of bad faith where the expulsion immediately followed the plaintiff's threat to sue for records under the partnership agreement that would have indicated wrongdoing by the manager who was instrumental in the expulsion despite earlier assurances to the plaintiff that he would not be removed. Should this give rise to a remedy on behalf of the expelled partner or, like any other breach of fiduciary duty, on behalf of the partnership?

The courts generally do not require elaborate procedures unless these are provided for in the partnership agreement. *See, e.g., Fisher v. Parks,* 248 Ill. App. 3d 666, 618 N.E.2d 1202, 188 Ill. Dec. 632, *leave to appeal denied,* 248 Ill. App. 3d 666, 188 Ill. Dec. 632, 618 N.E.2d 1202 (1993).

4. **Expulsion of whistleblower.** Should expulsion be upheld if its effect is to interfere with enforcement of attorney ethical rules by penalizing a partner who sought to report misconduct? This basis of invalidating the expulsion would not be bad faith or a fiduciary breach in the traditional sense, but rather would be an ethical restriction on the partnership agreement for the protection of clients. In *Bohatch v. Butler & Binion,* 977 S.W.2d 543 (Tex. 1998), the court rejected the argument that "public policy requires a limited duty to remain partners—*i.e.*, a partnership must retain a whistleblower partner." There was a strong dissent, as well as a concurring opinion suggesting that the expulsion was justified because the whistleblower's charges of overbilling by a partner were inaccurate. *Nosal,* discussed above in Note 3, provides some authority for protection of whistleblowers since the court found a triable issue of bad faith expulsion of a partner who was attempting to uncover the manager's wrongdoing.

Expulsion of whistleblowers presents difficult policy issues. As the court noted in *Bohatch*, ethical restrictions on expulsion would override the firm's strong interests in maintaining internal efficiency. Moreover, it is not clear that restricting expulsion would help clients. The firm itself is best situated to protect clients by monitoring its partners, and restricting expulsion might actually interfere with the firm's ability to serve its clients by disciplining its members. It is arguably enough to invalidate a whistleblower's expulsion that, as in *Nosal*, it is in bad faith or breach of fiduciary duty in the traditional sense of benefiting only the partner who is charged with the wrong while eliminating a partner who had spotted a problem. The expulsion in *Bohatch* arguably did not hurt the firm because the plaintiff's allegations were incorrect. However, a test that would distinguish sharply between correct and incorrect allegations, like that suggested by the concurring judge in *Bohatch*, might excessively deter whistleblowing activity by punishing reasonable errors.

C.   Post-dissolution Work-in-Process and Competition

As discussed in § 9.04, an important issue in connection with dissolution of professional firms is the allocation of fees from cases or other work pending as of the time of dissolution. The rule under the UPA, which allocates the fee according to the pre-dissolution shares may not be what the parties want, particularly since it gives no credit for post-dissolution changes in the allocation of responsibility for the cases. Thus, the partnership agreement normally does, and certainly should, deal with this issue. Even if it does, there are often questions concerning interpretation and the duties of the leaving partners to the dissolved partnership. The following cases illustrate these issues and how the courts approach resolving them.

Meehan v. Shaughnessy
404 Mass. 419, 535 N.E.2d 1255 (1989)

HENNESSEY, Chief Justice.

The plaintiffs, James F. Meehan (Meehan) and Leo V. Boyle (Boyle), were partners of the law firm, Parker, Coulter, Daley & White (Parker Coulter). After Meehan and Boyle terminated their relationship with Parker Coulter to start their own firm, they commenced this action both to recover amounts they claim the defendants, their former partners, owed them under the partnership agreement, and to obtain a declaration as to amounts they owed the defendants for work done at Parker Coulter on cases they removed to their new firm. The defendants (hereinafter collectively Parker Coulter) counterclaimed that Meehan and Boyle violated their fiduciary duties, breached the partnership agreement, and tortiously interfered with their advantageous business and contractual relationships. As grounds for these claims, Parker Coulter asserted that Meehan and Boyle engaged in improper conduct in withdrawing cases and clients from the firm, and in inducing employees to join the new firm of Meehan, Boyle & Cohen, P.C. (MBC). Parker Coulter also filed a third-party action with similar claims against MBC and against Cynthia J. Cohen (Cohen), a former junior partner, and Steven H. Schafer (Schafer), a former associate, who, among others, left the firm to join MBC.

After a jury-waived trial, a Superior Court judge rejected all of Parker Coulter's claims for relief, and found that Meehan and Boyle were entitled to recover amounts owed to them under the partnership agreement. The judge also found, based on the partnership agreement and a quantum meruit theory, that Parker Coulter was entitled to recover from Meehan and

Boyle for time billed and expenses incurred on the cases Meehan and Boyle removed to their own firm. Parker Coulter appealed from the judgment, and we granted direct appellate review.

Although we are in agreement with most of the judge's reasoning and conclusions which he reached after lengthy and painstaking proceedings, we nevertheless reverse the judgment entered below and remand for further findings and a hearing, consistent in all respects with this opinion. This result follows from our conclusion, infra, that the judge erred in deciding that Meehan and Boyle acted properly in acquiring consent to remove cases to MBC.

We summarize the facts as found by the judge. Aside from certain conclusions which the judge reached, and which we address in more detail below, the parties agree that these findings were warranted by the evidence. Parker, Coulter, Daley & White is a large partnership which specializes in litigation on behalf of both defendants and plaintiffs. Meehan joined the firm in 1959, and became a partner in 1963; his practice focuses primarily on complex tort litigation, such as product liability and aviation defense work. Boyle joined Parker Coulter in 1971, and became a partner in 1980; he has concentrated on plaintiffs' work. Both have developed outstanding reputations as trial lawyers in the Commonwealth. Meehan and Boyle each were active in the management of Parker Coulter. They each served, for example, on the partnership's executive committee and, as members of this committee, were responsible for considering and making policy recommendations to the general partnership. Boyle was also in charge of the "plaintiffs department" within the firm, which managed approximately 350 cases. At the time of their leaving, Meehan's interest in the partnership was 6% and Boyle's interest was 4.8%.

Meehan and Boyle had become dissatisfied at Parker Coulter. On June 27, 1984, after unsuccessfully opposing the adoption of a firm-wide pension plan, the two first discussed the possibility of leaving Parker Coulter. Another partner met with them to discuss leaving but told them their proposed firm would not be suitable for his type of practice. On July 1, Meehan and Boyle decided to leave Parker Coulter and form their own partnership.

Having decided to establish a new firm, Meehan and Boyle then focused on whom they would invite to join them. The two spoke with Cohen, a junior partner and the de facto head of Parker Coulter's appellate department, about joining the new firm as a partner. They arranged to meet with her on July 5, and told her to keep their conversations confidential. The day before the July 5 meeting, Boyle prepared two lists of what he considered to be his cases. The lists contained approximately eighty to 100 cases, and for each case indicated the status, fee arrangement, estimated settlement value, and potential fee to MBC. Boyle gave these lists to Cohen for her to examine in preparation for the July 5 meeting.

At the July 5 meeting, Meehan and Boyle outlined to Cohen their plans for the new firm, including their intent to offer positions to Schafer, Peter Black (Black), and Warren Fitzgerald (Fitzgerald), who were associates at Parker Coulter. Boyle stated that he hoped the clients he had been representing would go with him to the new firm; Meehan said he would take the aviation work he had at Parker Coulter with him. Both stated that they felt others at Parker Coulter were getting paid as much as or more than they were, but were not working as hard. Cohen decided to consider the offer from Meehan and Boyle, and agreed to keep the plans confidential until formal notice of the separation was given to the partnership. Although the partnership agreement required a notice period of three months, the three decided to give only thirty days' notice. They chose to give shorter notice to avoid what they believed would be an uncomfortable situation at the firm, and possible retaliatory measures by the partnership. Meehan and Boyle had agreed that they would leave Parker Coulter on December 31, 1984, the end of Parker Coulter's fiscal year.

During the first week of August, Cohen accepted the offer to join the new firm as a partner. Her primary reason for leaving Parker Coulter to join MBC was that she enjoyed working with Meehan and Boyle.

In July, 1984, Boyle offered a position at MBC to Schafer, who worked closely with Boyle in the plaintiffs department. Boyle told Schafer to organize his cases, and "to keep an eye towards cases to be resolved in 1985 and to handle these cases for resolution in 1985 rather than 1984." He also told Schafer to make a list of cases he could take with him to MBC, and to keep all their conversations confidential.

Late in the summer of 1984, Meehan asked Black and Fitzgerald to become associates at MBC. Fitzgerald had worked with Meehan in the past on general defense work, and Black worked with Meehan, particularly in the aviation area. Meehan was instrumental in attracting Black, who had previously been employed by U.S. Aviation Underwriters (USAU), to Parker Coulter. Although Black had already considered leaving Parker Coulter, he was concerned about whether USAU would follow him to a small firm like MBC, and wanted to discuss his leaving Parker Coulter with the vice president of USAU. In October, 1984, Black and Meehan met with the USAU vice president in New York. They later received assurances from him that he would be interested in sending USAU business to the proposed new firm. Black then accepted the offer to join MBC. Fitzgerald also accepted. Schafer, Black, and Fitzgerald were the only associates Meehan, Boyle, and Cohen approached concerning the new firm.

During July and the following months, Meehan, Boyle, and Cohen made arrangements for their new practice apart from seeking associates. They began to look for office space and retained an architect. In early fall, a lease was executed on behalf of MBC in the name of MBC Realty Trust. They also retained an attorney to advise them on the formation of the new firm.

Boyle was assigned the task of arranging financing. He prepared a personal financial statement and obtained a bank loan in September, 1984. During that fall, two other loans were made on MBC's credit. Cohen, at the request of an accountant, had been trying to develop projections of MBC's expected revenue in order to obtain long-term financing. The accountant requested a list of cases with indications as to MBC's expected fees for this purpose. In November, Boyle updated and revised the list of cases he expected to take to MBC which he had compiled in July. The November list contained approximately 135 cases. The increase in Boyle's caseload from July to November resulted in part from the departure of a Parker Coulter attorney in early September, 1984. Boyle was in charge of reassigning the cases this attorney worked on. Although another attorney requested transfer of some of these cases, Boyle assigned none to that attorney, and assigned most of the cases to himself and Schafer. Meehan, Cohen, and Black also prepared lists of cases which they anticipated they would remove, and included the potential fee each case would generate for MBC.

Toward the end of November, Boyle prepared form letters to send to clients and referring attorneys as soon as Parker Coulter was notified of the separation. He also drafted a form for the clients to return to him at his home address authorizing him to remove cases to MBC. An outside agency typed these materials on Parker Coulter's letterhead. Schafer prepared similar letters and authorization forms.

While they were planning their departure, from July to approximately December, Meehan, Boyle, Cohen, Schafer, Black, and Fitzgerald all continued to work full schedules. They settled cases appropriately, made reasonable efforts to avoid continuances, tried cases, and worked on discovery. Each generally maintained his or her usual standard of performance.

Meehan and Boyle had originally intended to give notice to Parker Coulter on December 1, 1984. Rumors of their leaving, however, began to circulate before then. During the period from July to early fall, different Parker Coulter partners approached Meehan individually on three separate occasions and asked him if the rumors about his leaving were true. On each occasion, Meehan denied that he was leaving. On November 30, 1984, a partner, Maurice F. Shaughnessy (Shaughnessy), approached Boyle and asked him whether Meehan and Boyle intended to leave the firm. Shaughnessy interpreted Boyle's evasive response as an affirmation of the rumors. Meehan and Boyle then decided to distribute their notice that afternoon, which stated, as their proposed date for leaving, December 31, 1984. A notice was left on the desk of each partner. When Meehan, Boyle, and Cohen gave their notice, the atmosphere at Parker Coulter became "tense, emotional and unpleasant, if not adversarial."

On December 3, the Parker Coulter partners appointed a separation committee and decided to communicate with "important sources of business" to tell them of the separation and of Parker Coulter's desire to continue representing them. Meehan and Boyle asked their partners for financial information about the firm, discussed cases and clients with them, and stated that they intended to communicate with clients and referring attorneys on the cases in which they were involved. Sometime during the week of December 3, the partners sent Boyle a list of cases and requested that he identify the cases he intended to take with him.

Boyle had begun to make telephone calls to referring attorneys on Saturday morning, December 1. He had spoken with three referring attorneys by that date and told them of his departure from Parker Coulter and his wish to continue handling their cases. On December 3, he mailed his previously typed letters and authorization forms, and by the end of the first two weeks of December he had spoken with a majority of referring attorneys, and had obtained authorizations from a majority of clients whose cases he planned to remove to MBC.

Although the partners previously were aware of Boyle's intention to communicate with clients, they did not become aware of the extent of his communications until December 12 or 13. Boyle did not provide his partners with the list they requested of cases he intended to remove until December 17. Throughout December, Meehan, Boyle, and Schafer continued to communicate with referring attorneys on cases they were currently handling to discuss authorizing their transfer to MBC. On December 19, 1984, one of the partners accepted on behalf of Parker Coulter the December 31 departure date and waived the three-month notice period provided for by the partnership agreement. Meehan, Boyle, and Cohen formalized their arrangement as a professional corporation on January 1, 1985.

MBC removed a number of cases from Parker Coulter. Of the roughly 350 contingent fee cases pending at Parker Coulter in 1984, Boyle, Schafer, and Meehan removed approximately 142 to MBC. Meehan advised Parker Coulter that the 4,000 asbestos cases he had attracted to the firm would remain, and he did not seek to take certain other major clients. Black removed thirty-five cases; Fitzgerald removed ten; and Cohen removed three. A provision in the partnership agreement in effect at the separation provided that a voluntarily retiring partner, upon the payment of a "fair charge," could remove "any matter in which the partnership had been representing a client who came to the firm through the personal effort or connection of the retiring partner," subject to the right of the client to stay with the firm. Approximately thirty-nine of the 142 contingent fee cases removed to MBC came to Parker Coulter at least in part through the personal efforts or connections of Parker Coulter attorneys other than Meehan, Boyle, Cohen, Schafer, Black, or Fitzgerald. In all the cases removed to MBC, however, MBC attorneys had direct, existing relationships with the clients. In all the removed cases, MBC attorneys communicated with the referring attorney or with the client directly by telephone or letter. In each case, the client signed an authorization.

Schafer subsequently separated his practice from MBC's. He took with him a number of the cases which had been removed from Parker Coulter to MBC.

Based on these findings, the judge determined that the MBC attorneys did not manipulate cases, or handle them differently as a result of their decision to leave Parker Coulter. He also determined that Parker Coulter failed to prove that the clients whose cases were removed did not freely choose to have MBC represent them. Consequently, he concluded that Meehan and Boyle neither violated the partnership agreement nor breached the fiduciary duty they owed to their partners. In addition, the judge also found that Meehan and Boyle did not tortiously interfere with Parker Coulter's relations with clients or employees. He similarly rejected Parker Coulter's claims against Cohen and Schafer.

1. Statutory Considerations; the Partnership Agreement.

* * * Where a partnership agreement provides that the partnership is to continue indefinitely, and the partnership is therefore "at will," a partner has the right to dissolve the partnership, and the dissolution occurs "[w]ithout violation of the agreement between the partners." G.L. c. 108A, § 31(1). * * *

The Parker Coulter partnership agreement provided for rights on a dissolution caused by the will of a partner which are different from those c. 108A [UPA] provides.[7]

Because going concerns are typically destroyed in the dissolution process of liquidation and windup, see J. CRANE & A. BROMBERG, PARTNERSHIP 419 (1968), the agreement minimizes the impact of this process. The agreement provides for an allocation to the departing partner of a share of the firm's current net income, and a return of his or her capital contributions. In addition, the agreement also recognizes that a major asset of a law firm is the expected fees it will receive from unfinished business currently being transacted. Instead of assigning a value to the departing partner's interest in this unfinished business, or waiting for the unfinished business to be "wound up" and liquidated, which is the method of division c. 108A provides, the agreement gives the partner the right to remove any case which came to the firm "through the personal effort or connection" of the partner, if the partner compensates the dissolved partnership "for the services to and expenditures for the client."[8]

---

[7]   Chapter 108A is intended to be a type of "form contract." See 1 A.R. BROMBERG & L.E. RIBSTEIN, PARTNERSHIP § 1.01(d) (1988). Parties are therefore allowed the freedom to provide for rights at dissolution and during the wind-up period which are different from those provided for in the statute. See G.L. c. 108A, § 38(1).

[8]   The agreement expressly protects a client's right to choose his or her attorney, by providing that the right to remove a case is "subject to the right of the client to direct that the matter be retained by the continuing firm of remaining partners."

Once the partner has removed a case, the agreement provides that the partner is entitled to retain all future fees in the case, with the exception of the "fair charge" owed to the dissolved firm.[9]

Although the provision in the partnership agreement which divides the dissolved firm's unfinished business does not expressly apply to the removal of cases which did not come to Parker Coulter through the efforts of the departing partner, we believe that the parties intended this provision to apply to these cases also. We interpret this provision to cover these additional cases for two reasons. First, according to the Canons of Ethics and Disciplinary Rules Regulating the Practice of Law (S.J.C. Rule 3:07, Canon 2, as amended through 398 Mass. 1108 [1986]), a lawyer may not participate in an agreement which restricts the right of a lawyer to practice law after the termination of a relationship created by the agreement. One reason for this rule is to protect the public. [citation omitted] The strong public interest in allowing clients to retain counsel of their choice outweighs any professional benefits derived from a restrictive covenant. Thus, the Parker Coulter partners could not restrict a departing partner's right to remove any clients who freely choose to retain him or her as their legal counsel. Second, we believe the agreement's carefully drawn provisions governing dissolution and the division of assets indicate the partners' strong intent not to allow the provisions of c. 108A concerning liquidation and wind-up to govern any portion of the dissolved firm's unfinished business. Therefore, based on the partners' intent, and on the prohibition against restrictive covenants between attorneys, we interpret the agreement to provide that, upon the payment of a fair charge, any case may be removed regardless of whether the case came to the firm through the personal efforts of the departing partner. This privilege to remove, as is shown in our later discussion, is of course dependent upon the partner's compliance with fiduciary obligations.

Under the agreement, therefore, a partner who separates his or her practice from that of the firm receives (1) the right to his or her capital contribution, (2) the right to a share of the net income to which the dissolved partnership is currently entitled, and (3) the right to a portion of the firm's unfinished business, and in exchange gives up all other rights in the dissolved firm's remaining assets. As to (3) above, "unfinished business," the partner gives up all right to proceeds from any unfinished business of the dissolved firm which the new, surviving firm retains. Under the agreement, the old firm's unfinished business is, in effect, "wound up" immediately; the departing partner takes certain of the unfinished business of the old, dissolved Parker Coulter on the payment of a "fair charge," and the new, surviving Parker Coulter takes the remainder of the old partnership's unfinished business.[11]

---

[9]   The agreement provides that this "fair charge" is a "receivable account of the earlier partnership . . . and [is] divided between the remaining partners and the retiring partner on the basis of which they share in the profits of the firm at the time of the withdrawal." This fair charge is thus treated as an asset of the former partnership. Because the partnership, upon the receipt of the fair charge, gives up all future rights to income from the removed case, the partnership's collective interest in the case is effectively "wound up." The fair charge, therefore, is a method of valuing the partnership's unfinished business as it relates to the removed case.

[11]   A more equitable provision would require that the new, surviving partnership also pay a "fair charge" on the cases it takes from the dissolved partnership. This "fair charge" from the new firm, as is the "fair charge" from the departing partner, would be an asset of the dissolved partnership, in which the departing partner has an interest.

The two entities surviving after the dissolution possess "new business," unconnected with that of the old firm, and the former partners no longer have a continuing fiduciary obligation to windup for the benefit of each other the business they shared in their former partnership.

In sum, the statute gives a partner the power to dissolve a partnership at any time. Under the statute, the assets of the dissolved partnership are divided among the former partners through the process of liquidation and windup. The statute, however, allows partners to design their own methods of dividing assets and, provided the dissolution is not premature, expressly states that the partners' method controls. Here, the partners have fashioned a division method which immediately winds up unfinished business, allows for a quick separation of the surviving practices, and minimizes the disruptive impact of a dissolution.

2. Fiduciary Duties; Breach.

We now consider Parker Coulter's claims of wrongdoing. Parker Coulter claims that the judge erred in finding that Meehan, Boyle, Cohen, and Schafer fulfilled their fiduciary duties to the former partnership. In particular, Parker Coulter argues that these attorneys breached their duties (1) by improperly handling cases for their own, and not the partnership's benefit, (2) by secretly competing with the partnership, and (3) by unfairly acquiring from clients and referring attorneys consent to withdraw cases to MBC. We do not agree with Parker Coulter's first two arguments but agree with the third. * * *

Parker Coulter . . . argues that the judge's findings compel the conclusion that Meehan and Boyle breached their fiduciary duty not to compete with their partners by secretly setting up a new firm during their tenure at Parker Coulter. We disagree. We have stated that fiduciaries may plan to compete with the entity to which they owe allegiance, "provided that in the course of such arrangements they [do] not otherwise act in violation of their fiduciary duties." [citation omitted] Here, the judge found that Meehan and Boyle made certain logistical arrangements for the establishment of MBC. These arrangements included executing a lease for MBC's office, preparing lists of clients expected to leave Parker Coulter for MBC, and obtaining financing on the basis of these lists. We believe these logistical arrangements to establish a physical plant for the new firm were permissible . . . especially in light of the attorneys' obligation to represent adequately any clients who might continue to retain them on their departure from Parker Coulter. Canons of Ethics and Disciplinary Rules Regulating the Practice of Law (S.J.C. Rule 3:07, Canon 7, as appearing in 382 Mass. 784 [1981]). There was no error in the judge's determination that this conduct did not violate the partners' fiduciary duty.

Lastly, Parker Coulter argues that the judge's findings compel the conclusion that Meehan and Boyle breached their fiduciary duties by unfairly acquiring consent from clients to remove cases from Parker Coulter. We agree that Meehan and Boyle, through their preparation for obtaining clients' consent, their secrecy concerning which clients they intended to take, and the substance and method of their communications with clients, obtained an unfair advantage over their former partners in breach of their fiduciary duties.

A partner has an obligation to "render on demand true and full information of all things affecting the partnership to any partner." G.L. c. 108A, § 20. [citation omitted] On three separate occasions Meehan affirmatively denied to his partners, on their demand, that he had any plans for leaving the partnership. During this period of secrecy, Meehan and Boyle made preparations for obtaining removal authorizations from clients. Meehan traveled to

New York to meet with a representative of USAU and interest him in the new firm. Boyle prepared form letters on Parker Coulter's letterhead for authorizations from prospective MBC clients. Thus, they were "ready to move" the instant they gave notice to their partners. [citation omitted]

On giving their notice, Meehan and Boyle continued to use their position of trust and confidence to the disadvantage of Parker Coulter. The two immediately began communicating with clients and referring attorneys. Boyle delayed providing his partners with a list of clients he intended to solicit until mid-December, by which time he had obtained authorization from a majority of the clients.

Finally, the content of the letter sent to the clients was unfairly prejudicial to Parker Coulter. The ABA Committee on Ethics and Professional Responsibility, in Informal Opinion 1457 (April 29, 1980), set forth ethical standards for attorneys announcing a change in professional association. Because this standard is intended primarily to protect clients, proof by Parker Coulter of a technical violation of this standard does not aid them in their claims. [citation omitted] We will, however, look to this standard for general guidelines as to what partners are entitled to expect from each other concerning their joint clients on the division of their practice. The ethical standard provides that any notice explain to a client that he or she has the right to decide who will continue the representation. Here, the judge found that the notice did not "clearly present to the clients the choice they had between remaining at Parker Coulter or moving to the new firm." By sending a one-side announcement, on Parker Coulter letterhead, so soon after notice of their departure, Meehan and Boyle excluded their partners from effectively presenting their services as an alternative to those of Meehan and Boyle.

Meehan and Boyle could have foreseen that the news of their departure would cause a certain amount of confusion and disruption among their partners. The speed and preemptive character of their campaign to acquire clients' consent took advantage of their partners' confusion. By engaging in these preemptive tactics, Meehan and Boyle violated the duty of utmost good faith and loyalty which they owed their partners. Therefore, we conclude that the judge erred in deciding that Meehan and Boyle acted properly in acquiring consent to remove cases to MBC. * * *

3. Consequences of Breach.

* * * For Parker Coulter to recover any amount in addition to what it would be entitled to receive upon dissolution under the partnership agreement or the statute, there must be a causal connection between its claimed losses and the breach of duty on the part of the MBC attorneys. [citation omitted] We have concluded that the MBC attorneys unfairly acquired consent from clients. Parker Coulter, therefore, is entitled to recover only those amounts which flow from this breach of duty. * * *

In these circumstances, it is appropriate to place on the party who improperly removed the case the burden of proving that the client would have consented to removal in the absence of any breach of duty. [citation omitted] We have recognized that shifting the burden of proof may be justified on policy grounds because it encourages a defendant both to preserve information concerning the circumstances of the plaintiff's injury and to use best efforts to fulfill any duty he or she may owe the plaintiff. * * *

We conclude that Meehan and Boyle had the burden of proving no causal connection between their breach of duty and Parker Coulter's loss of clients. [citation omitted] Proof of the circumstances of the preparations for obtaining authorizations and of the actual communications with clients was more accessible to Meehan and Boyle than to Parker Coulter. Furthermore, requiring these partners to disprove causation will encourage partners in the future to disclose seasonably and fully any plans to remove cases. This disclosure will allow the partnership and the departing partner an equal opportunity to present to clients the option of continuing with the partnership or retaining the departing partner individually.[16]

We remand the case to the Superior Court for findings consistent with our conclusion that the MBC attorneys bear the burden of proof. * * *

To guide the judge on remand in his reexamination of the record and his subsidiary findings, we briefly outline factors relevant to determining whether a client freely chose MBC and, thus, whether the MBC attorneys met their burden of disproving a causal relationship between their preemptive tactics and the removal of the case. * * * [T]he parties expressly bargained with each other that they would allow a client a free choice. To give effect, therefore, to the entire agreement of the parties before us, there must be some examination of a client's reasons for choosing to retain MBC.

* * * Circumstantial factors relevant to whether a client freely exercised his or her right to choose include the following: (1) who was responsible for initially attracting the client to the firm; (2) who managed the case at the firm; (3) how sophisticated the client was and whether the client made the decision with full knowledge; and (4) what was the reputation and skill of the removing attorneys. Therefore, the judge is to reexamine the record and his subsidiary findings in light of the factors we have identified, and to reach a conclusion as to whether Meehan and Boyle have met their burden of proof on each of the removed cases. With the burden of proof on Meehan and Boyle, Parker Coulter will prevail if the evidence is in balance. [citation omitted]

In those cases, if any, where the judge concludes, in accordance with the above analysis, that Meehan and Boyle have met their burden, we resolve the parties' dispute over fees solely under the partnership agreement. * * * [I]n accordance with the partnership agreement, Meehan and Boyle must reimburse their former partnership for time billed and expenses incurred at that firm on all cases which were fairly removed. We further conclude that, under the agreement, Meehan and Boyle have the right to retain all fees generated by these cases in excess of the fair charge.

We now address the correct remedy in those cases, if any, which the judge determines Meehan and Boyle unfairly removed. In light of a conclusion that Meehan and Boyle have failed to prove that certain clients would not have preferred to stay with Parker Coulter, granting Parker Coulter merely a fair charge on these cases pursuant to the partnership agreement would not make it whole. We turn, therefore, to c. 108A. Section 21 of c. 108A provides: "Every partner must account to the partnership for any benefit, and hold as trustee for it any profits derived by him without the consent of the other partners from any transaction connected with the formation, conduct or liquidation of the partnership . . . ." We have consistently applied this statute, and held that a partner must account for any profits which flow from a breach of fiduciary duty. * * *

---

[16]   As between the attorneys, a mutual letter, from both the partnership and the departing partner, outlining the separation plans and the clients' right to choose, would be an appropriate means of opening the discussion between the attorneys and their clients concerning the clients' choice of continuing representation.

Meehan and Boyle breached the duty they owed to Parker Coulter. If the judge determines that, as a result of this breach, certain clients left the firm, Meehan and Boyle must account to the partnership for any profits they receive on these cases pursuant to c. 108A, in addition to paying the partnership a fair charge on these cases pursuant to the agreement. The "profit" on a particular case is the amount by which the fee received from the case exceeds the sum of (1) any reasonable overhead expenses MBC incurs in resolving the case, [citation omitted] and (2) the fair charge it owes under the partnership agreement. We emphasize that reasonable overhead expenses on a particular case are not the equivalent of the amount represented by the hours MBC attorneys have expended on the case multiplied by their hourly billing rate. * * * Meehan's and Boyle's former partners are . . . entitled to their portion of the fair charge on each of the unfairly removed cases (89.2%), and to that amount of profit from an unfairly removed case which they would have enjoyed had the MBC attorneys handled the case at Parker Coulter (89.2%).

The MBC attorneys argue that any remedy which grants Parker Coulter a recovery in excess of a fair charge on cases removed impermissibly infringes on an attorney's relationship with clients and reduces his or her incentive to use best efforts on their behalf. We agree that punitive measures may infringe on a client's right to adequate representation, and to counsel of his or her own choosing. [citation omitted] We believe, however, that the remedy we impose does not suffer from the MBC attorneys' claimed defects. Under the constructive trust we impose, Meehan and Boyle will receive a share of the fruits of their efforts in the unfairly removed cases which is the same as that which they would have enjoyed at Parker Coulter. We note, moreover, that incentives other than profit motivate attorneys. These incentives include an attorney's ethical obligations to the client and the profession, and a concern for his or her reputation. *See generally* 2 A.R. BROMBERG & L.E. RIBSTEIN, PARTNERSHIP § 7.08, at 7:85 (1988).

Furthermore, the MBC attorneys' argument would provide us with no mechanism to enforce the partners' fiduciary duties. Imposition of a narrowly tailored constructive trust will enforce the obligations resulting from a breach of duty and will not harm the innocent clients. We conclude, therefore, that Meehan and Boyle hold in a constructive trust for the benefit of the former partnership the profits they have derived or may derive from any cases which they unfairly removed. * * *

Notes and Questions

1. **Competition for clients.** *Meehan* illustrates some important lessons in drafting an agreement for a professional partnership to deal with the departure of partners and the removal of clients. Drafting and interpreting such an agreement requires an analysis of the contract itself, the background provisions of the partnership statute, and the partners' fiduciary duties among themselves and ethical duties to clients. The cases indicate that duties among the partners and to clients may sometimes conflict in that enforcing strict competition duties among the partners may leave the clients without the lawyer of their choice, or reduce the lawyers' incentives to act for the client. The conflict may be resolved by enforcing an ethical restriction on the permissible terms of the partnership agreement. These issues are discussed below in § 9.06(D).

2. **Duty not to take clients.** The *Meehan* agreement did not explicitly deal with clients who were not recruited by the "taking" partner. Should the agreement have been extended to deal with this situation, or instead interpreted as precluding partners from taking such clients? What result if the agreement had explicitly prohibited the partners from taking even clients that they had not recruited?

3. **Incomplete partnership agreements.** What if the agreement incompletely allocates, or does not mention, work in process? Should it be interpreted as providing for compensation for both the partner who leaves work in process with the firm and the firm that loses the work to the leaving partner, for neither, or for one or the other? The *Meehan* agreement required MBC to pay something (*i.e.*, a "fair charge") for cases they took with them but did not provide for, and the court did not require, payment of MBC for the clients the old firm retained. *See* note 11 to the court's opinion. In *Kelly v. Smith*, 611 N.E.2d 118 (Ind. 1993), the agreement provided in detail for calculation of the value of the withdrawing partner's interest in the partnership but did not mention work in process. The majority provided for something like the "fair charge" agreement the parties explicitly provided for in *Meehan*, while the dissent suggested an even more extensive obligation to share all fees from these cases. For a similar result, *see Schrempp and Salerno v. Gross*, 247 Neb. 685, 529 N.W.2d 764, 767-68 (1995), in which the court held that the following agreement unambiguously provided that the withdrawing partner had to compensate the partnership for post-withdrawal fees:

> Upon withdrawal from the Partnership, the withdrawing Partner shall be paid by the Partnership an amount equal to the balance as of the date of withdrawal of the withdrawing Partner's cash operating account (adjusted for Partnership profits and losses to the date of withdrawal) plus an amount equal to the unvested portion of the withdrawing Partner's share of any Partnership Pension, Profit Sharing or Keogh Plan. The foregoing amounts shall be in full payment for all sums due and owing to the withdrawing Partner and his interest in all work in process, clients of the partnership, client files, and papers, books, and records relating to Partnership clients shall terminate.

Kahn v. Seely, 980 S.W.2d 794 (Tex. App. 1998), held that an agreement providing for allocation of responsibility for cases did not reflect an agreement to compensate for post-dissolution services, so that the default no-compensation rule applied.

Did the results in these cases reflect the parties' likely intent? What does the agreement's silence imply? How might the agreements have been drafted in these cases to deal with work-in-process?

5. **Partners' fiduciary duties.** *Meehan* held that MBC had duties in addition to those prescribed by the partnership agreement regarding their taking of clients. In other words, the court interpreted the agreement as allocating fees only from those clients who were *properly* removed from the firm. The case provides some guidance on what, exactly, partners should do when departing their firms. *See also Fred Siegel Co., L.P.A. v. Arter & Hadden*, 85 Ohio St. 3d 171, 707 N.E.2d 853 (1999), holding that a departing partner's use of the firm's client list may constitute appropriation of a trade secret and, together

with the partner's use of wrongfully disclosed information, may support a claim of tortious interference with contract. The court also held that the partner's conduct may be wrongful even if he complied with ethical rules concerning informing clients of his departure from the firm. *See generally* Hillman, *Loyalty in the Firm, A Statement of General Principles on the Duties of Partners Withdrawing from Law Firms,* 55 WASH. & LEE L. REV. 997 (1998)

6. **Contractual waiver of non-competition duty.** Might the partners have contracted to restrict competition duties—that is, to permit partners to remove clients without giving their former partners an opportunity to compete for the business. If so, how? *See* § 8.06, above. Might such an agreement have violated ethical duties to the clients?

D. Withdrawal Compensation and Ethical Rules

As illustrated by *Meehan* in section C, post-dissolution competition by professional partners can pose vexing problems. In attempting to resolve these problems by advance agreement, law partners are met by the additional hurdle of ethical restrictions on attorney non-competes. Several cases have invalidated on ethical grounds not only direct restrictions on taking clients and recruiting attorneys, but also at least some attempts to deter lawyers from leaving by reducing their exit compensation. The leading case is *Cohen v. Lord Day & Lord,* 75 N.Y.2d 95, 551 N.Y.S.2d 157, 550 N.E.2d 410 (1989) (agreement denying withdrawing law partner distributions from post-dissolution receipts held unethical restriction on competition). Other prominent cases include *Jacob v. Norris, McLaughlin & Marcus,* 128 N.J. 10, 607 A.2d 142 (1992), and *Denburg v. Parker Chapin,* 82 N.Y.2d 375, 624 N.E.2d 995, 604 N.Y.S.2d 900, 624 N.E.2d 995 (1993). These cases were challenged by the following case.

Howard v. Babcock
6 Cal. 4th 409, 25 Cal. Rptr. 2d 80, 863 P.2d 150 (1994)

MOSK, Justice.
We granted review to decide whether an agreement between law partners is enforceable if it requires withdrawing partners to forego certain contractual withdrawal benefits if they compete with their former law firm. We conclude that an agreement among law partners imposing a reasonable toll on departing partners who compete with the firm is enforceable. We reverse the judgment of the Court of Appeal to the extent it holds the agreement unenforceable and orders an accounting to plaintiffs on that basis. We order the matter remanded to the trial court for a determination whether under the facts of this case the terms of the agreement are reasonable.

I

In 1982, partners in the law firm of Parker, Stanbury, McGee, Babcock & Combs executed a partnership agreement. Article X of the agreement provided in pertinent part that: "Should more than one partner, associate or individual withdraw from the firm prior to age sixty-five (65) and thereafter within a period of one year practice law . . . together or in combination with others, including former partners or associates of this firm, in a practice engaged in the handling of liability insurance defense work as aforesaid within the Los Angeles or Orange County Court system, said partner or partners shall be subject, at the sole discretion of the remaining non-withdrawing partners to forfeiture of all their rights to withdrawal benefits other than capital as provided for in Article V herein."[1]

Article V provided that a general partner who withdraws from the partnership shall be paid his or her capital interest, and a sum "equal to the share in the net profit of the firm that the withdrawn . . . partner would have received during the first twelve months following the withdrawal . . . if he had remained with the firm . . . during the said twelve month period." Plaintiffs Howard, Moss and Loveder and defendants Babcock, Combs, Kinnett, Waddell, Bergsten and Schaertel signed the partnership agreement.

In January 1984, participating partners Loveder and Schaertel were elevated to general partners and Osborne and Cicotte were admitted as participating partners. Strickroth and Mori were admitted as participating partners in 1985 and Barrett was admitted as a participating partner in 1986. The partnership agreement was not amended, nor did the new partners admitted after 1982 ever sign it.

On December 8, 1986, plaintiffs (Howard, Moss, Loveder and Strickroth) notified the remaining members of the firm that they were terminating their relationship with the firm, and that they would begin practice in competition with the firm in January 1987. They asserted that article X was unenforceable. Defendants notified plaintiffs that they would withhold a portion of plaintiffs' withdrawal benefits because of plaintiffs' violation of article X. Plaintiffs replied that the partnership agreement was no longer effective, and published notice of dissolution of the firm, effective December 31, 1986.

On January 2, 1987, plaintiffs entered business in Orange County as a general partnership under the name of Howard, Moss, Loveder & Strickroth, handling, among other cases, liability defense work for insurance companies and self-insured companies. Defendants operated as a new general partnership under the name of Parker, Stansbury, McGee, Babcock & Combs.

The assets of the original Parker firm on December 31, 1986, included the capital of the firm, namely, the profits shown on the balance sheet; the accounts receivable, that is, work performed and billed, but in which the bill had not been paid; and the unfinished business, that is, open files that required additional work that would be billed in the future.

Defendants tendered payment to plaintiffs for their share of the capital of the firm, but refused to compensate them for the accounts receivable or to acknowledge that they had any interest in the work in progress or unfinished business of the firm.

Clients of the original Parker firm substituted the Howard firm in approximately 200 cases. * * *

[At trial, the court decided that article X was valid and enforceable and entered judgment ordering plaintiffs to pay defendants the sum of $382,686 and finding that defendants owed plaintiffs nothing.]

---

[1]   Article X also provided that if only one partner withdraws, he or she is subject to forfeiture of 75 percent of withdrawal benefits for competition in Orange County or Los Angeles County, and 25 percent of withdrawal benefits if he or she competes in specified other counties.

II

California has a settled policy in favor of open competition. [citation omitted] Nonetheless, it has long been the law of this state that a partnership agreement may provide against competition by withdrawing partners in a limited geographical area. * * *

Not every agreement between partners in restraint of competition is permitted. We have held that the common law "rule of reason" should apply to evaluate the noncompetition agreement under Business and Professions Code section 16602. * * *

[W]e conclude that the statute applies to partners in law firms.

This conclusion does not end our inquiry, however. This court has the authority to prescribe rules of professional conduct for attorneys as part of its inherent power to regulate the practice of law. [citation omitted] It is in our power to impose a higher standard of conduct on lawyers than that applicable to other professionals. [citation omitted]

The Court of Appeal, plaintiffs, and the State Bar of California, as amicus curiae, maintain that we have already promulgated a rule of professional conduct imposing just such a higher standard, a rule that prohibits partners in law firms from entering into noncompetition agreements. They refer us to rule 1-500 of the Rules of Professional Conduct (rule 1-500).[5]

We are not persuaded that this rule was intended to or should prohibit the type of agreement that is at issue here. An agreement that assesses a reasonable cost against a partner who chooses to compete with his or her former partners does not restrict the practice of law. Rather, it attaches an economic consequence to a departing partner's unrestricted choice to pursue a particular kind of practice.

We agree with the Court of Appeal in *Haight* [*Haight, Brown & Bonesteel v. Superior Court* (1991), 234 Cal. App. 3d 963, 969, 285 Cal. Rptr. 845,] declaring an agreement between law partners that a reasonable cost will be assessed for competition is consistent with rule 1-500. Rejecting an interpretation of rule 1-500 like that proffered by plaintiffs here, the court stated: "We do not construe rule 1-500 in such a narrow fashion. * * * The rule does not . . . prohibit a withdrawing partner from agreeing to compensate his former partners in the event he chooses to represent clients previously represented by the firm from which he has withdrawn. Such a construction represents a balance between competing interests. On the one hand, it enables a departing attorney to withdraw from a partnership and continue to practice law anywhere within the state, and to be able to accept employment should he choose to do so from any client who desires to retain him. On the other hand, the remaining partners remain able to preserve the stability of the law firm by making available the withdrawing partner's share of capital and accounts receivable to replace the loss of the stream of income from the clients taken by the withdrawing partner to support the partnership's debts." (*Haight, supra,* at pp. 969-970, 285 Cal. Rptr. 845.) Concluding that the agreement was not invalid on its face, the court held that the validity of the agreement depended on whether it "amounts to an agreement for liquidated damages or an agreement resulting in a forfeiture." (*Id.* at p. 972, 285 Cal. Rptr. 845.)

---

[5]   Rule 1-500 is based on American Bar Association (ABA), Model Code of Professional Responsibility, former Disciplinary Rule 2-108 (1 WITKIN, CAL. PROCEDURE (3d ed. 1985) Attorneys, § 50, p. 70), now numbered rule 5.6 of the ABA Model Rules of Professional Conduct. * * *

The *Haight* court's construction is consistent with Business and Professions Code section 16602, permitting agreements between partners restricting competition. Further, our interpretation of the rule must be illuminated by our recognition that a revolution in the practice of law has occurred requiring economic interests of the law firm to be protected as they are in other business enterprises. We are confident that our recognition of a new reality in the practice of law will have no deleterious effect on the current ability of clients to retain loyal, competent counsel of their choice.

"The traditional view of the law firm as a stable institution with an assured future is now challenged by an awareness that even the largest and most prestigious firms are fragile economic units . . . ." (HILLMAN, LAW FIRM BREAKUPS (1990) § 1.1, at p. 1.) Not the least of the changes rocking the legal profession is the propensity of withdrawing partners in law firms to "grab" clients of the firm and set up a competing practice. [citations omitted] In response, many firms have inserted noncompetition clauses into their partnership agreements. [citation omitted] These noncompetition clauses have grown and flourished, despite, or in defiance of, the consistent holding of many courts across the nation that a noncompetition clause violates the rules of professional conduct of the legal profession. It is evident that these agreements address important business interests of law firms that can no longer be ignored.

The firm has a financial interest in the continued patronage of its clientele. [citation omitted] In earlier times, this investment was fairly secure, because the continued loyalty of partners and associates to the firm was assumed. [citation omitted] But more recently, lateral hiring of associates and partners, and the secession of partners from their firms has undermined this assumption. [citation omitted] Withdrawing partners are able to announce their departure to clients of the firm, and many clients defect along with the attorneys with whom they have developed good working relationships. The practical fact is that when partners with a lucrative practice leave a law firm along with their clients, their departure from and competition with the firm can place a tremendous financial strain on the firm. [citation omitted] * * *

Recognizing these sweeping changes in the practice of law, we can see no legal justification for treating partners in law firms differently in this respect from partners in other businesses and professions.

We are aware that many courts have interpreted the rules of professional conduct of their states, often stated in identical or very similar terms with the language of our rule 1-500, as prohibiting all agreements restricting competition among lawyers, including those that merely assess a cost for competition. * * *

However, we disagree with the analysis proffered by these courts to justify such an interpretation. Some courts, including the Court of Appeal in this case, reason that an attorney should have freedom to choose when, where and for whom to practice law; an anticompetitive covenant restricts that freedom. (*See, e.g., Cohen v. Lord, Day & Lord, supra*, 551 N.Y.S.2d at p. 158, 550 N.E.2d at p. 411.) Second, many courts reiterate that the practice of law is not a business, and clients are not commodities. These courts assert as an absolute rule that clients must have free choice of attorneys; to the extent that a restriction or toll on competition between lawyers is effective, it limits the ability of clients to have access to the attorney of their choice and is therefore improper. (*See, e.g., Jacob v. Norris, McLaughlin & Marcus, supra*, 607 A.2d at p. 147.)

Upon reflection, we have determined that these courts' steadfast concern to assure the theoretical freedom of each lawyer to choose whom to represent and what kind of work to undertake, and the theoretical freedom of any client to select his or her attorney of choice is inconsistent with the reality that both freedoms are actually circumscribed. Putting aside lofty assertions about the uniqueness of the legal profession, the reality is that the attorney, like any other professional, has no right to enter into employment or partnership in any particular firm, and sometimes may be discharged or forced out by his or her partners even if the client wishes otherwise. Nor does the attorney have the duty to take any client who proffers employment, and there are many grounds justifying an attorney's decision to terminate the attorney-client relationship over the client's objection. [citation omitted] Further, an attorney may be required to decline a potential client's offer of employment despite the client's desire to employ the attorney. For example, the attorney may have a technical conflict of interest because another attorney in the firm previously represented an adverse party. (Rules Prof. Conduct, rules 3-300, 3-310.) Finally, the client in the civil context, of course, ordinarily has no "right" to any attorney's services, and only receives those services he or she can afford.

Moreover, the contemporary changes in the legal profession to which we have already alluded make the assertion that the practice of law is not comparable to a business unpersuasive and unreflective of reality. Commercial concerns are now openly recognized as important in the practice of law. Indeed, we question whether any but the wealthy could enter the profession if it were to be practiced without attention to commercial success. In any event, no longer can it be said that law is a profession apart, untouched by the marketplace. Not only has law firm culture changed but, as in other businesses, lawyers now may advertise their services and may even communicate by letter with persons unknown to them, suggesting the possibility of employment. (*Shapero v. Kentucky Bar Assn.* (1988) 486 U.S. 466, 108 S.Ct. 1916, 100 L.Ed.2d 475; *Bates v. State Bar of Arizona* (1977) 433 U.S. 350, 97 S.Ct. 2691, 53 L.Ed.2d 810). Thus the general rules and habits of commerce have permeated the legal profession.

The same relaxation of the traditional rule against treating a law practice as comparable to a business can be seen in the development of the rules regarding sale of goodwill in a law firm. Although in 1988 the court in *Fraser v. Bogucki* (1988) 203 Cal. App. 3d 604, 250 Cal. Rptr. 41, rejected the concept of sale of goodwill in a law practice because it would treat clients as a commodity, the rules of professional conduct have since been amended expressly to permit the sale of goodwill in certain circumstances. (*See* Rules Prof. Conduct, rule 2-300.) Of course the rule requires notification to clients that the practice has been sold and that they have the right to hire new counsel, but the change does undercut the pristine view that clients are not deemed to be assets with a financial value.

Further, we question the premise that an agreement such as is at issue here would necessarily discourage withdrawing partners from continuing to represent clients who choose to employ them. Unless the penalty were unreasonable, it is more likely that the agreement would operate in the nature of a tax on taking the former firm's clients—a tax that is not unreasonable, considering the financial burden the partners' competitive departure may impose on the former firm. The sum to be forfeited by the withdrawing partners may be seen as comparable with a liquidated damage clause, an accepted fixture in other commercial contexts.[8]

---

[8]   We note too that in some respects, the "no-compensation rule" of partnership law, whereby departing partners are compensated for winding up the unfinished business of the partnership according to their partnership interest, may be just as much a disincentive on the withdrawing partner to continue to represent clients of the firm as an anticompetitive penalty, and yet this is not considered to be a violation of rule

In fact, it has been argued that a noncompetition agreement, or a penalty for competition, may actually serve clients as well as the financial well-being of the law firm. Without such an agreement, "[t]he culture of mistrust that results from systemic grabbing is very likely to damage, if not destroy, the law firm's stability. It is clear that when law firms dissolve, work on behalf of clients is undeniably disrupted. But even where a law firm does not self-destruct, it is easy to comprehend the disastrous impact on clients. Law firms have an affirmative obligation to the client to provide an atmosphere most conducive to the development of the attorney-client relationship and to the efficient, diligent completion of work. In an environment of pervasive lateral hiring, partners may be loath to financially or otherwise support the development of a colleague's relations with particular clients because the colleague may later exclusively usurp the benefits of that relationship. In addition, partnerships may be less willing to invest monies necessary to provide the equipment, library and other resources necessary to serve a client well if a partner could both leave a firm free of the mutually incurred liability, and also take the future income of the firm." [Penasack, *Abandoning the Per Se Rule Against Law Firm Agreements Anticipating Competition: Comment on Haight, Brown & Bonesteel v. Superior Court of Los Angeles County* (1992) 5 GEO. J. LEGAL ETHICS 889, 890-891, fns. omitted.]

It seems to us unreasonable to distinguish lawyers from other professionals such as doctors or accountants, who also owe a high degree of skill and loyalty to their patients and clients. The interest of a patient in a doctor of his or her choice is obviously as significant as the interest of a litigant in a lawyer of his or her choosing. Yet for doctors, reasonable noncompetition agreements binding upon withdrawing partners are permitted. [citation omitted]

We are confident that the interest of the public in being served by diligent, loyal and competent counsel can be assured at the same time as the legitimate business interest of law firms is protected by an agreement placing a reasonable price on competition. We hold that an agreement among partners imposing a reasonable cost on departing partners who compete with the law firm in a limited geographical area is not inconsistent with rule 1-500 and is not void on its face as against public policy.

We seek to achieve a balance between the interest of clients in having the attorney of choice, and the interest of law firms in a stable business environment. We have recognized that restraint of competition among partners is permissible only to the extent it protects the reasonable interests of the business seeking the restraint. [citation omitted] We consider it obvious that an absolute ban on competition with the partnership would be per se unreasonable, and inconsistent with the legitimate concerns of assuring client choice of counsel and assuring attorneys of the right to practice their profession. We agree with the court in *Haight, supra,* 234 Cal. App. 3d 963, 285 Cal. Rptr. 845, however, that to the extent the agreement merely assesses a toll on competition within a specified geographical area, comparable to a liquidated damage clause, it may be reasonable. [citation omitted]

As we have said with respect to liquidated damage clauses, "a contractual provision specifying damages for breach [of contract] is valid only if it 'represent[s] the result of a

---

1-500. (*Jewel v. Boxer* (1984) 156 Cal. App. 3d 171, 203 Cal. Rptr. 13; CORP. CODE, § 15018, subd. (f); *see also Rosenfeld, Meyer & Susman v. Cohen* (1983) 146 Cal. App. 3d 200, 219, 194 Cal. Rptr. 180; Note, *Winding Up Dissolved Law Partnerships: The No-Compensation Rule and Client Choice* (1985) 73 CAL. L. REV. 1597, 1598-1599.)

reasonable endeavor by the parties to estimate a fair average compensation for any loss that may be sustained.' [citation omitted] An amount disproportionate to the anticipated damages is termed a 'penalty.' A contractual provision imposing a 'penalty' is ineffective, and the wronged party can collect only the actual damages sustained." [citation omitted] Under this standard, a partner's agreement to pay former partners, or to forego benefits otherwise due under the contract, in an amount that at the time of the agreement is reasonably calculated to compensate the firm for losses that may be caused by the withdrawing partner's competition with the firm, would be permitted.

We have reviewed the arguments of the dissenting opinion with appropriate concern. It is not our intent to relegate clients to the position of commodities, nor to elevate commercial concerns over the lawyer's bedrock duty of loyal and vigorous advocacy on behalf of the client. Rather, we have exercised our duty to regulate the practice of law with a care to understanding the world as it is, uninfluenced by rhetoric that appears to obscure, rather than clarify, the problem. We are confident that our opinion will leave the lawyer's professional duties to his or her clients undisturbed, and that clients will enjoy the same degree of choice in retaining attorneys as they have always possessed.

III

The judgment of the Court of Appeal is reversed to the extent it holds article X unenforceable and orders an accounting to plaintiffs on that basis. The judgment of the Court of Appeal is otherwise affirmed. We direct that the Court of Appeal remand the matter to the trial court for a determination, consistent with our opinion, whether the terms of article X are reasonable, and for any further award on the accounting causes of action made necessary by that determination.

KENNARD, Justice, dissenting.

Should an attorney who leaves a law firm be free to compete with that firm? In this state, as in many others, attorneys are bound by a rule of ethics that prohibits them from entering into agreements that "restrict" their right to practice law after leaving a firm. (Rules Prof. Conduct of State Bar, rule 1-500.) The rule serves to eliminate unnecessary and artificial restrictions on clients' ability to select their attorneys. Yet, the majority, contrary to the unambiguous language of the rule, holds that this rule does not bar law firms from entering into noncompetition agreements with their attorneys if such agreements are "reasonable." I disagree. * * *

Although the law is a business in the sense that an attorney in a law firm earns a living by practicing law, it is also and foremost a profession, with all the responsibilities that word implies. The ethical rule that this court is called upon to interpret exists to enforce the traditional and sound view that service to clients, including protection of the clients' ability to employ the attorneys they have come to trust, is more important than safeguarding the economic interests of established attorneys and law firms. I would enforce the rule according to the ordinary meaning of its terms to bar all agreements by which established firms seek to protect themselves against competition from attorneys who leave the firm. * * *

IV.

* * * I have no quarrel with the majority's assertions that former partners sometimes "take" clients from law firms, that law firms have a financial interest in their clientele, or that law firms may be economically injured by the loss of clients.

But the purpose of rules of professional ethics is to restrain and guide the conduct of attorneys and to protect the public, not to protect the financial interests of law firms. (*Ames v. State Bar, supra*, 8 Cal. 3d at p. 917, 106 Cal. Rptr. 489, 506 P.2d 625.) Accordingly, I cannot accept the majority's view that the protection of law firms justifies devaluing the rights of clients. There is no reason to assume that the controlling partners of established law firms have a moral entitlement to protection from competition.

Indeed, a withdrawing partner's decision to leave a firm may be fully justified. For example, the withdrawal may be the result of unwillingness by nonproductive partners to fairly share income with productive partners, associates, and other personnel in the law firm. In other words, there is as much reason to assume that the withdrawal is caused by the remaining partners' undue emphasis on maximizing profits as there is to assume that fault lies with the withdrawing attorney.[2]

Nor can I share the majority's view that noncompetition agreements are justified because "[t]he firm's capital finances the development of a clientele and the support services and training necessary to satisfactorily represent the clientele." Clients remain loyal to a firm for many reasons that have no connection to existing partners' capital. The labor and efforts of attorneys and other employees of law firms contribute much more to the recruitment, retention, and development of clients than the capital of a law firm. Indeed, if a client chooses to be represented by a departing attorney rather than the law firm, that choice is generally based on the client's trust and confidence in the withdrawing attorney. * * *

Although other businesses and professions permit noncompetition agreements, the rules applicable to other professions do not necessarily provide guidance for the legal profession. The nature, ideals, and practices of the various professions are different. Moreover, ethics is not a subject in which the objective is to achieve consensus at the level of the lowest common denominator. In my view, attorneys should strive to, and should be required to, meet the highest ethical standards. * * *

If the practice of law is to remain a profession and retain public confidence and respect, it must be guided by something better than the objective of accumulating wealth. Here, in refusing to enforce a rule of ethics that prohibits attorneys from entering into agreements that restrict their right to practice law after leaving a firm, the majority diminishes the rights of clients in favor of the financial interest of law firms based on its one-sided view of the realities and equities of the practice of law.

---

[2]   The majority has made no effort to show that because of the economic "revolution" in the practice of law it asserts has taken place, law firms in jurisdictions that do not allow restrictive covenants have suffered greatly. I am doubtful such evidence exists.

Notes and Questions

1. **Reasons for restrictions on competition and reduced exit compensation.** As discussed in *Howard,* law and other professional firms may have strong reasons for preventing partners from leaving. For a discussion of some of the interests at stake in adjusting withdrawal competition, *see* Ribstein, *A Theoretical Analysis of Professional Partnership Goodwill,* 70 NEB. L. REV. 36 (1991). For a discussion of the ethics and economics of non-competition agreements in law firms, *see* Ribstein, *Ethical Rules, Agency Costs and Law Firm Structure,* 84 VA. L. REV. 1707 (1998). Consider the following:

(a) Leaving partners may take the firm's valuable assets. For example, the firm may have invested funds in recruiting and keeping clients that have not been recouped as fees by the time the clients leave with the partners. Or the firm may have paid salaries and other expenses in connection with pending cases the partners take with them. Leaving partners may also take information about forms, practices and procedures that the firm has developed but cannot copyright. While ethical restrictions do not prevent the firm from demanding compensation for these assets, there is a formidable valuation problem.

(b) Firm value may be destroyed by threats to the firm's continuity. The prospective longevity of the firm also may determine its ability to attract new business and new lawyers, as well as to incur long term debt for office space and equipment.

(c) It may be necessary to keep lawyers from leaving in order to enforce a risk-sharing bargain among lawyers in different specialties. One reason why lawyers form law firms may be for protection from the jarring effects of fluctuations in the demand for their particular specialties. *See* Gilson & Mnookin, *Sharing Among the Human Capitalists: An Economic Inquiry into the Law Firm and How Partners Split Profits,* 37 STAN. L. REV. 313 (1985). This sharing deal could fall apart if a lawyer could benefit from the deal when his specialty is in decline, and then leave without penalty when he is again in demand. Note that the ethical rules applied in the principal case would not prevent the assessment of damages against leaving partners for any of these injuries. But computing damages may present formidable problems. As a result, cutting off exit compensation or restricting competition altogether may, in some situations, be the most effective remedy. Thus, *Howard* treats exit compensation reductions as liquidated damages.

2. **Partners' interest in mobility.** A competing interest in enforcing non-competition agreements is the partners' need to be able to leave the firm and reinvest their human capital elsewhere. If the lawyers are prevented from leaving by stringent limits on their exit compensation, they can be exposed to exploitation. For example, their co-partners might divvy up the firm's financial pie without properly rewarding those

who contributed the most. Also, lawyers may have personal reasons for leaving that are beyond their control, such as a need to join a working spouse in another city. However, it is far from clear that this interest must be protected by mandatory rules. The interests of the firm and of its individual partners converge to a significant extent. Thus, a lawyer who does not know whether she will be leaving or staying would want to bind others to the firm if this is in the firm's interests. A lawyer who believes that the restriction may be costly (*see* Note 6, below) can bargain to be compensated for agreeing to the restriction or draft around it or refuse to join the firm.

3. **Protecting clients.** The main interest at stake regarding enforceability of non-competition agreements is, of course, that of the client. From this perspective, there is an agency cost problem between lawyers and clients just as there is between other agents and principals. Clients would like to be able to have full control over lawyer choice, partly as a matter of disciplining their agents. But lawyers may bind themselves to agreements that have the effect of restricting clients' choice where this is in the lawyers', but perhaps not the clients', long run interests. These agreements may solve agency cost and opportunism problems within the firm (*see* Notes 1-2, above) but increase such problems between lawyers and clients. Ethical rules enforcing professionalism require the lawyers to put clients' interests first. Note that competition restrictions are likely to affect different kinds of clients in different ways. A large corporate client may prefer that the lawyers with whom it has the primary relationships within the firm owe it their primary allegiance. These clients usually have in-house legal departments that can evaluate lawyers' work and do not need to rely on monitoring by the law firm. An exit restriction reduces the lawyer's incentive to maintain a personal client base and increases the lawyer's incentives to maximize the interests of the firm as a whole, including by monitoring co-partners. Smaller clients may rely more on monitoring within the law firm and may be hurt by arrangements that decrease law partners' incentives to maximize the interests of the firm as a whole, including monitoring each other. Assuming some clients may be hurt by restricting exit or competition, is the solution simply to disclose these arrangements to clients and let them decide whether to hire the firm? Would any but the largest corporate clients be able to evaluate these disclosures?

4. **The larger interests: Professionalism and social responsibility.** As indicated by the *Howard* dissent, there is a concern that enforcing non-competition agreements will make lawyers look too much like ordinary business people and not enough like professionals. This would erode the rationale for other special protections of the legal profession, such as restrictions on who can practice law and who can own law firms. On the other hand, one could argue that allowing lawyers to move around with portfolios of clients actually makes law look more like a business. Large firms that have long-term relationships with many clients have served as powerful intermediaries between corporations and social interests. These firms have the clout to insist that clients play by social rules rather than being ruled by their clients' interests. The more corporate clients can control individual lawyers rather than having to deal with large firms, the less corporate firms can continue to serve this function. *See* Gilson, *The Devolution of the Legal Profession: A Demand Side Perspective,* 49 MD. L. REV. 869 (1990).

5. **Drafting considerations.** Consider the lessons from *Howard* for drafting exit competition provisions in California. The parties must stay within contract rules governing enforceability of liquidated damage provisions. Even in states like New Jersey and New York, which invalidate restrictions on exit, the partners might effectively impede departure by assessing *actual* damages caused by the leaving partner. Thus, in *Jacob v. Norris, McLaughlin & Marcus,* 128 N.J. 10, 607 A.2d 142 (N.J. 1992), the court noted that ethical rules do not wholly prohibit adjusting the withdrawing partner's compensation for the value of her interest to reflect the damage to the firm caused by the withdrawal. Indeed, the UPA default rule on work in process discussed in § 9.04(E) is itself a kind of penalty for departure. The main difference between California and more restrictive states therefore may be the precision necessary in drafting damage provisions. Also, some kinds of provisions may not be considered restrictions on competition. An example might be a provision that gives an extra bonus to a partner who leaves to enter certain types of noncompetitive positions, such as teaching or a judgeship. What about giving a compensation committee complete discretion to determine exit compensation, even if they might or do consider the competitive nature of the departure? *See Rutowski v. Hill, Betts & Nash,* 613 N.Y.S.2d 874 (N.Y.A.D. 1994), holding that denial of discretionary bonus payments did not violate *Cohen.*

6. **Planning considerations.** Apart from *how* to draft an exit restriction, there is the important planning consideration of *whether* to include one in the agreement. As indicated in Note 2, some lawyers may have reasons to be concerned about these restrictions. The restriction may be costly for lawyers who are not being compensated for the value they add to the firm because of their "rainmaking" (client recruitment) or specialized legal skills. Accordingly, lawyers may be particularly concerned about exit restrictions under profit-sharing arrangements that are based other than on what partners are contributing to the bottom line, unless the firm's overall profitability is so high that even such "inequitable" sharing earns the partners more than they would make in other employment. It follows that the exit rule may need to be linked with the profit sharing rule (*see* § 4.03(b)(1), above).

CHAPTER 10
THE SEARCH FOR THE INCORPORATED PARTNERSHIP

10.01 Introduction

The general partnership form of business discussed in Chapters 3-9 above is well suited in several respects to closely held firms. The partnership statutes provide by default for rules owner-managers would want, including equal allocation of financial rights (Chapter 4), direct member participation in management (Chapter 5), restricted transferability of management rights (Chapter 7) and the ability to leave the firm via dissolution or buyout (Chapter 9). These rules also are easily altered by the partnership agreement to suit the variations in owner participation in the management of closely held firms.

The fly in the partnership ointment, however, is the owners' personal liability for partnership debts discussed in Chapter 6. While the firm easily can change management and finance rules and can contract directly with creditors for nonrecourse liability, the owners' personal liability is "sticky" when it comes to contracting with voluntary trade creditors and tort creditors such as retail customers and accident victims. In these situations, the firm may want to simply declare to the world that its owners' liability is limited to the firm's assets.

Firms traditionally have gotten this sort of broad limited liability by incorporating. Corporate shareholders are liable only up to their investments in the firm and are not otherwise at risk from corporate activities unless they agree to be liable or to do something for which they can be held personally responsible. But although incorporation offers the significant advantage of limited liability, corporate default rules are both unsuited to closely held firms and difficult for such firms to completely discard. Moreover, as discussed in more detail in § 10.04, corporate-type "double" taxation is a real cost for closely held firms and is not easy for closely held corporations to avoid.

These problems have led to the search for "incorporated partnerships"—that is, business forms that combine partnership-type governance rules with limited liability. Section 10.02 discusses an important driving force of this search—the need for limited liability. Sections 10.03 and 10.04 discuss the main drawbacks of incorporation for closely held firms—unsuitable default rules and double taxation. Section 10.05 discusses the factors that have impeded the search for the incorporated partnership—the uncertain federal income status of such firms, and policy concerns about extending the scope of limited liability beyond incorporated firms. Chapters 11-14 show the extent to which new business forms have overcome these problems.

10.02 The Benefits of Limited Liability

Although personal liability meshes with other partnership default features (*see* § 6.01), it is not necessarily right for all partnership-type firms. If the owners delegate control to managers, they may no longer be in a good position to monitor the riskiness of the firm's activities or its level of capitalization. At the same time, the creditors may not gain much from personal liability if they are otherwise assured of being able to collect out of the firm's assets. The costs and benefits of limited liability may change over time. Lloyd's, the famous British insurance market, long has been operated on the basis of syndicates in which underwriters agree to insure risks on behalf of the syndicates' investors, or Names, who each cover a portion of their risk to the extent of their personal wealth. The Names traditionally were thought to be willing and able to monitor the underwriters. *See* Winton, *Limitation of Liability and the Ownership Structure of the Firm,* 48 J. FIN. 487 (1993). Moreover, the Lloyds' market has featured several monitoring and incentive devices, such as a small group of trusted brokers who sell risks to the underwriters. As a result, the Names earned good returns on modest capital investments over the years. However, in recent years the number of Names has gone up and the quality of their monitoring apparently has declined. At the same time, there has been an explosion of asbestos and other "long tail" claims. As a result, the Names are now clamoring to limit their liability. *See* ADAM RAPHAEL, ULTIMATE RISK (1995). A similarly sharp change in the cost of personal liability for professional firms as a result of savings and loan and other massive liabilities may explain moves toward limited liability in these areas. *See* Chapter 13.

10.03 Corporate Governance and the Closely Held Firm

This section shows some governance-related reasons why partnership-type firms in search of limited liability may not be happy with the corporate form—the unsuitability of corporate default rules and the problems of waiving these defaults. For a discussion of potential advantages of incorporation, even for closely held firms, *see* Keatinge, *Corporations, Unincorporated Organizations, and Unincorporations: Check the Box and the Balkanization of Business Organizations,* 1 J. SMALL & EMERGING BUS. L. 201 (1997).

A.   Corporate Default Rules

Corporate statutes provide for several features that are unsuited to "closely held" firms. For purposes of this discussion, "closely held" is intended to mean firms that combine (1) owners' direct participation in management; (2) restricted transferability of management rights; and (3) a lack of a public market for the firm's shares. These features vary among firms but generally travel together, since the existence of a public market is a function of transferability, and owners are more likely to want "voice" in management the less they are able to "exit" the firm. (The classic work on the tradeoff between voice and exit is HIRSCHMAN, EXIT, VOICE AND LOYALTY (1970)).

1.   Management

Corporation statutes (*e.g.,* DEL. G.C.L. § 141(a)) provide for management "by or under the direction of a board of directors." This management power extends to day to day affairs as well as such important matters as the power to declare dividends (*e.g., id.* § 170). Shareholders select the directors and make important decisions, including amending the articles of incorporation (*e.g., id.* § 242(c)(1)), merger (*id.* § 251), sale of all or substantially all of the corporation's assets (*id.* § 271) and dissolution (*id.* § 275). In each case, however, the shareholders can act only after the directors have first resolved to take the action. Also, unlike partners, shareholders normally lack both actual and apparent authority to create corporate liabilities. This structure obviously contrasts sharply with the partnership standard form, which provides for equal participation of all partners in management decisions. Although partners often delegate some power to managers (*see* Chapter 5), they rarely delegate anything like the power directors have to effectively veto corporate events such as dissolutions, amendments and asset sales.

2.   Shareholder Voting

Corporate shareholders have one vote per share. Since shares usually are sold for cash or other property and not services, this effectively allocates voting power according to owners' capital investments. By contrast, the partnership default voting rule is one-partner-one-vote, which reflects partners' multifarious service, capital and credit contributions. *See* Chapter 4.

3. Transferability

Shareholders generally can sell their complete bundle of ownership rights in the firm, including both management and financial rights. Indeed, this shareholder power is sometimes regarded as a basic property right. *See Rafe v. Hindin*, 29 A.D.2d 481, 288 N.Y.S.2d 662 (1968), *aff'd mem.*, 23 N.Y.2d 759, 296 N.Y.S.2d 955, 244 N.E.2d 469 (1968). This contrasts with the rule discussed in Chapter 7 that partners can transfer only financial rights and can veto admission of new members. In a closely held firm, owner-managers will want to be able to determine the identity of co-managers, who have important rights to create liabilities for which the owners may be held personally responsible.

4. Dissociation and Dissolution

Corporate entities survive while the members come and go. A corporation normally can be dissolved only by majority vote after a director resolution (*see, e.g.,* DEL. G.C.L. § 275). By contrast, as discussed in Chapter 9, under partnership default rules individual partners can compel the firm to liquidate, or at least to buy out their interests, at any time. This provides some liquidity for otherwise non-transferable partnership interests.

B. Waiver of Corporate Defaults

Corporate law at first required strict adherence to corporate law norms even for closely held firms. The law on this issue is normally covered in detail in the corporations course. For present purposes it is enough to note that corporate statutory rules were not explicitly subject to contrary agreement and the courts took this literally. *See, e.g., McQuade v. Stoneham*, 263 N.Y. 323, 189 N.E. 234 (1934) (management by the board); *Rafe v. Hindin*, 29 A.D.2d 481, 288 N.Y.S.2d 662 (1968), *aff'd mem.*, 23 N.Y.2d 759, 244 N.E.2d 469, 296 N.Y.S.2d 955 (1968) (transferability of stock).

Corporate law evolved in this respect first by a judicial loosening of the statutory rules and then by statutory change. Important cases include *Ringling v. Ringling Bros.—Barnum & Bailey Combined Shows, Inc.*, 29 Del. Ch. 318, 49 A.2d 603 (Del. Ch. 1946), *modified*, 29 Del. Ch. 610, 53 A.2d 441 (Del. 1947) (enforcing shareholder voting agreement that effectively gave disproportionate power to minority shareholder); *Clark v. Dodge*, 269 N.Y. 410, 199 N.E. 641 (1936) (enforcing director control agreement giving substantial power to shareholder where there were no non-party shareholders and the board retained some power).

Corporate statutes came to recognize the enforceability of variations on corporate norms such as shareholder voting agreements (*see, e.g.,* DEL. G.C.L. § 218). However, the legislatures did not want to make some types of variability, particularly dispensing with the board of directors, available to publicly held corporations. Thus, most of these statutes could be used only by "close corporations," usually defined in terms of some combination of number of shareholders, absence of a public offering or listing on a securities exchange, and use of stock transfer restrictions. *See, e.g.,* DEL. G.C.L. §§ 341-356; N.C. GEN. STATS. § 55-73(b); MBCA § 7.32.

The effect of these statutes is sometimes unclear. In particular, when shareholders enter into an agreement that is enforceable only in "close corporations" but fail to elect or qualify as a close corporation under the applicable statute, courts might enforce the agreement anyway, consistent with the general trend toward liberalization of corporate requirements. *See, e.g., Zion v. Kurtz,* 50 N.Y.2d 92, 405 N.E.2d 681 (1980). Indeed it may not always be clear whether the statute has been violated, since even a non-qualifying or non-electing corporation may be able to argue that the basic corporation statute had been sufficiently liberalized to allow variation. For example, in *Lehrman v. Cohen,* 222 A.2d 800, 806 (Del. 1966), the court held that a deadlock breaking arrangement in a public corporation did not impermissibly bypass the board's management power. This authority may remain available even to non-complying close corporations under DEL. G.C.L. § 356, which provides that the close corporation provisions are not exclusive.

C.   Filling the Gaps

Questions arose concerning what default rules should fill the gaps in the parties' contracts. The parties to relatively informal closely held firms frequently know only that they want to form a firm and have limited liability. They do a "bare bones" incorporation, perhaps without consulting a lawyer, little realizing that they have selected a form whose default rules do not fit their situation. It is not clear whether issues the parties left open should be answered by applying corporate default rules, since the parties did elect to incorporate, or instead by *partnership* default rules which are normally better suited for closely held firms. In particular, should an owner be able to exit the firm by means of buyout or dissolution just as a partner can?

Legislatures answered this question by enacting close corporation dissolution and buyout remedies. These provisions do not quite apply the partnership exit-at-will approach, but instead require owners to prove that they *need* to leave, as because they are "oppressed." The courts came to interpret these provisions as calling for enforcement of the parties' "reasonable expectations." *See, e.g., Gardstein v. Kemp & Beatley,* 64 N.Y.2d 63, 484 N.Y.S.2d 799, 473 N.E. 2d 1173 (1984). But it was often far from clear whether the parties got what they bargained for. For example, *Gardstein* held that long-time employee-shareholders who were fired by their employer were entitled to a continuation of payments they received while they worked for the company. This "expectation" was far from clear in the case. The employees may have expected the company to buy their shares when they left, but this would still require the court to determine the value—which in turn would depend on whether the employees were entitled to a continuation of distributions.

Close corporations that were formed under statutes that did not provide for these special buyout and dissolution remedies presented additional challenges. Even in this situation, a leading case held that a *minority* shareholder was entitled to a buyout at the same price the corporation paid the *controlling* shareholder. *See Donahue v. Rodd Electrotype Co.,* 367 Mass. 578, 328 N.E.2d 505 (1975). The court stressed how much the firm looked like a partnership, in which owners need to be able to exit the firm, but made little of the fact that the parties chose to incorporate.

The courts have tended to draw the line at situations in which the parties could have formed under close corporation provisions of the corporation statute which provided remedies to deal with issue at hand, but did not do so. *See, e.g, Toner v. Baltimore Envelope Co.,* 304 Md. 256, 498 A.2d 642 (1985); *Sundberg v. Lampert Lumber Co.,* 390 N.W.2d 352 (Minn. App. 1986). Also, a court refused to apply special close corporation remedies to a firm that was not a close corporation under the Delaware statute, and could have but did not contractually resolve the issue. *See Nixon v. Blackwell,* 626 A.2d 1366 (Del. 1993).

In the final analysis, it was never clear what the courts should or will do when they had to fit the square peg of a closely held firm into the round hole of incorporation.

10.04 Double Taxation and the Corporation

The tax treatment of partnerships is more favorable than that for corporations for many types of firms. The differences flow from the fact that a corporation is treated more as a separate entity for many tax purposes than is a partnership.

A corporation that is subject to Subchapter C of the Internal Revenue Code (*compare* Subchapter S corporations, below) is taxed on *profits* when they are earned by the business at the corporate tax rate, a rate that may or may not be higher than the rate applicable to an individual investor. Its shareholders, however, are taxed only on what is distributed to them as *dividends*. Even if the corporation does not distribute earnings, the shareholders still may be taxed on them in effect when they sell their shares at a gain, since the selling shareholders normally are taxed on their gains, which may partly reflect accumulated earnings. A corporation that *loses* money in a given year does not get a commensurate reduction in tax unless it can carry the loss back or forth to previous or succeeding years to offset taxable earnings in those years. Shareholders who incur capital losses on selling their shares at a price lower than their purchase price may be able to deduct these losses against their capital gains, if any.

By comparison, a partnership's *profits* are earned for tax purposes directly by the partners. Accordingly, they are taxed only once to the partners, in the year when the profits are earned, at the partners' individual tax rate, and not again when they are distributed to the partners. Similarly, partners may be able to deduct partnership *losses* against their non-partnership income. (However, partners' ability to "shelter" income with losses from partnership investments is continually narrowing. For example, the partners cannot deduct "passive losses" they incur from firms they do not actively manage. *See* I.R.C § 469.)

Single level partnership taxation is an advantage for most firms, particularly as long as capital gains are taxed at ordinary income rates (so there is no break for retaining earnings). It is particularly well suited to professional and other firms that distribute most of their earnings each year. It may also suit firms whose owners participate directly in management. On the other hand, corporate taxation may be better for firms with passive owners. Under corporate taxation, transactions by the firm, such as the purchase and sale of corporate property, generate corporate-level tax consequences which do not hit the owners until they sell their shares. Because corporate taxation reduces managers' ability to affect the tax the owners owe, it is better suited for firms in which the owners do not directly participate in management. *See* Kanda & Levmore, *Taxes, Agency Costs and The Price of Incorporation,* 77 Va. L. Rev. 211 (1991). The story is more mixed when distributions are taken into account. Because shareholders pay tax on distributions, managers' decisions regarding when to distribute income have a direct tax impact on shareholders. But partners conversely suffer from managers' decision to *retain* earnings. *See* Snoe, *The Entity Tax and Corporate Integration: An Agency Cost Analysis and a Call for a Deferred Distributions Tax,* 48 U. Miami L. Rev. 1 (1993).

A corporation can get some of the tax advantages of partnership if it elects to be taxed under Subchapter S of the Internal Revenue Code. Income and losses in a Subchapter S corporation "flow through" to the shareholders almost like they do in a partnership. However, Subchapter S is subject to eligibility and operational restrictions, including the following:

(a) The shareholders in a close corporation may elect Subchapter S status if they vote unanimously to do so and (1) there are no more than 75 shareholders; (2) all are either individuals (U.S. citizens or resident aliens), estates, or certain types of trusts; (3) there is only one class of stock.

(b) The one-class-of-stock restriction means that, while there may be differences in voting rights, the shares must have the same dividend and liquidation rights. This eliminates capital structures that combine, for example, preferred and common stock, although "straight debt" is permitted. It is much less flexible than the allocations of income and other items permitted in partnerships under Subchapter K (*see* § 4.04, above).

(c) If an S corporation distributes appreciated property to a shareholder, the shareholder may have to recognize taxable gain, while gain would not be taxable in a partnership's property distribution back to a partner.

(d) An S corporation shareholder can increase the "basis" in her shares (which later determines how much the shares have appreciated or depreciated for tax purposes) through debt only if this is in the form of loans to the corporation (*see* IRC § 1367(b)). By contrast, partners' basis reflects their shares in the liabilities of the partnership (*see* IRC

§ 752(a)). This may be significant in computing the owners' taxable gain on sale of their interests in the firm.

(e) There is the danger that a corporation that initially qualifies for Subchapter S status may lose this status if its characteristics change, as where the stock is transferred to an ineligible shareholder or so as to create more than thirty-five shareholders. Although the shareholders can minimize this problem by proper planning, they do not always have adequate foresight. A court may fill the gap. In *A.W. Chesterton Company, Inc. v. Chesterton*, 128 F.3d 1 (1st Cir. 1997), the court enjoined a close corporation shareholder from a share transfer to two corporations that would have caused Subchapter S status to terminate. The court reasoned that would be a breach of fiduciary duty even though it was not expressly prohibited by the transfer restrictions in the corporation's articles of organization.

10.05 Unincorporated Limited Liability Forms

This Chapter has shown why firms would search for an alternative to the corporate and general partnership business forms. This section discusses two main reasons why this search has been unsuccessful until recently—tax restrictions on business form, and policy concerns about limited liability.

A. Tax Constraints

Until recently, the form of unincorporated businesses was restricted by complex tax rules that determined whether a firm was a "partnership" or a "corporation" for tax purposes. These so-called "Kintner rules" are discussed in subsection 1. Theoretical and practical problems with the Kintner rules are discussed in subsections 2 and 3. Subsection 4 discusses an important change that permits most closely held U.S. firms simply to elect whether to be taxed as corporations or partnerships. Despite this change, it is worth describing the Kintner rules because they help explain the current shape of business associations—and particularly the LLC.

1. The Kintner Rules

Whether a business is taxed as a corporation or a partnership is answered in most cases with reference to the definitions in the Internal Revenue Code of "corporation" (§ 7701(a)(3)) and "partnership" (§ 7701(a)(2)). The term "corporation" includes "association[s]," or businesses that resemble corporations even if they have not actually been organized pursuant to state corporation law. *See Morrissey v. Commissioner,* 296

U.S. 344 (1935). "Partnership" is a residual category which includes most of what is not a "corporation," trust or estate.

For many years, Treasury Regulations § 301.7701-2 governed the determination of what constitutes an "association" under the above rules through what are commonly referred to as the "Kintner regulations," referring to a series of cases led by *United States v. Kintner,* 216 F.2d 418 (9th Cir. 1954). Since the IRS was in that case concerned with stopping what it believed were essentially partnerships from attaining certain tax advantages of incorporation, including the ability to shelter income in corporate pension plans, the Kintner regulations were weighted in favor of finding that a business organization is *not* a corporation. This weighting worked against the IRS in cases involving firms that want to be treated as partnerships for tax purposes.

The Kintner regulations judged corporate resemblance in terms of what the IRS believed to be the distinguishing characteristics of corporations and partnerships: continuity of life, corporate-type management, limited liability, and free transferability of interests. The regulations provided that a business organization is a corporation for tax purposes only if it has at least three of these corporate characteristics. (It is important to keep in mind that "publicly traded" firms are normally taxed as corporations even if they are partnerships under state law. *See* § 11.12, below.)

The following is a brief summary of the four corporate characteristics set forth in the Kintner regulation.

Continuity of life. Under the Kintner regulations, a partnership generally does not have continuity of life because the organization may be dissolved through withdrawal or bankruptcy of a partner or in a number of other ways. However, the firm has continuity of life if, following a partner's or member's dissociation, it may be continued by a vote of fewer than a "majority in interest" of the other members or partners.

Centralized management. Corporate management is typically by directors who do not own significant interests in the corporation, while partners directly participate in management. Thus, a partnership adopting the partnership default rules on management would *not* be deemed to have centralized management under the Kintner regulations. Even if management is delegated to a few managing partners or members, or to general partners in a limited partnership, the partnership does not have *corporate-type* centralized management if the managers have significant ownership interests in the firm or lack exclusive power to bind the firm in transactions with third parties.

Limited liability. Corporate shareholders have limited liability while general partners traditionally did not, at least until the advent of the limited liability partnership discussed in Chapter 13. Although limited partners in limited partnerships have limited liability much like that of corporate shareholders, a limited partnership is deemed to lack corporate-type liability because it has general partners who are liable by statute for all of the firms' debts. At least for purposes of obtaining an IRS ruling, even a limited partnership with a corporate general partner does not automatically have corporate-type limited liability as long as the general partner meets certain net worth requirements.

Free transferability of interests. General partnerships lack the free transferability of ownership interests that characterizes the typical corporation because, as discussed in Chapter 7, partners generally cannot transfer management rights without the consent of the other partners. However, a partnership may be considered to have corporate-type free transferability if the partners agree that no consent is required for transfers or if any required consent must be freely given.

2. Rationale for the Corporate/Partnership Distinction

The obvious problem with the Kintner rules was that it was not clear why a firm that is not incorporated under state law nevertheless should be considered a corporation for income tax purposes. In other words, what is it about an unincorporated firm that should make it a tax "corporation"? The rules may be based on the fact that corporate features make a firm look more like an "entity" and therefore more appropriate for "entity"-like tax treatment. But there are several flaws with this argument. Even partnerships are "entities" in many critical respects, as RUPA § 201 recognizes. More generally, as discussed above in § 1.02(E), "aggregate" and "entity" are only descriptions of, rather than rationales for, default statutory features. Since these features can be waived by contrary agreement, they are not inherent aspects of firms that are labeled "partnerships" or "corporations."

The corporate tax might once properly have been attributed to the corporate "privilege" of limited liability. Although the corporate tax is not designed to compensate for or to reduce any social costs that limited liability might entail, it does at least encourage limited liability firms to delay the shareholder-level tax by retaining earnings. This would provide creditors with an extra capital cushion to mitigate the risks of limited liability. Conversely, if limited liability firms can be taxed as partnerships they have a strong incentive to distribute all of their earnings since owners are taxed on these funds as soon as they are earned by the firm. As discussed in § 10.04, policy concerns about limited liability that could be exacerbated by partnership taxation may partly explain why recognition of limited liability unincorporated firms was slow in coming.

Finally, the corporate/partnership distinction makes some sense insofar as corporate taxation is better suited to firms in which control and management is separated, as discussed in § 10.04. However, as discussed there, owner-manager separation creates problems for corporate taxation from the standpoint of distributions. More importantly, centralization of management is only one of the four Kintner factors. Thus, many tax "partnerships," including limited partnerships, LLCs and other firms that are subject to partnership taxation, may have the same types of owner-manager conflicts as big corporations. In other words, under the Kintner rules firms cannot freely choose their method of taxation to suit their management structure. In any event, it is not clear that tax rules *should* address conflicts of interest within firms. Firms can solve these problems themselves by internal rules, such as requiring member votes on matters such as distributions.

3. Practical Problems with the Corporate/Partnership Distinction

Even if it made sense to base the corporate tax on "corporate," as distinguished from "partnership," characteristics, in evaluating this approach it is also necessary to take into account possible costs of the system. *See* Ribstein, *The Deregulation of Limited Liability and the Death of Partnership,* 70 WASH. U. L.Q. 417 (1992).

First, the Kintner rules imposed extra governance costs on firms by encouraging them to adopt only two Kintner characteristics in order to avoid the extra tax costs of incorporation even if some other combination of governance terms would be better for the firm from a non-tax standpoint. For example, a firm that manages investment capital is likely to want to raise capital from passive investors (because people with money to invest are not necessarily the same as those with management skills) and delegate management to one or more managers. The investors would not want to be personally liable for the firm's debts, since this would force them to pay close attention to the business. If such a firm combined centralized management and limited liability, it would have to avoid both free transferability and continuity of life in order to be classified as a tax partnership. Under the Kintner rules, the firm would probably have to dissolve upon the death, insanity, bankruptcy, retirement, resignation, or expulsion at least of a manager, subject to a vote to continue by at least a majority of the remaining members. Yet such a rule exposes the firm to the potential disruption of an untimely liquidation and empowers individual members or minority factions to extract concessions from the majority as the price of letting them continue. The firm nevertheless may adopt the "partnership" dissolution rule to get the significant benefits of being taxed as a partnership. Thus, the tax rule forces the firm to adopt an inefficient governance structure.

Second, even if many non-corporate firms were willing to adopt two or more corporate characteristics, legislators would be reluctant to enact statutes that provide for these features out of concern for misleading less sophisticated firms and their lawyers as to tax classification. Thus, tax law inhibited the development and evolution of forms of business such as joint stock companies, partnership associations and business trusts which combine two or more corporate characteristics.

4. The "Check-the-Box" Approach

Finally recognizing the theoretical and practical problems with the Kintner rules, the I.R.S. adopted a rule that drops the four-factor approach in favor of letting unincorporated firms choose to be taxed as either corporations or partnerships—that is, to "check a box." *See* Simplification of Entity Classification Rules, 26 C.F.R. pt. 1, 301, 602 (December 10, 1996, effective January 1, 1997). The rules provide that a domestic "eligible entity" (foreign entities are covered separately), which includes business firms other than corporations, joint stock companies, insurance companies or banks, is not treated as a corporation for income tax purposes unless it elects this treatment. An eligible entity with two or more members is a partnership for income tax purposes unless it elects to be a corporation. An eligible entity with one member is taxed directly and the entity is ignored unless the entity elects to be a corporation for tax purposes.

B.   Limited Liability

Non-partnership alternatives to incorporation may have been unavailable not only because of the constraints imposed by the Kintner rules but also because of legislators' concerns about making limited liability available beyond the corporate form. In particular, there is a concern for the interests of involuntary creditors (*i.e.*, tort victims) who are not in a position to demand compensation for the extra risks they take under limited liability.

One explanation for permitting owners of firms to limit their liability to involuntary creditors is that the benefits to owners of limited liability discussed in § 10.01 outweigh the potential benefits to tort plaintiffs of personal liability. Whether this is actually the case depends on the extent to which limited liability lets firms' owners ignore potential risks to tort victims because they don't have to pay the full costs of these risks. Indeed, it is not clear why small firms would want to have limited liability *other than* to injure tort creditors. Limited liability is particularly easy to understand in public corporations, since it is difficult to establish a liquid market in which owners are personally liable for the firm's debts. *See* EASTERBROOK & FISCHEL, THE ECONOMIC STRUCTURE OF CORPORATE LAW, Ch. 2 (1992). As discussed in § 10.01, it may also be easy to see why centralized-management firms would find personal liability of owners to be costly. But in very closely held owner-managed firms it may be hard to understand why owners would want to pay the extra credit costs of limited liability. A possible answer is that the firms are *not* paying the higher costs of credit, but rather are shifting business risks to involuntary creditors who cannot demand extra compensation for the extra risks of dealing with firms whose owners do not bear the full costs of their actions. Indeed, a concern for tort creditors underlies criticism of limited tort liability in all kinds of firms. *See* Halpern, Trebilcock & Turnbull, *An Economic Analysis of Limited Liability in Corporation Law*, 30 U. TOR. L.J. 117 (1980); Leebron, *Limited Liability, Tort Victims, and Creditors,* 91 COLUM. L. REV. 1565 (1991).

This problem of involuntary creditors may not, however, be as serious as it might seem at first glance. Firms have incentives to insure against tort liabilities in order to reduce their credit costs to voluntary creditors. *See* EASTERBROOK & FISCHEL, *supra*; Ribstein, *The Deregulation of Limited Liability and the Death of Partnership,* 70 WASH. U. L.Q. 417 (1992). If the firm does insure, its insurance rates, and the availability of insurance, depend on how carefully the firm manages tort risks. Even holding investors personally liable may not actually cause them to do much more monitoring in firms in which ownership and management are separated. *See* Thompson, *Unpacking Limited Liability: Direct and Vicarious Liability of Corporate Participants for Torts of the Enterprise,* 47 VAND. L. REV. 1 (1994). Moreover, personal liability may not do tort creditors much good, given the costs of tracking down, suing and recovering from owners discussed in Chapter 6.

Even if limited liability to tort creditors is a problem, and even if it is particularly a problem in closely held firms, the important question for present purposes is why it should be confined to closely held *corporations*. One reason may be that in a standard-form corporation, distribution and other management decisions are made by non-owner directors whose interests are aligned somewhat with creditors because their jobs are at stake if the corporation goes broke. This may help explain policymakers' reluctance to let firms combine limited liability with the partnership management structure. Yet the owner-shareholder-director of a very closely held corporation hardly fits the standard corporate model.

Another reason for not allowing partnership-type firms to have limited liability is that firms that are taxed as partnerships have an extra incentive to distribute all of their earnings, retaining none for creditors. This, indeed, might be a reason to link limited liability and corporate taxation. While limited liability was only one of the Kintner factors (*see* § 10.04), until the breakthrough revenue ruling that gave rise to LLCs (*see* Chapter 12), it was not clearly recognized that a tax partnership could have full limited liability—that is, not even a single general partner. Given this tax uncertainty, state legislators had little incentive to take the lead in developing this form.

10.06 Conclusion

In general, then, there are good reasons for firms to want to be "incorporated partnerships." However, at least as of the late 1980s, there were also impediments based on the tax distinction between corporations and partnerships and reticence about extending limited liability to partnership-type firms. The following chapters show how these impediments have been rapidly disappearing, paving the way for the limited liability company, the limited liability partnership and other partnership-type firms with limited liability.

CHAPTER 11
THE LIMITED PARTNERSHIP

11.01 Background and History

A limited partnership has general partners whose rights and duties are mostly subject to the general partnership statute, as well as limited partners who have limited liability and whose rights and obligations are governed by statutory provisions that are primarily aimed at protecting creditors. This combination of terms presents some complicated problems in applying both partnership law and regulatory and tax rules. In particular, limited partnerships, unlike general partnerships, are regulated by the securities laws, and may be subject to corporate tax.

Limited partnerships were developed to accommodate a business need for a form of business that permitted non-loan investments of capital without personal liability. As discussed in Chapter 3, creditors of partnerships who seek unusual protection from and compensation for credit risk take the chance of being held liable as general partners. The precursor to the modern limited partnership was the European "commenda" in which a "commendator" provided funds to a "commmendatarius" or "tractator" and received some of the profits without liability for losses or liability for usury or for violating rules against clergy and others participating in trade." *See* HOLDSWORTH, HISTORY OF ENGLISH LAW 195 (2d ed. 1937).

The first limited partnership statutes were adopted in New York (1822), Connecticut (1822), and Pennsylvania (1836), and then in other eastern states as a way of avoiding partnership liability based on profit sharing. The original acts, such as New York's, imposed broad creditor protection provisions concerning such matters as limited partner contributions (cash only) and formalities. Early cases strictly applied these restrictions.

The Uniform Limited Partnership Act (1916) (ULPA) was intended to relieve this strictness. *See* Official Comment to ULPA § 1, 6 U.L.A. 563-64 (1969). ULPA included provisions such as enforcing the limited liability shield with only substantial compliance with formalities and allowing a limited partner's contribution to be in property rather than only in cash as under the prior law. Consistent with the tenor of these changes, *Giles v. Vette,* 263 U.S. 553 (1924), held that the statute should be liberally interpreted in favor of limited liability.

ULPA was widely adopted and then replaced by the Revised Uniform Limited Partnership Acts of 1976 and 1985. The Revised Uniform Limited Partnership Act (1976) was spurred by the use of the limited partnership as a sophisticated tax shelter vehicle by large, multi-state firms. As discussed below, it narrowed limited partners' "control" liability by requiring more participation in control and providing for a "safe harbor" of things limited partners may do without taking part in control (§ 303).

The 1985 version of the Revised Uniform Limited Partnership Act (here referred to simply as "RULPA") was motivated by adverse experience with the 1976 version and its modification in major business jurisdictions such as California and Delaware.

Among other changes, the 1985 Act modifies the "control rule" by adding a reliance requirement (*see* § 303, discussed in § 11.05(B)(2), below). Most states now have statutes based on 1985 RULPA.

A revision of RULPA, referred to here as "Re-RULPA" is underway as this book is being written. The drafts are available through http://www.law.upenn.edu/bll/ulc/ulc_frame.htm. For a preliminary analysis of the project, *see* Ribstein, *Limited Partnerships Revisited,* 67 U. CIN. L. REV. 953 (1999). Changes being proposed in the drafts are discussed throughout this chapter. References to "Re-RULPA" are to the status of the act as of summer, 2000. Section numbers are not given because they are likely to change throughout the revision process.

Although limited partnerships were widely used by publicly held firms in the 1970s and 1980s for tax shelter investments in oil and gas, real estate and other activities, changes in federal income tax legislation and interpretation have sharply reduced the utility of limited partnerships for publicly held businesses and the tax advantages of limited partnerships for all kinds of business. These tax changes and the collapse of the market for interests in publicly held limited partnerships left a legacy of fiduciary and disclosure litigation over failed limited partnerships and a new federal disclosure law. *See* § 11.12, below.

11.02 Linkage with General Partnership Law

An important aspect of limited partnership law is its "linkage" with partnership law. *See* Ribstein, *Linking Statutory Forms,* 58 J. L. & CONTEMP. PROB. 187 (1995); Vestal, *A Comprehensive Uniform Limited Partnership Act? The Time Has Come,* 28 U.C. DAVIS L. REV. 1195 (1995). UPA § 6(2) provides for application of the UPA to limited partnerships "except in so far as the statutes relating to such partnerships are inconsistent herewith." ULPA § 1 explicitly defines a limited partnership as a "partnership," and § 9 provides that "a general partner shall have all the rights and powers and be subject to all the restrictions and liabilities of a partner in a partnership without limited partners" except that a general partner has no power to bind the partnership as to certain acts without the limited partners' consent. RULPA § 101(7) defines a limited partnership as a "partnership," § 403 provides that a general partner has rights, powers, restrictions and liabilities of a general partner, and § 1105 provides that "in any case not provided for in this Act, the provisions of the Uniform Partnership Act govern."

RUPA does not explicitly apply to limited partnerships and § 101(4) defines "partnership" to exclude limited partnerships. Thus, in states that adopt RUPA but not RULPA, general partnership law applies to limited partnerships mainly by virtue of the RULPA provisions listed above, assuming this language is interpreted as referring to the current partnership law rather than the superseded UPA-based statute. Also, RUPA creates an additional link with limited partnership law through its provisions for mergers and conversions of limited and general partnerships (*see* § 11.10, below).

As discussed throughout this Chapter, these provisions mean in effect that limited partnership law is a combination of (1) limited partnership act provisions on limited partners; (2) UPA and RUPA provisions on general partners; and (3) an uncertain combination limited and general partnership law on issues such as dissolution that are incompletely covered in the limited partnership statutes. From a policy standpoint, this method of "linking" general and limited partnerships has both advantages and disadvantages. It makes the large body of partnership law discussed in Chapters 3 through 9 available to limited partnerships, which provides some certainty and predictability. But the dark side of linkage is that, as discussed throughout this chapter, these cases may be inappropriate in the distinct limited partnership setting.

One of the most significant decisions made so far in Re-RULPA is to make it a "stand-alone" act. However, a type of linkage remains in the form of importing RUPA language into the limited partnership act.

11.03 Formation: Formalities and Consequences of Non-Compliance

Unlike a general partnership, which can exist on the basis of a very informal agreement, forming a limited partnership requires the additional step of filing a certificate with the state. Limited partnership certificates provide notice both of the firm's limited liability status and of certain terms of the relationship, including the identity of the general partners to whom creditors can look for satisfaction of debts. The certificate is not intended to be controlling among the partners. See the *Fox* case excerpted on p. 312, below.

ULPA § 11 and RULPA § 304 protect "erroneous" limited partners—*i.e.,* parties who have contributed to the capital of a partnership erroneously believing that they have become limited partners. Section 304 has been held to apply even where the partnership was formed and always represented as a general partnership but the defendant partner, who received part of her interest on divorce, asserted that she understood it to be a limited partnership. *See Briargate Condominium Assoc. v. Carpenter,* 976 F.2d 868 (4th Cir. 1992) (N.C. law). The court vacated a judgment in favor of the creditor and remanded for determination whether the defendant had the necessary "good faith" belief that she was a limited partner.

11.04 Partners' Financial Rights

Limited partnership agreements in general, and the financial provisions of these agreements in particular, normally are heavily lawyered and tax-driven. The discussion of partnership capital accounts in § 4.04 generally applies here, although limited partnership financial arrangements may be much more complex. The default provisions of the statutes, by contrast, mainly provide simple default rules for the relatively informal firms that have not agreed in detail on these matters. They also provide some minimal protection for creditors who, like creditors of corporations, cannot necessarily seek recovery from owners' personal assets.

A.   Contributions

One becomes a limited partner by contributing to capital. *See Allen v. Amber Manor Apartments Partnership*, 95 Ill. App. 3d 541, 51 Ill. Dec. 26, 420 N.E.2d 440, 447 (1981). Although the law once restricted the form of the contribution, these restrictions have all but disappeared. RULPA § 501 now provides that a contribution can even be in the form of a promise to contribute services. Partners may agree to make additional contributions.

B.   Sharing of Distributions

RULPA §§ 503 and 504 provide that limited and general partners share profits, losses and distributions according to their capital contributions to the firm in the absence of contrary agreement. This apparently overrides UPA § 18(a) and RUPA § 401(b), discussed in Chapter 4, which provide for equal sharing of profits, losses and distributions. Re-RULPA plans to eliminate the allocation of profits and losses as unnecessary. The general partnership rule of equal sharing of financial rights should not apply to limited partnerships since, in the absence of contrary agreement, the parties probably would expect the general partners to receive something extra in return for their contributions of services and credit. Thus, the presumption of non-compensation that applies to general partners has been held not to apply to limited partners. *Szturm v. Huntington Blizzard Hockey Associates Ltd. Partnership*, 516 S.E.2d 267 (W. Va. 1999). Financial rights are almost invariably provided for in detail in the limited partnership agreement. Some issues concerning drafting the partnership agreement are covered in the analogous context of LLCs in § 12.03.

C.   Creditors' Rights

As a tradeoff for their limited liability, limited partners may be liable to creditors for failing to honor contribution obligations or for removing too much money from the firm. Creditors may have rights, directly or through a bankruptcy trustee, to collect on contributions partners owe the firm. *See* RULPA § 502. This extends even to compromised contribution obligations that creditors have relied on. *See id.* § 502(c). Partners can themselves be creditors of limited partnerships and obtain liens superior to those of other partnership creditors subject to other law, including bankruptcy law. *See Szturm v. Huntington Blizzard Hockey Associates Ltd. Partnership,* 516 S.E.2d 267 (W. Va. 1999).

Partners' liability to creditors may arise under the partnership agreement, as where the agreement provides for assessments of additional contributions. For example, *In re Securities Group*, 74 F.3d 1103 (11th Cir. 1996) held in favor of such liability for limited partners who had sold their interests before these assessments were called. *Builders Steel Co., Inc. v. Hycore, Inc.,* 877 P.2d 1168 (Okla. App. 1994), held that limited partners were liable to creditors for assessments noted in the certificate and refused to enforce the certificate's further statement that creditors may not rely on the assessments because of the limitations in RULPA § 208 on the effect of the articles as notice to third parties. Thus, the certificate was notice of the limited partners' obligations but not of the limitations on those obligations. *But see In re Villa West Associates*, 146 F.3d 798 (10th Cir. 1998), holding that an agreement to make additional capital contributions triggered only dilution rather than money damages. The court reasoned that a broader reading would be inconsistent with the partnership agreement, which provided: "[n]o Limited Partner shall be personally liable for any of the debts of the Limited Partnership or any of the losses thereof beyond the amount committed by him to the capital of the Limited Partnership." The court interpreted "amount committed" as a definite sum.

RULPA § 607 makes wrongful distributions that violate the partnership agreement or by insolvent firms. RULPA § 608 provides for liability for wrongful distributions, as well as for distributions that were rightful at the time of the distribution but constitute a return of partners' contributions and become necessary to discharge liabilities to pre-distribution creditors. *See also* ULPA § 17. This rule imposes on limited partners the risk of liability caused by an unpredictable reversal in the partnership's fortunes (although this risk is limited to one year under RULPA). Liability for distributions makes the limited partnership an awkward vehicle for informal firms that do not keep careful accounts and valuations that would reveal when distributions violate statutory restrictions, and professional firms that normally distribute all of their annual earnings to partners. Moreover, the restrictions on distributions provide little protection for creditors beyond the background law of fraudulent conveyances.

Re-RULPA would revise these provisions by adopting provisions based on the Model Business Corporation Act and the Uniform Limited Liability Company Act. A significant change is that partners would no longer be liable for distributions that were rightful when made.

Partners' distribution liabilities, like their contribution liabilities, may depend on the partnership agreement. This introduces a cautionary planning note, as demonstrated by the next case.

Henkels & McCoy, Inc. v. Adochio
138 F.3d 491 (3rd Cir. 1997)

ROSENN, Circuit Judge.

This appeal presents an important question pertaining to the obligation of limited partners to return capital contributions distributed to them in violation of their partnership agreement which required that they establish reasonably necessary reserves. The issue is rendered complex by an interrelated maze of corporations and partnerships devised by the limited partners and the general partner in their efforts to develop two separate real estate projects. One of these, Timber Knolls, was aborted shortly after conception, and the other, Chestnut Woods, became the genesis of protracted litigation and of this appeal.

The defendants-appellants are limited partners of Red Hawk North Associates, L.P. (Red Hawk), a New Jersey limited partnership. G & A Development Corporation (G & A) is the general partner of Red Hawk. Cedar Ridge Development Corporation (Cedar Ridge), a New Jersey corporation, and Red Hawk entered into a joint venture agreement, the Chestnut Woods Partnership (Chestnut Woods), to develop, construct, and market residential homes in Bucks County, Pennsylvania. Red Hawk and Cedar Ridge are both general partners of Chestnut Woods. Under the joint venture agreement, Red Hawk would provide the funding and Cedar Ridge would provide the land which it previously had agreed to purchase. Cedar Ridge would act as the managing partner and general contractor.

On December 29, 1989, Cedar Ridge, as general contractor for Chestnut Woods, entered into a written subcontract with Henkels & McCoy, Inc. (Henkels), the plaintiff herein, to have it furnish the labor, materials, and equipment for the installation of the storm and sanitary sewer systems for the project. Cedar Ridge agreed to pay Henkels a fixed-price of $300,270 under the contract. Henkels completed the installation of the storm and sewer systems but Chestnut Woods defaulted in making the payments due under the contract. Henkels, a Pennsylvania corporation, then filed three actions in the United States District Court for the Eastern District of Pennsylvania; Henkels filed the first in December 1990 against Cedar Ridge and Red Hawk, trading as Chestnut Woods, for the balance due on the contract plus interest. The court entered a default judgment which was not satisfied in whole or part.

Henkels then filed suit against G & A in its capacity as a general partner of Red Hawk and obtained a default judgment in the same amount as it had obtained against Cedar Ridge and Red Hawk. Efforts to obtain payment on this judgment also proved fruitless and counsel for the defendants advised plaintiff's counsel by letter dated October 26, 1993 that Red Hawk was worthless. Henkels's counsel also had been advised that G & A was unable to pay the judgment out of its assets.

Henkels finally brought this suit against the nineteen limited partners of Red Hawk (the Partners), standing in the shoes of the Red Hawk limited partnership; sixteen of the partners are parties to this appeal. Henkels sought, inter alia, to compel replacement of certain capital distributions made by Red Hawk to the limited partners aggregating $492,000 during the period that Cedar Ridge was obligated under its contract with Henkels to pay Henkels $300,270. Henkels alleged that the capital distributions were made in violation of the Red Hawk limited partnership agreement and § 42:2A-46(b) of the New Jersey Uniform Limited Partnership Law of 1976 (New Jersey ULPL).

* * *

As a preliminary matter, we must first address the Red Hawk Partners' argument that Henkels was not a creditor who had extended credit to Red Hawk at the time of the 1989 capital distributions, and therefore the Partners were not liable to Henkels. The Partners base their argument on Section 42:2A-46(a) of New Jersey's ULPL [RULPA §608(a)] [quoting language]. * * * The Partners' reliance on this section is, however, misguided for several reasons: first, and most importantly, Henkels brought suit under Section 42:2A-46(b) [RULPA §608(b)] not (a); second, subsection (b) is not in any way dependent upon nor does it even make cross reference to subsection (a); third, subsection (b) does not require that Henkels have extended credit or have been a creditor, nor does it even mention the word "creditor." Finally, subsection (b) addresses an entirely different concern than subsection (a): contributions made in violation of a partnership agreement or the New Jersey ULPL as opposed to distributions made without such violations but to the prejudice of creditors. Accordingly, Section 42:2A-46(a) is irrelevant to the issues raised on this appeal.

Our analysis does not end with this conclusion, however, because as just mentioned, Henkels does allege that the distributions made by G & A to the Partners were illegal under Section 42:2A-46(b) . . . . Henkels specifically alleges that the distributions violated the New Jersey ULPL because they were made in violation of the Red Hawk partnership agreement. Accordingly, we confine our analysis to the relevant sections of the partnership agreement in conjunction with Section 42:2A-46(b) [quoting language] Section 12(a) of the Red Hawk partnership agreement specifically provided that cash receipts be used for the establishment of reasonable reserves (for creditors) before such receipts be distributed to the Partners.[5] The Partners contend that the distributions were not made in violation of the partnership agreement because Henkels, under the sewer subcontract, at most was a creditor of only Cedar Ridge, not of either Chestnut Woods or Red Hawk. Thus Red Hawk, they argue, was not required to establish reserves. Pursuant to this reasoning, the Partners assert that because Henkels was not a creditor, they did not receive the 1989 distributions in violation of the partnership agreement and thus did not violate the New Jersey ULPL.

[The court held that the lower court did not err in finding that Henkels was a creditor of Red Hawk despite dealing only with Cedar Ridge because Cedar Ridge acted as the managing partner of Chestnut Woods, which was an undisclosed principal.]

* * *

The Partners also argue that the district court erred in finding that Henkels was a creditor of Red Hawk, because, even assuming arguendo that a contractual relationship existed between Red Hawk and Henkels, Henkels had not extended any credit to Cedar Ridge, Chestnut Woods, or Red Hawk. The unpaid invoices at issue here are from August, September, and November 1989, whereas the distributions to the Red Hawk Partners were made prior, in January, April, and July 1989. Therefore, the Partners claim that this is in itself prima facie proof that Henkels was not a creditor—i.e., Henkels was not owed any money at the time of the distributions. These arguments, however, take a very narrow and ultimately erroneous legal view of the contractual relationship with Henkels and even a more constricted view of the definition of creditor.

Although the term creditor is undefined in the New Jersey ULPL and there is no New Jersey case law interpreting the term in this context, the term creditor is not foreign to New Jersey law. For instance, many New Jersey statutes define creditor very broadly to include "the holder of any claim, of whatever character, . . . whether secured or unsecured, matured or unmatured, liquidated or unliquidated, absolute or contingent." * * * In addition, the generic common law definition of creditor is very broad and includes every one having [the]

---

[5]   Section 12, in pertinent part, provides that:

(a) Application of Cash Receipts. Cash receipts shall be applied in the following order of priority:

. . .

(iv) to the establishment of such reserves as the General Partner shall reasonably deem necessary; and

(v) to distributions to the Partners . . .

right to require the performance of *any* legal obligation [or] contract, . . . or a legal right to damages growing out of [a] contract or tort, and includes not merely the holder of a fixed and certain present debt, but *every one* having a right to require the performance of *any* legal obligation [or] contract, . . . or a legal right to damages growing out of [a] contract or tort." BLACK'S LAW DICTIONARY 368 (6th ed. 1990) (emphasis added). Finally, the failure of the statute to define creditor is indicative of the New Jersey legislature's intent that the term "creditor" be construed consistent with the New Jersey ULPL's broad remedial purpose and its common usage. *See* N.J. STAT. ANN. § 1:1-1 (General rules of construction). * * *

Pursuant to the subcontract agreement, Henkels had a claim to payment for a fixed contract price to be paid in installments upon progressive completion of the sewer work. Although the Partners argue that Henkels did not have a claim at the time of the 1989 distributions, the contract between Henkels and Cedar Ridge was entered into on December 29, 1988. Thus, Henkels and Cedar Ridge had definite obligations to each other under the contract over a week prior to the first distribution by the general partner to the Red Hawk limited partners. Those obligations required Henkels to make the site improvements and Cedar Ridge to make scheduled payments as performance was rendered. In addition, G & A made the bulk of the distributions after Henkels had commenced work and was incurring costs and expenses in fulfilling its commitments under the contract. Thus Chestnut Woods and Red Hawk had incurred liability as early as December 29, 1988, although the bulk of the payment matured the month after the last distribution by Red Hawk to the Partners. The Partners' overly narrow definition of creditor is inconsistent with the obvious financial realities that existed at the time, the generally accepted common law meaning of the term, the broad definition used in other New Jersey statutory contexts, and the broad remedial purpose of the statute. Accordingly, we hold that under this broad definition and consistent with the principles of agency and partnership law previously discussed, Henkels was not only a creditor of Cedar Ridge, but of Chestnut Woods, and thus Red Hawk and its partners.

The Partners further argue that even if we conclude that Henkels was a creditor of Chestnut Woods, Red Hawk was not "jointly and severally" liable for the partnership's debts, but only "jointly" liable, as it was only a partner in Chestnut Woods. The Partners find this significant and contend that as a partner Red Hawk was only contingently liable as a guarantor of collection, not as a guarantor of payment. Furthermore, the Partners contend that even then Red Hawk was not liable until Henkels had obtained a judgment against the Chestnut Woods partnership, was unable to collect, and then sought payment from Chestnut Woods's partner, Red Hawk. Therefore, the Partners conclude, Henkels was not a creditor of Red Hawk until this eventuality ultimately did occur in October 1991—more than two years after the distributions. Thus, they assert there was no violation of Section 42:2A-46(b) or the partnership agreement. Although the Partners make much of the distinction between "joint" and "joint and several liability," and between "guarantor of collection " and "guarantor of payment," the distinctions between these terms are illusory here and are not dispositive. * * * Although the Partners' individual assets were only contingently at risk, [after partnership assets are exhausted] the Partners nonetheless were liable to Henkels from the time the contract was signed and, as ultimately did happen, their assets did become available when the Red Hawk partnership's assets proved insufficient to meet its debt with Henkels.

Accordingly, we hold that the district court's finding that Henkels was a creditor of Red Hawk was correct. *See Henkels & McCoy,* 906 F. Supp. at 252-53. At the time of the

1989 distributions, Henkels was a creditor of Red Hawk and the individual Red Hawk partners were liable for that debt.[8]

III.

Although Henkels was a creditor of Red Hawk, the 1989 distributions were in violation of the partnership agreement only if, as Henkels argues, Red Hawk's distributions constituted a failure to abide by the partnership agreement's requirement to establish reasonably necessary reserves. The Partners, however, contend that the district court made several errors in interpreting the Red Hawk partnership agreement which resulted in its finding that the distributions were in violation of the agreement by failing to establish such reasonable reserves.

Section 9(b) of the partnership agreement grants the general partner, G & A, certain rights and powers, including, under subsection (ix), the power "to establish reasonable reserve funds from income derived from the Partnership's operations to provide for future . . . debt service or similar requirements." The Partners argue that this subsection is the only subsection of the agreement that permits or authorizes the general partner to reserve funds. Thus, according to the Partners, all reserves had to be (1) authorized by this subsection, (2) taken from income derived from operations, and (3) used for debt service. Therefore, had G & A reserved funds against the Henkels contract, the Partners contend that such reserves would have been taken in violation of this subsection of the partnership agreement because the funds would not have been derived from operations but from distributions of capital.

The Partners' argument fails, however, because it selectively presents the language of Sections 9 and 12 and omits other relevant language which demonstrates that the Partners greatly overemphasize the significance of subsection (ix). First, the express language of Section 9(b) provides that the general partner possess all "rights and powers required for or appropriate to its management of the partnership's business which, by way of illustration but not by way of limitation, shall include the following: . . . (ix) to establish reasonable reserve funds from income derived from the partnership's operations to provide for future . . . debt service or similar requirements." This unambiguous language demonstrates that G & A had the right and power to establish reserves, even if not expressly authorized under subsection (ix), if it deemed them required or appropriate for the management of Red Hawk's business. The list of rights and powers in subsection (ix) is merely illustrative and is not an exclusive limitation on the general partner's rights and powers.

Equally important, as the district court properly found, the distributions at issue here were not taken from income derived from operations, but were merely returns of capital of the aborted Timber Knolls partnership, which, as Red Hawk admits, "never got off

---

[8]   The dissent would extend our holding far beyond its limit. It concludes that the majority holds "by necessary implication . . . that a distribution could not be made to Red Hawk partners unless cash reserves had been established to fund the payment of all anticipated future liabilities of the joint venture partnerships (owned in part by others) that might accrue over some unspecified period of time . . . ." We are not called upon in this case to decide whether reserves are required for "all anticipated future liabilities" and therefore the majority does not decide that question, either directly or by implication. The focus of our holding is merely that when there is clear liability under an existing contract, the equity partners cannot ignore that liability, recapture their capital investments, and leave the creditor spinning in the wind.

the ground." Income from "operations," as used in this subsection, refers to income derived from the active, normal, on-going activities of the partnership. Timber Knolls never functioned, and thus there never was any income from operations. Therefore, subsection (ix) is not applicable to the distributions at issue here.[9] It is completely irrelevant because the distributions constituted capital funds retrieved by Red Hawk from its abandoned project, Timber Knolls. Although the Partners emphasize that the funds were derived from the Timber Knolls project, Subsection (ix) only addresses the reserving of funds derived from operations; the germinating project is immaterial.

Finally, as previously discussed, Henkels qualified as a creditor of Red Hawk at the time the distributions were made. Therefore, pursuant to Section 12(a) of the Red Hawk limited partnership agreement governing the distribution of all cash receipts, the Red Hawk general partner was required to establish reasonable reserves from the cash received on the Timber Knolls promissory notes to meet its ongoing liability before distributing such cash to the individual limited partners. We, therefore, turn to the issue as to what would constitute a "reasonable" reserve to meet the outstanding liability under the Henkels subcontract.

* * *

The Partners . . . propose that the highly deferential corporate "business judgment" standard is the appropriate standard. However, as Henkels correctly argues, the business judgment rule also is inapposite in the partnership context because it is a function of the unique corporate setting.

* * * Regardless of what standard the New Jersey courts will ultimately adopt, under any standard and using any definition of reasonable reserves, the Red Hawk general partner's failure to establish any reserves in the face of the fixed obligation and imminent payments due under the contract with Henkels and the operations of the Chestnut Woods development was callous and not reasonable.

It is undisputed that of the approximately $500,000 monies received by Red Hawk in 1989, the Red Hawk general partner (G & A) did not set aside any of these funds to establish reserves, even in the face of a contracted liability. Red Hawk argues, however, that this was not unreasonable because (1) the Red Hawk partnership had no liabilities and $3 million in assets at the time of the distributions; (2) Henkels had not yet invoiced Chestnut Woods; (3) the financial outlook of Red Hawk (& Chestnut Woods) was healthy; and (4) the express terms of the partnership agreement prohibited the taking of such reserves. Each of these contentions is without merit.

First, the $3 million of assets included on Red Hawk's January 1, 1989 balance sheet is somewhat illusory. Of the $3 million in assets, a scant $22,000 was in the form of cash or other liquid assets. The remaining were almost exclusively illiquid: the $800,000 investment in the Chestnut Woods project itself which consisted of land and infrastructure and the $2.1 million Timber Knolls notes receivable from Cedar Ridge—which were substan-

---

[9]   This point is significant in interpreting Section 12(a) as well. Following the order of priority for the distributions of cash receipts in Section 12(a)(i)-(v) is a provision which prohibits the general partner from "retain[ing] and invest[ing] any Cash Receipts *derived from the operations* of the Property, except . . . (2) for investments of reserves permitted to be established under clause (ix) of Paragraph 9(b)." Because the cash receipts used to fund the distributions were *not* derived from income from operations of Red Hawk property, this prohibition is not relevant to this appeal.

tially distributed to the limited partners. Neither of these assets were readily available to satisfy Red Hawk obligations, especially not after the payments on the notes were distributed to the partners. Moreover, Red Hawk repeatedly left almost no money in its checking account after each distribution to the Partners, other than several thousand dollars to cover incidental operating expenses. Additionally, the absence of any formal liabilities from its balance sheet and the failure of Henkels to physically invoice Cedar Ridge did not mean that Red Hawk had no liabilities; it simply was an "off-balance sheet" liability. In the accounting profession, an "off-balance sheet" liability is a financial obligation that is not formally recognized in an entity's accounting statements because no "accounting" obligation arises until the exchange transaction is completed; nonetheless, they do have real current and future cash flow consequences. *See* Accountant's Handbook, 10.29 (7th ed.1991). Under the broad definition of creditor established above, Red Hawk had an unmatured, fixed, off-balance sheet liability to Henkels.

Although by itself this may be not determinative, more telling is the Partners' failure to identify any other source of funds from which the Red Hawk Partnership would be able to meet its obligations, including its contract obligation to Henkels. * * * Without any other source of cash or liquid assets, short of liquidating the Chestnut Woods property itself, it clearly was unreasonable for G & A to distribute to the Partners Red Hawk's only available source of payment without setting aside any reserves to meet the Henkels debt. [10]

Second, and equally telling, G & A knew, or at least had ample notice, that the financial outlook of Red Hawk and Chestnut Woods was not as rosy at the time of the distributions as the Partners attempt to assert now. For example, the Partners fail to mention or accurately state many of the following facts: (1) Red Hawk and G & A, in December 1988, received notification from Cedar Ridge that four separate and distinct types of delays in the Chestnut Woods project were resulting in additional financial burdens to it; (2) Cedar Ridge also informed Red Hawk that these financial burdens were worrisome given the decline already experienced in the housing market; (3) Red Hawk had a scant $22,000 in cash or other liquid assets on hand as of January 1, 1989; (4) Chestnut Woods had an equally scant $12,000 in cash or other liquid assets on hand as of January 1, 1989; (5) Chestnut Woods' January 1, 1989 balance sheet showed over $1.7 million in current liabilities, with the land and construction in progress of Chestnut Woods comprising over 90% of its $2.4 million in assets, leaving meager resources available to pay for the planned 1989 site improvements, such as the $300,000 of sewer systems from Henkels; (6) as of March 7, 1989, Red Hawk had, at a minimum, imputed knowledge from its bank's written notice that interest on the Chestnut Woods mortgage would no longer be paid out of the interest reserve fund and that

---

[10]   As we noted above, under the New Jersey partnership statute and fundamental principles of agency law, every partner is an agent of the partnership and the act of every partner binds the partnership for the purpose of its business. Accordingly, the liability of the Red Hawk partnership to Henkels was committed by written contract between Henkels and Red Hawk's partner, Cedar Ridge, in December 1988, before any retrieval by the Partners of their capital investment in Timber Knolls. In addition, Red Hawk's project, Chestnut Woods, had current liabilities as of January 1, 1989, according to its tax returns, which disclosed debts of over $1.7 million. These liabilities also were in place prior to the retrieval of the Partners' investments in Red Hawk. Nevertheless, the dissent would relieve the Partners of any liability under the contract to creditor Henkels on the theory that from January to August 1989, Red Hawk "had no significant liabilities of any kind."

Cedar Ridge was responsible to pay interest out of its own funds due to "the past unfortunate circumstances [which] caused slower than expected [progress on the Chestnut Woods project,]" and which caused the remaining interest reserve to become substantially depleted and potentially "insufficient to carry this loan;" and (7) the August 1989 $2.7 million appraisal of the Chestnut Woods project was merely a potential future retail estimate and contained the express caveat that this "value estimate[ ] assume[s] that all site improvements will be completed in a workmanlike manner and within a reasonable period of time."

* * *

Although neither Henkels nor the district court attempted to determine what level of reserves was reasonable, no determination was needed because Red Hawk and G & A failed to establish any reserves. It is patently obvious that at least some level of reserves was reasonably necessary, and that the general partner's distributions and failure to reserve any money for the Henkels contract obligation, in light of Chestnut Woods' and Red Hawk's precarious financial condition, was unreasonable. Thus, the district court did not need to determine what level of reserves was reasonable; it clearly had an ample factual basis upon which to determine that the complete failure to establish any reserves was a violation of the Red Hawk partnership agreement's requirement that G & A establish some level of reserves before making distributions to the Partners. Accordingly, we hold that Red Hawk's failure to establish any reserves in light of both partnerships' then existing financial condition was not reasonable.

IV.

* * * The Partners are therefore obligated to return the improper capital distributions to Red Hawk. Because the plaintiff stands in the shoes of Red Hawk for the purpose of recovering these funds on behalf of the partnership * * *

STAPLETON, Circuit Judge, Dissenting:

The critical issue posed by this appeal is one of intent—the intent of the Red Hawk partners when they negotiated their partnership agreement. Given the text of that agreement and the context in which it was executed, I believe the district court clearly erred when it interpreted Section 12(a)(iv) as precluding the three challenged payments to Red Hawk's limited partners.

* * *

The Red Hawk Partnership Agreement . . . provided for a mandatory pass-through of cash receipts, whether generated by the joint ventures in the regular course of business or otherwise, after the general partner had paid all of the currently due debt obligations of Red Hawk and had set aside specifically limited reserves. Any reserves were expressly limited to such revenue from operations as the general partner, in its discretion, considered appropriate for the purpose of paying anticipated administrative expenses and, in the event of the distribution of joint venture property in kind, anticipated property management expenses. Section 12(a) of the agreement thus provided:

(a) Application of Cash Receipts. Cash Receipts shall be applied in the following order of priority:
   (i) to the extent required, to the creditors of the Partnership, except to any Partner or any Affiliate thereof;

    (ii) to the extend required, to the payment of any debts or liabilities to any Partner or any Affiliate thereof (other than a loan to the Partnership by the Partner);

    (iii) to the payment in full of any loans to the Partnership by a Partner;

    (iv) to the establishment of such reserves as the General Partner shall reasonably deem necessary; and

    (v) to distributions to the Partners in accordance with Paragraphs 12(b) and (c) hereof.

Notwithstanding the foregoing, the General Partner shall not retain and invest any Cash Receipts derived from the operations of the Property, except (1) to defray expenditures for any repair or improvement to any Property, which it, in its sole discretion, deems appropriate or (2) for investments of reserves permitted to be established under clause (ix) of Paragraph 9(b) hereof, nor shall the General Partner invest the net proceeds derived and retained by the Partnership from the sale or other disposition of any Property (including any total condemnation or destruction of any portion of the Property) except as otherwise provided herein.

    * * * Section 9 . . . imposes no duty on the General Partner to set aside reserves for any purpose. In subsection (b)(ix), the subsection referenced in Section 12(a), the general partner is given the authority "to establish reasonable reserve funds from income derived from the Partnership's operations to provide for future maintenance, repair, replacement, debt service or similar requirements."

    Read in the context of the Agreement and the expectations of the Partners, it is apparent that the dominant portion of Sections 12(a) is the paragraph commencing with the clause "Notwithstanding the foregoing." Indeed, that lead clause requires that this paragraph be given controlling significance over the preceding text. It mandates disbursement to the partners of all cash whether received by Red Hawk in the course of the normal operations of the joint venture properties or whether received by it from dispositions of joint venture property other than in the course of its regular business operations. The two exceptions recognize that the General Partner, in its sole discretion, should have the ability to retain cash derived from operations to establish reasonable reserves for property repairs and improvement, debt service, and other operating expenses.

    The subordinate portion of Section 12(a) that precedes the "notwithstanding" clause establishes the priorities among various interests that may compete for distributions of cash receipts. The purpose of subsection 12(a)(iv), in particular, is (1) to recognize the possibility that the General Partner may wish to withhold some funds pursuant to the two express exceptions from the flow through mandate; and (2) to emphasize that the General Partner's authority to do so is limited to such reserves as it might "reasonably deem necessary." Thus, subsection 12(a) is designed both to recognize the possibility of retention of cash receipts for authorized reserves at the discretion of the General Partner and, at the same time, to assure the limited partners that there will be no accumulation of even funds for reserves when the general partner, in the exercise of business judgment, could not reasonably regard them as necessary for the designated purposes.

* * *

Our court today holds that the Red Hawk partners, although mandating a pass-through to themselves of cash receipts, intended in Section 12(a) of their partnership agreement voluntarily to impose on themselves a very significant restriction for the benefit of joint venture creditors. This voluntary restriction, the court holds by necessary implication, was intended to be sufficiently broad that a distribution could not be made to Red Hawk partners unless cash reserves had been established to fund the payment of all anticipated future liabilities of the joint venture partnerships (owned in part by others) that might accrue over some unspecified period of time, even though those other partnerships were expected to pay their own liabilities with their own or borrowed funds. The record suggests no reason, however, why the partners, when setting up the Red Hawk partnership, would have imposed such an unnecessary and ill-defined burden on themselves, and the text of Section 12(a) does not require such a conclusion that they did.

The court resolves the central issue in this appeal in one sentence: Section 12(a)(iv) "of the Red Hawk partnership agreement specifically provided that cash receipts be used for the establishment of reasonable reserves (for creditors) before such receipts be distributed to the [limited partners]." Because Red Hawk's general partner had reason to believe that Henkels might submit invoices in the future for site improvement work, the court accordingly concludes that the three challenged distributions violated Section 12(a)(iv).

In my view, the court errs for at least five reasons: (1) In context, Section 12(a)(iv) was intended for the protection of the limited partners, not as a creditor protection device even for creditors of Red Hawk; (2) Section 12(a)(iv), even if viewed as a creditor protection provision, was not intended for the protection of joint venture creditors for whom the joint ventures were to make other provision; (3) the challenged distributions were a return of capital that the partners had agreed to devote to an abandoned venture, and it is not reasonable to find an intent in Section 12(a)(iv) to commit that capital contribution to the creditors of a different, fully capitalized venture; (4) Section 12(a)(iv) permits the general partner to retain reserves only from "Cash Receipts derived from the operations of the Property" and the challenged distributions did not come from funds generated by operations; and (5) even if Section 12(a)(iv) could reasonably be read to require Red Hawk's general partner to set aside funds for creditors in Henkels' position whenever a reasonable general partner exercising business judgment would do so, this record provides no basis for a conclusion that the failure of Red Hawk's general partner to set aside funds for Henkels in January through July of 1989 was a decision beyond the bounds of business judgment.

I would reverse and remand with instructions to enter judgment for the defendants.

Questions

1. Do you agree with the majority or the dissent concerning whether Red Hawk and G & A breached an obligation to establish reserves?

2. Why does it matter under RULPA § 608(b) whether Henkels was a creditor at the time of the distribution?

3. Assuming the reserve obligation was breached, should the creditors have a right of action or was the obligation intended for the limited partners' protection as the dis-

sent argues? How does a reserve requirement protect the limited partners? Does the intent matter under the statute?

4. How should the agreement have been drafted in light of the court's opinion to accomplish what the limited partners sought without the risk of liability to creditors? Would it be enough simply to add that any obligations in the agreement are not for the benefit of creditors? *Cf. Builders Steel Co., Inc. v. Hycore, Inc.*, p.295, above. Given the potential for liability, would the limited partners have been better off simply providing for a limitation on amounts the general partners could withhold for payment of debts rather than for the establishment of reserves?

11.05 Partners' Management and Control Rights

Like many other features of limited partnerships, separate management and voting rules apply to the separate classes of interests owned by general and limited partners.

A.   General Partners

A general partner in a limited partnership has the same rights and powers as a general partner in a general partnership described in Chapter 3 (*see* RULPA § 403). This includes the right to vote and participate equally in management and the general partner's power to bind the partnership, illustrated by the following case.

Luddington v. Bodenvest Ltd.
855 P.2d 204 (Utah 1993)

HOWE, Associate Chief Justice:

Bodenvest Ltd., a Utah limited partnership, appeals from a decree of foreclosure entered on a cross-claim filed against it by Foothill Thrift.

Until it filed bankruptcy in February 1987, Granada, Inc. was Bodenvest's general partner. Granada's common stock was owned by C. Dean Larsen, who was its president and one of its directors. Bodenvest's limited partners were retirement trusts established by various Utah medical practitioners. The primary purpose of the partnership, as stated in paragraph 2.1 of its certificate and agreement, was "to acquire a parcel of undeveloped real property containing approximately seventy-two (72) acres located in West Jordan, Salt Lake County, Utah . . . and the Partnership shall hold the subject for investment, and may from time to time sell parcels of said property to investors or may retain and sell the total parcel of property to one Buyer." In paragraph 15.2B, the general partner is given the power to borrow money and, if security is required therefor, "to mortgage or lien any portion of the property of the Partnership . . . as [the general partner] deems, in his absolute discretion, to be in the best interests of the Partnership."

* * * In 1985, part of the land was sold for a hospital, netting Bodenvest $203,000. Following this sale, the assets of Bodenvest were comprised of the remaining 50.3 acres and the $203,000 cash. * * *

In late 1984, Granada, by and through Larsen, began a series of three transactions in which the remaining 50.3 acres were encumbered to secure loans for the sole benefit of Granada or for Granada and Bodenvest. The first of these transactions was a $455,300 loan from Petersen Investors to Granada. The loan was secured by a trust deed on the 50.3 acres. Subsequently, a second trust deed on the property was recorded to secure a $150,000 loan to Bodenvest and Granada from the Dean F. Luddington Retirement Trust. A third trust deed (the one at issue in this case) was executed in April 1986 to Foothill Thrift by Granada to secure a ninety-day loan for $252,083 to meet Granada's business obligations. The trust deed became a first lien after Larsen arranged to have the Petersen Investors and the Luddington trust deeds reconveyed or subordinated. There is no evidence that the Bodenvest limited partners knew there were any encumbrances on the property until after Granada filed for bankruptcy many months later. Also, apparently without the knowledge of the limited partners, Granada borrowed $192,925 of Bodenvest's $203,000 cash proceeds. The loan, which was not evidenced by a promissory note, was entirely unsecured and has never been repaid.

When Foothill prepared the documentation for the $252,083 business loan, it had the property appraised at approximately $762,000. Foothill did not obtain a loan application or any financial information from Bodenvest. It did, however, obtain a recent personal financial statement from Larsen and a one-year unaudited financial statement from Granada. The loan documents were all signed by Larsen in various capacities. The promissory note was signed by Larsen individually and for Granada as its president. The trust deed on the Bodenvest property was signed by Larsen as president of Granada, the general partner. A hypothecation statement was signed by Larsen for Granada as general partner of Bodenvest. In neither the trust deed nor the hypothecation statement is there any express reference to the promissory note. Foothill issued its check dated April 23, 1986, for $252,083, payable only to Granada. The evidence is undisputed that there was no benefit to Bodenvest from the loan, nor did Bodenvest guarantee the Granada-Larsen promissory note. Furthermore, Foothill makes no claim that Bodenvest subsequently ratified the transaction.

The principal and accrued interest were due in ninety days. Granada made no payment when the note fell due on July 22, 1986. On September 2, Granada made a $55,795.34 partial payment, and Foothill agreed to renew the note. * * * No further payments of either principal or interest were made by the maturity date, June 8, 1987.

Granada filed bankruptcy on February 13, 1987, and Larsen filed personal bankruptcy the following month. Both listed Foothill as a creditor. In May of 1987, the Dean F. Luddington Trust commenced this action against Larsen for fraud and legal malpractice, and against the other defendants, including Foothill Thrift and Bodenvest, seeking foreclosure of its trust deed. Foothill cross-claimed against Bodenvest for foreclosure.

A decree of foreclosure in favor of Pacific America Construction, Inc., successor to Foothill Thrift, was entered on Foothill's cross-claim. The decree rests primarily on three findings of fact as to Granada's authority to execute the trust deed to Foothill. In those findings, the trial court found authority in the hypothecation statement given in connection with the transaction which in turn was authorized by the certificate and agreement of the partnership. Additionally, the court based its finding of apparent authority for Granada's act on the fact that the limited partners had allowed Larsen to sign the certificate and agreement for them. The certificate and agreement was a public document. The court also noted that the Foothill officer who made the loan was unaware that Larsen and Granada had no authority to execute and deliver the trust deed on behalf of Bodenvest.

Bodenvest appeals . . . assailing the findings of fact as insufficient to support the legal conclusion that Granada's act of encumbering the property was binding on Bodenvest. We begin our analysis by examining the Code provisions related to limited partnerships. UTAH CODE ANN. § 48-2-9 [RULPA § 403], which was in effect at the time of the events in this case, defines the rights, powers, and liabilities of a general partner. * * *

The trial court stated in finding of fact 10 that Granada had actual authority to execute the trust deed to Foothill because "Bodenvest (by its General Partner Granada, through its President, Larsen) consented and agreed to encumber the Bodenvest real property as evidenced by a hypothecation statement dated April 23, 1986, executed by Bodenvest." The hypothecation statement reads:

> For valuable consideration, and as an inducement to Foothill Thrift to loan money and grant credit from time to time to Bodenvest Ltd., a Utah limited partnership by Granada, Inc., general partner C. Dean Larsen, president, the undersigned promises to execute, acknowledge and deliver to Foothill Thrift as Beneficiary, a trust deed of even date hypothecating title and interest in and to that certain property located in Salt Lake County, State of Utah . . . .

The statement was signed by Larsen as Granada's president and Bodenvest's general partner. There is a fatal flaw in the hypothecation statement that prevents Foothill from relying upon it as authority for Granada to encumber the partnership property. That flaw is that the statement is given as an inducement to Foothill "to loan money and grant credit from time to time to Bodenvest Ltd." The loan of money here was not to Bodenvest. It was not a signatory on the promissory note. Bodenvest's name was not on the check disbursing the loan proceeds; the check was made solely to Granada. In short, the hypothecation statement did not authorize Granada to encumber partnership property to secure a loan to the general partner. * * * [I]t affords no basis for the trial court's finding that Foothill "intended that the hypothecation statement be authority from Bodenvest to encumber its property for the April [1986] Note executed by Granada and Larsen."

Foothill argues that, despite the defect in the hypothecation agreement, the certificate and agreement of limited partnership authorized Bodenvest to engage in business other than acquiring and selling the 72 acres of land; that Bodenvest had previously borrowed from and loaned money to other partnerships controlled by Granada; and that its books showed accrued interest owing to it on money it had loaned. Foothill refers us to paragraph 15.21 of the limited partnership agreement, which authorized Bodenvest to borrow money and secure the loan by hypothecating its assets. It also provides that the lender is not required to ascertain the purposes for which the loan is sought and that as between the lender and Bodenvest, it shall be conclusively presumed that the proceeds of the loan will be used for authorized partnership purposes. While all the foregoing is correct, it does not aid Foothill. In the Foothill transaction, Bodenvest was neither a lender nor a borrower. It simply provided the security for a loan made to its general partner and its president. Nothing in the certificate and agreement or in partnership law supports the use of partnership assets for such a purpose. * * *

However, even though an agent's act is not actually authorized by the principal, the principal may nevertheless be liable to a third party based on the doctrine of apparent authority. * * *

When Bodenvest was organized in 1976, a certificate and agreement of limited partnership was executed by the general partner and by the limited partners pursuant to statute. The document was filed in the office of the clerk of Salt Lake County, where its principal place of business was to be located. The general partner, Granada, executed the certificate and agreement by and through its president, Larsen. The limited partners did not sign individually. Their names were listed, and Larsen signed for them "as trustee or administrator." In finding of fact 20, the trial court stated that because the limited partners had allowed Larsen to sign the certificate and agreement on their behalf, they had thereby imbued him with apparent authority to execute the trust deed to Foothill Thrift. That finding of fact reads: "The Limited Partners of Bodenvest allowed Larsen to sign the Certificate and Agreement of Limited Partnership (Exhibit "P-1") which became a public, recorded document telling the world that Larsen was clothed with actual or apparent authority on behalf of such Limited Partners in matters related to Bodenvest. * * * "

There are several problems with the application of apparent authority in this case. First, most of the original limited partners who allowed Larsen to sign the certificate and agreement for them in 1976 were no longer members of the partnership at the time of the Foothill transaction in 1986. Many of them had withdrawn from Bodenvest and had been replaced by other retirement trusts. Second, there is no evidence that Larsen purported to give the consent of the limited partners to the Foothill transaction. He did not attempt to sign for them as he had done on the certificate and agreement. Nor does Foothill contend that it actually relied on Larsen's signing for the partners in 1976 as an expression of their consent to this transaction ten years later. Third, it does not follow that because the limited partners once allowed Larsen to sign for them, Granada was somehow authorized to engage in subsequent unauthorized acts on behalf of the partnership. The certificate and agreement, the same document that Foothill contends empowered Granada to act on behalf of the limited partners, also limits such power. The certificate and agreement clearly gives Bodenvest the power to borrow money and pledge partnership property as security, upon such terms and in such amounts as the general partner deems, in its absolute discretion, to be in the best interests of the partnership. As we have already observed, the general partner did not borrow money for the partnership. Bodenvest was not a signatory on the promissory note and did not receive any of the loan proceeds. Additionally, section 15.3 of the certificate and agreement provides: "The general partner shall have all the rights and powers and be subject to all the restrictions and liabilities of a partner in a partnership without limited partners, except that the general partner has no authority to: . . . ; (B) Do any act which would make it impossible to carry on the ordinary business of the partnership; . . . ; (D) Possess partnership property or assign the rights of the partnership in specific partnership property for other than a partnership purpose."

Encumbering the property to provide security for a loan to the general partner arguably violates subparagraph B by jeopardizing the continuation of the business of the partnership, which was to acquire and later sell the 72 acres of land. It is even more clear, however, that subparagraph D was violated since the encumbrance of the partnership property was for other than a partnership purpose. Section 48-2-9 provides that a general partner has authority to do those acts prohibited in subparagraphs B and D only with the written consent or ratification of the specific act by all the limited partners. No attempt was made here to obtain such consent.

Foothill also contends that the failure of the limited partners to object when Larsen on two prior occasions encumbered partnership property to secure loans to Granada constituted apparent authority. Although the trial court made no finding on this point, we will consider it as possible support for the trial court's legal conclusion. * * * Foothill argues that these prior transactions made its transaction "appear to be a routine Bodenvest partnership transaction." There are several problems with this argument. First, only one of the prior transactions, the Petersen loan, was solely for Granada; the Luddington loan was for Granada and Bodenvest jointly. Second, the limited partners were not aware of either of these loans. In order to support a theory of apparent authorization by the limited partners' failure to object, Foothill would have to prove that the partners were aware of the prior transactions. Otherwise, the failure to object cannot be construed as apparent authority.

Even if we were to agree with Foothill that Granada had apparent authority because Larsen signed the certificate and agreement for the partners or because the limited partners failed to object when the Bodenvest property was encumbered on two prior occasions, it is clear that Foothill was not reasonable in relying on any apparent authority in this instance. Section 48-1-6(2) [UPA § 9(2)] provides, "An act of a partner which is not apparently for the carrying on of the business of the partnership in the usual way does not bind the partnership, unless authorized by the other partners." Therefore, Foothill could rely on any apparent authority only to the extent that it was being exercised in pursuance of partnership business "in the usual way." Clearly, there was nothing "usual" about the Foothill transaction. As heretofore observed, the encumbering of its property to secure loans made to others was not the usual business of Bodenvest. * * * It should have been readily apparent to Foothill that there was no benefit to Bodenvest in encumbering its property.

Finding of fact 20, that Larsen had apparent authority to engage in the Foothill transaction, is clearly erroneous and must be set aside. Utah R.Civ.P. 52(a). Additionally, finding of fact 11, that the loan officer at Foothill "had no knowledge from Larsen or any limited partner of Granada that Larsen had no authority to execute and deliver the Foothill Trust Deed," does not support the decree of foreclosure. This lack of knowledge does not assist Foothill because the transaction was not for the carrying on of Bodenvest's business "in the usual way." See UTAH CODE ANN. § 48-1-6(1), (2) [UPA § 9(1), (2)].

In summary, the findings of fact that Granada had actual and apparent authority to encumber the partnership property to Foothill are clearly erroneous and must be set aside. The trust deed executed and delivered to Foothill to secure a loan to the general partner and its president was totally without authorization by the partnership owner. The decree of foreclosure is reversed, and the case is remanded to the trial court for further proceedings consistent with this opinion.

ZIMMERMAN, Justice: (dissenting).

I cannot join the majority in concluding that the trial court's findings are clearly erroneous. Considering the evidence in a light most favorable to the trial court, I find it sufficient to support the trial court's action. I fear that the majority has appraised the circumstances surrounding the loan in the bright gleam of hindsight rather than as the lender legitimately could have seen them at the time of the loan. I understand the sympathy one might feel for those who would be harmed by a ruling upholding the validity of Foothill's security interest, but sympathy alone cannot warrant imposing, de facto, an extraordinarily high duty of inquiry on the lender to police the internal operations of a partnership that had the misfortune of having Granada as a general partner.

Notes and Questions

1. **Application of general partnership statute.** *Luddington* illustrates the linkage with general partnership law regarding general partners' authority to bind the firm. *See also Connecticut Nat. Bank v. Cooper,* 232 Conn. 405, 656 A.2d 215 (1995), which applied the UPA provision that a restriction on a partner's authority binds a third party who knows of it to a general partner in limited partnership.

2. **Scope of general partner's authority: Self-dealing transactions.** Although the UPA and RUPA provide the basic rules on general partners' authority, it is not clear whether these rules should be *applied* the same way in limited and general partnerships. Because limited partners are usually passive (*see* subsection (B), below) and therefore delegate most management functions to the general partners, the generals' authority might be expected to be quite broad. On the other hand, this would leave the limited partners exposed to general partners' self-dealing, as in *Luddington.* The self-dealing problem is amplified by the fact that many general partners serve as promoters for several syndications. Several cases, as in *Luddington,* have put the loss on sophisticated third party lenders when the lender should have known of a problem with binding the limited partnership to the transactions. *See, e.g., Anchor Centre Partners, Ltd. v. Mercantile Bank, N.A.,* 803 S.W.2d 23 (Mo. 1991); *Green River Assocs. v. Mark Twain Kansas City Bank,* 808 S.W.2d 894 (Mo. App. 1991). On the other hand, in *Standish v. Sotavento Corp.,* 58 Conn. App. 789, 755 A.2d 910 (2000), the court held that the loan was binding where the creditor had no knowledge that the general partner intended to use the loan for unauthorized purposes. Do you agree with the majority or the dissent under the facts in *Luddington*? Who was the cheaper cost avoider here—the limited partners or the lender? Should it make a difference if the limited partners know that the general partner is engaged in some wrongdoing, such as commingling personal and partnership funds in the same account, if the partners do not also know of the partnership transactions at issue in the case? Note that the limited partners' knowledge of the general partner's activities might establish estoppel or ratification even if it does not establish apparent authority. *See* Notes 3-5, p. 30. For a discussion of cases like those discussed in this Note, *see* DeMott, *Our Partners' Keepers? Agency Dimensions of Partnership Relationships,* 58 J. LAW & CONTEMP. PROB. 109, 131-34 (Spring 1995).

3. **Planning considerations.** What more should the lender have done to ensure that the limited partnership would be bound in *Luddington*?

4. **The role of the partnership agreement.** The partners may attempt to expand general partners' authority in the partnership agreement in order to minimize third parties' costs of dealing with the firm and, therefore, the firm's cost of doing business. What weight should the court place on the partnership agreement provision in *Luddington* that

the lender is not required to ascertain the loan's purpose and that the lender is entitled to a conclusive presumption that the proceeds will be used for an authorized partnership purpose?

The partners also may *limit* the scope of the general partners' authority. This may be particularly important in light of the limited partners' passive role in the firm (*see* the next section) and their consequent inability to determine the generals' activities on an ongoing basis. For example, an agreement for a venture capital partnership may limit, among other things, the amount that the partnership may invest in any one firm or class of investments, how much it may borrow, reinvestments of earnings, general partners' investments of personal funds, and raising of new funds. *See* Gompers & Lerner, *The Use of Covenants: An Empirical Analysis of Venture Partnership Agreements,* 39 J. Law & Econ. 463 (1996). Such provisions may have implications for the scope of general partners' authority in transactions with third parties.

B.   Limited Partners

While the UPA and RUPA provide most of the law relating to general partners in limited partnerships, limited partnership statutory provisions focus on limited partners' rights and liabilities.

1. Voting Rights

RULPA § 302 provides that the partnership agreement may grant voting rights to limited partners. This suggests that, unlike corporate shareholders, the limited partners have no voting rights in the absence of contrary agreement. Note, however, that UPA § 21 provides that *all* partners must consent to self-dealing and RULPA § 101(8) defines "partner" to include both limited and general partners. These provisions together arguably require approval of self-dealing by both general and limited partners. In any event, limited partnership agreements do normally provide for some limited partner voting rights. Consider the following case.

Fox v. I-10, Ltd.
957 P.2d 1018 (Colo. 1998)

Justice Kourlis delivered the Opinion of the Court.

William Fox, individually, and as trustee for a pension plan and a profit sharing plan, (Fox) is a limited partner in I-10 Ltd. (the Partnership or I-10). Fox appeals a judgment of the court of appeals holding that the amendment provisions in the partnership agreement and applicable statutes allowed the limited partners to increase their capital contribution obligation by majority vote. We . . . now conclude that the majority vote provision plainly allows amendment of the limited partners' capital contributions; and this provision is not contrary to statutory provisions requiring capital contributions to be set forth in a certificate of limited partnership.

I.

In 1982, Fox purchased approximately 20% of the available limited partnership units in a Colorado limited partnership known as I-10 Ltd. Fox and several other limited partners (LPs) executed a limited partnership agreement with the general partner, MSP Investment Co., (MSP) dated November 1, 1982 (the Agreement). The purpose of the Partnership was to acquire, develop and hold for resale 305 acres of land in Pima County, Arizona.

Article 4.09 of the Agreement provided:

Additional Assessments. If at any time after the formation of the Partnership the General Partner determines that additional contributions to the capital of the Partnership are necessary or desirable for any purpose, the General Partner shall mail a notice to each Limited Partner specifying the aggregate amount of additional capital to be contributed to the Partnership, such Limited Partner's pro rata share of the additional capital required, the purpose for the assessment, the intended use of the proceeds thereof, and the penalty to be imposed for failure to meet the assessment . . . . The total additional capital contribution required to be made by each Limited Partner hereunder shall not exceed an amount equal to four hundred percent (400%) of the initial capital contribution to the Partnership of each Limited Partner.

Article 7.00 dealing with amendments set forth two methods of amending the agreement depending upon the nature of the proposed change. Article 7.01 allowed the general partner, in its sole discretion, and as attorney in fact for the limited partners, to make certain "routine amendments" without the need for any partnership vote. These types of amendments related mainly to administrative matters such as preservation of proper status for federal income tax purposes.

Article 7.02 encompassed all other, non-routine amendments, and provided that, except for amendments affecting MSP's rights, all other amendments to the agreement would be made by majority vote:

Other Amendments. All amendments, other than those set forth in paragraph 7.01 hereof, shall be proposed in writing by the General Partner or by Limited Partners owning not less than twenty-five percent (25%) of the Limited Partners' aggregate Interest in the Partnership for voting purposes. Any proposed amendment shall not become effective until it has been considered at a meeting of the Limited Partners duly held for that purpose and has received the affirmative vote of a majority of the Limited Partners' aggregate Interest in the Partnership and the approval of the General Partner. Notwithstanding the foregoing provisions of this paragraph to the contrary, no amendment shall be made to this Agreement which would deprive the General Partner of its Interest in the Partnership, or of any compensation or reimbursement of expenses due to the General Partner as provided herein.

In May of 1983, the Partnership filed a certificate of limited partnership in accordance with then-existing requirements under The Colorado Uniform Limited Partnership Act

(CULPA). *See* § 7-62-201, 3 C.R.S. (1973) (repealed 1986). This previous version of the statute required a limited partnership to specify in the certificate the amount each partner had contributed and had agreed to contribute in the future. *See* § 7-62-201(e), 3 C.R.S. (1973) (repealed 1986) (hereafter Section 201(e)). In addition, the certificate was to include a description of the "times at which or events on the happening of which any additional contributions agreed to made by each partner are to be made." § 7-62-201(f), 3 C.R.S. (1973) (repealed 1986) (hereafter Section 201(f)). CULPA was amended in 1986, and these items are no longer required in the certificate.

In accordance with these statutory provisions, the original certificate reflected that Fox had contributed a total of $85,000 to the Partnership and had agreed to potential future assessments not exceeding $340,000 (400% of $85,000). The certificate also stated that article 4.09 of the Agreement governed the times at which, or events upon the happening of which, the partners had agreed to make additional contributions. The Partnership attached a copy of article 4.09 as an exhibit to the certificate.

Over the next few years, the Partnership found it necessary for various reasons to amend the Agreement several times. In February 1986, MSP sent a letter and a proxy to the limited partners proposing certain amendments to the Agreement. Efforts to sell the property had failed, and MSP sought amendments that would, among other things, change the purpose of the Partnership to include a possible land exchange with the State of Arizona, and amend article 4.09 to increase potential assessments from 400% to 600% of the original investment.

In its letter, MSP focused on the proposed change in purpose and noted that such a change could only be accomplished if each partner agreed. This was true because article 2.04 of the Agreement required 100% of all outstanding interests in the Partnership to consent to any action of the general partner that was inconsistent with the existing "principal business and purpose of the Partnership." Because the Agreement did not contemplate a land exchange, MSP recognized that it had to obtain consent of all the partners to make this change.

In the proxy accompanying the letter, MSP set out all the proposed amendments to the Agreement, including, among others, the capital contribution increase, and specified that amendment would be accomplished by majority vote as required in article 7.02 of the Agreement.

At a meeting in March of 1986, MSP and all of the limited partners, including Fox, voted to amend paragraph 4.09 and increase the contribution cap to 600%. The Partnership filed an amended certificate reflecting the new cap and adjusting the total potential contributions accordingly. As with the original certificate, the amended certificate also stated that article 4.09 governed the times and events that could trigger obligations under the new cap.

The Partnership thereafter was unable to secure a suitable exchange or sale of its land, and by 1993 needed additional cash to finish paying its mortgage. MSP again proposed to amend article 4.09 of the Agreement by increasing the contribution cap to 800%. At a meeting in December of 1993, a majority of the partners (all partners except Fox) voted to amend article 4.09 and increase the cap to 800%. Fox voted against the amendment. Shortly after the majority vote, MSP sent Fox a notice of additional assessment for amounts in excess of the previous 600% cap. Fox paid the assessment up to 600% of his initial contribution, but refused to make further contributions. Fox then filed an action in the district court seeking a declaratory judgment that he had no obligation beyond the 600% cap, and seeking an injunction preventing the Partnership from declaring him in default under the terms of the Agreement.

The district court granted summary judgment for Fox and entered an order declaring that the Agreement did not permit an increase in the limited partners' capital contribution by majority vote. The district court also found that even if the Agreement were to permit such an amendment, it would be contrary to the provisions of CULPA. The court of appeals reversed, holding that the language of the Agreement did, in fact, allow this amendment by majority vote, and that the statutes did not prohibit it. We agree.

II.

* * * Our courts have repeatedly recognized the sanctity of contracts and the court's role in enforcing them. Quoting the United States Supreme Court, we have held that:
the right of private contract is no small part of the liberty of the citizen, and . . . the usual and most important function of courts of justice is rather to maintain and enforce contracts, than to enable parties thereto to escape from their obligation. * * * [citation omitted] The court's duty is to interpret and enforce contracts as written between the parties, not to rewrite or restructure them. [citations omitted] The court will not interfere with the valid bargain of the parties:

> The impossibility of courts attempting to act as business clearing houses for the readjustment of legitimate profits and losses occurring in the marts of trade and commerce is obvious at a glance. To attempt it . . . would be an unwarranted inter-ference with the freedom of action of business men in their private affairs.

[citation omitted]

Parties to a contract, therefore, may agree on whatever terms they see fit so long as such terms do not violate statutory prohibitions or public policy. * * *

III.

Hence, we look first to the terms of the Agreement itself to determine whether Fox can be required, by majority vote, to increase his capital contribution. Fox asserts that there is tension between article 4.09, placing a definitive cap on contributions, and article 7.02, allowing amendment of the Agreement by majority vote, thereby creating an ambiguity with respect to the parties' intent. We do not agree.

Article 7.02 plainly states that "[a]ll amendments, other than those [routine amendments] set forth in paragraph 7.01" may be accomplished by majority vote. Article 7.02 goes on to specify that certain items are excluded from amendment by the majority vote procedure set out therein. Increase in capital contributions is not among the exclusions of article 7.02. Furthermore, article 2.04 specifically requires unanimous consent of the limited partners prior to allowing the general partner to take certain actions. Hence the parties clearly excluded certain items from amendment by majority vote, but did not exclude a change in capital contributions from this method of amendment. Neither the language in article 4.09, nor any other language in the Agreement, creates doubt about whether article 7.02 provides the proper procedure for amending article 4.09.

Fox argues that the ceiling on a limited partner's capital contribution is such a fundamental aspect of a limited partnership that, as a matter of law, it may not be amended by majority vote regardless of what the Agreement might state. In other words, an LP's liability is "limited" by virtue of the very nature of limited partnerships and this fundamental precept cannot be altered without consent of the limited partner. We agree that the limit on an LP's liability represents a defining characteristic of a limited partnership interest. An LP's liability is limited by operation of law with respect to creditors of the partnership. * * * An LP's liability to the partnership is also limited, but this limitation is defined, not by operation of law, but by the partnership agreement as the amount of capital which an LP agrees to contribute. [citation omitted] While LPs may not, for example, agree among themselves to treat each other internally as general partners and still preserve their limited liability status with respect to creditors, there is no fundamental tenet of limited partnership law that prevents LPs from voluntarily agreeing, by majority vote or otherwise, to increase their capital contribution to the partnership.

The Washington Court of Appeals faced a remarkably similar situation in *Diamond Parking Inc. v. Frontier Bldg. Ltd. Partnership*, 72 Wash.App. 314, 864 P.2d 954 (1993). In that case the partnership agreement allowed for amendment by a 70% vote. *See id.* at 957. The holders of seventy-four percent of the partnership interests voted to restructure the partnership so as to increase the interests of those LPs who contributed additional capital. See *id.* The court enforced this amendment provision in the agreement noting that the "partnership agreement is the law of the partnership." *See id.* We find the Washington court's words particularly apposite to the instant case that a party "[h]aving elected to join the partnership with this type of majority voting provision . . . cannot now complain merely because the partnership adopted an amendment of which he did not approve." *Id.*

We thus conclude that the plain language of the Agreement allows a majority of the partners to vote to amend the capital contribution amount, and no "fundamental right" invalidates that contractual term. Rather, if any fundamental right is implicated, it is the fundamental right to enter into a contract and expect its terms to be enforced.

IV.

We now turn to the provisions of CULPA and consider whether it imposes other obligations on the parties, or supersedes the Agreement. * * *

* * * Section 201(f) requires the certificate to specify the events that can trigger additional capital contributions. Fox asserts that if majority vote of the partners constituted such an event, the statute mandated that it be so identified on the certificate. I-10's original and amended certificates state that article 4.09 governed the times or events upon which partners had agreed to make future contributions. Hence, Fox argues that majority vote cannot be an event triggering capital contributions because the certificate and amended certificates do not so state. * * *

We conclude that Section 201(f) required the partners to record those contributions the parties had already agreed to, i.e., 400% of the initial contribution, and Section 202(2)(a) required the partners to record any change in the obligation accomplished by amendment, i.e., 600%, and then 800% of the initial contribution.

* * * [E]ven if we were to conclude that I-10's certificates contained an error of this type, such an error would not supersede the partners' contractual obligations. Fox is not a creditor of I-10 seeking to prove that he was harmed by an error in the certificate, but rather a party to a contract seeking to elevate the certificate over contractual obligations.

V.

The Agreement, by its plain language, allows the parties to amend article 4.09 by majority vote. Neither a "fundamental right" of limited partnership nor CULPA precludes parties from agreeing to such an amendment procedure. Additionally, I-10 did not violate the certificate requirements of Sections 201(e) and (f), and in any event, the partners' rights and obligations inter se are governed by the partnership agreement, not by the certificate. Accordingly, we hereby affirm the court of appeals' decision reversing the district court's judgment, and remand for further proceedings consistent with the views expressed in this opinion.

Notes and Questions

1. **Limited partnerships vs. general partnerships.** Do you suppose that the court would have reached the same result in an analogous case involving the right to vote on a fundamental change in rights by general partners in a general partnership? Compare the discussion in § 5.04(A), above. What might justify a different result?

2. **Proxy voting.** The agreement also may provide for proxy voting, at least where the statute permits the agreement to so provide. *See Christman v. Brauvin Realty Advisors, Inc.*, 82 F. Supp. 2d 823 (N.D. Ill. 1998) (Delaware law). However, that case held that proxy voting was not permitted under agreement providing for voting by written ballot without provision of proxy voting. The court noted, 82 F. Supp. 2d at 834, n. 8, that it would have permitted proxy voting if the agreement had not including specific voting provisions. Does this interpretation seem reasonable?

2. Management Rights: The Control Rule

Limited partners may not participate in management without risking personal liability for the firm's debts. Specifically, ULPA § 7, applied in the following case, provides that a limited partner will be denied limited liability if "in addition to the exercise of his rights and powers as a limited partner, he takes part in the control of the business." Its successor, RULPA § 303, preserves the basic concept but narrows the liability by providing for a safe harbor and a reliance requirement.

Gast v. Petsinger
288 Pa. Super. 394, 323 A.2d 371 (1974)

HOFFMAN, JUDGE:

This appeal is from a summary judgment involving a contract dispute. Appellant charges in his Complaint that he was employed by LNG Services as a project engineer in 1968. For over a year, he was paid his agreed salary of $15,000.00 per year. From October of 1969 until March of 1971, when he severed his employment from the business, he continued in

his capacity without pay. Upon tendering notice of termination of employment, appellant submitted a claim for back pay and expenses. This amount was never paid and a suit in assumpsit was thereupon instituted. The Complaint states that the business known as LNG Services is formally a limited partnership. The only named general partner is the defendant, Robert E. Petsinger. Nevertheless, appellant claims that the other named individual defendants, while ostensibly limited partners, were, by virtue of their participation in the enterprise, acting as general partners, and should therefore be liable for the monies due him.
* * *

[T]he Court entered an Order granting defendants' Motion of Summary Judgment. The plaintiff-appellant has appealed to this Court asserting that the Answers to Interrogatories and his own Deposition supported by documentary evidence establish certain involvement in the partnership by the named defendants that presents a factual dispute on the question of "control" which should be submitted to a jury.

We have examined the record in this case and find the following to be the degree and kind of participation of the Limited Partners in LNG Services:

1. All Limited Partners have the following rights and powers as described in the Limited Partnership Agreement:

    (a) the right to receive distributions from time-to-time and upon dissolution;

    (b) the right to prevent the transfer of assets and other acts "outside the ordinary business of the partnership" unless an aggregate of 50% in interest give written consent to the transfers or acts;

    (c) the right to examine the books and records of the partnership at the principal office of the partnership;

    (d) the right to attend meetings "for the purpose of receiving the report of the General Partner and for taking any action referred to . . ." in clause (b), *supra*;

    (e) the right to transfer, sell or assign their interests to third parties;

    (f) and, upon the death of a Limited Partner, to have his or her share of the profits and distributions inure to his or her Estate.

2. According to the Limited Partnership Agreement, "the management and control of the Partnership's day-to-day operation and maintenance of the property of the Partnership shall rest exclusively with the General Partner." Consistent with statutes regulating limited partnerships, the Agreement places the "control" of the business in the hands of the General Partner. The Limited Partners, by virtue of their capital contributions, have the powers mentioned above, and are prohibited from taking any "part in the conduct or control of the Partnership and its business and shall have no right or authority to act for, or bind, the Partnership." * * *

The organization of LNG Services is in conformance with the Uniform Limited Partnership Act (59 P.S. § 171 *et seq.*) The certificate is in good order, and the Agreement delineates the powers, rights and liabilities of the General and Limited Partners in express terms. None of the powers mentioned therein exceed the degree of "control" which converts the status of a limited partner to that of general partner. * * *

Only Dr. Garwin and Jerome Apt, Jr., appear to have acted in capacities which require some discussion and evaluation. In addition to receiving reports and attending meetings wherein status reports and additional capital investments were discussed, Dr. Garwin was employed by the Partnership as an independent engineering consultant with respect to certain projects undertaken by LNG Services for which service he was retained by the General Partner and in which, he and the General Partner assert, he remained subject to the supervision and control of Petsinger, the General Partner. Apt was also engaged from time to time as an independent consultant on certain projects. These individuals were described as "Project Managers" on several booklets which were attached to appellant's deposition as exhibits.

Accepting all the facts as asserted by the plaintiff as true, as we must do in determining the propriety of a summary judgment, we do not believe that, at least with respect to several of the appellees, this case so clearly was devoid of a single factual issue as to remove the matter from the deliberation of a jury. * * *

The key issue before the lower court was whether the appellant had presented an arguable case demonstrating that some or all of the appellees had "take[n] part in the control of the business." The question of "control" has not been squarely met in Pennsylvania. We are, however, guided by decisions in a number of jurisdictions following the ULPA which have construed the term in various factual contexts. One excellent Harvard Law Review article examining this problem identifies the problem and the important factors to consider. "Investing Partners want to limit their liability in connection with the enterprise. They will not participate in managing the partnership's ordinary investment activities. * * * [H]owever, as a practical matter, it is unlikely that major commitments of capital would be made without informing and perhaps consulting with Investing Partners." Alan L. Feld, *The "Control" Test for Limited Partnerships*, 82 HARV. L. REV. 1471, 1474.

State and federal courts have taken a similar view. The courts have held, without satisfactorily describing the standards by which to judge a limited partner's activities, that the following did not constitute taking part in the "control" of the business: acting as a foreman in the employ of the partnership, with the power to purchase parts as necessary without consulting the general partner, but without the power to extend credit without prior approval from the general partner or deal with the partnership account, *Silvola v. Rowlett,* 129 Colo. 522, 272 P.2d 287 (1954); acting as a member of the board of directors of the partnership (although the Court noted that he never did actually serve as such), *Rathke v. Griffith,* 36 Wash.2d 394, 218 P.2d 757 (1950); acting as sales manager in a new car sales department of the partnership without power to hire or fire, and, with power to order cars only with the general partner's approval, *Grainger v. Antoyan,* 48 Cal.2d 805, 313 P.2d 848 (1957); and, participating in the choice of key employees and giving a certain degree of "advice," *Plasteel Products Corporation v. Helman,* 271 F.2d 354 (1st Cir. 1959).

An analysis of each of the cases reveals that they were decided on their own facts and are of little use in forming rules or standards. In each case, it was not the position of the limited partner that was stated as permissible, but the actual role and degree of participation that each had in relation to the general partner. A reading of those cases reinforces the belief of this Court that the determination must be made on an ad hoc basis, and while employment may not be conflicting with the status of a limited partner, the "control" that partner has in the day-to-day functions and operations of the business is the key question. Does the limited partner have decision-making authority that may not be checked or nullified by the general partner? As Alan Feld notes in his article: "[While] some cases would permit the limited partner to 'advise' the general partners . . . it is not at all clear that Investing Partners may do so without fear of liability in view of the weight their advice is likely to carry, both because of the size of their investment and because they are 'carrying' Managing Partners' interests. The determination of control is a factual one and this relationship may, as a practical matter, give any 'advice' the color of a command in the partnership." 81 HARV. L. REV. 1471, 1477.

Here, the appellant testified that partners Apt and Garwin acted in the partnership as "Project Managers." He stated in his deposition that the appearance of their names on brochures and reports, the obvious weight their "advice" carried in their recommendations and report on key projects, and their managerial responsibilities, all contributed to a belief that they exercised "control." The defendant Petsinger, the General Partner, confirms the fact that these two individuals acted as independent "consultants" on various "projects." He denies their authority or right to control the business decisions. His statement as defendant is conclusionary, and since we are reviewing this appeal on a summary judgment, the inference most favorable to the plaintiff must be made.

It may be true that once all the facts are in the appellees, Apt and Garwin, will have been found not to have exercised the degree of "control" necessary to impose general liability upon them. We agree that the nature of the business of LNG Services, described as having as its purposes "the management of the development, engineering, and technical advice relating to the development or uses for liquefied natural gas, etc., . . ." required the utilization of expert opinion of technical minds. It is not apparent from the face of the record that the technical skills and training of Apt and Garwin did not by virtue of their retention as "Project Managers" place them in a position where their "advice" did influence and perhaps, control the decisions of the General Partner, whose particular expertise is unknown.

With respect to the appellees, John J. McMullen Associates, Inc., J. Judson Brooks, John C. Oliver, Jr., W. D. George, Jr., Alexander M. Laughlin, Charles Manning, and Joan M. Apt, we affirm the order of the court below granting defendants' motion for summary judgment. None of the above-named partners is shown to have engaged in any activity or participated beyond those lawfully and expressly stated in the Limited Partnership Agreement. With respect to the appellees, Jerome Apt, Jr., and Dr. Leo Garwin, we reverse the order and judgment of the court below, and remand the case for further proceedings consistent with this opinion.

Notes and Questions

1. **RULPA "safe harbor."** RULPA § 303 contains a list of powers that can be granted to limited partners without triggering the control rule, including the power to "consult[] with and advis[e][] a general partner with respect to the business" and to propose, approve, or disapprove "matters related to the business of the limited partnership . . . , which the partnership agreement states in writing may be subject to the approval or disapproval of limited partners." What powers are *not* included in this safe harbor?

2. **RULPA reliance requirement.** RULPA § 303 also provides that, even when a limited partner is participating in control and this participation is not within one of

the safe harbor provisions, the third party may recover from the limited partner only if he has been misled by the limited partner's participation in control. The reliance requirement was applied recently in *In re Ridge II,* 158 B.R. 1016 (C.D. Cal. 1993).

3. **Limited partner as officer, director or shareholder of corporate general partner.** This is an important modern context for application of the control rule. *See* IV BROMBERG & RIBSTEIN ON PARTNERSHIP § 15.14(m). If the third party proves that the limited partner took part in control of the limited partnership, some courts hold that the limited has control liability unless she shows that she acted solely in the corporate capacity. *See Tapps of Nassau Supermarkets Inc. v. Linden Boulevard L.P.,* 661 N.Y.S.2d 223 (App. Div. 1997); *Gonzalez v. Chalpin,* 77 N.Y.2d 74, 77, 564 N.Y.S.2d 702, 703 (1990). For example, in *Tapps,* the court denied summary judgment where the limited signed some correspondence in her representative capacity but was the only person with whom plaintiff dealt and substituted a new general partner, which she solely controlled without amending the certificate. Other courts apparently put the burden on the third party to show that the limited acted solely as a partner. *See Bank Leumi Le Israel v. Lippe,* 1986 WL 14653 (N.D. Ill. Dec. 16, 1986); *Frigidaire Sales Corp. v. Union Properties, Inc.,* 88 Wash. 2d 400, 562 P.2d 244, 247 (1977). In order to protect against liability, the limited partner should clearly indicate that she is acting in corporate capacity.

4. **Explaining the control rule.** Why hold limited partners liable for participating in control? Corporate shareholders have no such liability. RULPA § 303 suggests that the basis is misleading creditors. But then the control rule does not seem necessary in light of estoppel or purported partner liability under UPA § 16 or RUPA § 308. Moreover, it is hard to see how a creditor could be misled to believe that a person was a general partner even if not so identified in the certificate. Alternatively, the control rule might be explained as ensuring that only those with personal liability exercise management powers. General partners' personal liability helps to align their interests with creditors by giving them an incentive to keep the firm from becoming insolvent. Moreover, general partners may be unwilling to agree to be personally liable for the firm's debts without some assurance that they will be able to guard their exposure by continuing to manage the firm. The control rule may work better than a provision in the limited partnership agreement forbidding the limited partners from managing. The rule gives limited partners the opportunity to take over the firm, particularly if it is near insolvency, as long as they are willing to pay the price by being subject to vicarious liability.

5. **The future of the control rule.** The control rule has been gradually whittled away by the expanding "safe harbor" exceptions and the reliance requirement discussed in Notes 2 and 3. This may be a part of the general story of evolution toward limited liability discussed in Chapters 10-14, which includes close corporation statutory provisions and the development of the LLC and the LLP. Two states have already eliminated the control rule. *See* GA. CODE ANN. § 14-9-303; MO. REV. STAT. § 359.201. Re-RULPA eliminates the control rule. (Moreover, Re-RULPA's proposed elimination of default personal liability for general partners discussed below in § 11.06 takes the teeth out of any control liability.) Should the control rule have any future? Some firms might want to "bond" their managers with personal liability as explained in Note 3 to make it easier

to borrow. Although members of all types of firms can agree to be liable for at least some debts, only in limited partnerships can managers make a binding commitment to be liable for all of the firm's debts, both now and in the future. (Of course, this commitment is diluted to some extent both by the incorporation of general partners, and by the ease with which limited partnerships can convert to the LLC or LLP form, as discussed in Chapters 12 and 13.) Can you think of particular types of firms that might choose this feature?

Problem

Assume you are drafting a limited partnership agreement for a partnership that will own and manage residential apartments. A general partner will manage for a fee, and there will be ten limited partners. Draft the provisions of the agreement that relate to general and limited partners' rights to participate in management and control.

11.06 Partners' Liability for Partnership Debts

General partners' liability under the general partnership act until recently has applied by "linkage" to general partners in limited partnerships. Under UPA § 15 general partners have joint or joint and several liability, depending on the type of liability. RUPA § 307 provides not only for joint and several liability for all debts, but also that creditors must exhaust remedies against the partnership. *See generally* Chapter 6, above. RUPA's exhaustion requirement may or may not extend to creditors' efforts to enforce *limited* partners' liability for distributions, discussed above in § 11.04. *See In re Sharps Run Associates, L.P.,* 157 B.R. 766 (D.N.J. 1993) (allowing direct recovery from limited partners).

This is in the process of changing. As discussed below in §13.06, limited partnerships can register as limited liability partnerships and become "limited liability limited partnerships," with limited liability for the general partners. Re-RULPA makes this the *default* rule in limited partnerships, so that general partners in limited partnerships would not be liable for partnership debts unless the certificate provides otherwise, with the general partner's consent. However, the Act is being drafted to include rules appropriate for limited partnerships with both types of general partners.

How, if at all, would a limited partnership with a limited-liability general partner differ from a limited liability company?

11.07 Partners' Property Rights

The property rights of both limited and general partners are modeled after those of general partners in general partnerships. Thus, the partners own both management and financial rights, but cannot freely transfer the former type of right.

A.   Transferability of Interests

RULPA § 702, like the UPA and RUPA (*see* Chapter 7, above), by default provides for free transferability only of partners' economic, and not management, rights. This seems odd for limited partners who, like corporate shareholders, have little direct voice in the firm. They would therefore have more need to be able to protect themselves by exiting the firm, and less need to veto the admission of new limited partners.

B.   Rights of Partners' Creditors

Creditors' rights against general partners' partnership interests are provided for in UPA § 28 and RUPA § 504, discussed above in Chapter 7. ULPA § 22 provides for a charging order against limited partners' interests, by implication thereby deferring to general partnership law regarding general partners. RULPA § 703 provides for a charging order against all partners, apparently precluding application of the UPA as to this remedy. However, the issue is complicated by the fact that the RULPA provision is similar but not identical to the general partnership provisions. This raises a question concerning the extent to which general partnership law, discussed in § 7.03, is linked to limited partnership law. The linkage issue is discussed in the following case.

Baybank v. Catamount Construction, Inc.
141 N.H. 780, 693 A.2d 1163 (1997)

JOHNSON, Justice.

The defendants, Catamount Construction, Inc., Sunset Construction Co., Eugene R. Connor, M. Patricia Connor, John H. Connor, and Marilyn A. Connor, appeal an order of the Superior Court (Perkins, J.) granting plaintiff Baybank a charging order and other relief against two of the defendants' interests in a limited partnership. We affirm in part, reverse in part, vacate in part, and remand.

Baybank obtained a judgment in superior court against defendants Eugene and John Connor (the Connors) as guarantors on a promissory note made by defendant Catamount Construction, Inc. In an effort to satisfy its judgment, Baybank sought to reach the Connors' interests in East Street Associates Limited Partnership (East Street), in which the Connors are limited partners. Baybank requested a charging order against the Connors' interests in East Street, the appointment of a receiver for any monies due the Connors as limited partners in East Street, and, if the judgment was not satisfied within fourteen days, dissolution of East Street. The Connors responded by conceding that Baybank would be entitled to a charging order under RSA chapter 304-B, but objecting to the additional relief sought. The superior court granted Baybank a charging order and further ordered that "East Street Limited Partnership be dissolved and a receiver appointed to dispose of [the Connors'] interest in the limited partnership to satisfy the judgment debt."

On appeal, the defendants challenge the trial court's authority to order the additional relief, particularly the dissolution of East Street. Specifically, the defendants contend that the trial court erred in importing creditors' rights and remedies found in RSA chapter 304-A, the Uniform Partnership Act (UPA), into RSA chapter 304-B, the Uniform Limited Partnership Act (ULPA).

The trial court ruled that it had broad equitable power to grant the additional relief under RSA 304-A:28, I [UPA § 28(1)]. * * * Citing RSA 304-A:6 [UPA § 6] . . . the trial court concluded that it should apply the UPA to East Street to the extent that the UPA did not conflict with the ULPA. RSA 304-A:6, II (1995). Finding no conflict between RSA 304-A:28 and anything in the ULPA, the court applied the UPA provision to East Street.

In addition, the trial court based its order of dissolution on RSA 304-A:32, II(b) [UPA § 32(2)(b)]. * * * The defendants urge us to hold that the rights of judgment creditors of limited partners are limited to those set forth in RSA chapter 304-B, and that it was error for the trial court to import any of the remedial provisions of RSA chapter 304-A into RSA chapter 304-B. We decline to adopt this position as we are persuaded by the weight of authority from other jurisdictions and scholarly commentary that the legislature did not intend to preclude a creditor with a charging order on a limited partnership interest from enforcing that interest if necessary. We are also convinced, however, that the legislature did not intend such a creditor to have the remedies ordered by the trial court.

The statutory remedy of a charging order was designed to prevent the personal creditors of a limited partner from disrupting the partnership business by seizing partnership assets on execution. [citations omitted] The statutory remedy forces a judgment creditor to look solely to the debtor's partnership interest . . . rather than to partnership assets.
* * *

The defendants conceded that their interests in East Street could have been charged under RSA chapter 304-B. We therefore affirm the portion of the trial court's order that charged the Connors' interests in East Street. The question before us is whether the additional remedies, particularly dissolution, ordered by the trial court are available to a creditor of a limited partner. * * * The ULPA provides that "[i]n any case not provided for in this chapter the provisions of the Uniform Partnership Act, RSA 304-A, shall govern." RSA 304-B:63 (1995) [RULPA §1105]. Although the parties disagree on whether the later-enacted RSA 304-B:63 applies to the exclusion of RSA 304-A:6, we find it unnecessary to decide this issue since we would arrive at our holding in this case regardless of which provision we applied.

We first address the defendants' contention that the appointment of a receiver and sale of a charged partnership interest are unauthorized under [RULPA § 703] . . . RSA 304-B:41. As observed by the court in *Madison Hills Ltd. v. Madison Hills, Inc.,* 35 Conn. App. 81, 644 A.2d 363, 367, *cert. denied,* 231 Conn. 913, 648 A.2d 153 (1994), this section does not provide a method for enforcing the charging order. The significance of this omission becomes apparent in a case such as that before us, in which Baybank alleges that a charging order alone would never divert enough money to Baybank to satisfy even the accruing interest on the judgment debt. It is in precisely such situations that courts have been most inclined to enforce the creditor's rights through foreclosure on the charged interest. *See Centurion Corp. [Centurion Corp. v. Crocker Nat. Bank,* 208 Cal. App. 3d 1, 255 Cal. Rptr. 794 (1989)], 255 Cal. Rptr. at 798. We therefore find that RSA 304-B:41 does not "provide [ ] for," within the meaning of RSA 304-B:63, a case such as this, and that the legislature intended that reference be made to the UPA for the means of enforcing the creditor's rights in the charged partnership interest. *See Madison Hills,* 644 A.2d at 368 (finding that where only the UPA, and not the ULPA, provides means of enforcing a charging order, the charging order provision of the ULPA "relies on rather than conflicts with" the UPA provision).

We also find that RSA 304-B:41 is not inconsistent with the remedial provisions of RSA 304-A:28, since, as the *Madison Hills* court noted, "the purpose of the charging order provisions under both statutes is to balance the need to protect the orderly operation of the partnership and the rights of creditors." *Id.* 644 A.2d at 368-69. In most cases, neither the appointment of a receiver to collect the debtor partner's share of distributed profits, nor the sale of the debtor partner's interest in the partnership, as opposed to partnership assets, would unduly interfere with the running of the partnership business. *See Hellman v. Anderson,* 233 Cal. App. 3d 840, 284 Cal. Rptr. 830, 837-38 (1991) (making a similar observation in regard to general partnerships). Thus, we hold that a court may properly look to RSA 304-A:28 for the means to enforce a charging order under RSA 304-B:41 when the latter remedy alone would be insufficient. *See Madison Hills,* 644 A.2d at 368 (finding that "the remedy provisions of the UPA are available to judgment creditors under the ULPA"). *But see In re Stocks,* 110 B.R. 65, 67 (Bankr. N.D. Fla.1989) (finding no right under Florida ULPA to foreclose on charged limited partnership interest).

The trial court, however, did not actually grant the type of relief contemplated by RSA 304-A:28. Although the trial court purported to order the appointment of a receiver "to dispose of the guarantors' interest in the limited partnership to satisfy the judgment debt," such relief would have been unnecessary in light of the trial court's order that the partnership be dissolved. In fact, it appears that the receiver and court-ordered sale were not intended to be in aid of the charging order but in aid of dissolution.

A review of the transcript of the hearing on Baybank's motion reveals that what was really at issue was Baybank's attempt to liquidate the primary asset of the limited partnership, a piece of real estate located in Tewksbury, Massachusetts, and satisfy its judgment out of the proceeds thereof. At one point, counsel for Baybank stated,

> the basic process that we're asking the court to do is to award the charging order for the judgment amount which is what the defendants confessed that we're entitled to, but then to go the next step which is to order—to make sufficient findings to order that a judicial dissolution of this partnership, given its history, given its stated purpose under oath, given its ultimate frustration of that purpose, to dissolve that partnership, *to allow the underlying property or the interest in the partnership and then the underlying property to be sold so that the cash gets freed up,* the debt gets paid so the interest ticker now does not outstrip the income that can be earned from the partnership. * * *

(Emphasis added.) Such an application of partnership property to pay the personal debts of a partner, however, is precisely what the charging order provisions of the ULPA and the UPA are intended to prevent. Neither the ULPA nor the UPA charging order provision allowsa creditor such as Baybank to satisfy its judgment out of partnership assets. [citations omitted]

Nor is Baybank entitled to the dissolution of East Street. The trial court erred by ordering dissolution under RSA 304-A:32, II(b). First, that provision allows the court to order dissolution "on the application of the purchaser of a partner's interest under RSA 304-A:27 [UPA § 27] or RSA 304-A:28." RSA 304-A:32, II. Baybank is not such a purchaser, however, because the defendants' partnership interests were never foreclosed upon. Baybank is merely a creditor with a charging order on the defendants' limited partnership interests and, as such, is not entitled under the terms of RSA 304-A:32, II, to petition for dissolution of East Street.

Moreover, on the issue of judicial dissolution, the ULPA is neither silent nor consistent with the UPA, which leaves no occasion to import the provisions of RSA 304-A:32 into RSA chapter 304-B. Judicial dissolution of a limited partnership is provided for in RSA 304-B:45, which states that "[o]n application by or for a partner, the superior court may decree dissolution of a limited partnership whenever it is not reasonably practicable to carry on the business in conformity with the partnership agreement." RSA 304-B:45 (1995). Thus, the availability of judicial dissolution under the terms of the ULPA is much more limited than under the UPA. *Cf.* RSA 304-A:32 (1995). Limited recourse to judicial dissolution for limited partnerships reflects basic structural differences between the two types of entities. *See* A. BROMBERG, CRANE AND BROMBERG ON PARTNERSHIP § 90B(a), at 516 (1968) (noting that there are differences between dissolution of general and limited partnerships and finding it "not surprising that in some aspects of continuity, limited partnerships resemble corporations more closely than they do general partnerships"). In short, the ULPA is inconsistent with the UPA on this issue, and the trial court therefore erred in applying the UPA.

Baybank argues that even if the superior court erred in basing its order of dissolution on RSA 304-A:32, II(b), the same result could have been reached under either RSA 304-B:45 [UPA § 32(1)] or RSA 304-A:32, I(f) [UPA § 32(1)(f)], which provides that a court may order dissolution on application by or for a partner when "[o]ther circumstances render a dissolution equitable." Thus, Baybank urges us to affirm the trial court's order on the ground that a correct result reached on mistaken grounds should be sustained if there are valid alternative grounds to support it. [citation omitted] We conclude, however, that dissolution was not authorized under either RSA 304-B:45 or RSA 304-A:32, I.

First, as with RSA 304-A:32, II, we find no occasion to import the provisions of RSA 304-A:32, I, into the ULPA, which speaks plainly and comprehensively on the issue of dissolution of a limited partnership. As for RSA 304-B:45, it requires that a petition for dissolution be made "by or for a partner." Baybank, as a judgment creditor, lacked standing to seek judicial dissolution under this section. As a creditor holding a charging order, Baybank has, to the extent of the interest charged, "only the rights of an assignee of the partnership interest." RSA 304-B:41. Under RSA 304-B:40 [RULPA § 702], "[a]n assignment of a partnership interest does not . . . entitle the assignee to become or to exercise any rights of a partner." This explicit statutory limitation on the rights of assignees precludes Baybank from acting "by or for" the Connors in petitioning for dissolution of East Street.

Nor do we believe, as Baybank argues, that a receiver appointed under RSA 304-A:28 could petition "by or for a partner" for dissolution. * * * It is the court, not the receiver, that is authorized by the statute to "make all other orders, functions, accounts and inquiries." RSA 304-A:28, I. * * *

Moreover, even if Baybank could petition on behalf of the Connors for dissolution of East Street, we find that the conditions for judicial dissolution under RSA 304-B:45 are not met in this case. Baybank argues that it is not reasonably practicable for East Street to carry on its business in conformity with its partnership agreement because East Street does not generate and distribute to its limited partners enough income to meet even the interest payments on the Connors' judgment debt. Even if we were to accept Baybank's statement that "the purpose of every partnership is to make a profit for its partners," however, we fail to see how East Street's alleged inability to distribute enough income to its partners to enable them to pay their personal debts renders the partnership unprofitable.

Finally, Baybank argues that allowing the Connors to use East Street as a shield against their personal creditors would be contrary to reason and against public policy. Baybank therefore asks us to read an exception into the statutory scheme to address the Connors' alleged attempt to defraud Baybank by transferring the Tewksbury property into East Street. We decline to do so. We note that the case upon which Baybank primarily relies, *Taylor* [*v. S & M Lamp Co.,* 190 Cal. App. 2d 700, 12 Cal. Rptr. 323, 328 (Dist. Ct. App. 1961)], involved an alleged fraudulent transfer of property out of a partnership, not into one. *Id.* 12 Cal. Rptr. at 330. In that case, the issue was the frustration of the charging order remedy when the fraudulent transfer of partnership assets ensured that there would be no profits or surplus from which the charging creditor could be satisfied. *Id.*

In the instant case, the value of the Connors' partnership interests, the only assets to which Baybank is entitled to look for satisfaction of its judgment, has not been placed beyond Baybank's reach. The purposes of RSA 304-B:41 and RSA 304-A:28 have not been frustrated. To the extent that Baybank believes the initial conveyance of the Tewksbury property from the Connors to East Street to have been fraudulent, its recourse lies in fraudulent conveyance law, not in a judicially created exception to the partnership statutes.

. . . We hold that the trial court erred in ordering dissolution of East Street, and we reverse that portion of the trial court's order. Since it appears that the trial court ordered the appointment of a receiver solely to assist in the dissolution of East Street, rather than for purposes authorized under the ULPA, by reference to UPA, we vacate that portion of the trial court's order and remand for further proceedings not inconsistent with this opinion.

Notes and Questions

1. **Linkage between general and limited partnership law: Foreclosure.** Evaluate the court's conclusion that the UPA foreclosure remedy should be applied to limited partners' creditors because it is not inconsistent with the ULPA provision. Note that, although the limited partnership statute does not include a remedy provision, it does make the creditor an assignee. By contrast, a charging creditor under the UPA probably is not an assignee *unless* it obtains foreclosure. *See* Note 2, p. 158. It follows that foreclosure may have been omitted from the limited partnership statute because it is unnecessary.

2. **Linkage: Dissolution.** Foreclosure is important in general partnerships mainly because letting a creditor buy the interest and thereby be in a position to compel dissolution may be the only way a partner's creditor can compel the firm to distribute enough assets to pay off the debt. *See* Note 2, p. 158. Foreclosure alone, however, does the creditor little good, particularly since, as just noted, the charging creditor is an assignee under the limited partnership statute even without foreclosure. Thus, does it makes sense to apply the UPA creditor-enforcement mechanism to the extent of permitting foreclosure but not to the extent of permitting dissolution when charging alone will not pay the debt? On the one hand, RULPA § 802 literally permits only *partners* to force judicial dissolution. RULPA's silence on assignees' rights in the context of a general provision on judi-

cial decrees arguably means that limited partners' assignees have no right to obtain a decree. On the other hand, RULPA § 802 may not apply at all to assignees, in which event the UPA provision on assignees would apply. This sort of confusion regarding linkage is a good reason for having a "stand-alone" limited partnership statute.

3. **Re-RULPA and De-linkage**: As noted at the beginning and throughout this Chapter, Re-RULPA is being drafted as a "stand-alone" statute. The current version provides for foreclosure of charging orders but carries over RULPA's provision for judicial dissolution only "on application by or for a partner." Why not provide, as do UPA § 31(2) and RUPA § 801(6), for dissolution on application by an assignee or transferee, including a charging creditor? *See* Section 7.03, above. Is there some distinction between limited and general partnerships that justifies different treatment in this respect?

4. **Fraudulent conveyances.** With respect to Baybank's fraudulent conveyance point, under the court's interpretation of the charging creditor's rights partners may be able to put their assets out of their creditors' reach by transferring them to a limited partnership. This becomes a potential issue in "family" limited partnerships which are used for estate planning purposes (*see* Section 11.09, below) but which also can have "asset protection" implications. In *Firmani v. Firmani,* 332 N.J. Super 118, 752 A.2d 854 (2000), a man whose $25,000 debt to his former wife was shortly to become due transferred his residence, in which he had $83,000 in equity, for a dollar to a family partnership. Pursuant to the partnership agreement, the husband held a one percent interest as the general partner and a 94% interest as a limited partner, with his second wife, three children, and stepson receiving the remaining interest. The first wife sued to set aside the conveyance as a fraudulent transfer—that is, a fraud on her as a creditor. The following is an excerpt from the court's opinion, 332 N.J. Super. at 120-24, 752 A.2d at 856-58:

> N.J.S.A. 25:2-26 [the fraudulent conveyance statute] sets forth a non-exhaustive list of eleven factors, referred to as "badges of fraud," that a court may consider in determining whether a party has established an actual intent to hinder, delay, or defraud under N.J.S.A. 25:2-25(a):
> a. The transfer or obligation was to an insider;
> b. The debtor retained possession or control of the property transferred after the transfer;
> c. The transfer or obligation was disclosed or concealed;
> d. Before the transfer was made or obligation was incurred, the debtor had been sued or threatened with suit;
> e. The transfer was of substantially all the debtor's assets;
> f. The debtor absconded;
> g. The debtor removed or concealed assets;
> h. The value of the consideration received by the debtor was reasonably equivalent to the value of the asset transferred or the amount of the obligation incurred;
> i. The debtor was insolvent or became insolvent shortly after the transfer was made or the obligation was incurred;

j.   The transfer occurred shortly before or shortly after a substantial debt was incurred; and

k.   The debtor transferred the essential assets of the business to a lienor who transferred the assets to an insider of the debtor.

* * *

We are satisfied that the undisputed facts show that Firmani's conveyance of the Haddonfield property to the Family Partnership manifested at least five of the "badges of fraud" set forth in N.J.S.A. 25:2-26. Defendant was the sole general partner and primary limited partner of the Family Partnership prior to the conveyance, and therefore the conveyance was made to an insider. N.J.S.A. 25:2-26(a); [citation omitted]. By continuing to use the Haddonfield property as a residence and place of business, and as the sole general partner with a total ninety-five percent interest in the Family Partnership, defendant clearly retained possession or control of the property after the conveyance. N.J.S.A. 25:2- 26(b). * * * By putting plaintiff in a position where she could only recover the money owed through the Limited Partnership charging process, defendant "removed . . . assets." N.J.S.A. 25:2-26(g); . . . . Finally, because Firmani's obligation to pay the remaining $25,000 he owed plaintiff became due on December 12, 1994, the conveyance to the Family Partnership occurred shortly after a substantial debt was incurred. N.J.S.A. 25:2-26(j).

Defendants failed to present any substantial evidence to counter the strong inference of fraudulent intent established by these badges of fraud. Firmani submitted a certification which asserted that he established the Family Partnership and conveyed the Haddonfield property to this entity for "estate planning purposes." However, we are unable to discern from Firmani's certification how the transaction could have served any estate planning purposes, except by increasing the total amount of his estate by the $25,000 he seeks to avoid paying plaintiff and by the amounts of the judgments that certain casinos have against him. In any event, N.J.S.A. 25:2-25(a) does not require that an intent to hinder, delay, or defraud a creditor be the exclusive motivation behind a transfer in order for the transfer to be deemed fraudulent.

Defendants also argue that "finally, and of greatest significance, the transfer did not deprive Ms. Firmani of assets sufficient to satisfy her judgment. The transfer merely changed the type of asset against which she could assert her lien." In *Shapiro v. Wilgus,* 287 U.S. 348, 354, 53 S.Ct. 142, 144, 77 L. Ed. 355, 358 (1932), the United States Supreme Court observed that "[a] conveyance is illegal if made with an intent to defraud the creditors of the grantor, but equally it is illegal if made with an intent to hinder or delay them." Under the Uniform Limited Partnership Law, N.J.S.A. 42:2A-1 to -72, the rights of a judgment creditor of a partner are defined by N.J.S.A. 42:2A-48 [RULPA § 703]

Thus, even if plaintiff were able to secure a charge against Firmani's partnership interest, she would have to wait until a distribution was made before she could collect any money, and Firmani, as the sole general partner, has sole discretion as to distributions. The partnership is not set to terminate until December 31, 2030, and the partnership agreement allows for an extension beyond that date. Moreover, Firmani has sole discretion to dissolve the partnership, and even upon his death, the other partners retain the right to vote to continue the partnership. Consequently, the conveyance of the Haddonfield property from Firmani to the Family Partnership serves to greatly hinder and delay plaintiff's ability to collect the debt Firmani owes her.

In sum, Firmani's conveyance of the Haddonfield property clearly manifested at least five badges of fraud. The dubious and weak justifications for the transaction offered by Firmani were insufficient to rebut the inference of actual fraudulent intent provided by these badges of fraud. Therefore, the trial court correctly concluded that the conveyance was fraudulent. * * *

11.08 Fiduciary Duties and Remedies

Fiduciary duties in general partnerships were discussed above in Chapter 8. As discussed in this section, unique issues are presented in limited partnerships concerning duties of both general and limited partners, remedies, and linkage with general partnership law.

A.   Fiduciary Duties of General Partners

ULPA and RULPA do not explicitly provide for fiduciary duties. As noted in § 11.02, above, the limited partnership acts provide that general partners in limited partnerships have the rights, powers, duties and liabilities of general partners in general partnerships. Thus UPA § 21 and RUPA § 404, discussed above in Chapter 8, govern the fiduciary duties of general partners in limited partnerships. *See* the *Appletree* and *Labovitz* cases excerpted above in Chapter 8. Re-RULPA essentially continues this result by including the RUPA duties in the limited partnership statute.

How these duties are applied should, however, depend on the context, including whether the firm is a limited or general partnership. Because of limited partners' enforced passivity and the conflicts inherent in the differing interests of members who are, and are not, personally liable for the firm's debts, there may be a greater need in limited than in general partnerships for rules restricting self-interested conduct by managers. *See* Note, *Regulating Rollups: General Partners' Fiduciary Obligations in Light of the Limited Partnership Rollup Reform Act of 1993,* 47 STAN. L. REV. 85 (1994). Thus, the courts often characterize the fiduciary duties of general partners in limited partnerships more along corporate than partnership lines, particularly regarding the duty of care. For cases analogizing general partners to corporate directors for this purpose *see Wyler v. Feuer,* 85 Cal. App. 3d 392, 149 Cal. Rptr. 626 (1979); *Trustees of General Electric Pension Trust v. Levenson,* 1992 WL 41820 (Del. Ch. 1992). But the corporate director analogy may not be any more appropriate. Fiduciary duties may be less necessary in limited partnerships than in corporations to constrain managers' actions that are careless or not strongly self-interested because general partners are motivated to act in the firm's interests by their ownership interests and personal liability.

RULPA Section 107, which permits a partner to deal with the partner as a third party "subject to other applicable law" does *not* affect a general partner's fiduciary duty to the firm. *See BT-I v. Equitable Life Assurance Society of the United States*, 75 Cal. App. 4th 1406, 76 Cal. App. 4th 684E, 89 Cal. Rptr. 2d 811, 817-18 (1999), discussed on p. 201, above. The court held that this was intended to leave *creditors'* rights against partners subject to general fraudulent conveyance law rather than to sanction self-dealing.

Waiver of fiduciary duties in limited partnerships presents issues similar to those in general partnerships, discussed in Section 8.06, above. Waivability in limited partnerships has been given a strong boost by a Delaware statutory provision (there is a similar provision in the Delaware LLC statute). The statute provides (6 DEL. CODE § 17-1101):

(c) It is the policy of this chapter to give maximum effect to the principle of freedom of contract and to the enforceability of partnership agreements.

(d) To the extent that, at law or in equity, a partner has duties (including fiduciary duties) and liabilities relating thereto to a limited partnership or to another partner, (1) any such partner acting under a partnership agreement shall not be liable to the limited partnership or to any such other partner for the partner's good faith reliance on the provisions of such partnership agreement, and (2) the partner's duties and liabilities may be expanded or restricted by provisions in a partnership agreement.

For a discussion of this provision *see* Ribstein, *Unlimited Contracting in the Delaware Limited Partnership and Its Implications for Corporate Law*, 17 J. CORP. L. 299 (1991).

Although this provision explicitly authorizes only agreements that expand or restrict, rather than eliminate fiduciary duties (*see* Demott, *Fiduciary Preludes: Likely Issues for LLCs*, 66 U. COLO. L. REV. 1043, 1057 (1995)), Delaware and other courts have recognized the provision's strong authorization of contracts and have broadly applied it. *See Elf Atochem North America, Inc. v. Jaffari,* 727 A.2d 286 (Del. 1999) (enforcing choice of forum and arbitration provision); *U.S. Cellular Inv. Co. of Allentown v. Bell Atlantic Mobile Sys., Inc.,* 677 A.2d 497 (Del. 1996) (no cause of action in absence of allegation of knowing breach of the agreement); *Sonet v. Timber Co., L.P.,* 722 A.2d 319 (Del. Ch. 1998) (agreement giving general partner "sole discretion" preempted fiduciary duty in connection with merger converting limited partnership into real estate investment trust); *Kahn v. Icahn,* 1998 WL 832629 (Del. Ch. Nov. 12, 1998) (general partner could compete with partnership under agreement authorizing the partner to compete and engage in other business ventures); *Whalen v. Connelly,* 545 N.W.2d 284 (Iowa 1996) (not breach for general partner or its "affiliate" to engage in riverboat gambling projects in other states without offering limited partner opportunity to participate since the partnership agreement permitted general partners to engage in other similar activities); *Rothmeier v. Investment Advisers, Inc.*, 556 N.W.2d 590 (Minn. App. 1996) (not breach to terminate employee who investigated employer's compliance with securities laws without evidence that the investigation was an improper motivating factor in the termination). The *Sonet* and *Kahn* cases include particularly strong statements of the contractual nature of fiduciary duties.

B.   Fiduciary Duties of Limited Partners

Fiduciary duties of *limited* partners are dealt with neither in the general partnership statutes nor RULPA. This raises a "linkage" issue: Limited partners' duties may depend on whether they are characterized as "partners" and thereby subject to the duties of imposed on general partners under the UPA or RUPA. Linkage is problematic here because, unlike general partners, limited partners do not exercise the sort of control that generally triggers fiduciary duties, particularly given limited partners' enforced passivity under the "control rule." Moreover, they may owe fiduciary duties to the extent that they act outside limited partners' usual role—a circumstance that is now increasingly likely in view of the decline and possible elimination of the "control rule" (see Note 5, p. 321-22). *See Goldwasser v. Geller*, 684 N.Y.S.2d 210 (A.D. 1999) (limited partners who arranged a settlement with general partners took over managerial control and assumed a fiduciary duty to a co-limited partner). *See also KE Property Management Inc. v. 275 Madison Management Corp.*, 1993 WL 285900 (Del. Ch.), 19 DEL. J. CORP. L. 805 (1993), noting that the applicable Uniform Partnership Act provides that all partners owe fiduciary duties and that "to the extent that a partnership agreement empowers a limited partner discretion to take actions affecting the governance of the limited partnership, the limited partner may be subject to the obligations of a fiduciary, including the obligation to act in good faith as to the other partners." (But the court declined to speculate that the limited partner was engaged in wrongdoing because its ulterior motive in removing the general partner was to prevent the general partner from putting the partnership in bankruptcy, which would prevent the limited's affiliate from foreclosing on its mortgage.) The current version of Re-RULPA provides for fiduciary duties for a limited partner who exercises a general partner's management power pursuant to the partnership agreement.

For cases holding against limited partners' fiduciary duties where the partners were not participating in control see *In re Kids Creek Partners, L.P. v. Leighton Holdings, Ltd.*, 212 B.R. 898, 936-37 (Bankr. N.D. Ill. 1997) (limited partner was not involved in management by virtue of being the investment manager for the foreclosing lender, owner of 1% owner of the grandparent of the corporate general partner, and general partner of a general partnership that owned a minority share of the grandparent of the corporate general partner and a 32.88% limited partnership interest); *In re Villa West Associates*, 146 F.3d 798 (10th Cir. 1998) (limited partners did not breach a fiduciary duty to the partnership by failing to make capital contributions where they did not act as a dominant group, hold a position of confidence in or control the partnership); *In re Villa West Associates,* 193 B.R. 587 (D. Kan. 1996) (limited partners did not breach a fiduciary duty to other limited partners by acquiring a partnership indebtedness to reduce their liability on a guarantee without affording a similar opportunity to the other limited partners).

Even if the limited partner did not breach a fiduciary duty, it might be deemed to have acted in bad faith. *See* Section 8.05, above, distinguishing bad faith and fiduciary duty. Should the court have found bad faith in any of the above cases? Should a limited partner be deemed to be acting in bad faith merely because it is protecting its self-interest as an owner of the firm?

Given the ambiguities regarding limited partner duties, they arguably ought to be covered in the partnership agreement. The parties ought to be able to specify limited partner duties even in situations where the duties would not exist by default, as where the partner is not participating in control. *Cantor Fitzgerald, L.P. v. Cantor,* 2000 WL 307370 (Del. Ch., Mar 17, 2000), held that the agreement could impose fiduciary duties even on limited partners who do not participate in control, noting the need to instill commitment and discourage competition within a closely held limited partnership in the highly competitive industry of brokerage of Treasury bonds, and that the partnership relies on its partners for capital. The court interpreted § 1101(d), quoted above in § 11.08(A), to permit the agreement to impose fiduciary duties that would not exist apart from the agreement.

C. Remedies

ULPA is silent on partner remedies. RULPA §§ 1001-1004 provide for derivative suits. It is not clear whether the accounting remedy under UPA § 22 or RUPA § 405 discussed above in Chapter 8 applies to limited partnerships, or whether in UPA jurisdictions that remedy is a prerequisite to other relief as in general partnerships. RULPA's derivative suit provisions strongly suggest that the accounting remedy is not exclusive as to limited partner remedies, but otherwise leave unclear the impact of the derivative suit provisions on general partner remedies. *Dulles Corner Properties II Ltd. Partnership v. Smith,* 246 Va. 153, 431 S.E.2d 309 (1993), held that a general partner of a limited partnership could not bring an action at law against another general partner in the partnership's name without first obtaining dissolution and accounting. The court noted that RULPA gives a general partner the same rights in a limited partnership as in a general partnership, but did not discuss the possible impact of the RULPA derivative suit provisions.

From a policy standpoint, even if the accounting remedy should be exclusive in general partnerships, should the exclusivity rule apply to limited partnerships? Note that the remedy may be appropriate to deal with the complex litigation that can arise out of cross-claims between partners. But this is less likely to be a problem in limited partnerships, which typically have only one or two general partners, and whose limited partners are unlikely to have contribution obligations that give rise to cross claims.

11.09 Dissociation and Dissolution

The limited partnership statutes provide incompletely for partner dissociation and dissolution. As for many of the other issues discussed above, this creates potential confusion about the extent to which general partnership law applies.

A.   Dissociation of Limited Partners

The limited partnership statutes clearly govern concerning the causes and consequences of limited partner dissociation, which the general partnership acts do not provide for. ULPA § 16(2)(c) provides that a limited partner is entitled to demand return of her contribution before dissolution on six months notice "if no time is specified in the certificate for return of the contribution or for dissolution of the partnership." RULPA § 603 provides that a limited partner may withdraw from a limited partnership as provided in writing in the partnership agreement or on six months' notice in the absence of contrary agreement. RULPA § 604 provides that a withdrawing partner should be paid distributions to which he is entitled and, if not otherwise provided in the agreement, the fair value of his interest in the partnership.

These provisions raise tax issues in "family limited partnerships" in which a business owner makes family members limited partners in the business, at least partly in the hope of transferring the business to them without substantial estate or gift tax. Whether this strategy is successful depends on the tax value of the limited partnership interests. This, in turn, depends partly on whether the family can remove their interests at any time and be paid "fair value," or whether they must wait some indefinite or very long time for the firm to be liquidated. The longer into the future the interest in the business must be discounted, the lower the valuation, other things being equal. Internal Revenue Code (26 U.S.C.) § 2704 provides that an "applicable restriction" on liquidation rights can be disregarded in valuing the interest for tax purposes. Section 2704(b)(3)(B) provides that an "applicable restriction" does not include "any restriction imposed, or required to be imposed, by any Federal or State law." Treasury Regulation § 25.2704-2(b), 26 C.F.R. § 25.2704-2(b) defines "applicable restriction" as one that is "more restrictive than the limitations that would apply under the State law generally applicable to the entity in absence of the restriction." Putting all this together, a provision in a limited partnership agreement that prohibits withdrawal would be ineffective for tax purposes if it is more restrictive than an applicable state statute, such as one based on RULPA that provides for a default right to exit on designated notice.

Many limited partnership statutes deal with the tax problem by eliminating limited partners' default power under RULPA § 603 to withdraw and be paid the value of their interests. *See* Bromberg & Ribstein on Partnerships § 17.02(d)(2), n. 21. Re-RULPA proposes to eliminate the withdrawn partner's default right to payment for his interest.

These provisions make the limited partnership suitable for family limited partnerships as a tax planning device under the tax law discussed above. The illiquidity of the limited partner's interest, coupled with the weakness of the charging order remedy (*see* § 11.07(b)), also makes the family limited partnership potentially useful in protecting partners' assets from creditors. For a discussion of the fraudulent conveyance issue that might arise in this connection, *see* Note 4, p. 328-30.

B.   Dissociation of General Partners

RULPA § 402 specifies events of withdrawal of general partners of limited partnerships, § 602 provides for voluntary withdrawal of a general partner, and for damages for withdrawal in violation of the partnership agreement, and § 801 provides that a limited partnership is dissolved on an event of withdrawal of a general partner unless the partnership is continued by consent of all the partners or pursuant to the partnership agreement. As noted above, RULPA § 604 provides for distribution to withdrawing partners of the fair value of their interests. ULPA § 20 also provides that retirement, death or insanity of a general partner dissolves the partnership. These provisions seem to override analogous provisions on events of withdrawal in RUPA § 601 and UPA § 42 and RUPA § 701 provisions on distributions to withdrawing partners. *See generally* Chapter 9 above. However, the general and limited partnership provisions are close enough in effect that linkage issues as to dissociation probably will be rare.

Should general partnership law on general partner dissociation be applied to general partners in limited partnerships? General partners' exits arguably should be more restricted in limited than in general partnerships. Although general partners' exposure to liability justifies giving them a default exit right in both types of firms, the costs to the partnership from general partner withdrawal are likely to be greater in limited partnerships because the limited partners necessarily rely on the general partner's managerial skills. Moreover, the potential costs to the general partner are likely to be less in limited than in general partnerships because the limited partners' passivity makes it less likely they will opportunistically take advantage of a frozen-in partner. The following sections consider more specifically how, in light of these differences, the rules regarding general partner dissociation and dissolution differ in limited and general partnerships.

Re-RULPA, which delinks the limited and general partnership acts, proposes to eliminate the default right of payment to dissociated general partners, just as it does for limited partners as discussed above in Subsection A. Re-RULPA also proposes to eliminate the default rule of automatic dissolution on general partner dissociation as long as there is another general partner, while providing that the firm dissolves on notice of dissolution by the general partner or majority vote by the limited partners.

C.   Dissolution Causes

There are differences between general and limited partnership law regarding the causes of dissolution. For example, under UPA §§ 31-32, dissolution is caused by (1) termination of the term or undertaking; (2) express will either without violation of the agreement if there is no definite term or undertaking or in contravention, by expulsion; (3) unlawfulness of the business or the members' participation; (4) death of a member; (5) bankruptcy of a partner or the partnership; or (6) judicial decree in the event of a partner's insanity, incapacity, wrongful conduct, the business can only be carried on at a loss, dissolution is equitable under the circumstances, or by application by an assignee in a partnership at will.

By contrast, under RULPA § 801, dissolution occurs (1) at the time specified in the certificate; (2) on an event specified in writing in the partnership agreement; (3) on written consent of all partners; (4) on a partner's event of withdrawal as specified in the statute *unless* the other members agree to continue; or (5) on judicial decree on the single § 802 cause of "its not being reasonably practicable to carry on the business in conformity with the partnership agreement." Note that the partnership may "terminate" for tax purposes whether or not it dissolves under state law. *See* § 9.04(D).

Although limited partnership statutes explicitly cover dissolution and dissociation, general partnership law may apply to specific dissolution and dissociation issues that the limited partnership statutes do not cover. For example, the limited partnership acts do not make express will a dissolution cause. The RULPA provision on dissolution causes appears to cover all causes of dissolution of a limited partnership, and therefore to exclude inconsistent UPA causes. But the RULPA provision arguably only specifies dissolution causes that differ between limited and general partnerships. In particular, general partner *withdrawal* is treated differently in limited partnerships from general partnerships—that is, it does not necessarily dissolve the firm. However, the UPA might still apply to permit a general partner to *dissolve* by express will. The Official Comment to § 801, which states that it "merely collects in one place all of the events causing dissolution," could mean that the section is all-inclusive. Alternatively, the Comment's use of the word "merely" and its contrast of RULPA's dissolution provision with the dispersion of dissolution provisions in various sections of ULPA could mean only that it collects *limited* partnership-type causes, while also preserving causes provided for in the general partnership statutes. But there is no apparent policy reason why, by application of general partnership law, a general partner who could not necessarily dissolve a limited partnership by *withdrawing* should be able to do the same thing by *dissolving* by express will.

The delinked Re-RULPA proposes causes of dissolution that are similar to those in RULPA except concerning partner dissociation, which is discussed above in subsection B.

D. Consequences of Dissolution

ULPA § 23 and RULPA § 805 provide for distributions on dissolution, and RULPA § 803 provides for winding up. While these provisions would seem to control the consequences of dissolution of limited partnerships, this is not completely clear because, as with dissolution causes (*see* Section C) general partnership provisions are considerably more detailed. As discussed in Chapter 9, the UPA provides in detail for continuation and liquidation of the partnership, effect of partners' power to bind and exist-ing liabilities, partners' rights to wind up, liability of persons continuing the business, and rights of withdrawn partners as against the continuing partnership. It seems to fol-low that the limited partnership statute imports these dissolution consequences. Thus, one court applied the UPA on continuation of the partnership for purposes of winding up where there was no applicable limited partnership provision under ULPA. *See Cheyenne Oil Corp. v. Oil & Gas Ventures,* 42 Del. Ch. 100, 204 A.2d 743 (Del. Sup. 1964).

The few courts that have addressed the issue generally have refused to apply UPA consequences to *limited* partners. For example, *Porter v. Barnhouse,* 354 N.W.2d 227 (Iowa 1984), refused to apply the UPA § 42 which provides for a post-dissolution profit share to a *limited* partner on the ground that a limited partner, unlike a general, has no exposure to continuing liability and no property interest that is used in contin-uing the business.

11.10 Merger and Conversion

RUPA provides for conversion of general partnerships into limited partnerships and vice versa and for mergers of general with limited partnerships. *See* RUPA §§ 901-908. This suggests that general partnership law controls mergers and conversions involving limited partnerships. This ultimately could link the general with the limited partnership statute. Consider the following issues that may arise in linking general and limited partnership law.

(a) RUPA § 902(c) requires a general partnership that has converted to a limited partnership to file a certificate that includes certain information about the conversion. Although the applicable limited partnership statute includes specific formation provi-sions that otherwise would supersede RUPA, a court nevertheless might decide that RUPA applies because RULPA has no merger or conversion provisions. If so, the court might hold that the converted limited partnership was not properly formed even if it complied with the applicable limited partnership statute unless the parties to the conversion complied with the RUPA conversion provisions.

(b) RUPA § 902(e) provides that a general partner who becomes a limited part-ner continues to be liable as a general partner for some post-conversion liabilities to third parties who reasonably believe that the limited partner is a general partner. Thus, a lim-ited partner may be liable under RUPA even if she has fully complied with the condi-tions for limited liability under limited partnership law.

(c) RUPA § 906 requires unanimous partner approval of a merger plan if the applic-able limited partnership statute does not include merger provisions even if the general voting provisions of the limited partnership agreement or statute would not require una-nimity. This means that a merger can be validly approved under the limited partnership statute but not under general partnership law.

(d) RUPA §§ 905 and 907 prescribe the effects of conversions and mergers, respectively. For example, a partner of a party to the merger who does not become a partner of the surviving entity has a dissociated partner's rights under RUPA. However, under a limited partnership statute that does not include merger or conversion provisions, the merger or conversion may be deemed to have the same effect as dissolution on the partners' rights.

Re-RULPA proposes a new Article that would permit conversions to and from, and mergers with, many different types of business associations.

11.11 Taxation of Limited Partnerships

Flow-through partnership taxation is an important reason for selecting the limited partnership form. Limited partnerships originally were constrained by the Kintner rules for partnership tax classification discussed in § 10.05(A)(1). These rules now are of only historical interest in light of the new "check-the-box" tax classification system discussed in § 10.04(A)(4) permitting firms to elect whether to be taxed as partnerships or as corporations. This is likely to eliminate the need for such tax-motivated statutory provisions as restrictions on the transferability of limited partner interests and statutory and contractual provisions for some kind of dissolution just to ensure that the partnership lacks continuity of life.

Internal Revenue Code (26 U.S.C.) § 7704 subjects to corporate tax treatment a "publicly traded partnership" which has ninety per cent or more "passive-type income"—that is, interest, dividends, rents and income from sale of real property or natural resource production. The section defines "publicly traded partnership" as a partnership that has interests which are either "traded on an established securities market" or "readily tradable on a secondary market (or the substantial equivalent thereof)." This definition is broad enough to reach even businesses that are closely held by conventional standards. A limited partnership that meets the qualifications of a "publicly traded partnership" will be taxed as a corporation.

Question

Given the tax-motivated nature of the limited partnership, is this form of business still necessary in light of check the box? In answering this question, consider the functions of the limited partnership management structure, the "control rule" discussed in § 11.05(B)(2), and general partner liability for partnership debts. What if the control rule and general partner liability are eliminated as Re-RULPA proposes?

11.12 Application of the Securities Laws

Limited partnership interests normally are treated as "securities" under the federal securities laws. *See* § 8.02(B), above. Indeed, in the 1970s and 1980s, this was an important segment of the securities markets. One popular type of transaction during the 80s was the "rollup" of privately held limited partnerships into publicly traded so-called "master" limited partnerships in which most interests were held by assignees of limited partners to escape the transfer restrictions discussed above in § 11.07(A). An SEC study reported that between 1985 and 1990 there were registration statements for 65 limited partnership rollups involving approximately 1.2 million investors and a total value of approximately $6.9 billion. Securities and Exchange Commission, Supplemental SEC Staff Report Regarding Roll-ups (Mar. 18, 1991).

The decision to tax publicly traded partnerships as corporations (*see* § 11.11), other changes in tax rules that made such partnerships less attractive as tax shelters, and the collapse of the markets for the real estate and commodities in which the limited partnerships invested had crushing effects on the value and liquidity of interests in these partnerships. The rollups also suffered from questionable economics. The general partners took increased fees or interests off the top and paid investment advisors and others handsome fees. Also, some rollups significantly devalued investors' interests by removing their legal right to cash out of the partnerships.

All of this helped trigger litigation concerning the initial sale of limited partnership interests and the restructuring of existing limited partnerships into publicly traded partnerships. The most publicized claims involved marketing of limited partnerships by Prudential, which has already allocated about half a billion dollars for damage claims. The restructuring transactions triggered actions based not only on inadequate disclosure of the risks inherent in the investments, but also on breach of fiduciary duty in paying limited partners too little for their existing interests which were exchanged for new interests in master limited partnerships.

These claims gave rise to a new securities law, The Limited Partnership Rollup Reform Act of 1993, Pub. L. No. 103-202, 107 Stat. 2344, 2359-67 (1993). The Act, among other things, provides for disclosure requirements in connection with rollups, including a "comprehensible summary" of the transaction that prominently highlights the risks of the rollup in the soliciting materials; requires and regulates fairness opinions; and prohibits compensation of brokers based on the number of consenting votes they solicit or on the ultimate approval of the transaction; restricts certain changes in the financial or governance structure of the firm, such as exchange of contingent for non-contingent interests by general partners; and provides for dissenters' rights in certain situations.

For accounts of the master limited partnership boom, bust and resulting legislation, *see* Shneider, *A Historical View of Limited Partnership Roll-Ups: Causes, Abuses, And Protective Strategies*, 72 DEN. U. L. REV. 403 (1995); Note, *Regulating Rollups: General Partners' Fiduciary Obligations in Light of the Limited Partnership Rollup Reform Act of 1993*, 47 STAN. L. REV. 85 (1994).

Notes and Questions

Analyzing the need for federal regulation. The Rollup Reform Act provides an exceptional level of federal regulation in an area—internal business association governance and structure—that is generally regulated mainly by state law and federal disclosure rules. Are there problems with leaving this area of finance to state law that would not apply to corporations? Although the limited partnership laws provide less participation in governance to limited partners than the corporate statutes allow shareholders, this alone is not a complete explanation. As discussed in § 11.08, state fiduciary duty rules may to some extent compensate for limited partners' inability to participate in management. One possible justification for regulation may be the reduced role of sophisticated institutional investors in limited partnerships as compared with corporations. This is due partly to the fact that limited partnerships initially were marketed as tax shelters for individuals because pass-through tax treatment was of considerably less benefit to institutional investors. Does this suggest a problem with tax rules that influence the structure of investments and induce investors to ignore governance costs? *See* § 10.04(A).

CHAPTER 12
THE LLC

12.01 History and Overview

Like the limited partnership, the limited liability company (LLC) combines limited liability with partnership features, particularly those considered important for tax classification. Unlike the limited partnership, however, LLC statutes generally provide for a default rule of management directly by the members, while permitting the firm to elect management by managers. In either case, members, unlike limited partners (*see* § 11.05(B)), are not liable for participating in control. In a sense, therefore, the LLC is the logical next stage in the evolution of unincorporated limited liability firms.

The first LLC statute was adopted in Wyoming in 1977. The original Wyoming statute was missing some details, such as rules regarding fiduciary duties and the agency powers of members and managers, and borrowed mainly from Wyoming's corporate and limited partnership statutes. By 1988, eleven years after the enactment of the Wyoming statute, only one other state (Florida) had enacted an LLC statute and there were only 26 LLCs in Wyoming. *See* Fonfara & McCool, Comment, *The Wyoming Limited Liability Company: A Viable Alternative to the S Corporation and Limited Partnership?,* 23 LAND & WATER L. REV. 523 (1988).

LLCs truly arrived with Revenue Ruling 88-76, 1988-2 Cumulative Bulletin 361 (1988) in which the IRS classified a Wyoming LLC as a partnership for tax purposes. By mid-1996, all 51 U.S. jurisdictions had adopted LLC statutes, and tens of thousands of LLCs had been formed. The impact of Revenue Ruling 88-76 illustrates the importance of partnership tax classification to the development of the LLC. As discussed throughout this chapter, LLC statutory default rules always have been designed to help ensure that LLCs formed under the statute will be classified as partnerships for tax purposes.

The LLC form has evolved rapidly as LLC statutes have been enacted and amended since 1988. The choice of law provisions in LLC statutes discussed in § 12.05 give LLCs significant mobility. The evolution of the LLC may have been driven to some extent by competition among legislatures and local bar groups to attract foreign firms, or perhaps more importantly to prevent local firms from organizing elsewhere. *See* Goforth, *The Rise of the Limited Liability Company: Evidence of a Race Between the States, But Heading Where?,* 45 SYRACUSE L. REV. 1193 (1995).

As it has evolved, the LLC has become more of a distinct form, and less a hodgepodge of existing corporate and limited partnership rules. LLC statutes also have tended to move away from mandatory rules, such as rules that attempted to ensure that all firms formed under the statute would have partnership tax classification. Although this evolution has produced considerable variation among LLC statutes, some types of provisions, such as those concerning contributions and distributions, have become fairly uniform. In 1992 a committee of the American Bar Association promulgated a Prototype LLC Act. Some statutes, including those in Idaho and Arkansas, have been based closely on this statute.

A Uniform LLC Act ("ULLCA") was promulgated in 1995 and now forms the basis of some or all of several state statutes. For studies of the evolution of LLC law, *see* Ribstein & Kobayashi, *Uniform Laws, Model Laws and ULLCA,* 66 U. COLO. L. REV. 947 (1995); Ribstein, *Statutory Forms for Closely Held Firms: Theories and Evidence,* 73 WASH. U. L.Q. 369 (1995); Kobayashi & Ribstein, *Evolution and Uniformity,* 34 ECONOMIC INQUIRY 464 (July, 1996), *reprinted in* UNCERTAINTY AND ECONOMIC EVOLUTION (John Lott, ed. 1997). For a snapshot of where LLCs stood as of late 1995, *see* Ribstein, *The Emergence of the Limited Liability Company,* 51 BUS. LAW. 1 (1995). LLC statutes are analyzed in detail, with comparative charts, in RIBSTEIN & KEATINGE, RIBSTEIN & KEATINGE ON LIMITED LIABILITY COMPANIES (1992 & Supp.). Among other things, these charts reflect which statutes have borrowed provisions from ULLCA and the Prototype Act.

The LLC has become a much more recognizable form, with a growing amount of case law creating a unique LLC jurisprudence, and more settled tax law eliminating much of the early tax unpredictability. Thus, the reasons for continuing to use the close corporation form are declining. The main remaining reason might be that lawyers trained in the use of close corporations and comfortable with agreements tailored to this form may be reluctant to make the switch.

Problem

The flexibility, flow-through taxation and limited liability of the LLC form means that most firms that are now closely held corporations should at least consider adopting the LLC form. Nevertheless, some may mistrust the novelty of the LLC form or be concerned about specific features. The following planning problem is intended to provide a perspective from which to view the rest of this Chapter.

Your client is a computer software developer who is forming a software firm with some friends, all of whom currently work for other software firms. The client plans to raise just enough money from the friends to establish an initial product, and then to raise additional funds from a venture capital firm. In the long run, if the firm is successful it will probably have a public offering. You have concluded that the firm should be organized as an LLC under the local LLC statute to take advantage of flow-through taxation. You have concluded that the tax savings exceed the costs of forming an LLC. Your client, however, wants you to organize as a corporation. The main sticking points with the client are: (1) a corporate structure would permit the firm to reward the friends' hard work, risk and innovation with stock options; (2) a corporate structure would make it difficult for the venture capital firm to later squeeze out the entrepreneurs as the price of providing badly needed additional funding; and (3) incorporation would facilitate a later public offering.

How would you answer these objections to forming an LLC? What provisions of the LLC operating agreement would respond to the client's concerns enumerated above? Can you think of any other reasons why the firm should be incorporated? For some additional factual background, *see* Bankman, *The Structure of Silicon Valley Startups,* 41 UCLA L. REV. 1737 (1994).

12.02 Forming the LLC

The formation of LLCs involves two procedures—drafting the operating agreement and complying with the requisite formalities for the members to obtain limited liability. These topics will be discussed separately in the following sections.

A. Formal Prerequisites

LLCs, like limited partnerships and corporations, are formed by filing a certificate with the secretary of state or equivalent agency. If the formalities have not been met, the members might be treated as partners and held personally liable for the debts of the firm. In *New Horizons Supply Cooperative v. Haack*, 224 Wis. 2d 644, 590 N.W.2d 282 (1999), the court held that even without direct evidence of the filing of LLC articles the LLC was formed as against a third party creditor based on evidence that the Department of Revenue recognized the existence of the LLC. Some LLC statutes provide, as do many corporate statutes, for liability of those who act on behalf of an LLC that has not been formed. It has been held under one such statute that waiver and estoppel defenses apply, so that plaintiff cannot recover if he knew that the LLC had not been formed (the statute in question had been amended to so provide after the transaction at issue). *See Ruggio v. Vining*, 755 So. 2d 792 (Fla. App. 2000).

B. Conversions of Existing General Partnerships

An important use of the LLC probably will be by existing general partnerships that are seeking to obtain limited liability without having to abandon their existing governance arrangement. Nearly all LLC statutes allow mergers among LLCs, and most between LLCs and other types of business entities. *See, e.g.,* ULLCA § 904(a). Several LLC statutes permit general and limited partnerships, or many different types of business entities, to "convert" to the LLC form simply by making a filing. *See* RIBSTEIN & KEATINGE ON LIMITED LIABILITY COMPANIES, app. 11-1 (tabulating statutory provisions). This procedure does not involve the creation of a technically new "entity," and probably does not trigger tax consequences. *See* Rev. Rul. 95-37, 1995-17 I.R.B. 10 (ruling that this conversion is comparable to a conversion of a limited into a general partnership); Rev. Ruling 84-52, 1984-1 C.B. 157 (conversion of limited into general partnership or vice versa is not a taxable event). However, the fact that a converting partner is no longer liable for the firm's post-conversion debts may have important tax implications for what the partner can deduct on account of her partnership investment.

These statutes raise interesting, and perhaps troubling, questions about the impact of the change in form on existing contracts and creditors. To be sure, none of the statutes would permit a general partner simply to shed existing personal liability. But the former general partners may be able to shed their personal liability for pre-conversion leases and other long-term contracts if courts characterize rental payments and other amounts that accrue after the conversion as new LLC rather than old partnership debts. *See* § 9.05, above. Landlords and other long-term creditors might try to solve this problem by including "anti-assignment" provisions in their contracts that attempt to prevent changes in the nature of the entity that is obligated on the contract. However, most statutory conversion provisions purport to override even these contracts by stating that the entity is unchanged by the transaction and that all property and contracts remain with the converted entity.

Some recent cases deal with these issues. *Town of Vernon v. Rumford Associates IV*, 53 Conn. App. 785, 732 A.2d 779 (1999), held that although an entity that converted into an LLC that then filed for bankruptcy was technically the same entity as its predecessor under Connecticut law, the trial court did not improperly violate a stay of bankruptcy by awarding fees in a foreclosure against the converting entity because the LLC was not automatically a party to the foreclosure. The effect of the Connecticut statute was that the foreclosure action continued "as if the conversion had not occurred" against the predecessor which was not under bankruptcy protection. Note that while ULLCA § 903 provides that the converted entity is the same entity "for all purposes," DEL. CODE tit. 6 § 18-214 provides that the converted LLC is the same entity "for all purposes of the laws of the State of Delaware." Does this mean that the firm may not be the "same entity" for purposes of contracts and other laws?

The conversion provisions generally apply to conversions from partnership to LLC. What if a sole proprietor converts? In *C & J Builders and Remodelers v. Geisenheimer*, 249 Conn. 415, 733 A.2d 193 (1999), the court applied an arbitration clause in a sole proprietor's agreement to a successor LLC, relying in part on Connecticut statutory provisions relating to partnership-LLC conversions and reasoning that conversion provisions should be used as a source of legislative policy. It has also been held, relying in part on *Geisenheimer*, that a professional LLC formed by a sole proprietor lawyer in order to escape a malpractice/fraud judgment would be subject to successor liability for the debts of the sole proprietor. *Baker v. Dorfman*, 2000 WL 1010285 (S.D.N.Y., Jul 21, 2000).

C.   Limited Liability and Veil-Piercing

LLC statutes commonly provide that LLC members are not liable solely by reason of their membership in the LLC. This does not exclude liability for wrongful acts by individual members. For example, in *Pepsi-Cola Bot. Co. of Salisbury, Md. v.*

Handy, 2000 WL 364199 (Del. Ch., Mar 15, 2000), the court held: "[I]f a person makes material misrepresentations to induce a purchaser to purchase a parcel of land at a price far above fair market value, and thereafter forms an LLC to purchase and hold the land, can that person later claim that his status as an LLC member protects him from liability to the purchaser under § 18-303? I think not."

One of the most important open questions about LLC members' liability concerns the grounds on which courts will "pierce the veil" of LLCs and impose liability on LLC members that have complied with statutory formalities. Corporate veil piercing is based on equitable and common-sense grounds that should apply equally to LLCs, including misrepresentation of capitalization or of owners' responsibility for debts, deliberate undercapitalization in the form of excessive dividends, or commingling of the firm's and the owners' assets. Some LLC statutes confirm this by providing that the corporate veil-piercing standard applies to LLCs. These statutes do not necessarily mean, however, that it is irrelevant for veil-piercing that a firm is an LLC rather than a corporation. For example, while a court may hold that the failure to hold meetings or to issue shares is a sort of "tipping factor" supporting piercing the veil in a corporation, the same facts do not necessarily justify veil-piercing in the inherently less formal LLC context. Some LLC statutes confirm this by providing that an LLC's failure to observe certain formalities is not a ground for veil piercing. *See, e.g.,* CA Corp. Code § 1701(a). State statutory variations on veil-piercing statutes are tabulated in Ribstein & Keatinge on Limited Liability Companies, app. 12-1.

Several cases have dealt with veil-piercing in LLCs, generally applying corporate veil-piercing standards. In *Ditty v. Checkrite, Ltd., Inc.,* 973 F. Supp. 1320 (D. Utah 1997) the court refused to pierce the veil to reach the sole owner and officer, reasoning in part:

> That DeLoney played an active role in the firm's business is, at best, only marginally probative of the factors considered when determining whether to pierce the corporate veil. Further, there is no evidence that DeLoney & Associates was improperly organized under the Utah Limited Liability Company Act.

In *Hollowell v. Orleans Regional Hospital,* 1998 WL 283298 (E.D. La. May 29, 1998), at 9-10, *aff'd,* 217 F.3d 379 (5th Cir. 2000), the court said (footnotes and citations omitted):

> ORH is a limited liability company rather than a corporation. No case has yet explicitly held that the "veil" of protection from liability afforded by the limited liability company form of business in Louisiana may be "pierced" in the same manner as the "veil" of protection afforded Louisiana corporations. However, commentators throughout the nation appear to agree that the limited liability company "veil" may be "pierced" in the same manner as the corporate "veil." More specifically, several commentators appear to assume that indeed a Louisiana limited liability company's "veil" may be pierced. As Professor Kalinka notes in her Louisiana Civil Law Treatise on Louisiana Limited Liability Companies and Partnerships, "[t]he same policy considerations in piercing the veil of a corporation apply to an LLC." However, Professor

Kalinka cautions that the analyses between corporate veil piercing and limited liability company veil piercing may not completely overlap, noting that "[b]ecause the Louisiana LLC law requires fewer formalities such as annual elections of directors, keeping minutes, or holding meetings, failure to follow these formalities should not serve as grounds for piercing the veil of an LLC."

With this caveat in mind, this court holds that under Louisiana law the "veil" of protection afforded ORH by its Limited Liability Company form may be "pierced" if in fact ORH was operating as the "alter ego" of ORH's members or if ORH's members were committing fraud or deceit on third parties through ORH. Moreover, the veil provided by the corporate status of ORH's members may also be pierced in like fashion. These questions necessarily involve a fact-intensive review of the relationships among all of the members of ORH in order to make a determination of whether ORH was the "alter ego" of its members or, alternatively, whether ORH's members were using ORH to commit fraud. Accordingly, the court declines to grant summary judgment to any of the defendants, or in favor of the plaintiffs, on the plaintiffs' "veil piercing" claims.

The appellate court, in affirming, held simply that an LLC should be treated like a corporation for veil-piercing purposes. *See* 217 F.3d at 385, n. 7.

New Horizons Supply Cooperative v. Haack, 224 Wis. 2d 644, 590 N.W.2d 282 (Wis. App. 1999), held that it was error to pierce the veil based solely on the LLC's treatment as a partnership for tax purposes in the absence of sufficient evidence that LLC was defendant's "mere instrumentality" or was "used to evade an obligation, to gain an unjust advantage or to commit an injustice" under the corporate veil-piercing standard. But the court held an LLC member personally liable for the LLC's debts for failing to follow statutory procedures requiring notification of creditors. Finally, *Tom Thumb Food Markets, Inc. v. TLH Properties, LLC,* 1999 WL 31168 (Minn. App. Jan. 26, 1999), held that the record did not establish injustice or fundamental unfairness required to pierce the veil in the absence of intent to mislead regarding ownership of property, applying the Minnesota provision cited above.

Courts also may impose liability on LLC members and others for insufficiently identifying their status in transactions with third parties. *Water, Waste and Land v. Lanham*, 955 P. 2d 997 (Colo. 1998), imposed liability on an agent who disclosed only the initials "P.I.I." rather than the full name "Preferred Income Investors, LLC" in dealing with a third party. The court held that the agent was a partially disclosed principal. It interpreted a Colorado statute making the articles notice of facts they disclose as providing that, *if* the name is disclosed, the third party has constructive notice of the LLC's limited liability status and accordingly that managers and members are not liable solely as members.

The Delaware LLC statute provides some relief from veil-piercing liability. It explicitly permits a Delaware LLC to designate series of members, managers or LLC interests with separate rights, powers or duties with respect to specified property or obligations or profits and losses associated with this property or obligations as well as separate business purposes or investment objectives. *See* Del. Code Ann. § 18-215. Most importantly, liabilities may be charged to the property allocated only to one series and not to other series. This may have implications for related firms' ability to avoid veil-piercing liability.

D.   The Two-Member and "For Profit" Requirements

LLC statutes once generally required the LLC to have two members. This requirement was probably best explained by the partnership origins of the LLC. As discussed in Chapter 3, partnership is inherently an "association," which implies multiple members, and the partnership statutes require two or more members. However, as of this writing, only Massachusetts explicitly required LLCs to have two members. Note that, even if sole proprietorships *can* be LLCs, they may not *want* to be because the LLC form is not suited to this type of business. The best solution may be a special form of business designed for sole proprietorships. *See* § 14.05, below.

There is increasing recognition that LLCs may be formed other than to engage in business or to make a profit. Many LLC statutes provide that LLCs may be formed for any lawful "purpose" rather than "business." *See* Ribstein & Keatinge on Limited Liability Companies § 4.10. This helps pave the way for the use of LLCs to protect personal assets from creditors. *See* Ribstein, *Limited Liability Unlimited,* 24 Del. J. Corp. L. 407 (1999). The potential for fraudulent conveyance liability is discussed above in Note 4, p. 328-30.

E.   LLC Operating Agreements

Even if the LLC meets statutory requirements, it is not complete without an operating agreement among the members that sets forth the rules that govern their particular firm. This section discusses some general considerations that need to be taken into account in drafting the LLC operating agreement. Later sections will discuss specific issues that are covered by these agreements.

1.   Statutory Limitations on Operating Agreements

LLC statutes vary in the extent to which the agreement controls over inconsistent provisions in the statute. The most permissive is Delaware's statute, which explicitly gives "maximum effect . . . to the enforceability of limited liability company agreements." Del. Code, tit. 18, § 1101(b). By contrast, ULLCA § 103 provides that certain types of provisions, including fiduciary duty waivers, are unenforceable. Moreover, statutes may change over time, with formerly mandatory rules being changed into default rules.

2. Interpretation of Agreements and Statutes: Linkage with Other Forms

Compared to partnerships, there is relatively little case law interpreting LLC statutes or agreements. Courts undoubtedly will apply cases concerning other types of business associations, particularly since LLC statutes and agreements borrow language from those other forms. But as discussed throughout this chapter, courts should do so cautiously since there are important differences between LLCs and partnerships, limited partnerships and corporations. For example, an LLC is not exactly like a limited partnership since LLC statutes provide by default for direct member management. Even if the LLC opts out of member management and provides for centralized management by managers, the firm still differs from a limited partnership in that all members and managers have limited liability and there is no "control rule" conditioning the limited liability of non-managing members (although as discussed in Chapter 11, the revision of the Revised Uniform Limited Partnership Act may eliminate these differences between the two forms). This may affect other LLC default rules. For example, it arguably follows from the greater participation of LLC members in management that LLC managers' default fiduciary duties need not be as intense as those of general partners in limited partnerships.

12.03 Tax Considerations

As discussed in Chapter 10, an important reason for the development of new unincorporated limited liability business forms was to obtain the tax advantages of partnership over the more constrained "flow-through" taxation available under Subchapter S of the Internal Revenue Code. At one time an LLC had to follow the tax classification rules discussed in § 10.05(A) to be taxed under Subchapter K of the Internal Revenue Code. Under these rules, since an LLC normally had at least one corporate feature (limited liability) it would need to lack at least two of the other three corporate characteristics in order to be classified as a partnership for tax purposes. All this has now been changed by the IRS's "check-the-box" rule discussed in § 10.05(A)(4) which allows closely held domestic unincorporated firms to elect to be taxed as partnerships. Nevertheless, an understanding of the application of the Kintner rules to LLCs is helpful in showing how the LLC form has developed to this point. Legislatures have been careful to preserve the distinction between manager-managed and member-managed LLCs, and to provide for restricted continuity of life and transferability of management interests. In the wake of "check-the-box," many LLC statutes have been amended to blur the distinctions between corporations and partnerships. However, even if LLCs can now easily avoid corporate taxation, the form of the business may continue to matter for other tax purposes, such as which business owners are subject to self-employment tax. *See generally* Frost, *"Square Peg, Meet Round Hole": Classifying LLC Members as "General Partners" or "Limited Partners" for Federal Tax Purposes,* TAXES 676 (December, 1995).

12.04 Application of Regulatory Statutes

Regulatory statutes may play an important role in drafting, planning and forming the LLC. For example, the employment discrimination laws, which are discussed in section 3.03(A), also may apply to LLCs. The application of the bankruptcy laws is discussed below in Note 4, p. 362. This section discusses the application of federal and state securities laws and the possibly surprising application of a wide variety of other laws.

A. Securities Laws

If federal and state securities laws apply to LLCs, they would require such firms to go through a registration and disclosure process in order to sell their interests, and may subject LLCs to extensive administrative and civil liabilities under federal and state antifraud rules, in particular Section 10(b) of the Securities and Exchange Act of 1934. General partnership interests usually are not "securities" (*see* § 3.03(A)) while limited partnership interests usually are (*see* § 11.12). How should these laws apply to LLC interests?

Some state law rulings have held that LLC interests are securities under definitions similar to the federal definition, and some state statutes now explicitly define at least some types of LLC interests—particularly manager-managed LLCs—as "securities." *See* RIBSTEIN & KEATINGE ON LIMITED LIABILITY COMPANIES § 14.03.

As for treatment of LLCs under the federal securities laws, the meager results have been mixed. For cases holding that LLC interests were or may be securities *see SEC v. Parkersburg Wireless Ltd. Liability Corp.*, 991 F. Supp. 6 (D.D.C. 1997) (membership interests in wireless cable firm); *KFC Ventures, L.L.C. v. Metaire Medical Equipment Leasing Corp.*, 2000 WL 726877 (E.D. La., Jun 05, 2000) (refusing to dismiss securities law claim, holding that interests in manager-managed LLC may be securities). For cases holding that LLC interests were not securities, *see Great Lakes Chemical Corp. v. Monsanto Co.*, 96 F. Supp. 2d 376 (D. Del. 2000) (purchase of 100% of interests of manager-managed LLC, where operating agreement gave members power to remove managers and dissolve the firm); *Keith v. Black Diamond Advisors*, 48 F. Supp. 2d 326 (S.D.N.Y. 1999) ("member-managed" New York LLC, applying case law on partnership interests as securities discussed in § 3.03(B)).

An argument against treating LLC interests as "securities" runs like this: Because LLCs have the critical features of flexibility of management structure and members' opportunity to participate in control without jeopardizing their limited liability, LLC owners do not expect to be relying on the "efforts of others." Even if there are some differences between LLCs and general partnerships that arguably relate to the "security" characterization, particularly including the ability to centralize management, most investors probably expect LLCs to be like partnerships because they are so classified under all-important tax law. Moreover, considerations of certainty and predictability justify applying to LLCs the strong partnership-type presumption against characterizing the interests as securities. Otherwise, wary of making a mistake about the effect of subtle differences in members' management participation and sophistication, entrepreneurs would have to register *all* LLCs—and, for that matter, many non-LLC investments—regardless of the lack of a general need for securities law protection in this context. *See* Ribstein, *Form and Substance in the Definition of a "Security": The Case of Limited Liability Companies,* 51 WASH. & LEE L. REV. 807 (1994). For other views on whether LLC interests should be treated as "securities," *see* Goforth, *Why Limited Liability Company Membership Interests Should Not Be Treated As Securities And Possible Steps To Encourage The Result,* 45 HASTINGS L.J. 1223 (1994); Sargent, *Are Limited Liability Company Interests Securities?,* 19 PEPP. L. REV. 1069 (1992) (LLC interests normally should not be securities); Steinberg & Conway, *The Limited Liability Company as a Security,* 19 PEPP. L. REV. 1105 (1992) (LLC interests normally should be securities).

Policy considerations aside, from a planning standpoint it is important to keep in mind that centrally managed LLCs are more likely than member-managed firms to be characterized as securities under the "efforts-of-others" *Howey* factor (*see* § 3.03(B)) and state definitions that define LLC interests as securities unless all members participate in management. This meshes with tax law, which generally (but not always) makes it easier for owner-managed LLCs to be classified as partnerships. Yet LLCs need to balance tax and securities considerations against internal governance considerations. Centralized management may be convenient for many firms, particularly since the members' limited liability makes passivity feasible. Firms could resolve this conflict by electing member-management but designating managing members or non-member executives. While this approach may sacrifice some ability to focus agency power in the management group, this cost may be worth the regulatory and tax benefits of formally decentralizing management. For a discussion of the relationship of LLC management options and federal securities law, *see* Goforth, *Continuing Obstacles to Freedom of Choice for Management Structure in LLCs,* 1 J. SMALL & EM. BUS. LAW 165 (1997).

B.   Other Regulatory Statutes

As illustrated by the following case, the choice of the LLC form may be unexpectedly relevant in a wide variety of contexts in addition to those already mentioned.

Meyer v. Oklahoma Alcoholic Beverage Laws Enforcement Commission
890 P.2d 1361 (1995)

STUBBLEFIELD, Judge.

This is an appeal from the district court's reversal of the declaratory ruling of the Oklahoma Alcoholic Beverage Laws Enforcement Commission (ABLE) that a newly created form of business entity, a limited liability company (LLC), is not entitled to receive and hold a retail package store license. Wanda L. Meyer, holder of a retail package store license, initiated these proceedings when she petitioned ABLE requesting a declaratory judgment that she could hold the license as an LLC, a business entity authorized by the Oklahoma Legislature in 1992 through the adoption of the Oklahoma Limited Liability Company Act (OLLC Act), 18 O.S. SUPP. 1992 §§ 2000 through 2060. ABLE denied the petition, thus holding that an LLC is not eligible to hold a retail package store license.

Meyer, pursuant to the provisions of the Administrative Procedures Act, 75 O.S.1991 §§ 250-323, appealed the ABLE decision to the district court. That court focused on two provisions of the law: (1) The Oklahoma constitutional provision, which only prohibits licensing of "corporations, business trusts, and secret partnerships," OKLA. CONST., art. 28, § 10; and, (2) The provision in the LLC Act that authorized LLCs to "conduct business in any state for any lawful purpose, except the business of banking and insurance," 18 O.S. SUPP. 1992 § 2002 (footnote omitted). Based upon those provisions, and a conclusion that the provisions of the Oklahoma Alcoholic Beverage Control Act "do not prohibit an LLC from holding a package store license," the trial court reversed the ABLE ruling and ordered it to "issue such license to petitioner as a limited liability company."

ABLE appeals, claiming that the order of the lower court is contrary to law in that an LLC is not authorized to hold a package store license. ABLE further claims that it could not be ordered to grant a license when no application by Meyer, as an LLC, was made. * * *

The issue is one of first impression—whether an LLC, created pursuant to the OLLC Act, is eligible for issuance of a retail package store liquor license. Indeed, the issue could only have arisen after the 1992 legislative creation of the new form of business entity. LLCs were not a recognized business entity in this state at the time of adoption of our Constitution or at the time of adoption of the Oklahoma Alcoholic Beverage Control Act. However, both the Constitution and the Oklahoma Alcoholic Beverage Control Act do address qualifications of an applicant for a package store license. We conclude that the constitutional directives do prohibit the holding of a license by an LLC and, thus, the lower court did err in its conclusion. * * *

It is true, as noted by the trial court in its decision, that the specific constitutional prohibitions regarding license holders includes only corporations, business trusts, and secret partnerships. Of course, neither the framers nor amenders of the Constitution could have addressed the qualification or disqualification of LLCs as retail package store licensees, because the business entity did not exist in this state until 1992. Indeed, the testimony before ABLE indicated that the business form did not exist in this country until 1977. However, the Constitution did address all of the business formats as they existed at the time of adoption of the article on alcoholic beverage laws and enforcement and, significantly, section 4 names only individuals and partnerships as those entities to which a license may be issued.

Likewise, it is true that the Oklahoma Alcoholic Beverage Control Act does not prohibit an LLC from holding a license. However, what the Act does or does not prohibit is not dispositive because the Act does not purport to address the nature of the applicant—a matter controlled by the constitutional provisions. The Act does restate some of the disqualifications set forth in section 10 of the Constitution regarding residency, criminal conviction, etc., but does not purport to prohibit the licensing of corporations, business trusts and secret partnerships, which are specifically prohibited as licensees by the Constitution. It appears that qualification as a license holder, with regard to types of business entities, was left to the constitutional pronouncement.

When the legislature adopted the OLLC Act, it provided that "[a] limited liability company may be organized under this act and may conduct business in any state for any lawful purpose, except the business of banking and insurance." 18 O.S. SUPP. 1992 § 2002 (footnote omitted). Of course, such a legislative enactment could not countermand a constitutional prohibition, even if that had been the legislative intent. However, we do not believe the language of section 2002 indicates a legislative intent to extend the authority of LLCs in ways specifically prohibited elsewhere by statute, and particularly not to an act prohibited by the Oklahoma Constitution. Thus, we do not view section 2002 of the OLLC Act as sanction for the operation of a retail package store by an LLC.

If we interpreted section 2002 as argued by Meyer, then it could, in some respects, negate specific declarations of OKLA. CONST., art. 28, § 10. An LLC—neither a person, corporation nor partnership—is not specifically named in section 10 and, thus, if eligible as a licensee, its members would not be subject to the same restrictions regarding residence, violations of the liquor laws and status as a felon, which are imposed upon members of other permissible business entity licensees. Even the similar prohibitions in 37 O.S. 1991 § 527, are not drawn with this new business entity in mind and would not clearly apply to LLC members. Meyer apparently recognized this fundamental problem with the LLC business entity and by company rule restricted membership in keeping with the prohibitions of the Constitution and section 527. However, these restrictions are set out in fully amendable articles. 18 O.S. SUPP. 1992 § 2011. Furthermore, the question is not whether the members of this particular LLC are eligible applicants because those members are not the applicants. The applicant is the LLC, and the question is whether the business entity is a permissible license holder.

Meyer argues that an LLC is essentially a partnership. However, the act creating the business form is in Title 18, which is entitled "Corporations." Furthermore, a provision in our Uniform Partnership Act states that "any association formed under any other statute of this state . . . is not a partnership under this act, unless such association would have been a partnership in this state prior to adoption of this act." 54 O.S. 1991 § 206(2).

Meyer claims that its expert witness, the only witness in all the proceedings, testified that an LLC was a partnership. However, contrary to Meyer's contention, the witness's testimony was not so unequivocal. The totality of the testimony was that an LLC is a hybrid that has attributes of both corporations and partnerships. The witness indicated an LLC is more like a partnership, but noted the primary difference is that all owners/members have limited liability in an LLC—something not found in partnerships. We conclude that the limitation of liability of all LLC members is a substantial difference especially relevant to the provisions of our liquor laws.

Our examination of the pertinent constitutional provisions leads us to conclude that their evident purpose was the assignment of personal responsibility for compliance with the liquor laws. Thus, business forms that did not insure such personal responsibility were excluded from eligibility for licensing.

The OLLC Act does exactly what its name indicates. It creates a form of business that has as its most important feature the limitation of liability of its members. This liability limitation is also a shield from the very responsibility and accountability that the constitutional provisions regarding alcoholic beverage laws and enforcement sought to impose.

The trial court reversed the ABLE decision as contrary to law. Based upon the foregoing analysis, we conclude that there was no such error and that the trial court erred in reversing the ABLE decision. Because of our ruling, we do not need to address ABLE's contention that the trial court erred in ordering it to grant a license when an application had not been made.

The judgment of the trial court is REVERSED.

Notes and Questions

1. **LLCs under other regulatory statutes.** Several cases have examined the status of LLCs under regulatory statutes. In *R & R Marketing, L.L.C. v. Brown-Forman Corp.*, 307 N.J. Super. 474, 704 A.2d 1327 (1998), the appellate division held against summary judgment for a liquor company on a claim that it violated New Jersey's wholesaler anti-discrimination statute by refusing to supply two of its authorized distributors who combined their businesses into an LLC that was not itself an authorized distributor. The court relied in part on the legislature's purpose in enacting the LLC act to encourage capital investment in New Jersey. The Supreme Court, however, remanded to the appropriate administrative agency to determine, among other things, whether the restructuring materially altered the distribution rights that the supplier had granted to the constituent entities. 158 N.J. 170, 729 A.2d 1 (1999). *Exchange Point LLC v. SEC*, 1999 WL 386736 (S.D.N.Y. June 10, 1999) held that an LLC was not an individual or small partnership entitled to standing under the Right to Financial Privacy Act of 1978. The court relied on the plain meaning approach to interpreting the RFPA, as well as the LLC's liability protection, which implied a greater separation between the owners and the entity and therefore a weaker claim to privacy protection under the Act. *Fraser v. Major League Soccer, L.L.C.*, 97 F. Supp. 2d 130, 134 (D. Mass. 2000) held that an LLC should be treated like a corporation under the antitrust laws, citing the resemblance between LLC owners and shareholders in limited liability and other respects, and noting the holdings of other courts in other contexts, including *Exchange Point LLC*, above.

2. **Redrafting the statute.** Do you suppose the result in *Meyer* was what the legislature intended in drafting the LLC act? How might the legislature have made its intention clearer? Might the result have differed if the LLC statute had provided that LLCs can engage in any business that is open to partnerships, limited partnerships and corporations? Consider the approach of the following South Carolina provision (S.C. CODE § 33-44-1205) to issues like the one in *Meyer*: "Except (1) as otherwise required by the context, (2) as inconsistent with the provisions of this chapter, and (3) for this chapter . . . , the term 'partnership' or 'general partnership,' when used in any other statute or in any regulation, includes and also means 'limited liability company.'"

12.05 Choice of State Law

An LLC generally may choose the state law that will provide the default rules for management, financial, fiduciary duty and other internal governance matters. Indeed, choice of state law is an important initial planning consideration. Unlike general partnerships (*see* § 3.04, above), LLC statutes have adopted something like the corporate "internal affairs" rule, which applies the law of the state of organization wherever the LLC does business. Although all LLC statutes require foreign LLCs that are transacting business in the state to register or qualify, the choice-of-law provisions generally apply to any "foreign limited liability company" irrespective of registration or qualification. This means that there are now two main questions regarding choice of law for LLCs, which are discussed in the following subsections: (1) what is a "foreign LLC"? and (2) to what matters does the formation state law apply under foreign LLC statutory provisions?

A. Definition of Foreign LLC

Only a firm that is a "foreign limited liability company" may do business in a state subject to its formation-state law. Other types of firms are subject to the vagaries of the common law conflict of laws rules discussed in § 3.04. States take one of several general approaches to defining foreign LLCs that vary according to whether the firm may be one formed under the laws of a U.S. or non-U.S. jurisdiction, and whether the foreign jurisdiction's characterization of the firm as a "limited liability company" is accepted or whether the firm is defined in terms of particular characteristics, such as limited liability. *See* RIBSTEIN & KEATINGE ON LIMITED LIABILITY COMPANIES, app. 13-1 (tabulating statutory provisions). The approaches attempt to balance the costs and benefits of flexibility. An approach that looks to whether the firm is an LLC in a U.S. jurisdiction is no longer as potentially open-ended as it might once have been because state LLC statutes do not fundamentally vary. Applying this approach to LLCs formed in foreign countries, however, might open the door somewhat further.

In evaluating the various approaches, it is important to ask what problems the statutory definitions of foreign LLCs seek to address. Why not simply allow any firm to be characterized as a foreign LLC for choice-of-law purposes? This would amount to enforcing the parties' chosen law in all kinds of business associations. While there are strong policy arguments favoring such an approach (*see generally* Ribstein, *Choosing Law By Contract,* 18 J. CORP. L. 245 (1993); Ribstein, *Delaware, Lawyers and Choice of Law,* 19 DEL. J. C. L. 999 (1994)), some states may not be prepared to go this far.

B. Scope of Application of Formation—State Law

Most LLC statutes provide that the law of the organization jurisdiction governs the internal affairs, organization or liability of members of foreign LLC. A couple provide that the formation jurisdiction's law governs the internal affairs or organization of a foreign LLC but do not refer to member liability. *See* RIBSTEIN & KEATINGE ON LIMITED LIABILITY COMPANIES, app. 13-1 (tabulating statutory provisions). The apparent distinction among the provisions with regard to member liability is not as important as it might seem on the surface. Since all LLC statutes provide that members are not liable as such, the basic rule on liability does not depend on whether a jurisdiction applies its own or the formation state's law. As discussed below, however, the distinction may matter to the application of veil-piercing law.

The main questions about choice of law under foreign LLC provisions concern the application of formation-state law to dealings with third parties apart from whether members have limited liability. First, the statutes generally do not make clear which state's law controls members' power to bind the LLC in third-party transactions. Choice of law may be significant if, for example, the formation state law provides that a non-managing member cannot bind a manager-managed firm but the operation state statute does not make this clear. This may be a matter of internal affairs or organization or one of liability of the *members*. In either case, it is so bound up with the internal allocation of power that third parties would expect to look to formation state law. Moreover, authority issues normally do not implicate the sort of strong policies of the operation state that might apply to, for example, the scope of vicarious liability.

A second question concerns the extent to which the LLC is subject to regulatory law in the operation state that differs from comparable law in the formation state, such as the rules limiting the availability of the LLC form to professionals and other types of businesses. This sort of issue is almost certainly governed by the operation state's law. Many LLC statutes make this clear by providing that a foreign LLC does not have any greater rights or privileges than, or is subject to same limitations as, a domestic LLC or cannot engage in a transaction in which a domestic LLC cannot engage (*e.g.,* ULLCA § 1001(c)). *See* RIBSTEIN & KEATINGE ON LIMITED LIABILITY COMPANIES, app. 13-1 (tabulating statutory provisions). The special problems of professional firms are discussed below Note 7, p. 359.

A third specific problem concerns which state's law on veil-piercing applies. Even under statutes that apply formation state law on member liabilities, organization state law may apply on veil-piercing. The resolution of this issue ultimately depends on how courts characterize veil-piercing. Most veil-piercing arguably amounts either to liability for misrepresentations to third parties about the extent of capitalization or the nature of the entity or to a kind of fraudulent conveyance liability. Only in the relatively rare case that the courts pierce for initial undercapitalization or for failure to adhere to formalities unaccompanied by fraud is there a strong argument that veil-piercing should be treated as part of the basic liability limitation. It is relevant in this regard that some statutes restrict veil-piercing for non-compliance with formalities. *See* § 12.02(B), above.

The parties to an LLC might try to increase the probability that formation state law will be applied by providing in the operating agreement that the agreement and the parties' rights shall be determined according to the law of the formation state even if another state's law would be applied under conflict of laws principles in the absence of this provision. However, there is some chance a court will disregard the provision and apply the other state's law anyway.

12.06 Professional Firms as LLCs

One of the most important uses of the LLC form is by professional firms, particularly including law and accounting firms. Although the following discussion focuses on law firms, the issues covered arise with respect to other types of professional firms.

Law and other professional firms long have been able to organize as professional corporations, which are now permitted in every state. Under all of these statutes professionals are liable for their own acts. Many permit members to limit their personal liability for non-professional contract debts and for co-members' acts, at least if those acts are not done under the defendant's supervision or control. This liability echoes both the liability under ethical rules discussed below in this section and under LLP statutes discussed below in § 13.03(B).

The professional corporation was not a complete solution for law firms in search of limited liability because, as in other corporations, earnings may be taxed twice—at the corporate level when earned, and again at the shareholder level when distributed. This is particularly a problem for law and other professional firms, which tend to distribute most of their earnings. Large professional firms cannot take advantage of Subchapter S of the Internal Revenue Code (*see* § 10.02, above) because they have more than the statutory limit of 75 members.

The advent of the LLC, in which members can combine personal liability and flow-through taxation, was particularly significant for lawyers and accountants who were increasingly exposed to liability risk from securities and savings and loan litigation. However, as discussed in the following notes and questions, professionals' use of the LLC is subject to restrictions that do not apply to other types of firms. For general discussions of the law and policy relating to limiting liability in law firms, *see* Johnson, *Limited Liability for Attorneys: General Partners Need Not Apply*, 51 BUS. LAW 85 (1995); Fortney, *Am I My Partner's Keeper? Peer Review in Law Firms*, 66 U. COLO. L. REV. 329 (1995); Fortney, *Professional Responsibility and Liability Issues Related to Limited Liability Law Partnerships*, 39 S. TEX. L. REV. 399 (1998); Fortney, *Seeking Shelter in the Minefield of Unintended Consequences—The Traps of Limited Liability Law Firms*, 54 WASH. & LEE L. REV. 717 (1997); Goforth, *Limiting the Liability of General Partners in LLPs: An Analysis of Statutory Alternatives*, 75 OR. L. REV. 1139 (1996); Hamilton, *Registered Limited Liability Partnerships: Present at the Birth (Nearly)*, 66 U. COLO. L. REV. 1065 (1995); Ribstein, *Possible Futures for Closely Held Firms*, 64 U. CIN. L. REV. 319 (1996).

Notes and Questions

1. **LLC statutes.** Most states either explicitly authorize use of LLCs by professional firms, usually under separate provisions that apply to professional firms. Professional LLCs are likely to raise issues similar to those in professional partnerships. For a case interpreting a law firm LLC agreement on work-in-process (*see* § 9.06(C), above), *see* *Goldstein and Price, L.C. v. Tonkin & Mondl, L.C.,* 974 S.W.2d 543 (Mo. App. 1998). The court held that a withdrawing member was not entitled to share in a post-withdrawal contingency fee under an operating agreement providing for payment of a withdrawing member's capital contribution and share of billed and unpaid fees, but not for unbilled work in progress.

2. **Licensing statutes and court rules.** In order for a professional firm to determine whether it can use the LLC statute it must also check the relevant licensing statute or, in the case of lawyers, the local supreme court or bar rule. The Colorado Supreme Court, for example, allows law firms to be LLCs (*see* Supreme Court Rule 265 I.A.). In other states, the state bar regulates lawyer liability. Several states have issued opinions that explicitly authorize law firms to practice as LLCs. *See, e.g.,* Legal Ethics Committee of the District of Columbia Bar Opinion No. 235 (approved February 16, 1993), *amended by* Opinion No. 254 (March 21, 1995); New York County Lawyers' Ethics Opinion No. 703 (November 28, 1994); Assn. of the Bar of the City of N.Y., Formal Op. No. 1995-7 (May 31, 1995).

3. **Legal restrictions on the scope of limited liability.** Even if the general LLC statute completely limits members' liabilities for the firm's debts, professionals are subject to the professional corporation restrictions on liability limits discussed above.

4. **Ethical restrictions on scope of limited liability.** Even if there is no *legal* limitation on the scope of limited liability, there are restrictions under ethical rules. Under both the Model Code of Professional Responsibility § 6-102(a) and Model Rules of Professional Conduct, Rule 18(h), lawyers cannot limit their liability for their own malpractice. ABA Comm. on Ethics and Professional Responsibility, Formal Op. 96-401 (1996) held that Rule 1.8(h) does not apply to limitations on vicarious liability. Model Rule 5.1 provides that a law firm partner must "make reasonable efforts to ensure that the firm has in effect measures giving reasonable assurance that all lawyers in the firm conform to the Rules of Professional Conduct" and "a lawyer having direct supervisory authority over another lawyer shall make reasonable efforts to ensure that the other lawyer conforms to the Rules of Professional Conduct." The law partner or supervisor is responsible for another lawyer's violation of the rules if the lawyer "knows of the conduct at the time when its consequences can be avoided or mitigated but fails to take reasonable remedial action." It has been held that these rules do not give rise to vicarious liability. *See Stewart v. Coffman,* 748 P.2d 579, 581 (Utah Ct. App. 1988), *cert. granted,* 765 P.2d 1277 (Utah 1988), *cert. dismissed,* Aug. 19, 1988 (unpublished order). However, it is not clear that all courts will so hold. For a discussion of ethical rules as a basis of liability *see* Keatinge, *The Floggings Will Continue Until Morale Improves: the Supervising Attorney and His or Her Firm,* 39 S. Tex. L. Rev. 279, 292-94 (1998). For a discussion of ethical restrictions on limited liability *see* Wolfram, *Inherent Powers in the Crucible of Lawyer Self-Protection: Reflections on the LLP Campaign,* 39 S. Tex. L. Rev. 359 (1998) (arguing that Rule 1.8(h) does apply to limited liability and that courts' inherent powers to regulate the legal profession take precedence over statutory liability limitations).

5. **The ALI and limited liability.** Proposed in the midst of the rapid spread of LLC statutes, The American Law Institute, Restatement of the Law Governing Lawyers (Tentative Draft No. 7) (Apr. 7, 1994) stated that "A law firm and each of its principals is civilly liable for damages legally caused to a person by the wrongful act or omission of any principal or employee of the firm acting in the ordinary course of the firm's business or with actual authority." This proposed section was withdrawn after the ALI's 1994

meeting. The final version of the Restatement of the Law (Third) Law Governing Lawyers, Section 58 (1998) provides: "A principal of a law firm organized other than as a general partnership without limited liability as authorized by law is vicariously liable for the acts of another principal or employee of the firm to the extent provided by law."

6. **Notice.** A law firm that becomes an LLC may have to give detailed notice of the change. This issue is discussed below in § 13.05(E) in connection with the registration to become a limited liability partnership.

7. **Multistate professional firms.** The general rules on choice of law for LLCs may not apply to professional firms. This may pose special problems for large law or accounting firms that practice in many states. A multistate firm operating in a state that restricts the use of the LLC form by professionals (*see* Notes 1-2) may have to maintain separate names, letterheads, and the like for all of its clients in each state. Even if the firm takes these precautions, it might be misleading clients and violating the law in their home states because of what they must do in their states of operation. As a result of these problems, an interstate firm that cannot operate as an LLC in *every* state may not be able to operate as one in *any* state.

Even if the firm may practice everywhere as an LLC, its members' liability limitation may differ from state to state under the rules discussed in Notes 3 and 4. For example, if a firm that is based and organized in State A, which permits its members to limit their vicarious liability, commits malpractice and is sued in State B, which does not, it is not clear whether State A's liability limitation applies to State A lawyers, State B lawyers, both or neither. State B may regard this application of a local regulatory rule as not subject to the general "internal affairs" provision of the LLC statute discussed above in § 12.05. State B members may want to be indemnified, or at least compensated for their extra risk, by the State A members. Apart from the extra contracting costs of these special provisions, indemnification may be a problem for the State A lawyers, who may find themselves being held personally liable to creditors as a result of the indemnification despite the general liability limitation. *See* § 13.03(G)-(H) for analogous problems facing LLPs.

These problems make a strong argument for enforcing the formation state's professional firm liability rules. On the other hand, some might argue that this would lead to a "race to the bottom" in professional liability rules. The strength of this counter-argument depends largely on the policy arguments concerning limited liability in professional firms (*see* Note 8) and on whether clients should be bound to the contracts they make with lawyers regarding such liability.

8. **Policy issues.** In answering the issues raised by the above notes, it is helpful to confront the basic policy issue of whether professional firms *should* have limited liability. Since professionals often have personal wealth but the firm owns little marketable assets, unlimited liability arguably helps ensure that professionals will monitor their co-partners' work. Yet this may impose heavy burdens on professionals, particularly in relatively large firms where each partner may be quite remote from negligent conduct. *See* Ribstein, *The Deregulation of Limited Liability and the Death of Partnership,* 70 WASH. U. L.Q. 417, 434-435 (1992). Moreover, clients may get little benefit from professionals'

second-guessing their co-partners' professional decisions. Clients themselves, such as the corporate clients of large law firms, may be able to monitor their own cases through legal departments. And the larger law firms often have significant tangible assets and the intangible asset of reputation, both of which protect clients. Limited liability may restrict the size of law firms, thereby reducing their ability to provide this protection. *See* Ribstein, *Ethical Rules, Agency Costs and Law Firm Structure*, 84 VA. L. REV. 1707 (1998). In smaller firms, where minimum capitalization may be a problem, the professionals are usually directly liable for their own and their partners' malpractice. Finally, even if vicarious liability is appropriate for some firms, there is a further question whether firms should be able to decide for themselves whether vicarious liability should apply, or instead decide to become LLCs or LLPs.

12.07 Members' Financial Rights and Obligations

This Section discusses the financial structure of LLCs, including both rules allocating these rights internally and owners' obligations to creditors.

A.   Internal Allocation of Financial Interests

LLC statutes differ regarding default allocation of financial rights. Some have a rule of partnership-type equal allocation among the members. This provides a relatively simple default structure that firms can contract around. Most statutes follow a corporate/limited partnership model by allocating financial rights pro rata by contributions or the value of members' interests. This reflects the fact that financial contributions are more important in limited liability firms than they are in general partnerships, where members necessarily contribute their personal credit. However, LLCs differ from corporations in not using share certificates as a default method of allocating or reflecting financial interests (although many statutes expressly permit LLCs to issue share certificates).

Note that under any of these rules LLCs generally establish accounts and customize allocation of financial rights in the operating agreement along the general lines discussed for general partnerships in Chapter 4. See, especially, the discussion of partnership capital accounts in § 4.04. Some drafting considerations are discussed in the Notes below.

B.   Member Contributions

As in corporations and limited partnerships, but unlike general partnerships, one usually becomes an LLC member by making a contribution to the firm's capital. As in limited partnership statutes (*see* § 11.04(A)), such contributions usually are defined very broadly to include even obligations to perform services.

C.   Members' Liability to Creditors of the LLC

As noted at the beginning of this Chapter, an important aspect of LLCs is that they offer members corporate-type limited liability. However, LLC members may be liable to creditors under several circumstances, as where a court pierces the veil (*see* § 12.02(C)), when the members themselves have committed actionable wrongs, for debts the members contractually assume or guarantee, and on account of unpaid contributions or excessive distributions.

Some statutes include a variation on the guarantee by providing that members may agree to be held liable for *all* or some of the LLC's debts if, in addition to the member's agreement, the liability is stated in the articles of organization. *See* ULLCA § 303(c). This lets some members broadly erase the liability limitation without having to contract with individual creditors. A member's assumption of liability may have tax consequences in that the member who bears an economic risk of loss may increase her tax basis in the LLC for purposes of computing her gain on a later sale of the interest, and may be able to deduct tax losses relating to the indebtedness. *See* I.R.C. §§ 704(b) and 752. Whether the member bears the economic risk of loss depends (under Treas. Reg. § 1.752-2) on, among other things, whether the partner is entitled to reimbursement for the liability from another member, and on how contingent the member's obligation is.

LLC statutes, like statutes for other limited-liability firms, include rules designed to ensure that members leave some money in the firm for creditors. These rules are usually closely based on the limited partnership provisions discussed in § 11.04. Most provide that a member whose contribution obligation is compromised by consent of the other members nevertheless may have to honor the original promise for the benefit of creditors who extended credit in reliance on the contribution before being notified of the compromise. *See, e.g.,* ULLCA § 402(b).

Most statutes also provide for member liability for receiving distributions made by an insolvent LLC and, under some of the earliest statutes, by a solvent LLC that is later unable to pay its debts. Even without such rules, creditors may reach excessive distributions by insolvent firms under fraudulent conveyance law. Accordingly, the rules add little creditor protection while creating potential difficulties for informal firms or for firms that ordinarily distribute most of their income.

Notes and Questions

1. **Initial Contributions.** Operating agreements conventionally list the amounts, value and time of each member's initial contribution or contribution obligation. *See* paragraph 3.1 of the Chameleon agreement. Since these are equity investments, the agreement normally makes clear that the contributions earn no interest, by analogy to the partnership rule (*see* § 4.02). The agreement may also provide for enforcement of contribution obligations.

2. **Additional Contributions.** The operating agreement may provide for additional contributions. *See* paragraph 3.3 of the Chameleon agreement. Such contributions

may increase the voting power and financial rights of the members who make them. In corporations, this problem is addressed by giving shareholders "preemptive rights" to purchase additional shares. LLCs, which normally do not provide for shares, may provide comparable protection by providing that the members may make additional contributions only when they are called for by the managers, and then only in proportion to their existing financial shares. The agreement also may provide for a procedure by which additional contributions can be required or "assessed." Although this helps ensure future funding, it can impose sudden burdens on the members, help the majority to squeeze out the minority, and perhaps even provide a basis for creditor suits against the partners (*see* Note 3). In light of these dangers, assessment procedures are rarely used. Indeed, the agreement may make clear that members cannot be assessed beyond their initial contribution obligation.

3. **Creditors' rights to enforce contribution obligations.** Even where the members decide not to enforce contribution obligations, creditors may step in and claim that they are third party beneficiaries of members' original contribution promises. As discussed in § 11.04(C) concerning limited partnerships, creditors may be able to enforce assessments made against partners. Limited partnership case law may be applied in interpreting closely similar LLC creditor protection provisions. The members may try to block creditor rights by an operating agreement provision which says that the operating agreement is "not intended for the benefit of any creditor . . . ." However, *Builders Steel Co., Inc. v. Hycore, Inc.,* 877 P.2d 1168 (Okla. App. 1994), held that limited partners were liable to creditors for assessments noted in the certificate and refused to enforce the certificate's further statement that creditors may not rely on the assessments because of the limitations in RULPA § 208 on the effect of the articles as notice to third parties. How, then, can members minimize potential liabilities to creditors? How effective would it be if the members limited the amount, purposes, and conditions of the obligation? What if they limited the remedy to, for example, dilution or elimination of the defaulting member's interest, or provided that the defaulting member has no personal liability to any member for its obligation or failure to contribute? *See Chandler Medical,* Section 9.06(B), above. Can the creditor have any greater remedies against the defaulter than do the other members? Note that reducing enforcement of the members' obligations to contribute simultaneously diminishes the firm's ability to obtain the cash when it needs it. Mere dilution of the interest of the defaulting partner may not be much of a penalty in a cash-strapped firm that is not worth much at the time of the capital call. In contrast to the partnership situation involved in *Chandler Medical,* members who walk away from the firm probably need not fear that they will have personal liabilities in connection with the eventual liquidation.

4. **Application of bankruptcy law.** A bankrupt partnership's trustee in bankruptcy may enforce partners' contribution obligations, while creditors may be stayed, or more likely enjoined, from collecting partnership debts from individual partners. *See* Note 3, p. 139. Although an LLC is probably subject to the bankruptcy laws, it is not clear whether these partnership rules apply to LLCs. *See generally* RIBSTEIN & KEATINGE ON

LIMITED LIABILITY COMPANIES § 14.02. The application of the bankruptcy laws to LLCs is discussed further below in Note 7, p. 375.

5. **Capital Accounts.** Like partnership agreements (*see* § 4.04), LLC operating agreements normally provide for the maintenance of "capital accounts." *See* paragraph 3.4 of the Chameleon agreement. These accounts provide an individualized report of members' financial interests. In general, they reflect members' contributions, profits and other gains, distributions to the members, and members' shares of losses and other negative adjustments. Agreement provisions concerning capital accounts are often quite complex and heavily influenced by tax considerations.

6. **Allocations of profits and losses.** Even if the statute provides for per capita allocation among the partners as a default rule, the agreement normally provides for apportionment according to an agreed sharing ratio, which usually corresponds to members' financial contributions and may or may not be the same as the ratio of members' capital accounts. *See* paragraph 4.2 of the Chameleon agreement. Once again, this is heavily influenced by tax considerations. *See* § 4.04. Suppose LLC members want to allocate additional ownership interest to members as compensation for services? One method would be to establish multiple classes of interests, with one class being used as a kind of "stock option" to be awarded as compensation, analogous to the corporation. But it is important to note that the LLC capital structure is more flexible than that of the corporation. It is based solely on the operating agreement and can be customized at will. Thus, members can allocate different interests to different members reflecting, among other things, their differing service and capital contributions, and aligning voting and financial interests differently for each member.

7. **Interim Distributions.** Distributions made prior to members' withdrawal or dissolution are usually referred to as "interim distributions." Agreements may include several types of provisions concerning such distributions (*see* paragraph 4.4 of the Chameleon agreement):

(a) As with dividends on corporate common stock, interim distributions are normally left to the managers' discretion. *See Five Star Concrete, L.L.C. v. Klink, Inc.*, 693 N.E.2d 583 (Ind. App. 1998) (under operating agreement distributions to be determined by majority of members and were not necessarily equal to income allocated to members for tax purposes). The agreement may clarify the basis on which the decision is made—as when cash exceeds current and anticipated needs for operations, interest on debt and so forth. The partnership law discussed in §§ 4.03(B)(1) and 8.03 suggests that such provisions do not necessarily exculpate managers from liability for opportunistically making or refusing to make distributions.

(b) The agreement may clarify managers' duty to declare distributions, if possible, to fund members' tax liabilities for the firm's profits. Alternatively, to address potential problems with tax distributions, such as the LLC's need for operating cash, the agreement might provide for member voting on tax distributions, or for distributions only if the firm's CPA certifies that the firm will have a given surplus left after the distribution is made. Should these problems be dealt with by leaving distributions to the managers' discretion?

(c) The statutes normally provide that members are not entitled to distributions of property and cannot be forced to accept such distributions of property disproportionately to their ownership interests. Such distributions involve possible valuation and tax recognition issues. Nevertheless, the agreement may give managers discretion to make such "in kind" distributions. Again, fiduciary duty constraints may still apply.

(d) To the extent that a distribution exceeds a member's basis in the LLC interest, this may trigger a potential tax liability. The agreement may be drafted to prevent this from occurring.

(e) The agreement may include statutory limitations on distributions when liabilities exceed assets, to clarify that members have no rights among themselves to distributions in this situation irrespective of whether such distributions may otherwise be permitted by the agreement.

12.08 Management

The bifurcation between member-management and manager-management is one of the unique attributes of LLCs. As discussed below, this format raises several drafting and policy problems.

A.   The Management Election

Most LLC statutes provide that in the absence of contrary agreement the LLC is managed directly by members. *See* RIBSTEIN & KEATINGE ON LIMITED LIABILITY COMPANIES, app. 8-1 (tabulating statutory variations). This is the default rule that makes the most sense for informal firms that lack customized agreements.

Recognizing that many LLCs, like other limited liability firms such as corporations and limited partnerships, will want to adopt centralized management, LLC statutes all provide that LLCs can opt out of the management default by a provision in the articles or operating agreement. This ability to opt for centralized management distinguishes LLCs from general partnerships (*see generally* Chapter 5). Although a general partnership can have one or more managers, LLC statutes try to clarify the effect of centralized management, including who can bind the firm in third-party transactions and who has fiduciary duties. Under most statutes, members have partner-like authority to bind a member-managed LLC, managers have similar authority to bind manager-managed LLCs, and members have no authority as such to bind manager-managed LLCs. The effect of centralized management on fiduciary duties is discussed below in § 12.08.

B.   Effect of Articles and Operating Agreement

LLC statutes vary considerably concerning whether the manager-management election must be embodied in the articles or certificate. Some LLC statutes provide that the firm must elect manager-management by a provision in the articles or certificate. Others permit an election solely in the operating agreement. Still others require an election to be manager-managed to be made in the articles or certificate but also permit the operating agreement to provide for management power. Finally, some statutes, permit an election in the operating agreement but provide that only an election in the articles is effective concerning members' or managers' *agency* power to bind the firm in transactions with third parties. *See* RIBSTEIN & KEATINGE ON LIMITED LIABILITY COMPANIES, app. 8-1 (tabulating statutory provisions). Requiring the centralized-management election to be set forth in the articles gives some notice to third parties, whose rights may be affected by restrictions on non-managers' authority. However, making the articles controlling may mislead those who have relied on the operating agreement.

C.   The Role of Background Agency Rules

LLC statutes pose many questions concerning the allocation of authority among members and managers and, in particular, the application of background rules of apparent agency authority to LLCs. There are tradeoffs between LLC members' desire to limit the power of rogue members and third parties' desire to avoid excessive investigation costs. *See generally* § 2.02. This is not a matter of what is "fair" for either side, since rules that threaten the security of transactions will make third parties wary about dealing with LLCs, and LLCs ultimately will bear at least some of these costs.

First, it may not be clear whether the statutory default agency power of a member of a member-managed firm or manager of a manager-managed firm is effectively limited or expanded by the agreement. For example, can a single member or manager bind the firm in an extraordinary transaction, or is a third party bound by an operating agreement restriction on the member's or manager's authority? Delaware provides explicitly for broad member or manager authority to bind unless otherwise limited. *See* DEL. CODE ANN., tit. 6 § 18-402 (providing that each member or manager has the authority to bind the LLC unless otherwise provided in operating agreement). This makes the operating agreement control both actual and apparent authority of members and managers. Another alternative would be to permit LLCs to file documents like the statement of partnership authority provided for in Revised Uniform Partnership Act § 303, discussed above in § 5.04(C), which would bind the LLC, and would bind third parties in real estate transactions.

Second, it may not be clear whether a non-member or a member of a manager-managed LLC can bind the firm despite a statutory provision that purports to empower only members of member-managed firms or managers of manager-managed firms. The statute arguably should supplant the common law unless the statute explicitly makes agency law applicable, as in MD. CORPS. & ASS'NS Code § 4A-401(b). On the other hand, making the statute controlling in this regard would put a significant burden on third parties dealing with LLCs to know the statutory default rules, the form of management and the identity of members and managers.

Third, even if the statute controls regarding whether members and managers can bind the firm, it may not be clear who these members and managers are. The statutes do not require LLCs to disclose in filings or otherwise make a binding declaration of the names of managers and members other than the initial members or managers. Moreover, the identity of managers or members with agency power may be unclear even within the firm where the lines of authority are not definitively drawn and members exercise some management authority.

Why require firms to formally elect between manager and direct member management? Why not just let the operating agreement control members' and managers' power, like the Delaware statute discussed above?

One way LLCs may attempt to clarify who can bind the LLC is to designate corporate-type officers such as president, vice president or treasurer. However, even if officers are expressly provided for in the statute (*see, e.g.,* DEL. CODE ANN. § 18-407), the scope of their authority may not be clear even in corporations, much less if these officers are transplanted to the new LLC context.

For a case defining the scope of LLC managers' power, *see In re D & B Countryside, L.L.C. (D & B Countryside, L.L.C. v. S. P. Newell)*, (Bankr. E.D. Va. February 24, 1997), holding that the manager of a manager-managed LLC lacked authority to pledge the company's assets for personal loan, relying on limited partnership cases (*see* § 11.05(a), above). Although the original operating agreement gave the manager broad authority to deal for the company's benefit, he could not encumber the property for loans unrelated to the LLC's business. Also, the restated agreement limited the manager's authority to engage in loans that affected the company's assets and the granting of deeds of trust on LLC property in return for personal payments to the manager were not in ordinary course.

Notes and Questions: Drafting the Operating Agreement

1. **Effect of operating agreement.** As discussed above, it is important to examine the applicable statute to determine the extent to which an allocation of management power solely by the operating agreement, as distinguished from the articles or certificate, will be effective among the members and between the firm and third parties.

2. **Member-management.** In a member-managed LLC, the parties need to provide for the basis on which members will make decisions for the firm. For example, given the type of firm, should the partnership rules concerning equal participation in management, one-member-one-vote, and majority rule on ordinary, non-amending, decisions apply?

3. **Manager-management: power of managers.** Similarly, what rules should guide decisionmaking in a manager-managed LLC? *See* paragraphs 6.1 and 8.1 of the

Chameleon agreement. In particular, given the type of firm, on which issues should a member vote be required? Should managers have the general power to make "ordinary" decisions, or should these decisions be spelled out? Should the firm have officers, such as president, vice-president and treasurer? How should such persons be selected and what should be their authority?

4. **Manager-management: election and removal of managers.** One way the members can keep a "leash" on their managers is by provisions for periodic re-election or for removal. Removal may be more cost-effective in a relatively small firm than having to go through an election every year or so. If the members go this route, they must decide whether to require grounds for removal, and what member vote is sufficient. If the agreement is silent, the default provisions in the statute will apply. In *In re DeLuca (Broyhill v. DeLuca)*, 194 B.R. 65 (E.D. Va. 1996), the court applied the statutory majority-vote provision although the operating agreement required a unanimous vote to *elect* managers. The court reasoned that the unanimity provision was intended to prevent a person from being a manager without unanimous support, and that this was consistent with removal by only a majority vote.

5. **Amendments.** Assuming fewer than all of the members may make extraordinary decisions, should there be any limits on this power? Consider the following limitations on amendments (*see* paragraph 8.1 of the Chameleon agreement):

   (a) No amendment that would cause the LLC to be classified as a non-partnership for tax purposes.

   (b) Amendment is effective only if set forth in a written instrument.

   (c) Written consent by affected members is required to increase members' contribution obligations or change members' tax allocations or distribution rights.

6. **Meetings and formalities.** Should the operating agreement provide for meetings, notice of meeting, proxy voting, and other such details? *See* paragraph 8.3 of the Chameleon agreement. Such provisions may clarify members' rights and protect minority members, but may also have unexpected implications, such as giving disgruntled members a way to contest acts where formalities were omitted accidentally, or third parties a basis for "veil-piercing" claims. *See* § 12.02(C).

7. **Voting percentages.** To the extent that members have a vote, what percentage vote should be required to constitute approval? *See* paragraph 8.1 of the Chameleon agreement. Are there issues, such as amendment of the agreement or merger or dissolution, on which the firm should require supermajority or unanimity? It is necessary to balance the costs to the firm of being unable to take action or of being held up by a small minority against the costs to particular members of being subjected to the majority's will. The latter cost depends to some extent on members' ability to cash out of the firm whenever they want—that is, withdraw and receive compensation for the value of their interests. *See* § 12.10, below.

8. **Allocating voting power.** On what basis should the members vote—capital contributions, one-member-one-vote, or some other basis? The statutes are about evenly divided as to whether they provide by default for one-member-one-vote or for voting according to financial contributions. *See* RIBSTEIN & KEATINGE ON LIMITED LIABILITY COMPANIES, app. 8-1 (tabulating statutory provisions). A one-member-one-vote allocation seems suitable for the most informal firms, in which members may want to participate actively in management and in which it may be most difficult to determine the ratio of financial interests. The members may want to customize the vote allocation in their operating agreement. *See* paragraph 8.1 of the Chameleon agreement. This may raise interpretation issues. *In re DeLuca (JTB Enterprises, L.C. v. D & B Venture, L.C.)*, 194 B.R. 79 (E.D. Va. 1996), held that an operating agreement that did not allocate voting rights but did give each member a 50% membership interest despite their inequality in capital contributions varied the Virginia default rule of voting according to contributions, so that each member had an equal vote. Should the court have applied the statutory default voting rule since it was not explicitly waived? The Delaware statute provides for a way to use a single operating agreement to govern a series of LLCs with separate voting rights. *See* DEL. CODE ANN. tit. 6, § 18-215.

9. **Special voting arrangements.** The members may want to allocate voting rights to certain members on a basis other than the one generally chosen for allocation. They may, for example, provide for class voting—*i.e.,* that certain classes of interests have extra or inferior voting rights. No LLC statutes explicitly prohibit this and some explicitly allow it. Another possible alternative is a voting trust or agreement. In corporations these are ways for fewer than all of shareholders to bind themselves to exercise their voting power in a particular way. A voting trust in effect enforces such an agreement by delegating voting power to a trustee. Corporate statutes often include explicit provisions for enforcing these arrangements. *See, e.g.,* DEL. GEN. CORP. LAW § 218. LLC statutes normally do not. Moreover, most LLC statutes define the operating agreement as one or more agreements among all of the members. *See* ULLCA § 103(a). What is the effect of a voting trust or voting agreement under an ULLCA-type provision as to those who are not parties to the agreement or trust? How would you advise that such an arrangement be created?

10. **Members' authority to bind the firm.** What should the agreement say in order to limit non-managing members' power to bind the firm? *See* paragraphs 6.1 and 8.2 of the Chameleon agreement. The statutes generally provide that non-managing members have no authority to bind. Under such a provision, would it help in restricting who can bind the firm if the operating agreement identified the managers? The agreement might reinforce managers' exclusive agency power by providing that members who create unauthorized liabilities must indemnify the firm against damages resulting from the transactions. *See* paragraph 7.5 of the Chameleon agreement. Is an indemnification provision necessary under the Delaware statute, which provides that the operating agreement controls who can bind the firm?

11. **Protecting third parties.** The firm may want to include a provision that gives third parties some assurance that transactions with the firm will be binding in order

to encourage them to enter into transactions with this "new-fangled" organization. For example, the agreement could provide that any person may rely on a document signed by a manager as to the identity and authority of the manager or other facts. *See Luddington*, § 11.05(A). The LLC statute may provide an additional mechanism for third party reliance by including a provision like RUPA § 303, discussed above in § 5.04(C). Third parties who *must* know whether a transaction is authorized, such as title insurers, often insist on either signatures of all partners of a general partnership for deeds and deeds of trust or, if the law permits it (see p. 130-31, above), a recorded statement signed by all partners authorizing fewer signatures, even if the partnership agreement provides otherwise.

12. **Planning considerations.** In selecting a form of management, LLCs, like other types of firms, must trade off internal governance considerations against tax and regulatory considerations. Adopting direct management by members may help the firm avoid regulation under employment discrimination, securities and other laws. Yet centralized management may be desirable from an internal governance standpoint.

12.09 Transfer of Interests

Consistent with their partnership origins and their goal to ensure partnership tax classification, LLC statutes, like partnership statutes, do not provide by default for free transferability of management rights. Rather, most statutes define an LLC interest to include only financial rights, which are freely transferable in the absence of contrary agreement. *See* RIBSTEIN & KEATINGE ON LIMITED LIABILITY COMPANIES, app. 7-1 (tabulating statutory variations). Every statute provides by default that non-transferring members must approve a transfer of management rights, usually unanimously, although some by a majority or "majority in interest."

Apart from tax considerations, transfer restrictions—particularly the unanimity requirement for transfer of management rights—impose costs that may exceed their benefits. Given the limited liability of LLC members and the centralization of management in many LLCs, the transfer of management rights in an LLC is not the sort of momentous event that it may be in a general partnership. The "majority in interest" may create confusion, particularly under statutes that provide generally for voting based on member contributions or on some other basis.

LLC statutes commonly also provide for a creditor's charging order remedy similar to that provided for in general partnerships (*see* § 7.03) and often identical to that provided for limited partnerships (*see* § 11.07(B)). As to matters on which the statute is silent—for example, whether the interest can be foreclosed or as to the rights of a creditor-assignee—it is not clear whether a court should apply general partnership law, the possibly different law applied to limited partner interests, or some other rule. The analogous "linkage" problem for limited partnerships is discussed above in § 11.07(B). The difference between limited partnerships and LLCs is that the general partnership rule permitting assignees to obtain a judicial dissolution of the firm is less likely to apply to LLCs than to limited partnerships because an explicit linkage with partnership law applies in the latter case. This may have the practical effect of causing an LLC's members' creditors to have less power to compel the firm to make distributions than do a limited partner's creditors.

Notes and Questions: Drafting the Operating Agreement

1. **Voting rules on transfer of management rights.** Where the statute provides for a unanimity requirement, for the reasons discussed above the members may want to reduce the requirement to something like a majority or majority in interest in order to protect against excessive decision-making costs.

2. **Restrictions on sales of membership interests.** The agreement may provide that attempted sales of membership interests are ineffective in some particular circumstances (*see* paragraph 9.1 of the Chameleon agreement):

   (a) To ensure that the sale does not trigger undesirable tax consequences, such as causing a "termination" under I.R.C. § 708.

   (b) To ensure that that the sale does not violate federal or state securities registration requirements.

3. **Prohibitions and first options.** The members may want to prevent transfers of financial interests that would bring in potentially troublesome assignees. They may also want to share in any gains on sale, and to prevent members from giving up financial incentives while retaining management rights. As a result, the operating agreement may prohibit all transfers. On the other hand, such restrictions may impose costs on the members by freezing their financial rights in the firm. Thus, the agreement may give other members the first option to buy the shares at a price set in advance by the agreement or determined by the selling member or a third party offer. The agreement may exempt from these restrictions transfers to other members or to members of the transferor's immediate family, or transfers on death.

12.10 Fiduciary Duties

The general discussion of the nature of fiduciary duties in § 8.01 applies to LLCs. As detailed below in this section, the precise duties that apply to LLCs may differ from those in partnerships because fiduciary duties in any particular contractual relationship depend on the other terms of the parties' relationship, including members' direct and indirect power of control, their ability to protect themselves from the effects of bad decisions by transferring or liquidating their interests, and the economic impact of the decisions on the members. For example, managerial decisions may have less effect on LLC members than on partners because of limited liability. Members of default LLCs also differ from corporate shareholders in having greater power to participate in management, and from close corporation shareholders in having a greater ability to exit the firm through buyout or dissolution.

A. Disclosures to Members

The statutes often prescribe specific disclosure and information obligations, including the obligation to keep or to maintain access to certain records.

B. Managers' Duties

The duties of managers in manager-managed LLCs are "fiduciary" in nature in the strict sense that managers, as agents, have a duty to act unselfishly. LLC statutes generally define two types of manager duties—the duty of care and the duty of loyalty.

1. Duty of Care

Most LLC statutes provide that managers, like corporate directors, have a duty of care, which is described either as a duty to refrain from reckless conduct (*e.g.,* ULLCA § 409(c)) or as one based on language in the Model Business Corporation Act § 8.30 to act as a prudent person in similar circumstances with a right to rely reasonably on reports of others.

Borrowing from corporate law in this respect encourages courts to apply case law that may be inappropriate for LLC managers. Since LLC interests are not tradable in liquid securities markets, members are not likely to take the same sort of passive, hands-off attitude as corporate shareholders. At the same time, LLC members may be able powerfully to express their dissatisfaction with management by forcing the firm to repurchase their shares, perhaps even forcing liquidation. Even non-managing members may have more power to initiate and block actions than corporate shareholders have. Also, corporate duty of care decisions such as *Smith v. Van Gorkom,* 488 A.2d 858 (Del. 1985), tend to focus on whether the parties employed formal decision-making procedures. These elaborate procedures may not be justified in the smaller transactions and more informal context of LLCs.

2. Duty of Loyalty

LLC managers also have a duty of loyalty. Some statutes include a rule modeled on UPA § 21 which provides that managers can benefit from transactions with the firm only with the consent of other managers or members, usually by a disinterested majority vote. Others include a corporate-type conflict-of-interest provision requiring a vote by disinterested managers or members or a judicial fairness determination. *See* RIBSTEIN & KEATINGE ON LIMITED LIABILITY COMPANIES, app. 9-1 (tabulating statutory provisions). In either event, LLC managers' duty of loyalty probably includes the same elements as in other business associations—that is, duties to refrain from self-dealing transactions, selfish use of the firm's assets and usurping the firm's business opportunities. Once again, corporate standards may not transplant well to the LLC. For example, requiring wholly disinterested decision-making in a very closely held firm may impose excessive costs, particularly given the fact that LLC members may have more management power and ability to exit the firm than do corporate shareholders.

C. Members' Duties

Members who are not acting as managers should not have the fiduciary duties associated with the delegation of discretionary power. This is analogous to the fiduciary duties of limited partners discussed above in § 11.08(A)(2). Consistent with this principle, LLC statutes commonly provide in varying terms that members of member-managed firms have the same duties as managers of manager-managed LLCs, but that members in manager-managed LLCs have no fiduciary duties when acting solely as members. *See* RIBSTEIN & KEATINGE ON LIMITED LIABILITY COMPANIES, app. 9-1 (tabulating statutory provisions).

There may be some problems in applying this distinction between members and managers. Even a "member-managed" LLC may delegate some management power to particular members. The statutes may not make clear in this situation which members are "managers" with full fiduciary duties. ULLCA § 409(h) provides that a member who exercises some management rights has a manager's duties, while managers are relieved of liability to the extent of the authority delegated to the members. But it is not clear whether this refers only to powers exercised pursuant to a formal delegation, or to any authority *actually* exercised by members, or authority *delegated* to managers under the agreement regardless of who *exercises* the authority.

LLC statutes providing that members have no duties as such in manager-managed LLCs negate only *fiduciary* duties. This would still leave the members' fundamental contractual obligation of *good* faith. *See* § 8.05. Thus, members are not completely free to act self-interestedly in doing such things as voting on management acts, dissociating and compelling liquidation of the firm, and transferring their interests. Once again, compare § 11.08(A)(2) concerning the duties of limited partners. Nevertheless, ULLCA § 409(h)(1) provides that "a member who is not also a manager owes *no* duties to the company or to the other members solely by reason of being a member."

D. Waiver

Fiduciary duty waivers in partnerships are discussed in § 8.06. Similar considerations apply to LLCs, except that, because LLC members are not personally liable for the financial consequences of the firm's failure, there is arguably even less justification for protecting LLC members from their own contracts than there is for protecting partners.

LLC statutes vary considerably on the extent to which the members can waive default fiduciary duties by a provision in their operating agreement. *See* RIBSTEIN & KEATINGE ON LIMITED LIABILITY COMPANIES, app. 9-1 (tabulating statutory provisions). Most statutes permit waiver only of some types liability, such as negligence or misconduct. ULLCA § 103(b) is unusually detailed. Some statutes, including the Delaware act (DEL. CODE ANN., tit. 6, § 18-1101) give complete power to the members to waive fiduciary duties and other statutory provisions. An important case applying this provision is *Elf Atochem North America, Inc. v. Jaffari,* 727 A.2d 286 (Del. 1999), enforcing an LLC agreement providing for arbitration rather than a derivative remedy and for a California forum. The court noted that "only where the agreement is inconsistent with mandatory statutory provisions will the members' agreement be invalidated. Such statutory provisions are likely to be those intended to protect third parties, not necessarily the contracting members." 727 A.2d at 292. For a case applying Kansas' Delaware-like fiduciary duty waiver provision to hold that taking of business opportunities was governed by the operating agreement, *see Lynch Multimedia Corp. v. Carson Communications, L.L.C.,* 102 F. Supp. 2d 1261 (D. Kan. 2000).

Some alternatives for drafting fiduciary duty waivers in partnerships, which apply equally to LLCs, are discussed in the Notes on p. 201-204.

E.   Derivative Actions and Other Remedies

Litigation on behalf of the LLC generally must be authorized by whoever is managing the firm. This system breaks down, however, for suits against the managers. Many statutes authorize derivative suits modeled on RULPA §§ 1001-1004. *See* § 11.08(B), above. Others require a vote of disinterested members or managers to authorize litigation rather than authorizing a single member to sue on behalf of the firm. Some statutes provide for derivative suits in manager-managed firms. *See* RIBSTEIN & KEATINGE ON LIMITED LIABILITY COMPANIES, app. 10-1 (tabulating statutory provisions).

The main question concerning LLC derivative suits is whether they must be authorized by at least a majority of members. Most LLCs are likely to be closely held, so plaintiffs need not seek authorization from thousands of owners as would be necessary in a publicly held corporation or publicly traded limited partnership. Moreover, unlike shareholders, LLC members have a default remedy of being able to sell their interests back to the firm. These considerations may persuade courts to require member authorization under statutes that do not explicitly provide otherwise.

12.11 Member Dissociation

LLC statutes provide for certain events of member dissociation, including voluntary withdrawal, death, bankruptcy, and the figurative "death" of members that are business associations. About half, like ULLCA § 801, include lists of dissociation events as in RULPA § 402 (*see* § 11.09(A)), while most of the rest provide that certain dissociation events are causes of dissolution. *See* RIBSTEIN & KEATINGE ON LIMITED LIABILITY COMPANIES, app. 11-1 (tabulating statutory provisions). LLC statutes generally provide for two consequences of dissociation: payment for the value of the dissociating member's interest, and dissolution of the LLC. The latter is discussed in the next section.

Until recently, LLC statutes, like general partnership laws, gave members a default right to be paid at any time or on specified notice. Such a right provides liquidity for members of closely held firms who otherwise face transfer restrictions and thin markets for their interests. As discussed in Chapter 10, shareholder illiquidity in closely held corporations, and the vague and uncertain common law and statutory oppression and buyout remedies that were fashioned to deal with this illiquidity, are strong reasons for firms to abandon the close corporation and adopt a business form that is better adapted to closely held firms. On the other hand, giving each member a power to leave and be paid could force the sale of valuable assets or even liquidation in marginally capitalized firms, thereby giving minority members a weapon to use against the majority. Accordingly, as discussed in the Notes and Questions below, LLCs may contract out of the default buy-back right. Moreover, as discussed below in Note 5, the tax implications of buyout in family firms have led to a change in the default statutory buyout right, as it has in limited partnerships.

Notes and Questions

1. **Management and other rights of members who are voluntarily dissociated but have not yet been paid.** Ex-members who are still invested in the firm may be owed some fiduciary duties, although these may include only disclosure duties rather than a right to complain of post-dissociation mismanagement by the continuing members. *See* the discussions of the analogous partnership issues in §§ 7.02 and 9.04(B). There is an additional issue whether dissociated but unpaid members should have a right to participate in management. The incentives of a member who has declared an intention no longer to be associated with the firm are no longer aligned with those of the other members if the firm continues. Accordingly, a member who has dissociated in this sense should lose the right to participate in ongoing management, although not necessarily in winding up. Some LLC statutes follow the partnership model and exclude managers or members who dissolved wrongfully. *See* RIBSTEIN & KEATINGE ON LIMITED LIABILITY COMPANIES, app. 11-1 (tabulating statutory provisions). But the partnership model is inappropriate here because LLC statutes (apart from ULLCA § 801) generally do not make the partnership distinction between "wrongful" and "non-wrongful" dissolution. Note that a dissociated member who retains the right to participate in winding up also should retain the fiduciary duties that are associated with those rights. The parties can contract to clarify the rights of members who have been dissociated but not yet paid. For example, the operating agreement may provide that the former member shall have the rights and obligations of an assignee—that is, no right to participate in management. *See* paragraph 10.2 of the Chameleon agreement.

2. **Rights of an estate or other successor in interest of a dissociated member.** An estate or other successor, like other assignees (*see* § 12.05), probably should have no management rights unless the successor is admitted as a new member. However, like

former members, successors who have not been paid probably are owed fiduciary duties by continuing members, particularly including the duty to make full disclosure in connection with negotiating purchase of the interest.

3. **Management power of a dissociated member.** Like partners of dissolved partnerships (*see* § 9.06), an LLC member may continue to have the agency power to bind the firm as to third parties who are not notified of the dissolution. *See* ULLCA § 703.

4. **Contracting around the default withdrawal right.** The burden to the firm of letting members get their money back at any time may be greater for many firms than the burden to the members of having to wait for a return of their investment. LLCs differ from partnerships in this respect, where withdrawal serves the important purpose of freeing partners from a continuing personal liability for the firm's debts. Thus, if the statute does provide for an automatic buyout right, many firms may contract around it.

5. **Family LLCs and elimination of dissociation rights.** As in limited partnerships (*see* § 11.09(A)(1)), the statutory buyback right is further complicated by tax considerations. The more liquid the interest, the higher its value for estate and gift tax purposes. This is particularly a problem for "family LLCs" which, like family limited partnerships, are used for passing interests in family firms to younger members. Assuming, as is probably the case, that the family limited partnership rules discussed in § 11.09(A)(1) apply to LLCs, an operating agreement prohibition on withdrawal would be deemed to be more restrictive than an applicable state LLC statute that provides for a default right to exit on designated notice. Many statutes accordingly have eliminated default exit or buyout rights. Some statutes, such as ULLCA, provide for a power to dissociate but do not mandate a right to be paid on dissociation. *See* RIBSTEIN & KEATINGE ON LIMITED LIABILITY COMPANIES, app. 11-1 (tabulating statutory provisions).

6. **The locked-in manager.** Under a statute that eliminates the default exit right, or under an operating agreement that contracts around a default exit right, must a member-*manager* continue to act as a manager? In answering this question it is helpful to distinguish membership rights and managerial duties. The latter, like those in other employment contracts, are almost certainly not specifically enforceable. Thus, the member can, in effect, withdraw as a *manager* but not as a *member*. This could trigger a damage suit for failing to perform managerial obligations but not buyout or dissolution. This problem can be eliminated by permitting dissociation without buyout as many statutes do.

7. **Bankruptcy law.** One court has held that an LLC member's Chapter 11 reorganization does not terminate the member's interest, so that the member continues as such, and the member's rights effectively become part of the member's bankruptcy estate under Bankruptcy Code (11 U.S.C.) §§ 363, 365 and 541. *See In re Daugherty Construction, Inc.,* 188 B.R. 607 (D. Neb. 1995). The court applied the law relating to partnerships discussed in Note 4, p. 159. Another court, however, has refused to apply *Daugherty* and relied instead on a Virginia partnership decision holding that bankruptcy can terminate the member's interest. *See In re DeLuca (JTB Enterprises, L.C. v. D & B Venture, L.C.),* 194 B.R. 79 (E.D. Va. 1996). Bankruptcy law may cause less of a problem

for LLCs than for partnerships because at least the non-debtor members of an LLC are not left to shoulder the LLC's debts alone while carrying on with an insolvent member.

8. **Buy-out provisions.** The agreement may set forth the details of the buyout right by, among other things, identifying dissociation events that trigger buyout and clarifying how the buyout price is to be determined. *See* Article X of the Chameleon agreement. In *Five Star Concrete, L.L.C. v. Klink, Inc.,* 693 N.E. 2d 583 (Ind. App. 1998), the court noted the complexity of valuing a member's interest and held that the fairness of the particular valuation used (book value) could not be decided as a matter of law. Consider the following questions or options that may arise in connection with drafting the agreement:

(a) Should the buyout be based on a *sale* of the leaving partner's interest in the firm, or on a *liquidation* of that interest by the firm? See the discussion in § 9.04(D) of the tax distinction between these two transaction forms under I.R.C. § 736. Note that this provision may not be available to LLCs because it refers specifically to "general partners."

(b) Is the buyout price based on the value of the member's *interest in the firm*—that is, the price the member would receive if he sold his interest alone—or of the member's pro rata share of the *assets of the entire firm.* This is, in effect, the "minority discount" question. *See* § 9.04(A)(1), above.

(c) Should valuation problems be addressed by referring the issue to an appraiser? If so, how should the appraiser be selected, and what, if any, guidelines must the appraiser follow in making the valuation? For example, in *Klink, supra,* 693 N.E.2d at 587, n.5, the parties agreed that "[t]he fair market value shall be determined by a certified public accountant selected by the selling Member and a certified public accountant selected by the Company or purchasing Member, although all Members may select the same accountant. If the two accountants cannot agree as to the fair market value, the value shall be determined by a majority vote of said accountants and a third certified public accountant selected by said accountants."

(d) Should the parties instead try to eliminate disputes over valuation by, for example, determining the buyout price with reference to a specific amount? For example, the agreement could base the buyout price on the members' capital accounts or the firm's book value, in each case determined under generally accepted accounting principles. *See* paragraph 10.3 of the Chameleon agreement.

(e) To what extent may cash payment of the buyout price be delayed? This may be an important mechanism for avoiding liquidation of valuable assets of the firm as a whole in order to pay off an exiting member. At the same time, it is necessary to balance the exiting member's need for liquidity. These questions arise with respect to the time for payment, and whether and how the payment is to be secured. *See* paragraph 10.3 of the Chameleon agreement.

12.12 Dissolution

All LLC statutes provide that the LLC is dissolved on member dissociation unless the non-dissociating members vote to continue the firm. The statutes also provide for dissolution in other situations, including when the firm's agreed duration—often required to be specified in the articles or certificate—expires, when an agreed event or time occurs, on consent of all members and judicial decree.

The statutes also provide for mergers of LLCs. *See* § 12.02(b). *R & R Marketing, L.L.C. v. Brown-Forman Corp.,* 307 N.J. Super. 474, 704 A.2d 1327 (1998), held that two authorized liquor distributors who combined their businesses in an LLC that was not itself an authorized distributor retained statutory protection against discrimination by the supplier, analogizing the transaction to a corporate merger in which the authorizations would have passed to the merged entity.

Dissolution on member dissociation used to be an important tax feature because it avoided the corporate tax classification feature of continuity of life. Thus, most LLC statutes initially provided that the firm can be continued after member dissociation only on unanimous consent of the other members. ULLCA § 801 provides for an elaborate compromise of tax and other considerations by providing that In the wake of the new tax freedom under "check-the-box," many statutes have been amended to eliminate member dissociation as a default dissolution event. *See* RIBSTEIN & KEATINGE ON LIMITED LIABILITY COMPANIES, app. 11-1 (tabulating statutory provisions).

LLC statutory provisions regarding distributions to owners on dissolution vary mainly on whether they provide for a default rule. Most statutes, including ULLCA § 806, adopt the RULPA § 804 approach of providing by default for distribution first of amounts due for distributions, then contributions or other return of capital, then profits. *See* RIBSTEIN & KEATINGE ON LIMITED LIABILITY COMPANIES, app. 11-1 (tabulating statutory provisions). This is similar in effect to the approach under UPA § 40, discussed above in § 9.03, except that the UPA does not explicitly give priority to declared distributions. This difference may not matter to the extent that declared distributions are treated as debts of the firm, and thereby given priority over other amounts.

Most of the other statutes essentially rely on the parties' own accounting or agreement—adjusted capital accounts after satisfying liabilities for distributions, agreement on sharing of interim distributions, or the distribution of assets set forth in the operating agreement. Most LLCs probably have either an accounting system or an agreement on which to base an allocation. It is not clear under these statutes what a court should do where the parties have no agreement on which to base the distributions. But the uncertainty in this situation probably will not be much greater than that created by the effect of incomplete agreements where the statutory sharing ratio seems to contradict the parties' expectations.

LLC statutes generally require filings on dissolution and winding up—either when an event of dissolution occurs, when winding up has been completed and the firm has been terminated, or at both times. *See* RIBSTEIN & KEATINGE ON LIMITED LIABIL-ITY COMPANIES, app. 9-1 (tabulating statutory provisions). The filing on dissolution noti-fies third parties of the change in the power of the members and managers to bind the firm to going concern transactions and of the period of final collection of assets and pay-ment of claims, while the filing on termination could trigger the running of a statute of limitations on presentation of claims.

Notes and Questions: Drafting the Operating Agreement

1. **Liquidation procedure.** The agreement may control the procedure for liqui-dating the company, including by specifying a procedure for electing a person to han-dle the winding up, and by clarifying what may be done in winding up by way of selling assets, deferring sale for a reasonable time, and distributing assets in kind to the mem-bers. *See* paragraph 11.3 of the Chameleon agreement. *In re DeLuca (JTB Enterprises, L.C. v. D & B Venture, L.C.),* 194 B.R. 79 (E.D. Va. 1996), held that a Virginia statute which provided for winding up by members who have not wrongfully dissolved was var-ied by an operating agreement which provided for liquidation by any manager. Note the importance of making the distribution in accordance with the capital accounts in order to ensure that the members' agreement will be given tax effect. *See* § 4.04, above.

2. **Priority of distribution.** The operating agreement may control the distribution of assets, at least in terms of member priorities among themselves. For example, the agree-ment may provide for distribution to members in accordance with their capital account balances.

3. **Type of distribution.** The agreement also may govern whether the distributions to members are in property (*i.e.,* "in-kind") or cash. In-kind distributions may involve valuation problems in terms of equalizing distributions among members, and tax prob-lems in terms of how members share in taxable gains and losses on the property. Accordingly, most statutes provide that members need not accept and are not entitled to receive disproportionate in-kind distributions. The agreement may contract around this rule where, for example, in-kind distributions are not likely to be a serious prob-lem and prohibiting even minor deviations may cause logistical problems.

CHAPTER 13
THE LIMITED LIABILITY PARTNERSHIP

13.01 Background and History

An important development in limited liability business forms occurred in 1991 when Texas invented the "registered limited liability partnership" ("LLP"). An LLP is a general partnership which, by filing a registration, limits the partners' personal liability at least for their co-partners' wrongdoing. The initial statutes, including the Texas statute, did not limit the partners' liability for the firm's contract-type debts, but most now have extended the liability to include all types of debts (*see* § 13.02, below). Since most LLP statutes explicitly define "partnership" to include LLPs, general partnership default rules, including those on management, financial rights, transfer and dissolution, apply to LLPs. Nevertheless, as discussed throughout this Chapter, LLP partners' limited liability necessitates many adjustments in applying both general partnership law and non-partnership tax and regulatory law.

The development of the LLP was spurred by escalating lawyer and accountant liability for malpractice and for multi-million dollar securities law and other regulatory claims (particularly including those arising out of savings and loan litigation), some of which were not fully covered by insurance. Professionals' woes have been further exacerbated by large professional firm bankruptcies in the wake of over-expansion in the 1980s. *See* Hamilton, *Registered Limited Liability Partnerships: Present at the Birth (Nearly),* 66 U. COLO. L. REV. 1065, 1066-71 (1995); Johnson, *Limited Liability for Lawyers: General Partners Need Not Apply,* 51 BUS. LAW. 85, 85-91 (1995). As discussed in Chapter 12, LLCs were not a complete answer, because of uncertainties about the extent to which professional firms could do business in a non-"partnership" form and non-partnerships' exposure to employment discrimination claims.

The LLP form has rapidly evolved since the 1991 invention of LLPs in Texas. The landmarks in the development of LLP law include:

(a) The Texas statute, which limited partners' vicarious liability for other partners' wrongdoing but not for the firm's contract-type debts.

(b) The Delaware statute, which refined the members' limited liability and added provisions adapting loss-sharing among the partners.

(c) The Minnesota and New York statutes, adopted in 1994, which were the first to recognize limited liability for all debts.

(d) The Georgia statute, adopted in 1995, which was the first to recognize limited liability for all debts coupled with availability to all types of firms (the New York statute can be used only by professional firms) and an absence of restrictions on distributions like those in the Minnesota statute.

(e) The Model LLP Act, promulgated in 1995 by a committee of the American Bar Association, which adapts the Revised Uniform Partnership Act for use by LLPs. The National Conference of Commissioners on Uniform State Laws prepared LLP amendments to RUPA based substantially on the Model LLP Act. *See* Uniform Partnership Act (1997) *reprinted in* the Appendix (cited hereafter as "RUPA" or "amended RUPA"). Statutes based on these provisions have been adopted in many states.

These variations will be discussed below in this chapter. A substantial majority of the states have now adopted LLP provisions. State statutes are reproduced and discussed in detail in BROMBERG & RIBSTEIN ON LIMITED LIABILITY PARTNERSHIPS AND THE REVISED UNIFORM PARTNERSHIP ACT.

Problems

Like the LLC, the LLP presents a choice of form question. The following problems are intended to focus your thinking on this issue.

1. Would you advise the firm discussed in the Problem in § 12.01 to be an LLP?

2. Assume you are a partner in a small law firm that has ten partners and five associates. The firm is currently organized as a general partnership. What considerations about the firm and the applicable law would be important in determining whether to register the firm as an LLP?

13.02 Creation of an LLP

As noted in § 13.01, an LLP is a "partnership." Accordingly, an LLP must first be a partnership under the definition discussed in Chapter 3—that is, it must be an association of two or more persons who carry on a business for profit. This definition excludes, among other things, one-member and non-profit firms. In order to become an LLP the firm must also comply with certain statutory prerequisites. Under all statutes, this includes completing a registration process, discussed in Section A. Under several statutes, including Delaware and Texas, the firm must also comply with insurance or other financial responsibility requirements.

A.   LLP Registration Process

The LLP form offers particular advantages for existing general partnerships that wish to become limited liability firms. Partners can convert to the LLP form merely by filing an LLP registration. Subject to the significant qualifications discussed in Section B, below, this registration may be simpler in several respects than changing a general partnership into a limited liability form of business by dissolving and transferring assets to the new firm. (Note, however, that the conversion procedure provided for in some LLC statutes provides convenience comparable to LLP registration, except that they may not cut off partners' personal liability for all post-conversion debts. *See* § 12.02(A), above.)

1.   Vote on Registration

Most LLP statutes provide for registration by a vote of the partners. For variations in voting requirements, *see* BROMBERG & RIBSTEIN ON LIMITED LIABILITY PARTERNSHIPS AND THE REVISED UNIFORM PARTNERSHIP ACT, Chapter 2, Table 2-8. Although dissenting partners may be able to block the registration by exercising their statutory power to withdraw and compel liquidation of the partnership (*see* § 9.02), the partnership agreement often may prevent this tactic by penalizing withdrawal or providing a way for the non-dissenting partners to avoid liquidation. By contrast, when a partnership becomes an LLC or corporation in the conventional way, by dissolution and transfer of assets, dissenting partners can block the transaction either by vetoing the sale as an extraordinary event that requires a unanimous vote unless otherwise agreed (*see* Chapter 5), or by blocking continuation of the firm by insisting that the assets be sold and the proceeds applied to the payment of debts (*see* Chapter 9).

2.   Post-Registration Liability

LLP statutes provide that partners have limited liability from the time of registration, even as to creditors who were not aware of the registration. By contrast, if the firm had dissolved and reformed as an LLC or corporation, the partners might be personally liable for post-dissolution transactions to creditors who were not notified of the change of form (*see* § 9.06).

3.   Effect on Existing Contracts

An LLP registration does not cause the underlying partnership to dissolve. Accordingly, contracts and debts simply continue to bind the LLP unless by their terms they are expressly subject to an intervening LLP registration. By contrast, when a partnership dissolves and reforms as an LLC or corporation, the dissolution might terminate existing contracts, particularly if these contracts include clauses that preclude assignment by merger or sale to a third party, including another business entity. *See* BROMBERG

& RIBSTEIN ON PARTNERSHIP, § 7.14. The question of what are "existing" contracts is discussed in subsection 13.02(B)(4), below.

B.   Potential Problems of Registration

The apparent simplicity of LLP registration by existing firms masks several potential problems for such firms that are discussed in the following subsections.

1.   Effect on Dissenting Members

As discussed below in § 13.03, LLP registration can profoundly affect members who have monitoring or supervisory roles or who are involved in activities that have the highest risk of suit, such as law partners engaged in highly regulated securities or banking work. Nevertheless, LLP statutes generally permit approval of the registration by a less-than-unanimous vote. This may let a majority shift the liability burden to a dissenting minority. On the other hand, bargaining costs under a unanimity rule, including redrafting the agreement to indemnify "exposed" partners against liability (*see* subsection 4, below), may prevent some efficient LLP registrations from taking place. Note that a majority vote rule might in effect override a partnership agreement that provides either explicitly or by application of the statutory default rule for unanimity on amendments and other important matters. Might it be bad faith or a breach of fiduciary duty under the general principles discussed in Chapter 8 for the majority to impose registration on a dissenting minority? Does the fact that the statute explicitly authorizes registration by majority vote negate such an argument? RUPA eliminates these problems by providing for approval of registration by the vote necessary to amend the agreement.

2.   Creation of Two Classes of Liabilities

After registration, the firm has at least two classes of creditors (in addition to the tort-contract classification under many statutes as discussed below in § 13.03(A))—pre-registration creditors who can collect out of the assets both of the firm and the individual partners, and post-registration creditors who may or may not have claims against individual partners depending on the type of statute and the type of claim. Partners therefore have an incentive to pay pre-registration claims for which they have vicarious liability, leaving insufficient assets to cover the post-registration claims for which their liability is limited. This subjects the post-registration creditors to an extra, possibly unexpected, risk of a shortfall of assets.

3. Effect on Post-Registration Creditors

Trade creditors, clients and others who have done business with the firm prior to registration may expect the same liability rules to continue to apply to their transactions. If the firm had dissolved and reformed as an LLC or corporation, the creditors would continue to have the benefit of personal liability unless they had actual or constructive notice of the change (*see* § 9.06). Although LLP statutes require an LLP's name to include "LLP" or similar designation, they do not explicitly condition the liability limitation on use of the designation in all of the firm's dealings. Courts might, however, imply such a condition, or "pierce the veil" of limited liability of firms that do not adequately disclose their new LLP status. This is particularly a problem for law and other professional firms that have continuing relationships with clients. *See* Notes 2-4, p. 396-98, below.

4. Effect on Existing Contracts and Relationships

Since LLP registration continues the pre-existing partnership entity, it apparently does not affect the firm's contracts either among the partners or between the partnership and third parties. But there are many unanswered questions with respect to attributing liabilities to the pre- or post-registration period. Are post-registration loans pursuant to a pre-registration line of credit subject to the LLP liability limitation (under statutes that limit liability for contract debts)? Is a partner's malpractice covered by the registration if it was committed prior to registration but results in an injury afterward? Is a creditor who agreed to a lease or a line of credit prior to registration stuck with limited liability as to subsequent loans or rent?

One possible place to look for answers to these questions is cases that have considered whether new partners are personally liable, or former partners not liable, for interest or other payments on preexisting partnership contracts or debts that accrue after dissociation or admission. *See* § 9.05. The reasoning in these cases for and against liability, which is based on the creditors' expectations as to who would be liable on the loan, arguably also applies to the effect of the LLP liability limitation on post-registration charges or liabilities that accrue on pre-registration contracts or misconduct.

Creditors can, of course, deal with these issues in their agreements with the partnership. The problem, of course, is that older agreements could not have anticipated the LLP. Should language in a loan agreement or lease that provides that the contract is terminated in the event of a merger or other fundamental change be interpreted to include an LLP registration?

C. Choice of Law

As discussed in § 3.04, partners traditionally have not been able to contract for the applicable law to the same extent as corporate shareholders. In any event, choice of law has not been an important issue given the widespread adoption of the Uniform Partnership Act. RUPA promises to introduce non-uniformity and simplifies choice of law with its "chief executive office" rule. Most LLP statutes take this process further by applying to foreign LLPs the law of their state of formation, particularly including the law limiting the partners' liability. Like foreign LLC provisions, LLP statutes generally provide that a foreign LLP must register prior to transacting business in the state. The firm's formation state law applies even if it does not register, although the firm may be unable to sue in the state's courts and it may be served through the secretary of state (*see* RUPA §§ 1101, 1103). These provisions raise the same issues concerning which types of firms they refer to, and which formation state law is applied, as do comparable provisions for registering foreign limited partnerships and LLCs (*see* § 12.02(I), above).

Although the law of an LLP's formation state may generally apply under foreign LLP provisions, the law of a jurisdiction in which an LLP operates may apply on the following issues: (a) compliance with regulatory or licensing statutes, such as those regulating the liability of lawyers and other professionals (*see* §§ 12.02(J), above and 13.05(E), below); (b) the *partnership's* liability to third parties, including partners' power to bind the firm; (c) *partners'* liability for monitoring or participation in misconduct (*see* § 13.03(B), below); and (d) veil-piercing (*see* § 13.03(E), below), including whether corporate veil-piercing rules apply. *See Abu-Nassar v. Elders Futures, Inc.,* 1991 WL 45062 (S.D.N.Y. Mar. 28, 1991) (applying Lebanese law to determine the compliance of limited liability company with formalities of organization, but New York law to determine whether veil should be pierced).

A state that simply adds foreign LLP provisions to the original version of RUPA (without LLPAmendments) raises questions about whether to apply the law of the state of registration under the foreign LLP provision, the law of the chief executive office state under RUPA § 106, or the law selected in the agreement pursuant to RUPA § 103. Amended RUPA §§ 106(b) and 103(b)(9) clarify that the Act applies to firms that register under it even if the agreement provides for application of a different law. However, it is not clear under this provision what law would apply outside the registration state if the LLP registers in a non-Model Act state but operates in a Model Act state, or registers under the Model Act but operates in a non-Model Act state.

13.03 Limited Liability

LLP statutes raise numerous problems and offer several variations concerning the scope of the liability protection they offer registering partnerships.

A.   Scope of Limited Liability

Although most LLP statutes originally limited partners' liability for a particular category of claims—those based on the misconduct of their co-partners—most now limit liability for all types of claims. *See* BROMBERG & RIBSTEIN ON LIMITED LIABILITY PARTERNSHIPS AND THE REVISED UNIFORM PARTNERSHIP ACT, Chapter 3, table 3-1. Personal liability only for contract-type claims seems to make little sense because it limits liability precisely as to the involuntary creditors for whom limited liability is most troubling (*see* § 10.02, above). However, this type of provision has been defended on the ground that it met an immediate need of providing limited relief from potentially disastrous vicarious liability for such uncontrollable events as bank failures and punitive damage awards. *See* Hamilton, *Registered Limited Liability Partnerships: Present at the Birth (Nearly),* 66 COLO. L. REV. 85, 85-91 (1995). Since partners cannot easily control co-partners' negligence or other misconduct, the costs to the partnership of vicarious tort liability beyond monitoring failures may exceed the social benefits of such liability (*see* § 10.02). Personal liability for contracts is less of a problem because, as discussed below in Section C, the partners can always contract around the personal-liability default rule. On the other hand, personal liability for contract claims is arguably a poor default rule. Vicarious liability is likely to do larger creditors the most good, because they're the ones who can afford to do credit checks and comply with the exhaustion requirement (*see* § 6.01). These creditors, therefore, could be expected to contract for partners' personal liability when such liability would be in the creditors' interests. However, if the default rule were otherwise, it may not pay the partnership to try to contract around it for smaller claims. *See* Ribstein, *The Deregulation of Limited Liability and the Death of Partnership,* 70 WASH. U. L.Q. 365 (1992).

B. Supervisory Liability

LLP statutes generally provide that LLP partners are personally liable not only for their own misconduct, but also for the conduct of others in which they somehow participated or for which they had some monitoring responsibility. This liability is similar to that imposed in many states on members of professional corporations (*see* § 12.02(I)). Focusing liability on monitors makes some superficial sense since it places the liability on those who are in the best position to prevent the harm. But these statutory provisions raise sticky questions for partners who (a) have overall responsibility for a client, (b) serve on a committee that reviews tax and other opinions prepared by other lawyers in the firm, (c) provide specific expert advice on a matter that is generally handled by other lawyers in the firm, (d) serve on a management or compensation committee that violates employment discrimination laws in setting associate compensation, (e) participate in a case in which an associate or paralegal negligently misses a deadline for filing of a notice of appeal or mishandles service of process on the defendant, or (f) have no role in the misconduct other than finding out about it and not doing anything about it, and so would have been better off remaining as ignorant as possible. *See* BROMBERG & RIBSTEIN ON LIMITED LIABILITY PARTNERSHIPS AND THE REVISED UNIFORM PARTNERSHIP ACT § 3.04.

Because partners may be unable to avoid supervisory liability that is based on *non-negligent* conduct merely by taking reasonable precautions, they may refuse to engage in supervisory activities without extra protection or compensation. Thus, supervisory liability ironically may have the result of discouraging law firms' efforts to move toward greater peer review and internal monitoring. For a discussion of these trends, *see* Fortney, *Am I My Partner's Keeper? Peer Review in Law Firms,* 66 U. COLO. L. REV. 329 (1995).

In order to counter the effects of supervisory liability, partnerships may contract to indemnify or compensate the partners who take the risk. *See* § 13.03(F)-(G), below. These contracts may be costly to negotiate and draft and may negate the non-supervising partners' protection from liability. Moreover, supervisory liability can create conflicts of interest among the partners—such as incentives to withhold distributions that might pay the liabilities—that may necessitate adjustments in fiduciary duties. In light of these problems, statutes may eliminate supervisory liability, as does RUPA § 306.

Notes and Questions: Drafting the Partnership Agreement

How might the partnership agreement minimize the impact of supervisory liability? Consider the likely effect on partners' liability to third parties of the following provisions in the partnership agreement:

1. A managing partner is not liable for the others' errors unless they occur under the administrator's direct supervision.
2. A partner in a law or accounting partnership who has overall responsibility for a particular client is not thereby responsible for all work done on behalf of that client.
3. A specialist who gives advice on a particular matter does not thereby have any supervisory or monitoring responsibility in connection with that matter.

C.   Contracting for Liability

LLPs or individual partners can contract for liability that is broader than what the statutes provide for. For example, one or more partners might personally guarantee particular debts of the firm. Some statutes provide explicitly for liability for debts for which the partners agreed to be liable. *See* BROMBERG & RIBSTEIN ON LIMITED LIABILITY PARTNERSHIPS AND THE REVISED UNIFORM PARTNERSHIP ACT, Chapter 3, Table 3-1 (tabulating state statutory provisions). Some partners might agree to be liable for all debts. Where only managing partners do so, the firm may resemble a limited partnership under RULPA. Whether partners guarantee only certain debts or contract for liability for all of the firm's debts may matter for purposes of determining whether the firm has corporate-type limited liability for tax purposes. *See* § 13.05(A)(1), below.

D.   Veil-Piercing Rules

Courts may impose personal liability on partners of LLPs that have complied with all statutory formalities, just as they have on corporate shareholders, under a "piercing the veil" theory. As with LLCs (*see* § 12.02(C)), there is a question whether corporate-type veil-piercing rules apply to LLPs. The potential application of corporate veil-piercing law to LLPs raises the following questions, among others.

1.   In the absence of statutory insurance or bonding requirements or other statutory constraints on capitalization, is a professional firm inadequately capitalized whenever it does not maintain adequate means of meeting predictable malpractice claims?

2.   Is minimum compliance with statutory insurance or bonding requirements enough to avoid veil-piercing on inadequate capitalization grounds? *See Walkovszky v. Carlton*, 18 N.Y.2d 414, 223 N.E.2d 6, 276 N.Y.S.2d 585 (1966), a famous corporate veil-piercing case in which the court, in refusing to pierce veil for inadequate capitalization, cited defendant's compliance with statutory insurance requirement.

3.   What is the effect of failure to observe formalities? LLP statutes do not provide for formalities, such as directors' and owners' meetings, as do corporate and some LLC statutes. The Colorado and Minnesota LLP provisions state that the use of informal procedures is not alone a ground for piercing the veil.

4.   What is the effect of misleading creditors as to the firm's limited liability status or capitalization? Should the veil be pierced under statutes that provide for limited liability only in tort cases where the firm has engaged in misleading only as to contract-type creditors?

5.   Assuming that the LLP is adequately capitalized and followed all formal procedures, might an LLP's veil still be pierced when a *corporate* veil would *not be*—in particular, where a professional firm has registered as an LLP without adequately notifying existing clients of the change? *See* § 13.02(B)(3).

E.   Creditor Enforcement of Partner Liability

To recover on the partnership's contract debts from partners who have registered under a tort-only shield, creditors probably have to exhaust remedies against the partnership because this is normally characterized as "joint" liability. *See* § 6.01. However, exhaustion relates only to partners' *vicarious* liability for partnership debts, and not to partners' liability for their own debts. The latter category might include partners' statutory supervisory liability. *See* RUPA § 307(d)(5), which excuses exhaustion if "liability is imposed on the partner by law or contract independent of the existence of the partnership."

F.   Contribution

As discussed in §§ 6.03 and 9.03, contribution is the mechanism by which part-ners make up a shortfall in partnership assets in order to pay creditor claims. Under RUPA, partners do not have to contribute to the "pot" to pay off liabilities for which their liability is limited. RUPA § 306(c) provides that partners are "not personally liable, directly or indirectly, including by way of contribution or otherwise, for such a part-nership obligation solely by reason of being or so acting as a partner." RUPA § 807(b) excludes from consideration in determining whether a partner has a contribution oblig-ation liabilities for which the partner is not liable under the LLP liability limitation. The most important context for application of the principles discussed in this section is in bankruptcy court, since contribution obligations matter most for insolvent firms. In bank-ruptcy, the trustee exercises creditors' rights under state law, including the right to enforce the contribution obligations of a bankrupt partnership under UPA § 40(e) or RUPA § 807(f). Bankruptcy Code (11 U.S.C.) § 723(a) provides that partners are liable for defi-ciencies only "to the extent that under applicable nonbankruptcy law such general partner is personally liable for such deficiency."

The order in which liabilities are paid may be critical under RUPA For example, if an LLP has assets of $50,000, $50,000 in debts to third parties arising prior to reg-istration for which partners are personally liable under most LLP statutes, and $50,000 for liabilities for which some partners are not individually liable under the LLP provi-sions, the shortfall might be handled by: (a) paying the personal liability claims in full out of partnership property, leaving neither partnership property nor partner contribution obligations for the other claims; (b) paying the limited-liability claims in full out of part-nership property and the contract-type claims out of partner contributions; or (c) pro-rating the $50,000 short-fall between the limited-liability and personal-liability claims, so that partners would be personally liable for $25,000. The last alternative seems most sensible. However, it does not settle whether the partnership can pay off contract claims *before* liquidation. A bankruptcy court may or may not recapture such payments for the benefit of the creditors as a whole.

G.   Indemnification

Indemnification is the process by which partners settle responsibilities for liabil-ities among themselves. Indemnification should operate the same way in an LLP as in a non-LLP partnership *unless* the indemnification liability exceeds the partnership assets and thereby raises the issue of whether partners must contribute to make up the short-fall. The question is whether the partners have agreed otherwise in their pre-registra-tion partnership agreement. *See* § 13.04(C)(4), below.

13.04 Effect of LLP Registration on Partnership Default Rules and Partnership Agreements

This Section discusses how an LLP may differ from a non-LLP general partnership both in terms of the partnership default rules and the approaches to drafting partnership agreements discussed above in Chapters 4-9.

A.   Application of General Partnership Law: Linkage

Defining LLPs as "partnerships" creates a linkage with existing partnership law and practice which makes available to LLPs the whole body of partnership custom and precedent. *See* § 1.02(B). This arguably helps clarify the meaning of statutory provisions and contract terms. Over time, as LLC law develops, the linkage advantages of the LLP may decline and the LLC form may become dominant. On the other hand, strong linkage advantages may encourage most firms to use the LLP form and thereby prevent the development of analogous advantages for LLCs.

Linkage with partnership law is potentially valuable when three conditions are satisfied. First, linking to another body of law may aid interpretation. For example, it may not be very important whether courts can draw on precedents to interpret statutory provisions for formalities since these formalities may be straightforward enough as not to require a reservoir of interpretive materials. Second, partnership precedents or forms must actually reduce any interpretation or drafting problems. Fiduciary duties, for example, may be so case-specific that precedents are of little help. Third, linkage must result in the application of *appropriate* forms or precedents. Partnership cases or contract terms on such matters as governance rights and partner duties do not apply equally well in firms whose members have no personal liability. In other words, the dubious "advantage" of LLP registration insofar as linkage is concerned may be that it encourages courts to make inappropriate analogies. This Section discusses some specific rules that present potential problems from this perspective.

B.   Partners' Management Rights

Limited liability reduces the cost of delegating responsibility to agents. *See* Ribstein, *Limited Liability and Theories of the Corporation,* 50 MD. L. REV. 80 (1991). It follows that LLPs—particularly those that have across-the-board limited liability—may prefer to provide for centralized management. As discussed in Chapter 5, it is hard in general partnerships to restrict the authority of non-managing co-partners to bind the firm in transactions with third parties. There is also authority for restrictively interpreting agreements that purport to exclude non-managing partners from participating in decision-making, or that permit a majority of the partners to make important decisions or permit free transfer of management rights. The LLP liability shield undercuts much of the rationale for this restrictive interpretation. If partners' liability for contract-type claims is limited, the partners may not have enough need for a veto power to justify the potentially high decision-making costs of requiring unanimity.

C. Financial Rights and Obligations

The limited liability of partners in LLPs has obvious implications for the application of partnership financial rights and obligations based on the assumption that partners are liable for all debts and obligations of the partnership.

1. Default Rule: Equal Profit Shares

As discussed in Chapter 4, partners share profits equally in the absence of contrary agreement. This allocation assumes that the partners' individual liability for partnership debts coupled with their contributions of human capital compensate for any inequality in capital contributions. The assumption of compensating credit contributions does not apply to LLPs with across-the-board limited liability. Per capita may still be the best *default* rule, particularly for the most informal firms whose members really are making equal contributions. But the partners may want to provide in their agreements for financial sharing pro rata according to capital contributions. Moreover, the courts may be tempted to imply such an agreement where the partners' labor and financial contributions are unequal.

2. Agreements on Partner Compensation and Profit Shares

LLP registration may affect partnership agreements on compensation. As discussed in § 13.02, LLP registration may focus vicarious liability on "supervisory" partners. The partners may want to reflect this reallocation of risk in the allocation of profit shares. For example, a professional partnership may have a "lockstep" seniority-based compensation system that gives the highest compensation to the most senior partners who have the most wealth and, therefore, the largest liability risk under a vicarious liability system. *See* § 4.01(B). If the firm converts to an LLP, the partners may want to change their compensation method to one in which the partners in the more liability-prone positions are compensated for taking the largest risk of personal liability.

3. Distributions to Partners

LLP provisions introduce potential conflicts of interest regarding distributions to partners. First, there is a conflict between partners, who have an incentive to distribute assets to themselves, and creditors, who must rely on the partnership's assets and would rather their claims be paid. Second, there is a conflict between partners who are fully protected from vicarious liability and so have an incentive to distribute assets, and partners who are exposed to liabilities, such as those resulting from failure to supervise or arising prior to registration, who want the partnership to retain assets to pay claims that they would otherwise have to pay out of personal assets. The partnership agreement may deal with the conflict among the partners by mandating or restricting distributions rather than leaving them to the discretion of managers or a majority of the partners. A court might constrain managing partners' discretion through fiduciary duties. *See* § 13.04(D), below.

With respect to the potential conflict between partners and creditors, partnership statutes, unlike limited partnership, corporation, and LLC statutes, only a few LLP statutes regulate partnership distributions. *See* BROMBERG & RIBSTEIN ON LIMITED LIABILITY PARTNERSHIPS AND THE REVISED UNIFORM PARTNERSHIP ACT, Chapter 3, table 3-1. The usual partnership rule reflects the fact that, since creditors of partnerships need not rely on the firm's assets, they need no assurance that the firm will have assets available for the payment of debts. The situation changes, of course, in LLPs.

Should LLP statutes include limitations on distributions? Such limitations may be very costly for the professional partnerships that are the largest category of LLPs because these firms tend to distribute all of their earnings to the partners, because professionals contribute services to the firm in return for the distribution, and because the value of the firm's assets may be difficult to determine for insolvency purposes. Some statutes deal with this through special provisions for distributions that constitute payment of compensation to partners. *See* BROMBERG & RIBSTEIN ON LIMITED LIABILITY PARTNERSHIPS AND THE REVISED UNIFORM PARTNERSHIP ACT, § 4.04(d).

Creditors may prefer to deal with firms that are subject to regulation of distributions. Conflicts between owners and creditors are likely to be particularly intense in partnerships, whose owners directly control decisions on activities that affect creditors' risk, as distinguished from corporations, in which such non-owner directors make such decisions. Moreover, partners have a greater incentive than shareholders to distribute earnings because the former pay tax on partnership income whether it is distributed or not. If distribution limits matter to creditors perhaps they should be included in statutes because of the high costs of negotiating for them in individual contracts. On the other hand, creditors may not care much about statutory restrictions on distributions because they largely duplicate protection under fraudulent conveyance law. (Note, however, that the law of fraudulent transfers would have to be modified to accommodate LLPs. *See* § 13.05(D), below.) In very risky situations, creditors probably would negotiate extra protection regardless of what the statutes provided.

Some LLP statutes attempt to reduce risks to creditors of undercapitalized firms by requiring insurance. *See* BROMBERG & RIBSTEIN ON LIMITED LIABILITY PARTNERSHIPS AND THE REVISED UNIFORM PARTNERSHIP ACT, § 2.06 and Chapter 3, table 3-1. But since firms vary widely in size and riskiness, minimum statutory insurance will be either too much or too little for most firms. Even if legislators could determine an appropriate minimum amount, they would also have to regulate in detail such terms as deductibles, exclusions, co-insurance and the use of proprietary insurers. Many of the more recent LLP statutes avoid these difficulties by not including insurance requirements.

Courts might substitute for the lack of insurance requirements or distribution restrictions by "piercing the veil" of LLPs that have "inadequate capitalization" *See* § 13.02(E), above.

4. Indemnification, Contribution and Other Loss-Sharing Provisions

Indemnification and contribution in LLPs are discussed above in § 13.03(F)-(G) as important aspects of the partners' liability shield. The partnership agreement may vary these default rules, as by promising to indemnify partners who are in management and supervisory positions in order to induce them to take these positions (*see* § 13.02(B)) or by requiring wrongdoing partners to bear the losses they cause. These provisions must be designed to provide appropriate incentives for careful conduct. Alternatively, the agreement may allow indemnification to partners who incur liabilities by, for example, serving as a manager or on an oversight committee (*see* § 13.02(B)), but require partners to bear liabilities created by their own intentional wrongdoing, negligence or unauthorized acts.

The partners must be wary about indemnification and contribution provisions that unexpectedly create personal-liability contract claims. For example, the partnership agreement may provide that partners are personally liable on partners' claims for indemnification. This sort of provision simply backs up general partners' usual liability on partnership debts. But if the partnership registers as an LLP, the creditors of the wrongdoing partner might claim that they are subrogated to that partner's right to collect from the partnership and the individual partners. Should the pre-registration agreement be interpreted as waiving the statutory liability limitation? This interpretation would assume that the indemnified partners want the comfort of being able to sue their co-partners individually rather than risking being left holding the bag of partnership liabilities. Indeed, that protection is even more important if the indemnified partners are the only ones who are personally liable under the statute. On the other hand, perhaps the partners' election to register as an LLP should be interpreted as replacing the indemnification provision with the liability protection in the LLP statute on the theory that the partners have now shown that they want limited liability. RUPA § 306(c) addresses these questions by providing that the liability limitation "shall apply notwithstanding anything inconsistent in the partnership agreement that existed immediately before the vote required to become a limited liability partnership . . . ." Is this an appropriate solution to the problem?

D.   Fiduciary Duties

LLP status may affect the fiduciary duties that are appropriate for such firms. As discussed in § 8.01, fiduciary duties are "gap-filling" rules that the courts apply to deal with matters that the parties cannot easily cover in their agreements. It follows that the duties applied to a contractual relationship depend on the express and implied terms of the particular relationship. One such term is surely a partnership's registration as an LLP.

LLP status may create conflicts of interest that are unique to this type of firm. Partners who may be subject to supervisory liability may use their management power to refuse to distribute earnings that could be used to pay off the liability and thereby reduce their exposure. This could hurt other partners, who are taxed on earnings rather than on distributions. Because specific contracting to deal with this problem may be costly, courts could fill gaps by applying fiduciary duties to constrain conflicts of interest. However, it is not clear what such duties should be, since the interests of the exposed partners in retaining income are not obviously superior to those of the other partners in distributing it.

LLP status also affects the partners' duty of care. Partners who face potential supervisory liability to third parties have special incentives to exercise caution, and therefore arguably do not need to be subjected to an additional duty of care to their co-partners. On the other hand, supervisory liability may justify the creation of a special duty of care to discipline partners who deliberately stay away from supervising in order to avoid personal liability to creditors, even if such actions increase the firm's risk of liability.

Despite the potential need for special fiduciary duties for LLPs, courts may tend to carry over fiduciary duties from non-LLPs to LLPs and vice versa without taking sufficient account of the differences between the two types of firms. For example, courts may hold on the basis of non-LLP partnership law that there is no conflict of interest as long as partners share equally in distributions, and that the RUPA gross negligence duty of care applies regardless of the liability shield. This is a potential cost of using the LLP form to "link" with an existing body of partnership precedents and customs (*see* §§ 1.02(B) and 13.04(A)).

E.   Dissolution

As discussed in Chapter 9, there are strong arguments for abandoning dissolution-at-will even in non-LLP partnerships. LLP statutes that limit all partner liability undercut one of the strongest remaining arguments for liquidation-at-will—the need to pay off liabilities when partners leave. Also, as discussed in Chapter 9, partnership law lets any partner withdraw from the firm irrespective of contrary provisions in the partnership agreement. The main argument against enforcing agreements not to dissociate is that the partners' inability to stop their continuing responsibility for partnership claims could so burden partners that it is doubtful they actually consented to such an open-ended obligation. LLP provisions undercut this rationale for mandating dissociation at will.

13.05 Tax and Regulatory Aspects of LLPs

The fact that LLPs are "linked" with partnership law does not mean that LLPs will be treated like non-LLP general partnerships for all purposes. This section illustrates some potential distinctions between LLPs and other types of firms under tax and regulatory statutes.

A.   Tax Characterization

Tax characterization is discussed generally in Chapter 10. The tax classification of LLPs under the "Kintner rules" was somewhat tricky. However, the Kintner rules are now largely of historical interest in light of the IRS' "check-the-box" rule, which permits closely held unincorporated domestic firms to elect whether to be treated as partnerships or corporations for tax purposes. *See* § 10.04(A)(4).

B.   LLP and LLC Interests as "Securities" under Federal and State Securities Laws

As discussed in § 8.02, general partnership interests usually are *not* securities even if management is centralized to some extent in a management committee as long as the partners have significant powers to oversee management and can exercise these powers. On the other hand, as discussed in § 12.02(A)(4), LLC interests may or may not be securities. Even if LLC interests *are* "securities," LLPs should and probably will be treated differently for reasons analogous to those discussed above with regard to tax characterization: The general partnership default rule of equal member participation in management matters under the "efforts of others" *Howey* rule (*see* § 3.03(B) above). Although partnerships can centralize internal management power in management committees, at least non-RUPA-based partnerships may not be able easily to cut off the authority of non-managing members to bind the firm in transactions with third parties.

C.   Employment Discrimination Law

As discussed in § 3.03(A), partnerships, including LLPs, are potentially subject to the employment discrimination laws. As the *Simpson* case in that section makes clear, one who is designated as a partner in a partnership may or may not be treated as an employee depending on whether she has partner characteristics. The *Simpson* case noted the importance of partners' personal liability, although it doubted that the employee in that case would really have been subject to such liability. This suggests that a member of an LLP might be more likely than a member of a non-LLP to be treated as an employee, assuming all other facts concerning the relationship are the same. However, a member of an LLP might be less likely to be an employee than is a member of an LLC, again if the terms of the relevant partnership and operating agreements were otherwise the same.

D. Bankruptcy Law

The treatment of a bankrupt LLP or bankrupt LLP partners depends to some extent on whether an LLP is a partnership or a corporation under the Bankruptcy Code. Code (11 U.S.C.) § 101(9) says corporation "includes" an "(i) association having a power or privilege that a private corporation, but not an individual or a partnership, possesses; (ii) partnership association organized under a law that makes the capital subscribed responsible for the debts of such association; (iii) joint-stock company; (iv) unincorporated company or association; or (v) business trust." However, it "does not include limited partnership."

LLPs fit the definition of "corporation" in the sense that they have at least a form of limited liability, which is a "power or privilege that a private corporation possesses." However, state law generally controls which firms are treated as "partnerships" in bankruptcy. Thus, it is significant that LLPs are clearly defined as "partnerships" under LLP provisions. Indeed, even "limited partnerships" are excluded from the definition of "corporation." Moreover, the Code explicitly applies state law LLP liability limitations in determining partner contribution obligations in bankruptcy (*see* § 13.02(G), above), strongly suggesting that LLPs will be treated as partnerships under this provision.

If an LLP is a partnership for bankruptcy law purposes, the same bankruptcy rules that apply to partnerships also should apply to LLPs. However, the law of fraudulent transfers applies differently to LLPs than to other partnerships. Code § 548(b) provides that a transfer may be avoided if made by an "insolvent" partnership or the transfer rendered the partnership insolvent. "Insolvent" is defined under Code § 101(32)(B), as well as under § 2(c) of the Uniform Fraudulent Transfers Act and § 2(2) of the Uniform Fraudulent Conveyance Act so as to take into account general partners' nonpartnership property. This definition does not fit LLPs, particularly those with complete limited liability, because LLP partners may not have to contribute toward the payment of debts.

E. Professional Firms as LLPs

General partnership and LLP statutes do not bar partnerships or LLPs from engaging in professional practice. In fact, the New York and California statutes are *restricted* to use by professional firms. In other states, the LLP form was apparently designed for use by professional firms. LLPs clearly are defined as "partnerships," which literally qualifies them for use by professional firms even under professional registration statutes that permit only partnerships or general partnerships to register. Moreover, the LLP statutes generally carry over the supervisory liability and insurance requirements from the state's professional corporation statutes.

Although statutes apparently authorize professional firms to use the LLP form, in some states law firms also must comply with state bar or court rules. Several ethics opinions have authorized law firms to practice as LLPs, but use of the LLP form, or at least the enforceability of the LLP liability limitation, is still unclear in other states. *See* BROMBERG & RIBSTEIN ON LIMITED LIABILITY PARTNERSHIPS AND THE REVISED UNIFORM PARTNERSHIP ACT, § 7.04(a)-(b). The use of the LLP form to limit professionals' liability raises issues similar to those discussed in § 12.06 concerning LLCs. Some specific problems concerning LLPs are discussed in the following Notes.

Notes and Questions

1. **Notice to clients.** Converting an existing general partnership to an LLP (or, for that matter, an LLC) raises the question whether and how existing clients must be notified. Is it enough for the firm to avoid personal liability merely to add the "LLP" designation to its letterhead, or must it send a notice to existing clients informing them of the change? If the latter, how explicitly must the notice inform clients of the consequences of the change? Clients may not understand that their lawyers are limiting their vicarious liability or what this means. On the other hand, this problem is not much greater than for professional corporations whose names include a "PC" designation. As discussed in the following notes, the notice issue may arise under LLP statutes, the common law and ethical rules.

2. **Notice under LLP statutes.** Under LLP statutes, post-registration dealings with the client may be deemed to arise from a preexisting contract in the form of a general client relationship or representation in connection with a specific pending matter. For example, a court might analogize the registration to a dissolution and require notice to prior clients just as a dissolving partnership must give actual or constructive notice to pre-existing creditors in order to limit post-dissolution liabilities. *See* § 9.05(B), and particularly *Redman v. Walters* discussed in that subsection. On the other hand, one could argue that the LLP provisions, by avoiding a dissolution of the firm, are specifically intended to cut off this type of continuing liability. *See* § 13.02(A), above.

3. **Common law disclosure requirements.** A lawyer or accountant may be deemed to be the client's fiduciary, thereby triggering strong affirmative disclosure requirements. Moreover, failure to fully disclose the change in liability may trigger remedies for fraud or persuade a court to pierce the veil of the LLP and impose personal liability even if the statute would limit the members' liability.

4. **Ethical considerations concerning notice.** Some ethical opinions have held that the "LLP" designation in the name of the firm is enough notice to third parties without spelling out "registered limited liability partnership." D.C. Ethics Op. No. 254 (March 21, 1995); Mich. State Bar Standing Comm. on Prof. and Jud. Ethics, Op. R-17 (1994); N.Y. County Lawyers' Ethics Opinion No. 703 (November 28, 1994). This is sensible since, as discussed in Note 1, there is no greater likelihood of confusion with respect to "LLP" than there is with respect to "PC," and since so many firms have lim-

ited liability in some form that clients and others may no longer expect their lawyers and other professionals to be vicariously liable. But these opinions do not necessarily mean that a mere addition of initials will be enough to ensure that the firm has limited liability with respect to existing clients that were caught in the transition. Thus, the Bar of the City of New York Formal Opinion 1995-7 (May 31, 1995) noted that "lawyers may wish to consider whether [use of the initials] is adequate in all circumstances. In addition, lawyers changing to LLC or LLP form should be prepared to answer any client questions regarding the nature of the change and its ramifications." Also, the Kansas Bar Association Ethics/Advisory Services Committee in Opinion 94-03 (June 28, 1994) states that "while changing the form of practice from a professional corporation, a general partnership, or an LLC, to an LLP format is not an 'agreement' to limit liability, the committee believes a full discussion should take place with the firm's clients of what is happening to the firm regarding the attorney-client relationship." For a discussion of ethical and common law requirements of notice, *see* Fortney, *Professional Responsibility and Liability Issues Related to Limited Liability Law Partnerships.* 39 S. TEX. L. REV. 399 (1998) (concluding that firms must fully disclose to clients rather than merely including in their names the initials indicating the type of firm).

5. **Multistate professional LLPs.** As with multistate LLCs (*see* § 12.02(J)(3)), state variations in rules regarding professional practice by LLPs may impose significant costs for national law and accounting firms. For example, the "Big Six" accounting firms could not convert to LLPs until all states allowed accounting firms to practice in this form. *See* Rick Telberg, *Big 6 Race into LLPs,* 8 ACCOUNTING TODAY, n.14 at 1, 41 (Aug. 8, 1994).

6. **Policy issues.** As with LLCs, the ultimate question is whether restrictions on limited liability for professional firms are justified from a policy standpoint. *See* Note 8, p. 359-60.

13.06 Limited Liability Limited Partnerships

Some state limited liability partnership (LLP) acts allow limited partnerships to register as LLPs. *See* BROMBERG & RIBSTEIN ON LIMITED LIABILITY PARTNERSHIPS AND THE REVISED UNIFORM PARTNERSHIP ACT, Chapter 5 (tabulating statutory variations, including those concerning the issues discussed below). This would create a "limited liability limited partnership," or "LLLP." As discussed above in Section 11.06, RULPA may be revised to effectively make LLLP status the default rule for limited partnerships.

A.   Liability of LLLP Partners

LLLP general partners are liable to the same extent as LLP general partners. LLLP limited partners may be subject to LLP statutory provisions that impose supervisory liability. Moreover, several statutes provide that the LLP liability limitation also applies to limited partners who are liable for the partnership's debts under the limited partnership act. This reduces the effect of the "control rule," discussed above in Chapter 11. For example, a "family limited partnership" (*see* § 11.09(A), above) might use the LLLP to assign equity interests without management rights or vicarious liability to family members by making them limited partners. In this context, it may be enough to deny management rights to the family members and to restrict their authority to bind the firm without also giving a potential remedy to creditors if the family members do exercise management powers. The firm could accomplish almost the same thing by becoming an LLP and delegating management rights to the senior managers.

Is there a danger of misleading creditors by removing the "teeth" of the control rule? Also, should a limited partnership that is not subject to the control rule be treated differently from other limited partnerships in terms of applying the other rules discussed in Chapter 11? For example, limited partners who have been freed from the constraints of the control rule may no longer need the strong fiduciary protections given limited partners in standard limited partnerships (*see* § 11.08(A)). These issues, of course, will be eliminated if, as is currently planned, the revision of RULPA eliminates the control rule and makes LLLP status the default rule.

B.   LLP Statutes with No LLLP Provisions

What is the status of LLLPs under LLP statutes that do not explicitly provide for LLLPs? UPA § 6(2) provides that the partnership act applies to limited partnerships except to the extent that limited partnership provisions are inconsistent, while RULPA § 1105 provides that the general partnership statute applies "in any case not provided for in this Act." LLP provisions probably would not apply to *limited* partners under either the general partnership or the limited partnership statute since the LLP provisions would vary applicable provisions of the limited partnership statute. However, RULPA § 403(b) provides that a general partner of a limited partnership has the liabilities of a partner in a partnership without limited partners. Under this provision, the LLP provisions probably apply to general partners in limited partnerships.

C.   Foreign LLLPs

What is the status outside of its formation state of a limited partnership that is an LLLP in its formation state? Should the state of operation apply the same rules as the formation state, or should the firm have personal liability for general partners and controlling limited partners if these rules applied in the state of operation?

CHAPTER 14
NEW DIRECTIONS FOR
UNINCORPORATED FIRMS

14.01 New Business Forms: The Statutory Business Trust and Limited Partnership Association

New forms of unincorporated firms may be added, and indeed may become more important than, those discussed so far. This development may be spurred by jurisdictional competition as well as new tax flexibility. In particular, the IRS' "check-the-box" rule, discussed in § 10.04(A)(4), permits virtually any unincorporated non-"publicly traded" domestic firm to elect to be taxed as a partnership. Examples of statutes that take advantage of this flexibility include the Wyoming Statutory Trust (WYO. STAT. §§ 17-23-101–17-23-121, 17-23-201, 17-23-202, 17-23-301 and 17-23-302), the Colorado Limited Partnership Association (COLO. REV. STAT. §§ 7-63-101-7-63-117) and the Delaware Business Trust (DEL. CODE ANN., tit. 12, §§ 3801-3820). These statutes might well become obsolete because of changes in the wake of "check-the-box" in limited partnership and LLC statutes discussed above in Chapters 11 and 12. This Chapter speculates about more radical variations and about where the law of unincorporated firms may be headed.

14.02 Unincorporated Non-Profit Associations

Suppose you have formed very informal neighborhood association that you plan to operate on a non-profit basis, but have not made any filings. A "neighborhood watch" car operated by your association runs over a kid on a bicycle. The damages exceed the car owner's insurance, and the child's parents sue the "association." Who is liable? Consider the following case.

Progress Printing Corporation v. Jane Byrne Political Committee
235 Ill. App. 3d 292, 601 N.E.2d 1055, 176 Ill. Dec. 357 (1992)

[The facts in this case are set forth in the excerpt above in § 2.02.]

* * *

III.

The circuit court held that the candidate was personally liable because it was she who initially spoke with Stanley, telling him that Progress would perform printing for her campaign and it was she whom the work benefitted. * * *

[T]he question presented in this case is a straightforward one: whether under the circumstances, the candidate may be held personally liable for the Committee's debts.

The candidate argues that she is liable neither directly nor vicariously under the facts in the record and the applicable law. She argues that ratification, if any, was by the Committee, not her, because it was the Committee's funds that paid the bills, and the debts of a voluntary association are those of the association alone[.] * * *

Although the candidate characterizes this case as one of first impression in Illinois, a similar suit was filed against William Hale "Big Bill" Thompson in *Severinghaus Printing Co. v. Thompson* (1926), 241 Ill. App. 35. In *Severinghaus*, a printer sued Thompson for unpaid bills for campaign literature that had been furnished to the William Hale Thompson Republican Organization, which Thompson headed. Although the circuit court had directed a verdict for Thompson, the appellate court reversed, noting that the plaintiff had presented sufficient evidence that Thompson had approved and ratified the printing contracts, so a directed verdict was improper. The court noted that much support existed for the plaintiff printer's theory that "if a member of a voluntary association, the objects of which do not contemplate profit or loss in the business sense, expressly or impliedly authorizes a transaction in which an indebtedness is incurred by or on behalf of such association, or if he assents to or ratifies the contract on which such a liability is predicated, he is liable as a principal for the indebtedness." (241 Ill. App. at 39.) The court also observed that "in such cases the liability of the participating, assenting or ratifying members is joint and several, and that it is a question for the [factfinder] to determine to whom the credit was given and whether the members authorized or ratified the contract." (241 Ill. App. at 39.) Therefore, we see no legal bar generally to holding the candidate jointly and severally liable for the Committee's debts. More particularly, even if the candidate did not have actual knowledge of each transaction, which is questionable given her conversation with Martin about a very small order, her lack of awareness, as explained above, was the direct result of her own and Griffin's admitted failure to avail themselves of the opportunity to repudiate the purportedly unauthorized transactions upon receipt of the invoices. Therefore, like any member of a voluntary association who knows, or should have known under the circumstances, that a transaction has occurred and who then accepts its benefits for herself, the candidate here may be held liable for the Committee's debts.

Moreover, we are persuaded by the record here that although the Committee was in form a voluntary unincorporated association, it was in substance a sole proprietorship. The candidate was the chairman of the Committee and the other two officers were family members. Even though the candidate was not the Committee's treasurer, only she signed the Committee's checks. The Committee had but a single purpose, election of its chairman to public office. By the candidate's own testimony, it was she who was in charge of the campaign. She herself initiated the series of transactions here, and the materials at issue were ordered and used for her benefit and could have had no other purpose. Unlike, for example, a parent-teacher association or a softball team, the purpose of which is to advance the interests of the group as a whole, with control of the association shared among officers, the Committee was controlled by and for the benefit of one person, the candidate.

Under these circumstances, just as a court in equity may hold corporate officers and directors personally liable by "piercing the corporate veil," so too was it appropriate for the circuit court to find the candidate herself liable here because the Committee had no personality separate from the candidate, and substantial injustice would result from an opposite conclusion. [citation omitted] Had the candidate wished to avoid personal liability for campaign debts, she had the option under the Election Code of refraining from membership in the association. Alternatively, she could have chosen to incorporate the Committee, as she did later, the standard method for avoiding personal liability. The candidate chose not to incorporate, to be chairman of the Committee, to have no one other than family members as Committee officers, and to retain "the final word." This choice carries with it the potential for contractual liability to third parties. Accordingly, the circuit court's ruling that the candidate may be held individually liable on the record here was not against the manifest weight of the evidence. * * *

Notes and Questions

1. **Planning implications.** What, precisely, should Byrne have done to insulate herself from liability under the law applied in the case?

2. **Sole proprietorship.** *Progress Printing* raises the question of how a sole proprietor may limit her liability. This is discussed below in § 14.04.

3. **Non-Profit Corporations, Partnerships and LLCs.** Conventional business association standard forms are designed for for-profit business firms. As discussed in § 3.02, the partnership statutes apply only if the firm is a "business for profit." There are, of course, special statutes for non-profit corporations, which include special provisions to protect contributors. There are no such statutes for non-profit LLCs. One might want to use the LLC form to avoid some of the formalities and requirements of the non-profit corporation statutes (although not necessarily for tax advantages, because non-profit corporations can be organized as tax-exempts). However, it is not clear whether conventional LLCs can be organized as non-profits. At least in the absence of clear statutory authorization, non-profit LLCs might be regarded as "end-runs" around the requirements for non-profit corporations. Moreover, the LLC form is better suited to firms whose members have a right to its profits since it provides for members who make

capital contributions, receive distributions, and have fiduciary protection and information rights. On the other hand, LLC statutes usually allow LLCs to be organized for any "lawful purpose," which certainly could include operating a non-profit business. *See* RIBSTEIN & KEATINGE ON LIMITED LIABILITY COMPANIES, § 4.10.

4 **Non-profit associations: a uniform law.** The National Conference of Commissioners on Uniform State Laws in 1992 promulgated a Uniform Unincorporated Nonprofit Association Act. *See* Comment, *The Ramifications of Idaho's new Uniform Unincorporated Nonprofit Associations Act,* 31 IDAHO L. REV. 297-312 (1994). The Act (§ 1(2)) defines "nonprofit association" as "an unincorporated organization consisting of [two] or more members joined by mutual consent for a common, nonprofit purpose." This almost certainly includes a marriage. Indeed, gay couples who lack the legal right to marry in California have registered in California as unincorporated associations. *See* Memorandum to Commissioners on Uniform State Laws from ABA Ad Hoc Committee on Uniform Unincorporated Nonprofit Associations Act (July 28, 1992) at 5 (quoting letter from California Bar Association Committee). The Act does not provide for governance rights, but does provide for some formalities. For example, § 5 of the Act provides for the formal filing of a statement of authority that would clarify who has the power to transfer property, and requires any such statement set forth facts such as name and street address that would not apply to very informal organizations. How might *Progress Printing* have been decided under this law?

14.03 Publicly Traded Unincorporated Firms

This book has been almost exclusively concerned with closely held firms. However, unincorporated business associations also may be publicly held. As discussed in Chapter 11, many publicly traded limited partnerships were formed during the 1980s. Moreover, many widely held mutual funds have been formed as common law (Massachusetts) business trusts, and there are many widely held real estate investment trusts (REITs).

Broader use of publicly traded unincorporated firms has been limited to some extent by tax rules, under which publicly traded partnerships are taxed as corporations. (*See* § 11.11(B)). But there is no reason in principle why an unincorporated firm could not decide to become publicly traded, as long as it did not seek to be taxed as a partnership.

Publicly traded firms may decide to be partnerships or LLCs, rather than corporations, in order to escape corporate restrictions on contracting. Such firms may greater flexibility in opting out of fiduciary duties. *See* Ribstein, *Unlimited Contracting in the Delaware Limited Partnership and its Implications for Corporate Law,* 17 J. CORP. L. 299 (1991). They might replace corporate-type fiduciary duties with other constraints on managers. For example, the default rights of members to cash out their interests under partnership and LLC statutes may help to reduce the managers' ability to use the firm's property for private gain. Also, the members could contract to compel managers to make regular distributions without needing to be concerned about rules that prevent restrictions on directors' discretion in corporations that are not "close corporations." (*See*

§ 10.03(B)). Such constraints on managers would have an effect similar to that of a leveraged buyout, which forces managers to distribute income in the form of interest on the large debt that results from such a buyout. The advantage of the partnership or LLC form from this perspective is that the members' exit and distribution rights are not as likely to throw the firm into a costly bankruptcy as are obligations to creditors.

The use of the partnership or LLC form by publicly held firms may create problems that are the converse of those which arise from close corporations. The partnership and the LLC forms are designed primarily for closely held businesses. Just as the close corporation form was not suited for firms in which members participate directly in management and have no ability to exit freely (*see* § 10.02), partnership-type default rules such as direct management by members, no free transferability of management rights, and allocation of finances by customized agreement rather than through shares of stock may create problems for publicly traded firms unless they are suitably customized by agreement.

14.04 Unified Business Association Statutes

Some lawyers have proposed a unified contractual organization, in which all business associations in a state would be formed under a single statute, and firms could check off variations under this statute, such as concerning management form. *See* George W. Coleman and Robert R. Keatinge, Universal [Contractual] Organization Act, American Bar Association, Section of Business Law, Committees on Taxation and Partnerships and Unincorporated Business Organizations (August 7, 1995).

Is this a good idea? Consider the various functions of business association statutes discussed in Chapter 1 and throughout this book. Separate statutory forms arguably serve important non-tax functions, such as helping courts and contracting parties fill gaps in contracts with rules that fit specific types of relationships. As also discussed throughout this book, "linkage" between business forms involves both costs and benefits—it provides a common body of case and administrative law, but invites courts and others to treat disparate situations alike. For example, the proposal just cited suggests, among other things, common dissolution and dissociation provisions for all business associations. In light of the functions of separate business firms, should these be embodied in separate statutes?

14.05 The Unincorporated Limited Liability Sole Proprietorship

Progress Printing raises issues that bring us back to the starting point of this book—the sole proprietorship. The common law agency rules discussed in Chapter 2 provide that an owner who delegates discretion or power to an agent may be personally liable for at least some of those agent's acts on the owner's behalf. The sole owner may establish a corporation, which would then hire the agent. As long as a court does not "pierce the corporate veil," the liability would have to be paid out of the corporation's, and not the owner's, assets. Moreover, the owner could have the advantage of "flow-through" taxation by electing to be taxed under Subchapter S of the Internal Revenue Code. But because of restrictions on this form, it is not a complete answer for the sole proprietor. For example, as discussed in Chapter 10, a non-resident alien or a business association may not own a Subchapter S. Thus, a foreign firm or individual could not operate the firm as an S corporation U.S. "branch." The sole owner can obtain limited liability without incorporating by forming an LLC under virtually all statutes. The firm probably would be taxed as a sole proprietorship, which would be similar to partnership taxation.

But these other business forms are not particularly well suited to sole proprietorships. They all provide for ownership, management and dissociation rights of multiple owners, and many of the statutes also assume a separation between owners and managers. Although the proprietor obviously would want to vary these default provisions, it is not clear how the proprietor can enter into an "operating agreement" (*see* § 12.02(E)) that accomplishes this result. Thus, under these statutes the sole proprietorship is a square peg in a round hole.

Why not a statute that is designed explicitly for sole proprietors? Such a statute might be called a "LISP"—that is, a "Limited Liability Sole Proprietorship." The statute could provide that, by forming a sole proprietorship under the statute, the owner is not personally liable for the debts of the business—that is, for acts solely of agents (as distinguished from wrongdoing or negligence of the owner himself). It might also provide for formalities of organization, name, and so forth that are common to all limited liability firms. The statute would not, however, include default rules designed for multiple members or manager-member firms. Rather, the statute could include rules governing relations between the sole owner and agents or managers that would clarify the non-owner status and the rights of such people. For example, the statute could provide that non-owner managers have certain powers to bind the firm and to be compensated, provide for succession of ownership following the proprietor's death or retirement, and clarify that the owner owes no fiduciary duties in dealing with the LISP. *See* Ribstein, *The Loneliest Number: The Unincorporated Limited Liability Sole Proprietorship,* J. ASSET PROT. 46 (May/June 1996).

14.06 Limited Liability without Business Associations

The only way to ensure limited liability for parties to a relationship that would otherwise be a partnership or agency is to form a corporation or one of the other business associations discussed in this book. But there are many types of economic relationships, including joint ventures, franchises and joint operating agreements, in which the parties may be vicariously liable but that may not want the default rules that go with the existing forms of business association. A possible way out of this dilemma is statutes authorizing "Contractual Entities" whose owner liability and other terms would be governed solely by their filed operating agreements. For an article discussing such a proposal, *see* Ribstein, *Limited Liability Unlimited,* 24 DEL. J. CORP. L. 407 (1999).

14.07 Limited Liability as a Default Rule

The LLC, LLP and other unincorporated limited liability business forms mean that it is now possible for virtually any type of business—regardless of how it is organized—to have limited liability. In other words, the only "ticket" to limited liability is a simple filing rather than complying with structural rules. As a result of the simplicity of forming limited liability firms, personal liability is becoming more the exception than the rule. This would be even clearer if statutes permitted the "Contractual Entity" discussed in the previous section.

Why not dispense with the filing and provide that a firm has limited liability unless otherwise agreed with the creditors? What policy issues would this present? Does the filing serve any function other than notice to creditors? If not, why not simply require firms to clarify in their names (*e.g.,* by adding "Ltd" or some such designation) that they are limited liability firms? For a discussion of this and related issues, *see* Ribstein, *Limited Liability and Theories of the Corporation,* 50 MD. L. REV. 80 (1991).

Assuming there is no reason in principle why firms should have to make formal filings in order to have limited liability, what types of "firms" would have limited liability? Limited liability could become the rule for partnerships simply by amending the partnership statute to eliminate partners' personal liability for partnership debts. This would cover for-profit business firms with two or more members. What about one-owner firms? Suppose one decides to go through life as "Larry Ribstein, Ltd."? Also, what about non-profit firms? Reconsider the hypothetical at the beginning of § 14.01.

MEMNERSHIP AGREEMENT
OF THE CHAMELEON COMPANY

Introduction

This is a "chameleon" agreement which can be adapted for a particular business and type of firm by selecting options for some of the provisions. Because the agreement is intended to suit several different statutory forms, the parties are referred to as "memners"—*i.e.,* partner/members. The agreement is relatively simple and does not emphasize sophisticated firm-specific variations or tax-oriented provisions (although some tax issues are discussed in the Annotations). The agreement is not intended as a "form" agreement, but rather is intended to illustrate some functions of operating or partnership agreements, such as how the provisions relate to each other and how they relate to the standard form. The Annotations cite to discussions of these issues and more particularized drafting examples discussed in this book.

Memnership Agreement of the Chameleon Company

WHEREAS, the undersigned parties wish to form a [type of firm] pursuant to the _____Act by entering into this Agreement [and filing a Certificate of Formation of the Company with the office of the Secretary of State of _____].

Annotation: This provision makes clear what type of standard form the parties have selected. For a limited liability firm, such as an LLC, the provision would add language that indicates that the formation of the underlying firm is contingent on the filing that is necessary to ensure that the parties have limited liability. Thus, if there has been no filing, a court may find that the parties are not liable as partners of the would-be LLC or limited partnership.

NOW, THEREFORE, in consideration of the obligations set forth herein and for other good and valuable consideration, the receipt and sufficiency of which are hereby acknowledged, the Memners hereby agree as follows:

ARTICLE I: DEFINITIONS

Unless the context otherwise requires, the terms defined in this Article I shall, for the purposes of this Agreement, have the meanings herein specified.

1.1 "Agreement"

This Agreement, as amended, modified, supplemented or restated from time to time.

1.2 "Capital Account"

The account maintained for a Memner pursuant to paragraph 3.4.

1.3 "Contribution"

The Memner's contribution to the capital of the firm pursuant to paragraph 3.1.

1.4 "Company"

Chameleon Company, the [type of firm] formed under this agreement.

Annotation: Some agreements add to this definition that the Company is formed under and pursuant to the selected state statute. This is misleading, however, because it is the agreement that forms the company, while the act simply gives the company characteristics that it might not have under the agreement alone. Note that this provision states the name of the Company. Some agreements specify the name in a separate provision. However, to the extent that the name has a special legal effect, this is effect is established by the statute governing the form of business or an assumed name statute.

1.5 "Manager"

X or a person elected as a successor to X pursuant to paragraph 6.6.

Annotation: Note that, pursuant to paragraph 6.2, a third party is entitled to rely on representations of a person listed in Schedule A as a manager.

1.6 "Memner"

A person who (i) executed the initial version of this Agreement or who has been admitted as a substitute or new Memner pursuant to Article IX and (ii) is identified on Schedule A attached to and made a part of this agreement, as updated from time to time.

Annotation: This provision, together with the definition of Schedule A, below, clarify that one becomes a memner not only by complying with the admission procedures but also by being identified on Schedule A. This makes it relatively easy for both memners and third parties to identify the memners.

1.7 "Memnership Interest"

A Memner's rights in distributions and allocations of the profits, losses, gains, deductions, and credits of the Company.

Annotation: This tracks the typical statutory definition for unincorporated firms. It isolates memners' financial rights, which are freely transferable under paragraph 9.1, as distinguished from the rest of the memners' rights, particularly including management rights, which are not freely transferable under paragraph 9.3.

1.8 "Net Loss"

Any loss incurred by the Memners under the Company's method of accounting for federal income tax purposes.

Annotation: As this provision makes clear, "net loss" is defined for tax purposes. A separate definition may apply for purposes of the firm's internal accounting.

1.9 "Net Profit"

Any income or gain actually earned by the Memners or which, under the Company's method of accounting, must be deemed to have been earned by the Company and reported on Form 1065 for federal income tax purposes

Annotation: As for "net losses," the firm may have a separate definition for internal accounting purposes. Note that professional firms may provide that "net profits" does not include compensation paid to memners for professional services pursuant to a separate provision for such compensation. This distinguishes service firms, whose memners receive distributions as employees as well as owners, from capital-intensive firms whose distributions are based solely on their ownership interests.

1.10 "Sharing Ratio"

The voting and financial interest of a Memner set forth on Schedule A attached to and made a part of this agreement, as updated from time to time.

Annotation: Many firms have voting and financial percentages that differ from the initial capital account ratios. For example, in a limited partnership, general partners may have different ratios than limited partners to reflect their different liability and management roles, and there may be significant differences among memners of service-oriented firms to reflect their human capital contributions. Moreover, even if the "sharing ratios" start out the same as the capital account ratios, they may diverge over time where the firm incurs losses that reduce memners' capital accounts below zero.

ARTICLE II: FORMATION AND PURPOSE

2.1 Formation and Applicable Law

The Memners agree to form the Company as a [type of firm] under and pursuant to the provisions of the _____ Act [effective as of the date on which the certificate is filed]. This Agreement shall be construed under and in accordance with the laws of the State of _____ .

Annotation: This establishes both choice of entity and choice of law, and makes clear that the parties do not intend to form the agreement until filing if the firm is a form of business in which the critical feature of limited liability may depend on filing. *See* the Annotation to the introductory clause.

2.2 Registered Agent and Office

The Company's registered agent and office shall be _____ . At any time, the Manager may designate another registered agent and/or registered office.

2.3 Principal Place of Business

The principal place of business of the Company shall be at _____unless otherwise changed by the vote of the Memners as provided below.

2.4 Purpose and Powers

The Company is formed for the object and purpose of, and the nature of the business to be conducted and promoted by the Company is, engaging in any lawful act or activity for which limited liability companies may be formed under the ___ Act.

Annotation: This is a standard provision, but it may not be a good idea since it may broadly define the power of memners and managers to bind the firm and expand their fiduciary duties. As to the power to bind, *see Zimmerman*, § 5.03

ARTICLE III: CONTRIBUTIONS AND ACCOUNTS

3.1 Nature and Amount of Contributions

Memners shall make or have made cash contributions to the capital of the Company in the amounts set forth on Schedule A, as updated from time to time.

Annotation: Note that this provision says that the contributions are as set forth on Schedule A, which makes that listing conclusive. This should help eliminate potential disputes about whether the list of contributions is accurate. However, since this may frustrate memners' expectations, it cannot completely foreclose litigation that seeks to reform Schedule A (which is part of the agreement) to align it with an alleged underlying bargain. Requiring cash contributions eliminates valuation problems and reduces tax problems, such as those concerning allocation of tax liabilities for gain in the value of property. It may reduce some financing flexibility, particularly in a service-oriented firm in which the memners may contribute tools of the trade such as a law library.

3.2 Enforcement of Contribution Agreement

In the event any Memner fails to make the contribution such Memner has agreed to make, the manager shall give such Memner a Notice of the failure to meet the agreement. If the Memner fails to perform the agreement within ten Business Days of the giving of Notice, the Memner shall be deemed to be in default and shall be subject to suit in the court of appropriate jurisdiction in the state in which the Principal Office is located or the state of the Memner's address as reflected in this Company Agreement, or expulsion of the Memner pursuant to paragraph 10.1. Each Memner expressly agrees to the jurisdiction of such courts but only for the enforcement of agreements. The other Memners may pay any amount that is in default as a loan which bears interest at the prime rate or the maximum non-usurious rate, whichever is less, and which is secured by the defaulting Memner's interest in the Company. Until they are fully repaid, the paying Memners shall be entitled to all distributions to which the defaulting Memner would have been entitled. Notwithstanding the foregoing, no agreement or other obligation to make an additional contribution may be enforced by a creditor of the Company or other Person other than the Company unless the Memner expressly consents to such enforcement or to the assignment of the obligation to such creditor.

3.3 Additional Contributions

Memners may be required or permitted to make contributions in addition to the initial amounts set forth on Schedule A only when and to the extent required by the Manager and a majority of the sharing ratios. When such a determination is made, the Managers shall give Notice to all Memners in writing at least ten Business Days prior to the date on which such contribution is due which shall set forth the amount of additional contribution needed, the purpose for which the contribution is needed, and the date by which the Memners should contribute. The Memners shall be obligated to make the additional contribution in the proportions of their sharing ratios. In the event any one or more Memners do not make their additional contribution, the other Memners shall be given the opportunity to make the contributions in their sharing ratios, and such ratios shall be adjusted to reflect these additional contributions. The exclusive remedy against a Memner who fails to make a required contribution is expulsion pursuant to Paragraph 10.1, below.

Annotation: The firm—particularly a startup without established equity or credit—may have difficulty finding needed capital without giving up significant equity or control. The memners, who presumably already have a stake in and substantial information about the company, may be the best source of capital. On the other hand, mandatory capital contributions may permit managers or majority memners to squeeze out other memners. This provision is a compromise that encourages memners to contribute more but also lets them out if they want to go. *See* the *Chandler* case and related discussion in § 9.06(B). Note how this provision clarifies the issue in *Chandler* as to whether expulsion is the exclusive remedy.

3.4 Capital Accounts

An individual capital account shall be established and maintained for each Memner. The amount in a Memner's capital account initially shall be the amount of a Memner's initial capital contribution. A Memner's capital account shall be credited with any other capital contribution made by it, if and when made and with a Memner's distributive share of net profits determined pursuant to paragraph 4.1, and shall be charged with distributions to the Memner and with the net losses charged to the Memner pursuant to paragraph 4.1.

Annotation: The capital account is used for the purpose of determining distributions on dissociation pursuant to paragraph 11.3, but not for voting and profit/loss percentages under paragraphs 4.2 and 8.1. As discussed in § 4.04, capital accounts are very important for tax purposes. Indeed, operating or partnership agreements sometimes refer to the Treasury Regulations regarding maintenance of capital accounts.

3.5 Advances

If any Memner advances any funds to the Company in excess of the Memner's capital contributions, including any payment of liabilities of the firm, the amount of such advance shall not increase its capital account or its sharing ratio. The amount of any such advance shall be a debt obligation of the Company to such Memner and shall be repaid to it by the Company upon such terms and conditions as shall be determined by the Manager and Memners holding a majority of the voting percentage.

Annotation: The distinction between advances and capital contributions is discussed for partnerships in § 4.02. Similar rules apply to LLCs.

ARTICLE IV: PROFITS, LOSSES, AND COMPENSATION

4.1 Determination of Net Profits and Net Losses

Net profits, net losses and any such other items shall be determined on a daily, monthly or other basis, as determined by the Manager using any method that is permissible under applicable federal and state tax law.

Annotation: The agreement often provides for much more detail, particularly regarding complications that may arise under tax law. The accounting method is specified in paragraph 5.3.

4.2 Allocation of Net Profits and Net Losses

The Company's net profits and net losses, as well as other items of income, gain, deduction and credit, shall be allocated to each Memner's capital account in proportion to the Memners' sharing ratios, except that all allocations shall be made in accordance with applicable tax law and regulations.

Annotation: This provision attempts to ensure that financial allocations among the memners accord with their internal deal as reflected in the sharing ratios, while also having "substantial economic effect" under § 704(b) of the Internal Revenue Code. The parties may want to provide that memners shall not be obligated to restore capital account deficits. While this limits the parties' financial obligations, it may also create tax complications. The parties may have to provide for a "qualified income offset" to restore capital account deficits.

4.3 Compensation

No Memner shall receive any interest, salary or drawing with respect to its contributions or its capital account or for services rendered on behalf of the Company or otherwise in its capacity as a Memner (including as a Manager), except as otherwise specifically provided in this Agreement.

Annotation: The no-interest rule is the default rule under the partnership statute. *See* § 4.02(B). This provision may be revised to deal with professional and other service firms, in which the appropriate design of incentive compensation to the employee-memners is important. *See* § 4.03.

4.4 Interim Distributions

The Company shall distribute to the Memners from time to time, in the same proportion as the allocation of net profits pursuant to paragraph 4.1, cash which the Manager determines to be available out of net profits of the Company making allowance for a reasonable reserve to fund the Company's business operations, provided that distributions to the extent possible shall be sufficient to enable the Memners to fund their federal and state income tax liabilities attributable to their respective distributive shares of the taxable income of the Company.

Annotation: Distributions are important where the memners cannot freely sell their shares, and particularly where the memners are taxed directly on profits whether or not these profits are distributed. Leaving this to the discretion of the manager may entail significant agency costs. These potential costs are mitigated if the manager is a memner and by the memners' ability to remove the manager at will pursuant to paragraph 6.5. Note that LLC and limited partnership statutes usually provide for liability for excessive distributions. *See* §§ 11.04 and 12.07. Agreements under such statutes may have to provide that the distribution obligation is subject to these statutory limitations. Finally, the parties may want to provide that memners have no right to demand or obligation to receive disproportionate in-kind distributions. This is a default rule under RULPA § 605 and many LLC statutes.

ARTICLE V: MEMNERS' INFORMATION RIGHTS

5.1 Duty to Keep Books and Records

The Manager shall prepare and maintain, or cause to be prepared and maintained, at the Company's principal place of business, the books of account of the Company that shall show a true and accurate record of all costs and expenses incurred, all charges made, all credits made and received and all income derived in connection with the operation of the Company business.

Annotation: Financial information is important both to help memners participate in and monitor management and to help them keep track of tax information that is vital to memners who are taxed on a flow-through basis. The maintenance of financial records is the duty of managers, subject to the standard of care set forth in paragraph 7.1. Access to and disclosure of information is dealt with below in this Article.

5.2 Disclosure to Memners

The following financial information, which need not be examined and certified to by an independent certified public accountant, shall be transmitted by the Manager to each Memner within three (3) months after the close of each Fiscal Year:

(i)   balance sheet of the Company as of the beginning and close of such Fiscal Year;

(ii) statement of Company profits and losses for such Fiscal Year;

(iii) statement of such Memner's capital account as of the close of such Fiscal Year, and changes therein during such Fiscal Year; and

(v)   a statement indicating such Memner's share of each item of Company income, gain, loss, deduction or credit for such Fiscal Year for income tax purposes.

Annotation: This is the sort of information that is required by most LLC statutes. The provision allowing the firm to dispense with CPA certification involves an obvious balance between expense, which may be particularly important in a very small, informal firm, and accuracy, which may be particularly important in a manager-managed firm with remote investors.

5.3 Accounting Method

For both financial and tax reporting purposes and for purposes of determining profits and losses, the books and records of the Company shall be kept on the [accrual] method of accounting applied in accordance with generally accepted accounting principles consistently applied, and shall reflect all Company transactions and be appropriate for the Company's business.

Annotation: The cash method of accounting is more appropriate (and available) to service firms that may have a significant lag between billing and payment. The agreement often specifies the taxable and fiscal year of the firm. Tax rules may affect the availability of a particular accounting method or taxable year. For the importance of the firm's agreed accounting method and a brief discussion of applicable tax rules, *see* § 4.04.

5.4 Access to Records

Each Memner shall have access to a copy of this Agreement and of the Certificate and the books and records referred to in paragraph 5.1 at all reasonable times during business hours.

Annotation: Memners' access to records is not subject to a "purpose" requirement, since memners in a closely held firm generally can be expected to have strong reasons for seeing these records.

ARTICLE VI: MANAGEMENT AND CONTROL

6.1 Management by Manager

The Manager shall manage the Company in accordance with this Agreement except and to the extent that such power is expressly delegated to any other person by the Manager. The Manager and any person to whom the Manager has delegated authority pursuant to this paragraph are the sole agents in connection with the Company's business, and the actions of such persons taken in such capacity and in accordance with this Agreement shall bind the Company.

Annotation: It is important to distinguish actual and apparent authority. *See* §§ 2.03(A), 5.02, 11.05 and 12.08. The manager's actual authority is subject to paragraph 8.1 on memners' voting rights. Whether the managers have exclusive apparent authority to bind the firm, on the other hand, depends on whether the firm has a statement of partner authority (*see* § 5.04(C)) or has adopted centralized management under an LLC statute (*see* § 12.08).

6.2 Reliance by Third Parties

A person may rely upon a writing that is signed by a person who is designated as "Manager" on Schedule A as to the identity of the Manager or of any persons who are authorized to execute and deliver any instrument or document of or on behalf of the Company.

Annotation: This provision involves a balancing of the costs of third parties dealing with the Company (some of which ultimately are borne by the Company) and the memners' agency costs resulting from the actions of rogue managers. Note that under this provision third parties still bear the costs of relying on a bogus "Schedule A." The memners' agency costs are mitigated to some extent by the manager's duties pursuant to Article VII and the memners' removal power under paragraph 6.5.

6.3 Term of Manager

The Manager shall serve until the earliest of:

(i)   the dissociation of such Manager as a Memner pursuant to paragraph 10.1;

(ii) the resignation of such Manager as a Manager pursuant to paragraph 6.4; or

(iii) the removal of the Manager pursuant to paragraph 6.5.

Annotation: Resignation and removal are dealt with below in this Article. Dissociation as a memner ends the manager's term because the memners rely to some extent on the manager's incentives being aligned with them.

6.4 Resignation of Manager

A Manager may resign as Manager at any time, subject to any right of the Company to recover damages from the Manager for breach of any employment contract between the Company and the Manager. A Manager's resignation shall not in itself cause the Manager's dissociation as a Memner.

Annotation: The manager's continued service would not be specifically enforceable even without this provision. *See* § 12.10. The removed manager may choose to dissociate as a memner. Whether removal as a manager should cause dissociation depends on a balancing of several factors, including the potential decision-making costs of having a disgruntled former manager continue as a memner with full voting rights, the incentive effects of exposing managers to the risk not only of removal as a manager but expulsion from memnership and forced sale of her interest (*see also* the Annotation to paragraph 6.5), and the potential opportunism costs of giving memners the power to force both removal and expulsion.

6.5 Removal of Manager

A Manager may be removed as such at any time and for any reason, or for no reason, by Memners owning a majority of the sharing ratios, subject to any right of the Manager to recover damages from the Company for breach of any employment contract with the Company.

Annotation: The memners' removal power is an important constraint on managerial conduct. On the other hand, a manager who has no job security may lack incentives to acquire firm-specific human capital and may hesitate to take risks that might pay off for the memners. These considerations may be taken into account by entering into an employment contract that, for example, entitles managers to damages or severance pay if they are removed other than for a stated cause prior to the expiration of a specified term.

6.6 Election of Manager

Upon the termination of the term of a Manager pursuant to paragraph 6.3, a new Manager shall be elected by a vote of the Memners who own a majority of the sharing ratios.

Annotation: There may be a problem under this provision if the memners are deadlocked or for some other reason fail to elect a replacement. Such problems may be resolved through dissolution or dissociation.

6.7 Tax Matters

The Manager is hereby designated as "Tax Matters Memner" of the Company for purposes of § 6231(a)(7) of the Code and shall have the power to manage and control, on behalf of the Company, any administrative proceeding at the Company level with the Internal Revenue Service relating to the determination of any item of Company income, gain, loss, deduction or credit for federal income tax purposes. In this capacity, the Manager shall, within ten (10) days of the receipt of any notice from the Internal Revenue Service in any administrative proceeding at the Company level relating to the determination of any Company item of income, gain, loss, deduction or credit, mail a copy of such notice to each Memner.

ARTICLE VII: DUTIES AND LIABILITIES OF MEMNERS AND MANAGERS

7.1 Managers' Standard of Care

A Manager's duty of care in the discharge of the Manager's duties to the Company and the other Memners is limited to acting in good faith and refraining from engaging in grossly negligent, reckless or willful misconduct. In discharging its duties, a Manager shall be fully protected in relying in good faith upon the records required to be maintained under Article V and upon any report of or information supplied by any person.

Annotation: This relatively low duty of care is appropriate in light of the memners' strong voting, dissociation and removal rights. Good faith may include knowing that reports or information are false or that a person reporting or supplying information is untrustworthy.

7.2 Self-Dealing and Outside Transactions

A Manager has a duty not to engage in a transaction with the Company if the Manager has a direct or indirect interest in the transaction, unless either the transaction is fair to the Company or Memners owning a majority of the sharing ratios knowing the material facts of the transaction and the Manager's interest, authorize, approve, or ratify the transaction. A Manager may engage in or possess an interest in business ventures that are not transactions with the Company of any nature or description and the Company and the Memners shall have no rights in and to such ventures. The pursuit of any such venture shall not be deemed wrongful or improper even if it is similar to or competitive with the business of the Company or could be engaged in by the Company.

7.3 Company Property and Information

A Memner or Manager shall not use or appropriate Company property unless such use or appropriation is fair to the Company or is approved, authorized or ratified by Memners who own a majority of the sharing and who know the material facts of the transaction and the Manager's or Memners' interest. For purposes of this paragraph, "Company property" shall include information developed exclusively for the Company or opportunities expressly offered to the Company.

Annotation. These provisions restrict self-dealing and use of company property but not outside dealings. For discussions of waivers of fiduciary duty, *see* §§ 8.06 and 12.10(D). Outside dealings may be a problem, since the Company cannot easily discipline managers who do not get good deals for the Company, as distinguished from getting the Company into bad deals. However, the memners' removal power may be enough to deal with this problem. Moreover, the alternative of requiring disclosure of and memner consent to the taking of outside business invites litigation over the sufficiency of disclosure. Note that memners have a duty regarding Company property but not regarding self-dealing or outside business opportunities. Since memners do not manage, there is no need to constrain management-related misconduct. But memners should not be able to use their access to Company property and information to appropriate more than the share of financial benefits from the Company that is explicitly allocated to them under the financial provisions of the agreement.

7.4 Limitations on Memners' and Managers' Duties

Except as expressly provided in this Agreement:

(i)   No Memner or Manager shall have any duties or obligations, including fiduciary duties, and including duties and obligations existing in law or equity.

(ii)   Whenever in this Agreement a Manager is permitted or required to make a decision, the Manager shall be entitled to consider only such interests and factors as it desires, including its own interests, and shall have no duty or obligation to give any consideration to any interest of or factors affecting the Company or any other Person.

(iii)   A Memner or Manager does not violate a duty or obligation to the Company merely by engaging in conduct that furthers the Memner's or Manager's interest.

Annotation: This reinforces the above duty provisions and hopefully discourages courts from finding gaps in the agreement that can be filled with default fiduciary duties. The problems of fiduciary waivers and judicial gap filling are discussed for partnerships in Chapter 8. This discussion applies equally in this respect to LLCs and other types of firms.

7.5 Indemnification of Company

The Company shall be entitled to indemnification from a Memner or Manager of the Company on account of a liability of or payment by the Company that results from the Memner's breach of duty to the Company pursuant to this Article. If more than one Memner is responsible for such liability or payment, the liability or payment shall be allocated between the responsible Memners based upon any relative liability determined by a court or other tribunal or, in the absence of a determination regarding such allocation, equally.

7.6 Indemnification by Company

The Company shall indemnify a Memner or Manager of the Company who pays or incurs a liability or expense (including legal fees) in connection with or in a proceeding arising out of the business of the Company unless such payment, liability or expense resulted from such Memner's or Manager's breach of duty to the company pursuant to this Article.

7.7 Insurance

The Company may purchase and maintain insurance on behalf of the Manager, Memner and agents of the Company against any liability that may be asserted against or expenses that may be incurred by any such person in connection with the activities of the Company or such indemnities, regardless of whether the Company would have the power to indemnify such person against such liability under the provisions of this Agreement.

7.8 Advances

Any expenses for which a Memner or Manager may be entitled to indemnification under paragraph 7.6 shall be advanced by the Company prior to the final disposition of any action or proceeding upon receipt by the Company of an undertaking by or on behalf of the Memner or Manager to repay such amount if it shall be determined that such person is not entitled to be indemnified as authorized in paragraph 7.6.

Annotation: These provisions allocate responsibility within the firm in accordance with memners' and managers' duties under this Article. In a professional firm, these provisions will serve to share responsibility for professional malpractice, subject to a client's or patient's right to obtain damages directly from a negligent memner even if the firm lacks assets to indemnify the memner. Since these provisions apply only to indemnification and insurance by the Company, they involve company assets only and do not serve as a basis for imposing personal liability on the memners. Insurance may be broader than indemnity because it introduces a third-party monitor. The memners' and managers' power to enter into insurance contracts and contracts to indemnify agents who are not memners or managers is subject to Article VIII. These provisions do not cover agents because the Company agreement is intended only to describe the rights and obligations of the parties to the firm—*i.e.,* the memners and managers. Note that memners' right to be protected from liabilities may affect their economic risk, and therefore their tax basis and ability to deduct losses. *See* § 12.07(C).

Addendum for Professional Firms

Each Memner shall:

(i)   maintain that Memner's license and privilege to render professional services in accordance with his or her admission to practice law in the State and in the courts and administrative bodies in which such Memner shall have occasion to practice and shall at all times comply with the rules of practice of each such state;

(ii) devote substantially full time to the performance of professional services and the management of the Company;

(iii) charge reasonably for all professional services rendered by that Memner, following generally the policies of the Company as to fees charged, including services to any member of his or her own family, and relative, or any client, except that a Memner may render services without charge or at less than regular charge to members of his or her immediate family, the organized bar, or any civic, educational, religious or charitable organization or project;

(iv) accept directly or indirectly salaries, commissions, honoraria, fees or gratuities of any substantial significance (more than $50) from any client or prospective client of the Company, or from any school, college or university only to the extent authorized and under any conditions imposed by Memners who own a majority of the sharing ratios, other than the recipient Memner or Memners, after full disclosure.

Annotation: This provision balances the potential goodwill for the firm and benefits to memners against the costs to the Company of allowing memners to give away too much of the Company's main resource—the memners' time. This problem may be indirectly mitigated by compensation provisions that effectively align memners' incentives to work with the Company's interests. Note that the memners' consent to items under subparagraph (iv) may be conditioned on charging the item against distributions to which the memner would otherwise be entitled.

ARTICLE VIII: MEMNERS' VOTING AND CONTROL RIGHTS

8.1 Requirement of Memner Approval

A vote by Memners owning a majority of the sharing ratios shall be required to approve the following actions:

(i)   any purchase or sale of real estate;

(ii) any transaction that involves an obligation to pay or to receive from one or more persons an aggregate in excess of $50,000;

(iii) any amendment to this Agreement, provided that without the written consent of each Memner adversely affected thereby, no amendment of the Company Agreement shall be made that (a) increases the obligations of such Memner to make contributions, (b) alters the allocation to the affected Memner for tax purposes of any items of income, gain, loss, deduction or credit, or (c) alters the manner of computing the distributions of the affected Memner;

(iv) admission of a new Memner;

(v) any matter that is expressly required by this agreement to be approved by the Memners.

Annotation: Memner voting provisions involve a balance of the costs of high-vote requirements, including potential holdout problems, against the potential agency costs of allowing a majority to impose costs on a minority. *See generally* Chapter 5. The outcome of the balance depends, among other things, on how well aligned memner interests are likely to be on particular issues, and on dissatisfied memners' ability to exit the firm (*see* paragraph 10.1) and their fiduciary duties (*see* Article VII). Subsection (v) refers, among other things, to votes on conflict of interest transactions. "Expressly required" is intended to prevent courts from implying voting rights. $50,000 is obviously arbitrary.

8.2 No Management by Memners

Except as otherwise expressly provided in this Agreement, no Memner other than the Manager shall take part in the management or control of the business and affairs of the Company. Except and only to the extent expressly delegated by the Manager, no Memner or other person other than the Manager shall be an agent of the Company or have any right, power or authority to transact any business in the name of the Company or to act for or on behalf of or to bind the Company.

Annotation: This provision is a companion to paragraph 6.1 concerning the manager's power. Although the memners may vote to approve some actions by the managers, the non-managing memners lack any actual authority under the agreement to represent the firm in transactions with third parties. However, this provision does not necessarily limit the memners' apparent authority. *See* the Annotation to paragraph 6.1.

8.3 Meetings of the Memners

(i) Memners may vote on any matter in writing or at a Memners' meeting conducted pursuant to this paragraph.

(ii) Meetings of the Memners may be called at any time by the Manager or by Memners' owning 25% of the sharing ratios. Notice of any meeting shall be given to all Memners not less than two (2) days nor more than thirty (30) days prior to the date of such meeting. Each Memner may authorize any Person to act for it by proxy on all matters in which a Memner is entitled to participate, including waiving notice of any meeting, or voting or participating at a meeting. Every proxy must be signed by the Memner or its attorney-in-fact.

(iii) A Memners' meeting shall be conducted by the Manager or by such other Person that the Manager may designate. The Manager, in its sole discretion, shall establish all other provisions relating to meetings of Memners, including notice of the time, place or purpose of any meeting at which may matter is to be voted on by any Memners, waiver of any such notice, action by consent without a meeting, the establishment of a record date, quorum requirements, voting in person or by proxy or any other matter with respect to the exercise of any such right to vote.

Annotation: There is an initial question whether meetings should be required for memner voting. A meeting may be costly, but collegial discussion may be beneficial.

ARTICLE IX: TRANSFER OF MEMNER RIGHTS

9.1 Voluntary Assignment of Memnership Interest

(i) Subject to subparagraph (ii), a Memner or an assignee of a Memnership Interest may assign or otherwise transfer all or a portion of a Memnership Interest.

(ii) A Memner or assignee may not assign or otherwise transfer all or any part of a Memnership Interest (a) unless and until the Memner or assignee provides the Company with information and agreements that the Managers may reasonably require, including but not limited to any taxpayer identification number and any agreement that may be required by any Taxing Jurisdiction; or (b) if such assignment or transfer, alone or when combined with other transactions, would result in a termination of the Company within the meaning of Section 708 of the Internal Revenue Code.

(iii) Any attempted assignment or transfer of a Memnership Interest, or any part thereof, not in compliance with subparagraph (ii) of this paragraph shall be, and is declared to be, null and void ab initio.

Annotation: It is important to distinguish management rights, which are not assignable under this section, and the financial rights (*i.e.*, the "memnership interest"), which are subject to limitations. This is consistent with the usual default rules of partnerships and partnership-type firms discussed in Chapter 7 and in §§ 11.07 and 12.09. This paragraph applies only to voluntary transfers, and not to assignments which occur by reason of death or other events. The provisions of the remainder of this Article are generally consistent with the default provisions of most partnership and LLC statutes.

9.2 Rights of Assignees

The assignee of a Memnership Interest has no right to participate in the management of the business and affairs of the Company or to become a Memner. The assignee is only entitled to receive the distributions and the allocations provided for in this Agreement.

9.3 Admission of Substitute Memners

An assignee of a Memnership Interest shall be admitted as a substitute Memner only with the approval of the non-assigning Memners who own a majority of the sharing ratios. A substitute Memner has all the rights and powers, has the same capital account and sharing ratio, and is subject to all the restrictions and liabilities of the Memner who originally assigned the Memnership Interest. The admission of a substitute Memner, without more, shall not release the Memner originally assigning the Memnership Interest from any liability to the Company that may have existed prior to the approval.

9.4 Admission of New Memners

New Memners shall be admitted to the Company only upon and subject to conditions concerning contributions, sharing ratios and other matters that are approved by the affirmative vote of the Memners holding a majority of the sharing ratios.

Annotation: A new memner differs from a substitute memner in that the latter takes the initial memner's rights while the former has new rights described in the admission agreement. Unlike the admission of a substitute memner, the admission of a new memner may entail a revaluation of the firm's assets.

ARTICLE X: DISSOCIATION AND DISSOLUTION

10.1 Memner Dissociation

A Memner is dissociated upon one of the following events:

(i)   A Memner's bankruptcy, application for or consent to the appointment of a trustee, receiver, or custodian of its assets or making of a general assignment for the benefit of creditors; or

(ii) The entry of an order, judgment or decree by any court of competent jurisdiction appointing a trustee, receiver or custodian of the assets of a Memner unless the proceedings and the person appointed are dismissed within ninety (90) days;

(iii) A Memner's Interest's becoming subject to a charging order under § ____of the Act or a similar enforcement of any rights of a creditor of a Memner if that Memner fails to effectuate the release of those enforcement rights within ninety (90) days after actual notice of that creditor's action;

(iv) The death of a Memner; or

(v)   The withdrawal or retirement of a Memner, provided that such dissociation shall be effective when the Company receives written notice that a Memner has withdrawn or retired; or

(vi) Expulsion of a Memner for failure to make an agreed contribution pursuant to paragraph 3.3.

Annotation: As discussed in § 9.01, memners' powers to dissociate from a closely held firm provide significant liquidity, but also may threaten the firm's continuity. The degree of liquidity is significant for other memner rights and powers, including fiduciary duties and management rights. Note that dissociation for bankruptcy may be invalidated under bankruptcy law. *See* §§ 9.02(C) and 12.11. Written notice is required for voluntary dissociation to provide some predictability. Note that if some of the memners are business associations, trusts or estates the agreement may provide for events of dissociation based on dissolution or other types of figurative "death" of those types of memners. *See* RULPA § 402(7)-(10).

10.2 Consequences of Dissociation

Upon dissociation as a Memner, the Memner shall have only the rights of an assignee of a Memner's Interest pursuant to paragraph 9.2.

Annotation: This provision means, in effect, that a dissociated memner no longer can exercise voting or other management rights. This is consistent with the fact that the incentives of a bankrupt or expelled memner, an estate of a deceased memner or a memner who has announced her voluntary departure are no longer aligned with those of the other memners. On the other hand, such a memner may be subjected to agency or opportunism costs by the continuing memners. This is constrained to some extent by the fact that the memner must be paid off or become a secured creditor under paragraph 10.3. As to fiduciary duties to former partners, *see* § 9.04.

10.3 Distribution to Dissociated Memner

In the event of a Memner's dissociation pursuant to paragraph 10.1, the dissociated Memner or any successor of such Memner shall receive as full payment for his or her interest an amount equal to the capital account balance of the withdrawing Memner (the "purchase price"). The purchase price shall be payable all in cash or by a promissory note due and payable upon the expiration of five years bearing interest at the Prime Rate which shall be secured by either pledge of the interest for which said note is given as consideration or by other assets having an unencumbered value at least equal to the amount of the promissory note given hereunder, as the parties shall mutually agree.

Annotation: It may be difficult to determine the "fair market value" of a memner's interest. On the other hand, the amount provided for in this provision may be significantly lower than the fair market value, and accordingly reduces the liquidity of the memner's interest. This is counterbalanced to some extent by the reduction in dispute costs and the potential increase in the firm's continuity under the more definite standard in this section. Agreements for professional firms need to deal with work in process, clients and competition. *See* § 9.06.

ARTICLE XI: DISSOLUTION, LIQUIDATION, AND TERMINATION

11.1 Dissolution

The Company shall be dissolved and its affairs shall be wound up upon the occurrence of any of the following events:

(i) The termination of the term of the Manager pursuant to paragraph 6.3 unless the business of the Company is continued with the consent of non-dissociating Memners holding a majority of the sharing ratios of all the non-dissociating Memners and the Memners by such vote elect a new Manager;

(ii) the entry of a decree of judicial dissolution under Section ___ of the ___Act; or

(iii) the written determination of the Manager and the vote of the owners of a majority of the sharing interests.

Annotation: Note that under the UPA the partnership necessarily dissolves while the business of the firm may be continued. Under RUPA and LLC statutes, the firm itself may be continued. This difference necessitates slightly different wording for UPA-based agreements. Dissolution is not justified on dissociation of a passive memner, particularly since the installment payment procedure under paragraph 10.3 minimizes the economic consequences of a memner's departure and the memners can always decide to dissolve the firm under subparagraph (iii).

11.2 Notice of Dissolution

Upon the dissolution of the Company, the Manager shall promptly notify the Memners of such dissolution.

11.3 Liquidation

Upon dissolution of the Company, the Manager, as liquidating trustee, shall immediately commence to wind up the Company's affairs; provided, however, that a reasonable time shall be allowed for the orderly liquidation of the assets of the Company and the satisfaction of liabilities to creditors so as to enable the Memners to minimize the normal losses attendant upon a liquidation. The Memners shall continue to share profits and losses during liquidation in the same proportions as before liquidation. The [contributions of the Memners] and the distribution of the proceeds of liquidation shall be in the manner provided in § ____ of the _____ Act. In the event that the Manager is unable to perform in its capacity as liquidating trustee due to its bankruptcy, dissolution, death, adjudicated incompetence or any other termination of the Manager as an entity, the liquidating trustee shall be a Person approved by the owners of a majority of the sharing ratios of the remaining Memners.

Annotation: The bracketed language is appropriate for partnerships, given the partners' statutory contribution obligations. *See also* the Addendum to paragraph 11.4.

11.4 Termination

The Company shall terminate when all of the assets of the Company have been distributed in the manner provided for in this Article and the Certificate shall have been canceled in the manner required by the _____ Act.

Addendum for Partnership: Claims of the Memners

If the assets of the Company remaining after payment of or due provision for all debts, liabilities and obligations of the Company are insufficient to make distributions to Memners provided for in this Agreement, the Memners and former Memners shall have no recourse against the Company or any other Memner.

ARTICLE XII: MISCELLANEOUS

12.1 Binding Effect

This Agreement shall be binding upon and inure to the benefit of all of the parties and, to the extent permitted by this Agreement, their successors, legal representatives and assigns. This Agreement is expressly not intended for the benefit of any creditor of the Company or any third person. Except and only to the extent provided by applicable statute, no such creditor or third party shall have any rights under this Company Agreement, Admission Agreement or any agreement between the Company and any Memner with respect to any capital contribution or otherwise.

12.2 Severability

The invalidity or unenforceability of any particular provision of this Agreement shall not affect the other provisions hereof, and this Agreement shall be construed in all respects as if such invalid or unenforceable provision were omitted.

12.3 Integration

This Agreement constitutes the entire agreement among the parties hereto pertaining to the subject matter hereof and supersedes all prior agreements and understandings pertaining thereto.

APPENDIX

UNIFORM PARTNERSHIP ACT (1914)*

Part I
Preliminary Provisions

Part II
Nature of a Partnership

Part III
Relations Of Partners To Persons Dealing With The Partnership

Part IV
Relations of Partners To One Another

---

*   Drafted by the National Conference of Commissioners on Uniform State Laws and by it approved and recommended for enactment in all the states at its conference in Washington, D.C., October 14, 1914. This act has been reprinted through the permission of the National Conference of Commissioners on Uniform State Laws, and copies may be ordered from them at 676 North St. Clair Street, Suite 1700, Chicago, Illinois, 60611.

Part V
Property Rights Of A Partner

Part VI
Dissolution and Winding Up

Part VII
Miscellaneous Provisions

UNIFORM PARTNERSHIP ACT (1914)
PART I
PRELIMINARY PROVISIONS

SECTION 1.   Name of Act.
SECTION 2.   Definition of Terms.
SECTION 3.   Interpretation of Knowledge and Notice.
SECTION 4.   Rules of Construction.
SECTION 5.   Rules for Cases Not Provided for in This Act.

SECTION 1. *Name of Act.* This act may be cited as Uniform Partnership Act.

SECTION 2. *Definition of Terms.* In this act, "Court" includes every court and judge having jurisdiction in the case.

"Business" includes every trade, occupation, or profession.

"Person" includes individuals, partnerships, corporations, and other associations.

"Bankrupt" includes bankrupt under the Federal Bankruptcy Act or insolvent under any state insolvent act.

"Conveyance" includes every assignment, lease, mortgage, or encumbrance.

"Real property" includes land and any interest or estate in land.

SECTION 3. *Interpretation of Knowledge and Notice.*
(1) A person has "knowledge" of a fact within the meaning of this act not only when he has actual knowledge thereof, but also when he has knowledge of such other facts as in the circumstances shows bad faith.
(2) A person has "notice" of a fact within the meaning of this act when the person who claims the benefit of the notice:
  (a) States the fact to such person, or
  (b) Delivers through the mail, or by other means of communication, a written statement of the fact to such person or to a proper person at his place of business or residence.

SECTION 4. *Rules of Construction.*
(1) The rule that statutes in derogation of the common law are to be strictly construed shall have no application to this act.
(2) The law of estoppel shall apply under this act.
(3) The law of agency shall apply under this act.
(4) This act shall be so interpreted and construed as to effect its general purpose to make uniform the law of those states which enact it.
(5) This act shall not be construed so as to impair the obligations of any contract existing when the act goes into effect, nor to affect any action or proceedings begun or right accrued before this act takes effect.

SECTION 5. *Rules for Cases Not Provided for in This Act.* In any case not provided for in this act the rules of law and equity, including the law merchant, shall govern.

PART II
NATURE OF A PARTNERSHIP

SECTION 6.   Partnership Defined.
SECTION 7.   Rules for Determining the Existence of a Partnership.
SECTION 8.   Partnership Property.

SECTION 6. *Partnership Defined.*

(1) A partnership is an association of two or more persons to carry on as co-owners a business for profit.

(2) But any association formed under any other statute of this state, or any statute adopted by authority, other than the authority of this state, is not a partnership under this act, unless such association would have been a partnership in this state prior to the adoption of this act; but this act shall apply to limited partnerships except in so far as the statutes relating to such partnerships are inconsistent herewith.

SECTION 7. *Rules for Determining the Existence of a Partnership.* In determining whether a partnership exists, these rules shall apply:

(1) Except as provided by section 16 persons who are not partners as to each other are not partners as to third persons.

(2) Joint tenancy, tenancy in common, tenancy by the entireties, joint property, common property, or part ownership does not of itself establish a partnership, whether such co-owners do or do not share any profits made by the use of the property.

(3) The sharing of gross returns does not of itself establish a partnership, whether or not the persons sharing them have a joint or common right or interest in any property from which the returns are derived.

(4) The receipt by a person of a share of the profits of a business is prima facie evidence that he is a partner in the business, but no such inference shall be drawn if such profits were received in payment:

(a) As a debt by installments or otherwise,

(b) As wages of an employee or rent to a landlord,

(c) As an annuity to a widow or representative of a deceased partner,

(d) As interest on a loan, though the amount of payment vary with the profits of the business,

(e) As the consideration for the sale of the good-will of a business or other property by installments or otherwise.

SECTION 8. *Partnership Property.*

(1) All property originally brought into the partnership stock or subsequently acquired by purchase or otherwise, on account of the partnership, is partnership property.

(2) Unless the contrary intention appears, property acquired with partnership funds is partnership property.

(3) Any estate in real property may be acquired in the partnership name. Title so acquired can be conveyed only in the partnership name.

(4) A conveyance to a partnership in the partnership name, though without words of inheritance, passes the entire estate of the grantor unless a contrary intent appears.

PART III
RELATIONS OF PARTNERS TO PERSONS DEALING WITH THE PARTNERSHIP

SECTION 9.   Partner Agent of Partnership as to Partnership Business.
SECTION 10. Conveyance of Real Property of the Partnership.
SECTION 11. Partnership Bound By Admission of Partner.
SECTION 12. Partnership Charged With Knowledge of or Notice to Partner.
SECTION 13. Partnership Bound By Partner's Wrongful Act.
SECTION 14. Partnership Bound By Partner's Breach of Trust.
SECTION 15. Nature of Partner's Liability.
SECTION 16. Partner By Estoppel.
SECTION 17. Liability of Incoming Partner.

SECTION 9. *Partner Agent of Partnership as to Partnership Business.*

(1) Every partner is an agent of the partnership for the purpose of its business, and the act of every partner, including the execution in the partnership name of any instrument, for apparently carrying on in the usual way the business of the partnership of which he is a member binds the partnership, unless the partner so acting has in fact no authority to act for the partnership in the particular matter, and the person with whom he is dealing has knowledge of the fact that he has no such authority.

(2) An act of a partner which is not apparently for the carrying on of the business of the partnership in the usual way does not bind the partnership unless authorized by the other partners.

(3) Unless authorized by the other partners or unless they have abandoned the business, one or more but less than all the partners have no authority to:
   (a) Assign the partnership property in trust for creditors or on the assignee's promise to pay the debts of the partnership,
   (b) Dispose of the good-will of the business,
   (c) Do any other act which would make it impossible to carry on the ordinary business of a partnership,
   (d) Confess a judgment,
   (e) Submit a partnership claim or liability to arbitration or reference.

(4) No act of a partner in contravention of a restriction on authority shall bind the partnership to persons having knowledge of the restriction.

SECTION 10. *Conveyance of Real Property of the Partnership.*

(1) Where title to real property is in the partnership name, any partner may convey title to such property by a conveyance executed in the partnership name;

but the partnership may recover such property unless the partner's act binds the partnership under the provisions of paragraph (1) of section 9, or unless such property has been conveyed by the grantee or a person claiming through such grantee to a holder for value without knowledge that the partner, in making the conveyance, has exceeded his authority.

(2) Where title to real property is in the name of the partnership, a conveyance executed by a partner, in his own name, passes the equitable interest of the partnership, provided the act is one within the authority of the partner under the provisions of paragraph (1) of section 9.

(3) Where title to real property is in the name of one or more but not all the partners, and the record does not disclose the right of the partnership, the partners in whose name the title stands may convey title to such property, but the partnership may recover such property if the partners' act does not bind the partnership under the provisions of paragraph (1) of section 9, unless the purchaser or his assignee, is a holder for value, without knowledge.

(4) Where the title to real property is in the name of one or more or all the partners, or in a third person in trust for the partnership, a conveyance executed by a partner in the partnership name, or in his own name, passes the equitable interest of the partnership, provided the act is one within the authority of the partner under the provisions of paragraph (1) of section 9.

(5) Where the title to real property is in the names of all the partners a conveyance executed by all the partners passes all their rights in such property.

SECTION 11. *Partnership Bound by Admission of Partner.* An admission or representation made by any partner concerning partnership affairs within the scope of his authority as conferred by this act is evidence against the partnership.

SECTION 12. *Partnership Charged with Knowledge of or Notice to Partner.* Notice to any partner of any matter relating to partnership affairs, and the knowledge of the partner acting in the particular matter, acquired while a partner or then present to his mind, and the knowledge of any other partner who reasonably could and should have communicated it to the acting partner, operate as notice to or knowledge of the partnership, except in the case of a fraud on the partnership committed by or with the consent of that partner.

SECTION 13. *Partnership Bound by Partner's Wrongful Act.* Where, by any wrongful act or omission of any partner acting in the ordinary course of the business of the partnership or with the authority of his co-partners, loss or injury is caused to any person, not being a partner in the partnership, or any penalty is incurred, the partnership is liable therefor to the same extent as the partner so acting or omitting to act.

SECTION 14. *Partnership Bound by Partner's Breach of Trust.* The partnership is bound to make good the loss:

(a) Where one partner acting within the scope of his apparent authority receives money or property of a third person and misapplies it; and

(b) Where the partnership in the course of its business receives money or property of a third person and the money or property so received is misapplied by any partner while it is in the custody of the partnership.

SECTION 15. *Nature of Partner's Liability. All partners are liable*
(a) Jointly and severally for everything chargeable to the partnership under sections 13 and 14.
(b) Jointly for all other debts and obligations of the partnership; but any partner may enter into a separate obligation to perform a partnership contract.

SECTION 16. *Partner by Estoppel.*
(1) When a person, by words spoken or written or by conduct, represents himself, or consents to another representing him to any one, as a partner in an existing partnership or with one or more persons not actual partners, he is liable to any such person to whom such representation has been made, who has, on the faith of such representation, given credit to the actual or apparent partnership, and if he has made such representation or consented to its being made in a public manner he is liable to such person, whether the representation has or has not been made or communicated to such person so giving credit by or with the knowledge of the apparent partner making the representation or consenting to its being made.
(a) When a partnership liability results, he is liable as though he were an actual member of the partnership.
(b) When no partnership liability results, he is liable jointly with the other persons, if any, so consenting to the contract or representation as to incur liability, otherwise separately.
(2) When a person has been thus represented to be a partner in an existing partnership, or with one or more persons not actual partners, he is an agent of the persons consenting to such representation to bind them to the same extent and in the same manner as though he were a partner in fact, with respect to persons who rely upon the presentation. Where all the members of the existing partnership consent to the representation, a partnership act or obligation results; but in all other cases it is the joint act or obligation of the person acting and the persons consenting to the representation.

SECTION 17. *Liability of Incoming Partner.* A person admitted as a partner into an existing partnership is liable for all the obligations of the partnership arising before his admission as though he had been a partner when such obligations were incurred, except that this liability shall be satisfied only out of partnership property.

PART IV
RELATIONS OF PARTNERS TO ONE ANOTHER

SECTION 18. Rules Determining Rights and Duties of Partners.
SECTION 19. Partnership Books.
SECTION 20. Duty of Partners to Render Information.

SECTION 18. *Rules Determining Rights and Duties of Partners*. The rights and duties of the partners in relation to the partnership shall be determined, subject to any agreement between them, by the following rules:

    (a) Each partner shall be repaid his contributions, whether by way of capital or advances to the partnership property and share equally in the profits and surplus remaining after all liabilities, including those to partners, are satisfied; and must contribute towards the losses, whether of capital or otherwise, sustained by the partnership according to his share in the profits.

    (b) The partnership must indemnify every partner in respect of payments made and personal liabilities reasonably incurred by him in the ordinary and proper conduct of its business, or for the preservation of its business or property.

    (c) A partner, who in aid of the partnership makes any payment or advance beyond the amount of capital which he agreed to contribute, shall be paid interest from the date of the payment or advance.

    (d) A partner shall receive interest on the capital contributed by him only from the date when repayment should be made.

    (e) All partners have equal rights in the management and conduct of the partnership business.

    (f) No partner is entitled to remuneration for acting in the partnership business, except that a surviving partner is entitled to reasonable compensation for his services in winding up the partnership affairs.

    (g) No person can become a member of a partnership without the consent of all the partners.

    (h) Any difference arising as to ordinary matters connected with the partnership business may be decided by a majority of the partners; but no act in contravention of any agreement between the partners may be done rightfully without the consent of all the partners.

SECTION 19. *Partnership Books*. The partnership books shall be kept, subject to any agreement between the partners, at the principal place of business of the partnership, and every partner shall at all times have access to and may inspect and copy any of them.

SECTION 20. *Duty of Partners to Render Information*. Partners shall render on demand true and full information of all things affecting the partnership to any partner or the legal representative of any deceased partner or partner under legal disability.

SECTION 21. *Partner Accountable as a Fiduciary.*

    (1) Every partner must account to the partnership for any benefit, and hold as trustee for it any profits derived by him without the consent of the other partners from any transaction connected with the formation, conduct, or liquidation of the partnership or from any use by him of its property.

(2) This section applies also to the representatives of a deceased partner engaged in the liquidation of the affairs of the partnership as the personal representatives of the last surviving partner.

SECTION 22. *Right to an Account.* Any partner shall have the right to a formal account as to partnership affairs:

    (a) If he is wrongfully excluded from the partnership business or possession of its property by his co-partners,

    (b) If the right exists under the terms of any agreement,

    (c) As provided by section 21,

    (d) Whenever other circumstances render it just and reasonable.

SECTION 23. *Continuation of Partnership Beyond Fixed Term.*

(1) When a partnership for a fixed term or particular undertaking is continued after the termination of such term or particular undertaking without any express agreement, the rights and duties of the partners remain the same as they were at such termination, so far as is consistent with a partnership at will.

(2) A continuation of the business by the partners or such of them as habitually acted therein during the term, without any settlement or liquidation of the partnership affairs, is prima facie evidence of a continuation of the partnership.

PART V
PROPERTY RIGHTS OF A PARTNER

SECTION 24. Extent of Property Rights of a Partner.
SECTION 25. Nature of a Partner's Right in Specific Partnership Property.
SECTION 26. Nature of Partner's Interest in the Partnership.
SECTION 27. Assignment of Partner's Interest.
SECTION 28. Partner's Interest Subject to Charging Order.

SECTION 24. *Extent of Property Rights of a Partner.* The property rights of a partner are (1) his rights in specific partnership property, (2) his interest in the partnership, and (3) his right to participate in the management.

SECTION 25. *Nature of a Partner's Right in Specific Partnership Property.*

(1) A partner is co-owner with his partners of specific partnership property holding as a tenant in partnership.

(2) The incidents of this tenancy are such that:

    (a) A partner, subject to the provisions of this act and to any agreement between the partners, has an equal right with his partners to possess specific partnership property for partnership purposes; but he has no right to possess such property for any other purpose without the consent of his partners.

    (b) A partner's right in specific partnership property is not assignable except in connection with the assignment of rights of all the partners in the same property.

(c) A partner's right in specific partnership property is not subject to attachment or execution, except on a claim against the partnership. When partnership property is attached for a partnership debt the partners, or any of them, or the representatives of a deceased partner, cannot claim any right under the homestead or exemption laws.

(d) On the death of a partner his right in specific partnership property vests in the surviving partner or partners, except where the deceased was the last surviving partner, when his right in such property vests in his legal representative. Such surviving partner or partners, or the legal representative of the last surviving partner, has no right to possess the partnership property for any but a partnership purpose.

(e) A partner's right in specific partnership property is not subject to dower, curtesy, or allowances to widows, heirs, or next of kin.

SECTION 26. *Nature of Partner's Interest in the Partnership.* A partner's interest in the partnership is his share of the profits and surplus, and the same is personal property.

SECTION 27. *Assignment of Partner's Interest.*

(1) A conveyance by a partner of his interest in the partnership does not of itself dissolve the partnership, nor, as against the other partners in the absence of agreement, entitle the assignee, during the continuance of the partnership, to interfere in the management or administration of the partnership business or affairs, or to require any information or account of partnership transactions, or to inspect the partnership books; but it merely entitles the assignee to receive in accordance with his contract the profits to which the assigning partner would otherwise be entitled.

(2) In case of a dissolution of the partnership, the assignee is entitled to receive his assignor's interest and may require an account from the date only of the last account agreed to by all the partners.

SECTION 28. *Partner's Interest Subject to Charging Order.*

(1) On due application to a competent court by any judgment creditor of a partner, the court which entered the judgment, order, or decree, or any other court, may charge the interest of the debtor partner with payment of the unsatisfied amount of such judgment debt with interest thereon; and may then or later appoint a receiver of his share of the profits, and of any other money due or to fall due to him in respect of the partnership, and make all other orders, directions, accounts and inquiries which the debtor partner might have made, or which the circumstances of the case may require.

(2) The interest charged may be redeemed at any time before foreclosure, or in case of a sale being directed by the court may be purchased without thereby causing a dissolution:

(a) With separate property, by any one or more of the partners, or

(b) With partnership property, by any one or more of the partners with the consent of all the partners whose interests are not so charged or sold.

(3) Nothing in this act shall be held to deprive a partner of his right, if any, under the exemption laws, as regards his interest in the partnership.

PART VI
DISSOLUTION AND WINDING UP

SECTION 29. *Dissolution Defined.* The dissolution of a partnership is the change in the relation of the partners caused by any partner ceasing to be associated in the carrying on as distinguished from the winding up of the business.

SECTION 30. *Partnership Not Terminated by Dissolution.* On dissolution the partnership is not terminated, but continues until the winding up of partnership affairs is completed.

SECTION 31. *Causes of Dissolution.* Dissolution is caused:
(1) Without violation of the agreement between the partners,
    (a) By the termination of the definite term or particular undertaking specified in the agreement,
    (b) By the express will of any partner when no definite term or particular undertaking is specified,
    (c) By the express will of all the partners who have not assigned their interests or suffered them to be charged for their separate debts, either before or after the termination of any specified term or particular undertaking.
    (d) By the expulsion of any partner from the business bona fide in accordance with such a power conferred by the agreement between the partners;
(2) In contravention of the agreement between the partners, where the circumstances do not permit a dissolution under any other provision of this section, by the express will of any partner at any time;

(3) By any event which makes it unlawful for the business of the partnership to be carried on or for the members to carry it on in partnership;

(4) By the death of any partner;

(5) By the bankruptcy of any partner or the partnership;

(6) By decree of court under section 32.

SECTION 32. *Dissolution by Decree of Court.*

(1) On application by or for a partner the court shall decree a dissolution whenever:

   (a) A partner has been declared a lunatic in any judicial proceeding or is shown to be of unsound mind;

   (b) A partner becomes in any other way incapable of performing his part of the partnership contract;

   (c) A partner has been guilty of such conduct as tends to affect prejudicially the carrying on of the business;

   (d) A partner wilfully or persistently commits a breach of the partnership agreement, or otherwise so conducts himself in matters relating to the partnership business that it is not reasonably practicable to carry on the business in partnership with him;

   (e) The business of the partnership can only be carried on at a loss;

   (f) Other circumstances render a dissolution equitable.

(2) On the application of the purchaser of a partner's interest under sections 28 or 29 [should read 27 or 28];

   (a) After the termination of the specified term or particular undertaking;

   (b) At any time if the partnership was a partnership at will when the interest was assigned or when the charging order was issued.

SECTION 33. *General Effect of Dissolution on Authority of Partner.* Except so far as may be necessary to wind up partnership affairs or to complete transactions begun but not then finished, dissolution terminates all authority of any partner to act for the partnership,

   (1) With respect to the partners,

      (a) When the dissolution is not by the act, bankruptcy or death of a partner; or

      (b) When the dissolution is by such act, bankruptcy or death of a partner, in cases where section 34 so requires.

   (2) With respect to persons not partners, as declared in section 35.

SECTION 34. *Rights of Partner to Contribution from Co-partners after Dissolution.* Where the dissolution is caused by the act, death or bankruptcy of a partner, each partner is liable to his co-partners for his share of any liability created by any partner acting for the partnership as if the partnership had not been dissolved unless:

   (a) The dissolution being by act of any partner, the partner acting for the partnership had knowledge of the dissolution, or

   (b) The dissolution being by the death or bankruptcy of a partner, the partner acting for the partnership had knowledge or notice of the death or bankruptcy.

SECTION 35. *Power of Partner to Bind Partnership to Third Persons After Dissolution.*

(1) After dissolution a partner can bind the partnership except as provided in Paragraph (3).

   (a) By any act appropriate for winding up partnership affairs or completing transactions unfinished at dissolution;

   (b) By any transaction which would bind the partnership if dissolution had not taken place, provided the other party to the transaction

      (I) Had extended credit to the partnership prior to dissolution and had no knowledge or notice of the dissolution; or

      (II) Though he had not so extended credit, had nevertheless known of the partnership prior to dissolution, and, having no knowledge or notice of dissolution, the fact of dissolution had not been advertised in a newspaper of general circulation in the place (or in each place if more than one) at which the partnership business was regularly carried on.

(2) The liability of a partner under Paragraph (1)(b) shall be satisfied out of partnership assets alone when such partner had been prior to dissolution

   (a) Unknown as a partner to the person with whom the contract is made; and

   (b) So far unknown and inactive in partnership affairs that the business reputation of the partnership could not be said to have been in any degree due to his connection with it.

(3) The partnership is in no case bound by any act of a partner after dissolution

   (a) Where the partnership is dissolved because it is unlawful to carry on the business, unless the act is appropriate for winding up partnership affairs; or

   (b) Where the partner has become bankrupt; or

   (c) Where the partner has no authority to wind up partnership affairs; except by a transaction with one who

      (I) Had extended credit to the partnership prior to dissolution and had no knowledge or notice of his want of authority; or

      (II) Had not extended credit to the partnership prior to dissolution, and; having no knowledge or notice of his want of authority, the fact of his want of authority has not been advertised in the manner provided for advertising the fact of dissolution in Paragraph (1)(b)(II).

(4) Nothing in this section shall affect the liability under Section 16 of any person who after dissolution represents himself or consents to another representing him as a partner in a partnership engaged in carrying on business.

SECTION 36. *Effect of Dissolution on Partner's Existing Liability.*

(1) The dissolution of the partnership does not of itself discharge the existing liability of any partner.

(2) A partner is discharged from any existing liability upon dissolution of the partnership by an agreement to that effect between himself, the partnership creditor and the person or partnership continuing the business; and such agreement may be inferred from the course of dealing between the creditor having

knowledge of the dissolution and the person or partnership continuing the business.

(3) Where a person agrees to assume the existing obligations of a dissolved partnership, the partners whose obligations have been assumed shall be discharged from any liability to any creditor of the partnership who, knowing of the agreement, consents to a material alteration in the nature or time of payment of such obligations.

(4) The individual property of a deceased partner shall be liable for all obligations of the partnership incurred while he was a partner but subject to the prior payment of his separate debts.

SECTION 37. *Right to Wind Up.* Unless otherwise agreed the partners who have not wrongfully dissolved the partnership or the legal representative of the last surviving partner, not bankrupt, has the right to wind up the partnership affairs; provided, however, that any partner, his legal representative or his assignee, upon cause shown, may obtain winding up by the court.

SECTION 38. *Rights of Partners to Application of Partnership Property.*

(1) When dissolution is caused in any way, except in contravention of the partnership agreement, each partner, as against his co-partners and all persons claiming through them in respect of their interests in the partnership, unless otherwise agreed, may have the partnership property applied to discharge its liabilities, and the surplus applied to pay in cash the net amount owing to the respective partners. But if dissolution is caused by expulsion of a partner, bona fide under the partnership agreement and if the expelled partner is discharged from all partnership liabilities, either by payment or agreement under section 36(2), he shall receive in cash only the net amount due him from the partnership.

(2) When dissolution is caused in contravention of the partnership agreement the rights of the partners shall be as follows:

(a) Each partner who has not caused dissolution wrongfully shall have,
    (I) All the rights specified in paragraph (1) of this section, and
    (II) The right, as against each partner who has caused the dissolution wrongfully, to damages for breach of the agreement.

(b) The partners who have not caused the dissolution wrongfully, if they all desire to continue the business in the same name, either by themselves or jointly with others, may do so, during the agreed term for the partnership and for that purpose may possess the partnership property, provided they secure the payment by bond approved by the court, or pay to any partner who has caused the dissolution wrongfully, the value of his interest in the partnership at the dissolution, less any damages recoverable under clause (2)(a)(II) of this section, and in like manner indemnify him against all present or future partnership liabilities.

(c) A partner who has caused the dissolution wrongfully shall have:

(I) If the business is not continued under the provisions of paragraph (2)(b) all the rights of a partner under paragraph (1), subject to clause (2)(a)(II), of this section,

(II) If the business is continued under paragraph (2)(b) of this section the right as against his co-partners and all claiming through them in respect of their interests in the partnership, to have the value of his interest in the partnership, less any damages caused to his co-partners by the dissolution, ascertained and paid to him in cash, or the payment secured by bond approved by the court, and to be released from all existing liabilities of the partnership; but in ascertaining the value of the partner's interest the value of the good-will of the business shall not be considered.

SECTION 39. *Rights Where Partnership is Dissolved for Fraud or Misrepresentation.* Where a partnership contract is rescinded on the ground of the fraud or misrepresentation of one of the parties thereto, the party entitled to rescind is, without prejudice to any other right, entitled,

(a) To a lien on, or a right of retention of, the surplus of the partnership property after satisfying the partnership liabilities to third persons for any sum of money paid by him for the purchase of an interest in the partnership and for any capital or advances contributed by him; and

(b) To stand, after all liabilities to third persons have been satisfied, in the place of the creditors of the partnership for any payments made by him in respect of the partnership liabilities; and

(c) To be indemnified by the person guilty of the fraud or making the representation against all debts and liabilities of the partnership.

SECTION 40. *Rules for Distribution.* In setting accounts between the partners after dissolution, the following rules shall be observed, subject to any agreement to the contrary:

(a) The assets of the partnership are:

(I)   The partnership property,

(II) The contributions of the partners necessary for the payment of all the liabilities specified in clause (b) of this paragraph.

(b) The liabilities of the partnership shall rank in order of payment, as follows:

(I)   Those owing to creditors other than partners,

(II) Those owing to partners other than for capital and profits,

(III Those owing to partners in respect of capital,

(IV) Those owing to partners in respect of profits.

(c) The assets shall be applied in the order of their declaration in clause (a) of this paragraph to the satisfaction of the liabilities.

(d) The partners shall contribute, as provided by section 18(a) the amount necessary to satisfy the liabilities; but if any, but not all, of the partners are insolvent, or, not being subject to process, refuse to contribute, the other partners shall contribute their share of the liabilities, and, in the relative proportions in which they share the profits, the additional amount necessary to pay the liabilities.

(e) An assignee for the benefit of creditors or any person appointed by the court shall have the right to enforce the contributions specified in clause (d) of this paragraph.

(f) Any partner or his legal representative shall have the right to enforce the contributions specified in clause (d) of this paragraph, to the extent of the amount which he has paid in excess of his share of the liability.

(g) The individual property of a deceased partner shall be liable for the contributions specified in clause (d) of this paragraph.

(h) When partnership property and the individual properties of the partners are in possession of a court for distribution, partnership creditors shall have priority on partnership property and separate creditors on individual property, saving the rights of lien or secured creditors as heretofore.

    (i) Where a partner has become bankrupt or his estate insolvent the claims against his separate property shall rank in the following order:

        (I)   Those owing to separate creditors,

        (II) Those owing to partnership creditors,

        (III Those owing to partners by way of contribution.

SECTION 41. *Liability of Persons Continuing the Business in Certain Cases.*

(1) When any new partner is admitted into an existing partnership, or when any partner retires and assigns (or the representative of the deceased partner assigns) his rights in partnership property to two or more of the partners, or to one or more of the partners and one or more third persons, if the business is continued without liquidation of the partnership affairs, creditors of the first or dissolved partnership are also creditors of the partnership so continuing the business.

(2) When all but one partner retire and assign (or the representative of a deceased partner assigns) their rights in partnership property to the remaining partner, who continues the business without liquidation of partnership affairs, either alone or with others, creditors of the dissolved partnership are also creditors of the person or partnership so continuing the business.

(3) When any partner retires or dies and the business of the dissolved partnership is continued as set forth in paragraphs (1) and (2) of this section, with the consent of the retired partners or the representative of the deceased partner, but without any assignment of his right in partnership property, rights of creditors of the dissolved partnership and of the creditors of the person or partnership continuing the business shall be as if such assignment had been made.

(4) When all the partners or their representatives assign their rights in partnership property to one or more third persons who promise to pay the debts and who continue the business of the dissolved partnership, creditors of the dissolved partnership are also creditors of the person or partnership continuing the business.

(5) When any partner wrongfully causes a dissolution and the remaining partners continue the business under the provisions of section 38(2)(b), either alone or with others, and without liquidation of the partnership affairs, creditors of the dissolved partnership are also creditors of the person or partnership continuing the business.

(6) When a partner is expelled and the remaining partners continue the business either alone or with others, without liquidation of the partnership affairs, creditors of the dissolved partnership are also creditors of the person or partnership continuing the business.

(7) The liability of a third person becoming a partner in the partnership continuing the business, under this section, to the creditors of the dissolved partnership shall be satisfied out of partnership property only.

(8) When the business of a partnership after dissolution is continued under any conditions set forth in this section the creditors of the dissolved partnership, as against the separate creditors of the retiring or deceased partner or the representative of the deceased partner, have a prior right to any claim of the retired partner or the representative of the deceased partner against the person or partnership continuing the business, on account of the retired or deceased partner's interest in the dissolved partnership or on account of any consideration promised for such interest or for his right in partnership property.

(9) Nothing in this section shall be held to modify any right of creditors to set aside any assignment on the ground of fraud.

(10) The use by the person or partnership continuing the business of the partnership name, or the name of a deceased partner as part thereof, shall not of itself make the individual property of the deceased partner liable for any debts contracted by such person or partnership.

SECTION 42. *Rights of Retiring or Estate of Deceased Partner When the Business is Continued.* When any partner retires or dies, and the business is continued under any of the conditions set forth in section 41 (1, 2, 3, 5, 6), or section 38(2)(b) without any settlement of accounts as between him or his estate and the person or partnership continuing the business, unless otherwise agreed, he or his legal representative as against such persons or partnership may have the value of his interest at the date of dissolution ascertained, and shall receive as an ordinary creditor an amount equal to the value of his interest in the dissolved partnership with interest, or, at his option or at the option of his legal representative, in lieu of interest, the profits attributable to the use of his right in the property of the dissolved partnership; provided that the creditors of the dissolved partnership as against the separate creditors, or the representative of the retired or deceased partner, shall have priority on any claim arising under this section, as provided by section 41(8) of this act.

SECTION 43. *Accrual of Actions.* The right to an account of his interest shall accrue to any partner, or his legal representative, as against the winding up partners or the surviving partners or the person or partnership continuing the business, at the date of dissolution, in the absence of any agreement to the contrary.

PART VII
MISCELLANEOUS PROVISIONS

SECTION 44. When Act Takes Effect.
SECTION 45. Legislation Repealed.

SECTION 44. *When Act Takes Effect.* This act shall take effect on the _____ day of _____ one thousand nine hundred and _____ .

SECTION 45. *Legislation Repealed.* All acts or parts of acts inconsistent with this act are hereby repealed.

UNIFORM PARTNERSHIP ACT (1997)
WITH MARKED LIMITED LIABILITY
ACT AMENDMENTS (JULY 1996 APPROVAL DATE)*

[Article] 1
General Provisions

[Article] 2
Nature Of Partnership

[Article] 3
Relations of Partners to
Persons Dealing With Partnership

---

* This act has been reprinted through the permission of the National Conference of Commissioners on Uniform State Laws, and copies may be ordered from them at 676 North St. Clair Street, Suite 1700, Chicago, Illinois, 60611.

[Article] 4
Relations of Partners to Each Other and to Partnership

[Article] 5
Transferees and Creditors of Partner

[Article] 6
Partner's Dissociation

[Article] 7
Partner's Dissociation When Business Not Wound Up

[Article] 8
Winding Up Partnership Business

[Article] 9
Conversions And Mergers

[Article] 10
Limited Liability Partnership

[Article] 11
Foreign Limited Liability Partnership

[Article] 12
Miscellaneous Provisions

AMENDMENTS TO ADD
LIMITED LIABILITY PARTNERSHIP
PROVISIONS TO
UNIFORM PARTNERSHIP ACT (1994)

[ARTICLE] 1
GENERAL PROVISIONS

Section 101. Definitions.
Section 102. Knowledge and Notice.
Section 103. Effect of Partnership Agreement; Nonwaivable Provisions.
Section 104. Supplemental Principles of Law.
Section 105. Execution, Filing, and Recording of Statements.
Section 106. Governing Law.
Section 107. Partnership Subject to Amendment or Repeal of [Act].

SECTION 101. DEFINITIONS. In this [Act]:

(1) "Business" includes every trade, occupation, and profession.

(2) "Debtor in bankruptcy" means a person who is the subject of:
   (i) an order for relief under Title 11 of the United States Code or a compa-
        rable order under a successor statute of general application; or
   (ii) a comparable order under federal, state, or foreign law governing insol-
        vency.

(3) "Distribution" means a transfer of money or other property from a partner-
    ship to a partner in the partner's capacity as a partner or to the partner's trans-
    feree.

(4) "Foreign limited liability partnership" means a partnership that:
   (i) is formed under laws other than the laws of this State;
   (ii) has the status of a limited liability partnership under those laws.

(5) "Limited liability partnership" means a partnership that has filed a statement
    of qualification under Section 1001 and does not have a similar statement in
    effect in any other jurisdiction.

(6) "Partnership" means an association of two or more persons to carry on as co-
    owners a business for profit formed under Section 202, predecessor law, or
    comparable law of another jurisdiction.

(7) "Partnership agreement" means the agreement, whether written, oral, or
    implied, among the partners concerning the partnership, including amendments
    to the partnership agreement.

(8) "Partnership at will" means a partnership in which the partners have not agreed
    to remain partners until the expiration of a definite term or the completion of
    a particular undertaking.

(9) "Partnership interest" or "partner's interest in the partnership" means all of
    a partner's interests in the partnership, including the partner's transferable inter-
    est and all management and other rights.

(10) "Person" means an individual, corporation, business trust, estate, trust, partnership, association, joint venture, government, governmental subdivision, agency, or instrumentality, or any other legal or commercial entity.

(11) "Property" means all property, real, personal, or mixed, tangible or intangible, or any interest therein.

(12) "State" means a State of the United States, the District of Columbia, the Commonwealth of Puerto Rico, or any territory or insular possession subject to the jurisdiction of the United States.

(13) "Statement" means a statement of partnership authority under Section 303, a statement of denial under Section 304, a statement of dissociation under Section 704, a statement of dissolution under Section 805, a statement of merger under Section 907, a statement of qualification under Section 1001, a statement of foreign qualification under Section 1102, or an amendment or cancellation of any of the foregoing.

(14) "Transfer" includes an assignment, conveyance, lease, mortgage, deed, and encumbrance.

SECTION 102. KNOWLEDGE AND NOTICE.

(a) A person knows a fact if the person has actual knowledge of it.

(b) A person has notice of a fact if the person:

    (1) knows of it;

    (2) has received a notification of it; or

    (3) has reason to know it exists from all of the facts known to the person at the time in question.

(c) A person notifies or gives a notification to another by taking steps reasonably required to inform the other person in ordinary course, whether or not the other person learns of it.

(d) A person receives a notification when the notification:

    (1) comes to the person's attention; or

    (2) is duly delivered at the person's place of business or at any other place held out by the person as a place for receiving communications.

(e) Except as otherwise provided in subsection (f), a person other than an individual knows, has notice, or receives a notification of a fact for purposes of a particular transaction when the individual conducting the transaction knows, has notice, or receives a notification of the fact, or in any event when the fact would have been brought to the individual's attention if the person had exercised reasonable diligence. The person exercises reasonable diligence if it maintains reasonable routines for communicating significant information to the individual conducting the transaction and there is reasonable compliance with the routines. Reasonable diligence does not require an individual acting for the person to communicate information unless the communication is part of the individual's regular duties or the individual has reason to know of the transaction and that the transaction would be materially affected by the information.

(f) A partner's knowledge, notice, or receipt of a notification of a fact relating to the partnership is effective immediately as knowledge by, notice to, or receipt of a notification by the partnership, except in the case of a fraud on the partnership committed by or with the consent of that partner.

SECTION 103. EFFECT OF PARTNERSHIP AGREEMENT; NONWAIVABLE PROVISIONS.

(a) Except as otherwise provided in subsection (b), relations among the partners and between the partners and the partnership are governed by the partnership agreement. To the extent the partnership agreement does not otherwise provide, this [Act] governs relations among the partners and between the partners and the partnership.

(b) The partnership agreement may not:

   (1) vary the rights and duties under Section 105 except to eliminate the duty to provide copies of statements to all of the partners;

   (2) unreasonably restrict the right of access to books and records under Section 403(b);

   (3) eliminate the duty of loyalty under Section 404(b) or 603(b)(3), but:

      (i) the partnership agreement may identify specific types or categories of activities that do not violate the duty of loyalty, if not manifestly unreasonable; or

      (ii) all of the partners or a number or percentage specified in the partnership agreement may authorize or ratify, after full disclosure of all material facts, a specific act or transaction that otherwise would violate the duty of loyalty;

   (4) unreasonably reduce the duty of care under Section 404(c) or 603(b)(3);

   (5) eliminate the obligation of good faith and fair dealing under Section 404(d), but the partnership agreement may prescribe the standards by which the performance of the obligation is to be measured, if the standards are not manifestly unreasonable;

   (6) vary the power to dissociate as a partner under Section 602(a), except to require the notice under Section 601(1) to be in writing;

   (7) vary the right of a court to expel a partner in the events specified in Section 601(5);

   (8) vary the requirement to wind up the partnership business in cases specified in Section 801(4), (5), or (6);

   (9) vary the law applicable to a limited liability partnership under Section 106(b); or

   (10) restrict rights of third parties under this [Act].

SECTION 104. SUPPLEMENTAL PRINCIPLES OF LAW.

(a) Unless displaced by particular provisions of this [Act], the principles of law and equity supplement this [Act].

(b) If an obligation to pay interest arises under this [Act] and the rate is not specified, the rate is that specified in [applicable statute].

SECTION 105. EXECUTION, FILING, AND RECORDING OF STATEMENTS.

(a) A statement may be filed in the office of [the Secretary of State]. A certified copy of a statement that is filed in an office in another state may be filed in the office of [the Secretary of State]. Either filing has the effect provided in this [Act] with respect to partnership property located in or transactions that occur in this State.

(b) A certified copy of a statement that has been filed in the office of the [Secretary of State] and recorded in the office for recording transfers of real property has the effect provided for recorded statements in this [Act]. A recorded statement that is not a certified copy of a statement filed in the office of the [Secretary of State] does not have the effect provided for recorded statements in this [Act].

(c) A statement filed by a partnership must be executed by at least two partners. Other statements must be executed by a partner or other person authorized by this [Act]. An individual who executes a statement as, or on behalf of, a partner or other person named as a partner in a statement shall personally declare under penalty of perjury that the contents of the statement are accurate.

(d) A person authorized by this [Act] to file a statement may amend or cancel the statement by filing an amendment or cancellation that names the partnership, identifies the statement, and states the substance of the amendment or cancellation.

(e) A person who files a statement pursuant to this section shall promptly send a copy of the statement to every nonfiling partner and to any other person named as a partner in the statement. Failure to send a copy of a statement to a partner or other person does not limit the effectiveness of the statement as to a person not a partner.

(f) The [Secretary of State] may collect a fee for filing or providing a certified copy of a statement. The [officer responsible for recording transfers of real property] may collect a fee for recording a statement.

SECTION 106. GOVERNING LAW.

(a) Except as otherwise provided in subsection (b), the law of the jurisdiction in which a partnership has its chief executive office governs relations among the partners and between the partners and the partnership.

(b) The law of this State governs relations among the partners and between the partners and the partnership and the liability of partners for an obligation of a limited liability partnership.

SECTION 107. PARTNERSHIP SUBJECT TO AMENDMENT OR REPEAL OF [ACT].

A partnership governed by this [Act] is subject to any amendment to or repeal of this [Act].

[ARTICLE] 2
NATURE OF PARTNERSHIP

Section 201. Partnership As Entity.
Section 202. Formation of Partnership.
Section 203. Partnership Property.
Section 204. When Property Is Partnership Property.

SECTION 201. PARTNERSHIP AS ENTITY.

(a) A partnership is an entity distinct from its partners.

(b) A limited liability partnership continues to be the same entity that existed before the filing of a statement of qualification under Section 1001.

SECTION 202. FORMATION OF PARTNERSHIP.

(a) Except as otherwise provided in subsection (b), the association of two or more persons to carry on as co-owners a business for profit forms a partnership, whether or not the persons intend to form a partnership.

(b) An association formed under a statute other than this [Act], a predecessor statute, or a comparable statute of another jurisdiction is not a partnership under this [Act].

(c) In determining whether a partnership is formed, the following rules apply:

(1) Joint tenancy, tenancy in common, tenancy by the entireties, joint property, common property, or part ownership does not by itself establish a partnership, even if the co-owners share profits made by the use of the property.

(2) The sharing of gross returns does not by itself establish a partnership, even if the persons sharing them have a joint or common right or interest in property from which the returns are derived.

(3) A person who receives a share of the profits of a business is presumed to be a partner in the business, unless the profits were received in payment:

(i) of a debt by installments or otherwise;

(ii) for services as an independent contractor or of wages or other compensation to an employee;

(iii) of rent;

(iv) of an annuity or other retirement benefit to a beneficiary, representative, or designee of a deceased or retired partner;

(v) of interest or other charge on a loan, even if the amount of payment varies with the profits of the business, including a direct or indirect present or future ownership of the collateral, or rights to income, proceeds, or increase in value derived from the collateral; or

(vi) for the sale of the goodwill of a business or other property by installments or otherwise.

SECTION 203. PARTNERSHIP PROPERTY.
Property acquired by a partnership is property of the partnership and not of the partners individually.

SECTION 204. WHEN PROPERTY IS PARTNERSHIP PROPERTY.

(a) Property is partnership property if acquired in the name of:

    (1) the partnership; or

    (2) one or more partners with an indication in the instrument transferring title to the property of the person's capacity as a partner or of the existence of a partnership but without an indication of the name of the partnership.

(b) Property is acquired in the name of the partnership by a transfer to:

    (1) the partnership in its name; or

    (2) one or more partners in their capacity as partners in the partnership, if the name of the partnership is indicated in the instrument transferring title to the property.

(c) Property is presumed to be partnership property if purchased with partnership assets, even if not acquired in the name of the partnership or of one or more partners with an indication in the instrument transferring title to the property of the person's capacity as a partner or of the existence of a partnership.

(d) Property acquired in the name of one or more of the partners, without an indication in the instrument transferring title to the property of the person's capacity as a partner or of the existence of a partnership and without use of partnership assets, is presumed to be separate property, even if used for partnership purposes.

[ARTICLE] 3
RELATIONS OF PARTNERS TO
PERSONS DEALING WITH PARTNERSHIP

SECTION 301. PARTNER AGENT OF PARTNERSHIP. Subject to the effect of a statement of partnership authority under Section 303:

    (1) Each partner is an agent of the partnership for the purpose of its business. An act of a partner, including the execution of an instrument in the partnership name, for apparently carrying on in the ordinary course the partnership business or business of the kind carried on by the partnership binds the partnership, unless the partner had no authority to act for the partnership in the particular matter and the person with whom the partner was dealing knew or had received a notification that the partner lacked authority.

    (2) An act of a partner which is not apparently for carrying on in the ordinary course the partnership business or business of the kind carried on by the part-

nership binds the partnership only if the act was authorized by the other partners.

SECTION 302. TRANSFER OF PARTNERSHIP PROPERTY.

(a) Partnership property may be transferred as follows:

    (1) Subject to the effect of a statement of partnership authority under Section 303, partnership property held in the name of the partnership may be transferred by an instrument of transfer executed by a partner in the partnership name.

    (2) Partnership property held in the name of one or more partners with an indication in the instrument transferring the property to them of their capacity as partners or of the existence of a partnership, but without an indication of the name of the partnership, may be transferred by an instrument of transfer executed by the persons in whose name the property is held.

    (3) Partnership property held in the name of one or more persons other than the partnership, without an indication in the instrument transferring the property to them of their capacity as partners or of the existence of a partnership, may be transferred by an instrument of transfer executed by the persons in whose name the property is held.

(b) A partnership may recover partnership property from a transferee only if it proves that execution of the instrument of initial transfer did not bind the partnership under Section 301 and:

    (1) as to a subsequent transferee who gave value for property transferred under subsection (a)(1) and (2), proves that the subsequent transferee knew or had received a notification that the person who executed the instrument of initial transfer lacked authority to bind the partnership; or

    (2) as to a transferee who gave value for property transferred under subsection (a)(3), proves that the transferee knew or had received a notification that the property was partnership property and that the person who executed the instrument of initial transfer lacked authority to bind the partnership.

(c) A partnership may not recover partnership property from a subsequent transferee if the partnership would not have been entitled to recover the property, under subsection (b), from any earlier transferee of the property.

(d) If a person holds all of the partners' interests in the partnership, all of the partnership property vests in that person. The person may execute a document in the name of the partnership to evidence vesting of the property in that person and may file or record the document.

SECTION 303. STATEMENT OF PARTNERSHIP AUTHORITY.

(a) A partnership may file a statement of partnership authority, which:

    (1) must include:

        (i) the name of the partnership;

      (ii)   the street address of its chief executive office and of one office in this State, if there is one;

      (iii) the names and mailing addresses of all of the partners or of an agent appointed and maintained by the partnership for the purpose of subsection (b); and

      (iv) the names of the partners authorized to execute an instrument transferring real property held in the name of the partnership; and

  (2) may state the authority, or limitations on the authority, of some or all of the partners to enter into other transactions on behalf of the partnership and any other matter.

(b) If a statement of partnership authority names an agent, the agent shall maintain a list of the names and mailing addresses of all of the partners and make it available to any person on request for good cause shown.

(c) If a filed statement of partnership authority is executed pursuant to Section 105(c) and states the name of the partnership but does not contain all of the other information required by subsection (a), the statement nevertheless operates with respect to a person not a partner as provided in subsections (d) and (e).

(d) Except as otherwise provided in subsection (g), a filed statement of partnership authority supplements the authority of a partner to enter into transactions on behalf of the partnership as follows:

  (1) Except for transfers of real property, a grant of authority contained in a filed statement of partnership authority is conclusive in favor of a person who gives value without knowledge to the contrary, so long as and to the extent that a limitation on that authority is not then contained in another filed statement. A filed cancellation of a limitation on authority revives the previous grant of authority.

  (2) A grant of authority to transfer real property held in the name of the partnership contained in a certified copy of a filed statement of partnership authority recorded in the office for recording transfers of that real property is conclusive in favor of a person who gives value without knowledge to the contrary, so long as and to the extent that a certified copy of a filed statement containing a limitation on that authority is not then of record in the office for recording transfers of that real property. The recording in the office for recording transfers of that real property of a certified copy of a filed cancellation of a limitation on authority revives the previous grant of authority.

(e) A person not a partner is deemed to know of a limitation on the authority of a partner to transfer real property held in the name of the partnership if a certified copy of the filed statement containing the limitation on authority is of record in the office for recording transfers of that real property.

(f) Except as otherwise provided in subsections (d) and (e) and Sections 704 and 805, a person not a partner is not deemed to know of a limitation on the authority of a partner merely because the limitation is contained in a filed statement.

(g) Unless earlier canceled, a filed statement of partnership authority is canceled by operation of law five years after the date on which the statement, or the most recent amendment, was filed with the [Secretary of State].

SECTION 304. STATEMENT OF DENIAL. A partner or other person named as a partner in a filed statement of partnership authority or in a list maintained by an agent pursuant to Section 303(b) may file a statement of denial stating the name of the partnership and the fact that is being denied, which may include denial of a person's authority or status as a partner. A statement of denial is a limitation on authority as provided in Section 303(d) and (e).

SECTION 305. PARTNERSHIP LIABLE FOR PARTNER'S ACTIONABLE CONDUCT.

(a) A partnership is liable for loss or injury caused to a person, or for a penalty incurred, as a result of a wrongful act or omission, or other actionable conduct, of a partner acting in the ordinary course of business of the partnership or with authority of the partnership.

(b) If, in the course of the partnership's business or while acting with authority of the partnership, a partner receives or causes the partnership to receive money or property of a person not a partner, and the money or property is misapplied by a partner, the partnership is liable for the loss.

SECTION 306. PARTNER'S LIABILITY.

(a) Except as otherwise provided in subsections (b) _and (c),_ all partners are liable jointly and severally for all obligations of the partnership unless otherwise agreed by the claimant or provided by law.

(b) A person admitted as a partner into an existing partnership is not personally liable for any partnership obligation incurred before the person's admission as a partner.

(c) An obligation of a partnership incurred while the partnership is a limited liability partnership, whether arising in contract, tort, or otherwise, is solely the obligation of the partnership. A partner is not personally liable, directly or indirectly, by way of contribution or otherwise, for such an obligation solely by reason of being or so acting as a partner. This subsection applies notwithstanding anything inconsistent in the partnership agreement that existed immediately before the vote required to become a limited liability partnership under Section 1001(b).

SECTION 307. ACTIONS BY AND AGAINST PARTNERSHIP AND PARTNERS.

(a) A partnership may sue and be sued in the name of the partnership.

(b) An action may be brought against the partnership and, to the extent not inconsistent with Section 306, any or all of the partners in the same action or in separate actions.

(c) A judgment against a partnership is not by itself a judgment against a partner. A judgment against a partnership may not be satisfied from a partner's assets unless there is also a judgment against the partner.

(d) A judgment creditor of a partner may not levy execution against the assets of the partner to satisfy a judgment based on a claim against the partnership unless the partner is personally liable for the claim under Section 306 and:

   (1) a judgment based on the same claim has been obtained against the partnership and a writ of execution on the judgment has been returned unsatisfied in whole or in part;

   (2) the partnership is a debtor in bankruptcy;

   (3) the partner has agreed that the creditor need not exhaust partnership assets;

   (4) a court grants permission to the judgment creditor to levy execution against the assets of a partner based on a finding that partnership assets subject to execution are clearly insufficient to satisfy the judgment, that exhaustion of partnership assets is excessively burdensome, or that the grant of permission is an appropriate exercise of the court's equitable powers; or

   (5) liability is imposed on the partner by law or contract independent of the existence of the partnership.

(e) This section applies to any partnership liability or obligation resulting from a representation by a partner or purported partner under Section 308.

SECTION 308. LIABILITY OF PURPORTED PARTNER.

(a) If a person, by words or conduct, purports to be a partner, or consents to being represented by another as a partner, in a partnership or with one or more persons not partners, the purported partner is liable to a person to whom the representation is made, if that person, relying on the representation, enters into a transaction with the actual or purported partnership. If the representation, either by the purported partner or by a person with the purported partner's consent, is made in a public manner, the purported partner is liable to a person who relies upon the purported partnership even if the purported partner is not aware of being held out as a partner to the claimant. If partnership liability results, the purported partner is liable with respect to that liability as if the purported partner were a partner. If no partnership liability results, the purported partner is liable with respect to that liability jointly and severally with any other person consenting to the representation.

(b) If a person is thus represented to be a partner in an existing partnership, or with one or more persons not partners, the purported partner is an agent of persons consenting to the representation to bind them to the same extent and in the same manner as if the purported partner were a partner, with respect to persons who enter into transactions in reliance upon the representation. If all of the partners of the existing partnership consent to the representation, a partnership act or obligation results. If fewer than all of the partners of the existing partnership consent to the representation, the person acting and the partners consenting to the representation are jointly and severally liable.

(c) A person is not liable as a partner merely because the person is named by another in a statement of partnership authority.

(d) A person does not continue to be liable as a partner merely because of a failure to file a statement of dissociation or to amend a statement of partnership authority to indicate the partner's dissociation from the partnership.

(e) Except as otherwise provided in subsections (a) and (b), persons who are not partners as to each other are not liable as partners to other persons.

[ARTICLE] 4
RELATIONS OF PARTNERS TO EACH OTHER AND TO PARTNERSHIP

SECTION 401. PARTNER'S RIGHTS AND DUTIES.

(a) Each partner is deemed to have an account that is:

(1) credited with an amount equal to the money plus the value of any other property, net of the amount of any liabilities, the partner contributes to the partnership and the partner's share of the partnership profits; and

(2) charged with an amount equal to the money plus the value of any other property, net of the amount of any liabilities, distributed by the partnership to the partner and the partner's share of the partnership losses.

(b) Each partner is entitled to an equal share of the partnership profits and is chargeable with a share of the partnership losses in proportion to the partner's share of the profits.

(c) A partnership shall reimburse a partner for payments made and indemnify a partner for liabilities incurred by the partner in the ordinary course of the business of the partnership or for the preservation of its business or property;

(d) A partnership shall reimburse a partner for an advance to the partnership beyond the amount of capital the partner agreed to contribute.

(e) A payment or advance made by a partner which gives rise to a partnership obligation under subsection (c) or (d) constitutes a loan to the partnership which accrues interest from the date of the payment or advance.

(f) Each partner has equal rights in the management and conduct of the partnership business.

(g) A partner may use or possess partnership property only on behalf of the partnership.

(h) A partner is not entitled to remuneration for services performed for the partnership, except for reasonable compensation for services rendered in winding up the business of the partnership.

(i) A person may become a partner only with the consent of all of the partners.

(j) A difference arising as to a matter in the ordinary course of business of a partnership may be decided by a majority of the partners. An act outside the ordinary course of business of a partnership and an amendment to the partnership agreement may be undertaken only with the consent of all of the partners.

(k) This section does not affect the obligations of a partnership to other persons under Section 301.

SECTION 402. DISTRIBUTIONS IN KIND. A partner has no right to receive, and may not be required to accept, a distribution in kind.

SECTION 403. PARTNER'S RIGHTS AND DUTIES WITH RESPECT TO INFORMATION.

(a) A partnership shall keep its books and records, if any, at its chief executive office.

(b) A partnership shall provide partners and their agents and attorneys access to its books and records. It shall provide former partners and their agents and attorneys access to books and records pertaining to the period during which they were partners. The right of access provides the opportunity to inspect and copy books and records during ordinary business hours. A partnership may impose a reasonable charge, covering the costs of labor and material, for copies of documents furnished.

(c) Each partner and the partnership shall furnish to a partner, and to the legal representative of a deceased partner or partner under legal disability:

   (1) without demand, any information concerning the partnership's business and affairs reasonably required for the proper exercise of the partner's rights and duties under the partnership agreement or this [Act]; and

   (2) on demand, any other information concerning the partnership's business and affairs, except to the extent the demand or the information demanded is unreasonable or otherwise improper under the circumstances.

SECTION 404. GENERAL STANDARDS OF PARTNER'S CONDUCT.

(a) The only fiduciary duties a partner owes to the partnership and the other partners are the duty of loyalty and the duty of care set forth in subsections (b) and (c).

(b) A partner's duty of loyalty to the partnership and the other partners is limited to the following:

   (1) to account to the partnership and hold as trustee for it any property, profit, or benefit derived by the partner in the conduct and winding up of the partnership business or derived from a use by the partner of partnership property, including the appropriation of a partnership opportunity;

(2) to refrain from dealing with the partnership in the conduct or winding up of the partnership business as or on behalf of a party having an interest adverse to the partnership; and

(3) to refrain from competing with the partnership in the conduct of the partnership business before the dissolution of the partnership.

(c) A partner's duty of care to the partnership and the other partners in the conduct and winding up of the partnership business is limited to refraining from engaging in grossly negligent or reckless conduct, intentional misconduct, or a knowing violation of law.

(d) A partner shall discharge the duties to the partnership and the other partners under this [Act] or under the partnership agreement and exercise any rights consistently with the obligation of good faith and fair dealing.

(e) A partner does not violate a duty or obligation under this [Act] or under the partnership agreement merely because the partner's conduct furthers the partner's own interest.

(f) A partner may lend money to and transact other business with the partnership, and as to each loan or transaction, the rights and obligations of the partner are the same as those of a person who is not a partner, subject to other applicable law.

(g) This section applies to a person winding up the partnership business as the personal or legal representative of the last surviving partner as if the person were a partner.

SECTION 405. ACTIONS BY PARTNERSHIP AND PARTNERS.

(a) A partnership may maintain an action against a partner for a breach of the partnership agreement, or for the violation of a duty to the partnership, causing harm to the partnership.

(b) A partner may maintain an action against the partnership or another partner for legal or equitable relief, with or without an accounting as to partnership business, to:

(1) enforce the partner's rights under the partnership agreement;

(2) enforce the partner's rights under this [Act], including:

(i)   the partner's rights under Sections 401, 403, or 404;

(ii) the partner's right on dissociation to have the partner's interest in the partnership purchased pursuant to Section 701 or enforce any other right under [Article] 6 or 7; or

(iii) the partner's right to compel a dissolution and winding up of the partnership business under or enforce any other right under [Article] 8; or

(3) enforce the rights and otherwise protect the interests of the partner, including rights and interests arising independently of the partnership relationship.

(c) The accrual of, and any time limitation on, a right of action for a remedy under this section is governed by other law. A right to an accounting upon a dissolution and winding up does not revive a claim barred by law.

SECTION 406. CONTINUATION OF PARTNERSHIP BEYOND DEFINITE TERM OR PARTICULAR UNDERTAKING.

(a) If a partnership for a definite term or particular undertaking is continued, without an express agreement, after the expiration of the term or completion of the undertaking, the rights and duties of the partners remain the same as they were at the expiration or completion, so far as is consistent with a partnership at will.

(b) If the partners, or those of them who habitually acted in the business during the term or undertaking, continue the business without any settlement or liquidation of the partnership, they are presumed to have agreed that the partnership will continue.

[ARTICLE] 5
TRANSFEREES AND CREDITORS OF PARTNER

SECTION 501. PARTNER NOT CO-OWNER OF PARTNERSHIP PROPERTY. A partner is not a co-owner of partnership property and has no interest in partnership property which can be transferred, either voluntarily or involuntarily.

SECTION 502. PARTNER'S TRANSFERABLE INTEREST IN PARTNERSHIP. The only transferable interest of a partner in the partnership is the partner's share of the profits and losses of the partnership and the partner's right to receive distributions. The interest is personal property.

SECTION 503. TRANSFER OF PARTNER'S TRANSFERABLE INTEREST.

(a) A transfer, in whole or in part, of a partner's transferable interest in the partnership:
   (1) is permissible;
   (2) does not by itself cause the partner's dissociation or a dissolution and winding up of the partnership business; and
   (3) does not, as against the other partners or the partnership, entitle the transferee, during the continuance of the partnership, to participate in the management or conduct of the partnership business, to require access to information concerning partnership transactions, or to inspect or copy the partnership books or records.

(b) A transferee of a partner's transferable interest in the partnership has a right:
   (1) to receive, in accordance with the transfer, distributions to which the transferor would otherwise be entitled;
   (2) to receive upon the dissolution and winding up of the partnership business, in accordance with the transfer, the net amount otherwise distributable to the transferor; and

(3) to seek under Section 801(6) a judicial determination that it is equitable to wind up the partnership business.

(c) In a dissolution and winding up, a transferee is entitled to an account of partnership transactions only from the date of the latest account agreed to by all of the partners.

(d) Upon transfer, the transferor retains the rights and duties of a partner other than the interest in distributions transferred.

(e) A partnership need not give effect to a transferee's rights under this section until it has notice of the transfer.

(f) A transfer of a partner's transferable interest in the partnership in violation of a restriction on transfer contained in the partnership agreement is ineffective as to a person having notice of the restriction at the time of transfer.

SECTION 504. PARTNER'S TRANSFERABLE INTEREST SUBJECT TO CHARGING ORDER.

(a) On application by a judgment creditor of a partner or of a partner's transferee, a court having jurisdiction may charge the transferable interest of the judgment debtor to satisfy the judgment. The court may appoint a receiver of the share of the distributions due or to become due to the judgment debtor in respect of the partnership and make all other orders, directions, accounts, and inquiries the judgment debtor might have made or which the circumstances of the case may require.

(b) A charging order constitutes a lien on the judgment debtor's transferable interest in the partnership. The court may order a foreclosure of the interest subject to the charging order at any time. The purchaser at the foreclosure sale has the rights of a transferee.

(c) At any time before foreclosure, an interest charged may be redeemed:

(1) by the judgment debtor;

(2) with property other than partnership property, by one or more of the other partners; or

(3) with partnership property, by one or more of the other partners with the consent of all of the partners whose interests are not so charged.

(d) This [Act] does not deprive a partner of a right under exemption laws with respect to the partner's interest in the partnership.

(e) This section provides the exclusive remedy by which a judgment creditor of a partner or partner's transferee may satisfy a judgment out of the judgment debtor's transferable interest in the partnership.

[ARTICLE] 6
PARTNER'S DISSOCIATION

SECTION 601. EVENTS CAUSING PARTNER'S DISSOCIATION. A partner is dissociated from a partnership upon the occurrence of any of the following events:

    (1) the partnership's having notice of the partner's express will to withdraw as a partner or on a later date specified by the partner;

    (2) an event agreed to in the partnership agreement as causing the partner's dissociation;

    (3) the partner's expulsion pursuant to the partnership agreement;

    (4) the partner's expulsion by the unanimous vote of the other partners if:

        (i)   it is unlawful to carry on the partnership business with that partner;

        (ii) there has been a transfer of all or substantially all of that partner's transferable interest in the partnership, other than a transfer for security purposes, or a court order charging the partner's interest, which has not been foreclosed;

        (iii) within 90 days after the partnership notifies a corporate partner that it will be expelled because it has filed a certificate of dissolution or the equivalent, its charter has been revoked, or its right to conduct business has been suspended by the jurisdiction of its incorporation, there is no revocation of the certificate of dissolution or no reinstatement of its charter or its right to conduct business; or

        (iv) a partnership that is a partner has been dissolved and its business is being wound up;

    (5) on application by the partnership or another partner, the partner's expulsion by judicial determination because:

        (i)   the partner engaged in wrongful conduct that adversely and materially affected the partnership business;

        (ii) the partner willfully or persistently committed a material breach of the partnership agreement or of a duty owed to the partnership or the other partners under Section 404; or

        (iii) the partner engaged in conduct relating to the partnership business which makes it not reasonably practicable to carry on the business in partnership with the partner;

    (6) the partner's:

        (i)   becoming a debtor in bankruptcy;

        (ii) executing an assignment for the benefit of creditors;

        (iii) seeking, consenting to, or acquiescing in the appointment of a trustee, receiver, or liquidator of that partner or of all or substantially all of that partner's property; or

      (iv) failing, within 90 days after the appointment, to have vacated or stayed the appointment of a trustee, receiver, or liquidator of the partner or of all or substantially all of the partner's property obtained without the partner's consent or acquiescence, or failing within 90 days after the expiration of a stay to have the appointment vacated;

(7) in the case of a partner who is an individual:

     (i)   the partner's death;

    (ii)   the appointment of a guardian or general conservator for the partner; or

   (iii) a judicial determination that the partner has otherwise become incapable of performing the partner's duties under the partnership agreement;

(8) in the case of a partner that is a trust or is acting as a partner by virtue of being a trustee of a trust, distribution of the trust's entire transferable interest in the partnership, but not merely by reason of the substitution of a successor trustee;

(9) in the case of a partner that is an estate or is acting as a partner by virtue of being a personal representative of an estate, distribution of the estate's entire transferable interest in the partnership, but not merely by reason of the substitution of a successor personal representative; or

(10) termination of a partner who is not an individual, partnership, corporation, trust, or estate.

SECTION 602. PARTNER'S POWER TO DISSOCIATE; WRONGFUL DISSOCIATION.

(a) A partner has the power to dissociate at any time, rightfully or wrongfully, by express will pursuant to Section 601(1).

(b) A partner's dissociation is wrongful only if:

    (1)   it is in breach of an express provision of the partnership agreement; or

    (2)   in the case of a partnership for a definite term or particular undertaking, before the expiration of the term or the completion of the undertaking:

       (i)   the partner withdraws by express will, unless the withdrawal follows within 90 days after another partner's dissociation by death or otherwise under Section 601(6) through (10) or wrongful dissociation under this subsection;

      (ii)   the partner is expelled by judicial determination under Section 601(5);

     (iii) the partner is dissociated by becoming a debtor in bankruptcy; or

     (iv) in the case of a partner who is not an individual, trust other than a business trust, or estate, the partner is expelled or otherwise dissociated because it willfully dissolved or terminated.

(c) A partner who wrongfully dissociates is liable to the partnership and to the other partners for damages caused by the dissociation. The liability is in addition to any other obligation of the partner to the partnership or to the other partners.

SECTION 603. EFFECT OF PARTNER'S DISSOCIATION.

(a) If a partner's dissociation results in a dissolution and winding up of the partnership business, [Article] 8 applies; otherwise, [Article] 7 applies.

(b) Upon a partner's dissociation:
  (1) the partner's right to participate in the management and conduct of the partnership business terminates, except as otherwise provided in Section 803;
  (2) the partner's duty of loyalty under Section 404(b)(3) terminates; and
  (3) the partner's duty of loyalty under Section 404(b)(1) and (2) and duty of care under Section 404(c) continue only with regard to matters arising and events occurring before the partner's dissociation, unless the partner participates in winding up the partnership's business pursuant to Section 803.

[ARTICLE] 7
PARTNER'S DISSOCIATION WHEN BUSINESS NOT WOUND UP

SECTION 701. PURCHASE OF DISSOCIATED PARTNER'S INTEREST.

(a) If a partner is dissociated from a partnership without resulting in a dissolution and winding up of the partnership business under Section 801, the partnership shall cause the dissociated partner's interest in the partnership to be purchased for a buyout price determined pursuant to subsection (b).

(b) The buyout price of a dissociated partner's interest is the amount that would have been distributable to the dissociating partner under Section 807(b) if, on the date of dissociation, the assets of the partnership were sold at a price equal to the greater of the liquidation value or the value based on a sale of the entire business as a going concern without the dissociated partner and the partnership were wound up as of that date. Interest must be paid from the date of dissociation to the date of payment.

(c) Damages for wrongful dissociation under Section 602(b), and all other amounts owing, whether or not presently due, from the dissociated partner to the partnership, must be offset against the buyout price. Interest must be paid from the date the amount owed becomes due to the date of payment.

(d) A partnership shall indemnify a dissociated partner whose interest is being purchased against all partnership liabilities, whether incurred before or after the dissociation, except liabilities incurred by an act of the dissociated partner under Section 702.

(e) If no agreement for the purchase of a dissociated partner's interest is reached within 120 days after a written demand for payment, the partnership shall pay, or cause to be paid, in cash to the dissociated partner the amount the partnership estimates to be the buyout price and accrued interest, reduced by any offsets and accrued interest under subsection (c).

(f) If a deferred payment is authorized under subsection (h), the partnership may tender a written offer to pay the amount it estimates to be the buyout price and accrued interest, reduced by any offsets under subsection (c), stating the time of payment, the amount and type of security for payment, and the other terms and conditions of the obligation.

(g) The payment or tender required by subsection (e) or (f) must be accompanied by the following:

   (1) a statement of partnership assets and liabilities as of the date of dissociation;

   (2) the latest available partnership balance sheet and income statement, if any;

   (3) an explanation of how the estimated amount of the payment was calculated; and

   (4) written notice that the payment is in full satisfaction of the obligation to purchase unless, within 120 days after the written notice, the dissociated partner commences an action to determine the buyout price, any offsets under subsection (c), or other terms of the obligation to purchase.

(h) A partner who wrongfully dissociates before the expiration of a definite term or the completion of a particular undertaking is not entitled to payment of any portion of the buyout price until the expiration of the term or completion of the undertaking, unless the partner establishes to the satisfaction of the court that earlier payment will not cause undue hardship to the business of the partnership. A deferred payment must be adequately secured and bear interest.

(i) A dissociated partner may maintain an action against the partnership, pursuant to Section 405(b)(2)(ii), to determine the buyout price of that partner's interest, any offsets under subsection (c), or other terms of the obligation to purchase. The action must be commenced within 120 days after the partnership has tendered payment or an offer to pay or within one year after written demand for payment if no payment or offer to pay is tendered. The court shall determine the buyout price of the dissociated partner's interest, any offset due under subsection (c), and accrued interest, and enter judgment for any additional payment or refund. If deferred payment is authorized under subsection (h), the court shall also determine the security for payment and other terms of the obligation to purchase. The court may assess reasonable attorney's fees and the fees and expenses of appraisers or other experts for a party to the action, in amounts the court finds equitable, against a party that the court finds acted arbitrarily, vexatiously, or not in good faith. The finding may be based on the partnership's failure to tender payment or an offer to pay or to comply with subsection (g).

SECTION 702. DISSOCIATED PARTNER'S POWER TO BIND AND LIABILITY TO PARTNERSHIP.

(a) For two years after a partner dissociates without resulting in a dissolution and winding up of the partnership business, the partnership, including a surviving partnership under [Article] 9, is bound by an act of the dissociated partner which would have bound the partnership under Section 301 before dissociation only if at the time of entering into the transaction the other party:

    (1)   reasonably believed that the dissociated partner was then a partner;

    (2)   did not have notice of the partner's dissociation; and

    (3)   is not deemed to have had knowledge under Section 303(e) or notice under Section 704(c).

(b) A dissociated partner is liable to the partnership for any damage caused to the partnership arising from an obligation incurred by the dissociated partner after dissociation for which the partnership is liable under subsection (a).

SECTION 703. DISSOCIATED PARTNER'S LIABILITY TO OTHER PERSONS.

(a) A partner's dissociation does not of itself discharge the partner's liability for a partnership obligation incurred before dissociation. A dissociated partner is not liable for a partnership obligation incurred after dissociation, except as otherwise provided in subsection (b).

(b) A partner who dissociates without resulting in a dissolution and winding up of the partnership business is liable as a partner to the other party in a transaction entered into by the partnership, or a surviving partnership under [Article] 9, within two years after the partner's dissociation, only if the partner is liable for the obligation under Section 306 and at the time of entering into the transaction the other party:

    (1)   reasonably believed that the dissociated partner was then a partner;

    (2)   did not have notice of the partner's dissociation; and

    (3)   is not deemed to have had knowledge under Section 303(e) or notice under Section 704(c).

(c) By agreement with the partnership creditor and the partners continuing the business, a dissociated partner may be released from liability for a partnership obligation.

(d) A dissociated partner is released from liability for a partnership obligation if a partnership creditor, with notice of the partner's dissociation but without the partner's consent, agrees to a material alteration in the nature or time of payment of a partnership obligation.

SECTION 704. STATEMENT OF DISSOCIATION.

(a) A dissociated partner or the partnership may file a statement of dissociation stating the name of the partnership and that the partner is dissociated from the partnership.

(b) A statement of dissociation is a limitation on the authority of a dissociated partner for the purposes of Section 303(d) and (e).

(c) For the purposes of Sections 702(a)(3) and 703(b)(3), a person not a partner is deemed to have notice of the dissociation 90 days after the statement of dissociation is filed.

SECTION 705. CONTINUED USE OF PARTNERSHIP NAME. Continued
use of a partnership name, or a dissociated partner's name as part thereof, by partners

continuing the business does not of itself make the dissociated partner liable for an obligation of the partners or the partnership continuing the business.

[ARTICLE] 8
WINDING UP PARTNERSHIP BUSINESS

SECTION 801. EVENTS CAUSING DISSOLUTION AND WINDING UP OF PARTNERSHIP BUSINESS. A partnership is dissolved, and its business must be wound up, only upon the occurrence of any of the following events:

(1) in a partnership at will, the partnership's having notice from a partner, other than a partner who is dissociated under Section 601(2) through (10), of that partner's express will to withdraw as a partner, or on a later date specified by the partner;

(2) in a partnership for a definite term or particular undertaking:

   (i) within 90 days after a partner's dissociation by death or otherwise under Section 601(6) through (10) or wrongful dissociation under Section 602(b), the express will of at least half of the remaining partners to wind up the partnership business, for which purpose a partner's rightful dissociation pursuant to Section 602(b)(2)(i) constitutes the expression of that partner's will to wind up the partnership business;

   (ii) the express will of all of the partners to wind up the partnership business; or

   (iii) the expiration of the term or the completion of the undertaking;

(3) an event agreed to in the partnership agreement resulting in the winding up of the partnership business;

(4) an event that makes it unlawful for all or substantially all of the business of the partnership to be continued, but a cure of illegality within 90 days after notice to the partnership of the event is effective retroactively to the date of the event for purposes of this section;

(5) on application by a partner, a judicial determination that:

   (i) the economic purpose of the partnership is likely to be unreasonably frustrated;

   (ii) another partner has engaged in conduct relating to the partnership business which makes it not reasonably practicable to carry on the business in partnership with that partner; or

   (iii) it is not otherwise reasonably practicable to carry on the partnership business in conformity with the partnership agreement; or

(6) on application by a transferee of a partner's transferable interest, a judicial determination that it is equitable to wind up the partnership business:
    (i) after the expiration of the term or completion of the undertaking, if the partnership was for a definite term or particular undertaking at the time of the transfer or entry of the charging order that gave rise to the transfer; or
    (ii) at any time, if the partnership was a partnership at will at the time of the transfer or entry of the charging order that gave rise to the transfer.

SECTION 802. PARTNERSHIP CONTINUES AFTER DISSOLUTION.

(a) Subject to subsection (b), a partnership continues after dissolution only for the purpose of winding up its business. The partnership is terminated when the winding up of its business is completed.

(b) At any time after the dissolution of a partnership and before the winding up of its business is completed, all of the partners, including any dissociating partner other than a wrongfully dissociating partner, may waive the right to have the partnership's business wound up and the partnership terminated. In that event:
    (1) the partnership resumes carrying on its business as if dissolution had never occurred, and any liability incurred by the partnership or a partner after the dissolution and before the waiver is determined as if dissolution had never occurred; and
    (2) the rights of a third party accruing under Section 804(1) or arising out of conduct in reliance on the dissolution before the third party knew or received a notification of the waiver may not be adversely affected.

SECTION 803. RIGHT TO WIND UP PARTNERSHIP BUSINESS.

(a) After dissolution, a partner who has not wrongfully dissociated may participate in winding up the partnership's business, but on application of any partner, partner's legal representative, or transferee, the [designate the appropriate court], for good cause shown, may order judicial supervision of the winding up.

(b) The legal representative of the last surviving partner may wind up a partnership's business.

(c) A person winding up a partnership's business may preserve the partnership business or property as a going concern for a reasonable time, prosecute and defend actions and proceedings, whether civil, criminal, or administrative, settle and close the partnership's business, dispose of and transfer the partnership's property, discharge the partnership's liabilities, distribute the assets of the partnership pursuant to Section 807, settle disputes by mediation or arbitration, and perform other necessary acts.

SECTION 804. PARTNER'S POWER TO BIND PARTNERSHIP AFTER DISSOLUTION.

Subject to Section 805, a partnership is bound by a partner's act after dissolution that:
    (1) is appropriate for winding up the partnership business; or

(2) would have bound the partnership under Section 301 before dissolution, if the other party to the transaction did not have notice of the dissolution.

SECTION 805. STATEMENT OF DISSOLUTION.

(a) After dissolution, a partner who has not wrongfully dissociated may file a statement of dissolution stating the name of the partnership and that the partnership has dissolved and is winding up its business.

(b) A statement of dissolution cancels a filed statement of partnership authority for the purposes of Section 303(d) and is a limitation on authority for the purposes of Section 303(e).

(c) For the purposes of Sections 301 and 804, a person not a partner is deemed to have notice of the dissolution and the limitation on the partners' authority as a result of the statement of dissolution 90 days after it is filed.

(d) After filing and, if appropriate, recording a statement of dissolution, a dissolved partnership may file and, if appropriate, record a statement of partnership authority which will operate with respect to a person not a partner as provided in Section 303(d) and (e) in any transaction, whether or not the transaction is appropriate for winding up the partnership business.

SECTION 806. PARTNER'S LIABILITY TO OTHER PARTNERS AFTER DISSOLUTION.

(a) Except as otherwise provided in subsection (b) <u>and Section 306</u>, after dissolution a partner is liable to the other partners for the partner's share of any partnership liability incurred under Section 804.

(b) A partner who, with knowledge of the dissolution, incurs a partnership liability under Section 804(2) by an act that is not appropriate for winding up the partnership business is liable to the partnership for any damage caused to the partnership arising from the liability.

SECTION 807. SETTLEMENT OF ACCOUNTS AND CONTRIBUTIONS AMONG PARTNERS.

(a) In winding up a partnership's business, the assets of the partnership, including the contributions of the partners required by this section, must be applied to discharge its obligations to creditors, including, to the extent permitted by law, partners who are creditors. Any surplus must be applied to pay in cash the net amount distributable to partners in accordance with their right to distributions under subsection (b).

(b) Each partner is entitled to a settlement of all partnership accounts upon winding up the partnership business. In settling accounts among the partners, profits and losses that result from the liquidation of the partnership assets must be credited and charged to the partners' accounts. The partnership shall make a distribution to a partner in an amount equal to any excess of the credits over the charges in the partner's account. A partner shall contribute to the partnership an amount equal to any excess of the charges over the credits in the partner's account <u>but excluding from the calculation charges attributable to an obligation for which the partner is not personally liable under Section 306.</u>

(c) If a partner fails to contribute <u>the full amount required under subsection (b),</u> all of the other partners shall contribute, in the proportions in which those partners share partnership losses, the additional amount necessary to satisfy the partnership obligations <u>for which they are personally liable under Section 306.</u> A partner or partner's legal representative may recover from the other partners any contributions the partner makes to the extent the amount contributed exceeds that partner's share of the partnership obligations <u>for which the partner is personally liable under Section 306.</u>

(d) After the settlement of accounts, each partner shall contribute, in the proportion in which the partner shares partnership losses, the amount necessary to satisfy partnership obligations that were not known at the time of the settlement <u>and for which the partner is personally liable under Section 306.</u>

(e) The estate of a deceased partner is liable for the partner's obligation to contribute to the partnership.

(f) An assignee for the benefit of creditors of a partnership or a partner, or a person appointed by a court to represent creditors of a partnership or a partner, may enforce a partner's obligation to contribute to the partnership.

[ARTICLE] 9
CONVERSIONS AND MERGERS

SECTION 901. DEFINITIONS. In this [article]:

(1) "General partner" means a partner in a partnership and a general partner in a limited partnership.

(2) "Limited partner" means a limited partner in a limited partnership.

(3) "Limited partnership" means a limited partnership created under the [State Limited Partnership Act], predecessor law, or comparable law of another jurisdiction.

(4) "Partner" includes both a general partner and a limited partner.

SECTION 902. CONVERSION OF PARTNERSHIP TO LIMITED PARTNERSHIP.

(a) A partnership may be converted to a limited partnership pursuant to this section.

(b) The terms and conditions of a conversion of a partnership to a limited partnership must be approved by all of the partners or by a number or percentage specified for conversion in the partnership agreement.

(c) After the conversion is approved by the partners, the partnership shall file a certificate of limited partnership in the jurisdiction in which the limited partnership is to be formed. The certificate must include:
(1) a statement that the partnership was converted to a limited partnership from a partnership;
(2) its former name; and
(3) a statement of the number of votes cast by the partners for and against the conversion and, if the vote is less than unanimous, the number or percentage required to approve the conversion under the partnership agreement.

(d) The conversion takes effect when the certificate of limited partnership is filed or at any later date specified in the certificate.

(e) A general partner who becomes a limited partner as a result of the conversion remains liable as a general partner for an obligation incurred by the partnership before the conversion takes effect. If the other party to a transaction with the limited partnership reasonably believes when entering the transaction that the limited partner is a general partner, the limited partner is liable for an obligation incurred by the limited partnership within 90 days after the conversion takes effect. The limited partner's liability for all other obligations of the limited partnership incurred after the conversion takes effect is that of a limited partner as provided in the [State Limited Partnership Act].

SECTION 903. CONVERSION OF LIMITED PARTNERSHIP TO PARTNERSHIP.

(a) A limited partnership may be converted to a partnership pursuant to this section.

(b) Notwithstanding a provision to the contrary in a limited partnership agreement, the terms and conditions of a conversion of a limited partnership to a partnership must be approved by all of the partners.

(c) After the conversion is approved by the partners, the limited partnership shall cancel its certificate of limited partnership.

(d) The conversion takes effect when the certificate of limited partnership is canceled.

(e) A limited partner who becomes a general partner as a result of the conversion remains liable only as a limited partner for an obligation incurred by the limited partnership before the conversion takes effect. Except as otherwise provided in Section 306, the partner is liable as a general partner for an obligation of the partnership incurred after the conversion takes effect.

SECTION 904. EFFECT OF CONVERSION; ENTITY UNCHANGED.

(a) A partnership or limited partnership that has been converted pursuant to this [article] is for all purposes the same entity that existed before the conversion.

(b) When a conversion takes effect:
(1) all property owned by the converting partnership or limited partnership remains vested in the converted entity;

(2)   all obligations of the converting partnership or limited partnership continue as obligations of the converted entity; and

(3)   an action or proceeding pending against the converting partnership or limited partnership may be continued as if the conversion had not occurred.

SECTION 905. MERGER OF PARTNERSHIPS.

(a) Pursuant to a plan of merger approved as provided in subsection (c), a partnership may be merged with one or more partnerships or limited partnerships.

(b) The plan of merger must set forth:

(1)   the name of each partnership or limited partnership that is a party to the merger;

(2)   the name of the surviving entity into which the other partnerships or limited partnerships will merge;

(3)   whether the surviving entity is a partnership or a limited partnership and the status of each partner;

(4)   the terms and conditions of the merger;

(5)   the manner and basis of converting the interests of each party to the merger into interests or obligations of the surviving entity, or into money or other property in whole or part; and

(6)   the street address of the surviving entity's chief executive office.

(c) The plan of merger must be approved:

(1)   in the case of a partnership that is a party to the merger, by all of the partners, or a number or percentage specified for merger in the partnership agreement; and

(2)   in the case of a limited partnership that is a party to the merger, by the vote required for approval of a merger by the law of the State or foreign jurisdiction in which the limited partnership is organized and, in the absence of such a specifically applicable law, by all of the partners, notwithstanding a provision to the contrary in the partnership agreement.

(d) After a plan of merger is approved and before the merger takes effect, the plan may be amended or abandoned as provided in the plan.

(e) The merger takes effect on the later of:

(1)   the approval of the plan of merger by all parties to the merger, as provided in subsection (c);

(2)   the filing of all documents required by law to be filed as a condition to the effectiveness of the merger; or

(3)   any effective date specified in the plan of merger.

SECTION 906. EFFECT OF MERGER.

(a) When a merger takes effect:

(1)   the separate existence of every partnership or limited partnership that is a party to the merger, other than the surviving entity, ceases;

(2)   all property owned by each of the merged partnerships or limited partnerships vests in the surviving entity;

(3)   all obligations of every partnership or limited partnership that is a party to the merger become the obligations of the surviving entity; and

(4)   an action or proceeding pending against a partnership or limited partnership that is a party to the merger may be continued as if the merger had not occurred, or the surviving entity may be substituted as a party to the action or proceeding.

(b) The [Secretary of State] of this State is the agent for service of process in an action or proceeding against a surviving foreign partnership or limited partnership to enforce an obligation of a domestic partnership or limited partnership that is a party to a merger. The surviving entity shall promptly notify the [Secretary of State] of the mailing address of its chief executive office and of any change of address. Upon receipt of process, the [Secretary of State] shall mail a copy of the process to the surviving foreign partnership or limited partnership.

(c) A partner of the surviving partnership or limited partnership is liable for:

(1)   all obligations of a party to the merger for which the partner was personally liable before the merger;

(2)   all other obligations of the surviving entity incurred before the merger by a party to the merger, but those obligations may be satisfied only out of property of the entity; and

(3)   except as otherwise provided in Section 306, all obligations of the surviving entity incurred after the merger takes effect, but those obligations may be satisfied only out of property of the entity if the partner is a limited partner.

(d) If the obligations incurred before the merger by a party to the merger are not satisfied out of the property of the surviving partnership or limited partnership, the general partners of that party immediately before the effective date of the merger shall contribute the amount necessary to satisfy that party's obligations to the surviving entity, in the manner provided in Section 807 or in the [Limited Partnership Act] of the jurisdiction in which the party was formed, as the case may be, as if the merged party were dissolved.

(e) A partner of a party to a merger who does not become a partner of the surviving partnership or limited partnership is dissociated from the entity, of which that partner was a partner, as of the date the merger takes effect. The surviving entity shall cause the partner's interest in the entity to be purchased under Section 701 or another statute specifically applicable to that partner's interest with respect to a merger. The surviving entity is bound under Section 702 by an act of a general partner dissociated under this subsection, and the partner is liable under Section 703 for transactions entered into by the surviving entity after the merger takes effect.

SECTION 907. STATEMENT OF MERGER.

(a) After a merger, the surviving partnership or limited partnership may file a statement that one or more partnerships or limited partnerships have merged into the surviving entity.

(b) A statement of merger must contain:

(1)   the name of each partnership or limited partnership that is a party to the merger;

(2)   the name of the surviving entity into which the other partnerships or limited partnership were merged;

(3)   the street address of the surviving entity's chief executive office and of an office in this State, if any; and

(4)   whether the surviving entity is a partnership or a limited partnership.

(c) Except as otherwise provided in subsection (d), for the purposes of Section 302, property of the surviving partnership or limited partnership which before the merger was held in the name of another party to the merger is property held in the name of the surviving entity upon filing a statement of merger.

(d) For the purposes of Section 302, real property of the surviving partnership or limited partnership which before the merger was held in the name of another party to the merger is property held in the name of the surviving entity upon recording a certified copy of the statement of merger in the office for recording transfers of that real property.

(e) A filed and, if appropriate, recorded statement of merger, executed and declared to be accurate pursuant to Section 105(c), stating the name of a partnership or limited partnership that is a party to the merger in whose name property was held before the merger and the name of the surviving entity, but not containing all of the other information required by subsection (b), operates with respect to the partnerships or limited partnerships named to the extent provided in subsections (c) and (d).

SECTION 908. NONEXCLUSIVE. This [article] is not exclusive. Partnerships or limited partnerships may be converted or merged in any other manner provided by law.

[ARTICLE] 10
LIMITED LIABILITY PARTNERSHIP

Section 1001.   Statement of Qualification.
Section 1002.   Name.
Section 1003.   Annual Report.

SECTION 1001. STATEMENT OF QUALIFICATION.

(a) A partnership may become a limited liability partnership pursuant to this section.

(b) The terms and conditions on which a partnership becomes a limited liability partnership must be approved by the vote necessary to amend the partnership agreement except, in the case of a partnership agreement that expressly considers obligations to contribute to the partnership, the vote necessary to amend those provisions.

(c) After the approval required by subsection (b), a partnership may become a limited liability partnership by filing a statement of qualification. The statement must contain:

(1) the name of the partnership;

(2) the street address of the partnership's chief executive office and, if different, the street address of an office in this State, if any;

(3) if the partnership does not have an office in this State, the name and street address of the partnership's agent for service of process;

(4) a statement that the partnership elects to be a limited liability partnership; and

(5) a deferred effective date, if any.

(d) The agent of a limited liability partnership for service of process must be an individual who is a resident of this State or other person authorized to do business in this State.

(e) The status of a partnership as a limited liability partnership is effective on the later of the filing of the statement or a date specified in the statement. The status remains effective, regardless of changes in the partnership, until it is canceled pursuant to Section 105(d) or revoked pursuant to Section 1003.

(f) The status of a partnership as a limited liability partnership and the liability of its partners is not affected by errors or later changes in the information required to be contained in the statement of qualification under subsection (c).

(g) The filing of a statement of qualification establishes that a partnership has satisfied all conditions precedent to the qualification of the partnership as a limited liability partnership.

(h) An amendment or cancellation of a statement of qualification is effective when it is filed or on a deferred effective date specified in the amendment or cancellation.

SECTION 1002. NAME. The name of a limited liability partnership must end with "Registered Limited Liability Partnership", "Limited Liability Partnership", "R.L.L.P.", "L.L.P.", "RLLP," or "LLP".

SECTION 1003. ANNUAL REPORT.

(a) A limited liability partnership, and a foreign limited liability partnership authorized to transact business in this State, shall file an annual report in the office of the [Secretary of State] which contains:

(1) the name of the limited liability partnership and the State or other jurisdiction under whose laws the foreign limited liability partnership is formed;

(2) the street address of the partnership's chief executive office and, if different, the street address of an office of the partnership in this State, if any; and

(3) if the partnership does not have an office in this State, the name and street address of the partnership's current agent for service of process.

(b) An annual report must be filed between [January 1 and April 1] of each year following the calendar year in which a partnership files a statement of qualification or a foreign partnership becomes authorized to transact business in this State.

(c) The [Secretary of State] may revoke the statement of qualification of a partnership that fails to file an annual report when due or pay the required filing fee. To do so, the [Secretary of State] shall provide the partnership at least 60 days' written notice of intent to revoke the statement. The notice must be mailed to the partnership at its chief executive office set forth in the last filed statement of qualification or annual report. The notice must specify the annual report that has not been filed, the fee that has not been paid, and the effective date of the revocation. The revocation is not effective if the annual report is filed and the fee is paid before the effective date of the revocation.

(d) A revocation under subsection (c) only affects a partnership's status as a limited liability partnership and is not an event of dissolution of the partnership.

(e) A partnership whose statement of qualification has been revoked may apply to the [Secretary of State] for reinstatement within two years after the effective date of the revocation. The application must state:

  (1) the name of the partnership and the effective date of the revocation; and

  (2) that the ground for revocation either did not exist or has been corrected.

(f) A reinstatement under subsection (e) relates back to and takes effect as of the effective date of the revocation, and the partnership's status as a limited liability partnership continues as if the revocation had never occurred.

[ARTICLE] 11
FOREIGN LIMITED LIABILITY PARTNERSHIP

SECTION 1101. LAW GOVERNING FOREIGN LIMITED LIABILITY PARTNERSHIP.

(a) The law under which a foreign limited liability partnership is formed govern relations among the partners and between the partners and the partnership and the liability of partners for obligations of the partnership.

(b) A foreign limited liability partnership may not be denied a statement of foreign qualification by reason of any difference between the law under which the partnership was formed and the law of this State.

(c) A statement of foreign qualification does not authorize a foreign limited liability partnership to engage in any business or exercise any power that a partnership may not engage in or exercise in this State as a limited liability partnership.

SECTION 1102. STATEMENT OF FOREIGN QUALIFICATION.

(a) Before transacting business in this State, a foreign limited liability partnership must file a statement of foreign qualification. The statement must contain:

(1) the name of the foreign limited liability partnership which satisfies the requirements of the State or other jurisdiction under whose laws it is formed and ends with "Registered Limited Liability Partnership", "Limited Liability Partnership", "R.L.L.P.", "L.L.P.", "RLLP," or "LLP";

(2) the street address of the partnership's chief executive office and, if different, the street address of an office of the partnership in this State, if any;

(3) if there is no office of the partnership in this State, the name and street address of the partnership's agent for service of process; and

(4) a deferred effective date, if any.

(b) The agent of a foreign limited liability company for service of process must be an individual who is a resident of this State or other person authorized to do business in this State.

(c) The status of a partnership as a foreign limited liability partnership is effective on the later of the filing of the statement of foreign qualification or a date specified in the statement. The status remains effective, regardless of changes in the partnership, until it is canceled pursuant to Section 105(d) or revoked pursuant to Section 1003.

(d) An amendment or cancellation of a statement of foreign qualification is effective when it is filed or on a deferred effective date specified in the amendment or cancellation.

SECTION 1103. EFFECT OF FAILURE TO QUALIFY.

(a) A foreign limited liability partnership transacting business in this State may not maintain an action or proceeding in this State unless it has in effect a statement of foreign qualification.

(b) The failure of a foreign limited liability partnership to have in effect a statement of foreign qualification does not impair the validity of a contract or act of the foreign limited liability partnership or preclude it from defending an action or proceeding in this State.

(c) A limitation on personal liability of a partner is not waived solely by transacting business in this State without a statement of foreign qualification.

(d) If a foreign limited liability partnership transacts business in this State without a statement of foreign qualification, the [Secretary of State] is its agent for service of process with respect to a right of action arising out of the transaction of business in this State.

SECTION 1104. ACTIVITIES NOT CONSTITUTING TRANSACTING BUSINESS.

(a) Activities of a foreign limited liability partnership which do not constitute transacting business for the purpose of this [article] include:

(1) maintaining, defending, or settling an action or proceeding;

(2) holding meetings of its partners or carrying on any other activity concerning its internal affairs;

(3) maintaining bank accounts;

(4) maintaining offices or agencies for the transfer, exchange, and registration of the partnership's own securities or maintaining trustees or depositories with respect to those securities;

(5) selling through independent contractors;

(6) soliciting or obtaining orders, whether by mail or through employees or agents or otherwise, if the orders require acceptance outside this State before they become contracts;

(7) creating or acquiring indebtedness, with or without a mortgage, or other security interest in property;

(8) collecting debts or foreclosing mortgages or other security interests in property securing the debts, and holding, protecting, and maintaining property so acquired;

(9) conducting an isolated transaction that is completed within 30 days and is not one in the course of similar transactions; and

(10) transacting business in interstate commerce.

(b) For purposes of this [Article], the ownership in this State of income-producing real property or tangible personal property, other than property excluded under subsection (a), constitutes transacting business in this State.

(c) This section does not apply in determining the contacts or activities that may subject a foreign limited liability partnership to service of process, taxation, or regulation under any other law of this State.

SECTION 1105. ACTION BY [ATTORNEY GENERAL]. The [Attorney General] may maintain an action to restrain a foreign limited liability partnership from transacting business in this State in violation of this [article].

[ARTICLE] 12
MISCELLANEOUS PROVISIONS

SECTION 1201. UNIFORMITY OF APPLICATION AND CONSTRUCTION. This [Act] shall be applied and construed to effectuate its general purpose to make uniform the law with respect to the subject of this [Act] among States enacting it.

SECTION 1202. SHORT TITLE. This [Act] may be cited as the Uniform Partnership Act (1997).

SECTION 1203. SEVERABILITY CLAUSE. If any provision of this [Act] or its application to any person or circumstance is held invalid, the invalidity does not affect other provisions or applications of this [Act] which can be given effect without the invalid provision or application, and to this end the provisions of this [Act] are severable.

SECTION 1204. EFFECTIVE DATE. This [Act] takes effect . . . .

SECTION 1205. REPEALS. Effective January 1, 199 ___ , the following acts and parts of acts are repealed: [the State Partnership Act as amended and in effect immediately before the effective date of this Act].

SECTION 1206. APPLICABILITY.
(a) Before January 1, 199 ___ , this [Act] governs only a partnership formed:
  (1) after the effective date of this [Act], except a partnership that is continuing the business of a dissolved partnership under [Section 41 of the superseded Uniform Partnership Act]; and
  (2) before the effective date of this [Act], that elects, as provided by subsection (c), to be governed by this [Act].
(b) On and after January 1, 199 ___ , this [Act] governs all partnerships.
(c) Before January 1, 199 ___ , a partnership voluntarily may elect, in the manner provided in its partnership agreement or by law for amending the partnership agreement, to be governed by this [Act]. The provisions of this [Act] relating to the liability of the partnership's partners to third parties apply to limit those partners' liability to a third party who had done business with the partnership within one year preceding the partnership's election to be governed by this [Act], only if the third party knows or has received a notification of the partnership's election to be governed by this [Act].

SECTION 1207. SAVINGS CLAUSE. This [Act] does not affect an action or proceeding commenced or right accrued before this [Act] takes effect.

SECTION 1208. EFFECTIVE DATE. This [Act] takes effect . . . .

SECTION 1209. REPEALS. Effective January 1, 199 ___ , the following acts and parts of acts are repealed: [the Limited Liability Partnership amendments to the State Partnership Act as amended and in effect immediately before the effective date of these [Amendments]].

SECTION 1210. APPLICABILITY.
(a) Before January 1, 199 ___ , these [Amendments] govern only a limited liability partnership formed:
  (1) on or after the effective date of these [Amendments], unless that partnership is continuing the business of a dissolved limited liability partnership; and

    (2)   before the effective date of these [Amendments], that elects, as provided by subsection (c), to be governed by these [Amendments].

(b) On and after January 1, 199   , these [Amendments] govern all partnerships.

(c) Before January 1, 199   , a partnership voluntarily may elect, in the manner provided in its partnership agreement or by law for amending the partnership agreement, to be governed by these [Amendments]. The provisions of these [Amendments] relating to the liability of the partnership's partners to third parties apply to limit those partners' liability to a third party who had done business with the partnership within one year before the partnership's election to be governed by these [Amendments], only if the third party knows or has received a notification of the partnership's election to be governed by these [Amendments].

(d The existing provisions for execution and filing a statement of qualification of a limited liability partnership continue until either the limited liability partnership elects to have this [Act] apply or January 1, 199   .

SECTION 1211. SAVINGS CLAUSE. These [Amendments] do not affect an action or proceeding commenced or right accrued before these [Amendments] take effect.

UNIFORM LIMITED LIABILITY COMPANY ACT (1996)*

[Article] 1
General Provisions

[Article] 2
Organization

---

*   This act has been printed through the permission of the National Conference of Commissioners on Uniform State Laws, and copies may be ordered from them at 676 North St. Clair Street, Suite 1700, Chicago, Illinois, 60611.

[Article] 3
Relations Of Members and Managers to Persons Dealing With
Limited Liability Company

[Article] 4
Relations Of Members to Each Other and
to Limited Liability Company

[Article] 5
Transferees and Creditors Of Member

[Article] 6
Member's Dissociation

[Article] 7
Member's Dissociation When
Business Not Wound Up

[Article] 8
Winding Up Company's Business

[Article] 9
Conversions and Mergers

[Article] 10
Foreign Limited Liability Companies

[Article] 11
Derivative Actions

[Article] 12
Miscellaneous Provisions

UNIFORM LIMITED LIABILITY COMPANY ACT

[ARTICLE] 1
GENERAL PROVISIONS

Section 101. Definitions.
Section 102. Knowledge and Notice.
Section 103. Effect of Operating Agreement; Nonwaivable Provisions.
Section 104. Supplemental Principles of Law.
Section 105. Name.
Section 106. Reserved Name.
Section 107. Registered Name.
Section 108. Designated Office and Agent for Service of Process.
Section 109. Change of Designated Office or Agent for Service of Process.
Section 110. Resignation of Agent for Service of Process.
Section 111. Service of Process.
Section 112. Nature of Business and Powers.

SECTION 101. DEFINITIONS. In this [Act]:

(1) "Articles of organization" means initial, amended, and restated articles of organization and articles of merger. In the case of a foreign limited liability com-

pany, the term includes all records serving a similar function required to be filed in the office of the [Secretary of State] or other official having custody of company records in the state or country under whose law it is organized.

(2) "At-will company" means a limited liability company other than a term company.

(3) "Business" includes every trade, occupation, profession and other lawful purpose, whether or not carried on for profit.

(4) "Debtor in bankruptcy" means a person who is the subject of an order for relief under Title 11 of the United States Code or a comparable order under a successor statute of general application or a comparable order under federal, state or foreign law governing insolvency.

(5) "Distribution" means a transfer of money, property or other benefit from a limited liability company to a member in the member's capacity as a member or to a transferee of the member's distributional interest.

(6) "Distributional interest" means all of a member's interest in distributions by the limited liability company.

(7) "Entity" means a person other than an individual.

(8) "Foreign limited liability company" means an unincorporated entity organized under laws other than the laws of this State which afford limited liability to its owners comparable to the liability under Section 303 and is not required to obtain a certificate of authority to transact business under any law of this State other than this [Act].

(9) "Limited liability company" means a limited liability company organized under this [Act].

(10) "Manager" means a person, whether or not a member of a manager-managed company, who is vested with authority under Section 301.

(11) "Manager-managed company" means a limited liability company which is so designated in its articles of organization.

(12) "Member-managed company" means a limited liability company other than a manager-managed company.

(13) "Operating agreement" means the agreement under Section 103 concerning the relations among the members, managers and limited liability company. The term includes amendments to the agreement.

(14) "Person" means an individual, corporation, business trust, estate, trust, partnership, limited liability company, association, joint venture, government, governmental subdivision, agency, or instrumentality or any other legal or commercial entity.

(15) "Principal office" means the office, whether or not in this State, where the principal executive office of a domestic or foreign limited liability company is located.

(16) "Record" means information that is inscribed on a tangible medium or that is stored in an electronic or other medium and is retrievable in perceivable form.

(17) "Sign" means to identify a record by means of a signature, mark or other symbol, with intent to authenticate it.

(18) "State" means a State of the United States, the District of Columbia, the Commonwealth of Puerto Rico, or any territory or insular possession subject to the jurisdiction of the United States.

(19) "Term company" means a limited liability company in which its members have agreed to remain members until the expiration of a term specified in the articles of organization.

(20) "Transfer" includes an assignment, conveyance, deed, bill of sale, lease, mortgage, security interest, encumbrance and gift.

SECTION 102. KNOWLEDGE AND NOTICE.

(a) A person knows a fact if the person has actual knowledge of it.

(b) A person has notice of a fact if the person:
   (1) knows the fact;
   (2) has received a notification of the fact; or
   (3) has reason to know the fact exists from all of the facts known to the person at the time in question.

(c) A person notifies or gives a notification of a fact to another by taking steps reasonably required to inform the other person in ordinary course, whether or not the other person knows the fact.

(d) A person receives a notification when the notification:
   (1) comes to the person's attention; or
   (2) is duly delivered at the person's place of business or at any other place held out by the person as a place for receiving communications.

(e) An entity knows, has notice or receives a notification of a fact for purposes of a particular transaction when the individual conducting the transaction for the entity knows, has notice, or receives a notification of the fact, or in any event when the fact would have been brought to the individual's attention had the entity exercised reasonable diligence. An entity exercises reasonable diligence if it maintains reasonable routines for communicating significant information to the individual conducting the transaction for the entity and there is reasonable compliance with the routines. Reasonable diligence does not require an individual acting for the entity to communicate information unless the communication is part of the individual's regular duties or the individual has reason to know of the transaction and that the transaction would be materially affected by the information.

SECTION 103. EFFECT OF OPERATING AGREEMENT; NONWAIVABLE PROVISIONS.

(a) Except as otherwise provided in subsection (b), all members of a limited liability company may enter into an operating agreement, which need not be in writing, to regulate the affairs of the company and the conduct of its business, and to govern relations among the members, managers and company. To the extent the operating agreement does not otherwise provide, this [Act] governs relations among the members, managers and company.

(b) The operating agreement may not:

    (1) unreasonably restrict a right to information or access to records under Section 408;

    (2) eliminate the duty of loyalty under Section 409(b) or 603(b)(3), but the agreement may:

        (i) identify specific types or categories of activities that do not violate the duty of loyalty, if not manifestly unreasonable; and

        (ii) specify the number or percentage of members or disinterested managers that may authorize or ratify, after full disclosure of all material facts, a specific act or transaction that otherwise would violate the duty of loyalty;

    (3) unreasonably reduce the duty of care under Section 409(c) or 603(b)(3);

    (4) eliminate the obligation of good faith and fair dealing under Section 409(d), but the operating agreement may determine the standards by which the performance of the obligation is to be measured, if the standards are not manifestly unreasonable;

    (5) vary the right to expel a member in an event specified in Section 601(6);

    (6) vary the requirement to wind up the limited liability company's business in a case specified in Section 801(a)(3) or (a)(4); or

    (7) restrict rights of a person, other than a manager, member and transferee of a member's distributional interest, under this [Act].

SECTION 104. SUPPLEMENTAL PRINCIPLES OF LAW.

(a) Unless displaced by particular provisions of this [Act], the principles of law and equity supplement this [Act].

(b) If an obligation to pay interest arises under this [Act] and the rate is not specified, the rate is that specified in [applicable statute].

SECTION 105. NAME.

(a) The name of a limited liability company must contain "limited liability company" or "limited company" or the abbreviation "L.L.C.", "LLC", "L.C." or "LC". "Limited" may be abbreviated as "Ltd." and "company" may be abbreviated as "Co.".

(b) Except as authorized by subsections (c) and (d), the name of a limited liability company must be distinguishable upon the records of the [Secretary of State] from:

    (1) the name of any corporation, limited partnership or company incorporated, organized or authorized to transact business in this State;

    (2) a name reserved or registered under Section 106 or 107;

    (3) a fictitious name approved under Section 1005 for a foreign company authorized to transact business in this State because its real name is unavailable.

(c) A limited liability company may apply to the [Secretary of State] for authorization to use a name that is not distinguishable upon the records of the [Secretary of State] from one or more of the names described in subsection (b). The [Secretary of State] shall authorize use of the name applied for if:

   (1) the present user, registrant or owner of a reserved name consents to the use in a record and submits an undertaking in form satisfactory to the [Secretary of State] to change the name to a name that is distinguishable upon the records of the [Secretary of State] from the name applied for; or

   (2) the applicant delivers to the [Secretary of State] a certified copy of the final judgment of a court of competent jurisdiction establishing the applicant's right to use the name applied for in this State.

(d) A limited liability company may use the name, including a fictitious name, of another domestic or foreign company which is used in this State if the other company is organized or authorized to transact business in this State and the company proposing to use the name has:

   (1) merged with the other company;

   (2) been formed by reorganization with the other company; or

   (3) acquired substantially all of the assets, including the name, of the other company.

SECTION 106. RESERVED NAME.

(a) A person may reserve the exclusive use of the name of a limited liability company, including a fictitious name for a foreign company whose name is not available, by delivering an application to the [Secretary of State] for filing. The application must set forth the name and address of the applicant and the name proposed to be reserved. If the [Secretary of State] finds that the name applied for is available, it must be reserved for the applicant's exclusive use for a nonrenewable 120-day period.

(b) The owner of a name reserved for a limited liability company may transfer the reservation to another person by delivering to the [Secretary of State] a signed notice of the transfer which states the name and address of the transferee.

SECTION 107. REGISTERED NAME.

(a) A foreign limited liability company may register its name subject to the requirements of Section 1005, if the name is distinguishable upon the records of the [Secretary of State] from names that are not available under Section 105(b).

(b) A foreign limited liability company registers its name, or its name with any addition required by Section 1005, by delivering to the [Secretary of State] for filing an application:

   (1) setting forth its name, or its name with any addition required by Section 1005, the state or country and date of its organization and a brief description of the nature of the business in which it is engaged; and

   (2) accompanied by a certificate of existence, or a record of similar import, from the state or country of organization.

(c) A foreign limited liability company whose registration is effective may renew it for successive years by delivering for filing in the office of the [Secretary of State] a renewal application complying with subsection (b) between October 1 and December 31 of the preceding year. The renewal application renews the registration for the following calendar year.

(d) A foreign limited liability company whose registration is effective may qualify as a foreign company under its name or consent in writing to the use of its name by a limited liability company later organized under this [Act] or by another foreign company later authorized to transact business in this State. The registered name terminates when the limited liability company is organized or the foreign company qualifies or consents to the qualification of another foreign company under the registered name.

SECTION 108. DESIGNATED OFFICE AND AGENT FOR SERVICE OF PROCESS.

(a) A limited liability company and a foreign limited liability company authorized to do business in this State shall designate and continuously maintain in this State:

  (1) an office, which need not be a place of its business in this State; and

  (2) an agent and street address of the agent for service of process on the company.

(b) An agent must be an individual resident of this State, a domestic corporation, another limited liability company or a foreign corporation or foreign company authorized to do business in this State.

SECTION 109. CHANGE OF DESIGNATED OFFICE OR AGENT FOR SERVICE OF PROCESS.

A limited liability company may change its designated office or agent for service of process by delivering to the [Secretary of State] for filing a statement of change which sets forth:

  (1) the name of the company;

  (2) the street address of its current designated office;

  (3) if the current designated office is to be changed, the street address of the new designated office;

  (4) the name and address of its current agent for service of process; and

  (5) if the current agent for service of process or street address of that agent is to be changed, the new address or the name and street address of the new agent for service of process.

SECTION 110. RESIGNATION OF AGENT FOR SERVICE OF PROCESS.

(a) An agent for service of process of a limited liability company may resign by delivering to the [Secretary of State] for filing a record of the statement of resignation.

(b) After filing a statement of resignation, the [Secretary of State] shall mail a copy to the designated office and another copy to the limited liability company at its principal office.

(c) An agency is terminated on the 31st day after the statement is filed in the office of the [Secretary of State].

SECTION 111. SERVICE OF PROCESS.

(a) An agent for service of process appointed by a limited liability company or a foreign limited liability company is an agent of the company for service of any process, notice or demand required or permitted by law to be served upon the company.

(b) If a limited liability company or foreign limited liability company fails to appoint or maintain an agent for service of process in this State or the agent for service of process cannot with reasonable diligence be found at the agent's address, the [Secretary of State] is an agent of the company upon whom process, notice or demand may be served.

(c) Service of any process, notice or demand on the [Secretary of State] may be made by delivering to and leaving with the [Secretary of State], the [Assistant Secretary of State] or clerk having charge of the limited liability company department of the [Secretary of State], duplicate copies of the process, notice, or demand. If the process, notice, or demand is served on the [Secretary of State], the [Secretary of State] shall forward one of the copies by registered or certified mail, return receipt requested, to the company at its designated office. Service is effected under this subsection at the earliest of:

   (1) the date the company receives the process, notice or demand;

   (2) the date shown on the return receipt, if signed on behalf of the company; or

   (3) five days after its deposit in the mail, if mailed postpaid and correctly addressed.

(d) The [Secretary of State] shall keep a record of all processes, notices and demands served pursuant to this Section and record the time of and the action taken regarding the service.

(e) This Section does not affect the right to serve process, notice or demand in any manner otherwise provided by law.

SECTION 112. NATURE OF BUSINESS AND POWERS.

(a) A limited liability company may be organized under this [Act] for any lawful purpose, subject to any law of this State governing or regulating business.

(b) Unless its articles of organization provide otherwise, a limited liability company has the same powers as an individual to do all things necessary or convenient to carry on its business or affairs, including power to:

   (1) sue and be sued, and defend in its name;

   (2) purchase, receive, lease or otherwise acquire, and own, hold, improve, use and otherwise deal with real or personal property, or any legal or equitable interest in property, wherever located;

   (3) sell, convey, mortgage, grant a security interest in, lease, exchange and otherwise encumber or dispose of all or any part of its property;

(4) purchase, receive, subscribe for or otherwise acquire, own, hold, vote, use, sell, mortgage, lend, grant a security interest in or otherwise dispose of and deal in and with, shares or other interests in or obligations of any other entity;

(5) make contracts and guarantees, incur liabilities, borrow money, issue its notes, bonds and other obligations, which may be convertible into or include the option to purchase other securities of the limited liability company, and secure any of its obligations by a mortgage on or a security interest in any of its property, franchises or income;

(6) lend money, invest and reinvest its funds and receive and hold real and personal property as security for repayment;

(7) be a promoter, partner, member, associate or manager of any partnership, joint venture, trust or other entity;

(8) conduct its business, locate offices and exercise the powers granted by this [Act] within or without this State;

(9) elect managers and appoint officers, employees and agents of the limited liability company, define their duties, fix their compensation and lend them money and credit;

(10) pay pensions and establish pension plans, pension trusts, profit sharing plans, bonus plans, option plans and benefit or incentive plans for any or all of its current or former members, managers, officers, employees and agents;

(11) make donations for the public welfare or for charitable, scientific or educational purposes; and

(12) make payments or donations, or do any other act, not inconsistent with law, that furthers the business of the limited liability company.

[ARTICLE] 2
ORGANIZATION

SECTION 201. LIMITED LIABILITY COMPANY AS LEGAL ENTITY. A limited liability company is a legal entity distinct from its members.

SECTION 202. ORGANIZATION.

(a) One or more persons may organize a limited liability company, consisting of one or more members, by delivering articles of organization to the office of the [Secretary of State] for filing.

(b) Unless a delayed effective date is specified, the existence of a limited liability company begins when the articles of organization are filed.

(c) The filing of the articles of organization by the [Secretary of State] is conclusive proof that the organizers satisfied all conditions precedent to the creation of a limited liability company.

SECTION 203. ARTICLES OF ORGANIZATION.

(a) Articles of organization of a limited liability company must set forth:

   (1) the name of the company;

   (2) the address of the initial designated office;

   (3) the name and street address of the initial agent for service of process;

   (4) the name and address of each organizer;

   (5) whether the company is to be a term company and, if so, the term specified;

   (6) whether the company is to be manager-managed, and, if so, the name and address of each initial manager; and

   (7) whether one or more of the members of the company are to be liable for its debts and obligations under Section 303(c).

(b) Articles of organization of a limited liability company may set forth:

   (1) provisions permitted to be set forth in an operating agreement; or

   (2) other matters not inconsistent with law.

(c) Articles of organization of a limited liability company may not vary the non-waivable provisions of Section 103(b). As to all other matters, if any provision of an operating agreement is inconsistent with the articles of organization:

   (1) the operating agreement controls as to managers, members and members' transferees; and

   (2) the articles of organization control as to persons other than managers, members and their transferees who reasonably rely on the articles to their detriment.

SECTION 204. AMENDMENT OR RESTATEMENT OF ARTICLES OF ORGANIZATION.

(a) Articles of organization of a limited liability company may be amended at any time by delivering articles of amendment to the [Secretary of State] for filing. The articles of amendment must set forth the:

   (1) name of the limited liability company;

   (2) date of filing of the articles of organization; and

   (3) amendment to the articles.

(b) A limited liability company may restate its articles of organization at any time. Restated articles of organization must be signed and filed in the same manner as articles of amendment. Restated articles of organization must be designated as such in the heading and state in the heading or in an introductory paragraph the limited liability company's present name and, if it has been changed, all of its former names and the date of the filing of its initial articles of organization.

SECTION 205. SIGNING OF RECORDS.

(a) Except as otherwise provided in this [Act], a record to be filed by or on behalf of a limited liability company in the office of the [Secretary of State] must be signed in the name of the company by a:

    (1) manager of a manager-managed company;

    (2) member of a member-managed company;

    (3) person organizing the company, if the company has not been formed; or

    (4) fiduciary, if the company is in the hands of a receiver, trustee or other court-appointed fiduciary.

(b) A record signed under subsection (a) must state adjacent to the signature the name and capacity of the signer.

(c) Any person may sign a record to be filed under subsection (a) by an attorney-in-fact. Powers of attorney relating to the signing of records to be filed under subsection (a) by an attorney-in-fact need not be filed in the office of the [Secretary of State] as evidence of authority by the person filing but must be retained by the company.

SECTION 206. FILING IN OFFICE OF [SECRETARY OF STATE].

(a) Articles of organization or any other record authorized to be filed under this [Act] must be in a medium permitted by the [Secretary of State] and must be delivered to the office of the [Secretary of State]. Unless the [Secretary of State] determines that a record fails to comply as to form with the filing requirements of this [Act], and if all filing fees have been paid, the [Secretary of State] shall file the record and send a receipt for the record and the fees to the limited liability company or its representative.

(b) Upon request and payment of a fee, the [Secretary of State] shall send to the requester a certified copy of the requested record.

(c) Except as otherwise provided in subsection (d) and Section 207(c), a record accepted for filing by the [Secretary of State] is effective:

    (1) at the time of filing on the date it is filed, as evidenced by the [Secretary of State's] date and time endorsement on the original record; or

    (2) at the time specified in the record as its effective time on the date it is filed.

(d) A record may specify a delayed effective time and date, and if it does so the record becomes effective at the time and date specified. If a delayed effective date but no time is specified, the record is effective at the close of business on that date. If a delayed effective date is later than the 90th day after the record is filed, the record is effective on the 90th day.

SECTION 207. CORRECTING FILED RECORD.

(a) A limited liability company or foreign limited liability company may correct a record filed by the [Secretary of State] if the record contains a false or erroneous statement or was defectively signed.

(b) A record is corrected:

(1) by preparing articles of correction that:

(i) describe the record, including its filing date, or attach a copy of it to the articles of correction;

(ii) specify the incorrect statement and the reason it is incorrect or the manner in which the signing was defective; and

(iii) correct the incorrect statement or defective signing; and

(2) by delivering the corrected record to the [Secretary of State] for filing.

(c) Articles of correction are effective retroactively on the effective date of the record they correct except as to persons relying on the uncorrected record and adversely affected by the correction. As to those persons, articles of correction are effective when filed.

SECTION 208. CERTIFICATE OF EXISTENCE OR AUTHORIZATION.

(a) A person may request the [Secretary of State] to furnish a certificate of existence for a limited liability company or a certificate of authorization for a foreign limited liability company.

(b) A certificate of existence for a limited liability company must set forth:

(1) the company's name;

(2) that it is duly organized under the laws of this State, the date of organization, whether its duration is at-will or for a specified term, and, if the latter, the period specified;

(3) if payment is reflected in the records of the [Secretary of State] and if non-payment affects the existence of the company, that all fees, taxes and penalties owed to this State have been paid;

(4) whether its most recent annual report required by Section 211 has been filed with the [Secretary of State];

(5) that articles of termination have not been filed; and

(6) other facts of record in the office of the [Secretary of State] which may be requested by the applicant.

(c) A certificate of authorization for a foreign limited liability company must set forth:

(1) the company's name used in this State;

(2) that it is authorized to transact business in this State;

(3) if payment is reflected in the records of the [Secretary of State] and non-payment affects the authorization of the company, that all fees, taxes and penalties owed to this State have been paid;

(4) whether its most recent annual report required by Section 211 has been filed with the [Secretary of State];

(5) that a certificate of cancellation has not been filed; and

(6) other facts of record in the office of the [Secretary of State] which may be requested by the applicant.

(d) Subject to any qualification stated in the certificate, a certificate of existence or authorization issued by the [Secretary of State] may be relied upon as conclusive evidence that the domestic or foreign limited liability company is in existence or is authorized to transact business in this State.

SECTION 209. LIABILITY FOR FALSE STATEMENT IN FILED RECORD.
If a record authorized or required to be filed under this [Act] contains a false statement, one who suffers loss by reliance on the statement may recover damages for the loss from a person who signed the record or caused another to sign it on the person's behalf and knew the statement to be false at the time the record was signed.

SECTION 210. FILING BY JUDICIAL ACT.
If a person required by Section 205 to sign any record fails or refuses to do so, any other person who is adversely affected by the failure or refusal may petition the [designate the appropriate court] to direct the signing of the record. If the court finds that it is proper for the record to be signed and that a person so designated has failed or refused to sign the record, it shall order the [Secretary of State] to sign and file an appropriate record.

SECTION 211. ANNUAL REPORT FOR [SECRETARY OF STATE].
(a) A limited liability company, and a foreign limited liability company authorized to transact business in this State, shall deliver to the [Secretary of State] for filing an annual report that sets forth:
   (1) the name of the company and the state or country under whose law it is organized;
   (2) the address of its designated office and the name and address of its agent for service of process in this State;
   (3) the address of its principal office; and
   (4) the names and business addresses of any managers.
(b) Information in an annual report must be current as of the date the annual report is signed on behalf of the limited liability company.
(c) The first annual report must be delivered to the [Secretary of State] between [January 1 and April 1]of the year following the calendar year in which a limited liability company was organized or a foreign company was authorized to transact business. Subsequent annual reports must be delivered to the [Secretary of State] between [January 1 and April 1] of the ensuing calendar years.
(d) If an annual report does not contain the information required in subsection (a), the [Secretary of State] shall promptly notify the reporting limited liability company or foreign limited liability company and return the report to it for correction. If the report is corrected to contain the information required in subsection (a) and delivered to the [Secretary of State] within thirty days after the effective date of the notice, it is timely filed.

[ARTICLE] 3
RELATIONS OF MEMBERS AND MANAGERS
TO PERSONS DEALING WITH
LIMITED LIABILITY COMPANY

Section 301. Agency of Members and Managers.
Section 302. Limited Liability Company Liable for Member's or Manager's Actionable Conduct.
Section 303. Liability of Members and Managers.

SECTION 301. AGENCY OF MEMBERS AND MANAGERS.

(a) Subject to subsections (b) and (c):

  (1) each member is an agent of the limited liability company for the purpose of its business and an act of a member, including the signing of an instrument in the company's name, for apparently carrying on in the ordinary course the company's business or business of the kind carried on by the company binds the company, unless the member had no authority to act for the company in the particular matter and the person with whom the member was dealing knew or had notice that the member lacked authority.

  (2) an act of a member which is not apparently for carrying on in the ordinary course the company's business or business of the kind carried on by the company binds the company only if the act was authorized by the other members.

(b) Subject to subsection (c), in a manager-managed company:

  (1) a member is not an agent of the company for the purpose of its business solely by reason of being a member. Each manager is an agent of the company for the purpose of its business and an act of a manager, including the signing of an instrument in the company's name, for apparently carrying on in the ordinary course the company's business or business of the kind carried on by the company binds the company, unless the manager had no authority to act for the company in the particular matter and the person with whom the manager was dealing knew or had notice that the manager lacked authority.

  (2) an act of a manager which is not apparently for carrying on in the ordinary course the company's business or business of the kind carried on by the company binds the company only if the act was authorized under Section 404.

(c) Unless the articles of organization limit their authority, any member of a member-managed company or manager of a manager-managed company may sign and deliver any instrument transferring or affecting the company's interest in real property. The instrument is conclusive in favor of a person who gives value without knowledge of the lack of the authority of the person signing and delivering the instrument.

SECTION 302. LIMITED LIABILITY COMPANY LIABLE FOR MEMBER'S OR MANAGER'S ACTIONABLE CONDUCT. A limited liability company is liable for loss or injury caused to a person, or for a penalty incurred, as a result of a wrongful act or omission, or other actionable conduct, of a member or manager acting in the ordinary course of business of the company or with authority of the company.

SECTION 303. LIABILITY OF MEMBERS AND MANAGERS.

(a) Except as otherwise provided in subsection (c), the debts, obligations and liabilities of a limited liability company, whether arising in contract, tort or otherwise, are solely the debts, obligations and liabilities of the company. A member or manager is not personally liable for a debt, obligation or liability of the company solely by reason of being or acting as a member or manager.

(b) The failure of a limited liability company to observe the usual company formalities or requirements relating to the exercise of its company powers or management of its business is not a ground for imposing personal liability on the members or managers for liabilities of the company.

(c) All or specified members of a limited liability company are liable in their capacity as members for all or specified debts, obligations or liabilities of the company if:

   (1) a provision to that effect is contained in the articles of organization; and

   (2) a member so liable has consented in writing to the adoption of the provision or to be bound by the provision.

[ARTICLE] 4
RELATIONS OF MEMBERS TO EACH OTHER AND
TO LIMITED LIABILITY COMPANY

SECTION 401. FORM OF CONTRIBUTION. A contribution of a member of a limited liability company may consist of tangible or intangible property or other benefit to the company, including money, promissory notes, services performed or other agreements to contribute cash or property, or contracts for services to be performed.

SECTION 402. MEMBER'S LIABILITY FOR CONTRIBUTIONS.

(a) A member's obligation to contribute money, property or other benefit to, or to perform services for, a limited liability company is not excused by the member's death, disability or other inability to perform personally. If a member does not make the required contribution of property or services, the member is obligated at the option of the company to contribute money equal to the value of that portion of the stated contribution which has not been made.

(b) A creditor of a limited liability company who extends credit or otherwise acts in reliance on an obligation described in subsection (a), and without notice of any compromise under Section 404(c)(5), may enforce the original obligation.

SECTION 403. MEMBER'S AND MANAGER'S RIGHTS TO PAYMENTS AND REIMBURSEMENT.

(a) A limited liability company shall reimburse a member or manager for payments made and indemnify a member or manager for liabilities incurred by the member or manager in the ordinary course of the business of the company or for the preservation of its business or property.

(b) A limited liability company shall reimburse a member for an advance to the company beyond the amount of contribution the member agreed to make.

(c) A payment or advance made by a member which gives rise to an obligation of a limited liability company under subsection (a) or (b) constitutes a loan to the company upon which interest accrues from the date of the payment or advance.

(d) A member is not entitled to remuneration for services performed for a limited liability company, except for reasonable compensation for services rendered in winding up the business of the company.

SECTION 404. MANAGEMENT OF LIMITED LIABILITY COMPANY.

(a) In a member-managed company:
   (1) each member has equal rights in the management and conduct of the company's business; and
   (2) except as otherwise provided in subsection (c), any matter relating to the business of the company may be decided by a majority of the members.

(b) In a manager-managed company:
   (1) each manager has equal rights in the management and conduct of the company's business;
   (2) except as otherwise provided in subsection (c), any matter relating to the business of the company may be exclusively decided by the manager or, if there is more than one manager, by a majority of the managers; and
   (3) a manager:
      (i) must be designated, appointed, elected, removed or replaced by a vote, approval or consent of a majority of the members; and
      (ii) holds office until a successor has been elected and qualified, unless the manager sooner resigns or is removed.

(c) The only matters of a member or manager-managed company's business requiring the consent of all of the members are:

(1) the amendment of the operating agreement under Section 103;

(2) the authorization or ratification of acts or transactions under Section 103(b)(2)(ii) which would otherwise violate the duty of loyalty;

(3) an amendment to the articles of organization under Section 204;

(4) the compromise of an obligation to make a contribution under Section 402(b);

(5) the compromise, as among members, of an obligation of a member to make a contribution or return money or other property paid or distributed in violation of this [Act];

(6) the making of interim distributions under Section 405(a), including the redemption of an interest;

(7) the admission of a new member;

(8) the use of the company's property to redeem an interest subject to a charging order;

(9) the consent to dissolve the company under Section 801(b)(2);

(10) a waiver of the right to have the company's business wound up and the company terminated under Section 802(b);

(11) the consent of members to merge with another entity under Section 904(c)(1); and

(12) the sale, lease, exchange or other disposal of all, or substantially all, of the company's property with or without goodwill.

(d) Action requiring the consent of members or managers under this [Act] may be taken without a meeting.

(e) A member or manager may appoint a proxy to vote or otherwise act for the member or manager by signing an appointment instrument, either personally or by the member's or manager's attorney-in-fact.

SECTION 405. SHARING OF AND RIGHT TO DISTRIBUTIONS.

(a) Any distributions made by a limited liability company before its dissolution and winding up must be in equal shares.

(b) A member has no right to receive, and may not be required to accept, a distribution in kind.

(c) If a member becomes entitled to receive a distribution, the member has the status of, and is entitled to all remedies available to, a creditor of the limited liability company with respect to the distribution.

SECTION 406. LIMITATIONS ON DISTRIBUTIONS.

(a) A distribution may not be made if:

(1) the limited liability company would not be able to pay its debts as they become due in the ordinary course of business; or

(2) the company's total assets would be less than the sum of its total liabilities plus the amount that would be needed, if the company were to be dissolved, wound up and terminated at the time of the distribution, to satisfy the preferential rights upon dissolution, winding up and termination of

members whose preferential rights are superior to those receiving the distribution.

(b) A limited liability company may base a determination that a distribution is not prohibited under subsection (a) on financial statements prepared on the basis of accounting practices and principles that are reasonable in the circumstances or on a fair valuation or other method that is reasonable in the circumstances.

(c) Except as otherwise provided in subsection (e), the effect of a distribution under subsection (a) is measured:

   (1) in the case of distribution by purchase, redemption or other acquisition of a distributional interest in a limited liability company, as of the date money or other property is transferred or debt incurred by the company; and

   (2) in all other cases, as of the date the:

      (i) distribution is authorized if the payment occurs within 120 days after the date of authorization; or

      (ii) payment is made if it occurs more than 120 days after the date of authorization.

(d) A limited liability company's indebtedness to a member incurred by reason of a distribution made in accordance with this Section is at parity with the company's indebtedness to its general, unsecured creditors.

(e) Indebtedness of a limited liability company, including indebtedness issued in connection with or as part of a distribution, is not considered a liability for purposes of determinations under subsection (a) if its terms provide that payment of principal and interest are made only if and to the extent that payment of a distribution to members could then be made under this Section. If the indebtedness is issued as a distribution, each payment of principal or interest on the indebtedness is treated as a distribution, the effect of which is measured on the date the payment is made.

SECTION 407. LIABILITY FOR UNLAWFUL DISTRIBUTIONS.

(a) A member of a member-managed company or a member or manager of a manager-managed company who votes for or assents to a distribution made in violation of Section 406, the articles of organization, or the operating agreement is personally liable to the company for the amount of the distribution which exceeds the amount that could have been distributed without violating Section 406, the articles of organization, or the operating agreement if it is established that the member or manager did not perform the member's or manager's duties in compliance with Section 409.

(b) A member of a manager-managed company who knew a distribution was made in violation of Section 406, the articles of organization, or the operating agreement is personally liable to the company, but only to the extent that the distribution received by the member exceeded the amount that could have been properly paid under Section 406.

(c) A member or manager against whom an action is brought under this Section may implead in the action all:

    (1) other members or managers who voted for or assented to the distribution in violation of subsection (a) and may compel contribution from them; and

    (2) members who received a distribution in violation of subsection (b) and may compel contribution from the member in the amount received in violation of subsection (b).

(d) A proceeding under this Section is barred unless it is commenced within two years after the distribution.

SECTION 408. MEMBER'S RIGHT TO INFORMATION.

(a) A limited liability company shall provide members and their agents and attorneys access to its records, if any, at the company's principal office or other reasonable locations specified in the operating agreement. The company shall provide former members and their agents and attorneys access for proper purposes to records pertaining to the period during which they were members. The right of access provides the opportunity to inspect and copy records during ordinary business hours. The company may impose a reasonable charge, limited to the costs of labor and material, for copies of records furnished.

(b) A limited liability company shall furnish to a member, and to the legal representative of a deceased member or member under legal disability:

    (1) without demand, information concerning the company's business or affairs reasonably required for the proper exercise of the member's rights and performance of the member's duties under the operating agreement or this [Act]; and

    (2) on demand, other information concerning the company's business or affairs, except to the extent the demand or the information demanded is unreasonable or otherwise improper under the circumstances.

(c) A member has the right upon written demand given to the limited liability company to obtain at the company's expense a copy of any written operating agreement.

SECTION 409. GENERAL STANDARDS OF MEMBER'S AND MANAGER'S CONDUCT.

(a) The only fiduciary duties a member owes to a member-managed company and its other members are the duty of loyalty and the duty of care imposed by subsections (b) and (c).

(b) A member's duty of loyalty to a member-managed company and its other members is limited to the following:

    (1) to account to the company and to hold as trustee for it any property, profit or benefit derived by the member in the conduct or winding up of the company's business or derived from a use by the member of the company's property, including the appropriation of a company's opportunity;

(2) to refrain from dealing with the company in the conduct or winding up of the company's business as or on behalf of a party having an interest adverse to the company; and

(3) to refrain from competing with the company in the conduct of the company's business before the dissolution of the company.

(c) A member's duty of care to a member-managed company and its other members in the conduct of and winding up of the company's business is limited to refraining from engaging in grossly negligent or reckless conduct, intentional misconduct or a knowing violation of law.

(d) A member shall discharge the duties to a member-managed company and its other members under this [Act] or under the operating agreement and exercise any rights consistently with the obligation of good faith and fair dealing.

(e) A member of a member-managed company does not violate a duty or obligation under this [Act] or under the operating agreement merely because the member's conduct furthers the member's own interest.

(f) A member of a member-managed company may lend money to and transact other business with the company. As to each loan or transaction, the rights and obligations of the member are the same as those of a person who is not a member, subject to other applicable law.

(g) This Section applies to a person winding up the limited liability company's business as the personal or legal representative of the last surviving member as if the person were a member.

(h) In a manager-managed company:

(1) a member who is not also a manager owes no duties to the company or to the other members solely by reason of being a member;

(2) a manager is held to the same standards of conduct prescribed for members in subsections (b) through (f);

(3) a member who pursuant to the operating agreement exercises some or all of the rights of a manager in the management and conduct of the company's business is held to the standards of conduct in subsections (b) through (f) to the extent that the member exercises the managerial authority vested in a manager by this [Act]; and

(4) a manager is relieved of liability imposed by law for violation of the standards prescribed by subsections (b) through (f) to the extent of the managerial authority delegated to the members by the operating agreement.

SECTION 410. ACTIONS BY MEMBERS.

(a) A member may maintain an action against a limited liability company or another member for legal or equitable relief, with or without an accounting as to the company's business, to enforce:

(1) the member's rights under the operating agreement;

(2) the member's rights under this [Act]; and

(3) the rights and otherwise protect the interests of the member, including rights and interests arising independently of the member's relationship to the company.

(b) The accrual, and any time limited for the assertion, of a right of action for a remedy under this Section is governed by other law. A right to an accounting upon a dissolution and winding up does not revive a claim barred by law.

SECTION 411. CONTINUATION OF TERM COMPANY AFTER EXPIRATION OF SPECIFIED TERM.

(a) If a term company is continued after the expiration of the specified term, the rights and duties of the members and managers remain the same as they were at the expiration of the term except to the extent inconsistent with rights and duties of members and managers of an at-will company.

(b) If the members in a member-managed company or the managers in a manager-managed company continue the business without any winding up of the business of the company, it continues as an at-will company.

[ARTICLE] 5
TRANSFEREES AND CREDITORS OF MEMBER

SECTION 501. MEMBER'S DISTRIBUTIONAL INTEREST.

(a) A member is not a co-owner of, and has no transferable interest in, property of a limited liability company.

(b) A distributional interest in a limited liability company is personal property and, subject to Sections 502 and 503, may be transferred, in whole or in part.

(c) An operating agreement may provide that a distributional interest may be evidenced by a certificate of the interest issued by the limited liability company and, subject to Section 503, may also provide for the transfer of any interest represented by the certificate.

SECTION 502. TRANSFER OF DISTRIBUTIONAL INTEREST. A transfer of a distributional interest does not entitle the transferee to become or to exercise any rights of a member. A transfer entitles the transferee to receive, to the extent transferred, only the distributions to which the transferor would be entitled.

SECTION 503. RIGHTS OF TRANSFEREE.

(a) A transferee of a distributional interest may become a member of a limited liability company if and to the extent that the transferor gives the transferee the right in accordance with authority described in the operating agreement or all other members consent.

(b) A transferee who has become a member, to the extent transferred, has the rights and powers, and is subject to the restrictions and liabilities, of a member under the operating agreement of a limited liability company and this [Act]. A transferee who becomes a member also is liable for the transferor member's obligations to make contributions under Section 402 and for obligations under

Section 407 to return unlawful distributions, but the transferee is not obligated for the transferor member's liabilities unknown to the transferee at the time the transferee becomes a member.

(c) Whether or not a transferee of a distributional interest becomes a member under subsection (a), the transferor is not released from liability to the limited liability company under the operating agreement or this [Act].

(d) A transferee who does not become a member is not entitled to participate in the management or conduct of the limited liability company's business, require access to information concerning the company's transactions or inspect or copy any of the company's records.

(e) A transferee who does not become a member is entitled to:
   (1) receive, in accordance with the transfer, distributions to which the transferor would otherwise be entitled;
   (2) receive, upon dissolution and winding up of the limited liability company's business:
      (i) in accordance with the transfer, the net amount otherwise distributable to the transferor;
      (ii) a statement of account only from the date of the latest statement of account agreed to by all the members;
   (3) seek under Section 801(a)(5) a judicial determination that it is equitable to dissolve and wind up the company's business.

(f) A limited liability company need not give effect to a transfer until it has notice of the transfer.

SECTION 504. RIGHTS OF CREDITOR.

(a) On application by a judgment creditor of a member of a limited liability company or of a member's transferee, a court having jurisdiction may charge the distributional interest of the judgment debtor to satisfy the judgment. The court may appoint a receiver of the share of the distributions due or to become due to the judgment debtor and make all other orders, directions, accounts and inquiries the judgment debtor might have made or which the circumstances may require to give effect to the charging order.

(b) A charging order constitutes a lien on the judgment debtor's distributional interest. The court may order a foreclosure of a lien on a distributional interest subject to the charging order at any time. A purchaser at the foreclosure sale has the rights of a transferee.

(c) At any time before foreclosure, a distributional interest in a limited liability company which is charged may be redeemed:
   (1) by the judgment debtor;
   (2) with property other than the company's property, by one or more of the other members; or
   (3) with the company's property, but only if permitted by the operating agreement.

(d) This [Act] does not affect a member's right under exemption laws with respect to the member's distributional interest in a limited liability company.

(e) This Section provides the exclusive remedy by which a judgment creditor of a member or a transferee may satisfy a judgment out of the judgment debtor's distributional interest in a limited liability company.

[ARTICLE] 6
MEMBER'S DISSOCIATION

Section 601. Events Causing Member's Dissociation.
Section 602. Member's Power to Dissociate; Wrongful Dissociation.
Section 603. Effect of Member's Dissociation.

SECTION 601. EVENTS CAUSING MEMBER'S DISSOCIATION. A member is dissociated from a limited liability company upon the occurrence of any of the following events:

(1) the company's having notice of the member's express will to withdraw upon the date of notice or on a later date specified by the member;

(2) an event agreed to in the operating agreement as causing the member's dissociation;

(3) upon transfer of all of a member's distributional interest, other than a transfer for security purposes or a court order charging the member's distributional interest which has not been foreclosed;

(4) the member's expulsion pursuant to the operating agreement;

(5) the member's expulsion by unanimous vote of the other members if:

    (i) it is unlawful to carry on the company's business with the member;

    (ii) there has been a transfer of substantially all of the member's distributional interest, other than a transfer for security purposes, or a court order charging the member's distributional interest, which has not been foreclosed;

    (iii) within ninety days after the company notifies a corporate member that it will be expelled because it has filed a certificate of dissolution or the equivalent, its charter has been revoked, or its right to conduct business has been suspended by the jurisdiction of its incorporation, the member fails to obtain a revocation of the certificate of dissolution or a reinstatement of its charter or its right to conduct business; or

    (iv) a partnership or a limited liability company that is a member has been dissolved and its business is being wound up;

(6) on application by the company or another member, the member's expulsion by judicial determination because the member:

    (i) engaged in wrongful conduct that adversely and materially affected the company's business;

    (ii) willfully or persistently committed a material breach of the operating agreement or of a duty owed to the company or the other members under Section 409; or

    (iii) engaged in conduct relating to the company's business which makes it not reasonably practicable to carry on the business with the member;

(7) the member's:

- (i) becoming a debtor in bankruptcy;
- (ii) executing an assignment for the benefit of creditors;
- (iii) seeking, consenting to, or acquiescing in the appointment of a trustee, receiver or liquidator of the member or of all or substantially all of the member's property; or
- (iv) failing, within ninety days after the appointment, to have vacated or stayed the appointment of a trustee, receiver or liquidator of the member or of all or substantially all of the member's property obtained without the member's consent or acquiescence, or failing within ninety days after the expiration of a stay to have the appointment vacated;
- (8) in the case of a member who is an individual:
  - (i) the member's death;
  - (ii) the appointment of a guardian or general conservator for the member; or
  - (iii) a judicial determination that the member has otherwise become incapable of performing the member's duties under the operating agreement;
- (9) in the case of a member that is a trust or is acting as a member by virtue of being a trustee of a trust, distribution of the trust's entire rights to receive distributions from the company, but not merely by reason of the substitution of a successor trustee;
- (10) in the case of a member that is an estate or is acting as a member by virtue of being a personal representative of an estate, distribution of the estate's entire rights to receive distributions from the company, but not merely the substitution of a successor personal representative; or
- (11) termination of the existence of a member if the member is not an individual, estate or trust other than a business trust.

SECTION 602. MEMBER'S POWER TO DISSOCIATE; WRONGFUL DISSOCIATION.

- (a) Unless otherwise provided in the operating agreement, a member has the power to dissociate from a limited liability company at any time, rightfully or wrongfully, by express will pursuant to Section 601(1).
- (b) If the operating agreement has not eliminated a member's power to dissociate, the member's dissociation from a limited liability company is wrongful only if:
  - (1) it is in breach of an express provision of the agreement; or
  - (2) before the expiration of the specified term of a term company:
    - (i) the member withdraws by express will;
    - (ii) the member is expelled by judicial determination under Section 601(6);
    - (iii) the member is dissociated by becoming a debtor in bankruptcy; or
    - (iv) in the case of a member who is not an individual, trust other than a business trust, or estate, the member is expelled or otherwise dissociated because it willfully dissolved or terminated its existence.
- (c) A member who wrongfully dissociates from a limited liability company is liable to the company and to the other members for damages caused by the disso-

ciation. The liability is in addition to any other obligation of the member to the company or to the other members.

(d) If a limited liability company does not dissolve and wind up its business as a result of a member's wrongful dissociation under subsection (b), damages sustained by the company for the wrongful dissociation must be offset against distributions otherwise due the member after the dissociation.

SECTION 603. EFFECT OF MEMBER'S DISSOCIATION.

(a) Upon a member's dissociation:

    (1) in an at-will company, the company must cause the dissociated member's distributional interest to be purchased under [Article] 7; and

    (2) in a term company:

        (i) if the company dissolves and winds up its business on or before the expiration of its specified term, [Article] 8 applies to determine the dissociated member's rights to distributions; and

        (ii) if the company does not dissolve and wind up its business on or before the expiration of its specified term, the company must cause the dissociated member's distributional interest to be purchased under [Article] 7 on the date of the expiration of the term specified at the time of the member's dissociation.

(b) Upon a member's dissociation from a limited liability company:

    (1) the member's right to participate in the management and conduct of the company's business terminates, except as otherwise provided in Section 803, and the member ceases to be a member and is treated the same as a transferee of a member;

    (2) the member's duty of loyalty under Section 409(b)(3) terminates; and

    (3) the member's duty of loyalty under Section 409(b)(1) and (2) and duty of care under Section 409(c) continue only with regard to matters arising and events occurring before the member's dissociation, unless the member participates in winding up the company's business pursuant to Section 803.

[ARTICLE] 7
MEMBER'S DISSOCIATION WHEN
BUSINESS NOT WOUND UP

Section 701. Company Purchase of Distributional Interest.
Section 702. Court Action to Determine Fair Value of Distributional Interest.
Section 703. Dissociated Member's Power to Bind Limited Liability Company.
Section 704. Statement of Dissociation.

SECTION 701. COMPANY PURCHASE OF DISTRIBUTIONAL INTEREST.

(a) A limited liability company shall purchase a distributional interest of a:

    (1) member of an at-will company for its fair value determined as of the date of the member's dissociation if the member's dissociation does not result

in a dissolution and winding up of the company's business under Section 801; or

(2) member of a term company for its fair value determined as of the date of the expiration of the specified term that existed on the date of the member's dissociation if the expiration of the specified term does not result in a dissolution and winding up of the company's business under Section 801.

(b) A limited liability company must deliver a purchase offer to the dissociated member whose distributional interest is entitled to be purchased not later than 30 days after the date determined under subsection (a). The purchase offer must be accompanied by:

(1) a statement of the company's assets and liabilities as of the date determined under subsection (a);

(2) the latest available balance sheet and income statement, if any; and

(3) an explanation of how the estimated amount of the payment was calculated.

(c) If the price and other terms of a purchase of a distributional interest are fixed or are to be determined by the operating agreement, the price and terms so fixed or determined govern the purchase unless the purchaser defaults. If a default occurs, the dissociated member is entitled to commence a proceeding to have the company dissolved under Section 801(a)(4)(iv).

(d) If an agreement to purchase the distributional interest is not made within 120 days after the date determined under subsection (a), the dissociated member, within another 120 days, may commence a proceeding against the limited liability company to enforce the purchase. The company at its expense shall notify in writing all of the remaining members, and any other person the court directs, of the commencement of the proceeding. The jurisdiction of the court in which the proceeding is commenced under this subsection is plenary and exclusive.

(e) The court shall determine the fair value of the distributional interest in accordance with the standards set forth in Section 702 together with the terms for the purchase. Upon making these determinations, the court shall order the limited liability company to purchase or cause the purchase of the interest.

(f) Damages for wrongful dissociation under Section 602(b), and all other amounts owing, whether or not currently due, from the dissociated member to a limited liability company, must be offset against the purchase price.

SECTION 702. COURT ACTION TO DETERMINE FAIR VALUE OF DISTRIBUTIONAL INTEREST.

(a) In an action brought to determine the fair value of a distributional interest in a limited liability company, the court shall:

(1) determine the fair value of the interest, considering among other relevant evidence the going concern value of the company, any agreement among some or all of the members fixing the price or specifying a formula for determining value of distributional interests for any other purpose, the recommendations of any appraiser appointed by the court, and any legal constraints on the company's ability to purchase the interest;

    (2) specify the terms of the purchase, including, if appropriate, terms for installment payments, subordination of the purchase obligation to the rights of the company's other creditors, security for a deferred purchase price and a covenant not to compete or other restriction on a dissociated member; and

    (3) require the dissociated member to deliver an assignment of the interest to the purchaser upon receipt of the purchase price or the first installment of the purchase price.

(b) After the dissociated member delivers the assignment, the dissociated member has no further claim against the company, its members, officers or managers, if any, other than a claim to any unpaid balance of the purchase price and a claim under any agreement with the company or the remaining members that is not terminated by the court.

(c) If the purchase is not completed in accordance with the specified terms, the company is to be dissolved upon application under Section 801(b)(5)(iv). If a limited liability company is so dissolved, the dissociated member has the same rights and priorities in the company's assets as if the sale had not been ordered.

(d) If the court finds that a party to the proceeding acted arbitrarily, vexatiously or not in good faith, it may award one or more other parties their reasonable expenses, including attorney's fees and the expenses of appraisers or other experts, incurred in the proceeding. The finding may be based on the company's failure to make an offer to pay or to comply with Section 701(b).

(e) Interest must be paid on the amount awarded from the date determined under Section 701(a) to the date of payment.

SECTION 703. DISSOCIATED MEMBER'S POWER TO BIND LIMITED LIABILITY COMPANY. For two years after a member dissociates without the dissociation resulting in a dissolution and winding up of a limited liability company's business, the company, including a surviving company under [Article] 9, is bound by an act of the dissociated member which would have bound the company under Section 301 before dissociation only if at the time of entering into the transaction the other party:

    (1) reasonably believed that the dissociated member was then a member;

    (2) did not have notice of the member's dissociation; and

    (3) is not deemed to have had notice under Section 704.

SECTION 704. STATEMENT OF DISSOCIATION.

(a) A dissociated member or a limited liability company may file in the office of the [Secretary of State] a statement of dissociation stating the name of the company and that the member is dissociated from the company.

(b) For the purposes of Sections 301 and 703, a person not a member is deemed to have notice of the dissociation 90 days after the statement of dissociation is filed.

[ARTICLE] 8
WINDING UP COMPANY'S BUSINESS

SECTION 801. EVENTS CAUSING DISSOLUTION AND WINDING UP OF COMPANY'S BUSINESS.

(a) A limited liability company is dissolved, and its business must be wound up, upon the occurrence of any of the following events:

(1) an event specified in the operating agreement;

(2) consent of the number or percentage of members specified in the operating agreement;

(3) an event that makes it unlawful for all or substantially all of the business of the company to be continued, but any cure of illegality within 90 days after notice to the company of the event is effective retroactively to the date of the event for purposes of this Section;

(4) on application by a member or a dissociated member, upon entry of a judicial decree that:

(i) the economic purpose of the company is likely to be unreasonably frustrated;

(ii) another member has engaged in conduct relating to the company's business that makes it not reasonably practicable to carry on the company's business with that member;

(iii) it is not otherwise reasonably practicable to carry on the company's business in conformity with the articles of organization and the operating agreement;

(iv) the company failed to purchase the petitioner's distributional interest as required by Section 701; or

(v) the managers or members in control of the company have acted, are acting or will act in a manner that is illegal, oppressive, fraudulent or unfairly prejudicial to the petitioner;

(5) on application by a transferee of a member's interest, a judicial determination that it is equitable to wind up the company's business:

(i) after the expiration of the specified term, if the company was for a specified term at the time the applicant became a transferee by member dissociation, transfer or entry of a charging order that gave rise to the transfer; or

(ii) at any time, if the company was at will at the time the applicant became a transferee by member dissociation, transfer or entry of a charging order that gave rise to the transfer.

SECTION 802. LIMITED LIABILITY COMPANY CONTINUES AFTER DISSOLUTION.

(a) Subject to subsection (b), a limited liability company continues after dissolution only for the purpose of winding up its business.

(b) At any time after the dissolution of a limited liability company and before the winding up of its business is completed, the members, including a dissociated member whose dissociation caused the dissolution, may unanimously waive the right to have the company's business wound up and the company terminated. In that case:

(1) the limited liability company resumes carrying on its business as if dissolution had never occurred and any liability incurred by the company or a member after the dissolution and before the waiver is determined as if the dissolution had never occurred; and

(2) the rights of a third party accruing under Section 804(a) or arising out of conduct in reliance on the dissolution before the third party knew or received a notification of the waiver are not adversely affected.

SECTION 803. RIGHT TO WIND UP LIMITED LIABILITY COMPANY'S BUSINESS.

(a) After dissolution, a member who has not wrongfully dissociated may participate in winding up a limited liability company's business, but on application of any member, member's legal representative or transferee, the [designate the appropriate court], for good cause shown, may order judicial supervision of the winding up.

(b) A legal representative of the last surviving member may wind up a limited liability company's business.

(c) A person winding up a limited liability company's business may preserve the company's business or property as a going concern for a reasonable time, prosecute and defend actions and proceedings, whether civil, criminal or administrative, settle and close the company's business, dispose of and transfer the company's property, discharge the company's liabilities, distribute the assets of the company pursuant to Section 806, settle disputes by mediation or arbitration and perform other necessary acts.

SECTION 804. MEMBER'S OR MANAGER'S POWER AND LIABILITY AS AGENT AFTER DISSOLUTION.

(a) A limited liability company is bound by a member's or manager's act after dissolution that:

(1) is appropriate for winding up the company's business; or

(2) would have bound the company under Section 301 before dissolution, if the other party to the transaction did not have notice of the dissolution.

(b) A member or manager who, with knowledge of the dissolution, subjects a limited liability company to liability by an act that is not appropriate for winding up the company's business is liable to the company for any damage caused to the company arising from the liability.

SECTION 805. ARTICLES OF TERMINATION.

(a) At any time after dissolution and winding up, a limited liability company may terminate its existence by filing with the [Secretary of State] articles of termination stating:

(1) the name of the company;

(2) the date of the dissolution; and

(3) that the company's business has been wound up and the legal existence of the company has been terminated.

(b) The existence of a limited liability company is terminated upon the filing of the articles of termination, or upon a later effective date, if specified in the articles of termination.

SECTION 806. DISTRIBUTION OF ASSETS IN WINDING UP LIMITED LIABILITY COMPANY'S BUSINESS.

(a) In winding up a limited liability company's business, the assets of the company must be applied to discharge its obligations to creditors, including members who are creditors. Any surplus must be applied to pay in money the net amount distributable to members in accordance with their right to distributions under subsection (b).

(b) Each member is entitled to a distribution upon the winding up of the limited liability company's business consisting of a return of all contributions which have not previously been returned and a distribution of any remainder in equal shares.

SECTION 807. KNOWN CLAIMS AGAINST DISSOLVED LIMITED LIABILITY COMPANY.

(a) A dissolved limited liability company may dispose of the known claims against it by following the procedure described in this Section.

(b) A dissolved limited liability company shall notify its known claimants in writing of the dissolution. The notice must:

(1) specify the information required to be included in a claim;

(2) provide a mailing address where the claim is to be sent;

(3) state the deadline for receipt of the claim, which may not be less than 120 days after the date the written notice is received by the claimant; and

(4) state that the claim will be barred if not received by the deadline.

(c) A claim against a dissolved limited liability company is barred if the requirements of subsection (b) are met, and:

(1) the claim is not received by the specified deadline; or

(2) in the case of a claim that is timely received but rejected by the dissolved company, the claimant does not commence a proceeding to enforce the claim within 90 days after the receipt of the notice of the rejection.

(d) For purposes of this Section, "claim" does not include a contingent liability or a claim based on an event occurring after the effective date of dissolution.

SECTION 808. OTHER CLAIMS AGAINST DISSOLVED LIMITED LIABILITY COMPANY.

(a) A dissolved limited liability company may publish notice of its dissolution and request persons having claims against the company to present them in accordance with the notice.

(b) The notice must:

(1) be published at least once in a newspaper of general circulation in the [county] in which the dissolved limited liability company's principal office is located or, if none in this State, in which its designated office is or was last located;

(2) describe the information required to be contained in a claim and provide a mailing address where the claim is to be sent; and

(3) state that a claim against the limited liability company is barred unless a proceeding to enforce the claim is commenced within five years after publication of the notice.

(c) If a dissolved limited liability company publishes a notice in accordance with subsection (b), the claim of each of the following claimants is barred unless the claimant commences a proceeding to enforce the claim against the dissolved company within five years after the publication date of the notice:

(1) a claimant who did not receive written notice under Section 807;

(2) a claimant whose claim was timely sent to the dissolved company but not acted on; and

(3) a claimant whose claim is contingent or based on an event occurring after the effective date of dissolution.

(d) A claim not barred under this Section may be enforced:

(1) against the dissolved limited liability company, to the extent of its undistributed assets; or

(2) if the assets have been distributed in liquidation, against a member of the dissolved company to the extent of the member's proportionate share of the claim or the company's assets distributed to the member in liquidation, whichever is less, but a member's total liability for all claims under this Section may not exceed the total amount of assets distributed to the member.

SECTION 809. GROUNDS FOR ADMINISTRATIVE DISSOLUTION.

The [Secretary of State] may commence a proceeding to dissolve a limited liability company administratively if the company does not:

(1) pay any fees, taxes or penalties imposed by this [Act] or other law within 60 days after they are due;

(2) deliver its annual report to the [Secretary of State] within 60 days after it is due.

SECTION 810. PROCEDURE FOR AND EFFECT OF ADMINISTRATIVE DISSOLUTION.

(a) If the [Secretary of State] determines that a ground exists for administratively dissolving a limited liability company, the [Secretary of State] shall enter a record of the determination and serve the company with a copy of the record.

(b) If the company does not correct each ground for dissolution or demonstrate to the reasonable satisfaction of the [Secretary of State] that each ground determined by the [Secretary of State] does not exist within 60 days after service of the notice, the [Secretary of State] shall administratively dissolve the company by signing a certification of the dissolution that recites the ground for dissolution and its effective date. The [Secretary of State] shall file the original of the certificate and serve the company with a copy of the certificate.

(c) A company administratively dissolved continues its existence but may carry on only business necessary to wind up and liquidate its business and affairs under Section 802 and to notify claimants under Sections 807 and 808.

(d) The administrative dissolution of a company does not terminate the authority of its agent for service of process.

SECTION 811. RESTATEMENT FOLLOWING ADMINISTRATIVE DISSOLUTION.

(a) A limited liability company administratively dissolved may apply to the [Secretary of State] for reinstatement within two years after the effective date of dissolution. The application must:

    (1) recite the name of the company and the effective date of its administrative dissolution;

    (2) state that the ground for dissolution either did not exist or have been eliminated;

    (3) state that the company's name satisfies the requirements of Section 105; and

    (4) contain a certificate from the [taxing authority] reciting that all taxes owed by the company have been paid.

(b) If the [Secretary of State] determines that the application contains the information required by subsection (a) and that the information is correct, the [Secretary of State] shall cancel the certificate of dissolution and prepare a certificate of reinstatement that recites this determination and the effective date of reinstatement, file the original of the certificate, and serve the company with a copy of the certificate.

(c) When reinstatement is effective, it relates back to and takes effect as of the effective date of the administrative dissolution and the company may resume its business as if the administrative dissolution had never occurred.

SECTION 812. APPEAL FROM DENIAL OF REINSTATEMENT.

(a) If the [Secretary of State] denies a limited liability company's application for reinstatement following administrative dissolution, the [Secretary of State] shall serve the company with a record that explains the reason or reasons for denial.

(b) The company may appeal the denial of reinstatement to the [name appropriate] court within 30 days after service of the notice of denial is perfected. The company appeals by petitioning the court to set aside the dissolution and attaching to the petition copies of the [Secretary of State's] certificate of dissolution, the company's application for reinstatement and the [Secretary of State's] notice of denial.

(c) The court may summarily order the [Secretary of State] to reinstate the dissolved company or may take other action the court considers appropriate.

(d) The court's final decision may be appealed as in other civil proceedings.

[ARTICLE] 9
CONVERSIONS AND MERGERS

SECTION 901. DEFINITIONS. In this article:

(1) "Corporation" means a corporation under [the State Corporation Act], a predecessor law, or comparable law of another jurisdiction.

(2) "General partner" means a partner in a partnership and a general partner in a limited partnership.

(3) "Limited partner" means a limited partner in a limited partnership.

(4) "Limited partnership" means a limited partnership created under [the State Limited Partnership Act], a predecessor law, or comparable law of another jurisdiction.

(5) "Partner" includes a general partner and a limited partner.

(6) "Partnership" means a general partnership under [the State Partnership Act], a predecessor law, or comparable law of another jurisdiction.

(7) "Partnership agreement" means an agreement among the partners concerning the partnership or limited partnership.

(8) "Shareholder" means a shareholder in a corporation.

SECTION 902. CONVERSION OF PARTNERSHIP OR LIMITED PARTNERSHIP TO LIMITED LIABILITY COMPANY.

(a) A partnership or limited partnership may be converted to a limited liability company pursuant to this section.

(b) The terms and conditions of a conversion of a partnership or limited partnership to a limited liability company must be approved by all of the partners or by a number or percentage of the partners required for conversion in the partnership agreement.

(c) An agreement of conversion must set forth the terms and conditions of the conversion of the interests of partners of a partnership or of a limited partnership, as the case may be, into interests in the converted limited liability company or the cash or other consideration to be paid or delivered as a result of the conversion of the interests of the partners, or a combination thereof.

(d) After a conversion is approved under subsection (b), the partnership or limited partnership shall file articles of organization in the office of the [Secretary of State] which satisfy the requirements of Section 203 and contain:

    (1) a statement that the partnership or limited partnership was converted to a limited liability company from a partnership or limited partnership, as the case may be;

    (2) its former name;

    (3) a statement of the number of votes cast by the partners entitled to vote for and against the conversion and, if the vote is less than unanimous, the number or percentage required to approve the conversion under subsection (b); and

    (4) in the case of a limited partnership, a statement that the certificate of limited partnership is to be canceled as of the date the conversion took effect.

(e) In the case of a limited partnership, the filing of articles of organization under subsection (d) cancels its certificate of limited partnership as of the date the conversion took effect.

(f) A conversion takes effect when the articles of organization are filed in the office of the [Secretary of State] or at any later date specified in the articles of organization.

(g) A general partner who becomes a member of a limited liability company as a result of a conversion remains liable as a partner for an obligation incurred by the partnership or limited partnership before the conversion takes effect.

(h) A general partner's liability for all obligations of the limited liability company incurred after the conversion takes effect is that of a member of the company. A limited partner who becomes a member as a result of a conversion remains liable only to the extent the limited partner was liable for an obligation incurred by the limited partnership before the conversion takes effect.

SECTION 903. EFFECT OF CONVERSION; ENTITY UNCHANGED.

(a) A partnership or limited partnership that has been converted pursuant to this article is for all purposes the same entity that existed before the conversion.

(b) When a conversion takes effect:
  (1) all property owned by the converting partnership or limited partnership vests in the limited liability company;
  (2) all debts, liabilities and other obligations of the converting partnership or limited partnership continue as obligations of the limited liability company;
  (3) an action or proceeding pending by or against the converting partnership or limited partnership may be continued as if the conversion had not occurred;
  (4) except as prohibited by other law, all of the rights, privileges, immunities, powers and purposes of the converting partnership or limited partnership vest in the limited liability company; and
  (5) except as otherwise provided in the agreement of conversion under Section 902(c), all of the partners of the converting partnership continue as members of the limited liability company.

SECTION 904. MERGER OF ENTITIES.

(a) Pursuant to a plan of merger approved under subsection (c), a limited liability company may be merged with or into one or more limited liability companies, foreign limited liability companies, corporations, foreign corporations, partnerships, foreign partnerships, limited partnerships, foreign limited partnerships or other domestic or foreign entities.

(b) A plan of merger must set forth:
  (1) the name of each entity that is a party to the merger;
  (2) the name of the surviving entity into which the other entities will merge;
  (3) the type of organization of the surviving entity;
  (4) the terms and conditions of the merger;
  (5) the manner and basis for converting the interests of each party to the merger into interests or obligations of the surviving entity, or into money or other property, in whole or in part; and
  (6) the street address of the surviving entity's principal place of business.

(c) A plan of merger must be approved:
  (1) in the case of a limited liability company that is a party to the merger, by all of the members or by a number or percentage of members specified in the operating agreement;
  (2) in the case of a foreign limited liability company that is a party to the merger, by the vote required for approval of a merger by the law of the state or foreign jurisdiction in which the foreign limited liability company is organized;
  (3) in the case of a partnership or domestic limited partnership that is a party to the merger, by the vote required for approval of a conversion under Section 902(b); and
  (4) in the case of any other entities that are parties to the merger, by the vote required for approval of a merger by the law of this State or of the State or foreign jurisdiction in which the entity is organized and, in the absence of such a requirement, by all the owners of interests in the entity.

(d) After a plan of merger is approved and before the merger takes effect, the plan may be amended or abandoned as provided in the plan.

(e) The merger is effective upon the filing of the articles of merger with the [Secretary of State], or at such later date as the articles may provide.

SECTION 905. ARTICLES OF MERGER.

(a) After approval of the plan of merger under Section 904(c), unless the merger is abandoned under Section 904(d), articles of merger must be signed on behalf of each limited liability company and other entity that is a party to the merger and delivered to the [Secretary of State] for filing. The articles must set forth:

(1) the name and jurisdiction of formation or organization of each of the limited liability companies and other entities that are parties to the merger;

(2) for each limited liability company that is to merge, the date its articles of organization were filed with the [Secretary of State];

(3) that a plan of merger has been approved and signed by each limited liability company and other entity that is to merge;

(4) the name and address of the surviving limited liability company or other surviving entity;

(5) the effective date of the merger;

(6) if a limited liability company is the surviving entity, such changes in its articles of organization as are necessary by reason of the merger;

(7) if a party to a merger is a foreign limited liability company, the jurisdiction and date of filing of its initial articles of organization and the date when its application for authority was filed by the [Secretary of State] or, if an application has not been filed, a statement to that effect; and

(8) if the surviving entity is not a limited liability company, an agreement that the surviving entity may be served with process in this State and is subject to liability in any action or proceeding for the enforcement of any liability or obligation of any limited liability company previously subject to suit in this State which is to merge, and for the enforcement, as provided in this [Act], of the right of members of any limited liability company to receive payment for their interest against the surviving entity.

(b) If a foreign limited liability company is the surviving entity of a merger, it may not do business in this State until an application for that authority is filed with the [Secretary of State].

(c) The surviving limited liability company or other entity shall furnish a copy of the plan of merger, on request and without cost, to any member of any limited liability company or any person holding an interest in any other entity that is to merge.

(d) Articles of merger operate as an amendment to the limited liability company's articles of organization.

SECTION 906. EFFECT OF MERGER.

(a) When a merger takes effect:

    (1) the separate existence of each limited liability company and other entity that is a party to the merger, other than the surviving entity, terminates;

    (2) all property owned by each of the limited liability companies and other entities that are party to the merger vests in the surviving entity;

    (3) all debts, liabilities and other obligations of each limited liability company and other entity that is party to the merger become the obligations of the surviving entity;

    (4) an action or proceeding pending by or against a limited liability company or other party to a merger may be continued as if the merger had not occurred or the surviving entity may be substituted as a party to the action or proceeding; and

    (5) except as prohibited by other law, all the rights, privileges, immunities, powers and purposes of every limited liability company and other entity that is a party to a merger vest in the surviving entity.

(b) The [Secretary of State] is an agent for service of process in an action or proceeding against the surviving foreign entity to enforce an obligation of any party to a merger if the surviving foreign entity fails to appoint or maintain an agent designated for service of process in this State or the agent for service of process cannot with reasonable diligence be found at the designated office. Upon receipt of process, the [Secretary of State] shall send a copy of the process by registered or certified mail, return receipt requested, to the surviving entity at the address set forth in the articles of merger. Service is effected under this subsection at the earliest of:

    (1) the date the company receives the process, notice or demand;

    (2) the date shown on the return receipt, if signed on behalf of the company; or

    (3) five days after its deposit in the mail, if mailed postpaid and correctly addressed.

(c) A member of the surviving limited liability company is liable for all obligations of a party to the merger for which the member was personally liable before the merger.

(d) Unless otherwise agreed, a merger of a limited liability company that is not the surviving entity in the merger does not require the limited liability company to wind up its business under this [Act] or pay its liabilities and distribute its assets pursuant to this [Act].

(e) Articles of merger serve as articles of dissolution for a limited liability company that is not the surviving entity in the merger.

SECTION 907. [ARTICLE] NOT EXCLUSIVE. This [Article] does not preclude an entity from being converted or merged under other law.

[ARTICLE] 10
FOREIGN LIMITED LIABILITY COMPANIES

Section 1001. Law Governing Foreign Limited Liability Companies.
Section 1002. Application for Certificate of Authority.
Section 1003. Activities Not Constituting Transacting Business.
Section 1004. Issuance of Certificate of Authority.
Section 1005. Name of Foreign Limited Liability Company.
Section 1006. Revocation of Certificate of Authority.
Section 1007. Cancellation of Authority.
Section 1008. Effect of Failure to Obtain Certificate of Authority.
Section 1009. Action By [Attorney General].

SECTION 1001. LAW GOVERNING FOREIGN LIMITED LIABILITY COMPANIES.

(a) The laws of the state or other jurisdiction under which a foreign limited liability company is organized govern its organization and internal affairs and the liability of its managers, members and their transferees.

(b) A foreign limited liability company may not be denied a certificate of authority by reason of any difference between the laws of another jurisdiction under which the foreign company is organized and the laws of this State.

(c) A certificate of authority does not authorize a foreign limited liability company to engage in any business or exercise any power that a limited liability company may not engage in or exercise in this State.

SECTION 1002. APPLICATION FOR CERTIFICATE OF AUTHORITY.

(a) A foreign limited liability company may apply for a certificate of authority to transact business in this State by delivering an application to the [Secretary of State] for filing. The application must set forth:

(1) the name of the foreign company or, if its name is unavailable for use in this State, a name that satisfies the requirements of Section 1005;

(2) the name of the State or country under whose law it is organized;

(3) the street address of its principal office;

(4) the address of its initial designated office in this State;

(5) the name and street address of its initial agent for service of process in this State;

(6) whether the duration of the company is for a specified term and, if so, the period specified;

(7) whether the company is manager-managed, and, if so, the name and address of each initial manager; and

(8) whether the members of the company are to be liable for its debts and obligations under a provision similar to Section 303(c).

(b) A foreign limited liability company shall deliver with the completed application a certificate of existence or a record of similar import authenticated by the secretary of state or other official having custody of company records in the State or country under whose law it is organized.

SECTION 1003. ACTIVITIES NOT CONSTITUTING TRANSACTING BUSINESS.

(a) Activities of a foreign limited liability company that do not constitute transacting business in this State within the meaning of this article include:

    (1) maintaining, defending or settling an action or proceeding;

    (2) holding meetings of its members or managers or carrying on any other activity concerning its internal affairs;

    (3) maintaining bank accounts;

    (4) maintaining offices or agencies for the transfer, exchange and registration of the foreign company's own securities or maintaining trustees or depositories with respect to those securities;

    (5) selling through independent contractors;

    (6) soliciting or obtaining orders, whether by mail or through employees or agents or otherwise, if the orders require acceptance outside this State before they become contracts;

    (7) creating or acquiring indebtedness, mortgages or security interests in real or personal property;

    (8) securing or collecting debts or enforcing mortgages or other security interests in property securing the debts, and holding, protecting and maintaining property so acquired;

    (9) conducting an isolated transaction that is completed within 30 days and is not one in the course of similar transactions of a like manner; and

    (10) transacting business in interstate commerce.

(b) For purposes of this article, the ownership in this State of income-producing real property or tangible personal property, other than property excluded under subsection (a), constitutes transacting business in this State.

(c) This Section does not apply in determining the contacts or activities that may subject a foreign limited liability company to service of process, taxation or regulation under any other law of this State.

SECTION 1004. ISSUANCE OF CERTIFICATE OF AUTHORITY.
Unless the [Secretary of State] determines that an application for a certificate of authority fails to comply as to form with the filing requirements of this [Act], the [Secretary of State], upon payment of all filing fees, shall file the application and send a receipt for it and the fees to the limited liability company or its representative.

SECTION 1005. NAME OF FOREIGN LIMITED LIABILITY COMPANY.

(a) If the name of a foreign limited liability company does not satisfy the requirements of Section 105, the company, to obtain or maintain a certificate of authority to transact business in this State, must use a fictitious name to transact business in this State if its real name is unavailable and it delivers to the [Secretary of State] for filing a copy of the resolution of its managers, in the case of a manager-managed company, or of its members, in the case of a member-managed company, adopting the fictitious name.

(b) Except as authorized by subsections (c) and (d), the name, including a fictitious name to be used to transact business in this State, of a foreign limited liability company must be distinguishable upon the records of the [Secretary of State] from:

    (1) the name of any corporation, limited partnership, or company incorporated, organized or authorized to transact business in this State;

    (2) a name reserved or registered under Section 106 or 107; and

    (3) the fictitious name of another foreign limited liability company authorized to transact business in this State.

(c) A foreign limited liability company may apply to the [Secretary of State] for authority to use in this State a name that is not distinguishable upon the records of the [Secretary of State] from a name described in subsection (b). The [Secretary of State] shall authorize use of the name applied for if:

    (1) the present user, registrant or owner of a reserved name consents to the use in a record and submits an undertaking in form satisfactory to the [Secretary of State] to change its name to a name that is distinguishable upon the records of the [Secretary of State] from the name of the foreign applying limited liability company; or

    (2) the applicant delivers to the [Secretary of State] a certified copy of a final judgment of a court establishing the applicant's right to use the name applied for in this State.

(d) A foreign limited liability company may use in this State the name, including the fictitious name, of another domestic or foreign entity that is used in this State if the other entity is incorporated, organized or authorized to transact business in this State and the foreign limited liability company:

    (1) has merged with the other entity;

    (2) has been formed by reorganization of the other entity; or

    (3) has acquired all or substantially all of the assets, including the name, of the other entity.

(e) If a foreign limited liability company authorized to transact business in this State changes its name to one that does not satisfy the requirements of Section 105, it may not transact business in this State under the name as changed until it adopts a name satisfying the requirements of Section 105 and obtains an amended certificate of authority.

SECTION 1006. REVOCATION OF CERTIFICATE OF AUTHORITY.

(a) A certificate of authority of a foreign limited liability company to transact business in this State may be revoked by the [Secretary of State] in the manner provided in subsection (b) if:

    (1) the company fails to:

        (i) pay any fees, taxes and penalties owed to this State;

        (ii) deliver its annual report required under Section 211 to the [Secretary of State] within 60 days after it is due;

        (iii) appoint and maintain an agent for service of process as required by this [article]; or

        (iv) file a statement of a change in the name or business address of the agent as required by this [article]; or

    (2) a misrepresentation has been made of any material matter in any application, report, affidavit or other record submitted by the company pursuant to this [article].

(b) The [Secretary of State] may not revoke a certificate of authority of a foreign limited liability company unless the [Secretary of State] sends the company notice of the revocation, at least 60 days before its effective date, by a record addressed to its agent for service of process in this State, or if the company fails to appoint and maintain a proper agent in this State, addressed to the office required to be maintained by Section 108. The notice must specify the cause for the revocation of the certificate of authority. The authority of the company to transact business in this State ceases on the effective date of the revocation unless the foreign limited liability company cures the failure before that date.

SECTION 1007. CANCELLATION OF AUTHORITY. A foreign limited liability company may cancel its authority to transact business in this State by filing in the office of the [Secretary of State] a certificate of cancellation. Cancellation does not terminate the authority of the [Secretary of State] to accept service of process on the company for [claims for relief] arising out of the transactions of business in this State.

SECTION 1008. EFFECT OF FAILURE TO OBTAIN CERTIFICATE OF AUTHORITY.

(a) A foreign limited liability company transacting business in this State may not maintain an action or proceeding in this State unless it has a certificate of authority to transact business in this State.

(b) The failure of a foreign limited liability company to have a certificate of authority to transact business in this State does not impair the validity of a contract or act of the company or prevent the foreign limited liability company from defending an action or proceeding in this State.

(c) Limitations on personal liability of managers, members and their transferees are not waived solely by transacting business in this State without a certificate of authority.

(d) If a foreign limited liability company transacts business in this State without a certificate of authority, it appoints the [Secretary of State] as its agent for service of process for [claims for relief] arising out of the transaction of business in this State.

SECTION 1009. ACTION BY [ATTORNEY GENERAL]. The [Attorney General] may maintain an action to restrain a foreign limited liability company from transacting business in this State in violation of this [article].

[ARTICLE] 11
DERIVATIVE ACTIONS

SECTION 1101. RIGHT OF ACTION. A member of a limited liability company may maintain an action in the right of the company if the members or managers having authority to do so have refused to commence the action or an effort to cause those members or managers to commence the action is not likely to succeed.

SECTION 1102. PROPER PLAINTIFF. In a derivative action for a limited liability company, the plaintiff must be a member of the company when the action is commenced; and:

(1) must have been a member at the time of the transaction of which the plaintiff complains; or

(2) the plaintiff's status as a member must have devolved upon the plaintiff by operation of law or pursuant to the terms of the operating agreement from a person who was a member at the time of the transaction.

SECTION 1103. PLEADING. In a derivative action for a limited liability company, the complaint must set forth with particularity the effort of the plaintiff to secure initiation of the action by a member or manager or the reasons for not making the effort.

SECTION 1104. EXPENSES. If a derivative action for a limited liability company is successful, in whole or in part, or if anything is received by the plaintiff as a result of a judgment, compromise or settlement of an action or claim, the court may award the plaintiff reasonable expenses, including reasonable attorney's fees, and shall direct the plaintiff to remit to the limited liability company the remainder of the proceeds received.

[ARTICLE] 12
MISCELLANEOUS PROVISIONS

SECTION 1201. UNIFORMITY OF APPLICATION AND CONSTRUCTION. This [Act] shall be applied and construed to effectuate its general purpose to make uniform the law with respect to the subject of this [Act] among states enacting it.

SECTION 1202. SHORT TITLE. This [Act] may be cited as the Uniform Limited Liability Company Act (1996).

SECTION 1203. SEVERABILITY CLAUSE. If any provision of this [Act] or its application to any person or circumstance is held invalid, the invalidity does not affect other provisions or applications of this [Act] which can be given effect without the invalid provision or application, and to this end, the provisions of this [Act] are severable.

SECTION 1204. EFFECTIVE DATE. This [Act] takes effect [_____].

SECTION 1205. TRANSITIONAL PROVISIONS.

(a) Before January 1, 199 ____ , this [Act] governs only a limited liability company organized:

  (1) after the effective date of this [Act], unless the company is continuing the business of a dissolved limited liability company under [Section of the existing Limited Liability Company Act]; and

  (2) before the effective date of this [Act], which elects, as provided by subsection (c), to be governed by this [Act].

(b) On and after January 1, 199 ____ , this [Act] governs all limited liability companies.

(c) Before January 1, 199 ____ , a limited liability company voluntarily may elect, in the manner provided in its operating agreement or by law for amending the operating agreement, to be governed by this [Act].

SECTION 1206. SAVINGS CLAUSE. This [Act] does not affect an action or proceeding commenced or right accrued before the effective date of this [Act].

UNIFORM LIMITED PARTNERSHIP ACT (1985)*

Article 1
General Provisions

Article 2
Formation; Certificate of Limited Partnership

Article 3
Limited Partners

---

* Drafted by the National Conference of Commissioners on Uniform State Laws and by it approved and recommended for enactment in all the states at its annual conference meeting in Minneapolis, Minnesota, August 2-August 9, 1985. This act has been printed through the permission of the National Conference of Commissioners on Uniform State Laws, and copies may be ordered from them at 676 North St. Clair Street, Suite 1700, Chicago, Illinois, 60611.

Article 4
General Partners

Article 5
Finance

Article 6
Distributions and Withdrawal

Article 7
Assignment of Partnership Interests

Article 8
Dissolution

Article 9
Foreign Limited Partnerships

Article 10
Derivative Actions

Article 11

Miscellaneous

UNIFORM LIMITED PARTNERSHIP ACT (1976)
WITH 1985 AMENDMENTS

ARTICLE 1
GENERAL PROVISIONS

§ 101. Definitions

As used in this [Act], unless the context otherwise requires:

(1) "Certificate of limited partnership" means the certificate referred to in Section 201, and the certificate as amended or restated.

(2) "Contribution" means any cash, property, services rendered, or a promissory note or other binding obligation to contribute cash or property or to perform services, which a partner contributes to a limited partnership in his capacity as a partner.

(3) "Event of withdrawl of a general partner" means an event that causes a person to cease to be a general partner as provided in Section 402.

(4) "Foreign limited partnership" means a partnership formed under the laws of any state other than this State and having as partners one or more general partners and one or more limited partners.

(5) "General partner" means a person who has been admitted to a limited partnership as a general partner in accordance with the partnership agreement and named in the certificate of limited partnership as a general partner.

(6) "Limited partner" means a person who has been admitted to a limited partnership as a limited partner in accordance with the partnership agreement.

(7) "Limited partnership" and "domestic limited partnership" mean a partnership formed by two or more persons under the laws of this State and having one or more general partners and one or more limited partners.

(8) "Partner" means a limited or general partner.

(9) "Partnership agreement" means any valid agreement, written or oral, of the partners as to the affairs of a limited partnership and the conduct of its business.

(10) "Partnership interest" means a partner's share of the profits and losses of a limited partnership and the right to receive distributions of partnership assets.

(11) "Person" means a natural person, partnership, limited partnership (domestic or foreign), trust, estate, association, or corporation.

(12) "State" means a state, territory or possession of the United States, the District of Columbia, or the Commonwealth of Puerto Rico.

§ 102. Name

The name of each limited partnership as set forth in its certificate of limited partnership:

(1) shall contain without abbreviation the words "limited partnership";

(2) may not contain the name of a limited partner unless (i) it is also the name of a general partner or the corporate name of a corporate general partner, or (ii) the business of the limited partnership had been carried on under that name before the admission of that limited partner;

(3) may not be the same as, or deceptively similar to, the name of any corporation or limited partnership organized under the laws of this State or licensed or registered as a foreign corporation or limited partnership in this State; and

(4) may not contain the following words [here insert prohibited words].

§ 103. Reservation of Name

(a) The exclusive right to the use of a name may be reserved by:
- (1) any person intending to organize a limited partnership under this [Act] and to adopt that name;
- (2) any domestic limited partnership or any foreign limited partnership registered in this State which, in either case, intends to adopt that name;
- (3) any foreign limited partnership intending to register in this State and adopt that name; and
- (4) any person intending to organize a foreign limited partnership and intending to have it register in this State and adopt that name.

(b) The reservation shall be made by filing with the Secretary of State an application, executed by the applicant, to reserve a specified name. If the Secretary of State finds that the name is available for use by a domestic or foreign limited partnership, he [or she] shall reserve the name for the exclusive use of the applicant for a period of 120 days. Once having so reserved a name, the same applicant may not again reserve, the same name until more than 60 days after the expiration of the last 120-day period for which that applicant reserved that name. The right to the exclusive use of a reserved name may be transferred to any other person by filing in the office of the Secretary of State a notice of the transfer, executed by the applicant for whom the name was reserved and specifying the name and address of the transferee.

§ 104. Specified Office and Agent

Each limited partnership shall continuously maintain in this State:
- (1) an office, which may but need not be a place of its business in this State, at which shall be kept the records required by Section 105 to be maintained; and
- (2) an agent for service of process on the limited partnership, which agent must be an individual resident of this State, a domestic corporation, or a foreign corporation authorized to do business in this State.

§ 105. Records to be Kept

(a) Each limited partnership shall keep at the office referred to in Section 104(1) the following:
- (1) a current list of the full name and last known business address of each partner, separately identifying the general partners (in alphabetical order) and the limited partners (in alphabetical order);
- (2) a copy of the certificate of limited partnership and all certificates of amendment thereto, together with executed copies of any powers of attorney pursuant to which any certificate has been executed;
- (3) copies of the limited partnership's federal, state and local income tax returns and reports, if any, for the three most recent years;
- (4) copies of any then effective written partnership agreements and of any financial statements of the limited partnership for the three most recent years; and
- (5) unless contained in a written partnership agreement, a writing setting out:

    (i) the amount of cash and a description and statement of the agreed value of the other property or services contributed by each partner and which each partner has agreed to contribute;

    (ii) the times at which or events on the happening of which any additional contributions agreed to be made by each partner are to be made;

    (iii) any right of a partner to receive, or of a general partner to make, distributions to a partner which include a return of all or any part of the partner's contribution; and

    (iv) any events upon the happening of which the limited partnership is to be dissolved and its affairs wound up.

(b) Records kept under this section are subject to inspection and copying at the reasonable request and at the expense of any partner during ordinary business hours.

§ 106. Nature of Business

A limited partnership may carry on any business that a partnership without limited partners may carry on except [here designate prohibited activities].

§ 107. Business Transactions of Partner with Partnership

Except as provided in the partnership agreement, a partner may lend money to and transact other business with the limited partnership and, subject to other applicable law, has the same rights and obligations with respect thereto as a person who is not a partner.

ARTICLE 2
FORMATION; CERTIFICATE OF LIMITED PARTNERSHIP

Section 201. Certificate of Limited Partnership.
Section 202. Amendment to Certificate.
Section 203. Cancellation of Certificate.
Section 204. Execution of Certificates.
Section 205. Execution by Judicial Act.
Section 206. Filing in Office of Secretary of State.
Section 207. Liability for False Statement in Certificate.
Section 208. Scope of Notice.
Section 209. Delivery of Certificates to Limited Partners.

§ 201. Certificate of Limited Partnership

(a) In order to form a limited partnership, a certificate of limited partnership must be executed and filed in the office of the Secretary of State. The certificate shall set forth:

(1) the name of the limited partnership;

(2) the address of the office and the name and address of the agent for service of process required to be maintained by Section 104;

(3) the name and the business address of each general partner;

(4) the latest date upon which the limited partnership is to dissolve; and

(5) any other matters the general partners determine to include therein.

(b) A limited partnership is formed at the time of the filing of the certificate of limited partnership in the office of the Secretary of State or at any later time specified in the certificate of limited partnership if, in either case, there has been substantial compliance with the requirements of this section.

§ 202. Amendment to Certificate

(a) A certificate of limited partnership is amended by filing a certificate of amendment thereto in the office of the Secretary of State. The certificate shall set forth:
   (1) the name of the limited partnership;
   (2) the date of filing the certificate; and
   (3) the amendment to the certificate
(b) Within 30 days after the happening of any of the following events, an amendment to a certificate of limited partnership reflecting the occurrence of the event or events shall be filed:
   (1) the admission of a new general partner;
   (2) the withdrawl of a general partner; or
   (3) the continuation of the business under Section 801 after an event of withdrawal of a general partner.
(c) A general partner who becomes aware that any statement in a certificate of limited partnership was false when made or that any arrangements or other facts described have changed, making the certificate inaccurate in any respect, shall promptly amend the certificate.
(d) A certificate of limited partnership may be amended at any time for any other proper purpose the general partners determine.
(e) No person has any liability because an amendment to a certificate of limited partnership has not been filed to reflect the occurrence of any event referred to in subsection (b) of this section if the amendment is filed within 30-day period specified in subsection (b).
(f) A restated certificate of limited partnership may be executed and filed in the same manner as a certificate of amendment.

§ 203. Cancellation of Certificate

A certificate of limited partnership shall be cancelled upon the dissolution and the commencement of winding up of the partnership or at any other time there are no limited partners. A certificate of cancellation shall be filed in the office of the Secretary of State and set forth:
   (1) the name of the limited partnership;
   (2) the date of filing of its certificate of limited partnership;
   (3) the reason for filing the certificate of cancellation;
   (4) the effective date (which shall be a date certain) of cancellation if it is not to be effective upon the filing of the certificate; and
   (5) any other information the general partners filing the certificate determine.

§ 204. Execution of Certificates

(a) Each certificate required by this Article to be filed in the office of the Secretary of State shall be executed in the following manner:

    (1) an original certificate of limited partnership must be signed by all general partners;

    (2) a certificate of amendment must be signed by at least one general partner and by each other general partner designated in the certificate as a new general partner; and

    (3) a certificate of cancellation must be signed by all general partners.

(b) Any person may sign a certificate by an attorney-in-fact, but a power of attorney to sign a certificate relating to the admission, of a general partner must specifically describe the admission.

(c) The execution of a certificate by a general partner constitutes an affirmation under the penalties of perjury that the facts stated therein are true.

§ 205. Execution by Judicial Act

If a person required by Section 204 to execute any certificate fails or refuses to do so, any other person who is adversely affected by the failure or refusal may petition the [designate the appropriate court] to direct the execution of the certificate. If the court finds that it is proper for the certificate to be executed and that any person so designated has failed or refused to execute the certificate, it shall order the Secretary of State to record an appropriate certificate.

§ 206. Filing in Office of Secretary of State

(a) Two signed copies of the certificate of limited partnership and of any certificates of amendment or cancellation (or of any judicial decree of amendment or cancellation) shall be delivered to the Secretary of State. A person who executes a certificate as an agent or fiduciary need not exhibit evidence of his [or her] authority as a prerequisite to filing. Unless the Secretary of State finds that any certificate does not conform to law, upon receipt of all filing fees required by law he [or she] shall:

    (1) endorse on each duplicate original the word "Filed" and the day, month, and year of the filing thereof;

    (2) file one duplicate original in his [or her] office; and

    (3) return the other duplicate original to the person who filed it or his [or her] representative.

(b) Upon the filing of a certificate of amendment (or judicial decree of amendment) in the office of the Secretary of State, the certificate of limited partnership shall be amended as set forth therein, and upon the effective date of a certificate of cancellation (or a judicial decree thereof), the certificate of limited partnership is cancelled.

§ 207. Liability for False Statement in Certificate

If any certificate of limited partnership or certificate of amendment or cancellation contains a false statement, one who suffers loss by reliance on the statement may recover damages for the loss from:

(1) any person who executes the certificate, or causes another to execute it on his behalf, and knew, and any general partner who knew or should have known, the statement to be false at the time the certificate was executed; and

(2) any general partner who thereafter knows or should have known that any arrangement or other fact described in the certificate has changed, making the statement inaccurate in any respect within a sufficient time before the statement was relied upon reasonably to have enabled that general partner to cancel or amend the certificate, or to file a petition for its cancellation or amendment under Section 205.

§ 208. Scope of Notice

The fact that a certificate of limited partnership is on file in the office of the Secretary of State is notice that the partnership is a limited partnership and the persons designated therein as general partners are general partners, but it is not notice of any other fact.

§ 209. Delivery of Certificates to Limited Partners

Upon the return by the Secretary of State pursuant to Section 206 of a certificate marked "Filed," the general partners shall promptly deliver or mail a copy of the certificate of limited partnership and each certificate of amendment or cancellation to each limited partner unless the partnership agreement provides otherwise.

ARTICLE 3
LIMITED PARTNERS

Section 301. Admission of Limited Partners.
Section 302. Voting.
Section 303. Liability to Third Parties.
Section 304. Person Erroneously Believing Himself [or Herself] Limited Partner.
Section 305. Information.

§ 301. Admission of Limited Partners

(a) A person becomes a limited partner:
  (1) at the time the limited partnership is formed; or
  (2) at any later time specified in the records of the limited partnership for becoming a limited partner.
(b) After the filing of a limited partnership's original certificate of limited partnership, a person may be admitted as an additional limited partner:
  (1) in the case of a person acquiring a partnership interest directly from the limited partnership, upon compliance with the partnership agreement or, if the partnership agreement does not so provide, upon the written consent of all partners; and
  (2) in the case of an assignee of a partnership interest of a partner who has the power, as provided in Section 704, to grant the assignee the right to become a limited partner, upon the exercise of that power and compliance with any conditions limiting the grant or exercise of the power.

§ 302. Voting

Subject to Section 303, the partnership agreement may grant to all or a specified group of the limited partners the right to vote (on a per capita or other basis) upon any matter.

§ 303. Liability to Third Parties

(a) Except as provided in subsection (d), a limited partner is not liable for the obligations of a limited partnership unless he [or she] is also a general partner or, in addition to the exercise of his [or her] rights and powers as a limited partner, he [or she] participates in the control of the business. However, if the limited partner participates in the control of the business, he [or she] is liable only to persons who transact business with the limited partnership reasonably believing, based upon the limited partner's conduct, that the limited partner is a general partner.

(b) A limited partner does not participate in the control of the business within the meaning of subsection (a) solely by doing one or more of the following:

    (1) being a contractor for or an agent or employee of the limited partnership or of a general partner or being an officer, director, or shareholder of a general partner that is a corporation;

    (2) consulting with and advising a general partner with respect to the business of the limited partnership;

    (3) acting as surety for the limited partnership or guaranteeing or assuming one or more specific obligations of the limited partnership;

    (4) taking any action required or permitted by law to bring or pursue a derivative action in the right of the limited partnership;

    (5) requesting or attending a meeting of partners;

    (6) proposing, approving, or disapproving, by voting or otherwise, one or more of the following matters:

        (i) the dissolution and winding up of the limited partnership;

        (ii) the sale, exchange, lease, mortgage, pledge, or other transfer of all or substantially all of the assets of the limited partnership;

        (iii) the incurrence of indebtedness by the limited partnership other than in the ordinary course of its business;

        (iv) a change in the nature of the business;

        (v) the admission or removal of a general partner;

        (vi) the admission or removal of a limited partner;

        (vii) a transaction involving an actual or potential conflict of interest between a general partner and the limited partnership or the limited partners;

        (viii) an amendment to the partnership agreement or certificate of limited partnership; or

        (ix) matters related to the business of the limited partnership not otherwise enumerated in this subsection (b), which the partnership agreement states in writing may be subject to the approval or disapproval of limited partners;

(7) winding up the limited partnership pursuant to Section 803; or

(8) exercising any right or power permitted to limited partners under this [Act] and not specifically enumerated in this subsection (b).

(c) The enumeration in subsection (b) does not mean that the possession or exercise of any other powers by a limited partner constitutes participation by him [or her] in the business of the limited partnership.

(d) A limited partner who knowingly permits his [or her] name to be used in the name of the limited partnership, except under circumstances permitted by Section 102(2), is liable to creditors who extend credit to the limited partnership without actual knowledge that the limited partner is not a general partner.

§ 304. Person Erroneously Believing Himself [or Herself] Limited Partner

(a) Except as provided in subsection (b), a person who makes a contribution to a business enterprise and erroneously but in good faith believes that he [or she] has become a limited partner in the enterprise is not a general partner in the enterprise and is not bound by its obligations by reason of making the contribution, receiving distributions from the enterprise, or exercising any rights of a limited partner, if, on ascertaining the mistake, he [or she]:

(1) causes an appropriate certificate of limited partnership or a certificate of amendment to be executed and filed; or

(2) withdraws from future equity participation in the enterprise by executing and filing in the office of the Secretary of State a certificate declaring withdrawl under this section.

(b) A person who makes a contribution of the kind described in subsection (a) is liable as a general partner to any third party who transacts business with the enterprise (i) before the person withdraws and an appropriate certificate is filed to show withdrawl, or (ii) before an appropriate certificate is filed to show that he [or she] is not a general partner, but in either case only if the third party actually believed in good faith that the person was a general partner at the time of the transaction.

§ 305. Information

Each limited partner has the right to:

(1) inspect and copy any of the partnership records required to be maintained by Section 105; and

(2) obtain from the general partners from time to time upon reasonable demand (i) true and full information regarding the state of the business and financial condition of the limited partnership, (ii) promptly after becoming available, a copy of the limited partnership's federal, state, and local income tax returns for each year, and (iii) other information regarding the affairs of the limited partnership as is just and reasonable.

ARTICLE 4
GENERAL PARTNERS

§ 401. Admission of Additional General Partners

After the filing of a limited partnership's original certificate of limited partnership, additional general partners may be admitted as provided in writing in the partnership agreement or, if the partnership agreement does not provide in writing for the admission of additional general partners, with the written consent of all partners.

§ 402. Events of Withdrawal

Except as approved by the specific written consent of all partners at the time, a person ceases to be a general partner of a limited partnership upon the happening of any of the following events:

(1) the general partner withdraws from the limited partnership as provided in Section 602;

(2) the general partner ceases to be a member of the limited partnership as provided in Section 702;

(3) the general partner is removed as a general partner in accordance with the partnership agreement;

(4) unless otherwise provided in writing in the partnership agreement, the general partner: (i) makes an assignment for the benefit of creditors; (ii) files a voluntary petition in bankruptcy; (iii) is adjudicated a bankrupt or insolvent; (iv) files a petition or answer seeking for himself [or herself] any reorganization, arrangement, composition, readjustment, liquidation, dissolution, or similar relief under any statute, law, or regulation; (v) files an answer or other pleading admitting or failing to consent the material allegations of a petition filed against him [or her] in any proceeding of this nature; or (vi) seeks, consents to, or acquiesces in the appointment of a trustee, receiver, or liquidator of the general partner or of all or any substantial part of his [or her] properties;

(5) unless otherwise provided in writing in the partnership agreement [120] days after the commencement of any proceeding against the general partner seeking reorganization, arrangement, composition, readjustment, liquidation, dissolution, or similar relief under any statute, law, or regulation, the proceeding has not been dismissed, or if within [90] days after the appointment without his [or her] consent or acquiescence of a trustee, receiver, or liquidator of the general partner or of all or any substantial part of his [or her] properties, the appointment is not vacated or stayed or within [90] days after the expiration of any such stay, the appointment is not vacated;

(6) in the case of a general partner who is a natural person,

      (i) his [or her] death; or

     (ii) the entry of an order by a court of competent jurisdiction adjudicating him [or her] incompetent to manage his [or her] person or his [or her] estate;

  (7) in the case of a general partner who is acting as a general partner by virtue of being a trustee of a trust, the termination of the trust (but not merely the substitution of a new trustee);

  (8) in the case of a general partner that is a separate partnership, the dissolution and commencement of winding up of the separate partnership;

  (9) in the case of a general partner that is a corporation, the filing of a certificate of dissolution, or its equivalent, for the corporation or the revocation of its charter; or

(10) in the case of an estate, the distribution by the fiduciary of the estate's entire interest in the partnership.

§ 403. General Powers and Liabilities

(a) Except as provided in this [Act] or in the partnership agreement, a general partner of a limited partnership has the rights and powers and is subject to the restrictions of a partner in a partnership without limited partners.

(b) Except as provided in this [Act], a general partner of a limited partnership has the liabilities of a partner in a partnership without limited partners to persons other than the partnership and the other partners. Except as provided in this [Act] or in the partnership agreement, a general partner of a limited partnership has the liabilities of a partner in a partnership without limited partners to the partnership and to the other partners.

§ 404. Contributions by General Partner

A general partner of a limited partnership may make contributions to the partnership and share in the profits and losses of, and in distributions from, the limited partnership as a general partner. A general partner also may make contributions to and share in profits, losses, and distributions as a limited partner. A person who is both a general partner and a limited partner has the rights and powers, and is subject to the restrictions and liabilities, of a general partner and, except as provided in the partnership agreement, also has the powers, and is subject to the restrictions, of a limited partner to the extent of his [or her] participation in the partnership as a limited partner.

§ 405. Voting

The partnership agreement may grant to all or certain identified general partners the right to vote (on a per capita or any other basis), separately or with all or any class of the limited partners, on any matter.

ARTICLE 5
FINANCE

§ 501. Form of Contribution

The contribution of a partner may be in cash, property, or services rendered, or a promissory note or other obligation to contribute cash or property or to perform services.

§ 502. Liability for Contributions

(a) A promise by a limited partner to contribute to the limited partnership is not enforceable unless set out in a writing signed by the limited partner.

(b) Except as provided in the partnership agreement, a partner is obligated to the limited partnership to perform any enforceable promise to contribute cash or property or to perform services, even if he [or she] is unable to perform because of death, disability, or any other reason. If a partner does not make the required contribution of property or services, he [or she] is obligated at the option of the limited partnership to contribute cash equal to that portion of the value, as stated in the partnership records required to be kept pursuant to Section 105, of the stated contribution which has not been made.

(c) Unless otherwise provided in the partnership agreement, the obligation of a partner to make a contribution or return money or other property paid or distributed in violation of this [Act] may be compromised only by consent of all partners. Notwithstanding the compromise, a creditor of a limited partnership who extends credit or, otherwise acts in reliance on that obligation after the partner signs a writing which reflects the obligation and before the amendment or cancellation thereof to reflect the compromise may enforce the original obligation.

§ 503. Sharing of Profits and Losses

The profits and losses of a limited partnership shall be allocated among the partners, and among classes of partners, in the manner provided in writing in the partnership agreement. If the partnership agreement does not so provide in writing, profits and losses shall be allocated on the basis of the value, as stated in the partnership records required to be kept pursuant to Section 105, of the contributions made by each partner to the extent they have been received by the partnership and have not been returned.

§ 504. Sharing of Distributions

Distributions of cash or other assets of a limited partnership shall be allocated among the partners and among classes of partners in the manner provided in writing in the partnership agreement. If the partnership agreement does not so provide in writing, distributions shall be made on the basis of the value, as stated in the partnership records required to be kept pursuant to Section 105, of the contributions made by each partner to the extent they have been received by the partnership and have not been returned.

ARTICLE 6
DISTRIBUTIONS AND WITHDRAWAL

Section 601. Interim Distributions.
Section 602. Withdrawal of General Partner.
Section 603. Withdrawal of Limited Partner.
Section 604. Distribution Upon Withdrawal.
Section 605. Distribution in Kind.
Section 606. Right to Distribution.
Section 607. Limitations on Distribution.
Section 608. Liability Upon Return of Contribution.

§ 601. Interim Distributions

Except as provided in the Article, a partner is entitled to receive distributions from a limited partnership before his [or her] withdrawal from the limited partnership and before the dissolution and winding up thereof to the extent and at the times or upon the happening of the events specified in the partnership agreement.

§ 602. Withdrawal of General Partner

A general partner may with draw from a limited partnership at any time by giving written notice to the other partners, but if the withdrawl violates the partnership agreement, the limited partnership may recover from the withdrawing general partner damages for breach of the partnership agreement and offset the damages against the amount otherwise distributable to him [or her].

§ 603. Withdrawal of Limited Partner

A limited partner may withdraw from a limited partnership at the time or upon the happening of events specified in writing in the partnership agreement. If the agreement does not specify in writing the time or the events upon the happening of which a limited partner may withdraw or a definite time for the dissolution and winding up of the limited partnership, a limited partner may withdraw upon not less than six months' prior written notice to each general partner at his [other] address on the books of the limited partnership at its office in this State.

§ 604. Distribution Upon Withdrawal

Except as provided in this Article, upon withdrawal any withdrawing partner is entitled to receive any distribution to which he [or she] is entitled under the partnership agreement and, if not otherwise provided in the agreement, he [or she] is entitled to receive, within a reasonable time after withdrawal, the fair value of his [or her] interest in the limited partnership as of the date of withdrawal based upon his [or her] right to share in distributions from the limited partnership.

§ 605. Distribution in Kind

Except as provided in writing in the partnership agreement, a partner, regardless of the nature of his [or her] contribution, has no right to demand and receive any distribution from a limited partnership in any form other than cash. Except as provided in writing in the partnership agreement, a partner may not be compelled to accept a distribution of any asset in kind from a limited partnership to the extent that the percentage of the asset distributed to him [or her] exceeds a percentage of that asset which is equal to the percentage in which he [or she] shares in distributions from the limited partnership.

§ 606. Right to Distribution

At the time a partner becomes entitled to receive a distribution, he [or she] has the status of, and is entitled to all remedies available to, a creditor of the limited partnership with respect to the distribution.

§ 607. Limitations on Distribution

A partner may not receive a distribution from a limited partnership to the extent that, after giving effect to the distribution, all liabilities of the limited partnership, other than liabilities to partners on account of their partnership interests, exceed the fair value of the partnership assets.

§ 608. Liability Upon Return of Contribution

(a) If a partner has received the return of any part of his [or her] contribution without violation of the partnership agreement or this [Act], he [or she] is liable to the limited partnership for a period of one year thereafter for the amount of the returned contribution, but only to the extent necessary to discharge the limited partnership's liabilities to creditors who extended credit to the limited partnership during the period the contribution was held by the partnership.

(b) If a partner has received the return of any part of his [or her] contribution in violation of the partnership agreement or this [Act], he [or she] is liable to the limited partnership for a period of six years thereafter for the amount of the contribution wrongfully returned.

(c) A partner receives a return of his [or her] contribution to the extent that a distribution to him [or her] reduces his [or her] share of the fair value of the net assets of the limited partnership below the value, as set forth in the partnership records required to be kept pursuant to Section 105, of his contribution which has not been distributed to him [or her].

ARTICLE 7
ASSIGNMENT OF PARTNERSHIP INTERESTS

§ 701. Nature of Partnership Interest

A partnership interest is personal property.

§ 702. Assignment of Partnership Interest

Except as provided in the partnership agreement, a partnership interest is assignable in whole or in part. As assignment of a partnership interest does not dissolve a limited partnership or entitle the assignee to become or to exercise any rights of a partner. An assignment entitles the assignee to receive, to the extent assigned, only the distribution to which the assignor would be entitled. Except as provided in the partnership agreement, a partner ceases to be a partner upon assignment of all his [or her] partnership interest.

§ 703. Rights of Creditor

On application to a court of competent jurisdiction by any judgment creditor of a partner, the court may charge the partnership interest of the partner with payment of the unsatisfied amount of the judgment with interest. To the extent so charged the judgment creditor has only the rights of an assignee of the partnership interest. This [Act] does not deprive any partner of the benefit of any exemption laws applicable to his [or her] partnership interest.

§ 704. Right of Assignee to Become Limited Partner

(a) An assignee of a partnership interest, including as assignee of a general partner, may become a limited partner if and to the extent that (i) the assignor gives the assignee that right in accordance with authority described in the partnership agreement, or (ii) all other partners consent.

(b) An assignee who has become a limited partner has, to the extent assigned, the rights and powers, and is subject to the restrictions and liabilities, of a limited partner under the partnership agreement and this [Act]. An assignee who becomes a limited partner also is liable for the obligations of his [or her] assignor to make and return contributions as provided in Articles 5 and 6. However, the assignee is not obligated for liabilities unknown to the assignee at the time he [or she] became a limited partner.

(c) If an assignee of a partnership interest becomes a limited partner, the assignor is not released from his [or her] liability to the limited partnership under Sections 207 and 502.

§ 705. Power of Estate of Deceased or Incompetent Partner

If a partner who is an individual dies or a court of competent jurisdiction adjudges him [or her] to be incompetent to manage his [or her] person or his [or her] property, the partner's executor, administrator, guardian, conservator, or other legal representative may exercise all of the partner's rights for the purpose of settling his [or her] estate or administering his [or her] property, including any power the partner had to give an assignee the right to become a limited partner. If a partner is a corporation, trust or other entity and is dissolved or terminated, the powers of that partner may be exercised by its legal representative or successor.

ARTICLE 8
DISSOLUTION

Section 801. Nonjudicial Dissolution.
Section 802. Judicial Dissolution.
Section 803. Winding Up.
Section 804. Distribution of Assets.

§ 801. Nonjudicial Dissolution

A limited partnership is dissolved and its affairs shall be wound up upon the happening of the first to occur of the following:

(1) at the time specified in the certificate of limited partnership;
(2) upon the happening of events specified in writing in the partnership agreement;
(3) written consent of all partners;
(4) an event of withdrawal of a general partner unless at the time there is at least one other general partner and the written provisions of the partnership agreement permit the business of the limited partnership to be carried on by the remaining general partner and that partner does so, but the limited partnership is not dissolved and is not required to be wound up by reason of any event of withdrawal if, within 90 days after the withdrawal, all partners agree in writing to continue the business of the limited partnership and to the appointment of one or more additional general partners if necessary or desired; or
(5) entry of a decree of judicial dissolution under Section 802.

§ 802. Judicial Dissolution

On application by or for a partner the [designate the appropriate court] court may decree dissolution of a limited partnership whenever it is not reasonably practicable to carry on the business in conformity with the partnership agreement.

§ 803. Winding up

Except as provided in the partnership agreement, the general partners who have not wrongfully dissolved a limited partnership or, if none, the limited partners, may wind up the limited partnership's affairs; but the [designate the appropriate court] court may wind up the limited partnership's affairs upon application of any partner, his [or her] legal representative, or assignee.

§ 804. Distribution of Assets

Upon the winding up of a limited partnership, the assets shall be distributed as follows:

(1) to creditors, including partners who are creditors, to the extent permitted by law, in satisfaction of liabilities of the limited partnership other than liabilities for distributions to partners under Section 601 or 604;

(2) except as provided in the partnership agreement, to partners and former partners in satisfaction of liabilities for distributions under Section 601 or 604; and

(3) except as provided in the partnership agreement, to partners first for the return of their contributions and secondly respecting their partnership interests, in the proportions in which the partners share in distributions.

ARTICLE 9
FOREIGN LIMITED PARTNERSHIPS

§ 901. Law Governing

Subject to the Constitution of this State, (i) the laws of the state under which a foreign limited partnership is organized govern its organization and internal affairs and the liability of its limited partners, and (ii) a foreign limited partnership may not be denied registration by reason of any difference between those laws and the laws of this State.

§ 902. Registration

Before transacting business in this State, a foreign limited partnership shall register with the Secretary of State. In order to register, a foreign limited partnership shall submit to the Secretary of State, in duplicate, an application for registration as a foreign limited partnership, signed and sworn to by a general partner and setting forth:

(1) the name of the foreign limited partnership and, if different, the name under which it proposes to register and transact business in this State;

(2) the State and date of its formation;

(3) the name and address of any agent for service of process on the foreign limited partnership whom the foreign limited partnership elects to appoint; the agent must be an individual resident of this State, a domestic corporation, or a foreign corporation having a place of business in, and authorized to do business in, this State;

(4) a statement that the Secretary of State is appointed the agent of the foreign limited partnership for service of process if no agent has been appointed under paragraph (3) or, if appointed, the agent's authority has been revoked or if the agent cannot be found or served with the exercise of reasonable diligence;

(5) the address of the office required to be maintained in the state of its organization by the laws of that state or, if not so required, of the principal office of the foreign limited partnership;

(6) the name and business address of each general partner; and

(7) the address of the office at which is kept a list of the names and addresses of the limited partners and their capital contributions, together with an undertaking by the foreign limited partnership to keep those records until the foreign limited partnership's registration in this State is cancelled or withdrawn.

§ 903. Issuance of Registration

(a) If the Secretary of State finds that an application for registration conforms to law and all requisite fees have been paid, he [or she] shall:

   (1) endorse on the application the word "Filed", and the month, day, and year of the filing thereof;

   (2) file in his [or her] office a duplicate original of the application; and

   (3) issue a certificate of registration to transact business in this State.

(b) The certificate of registration, together with a duplicate original of the application, shall be returned to the person who filed the application or his [or her] representative.

§ 904. Name

A foreign limited partnership may register with the Secretary of State under any name, whether or not it is the name under which it is registered in its state of organization, that includes without abbreviation the words "limited partnership" and that could be registered by a domestic limited partnership.

§ 905. Changes and Amendments

If any statement in the application for registration of a foreign limited partnership was false when made or any arrangements or other facts described have changed, making the application inaccurate in any respect, the foreign limited partnership shall promptly file in the office of the Secretary of State a certificate, signed and sworn to by a general partner, correcting such statement.

§ 906. Cancellation of Registration

A foreign limited partnership may cancel its registration by filing with the Secretary of State a certificate of cancellation signed and sworn to by a general partner. A cancellation does not terminate the authority of the Secretary of State to accept service of process on the foreign limited partnership with respect to [claims for relief] [causes of actions] arising out of the transactions of business in this State.

§ 907. Transaction of Business Without Registration

(a) A foreign limited partnership transacting business in this State may not maintain any action, suit, or proceeding in any court of this State until it has registered in this State.

(b) The failure of a foreign limited partnership to register in this State does not impair the validity of any contact or act of the foreign limited partnership or prevent the foreign limited partnership from defending any action, suit, or proceeding in any court of this State.

(c) A limited partner of a foreign limited partnership is not liable as a general partner of the foreign limited partnership solely by reason of having transacted business in this State without registration.

(d) A foreign limited partnership, by transacting business in this State without registration, appoints the Secretary of State as its agent for service of process with respect to [claims for relief] [causes of action] arising out of the transaction of business in this State.

§ 908. Action by [Appropriate Official]

The [designate the appropriate official] may bring an action to restrain a foreign limited partnership from transacting business in this State in violation of this Article.

ARTICLE 10
DERIVATIVE ACTIONS

Section 1001. Right of Action.
Section 1002. Proper Plaintiff.
Section 1003. Pleading.
Section 1004. Expenses.

§ 1001. Right of Action

A limited partner may bring an action in the right of a limited partnership to recover a judgment in its favor if general partners with authority to do so have refused to bring the action or if an effort to cause those general partners to bring the action is not likely to succeed.

§ 1002. Proper Plaintiff

In a derivative action, the plaintiff must be a partner at the time of bringing the action and (i) must have been a partner at the time of the transaction of which he [or she] complains or (ii) his [or her] status as a partner must have devolved upon him [or her] by operation of law or pursuant to the terms of the partnership agreement from a person who was a partner at the time of the transaction.

§ 1003. Pleading

In a derivative action, the complaint shall set forth with particularity the effort of the plaintiff to secure initiation of the action by a general partner or the reasons for not making the effort.

§ 1004. Expenses

If a derivative action is successful, in whole or in part, or if anything is received by the plaintiff as a result of judgment, compromise, or settlement of an action or claim, the court may award the plaintiff reasonable expenses, including reasonable attorney's fees, and shall direct him [or her] to remit to the limited partnership the remainder of those proceeds received by him [or her].

ARTICLE 11
MISCELLANEOUS

Section 1101. Construction and Application.
Section 1102. Short Title.
Section 1103. Severability.
Section 1104. Effective Date, Extended Effective Date and Repeal.
Section 1105. Rules for Cases Not Provided for in This Act.
Section 1106. Savings Clause.

§ 1101. Construction and Application

This [Act] shall be so applied and construed to effectuate its general purpose to make uniform the law with respect to the subject of this [Act] among states enacting it.

§ 1102. Short Title

This [Act] may be cited as the Uniform Limited Partnership Act.

§ 1103. Severability

If any provision of this [Act] or its application to any person or circumstance is held invalid, the invalidity does not affect other provisions or applications of the [Act] which can be given effect without the invalid provision or application, and to this end the provisions of this [Act] are severable.

§ 1104. Effective Date, Extended Effective Date and Repeal

Except as set forth below, the effective date of this [Act] is _____ and the following acts [list existing limited partnership acts] are hereby repealed:

(1) The existing provisions for execution and filing of certificates of limited partnerships and amendments thereunder and cancellations thereof continue in effect until [specify time required to create central filing system], the extended effective date, and Sections 102, 103, 104, 105, 201, 202, 203, 204 and 206 are not effective until the extended effective date.

(2) Section 402, specifying the conditions under which a general partner ceases to be a member of a limited partnership, is not effective until the extended effective date, and the applicable provisions of existing law continue to govern until the extended effective date.

(3) Sections 501, 502 and 608 apply only to contributions and distributions made after the effective date of this [Act].

(4) Section 704 applies only to assignments made after the effective date of this [Act].

(5) Article 9, dealing with registration of foreign limited partnerships, is not effective until the extended effective date.

(6) Unless otherwise agreed by the partners, the applicable provisions of existing law governing allocation of profits and losses (rather than the provisions of Section 503), distributions to a withdrawing partner (rather than the provisions of Section 604), and distributions of assets upon the winding up of a limited partnership (rather than the provisions of Section 804) govern limited partnerships formed before the effective date of this [Act].

§ 1105. Rules for Cases Not Provided for in This [Act]

In any case not provided for in this [Act] the provisions of the Uniform Partnership Act govern.

§ 1106. Savings Clause

The repeal of any statutory provision by this [Act] does not impair, or otherwise affect, the organization or the continued existence of a limited partnership existing at the effective date of this [Act], nor does the repeal of any existing statutory provision by this [Act] impair any contract or affect any right accrued before the effective date of this [Act].